Y0-BZY-932

JDBC

ISBN 0-13-045323-4

90000

9 790130 453234

JDBC

DATABASE PROGRAMMING WITH J2EE™

ART TAYLOR

PH
PTR

PRENTICE HALL PTR
UPPER SADDLE RIVER, NJ 07458

Library of Congress Cataloging-in-Publication Data

Taylor, Art
  JDBC: database programming with J2EE/Art Taylor.
    p. cm.
  ISBN 0-13-045323-4
  1. Database design. 2. Relational databases. 3. Java (Computer program language) I.
  Title: Database programming with J2EE. II. title.

  QA76.9D26 T39 2003
  005.74—dc21

                    2002027068

Editorial/production supervision: *Kerry Reardon*
Composition and interior design: *Laurel Road Publishing Services*
Cover design director: *Jerry Votta*
Cover designer: *Nina Scuderi*
Art director: *Gail Cocker-Bogusz*
Manufacturing manager: *Alexis Heydt-Long*
Manufacturing buyer: *Maura Zaldivar*
Acquisitions editor: *Victoria Jones*
Editorial assistant: *Michelle Vincenti*
Marketing manager: *Debby VanDijk*
Project coordinator: *Anne R. Garcia*

Prentice Hall books are widely used by corporations
and government agencies for training, marketing, and resale.

For information regarding corporate and government bulk
discounts please contact:
Corporate and Government Sales (800) 382-3419 or corpsales@pearsontechgroup.com

Printed in the United States of America
10 9   8   7   6   5   4   3   2   1

ISBN 0-13-045323-4

Pearson Education LTD.
Pearson Education Australia PTY, Limited
Pearson Education Singapore, Pte. Ltd.
Pearson Education North Asia Ltd.
Pearson Education Canada, Ltd.
Pearson Educación de Mexico, S.A. de C.V.
Pearson Education–Japan
Pearson Education Malaysia, Pte. Ltd.

CONTENTS

CHAPTER 6   RETRIEVING AND MANIPULATING DATA: THE STATEMENT CLASS AND JDBC EXCEPTIONS   103

CHAPTER 9   TRANSACTIONS IN JDBC   203

CHAPTER 10 JDBC AND DYNAMIC QUERIES   217

CHAPTER 11   THE DATABASEMETADATA INTERFACE   245

CHAPTER 12 DATABASEMETADATA METHODS   267

CHAPTER 13 ADVANCED TOPICS JDBC IN ACTION: INTRODUCTION TO JDBC DESIGN PATTERNS   299

CHAPTER 14 TABLE BROWSER APPLICATION 339

CHAPTER 15 PERSISTING DATA OBJECTS WITH JDBC 365

CHAPTER 21 JDBC AND BLOBs 565

CHAPTER 22 ENTERPRISE JAVABEANS ARCHITECTURE 583

PREFACE

ABOUT THIS BOOK

This book was written with two major goals: cover the JDBC specification in detail and provide a series of examples that demonstrate how JDBC would be used in real world using J2EE.

These goals create two targets: one which is clear and focused and the other which is open-ended and vague. Writing about the JDBC API is fairly straightforward; take the classes, describe the methods and show examples that use the methods in the class. But writing about any possible Java database application is open-ended. A *database application* can be a text-based application reading from a file and updating a database. It can be an applet written using AWT, a GUI client written in Swing, or it can be a servlet or JSP page running in a Web server. It can be a distributed component written as an EJB.

So showing every possible Java database application was not an option. What was chosen were a set of examples that cover some common and some interesting approaches to Java database programming with J2EE. The result was a set of applications that included text-based applications, RMI, Java file i/o, the Swing GUI, Java Server Pages, Java servlets, JavaBeans and Enterprise JavaBeans.

With that in mind, this book is designed to accommodate the introductory developer, the Java developer who has just started working with Java, up to the intermediate and even advanced Java developer. The book begins by assuming some knowledge of Java and relational databases and presents a series of short examples and a few code *snippets*. The initial examples are not meant to be representative of how JDBC would be used in a complete application, but are meant to show specific JDBC API features and methods. By using short examples with most of the work being done within the `main` program block, the focus in these early chapters remains on the JDBC API and is not lost in a complex application.

Examples begin to progress in complexity with the later chapters. This is obviously based on the assumption that the reader is now more familiar with JDBC and database programming with Java and is ready to see JDBC in more complex, real-world examples. As mentioned previously, these later examples use Swing, RMI, JSPs, JavaBeans, servlets and EJBs and apply various Java design patterns to provide additional structure to the code.

This book covers the majority of the JDBC 3.0 specification. Examples were compiled and tested using JDK 1.4 using JDBC drivers based on the JDBC 2.1 specification.

The code examples in the book are available on the companion web site *http://www.phptr.com/taylor/jdbc/* in addition to other code examples and content. Be sure to check the web site to keep up to date on any corrections, changes or additional content.

WHO SHOULD READ THIS BOOK

The individual who should read this book should be familiar with the Java language but there is no requirement to be a Java guru. Instead, some knowledge of the language basics, familiarity with the syntax, understanding of object-oriented programming, Java exception handling, and class file layout should be sufficient.

The individual reading this book should also have some understanding of relational databases. Since the assumption is that the potential reader will most likely be a Java programmer who has had a JDBC project thrust upon them (or has wisely pursued such a project), the book will devote some coverage to relational databases in Chapter 2. The SQL language will be covered, including the basic syntax of Data Manipulation Language (DML) and some of the more advanced SQL features such as unions and complex joins.

ACKNOWLEDGEMENTS

I would like to thank to my editor, Victoria Jones, and all the support staff at Prentice Hall for their help in preparing this book. They've been patient, as always.

Additional thanks to the production staff at Laurel Road Publishing, for their patience and skill.

Randy Layman has been an excellent technical editor throughout. More than once he convinced me that some additional refactoring would create a better example.

These books do not just spring into existence overnight (though I wish they did). None of this would be possible without the support and endurance of my family through the many long hours of work. Thanks always to Carolyn, Hannah and Eric for being there and so much more.

CHAPTER 1

JDBC Today

INTRODUCTION

Since its inception in 1995 the Java language has continued to grow in popularity. Originally intended as a language for embedded systems, the Java language has moved far beyond that. Today Java is used by millions of developers in a myriad of development efforts, from distributed components such as Enterprise JavaBeans, to client-side GUI development with Swing and AWT. Java is used to create Web pages with Java Server Pages and servlets, and to develop Web applications with Java plug-in applets and Java Webstart.

A common thread running through these applications is that they all need data. As the marketing message of the Internet age constantly reminds us, information drives the enterprise. That information is consumed by applications, and the Java Database Connectivity (JDBC) API represents the tool of choice for Java applications to access that data.

JDBC DESIGN

Just as Java was designed to provide platform independence from hardware/software platforms, so too JDBC has been designed to provide some degree of database independence for developers. JDBC is designed to provide a *database-neutral* API for accessing relational databases from different vendors. Just as a Java application does not need to be aware of the operating system platform on which it is running, so too JDBC has been designed so that the database application can use the same methods to access data regardless of the underlying database product.

JDBC was developed to work with the most common type of database: the relational database. This is not to say that JDBC cannot be used with another type of database. In fact, there are JDBC drivers that allow the API to be used to connect to both high-end, mainframe databases, which are not relational, and to access flat files and spreadsheets as databases (which are definitely not relational). But the reality is that JDBC is most commonly used with relational databases.

THE RELATIONAL DATABASE

The technical definition of a relational database is a database that stores data as a collection of related *entities*. These entities are composed of *attributes* that describe the entity, and each entity has a collection of *rows*. Another way to think about a relational database is that it stores information on real-world *objects* (the entities). The information about the objects is contained in the *attributes* for the object.

Since real world objects have some type of relation to each other, we must have a facility for expressing relations between the objects in the database. The relationships between the database objects is described using a query language, the most popular of which is the Structured Query Language (SQL). (Chapter 2 will describe relational databases and SQL in more detail.)

The relational database is the predominant form of database in use today. Other database types include hierarchical, network, flat-file databases, and object databases. Though the hierarchical database is still common on many mainframe systems, it is not commonly used on other platforms.

JAVA AND RELATIONAL DATABASES

Since Java is an object-oriented language, it does not manage data as a relational database does. Data is modeled as objects in Java application design. These objects contain *attributes* (also referred to as *members*), which represent the details of the object. From an object design perspective, an object is not stored—it persists. Its life extends over multiple invocations of the application. These objects are manipulated using a procedural language with syntax similar to the C programming language.

All of this differs markedly from relational databases, which represent data with tables and columns and manipulate the data using the non-procedural SQL. What we are left with is an impedance mismatch between the object-oriented model of Java and the relational model of relational databases. Ultimately, we must reconcile this difference with our class design. This is a process known as object-relational (OR) mapping and can be done manually by applying certain design patterns, as we do later in this text, or can use various OR-mapping tools (for example, TopLink - `www.objectpeople.com`, CocoBase - `www.thought-inc.com`).

OBJECT DATABASES

From a pure object-oriented perspective, object databases provide a nice fit for object-oriented development. Object databases are available that provide APIs and query languages that can be used for Java. While these tools do provide a convenient facility for persisting objects in Java, they generally do not provide a standardized query language, and they begin to experience performance issues as the size of the data set grows larger and queries against the data become more complex.

Object database management systems (ODBMS) have always enjoyed some degree of popularity in some information technology (IT) sectors—for example, finance and research—but for various reasons, these databases do not currently enjoy the popularity of relational databases.

OBJECT-RELATIONAL MAPPING TOOLS AND JDO

An interesting alternative to both JDBC and object databases is the *Java Data Object* (JDO) API. JDO provides a vendor-neutral facility for persisting Java objects. Like the object database, this represents a natural, object-oriented approach to working with data in a Java application. Issues such as transaction support and query language capabilities are provided for in the JDO specification. Since the JDO specification is not specific to any vendor, a developer could create a Java application using JDO with SQL-Server and port it to use Oracle or DB2 without needing to change any code.

JDO is not necessarily a replacement for JDBC but is instead a complementary approach. JDO will provide for the OR-mapping between the object definitions of Java and the entities and attributes of the relational database, and JDBC will provide the low-level access to the database. JDO and JDBC could be used together in an application with JDO being used to manage a large number of persistent objects and JDBC being used to provide access to complex, legacy relational databases that prove too difficult and expensive to map into objects.

Limitations of OR-Mapping and JDO

On the surface, JDO and OR-mapping provide a very attractive approach, but there are potential issues. Data queries can become very complex even for a relatively simple application. The nonprocedural nature of SQL allows complex queries to be expressed relatively simply. It remains to be seen whether or not the query language of JDO will provide this expressive elegance.

There is significant technology and experience that relational databases have accumulated over the past 20 or more years that provide performance and usability benefits for the application developer. Additionally, a significant amount of existing data that Java applications must access is in relational databases.

RELATIONAL DATABASES AND SQL

One of the major benefits of relational databases is that they virtually all use standard SQL for a query language. Initially it was hoped that with SQL, applications that were developed to work with a database from one vendor could easily be ported to work with a database from another vendor. But that has not been the case. Database vendors, in an effort to distinguish themselves from one another, have extended the SQL language in many ways.

The extensions to SQL have been both problematic and beneficial. They have been problematic in that a standard was being extended by vendors and thus reducing the benefit of having a standard. But they have been a benefit in that the extensions were often very useful (Oracle's `decode` statement, for example).

Part of the extensions to existing SQL implementations are the Stored Procedure Languages (SPL). Since SQL is a nonprocedural language, it has difficulties managing certain complex operations where many layers of logic must be applied, such as applying complex business rules to large amounts of report data. SPLs are procedural languages like C or Java and can manage these complex logical operations by providing procedural language facilities, such as conditional statements and flow of control operators, and the ability to declare methods or functions.

These SPL implementations are complete programming languages that are implemented within the database engine. It may seem that the inclusion of a programming language in the database engine is redundant and unnecessary when we are working with a full-fledged programming language like Java. But the advantage of using an SPL to perform data processing is that the processing is done in the database engine. The data used in the SPL procedure resides in the memory space of the database engine, so there is no need to move the data across the network to a program in order to perform the processing. While this performance advantage may not be significant for the processing of 2,000 small rows of data, it does become significant where large pools of data are being processed— for example, the processing of a million rows of data. With large blocks of data, the use of an SPL can mean the difference between only 1 hour of processing for a million rows using an SPL procedure and 8 hours of processing required to extract the data from the database and process it within a program.

Many relational databases also provide database *triggers*. These triggers are associated with a database table and initiate various actions when database activity takes place against the table. Database *update triggers,* probably the most common type of trigger, are executed when a database insert, update, or delete is run against a database table. These triggers are an excellent means of enhancing database integrity and can be used to enforce business rules, replicate data, and provide auditing type facilities by logging table updates.

Other important extensions to relational databases include data fragmentation where data for a table is distributed across separate logical devices, thus improving performance for scans of a large number of rows from the table. Also, database replication where two different database servers running on two different machines remain completely synchronized provides significant benefits.

THE JDBC API

The JDBC API was released in 1997 following a series of specifications that were finalized in the previous year. The API was designed to make the Call Level Interface (CLI) access of relational databases vendor-neutral. Each relational database vendor had created its own version of a CLI for accessing its database. These CLIs were primarily created for the C programming language and later C++. To reduce confusion over these varying CLI implementations, the X/Open Consortium created a standard CLI specification.

JDBC is currently divided into two Java packages: `java.sql` and `javax.sql`. The `java.sql` package contains the core of the original JDBC API and the various improvements on that package that have been made over the years. The `javax.sql` package contains the extensions to the JDBC API that provide some very useful features that were originally added as part of the JDBC 2.0 standard extensions (yes, a contradiction in terms). Both the `java.sql` package and `javax.sql` package are part of the J2SE 1.4 release.

The JDBC specification provides a set of interfaces that database vendors must implement. Vendors have some flexibility in how they implement the JDBC specification. Four different types of implementations have been identified, as detailed in Table 1–1.

| Table 1–1 | JDBC Driver Types |

Driver	Description
Type 1	Implements JDBC by mapping JDBC calls to other CLI calls. Uses a binary library written in another language. Requires software on the client machine, for example, the JDBC-ODBC bridge driver.
Type 2	Driver is partially composed of Java code and partially in native code using another CLI . Requires some client-side binary code.
Type 3	Pure Java driver; uses middleware to convert JDBC calls to vendor-specific calls and protocol required to access the database.
Type 4	Pure Java driver that implements the native protocol. Does not require middleware or any client-side binary. Can be downloaded to a client if necessary.

There are four different types of JDBC drivers. The distinctions between these drivers are based primarily on the components of the driver, where the components must reside, and the language used to develop the components. Each database vendor uses a different set of calls and a different network protocol to access its database. These database vendors offer their own proprietary APIs and drivers to provide access to their databases, and with all JDBC driver types, JDBC calls must be *mapped* or converted to the vendor protocol. In the case of the Type 1 driver, this mapping has an additional layer of indirection through the binary library to the native CLI. The Type 3 driver provides this mapping through a middleware server component that communicates with the client-side driver and provides mapping and database communication. The Type 4 driver provides this mapping through pure Java code written to manage the vendor-specific protocol.

Type 1 and Type 2 drivers require binaries on the client machine. Type 3 and Type 4 drivers, however, are pure Java solutions that significantly reduce porting issues for JDBC driver providers.

Type 2 drivers require some binary code to reside on the client machine. JDBC calls are converted into vendor-specific protocol for the database vendor, potentially mapping the calls to a database driver (usually provided by the database vendor) written in some other language.

The type of driver generally recommended is the Type 4 driver. The fact that it is pure Java code enhances portability, which means driver developers are not stretched thin supporting multiple ports. The Type 4 driver also enjoys potential performance benefits from more efficient code, since JDBC calls do not need to be mapped to proprietary CLI calls (as in Type 2 drivers) and there is no middleware to add additional network overhead, as with Type 3 drivers.

PROGRAMMING FOR TODAY

Today's programming goes far beyond the simple needs of client-server or monolithic applications. In the age of the Internet, it is not unusual and is often necessary for an application to be composed of many different parts or *components* spread across multiple machines. This distributed programming requires a *multitiered* or *n-tiered* development approach.

Multitiered programming is also known as *distributed programming:* an application that is composed of multiple components working together. These multiple components may run on one server or on many servers—they are still collectively considered a complete application.

With this approach, a single application is composed of multiple components running on distinct architectural *tiers*. From a design perspective, the composition of these logical tiers, the work that will be performed on these tiers, should reflect the "responsibility" of the components. This benefits the development effort by providing a consistent structure to multitiered applications. A common approach to n-tiered development uses the following tiers.

- client tier
- presentation tier
- business tier
- resource tier

The *client tier* is responsible for interacting with the user. This interaction will include the display (or rendering) of the user interface and the initial processing of user input. In a Web application, the client tier is the Web browser.

The *presentation tier* is responsible for preparing the output to the client tier and interfacing with the business tier. The presentation tier should not execute any business logic. That is, it should not enforce the business rules of the enterprise; that work should be left to the business tier. In a Web application, the presentation tier is usually a Web server with the ability to process JSP or servlet pages.

The *business tier* is responsible for the execution of the business logic of the enterprise. This tier is expected to process requests from the presentation tier: requests that have been forwarded from the client tier. The business tier will interface with the resource tier to obtain the data that it needs to complete its processing.

The *resource tier* is responsible for managing the resources of the application. For most applications, this tier represents the database. This is where the application data that will persist will be stored and managed.

JDBC Code in N-Tiered Architectures

Java code using JDBC usually resides on the business tier. The code performing the data access on this tier should be isolated and encapsulated in a set of *black box* objects, objects which conceal their details and expose a concise interface.

Multitiered/distributed application architecture and Java design patterns will be explained in more detail in Chapter 13. What is worth noting at this point is that JDBC code will be used differently depending on the component we are writing and the architectural tier where that component will be placed. We can use Java design patterns to help guide this coding process.

Java Technologies for Distributed Programming

Sun Microsystems has packaged a number of Java technologies together under the marketing and distribution umbrella of the Java 2 Enterprise Edition (J2EE). This package is comprised of numerous APIs and technologies that represent the Java tools for developing distributed applications. To develop a Web application using Java technology, these are the tools to use. The core of J2EE includes the APIs listed in Table 1–2 (which include JDBC).

J2EE not only includes Java APIs, but requires servers to run the various components created using the Java APIs. For instance, servlets and JSP pages must run with a servlet server that provides what is known as a *servlet container*. The Java applet must in turn run within what is known as an *applet container*. Enterprise Java Beans (EJB) must run within an *EJB container*. J2EE and the technology behind it is covered in more detail in Chapter 22 and Chapter 23.

Sun has expanded on its J2EE architecture, in a large part in response to the overwhelming interest (whether justified or not) in *Web services*. A Web service is a service that makes itself available over the Internet using HTTP and involves the exchange of messages in XML format. Web services have been popularized to a large extent by Microsoft, which has made Web services a key part of its .Net architecture. Sun has expanded and refined its J2EE architecture to include additional services in what has been dubbed the Open Net Environment (ONE).

J2EE is a distributed component architecture and, as such, does not limit components to the exchange of messages in XML format. Instead, components can communicate with a variety of protocols, including the binary protocols of RMI-IIOP, and also including the asynchronous message passing of JMS or Message Beans and participation in SOAP transactions if the application server provides that. So, while not part of the current J2EE specification, Web services are part of what Sun considers a valid enterprise architecture.

Table 1–2	*J2EE APIs*

API/Java Technology	Description
servlets, JSP	Distributes HTML output over HTTP connection. JSP Java Server Pages extends the servlet API and includes a preprocessor that converts a JSP page into a servlet, which is then run in a servlet engine.
EJB	Enterprise Java Beans. A distributed component technology that provides a number of standard services, such as persistence, transactions, security, and others.
JMS	Java Messaging Service. Common access to message servers for asynchronous message communication.
JDBC	Provides communication with relational databases.
JavaMail	Access to POP3, IMAP, and other standardized mail servers.
JNDI	Java Naming and Directory Interface. Used to provide general lookup of objects and application properties.
JAF	Java Activation Framework. Used with JavaMail for viewing/editing of MIME content.
Java–IDL	Provides access to CORBA components using Java.
RMI, RMI-IIOP	Remote Method Invocation. Provides the ability to create remote objects and execute methods (passing parameters and receiving return values) with those remote objects.
JTS/JTA	Java Transaction API. An API that provides access to transaction controls. Uses Java Transaction Service as the low-level implementation (the service provider interface) for the transaction service.
Java-XML	XML-encoded documents provide much of the configuration information for J2EE. XML is becoming more important as a means of data encoding for data interaction. Provides parsers (JAXP), messaging (JAXMP), registries (JAXR) and RPC (JAX-RPC) APIs.

JAVA DESIGN PATTERNS

The concept of design patterns is often heard discussed in connection with Java application design. Design patterns are used to help guide the development process. Design patterns do not represent complete, template-like solutions, but instead represent recommendations on how to solve certain recurring problems with Java development.

The concept of design patterns can be traced back to work that Christopher Alexander did with building construction architecture in the 1980s. Alexander noted that certain problems would consistently recur in building design and that certain proven solutions could be used to solve these problems. He referred to these proven solutions as *design patterns*.

A group of academics picked up on this work and wrote a seminal book on the subject titled, appropriately enough, *Design Patterns: Elements of Reusable Object-Oriented Software*. The authors of this text, Erich Gamma, Richard Helm, Ralph Johnson, and John Vlissides, are often referred to as the Gang of Four, and thus the text is often referred to as the GoF book. The authors of this text very succinctly applied the concept of design patterns to the process of developing good, object-oriented code. They used the Smalltalk language, but the solutions can easily be applied to any full-featured object-oriented language that supports polymorphism and a facility similar to Java interfaces.

Chapter 13 covers design patterns that apply to JDBC programming in more detail. What is important to note at this point is that design patterns have a significant impact on how JDBC will be used in an application. It should also be noted that design patterns can be applied at several different levels of the development process. Gamma, Helm, Johnson, and Vlissides refer to design patterns as taking the form of creational, structural, or behavioral patterns in relation to how the patterns will be used.

A design pattern that is often noted is the Model, View, Controller (MVC) design pattern. The MVC design pattern was originally applied to the Graphical User Interface (GUI) programming and describes the responsibilities of different portions of the application, as shown in Table 1–3.

As applied to a GUI application, the *model* portion of the application manages the data, the *view* displays the controls of the application (input fields, tables, list boxes), and the *controller* represents the event handlers for user-generated events: button clicks, list box choices, and others. In a GUI application being developed with an object-oriented language, these components would represent objects (and the class definitions for the object) that would be designed to provide for the behaviors, the responsibilities described in Table 1–3.

Table 1–3   *MVC Design Pattern*

Component	Responsibility
Model	Manages the application state, the data the application is using.
View	Renders the portion of the application visible to the user.
Controller	Responds to user gestures and interfaces with the model to control the application.

Table 1–4	J2EE Components by Tier

Tier	MVC	Component
Client	View	Applet, HTML, Java Webstart
Presentation	Controller	servlet, JSP page
Business	Model	Enterprise JavaBean, JavaBean
Resource	n/a	SQL

But in order to apply this design pattern to a Web application, it is imperative that we identify which Web application components will implement the design. If we approach this design pattern using our multitiered architecture described earlier, we should expect that the view portion will be managed by the client tier, the controller will be managed the presentation tier, and the model will be managed by the business tier components. If we are using J2EE, our most likely candidate for each of these components is as follows (Table 1–4).

When viewed in this respect, the MVC pattern describes the responsibilities of the components being used and so would probably more accurately be described as an *architectural* design pattern. The MVC pattern alone does not describe how the specific components (the view component being used on the presentation tier, for example) would be designed. Other Java design patterns as shown later in this book do provide these details.

Using MVC as an architectural pattern, we do receive some high-level guidance about where JDBC code would be located. We would expect the JDBC calls to be placed in the components in the business tier. Located in that tier, the JDBC calls would retrieve data from the resource tier, and the Java code in the business tier would apply business logic and then return the data to the presentation tier, where it would be formatted for presentation to the user.

SUMMARY

This chapter introduced the topic of Java database programming in today's programming world. We have seen how Java has grown and progressed from a small side project at Sun Microsystems to the language of choice for enterprise application development. We have also seen how JDBC fits into this picture as being the API developed by Sun to provide access to relational databases using a vendor-neutral API.

There are some alternatives to JDBC, such as OR-mapping and the incipient JDO. But when existing relational databases with all their complexity must be accessed, JDBC is the tool of choice.

COMING UP NEXT

Chapter 2 examines the target of most JDBC applications: the relational database. The roots of the relational database are covered, and an introduction to the lingua franca of the query languages—SQL—will be provided. Following that chapter, we will begin our detailed discussion of the JDBC API.

The Relational Database and SQL

INTRODUCTION

The defined purpose of the JDBC API is to provide access to relational databases. Therefore, it stands to reason that some knowledge of the relational database, its theory, its structure, and the current state of the database industry is needed. In addition to that knowledge, an understanding of the Structured Query Language (SQL), which is used to access the database, is helpful.

Failure of developers to understand relational databases and the process of accessing the data in them can lead to applications that display poor performance. The process of choosing how to access the data in a relational database can affect performance. What is often cited as a *database problem* or a *machine problem* is in fact due to poor database programming in the application. Having a solid understanding of relational databases can help alleviate these problems.

RELATIONAL DATABASE CONCEPTS

The relational database model had its theoretical start in the late 1960s. In 1968, while at an IBM research institution, Dr. E. F. Codd began researching the concept of applying mathematical rigor to the world of database management systems. Codd's ideas were later published in a landmark paper, "A Relational Model of Data for Large Shared Data Banks" (Communications of the ACM, Volume 13, No. 6, June 1970). The ideas laid out in this paper had a sweeping influence on the nature of database systems for years to come. Today, they are the theoretical standard of all relational database systems.

The relational database is conceptually a collection of *tables*. Each table in the database represents a data *entity*, and each entity is a collection of data *attributes*. An entity is a distinguishable object (person, place, or thing) about which information is to be recorded.

An example of such an object is a car. An attribute is a characteristic or property associated with the distinguishable object. An example of attributes for a car entity would be the color of the car, the make of the car, the size of the engine, and the age of the car.

ENTITIES, ATTRIBUTES, AND RELATIONSHIPS

The process of designing a relational database involves first identifying the entities (the objects) to be modeled. In the design of a system to take catalog orders, for example, the entities would be objects such as a catalog item, an order for an item, the manufacturer of an item, and the customer who purchased an item. The attributes for these entities would be the characteristics, the features of the entity or object.

In the case of a catalog item, attributes would be a description of the item, the cost of the item, the weight of the item, the size of the item, and the manufacturer of the item. The attributes of another entity, such as the customer, would be the name of the customer and the address of the customer with the zip code. And the order would contain characteristics or attributes for the customer making the order, the item or items being ordered, and the cost of the order.

Entities can have *relationships*. Relationships are the connections between the objects being modeled. An order does not exist in its environment alone. There are customers who have made the order, and there are items on the order that represent items the customer has purchased. The customer and item entities are therefore related to the order entity (see Figure 2–1).

Relationships have several forms: one-to-one, one-to-many, and many-to-many. A one-to-one relationship indicates that for a particular entity, there is one and only one related entity. An example of a one-to-one relationship would be the relationship between a manufacturer and an item (see Figure 2–2). For any particular item record,

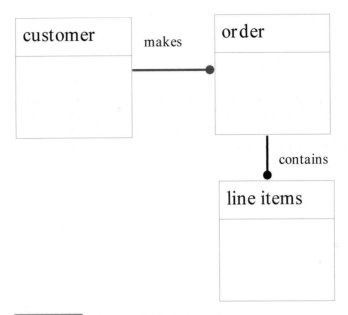

Figure 2–1   *Customer-Order Relationship*

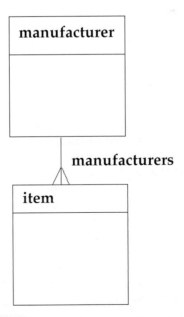

Figure 2–2   *Manufacturer-Item Relationship*

there is one and only one manufacturer record. (An alternative design could allow multiple manufacturers for an item, but for our purposes, a different manufacturer would entail a different item.)

A one-to-many relationship indicates that for a given entity record, there are one or more than one related entity records. This would be the case for the orders entity and the line items entities on the order (see Figure 2–3). For every unique order entity record (for instance, order #1), there could be multiple items purchased, and each of these items purchased would be represented by a line item record. Each line item has associated with it one order record (for instance, line item #10 is part of order #1) and an associated item record. This is also referred to as a master-detail relationship.

A many-to-many relationship indicates that for the multiple records in a given entity, there are one or more than one records in a related entity. An example of a many-to-many relationship is the relationship between cars and family members. A single family member can own more than one car, and a single car can be owned by more than one family member.

A relational database is often diagrammed using an entity-relationship diagram (ERD); these diagrams provide a series of specialized lines, boxes, and symbols to represent the relationships between entities (see figures 2-2 and 2-3).

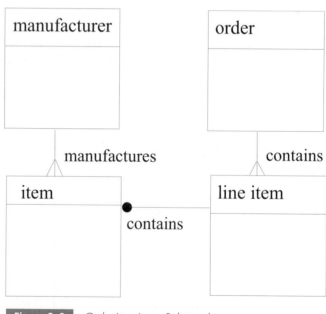

Figure 2–3   *Order-Line Items Relationship*

NORMALIZATION

Once the attributes and entities of the database have been identified, there is usually a process of *normalization* that the database developer must complete. Normalization generally involves the elimination of repeating attributes in an entity and the identification of attributes that belong in a particular entity and attributes that belong elsewhere. The database developer must usually go through several iterations of review and modification before the proper level of normalization has been achieved.

Several levels of normalization have been defined by Dr. Codd and other academics. Each level provides for examination and review of the entity and its attributes and a determination of what belongs and does not belong to that entity. The most common level of normalization is known as *third-normal form*, though an even more rigorous fourth-normal and fifth-normal form has been defined.

The normalization of a relational database is an important part of the database design process. Normalization reduces data redundancy and thus reduces the amount of data storage required for the data. A normalized design also reduces the difficulty of making the inevitable design modifications required of most databases.

CREATING THE DATABASE TABLES

At the end of the design process, the identified entities become the tables of the database and the identified attributes become the columns of the tables. These tables and columns are then manipulated using SQL. Each table can contain one or more rows of data.

For each row in the table, a column or a collection of columns should uniquely identify the row. This unique identifier is considered the *primary key*. If this unique identifier is contained in another table, then it would represent the foreign key in that table. The following code illustrates this concept.

```
— Customer Table

        customer_number (primary key)
     first_name
     last_name


— Customer Address Table

     customer_number (primary key, foreign key)
     address_type (primary key)
     address_line1
```

```
address_line2
city
state
```

In this example, a customer table and an address table are used to track one or more addresses for a customer. A customer could have only one address (a primary residence) or a customer could have multiple addresses (a primary residence, and for the privileged, one or more secondary residences such as a vacation home in Vale and another vacation home in Key West). The primary key for the `customer` table is the `customer_number` field. This number uniquely identifies each row in this table. For the related `customer_address` table, the `customer_number` is a *foreign key* because this number refers to a row in the customer table.

Because this example allows for the customer to have more than one address (a primary and secondary residence), the customer number in the customer address table does not uniquely identify each row in this table. If the customer had multiple addresses, with just the customer number as a key, there would be no way to identify which address was the primary residence and which address was the secondary residence.

Another key column is needed to create a primary key for the `customer_address` table; this is the reason for the `address_type` column. This column is a two character column that represents the type of customer address being examined. This column would be "P" for primary residence and "S1" for the first secondary residence, "S2" for the second secondary residence, and so on. This column combined with the `customer_number` column would uniquely identify each row in the customer address table.

RELATIONAL DATABASE TERMINOLOGY

The relational database is firmly planted on the theoretical foundation of relational algebra; thus the terminology of that discipline has found its way into the relational database industry. Some of the common terms and their meanings are explained in the following sections.

Relation

The term *relation* is a mathematical term for a table. A database with three tables would therefore be a database with three relations. The terms relation and table are often used interchangeably.

Domain

A domain is often used to describe a pool of values that are appropriate for an attribute (or column). For example, a single character column that stores the response to a true or false question with a valid answer of T or F would have a domain of T and F. A column that held the years of employment for a company that had been in existence for 12 years would have a domain of integer values in the range of 1 to 12 inclusive.

Join

In technical terms, a join builds a relation from two specified relations. To extract rows from two related tables having a corresponding primary key–foreign key relationship is to *join* the two tables.

Using the SQL `select` statement (which is different than the relational algebra SELECT and provides a number of the relational set operations with a single statement), a join between two tables with no join criteria results in the Cartesian product of the two tables: Every row in table A is joined with every row in table B. This is usually not the desired result, so a join condition expressing an equality condition between key columns of joined tables is usually part of a valid `select` statement. This equality join still produces a Cartesian product between the two tables, but the filter clause reduces the product to a useful result set.

Tuples

The term tuple is roughly equivalent to a record, but because of the sometimes fuzzy definition of a record in the early days of database management systems, the term tuple was used to apply to a specific flat record instance. In the case where a join of multiple tables retrieves specific columns from each table, the result is referred to in relational database terminology as a tuple (though it is very likely a programmer would refer to this result as a record regardless of academic opinion).

Unions

The union of two relations A and B is the set of all tuples in A, all tuples in B, or both. With the SQL `union` operation, duplicate rows are eliminated from the result by default. A `union all` operation is sometimes available to preserve duplicate rows in the result. Depending on how the statement is written, the results of a `union` statement can often be duplicated with a SQL `select` statement.

Master–Detail Relationships

A master–detail relationship exists when a record in one table relates to several records in another table (see Figure 2–3). Such is the case with an order where a single record contains the order information, such as the order number and the order date, and a related table stores the order line items, with each line item being stored as a separate record. With this example, the order information record would be referred to as the *master* (or header) record and the order line item records would be referred to as the *detail* records. This is also sometimes referred to as a parent–child relationship, with the master record being the parent record and the detail records being the child records. (The term *record* is used here in lieu of tuple because this is the most common usage of these terms.)

STRUCTURED QUERY LANGUAGE

The language of choice for the relational database is the Structured Query Language, usually referred to as SQL. Originally spelled SEQUEL and still pronounced that way by many, the SQL language was developed by IBM at its San Jose, California, research facility. Now widely adopted as a query language in the relational database industry, it is essentially the lingua franca of relational databases.

One of the strengths of SQL is that it expresses set logic clearly with an English-like syntax. This has enabled relational database users to quickly learn the language. With the knowledge of a few keywords and clauses, a user can quickly learn to access data in a SQL database. Data retrieval and formatting that would require a lengthy program be written in other languages can often be expressed in a single SQL statement. SQL statements are divided into two types: data definition language (DDL) statements and data manipulation language (DML) statements. The DDL statements include schema definition statements such as `create database`, `create table`, and `create view`. These statements create databases and tables and provide for the creation of different stored selections or views on that data. The DML statements include the `select`, `update`, and `delete` statements used for querying and updating the database.

Using JDBC, DDL statements are executed using the `executeUpdate` method in both the `Statement` and `PreparedStatement` classes. SQL DML statements are executed using both the `executeQuery` method and the `executeUpdate` statements. The `executeQuery` method is used for statements that return values such as the select statement. The `executeUpdate` statement is used for statements that do not return values, such as update statements and DDL statements (create table, create index).

Additional SQL statements exist for manipulation of the database. Many of these statements are database-vendor-specific. These statements perform additional functions such as changing the isolation level, the unloading and loading of data from external data sources, the definition of constraints, and the creation and execution of stored procedures.

SQL Standards

SQL has been standardized by the American National Standards Institute (ANSI). The original standard was issued in 1986. Later standards were released in 1992 and 1999. JDBC 3.0 is aligned with SQL 99, though not all database vendors have completely adopted the various features and data types of the SQL 99 standard.

While the wide acceptance of a standard has been useful, database vendors have been quick to extend SQL. These extensions, though useful, have diluted the benefit of a standard query language and have reduced the portability of database applications between databases of different vendors.

The JDBC API provides a number of methods to help improve the portability of an application and limit the impact of varied SQL implementations. JDBC *escape syntax* can be used to code SQL that varies between vendors, and various metadata classes provide detailed information on the SQL supported in the currently connected database.

The Call Level Interface (CLI)

Traditionally, programmatic access to a database was provided with a Call Level Interface (CLI) which defined a set of native language calls for database interaction. Using the CLI, the programmer could determine the state of the database, and use SQL statements to query and update the database. The JDBC API is technically a CLI, though the acronym CLI is not as widely used as it used to be.

Alternatives to using a CLI to access a database is to embed SQL directly into the native language code. The Oracle JSQL product uses this approach with the Java language. With JSQL, SQL statements and a few extensions are placed directly into a Java program. Extensions to SQL are used to provide interaction with the procedural Java language.

A CLI provides all of the functionality of an embedded SQL interface but with some added flexibility, especially in the area of dynamic data access. The CLI does not require the use of host variables, as an embedded SQL interface does, and is therefore a more natural form of programming for a developer familiar with the language.

Processing a dynamic SQL statement requires interaction with the native programming language, something which is difficult to express with an embedded SQL interface. But with a CLI native programming language, language variables can be used to store the dynamic information, allowing for a more natural programming style. Both ODBC and JDBC are CLI definitions. The ODBC CLI definition and JDBC are based on the SQL Access Group CAE specification (1992) and X/Open CLI definition.

SQL Statements

There are several core SQL statements that provide the bulk of the functionality of SQL. These statements are `select`, `update`, and `delete`. The `where` clause, which provides filter criteria to specify the specific tuples to extract or update and the table join criteria, is shared by these statements and is explained in more detail in the following sections.

The Select Statement

The SQL `select` statement is used to perform all queries on the database and can be used to provide filter values for other SQL statements. It can also be used to provide a value list for an `insert` statement. The syntax for the `select` statement is as follows:

```
select    <column list>
from        <table list>
where     <filter and join criteria>
```

The *column list* in the `select` clause identifies the columns that will be retrieved as part of the query. These column lists can sometimes contain expressions so that mathematical calculations can be made on columns. With this same functionality, several columns can be concatenated with other columns or with character string constants.

The *table list* in the `from` clause contains the list of tables from which the columns will be retrieved. Many versions of SQL support the ability to perform *outer joins* on the tables listed (retrieving partial joined rows even if the related row does not exist).

The optional `where` clause is used to express the *filter and join criteria* for the SQL statement being executed. The filter criteria is expressed as a series of Boolean expressions. An example of this statement follows.

```
select  orders.*, items.*
from    orders, items
where   orders.order_num = items.order_num
```

In this example, columns are selected from the `orders` table and the `items` table. This query effectively joins these two tables on the `order_num` column, as specified in the `where` clause.

Column Naming (Aliases)

Many SQL implementations allow substitute names or *aliases* to be used for the column names or expressions in the select list. The following query demonstrates.

```
select region, sales_amount base_sale,
sales_amount * ( 1 - discount_percent) discounted_sale
from sales
```

In this query, the sales table contains a column holding the dollar amount of the sale (`sales_amount`) and a column holding the discount percentage (`discount_percent`). To show the base price of the sale and the discounted price the select list must include an expression (which is allowed in most implementations). By placing a string next to the expression in the 'select' list we inform the SQL engine that we would like the name of the expression column to be the string, so that the name assigned to the 'discounted sales' expression is `discounted_sales`.

For clarity in this `select` statement, we also choose to assign a name to the `sales_amount` column that is different than the name of the column; we assign it the name of `base_sale`. The database server will now substitute that name alias for the automatically generated *column name* of the expression. The output of this query would be as follows.

```
Region    base_sale          discounted_sale
North       100.00             90.00
North        80.00             78.00
South       100.00             80.00
South        80.00             78.00
```

Table Aliases

Most relational databases will allow substitute names to be assigned to tables used in a query, sometimes referred to as *table name aliases*. These aliases can be used to clarify common columns in query where two joined tables share the same column. The following query provides an example.

```
select  cust.customer_id,
        first_name,
        last_name,
        address1,
        address2,
        city,
        state
from    customer cust, customer_address ca
where   cust.customer_id = ca.customer_id
```

Through the use of table aliases in the `from` clause, the `customer` table is assigned the substitute name `cust` and the `customer_address` table is assigned the substitute name of `ca`. The result is a query with a more concise, less tedious syntax. When using *correlated subqueries* (covered later in this chapter), the use of table aliases has the added benefit of allowing inner queries to access tables in the outer query.

Grouping Records

Results from a `select` statement can be grouped using the `group by` clause. These record groups can be used with aggregate functions to provide subtotals for groups of records. In most implementations of this statement, only columns or expressions in the `select` list can be used in the `group by` clause. If an expression is being used, either the expression alias (the name that has been given to the expression) must be used or, in some implementations, the ordinal position of the expression in the `select` list must be used. The following is an example

```
select region, sum( sales_amount) base_sales,
sum( ( sales_amount * ( 1 - discount_percent) ) ) discounted_sales
from sales
group by region
order by base_sale desc, discounted_sale desc, region
```

In this example, records are retrieved from the `sales` table and then grouped by region. For each region, the sales amount of the base sale is subtotaled, and the amount of the discounted sale is subtotaled. The results of the grouped query are then sorted in descending order (using the `desc` keyword in the `order by` clause) for `base_sales` and `discounted_sales`, thereby sorting the results from highest sales to lowest sales figures (a common approach in sales reporting). The output will be subtotaled (grouped) by region as shown below. With this example, using just five lines of SQL, a sales report has been prepared that would have undoubtedly taken more than five lines of procedural language code to create.

```
region      base_sales      discounted_sales
North       1000.00         800.00
South       5000.00         4000.00
West        10000.00        9000.00
```

When using a `group by` clause, the `where` clause provides filtering *before* the database records are grouped. The `having` clause can be combined with the `group by` clause to filter the grouped results after they have been filtered by the `where` clause expressions. To filter the query above for aggregated base sales of greater than $10,000, the following query could be used.

```
select region, sum( sales_amount) total_sales,
sum( ( sales_amount * ( 1 - discount_percent) ) ) discounted_sale
from sales
where sales_amount > 100
group by region
```

```
having total_sales > 10000
order by base_sale desc, discounted_sale desc, region
```

In this example, sales records are filtered by the `where` clause for sales greater than $100. After the sales have been grouped, they are filtered by the `hav-ing` clause for `total_sales` of greater than $10,000. The results are sorted as they were in the previous example, in descending order of the aggregated `base_sale` and `discounted_sale`.

Subqueries and Correlated Subqueries

Subqueries provide the capability of having a query within a query, thus allowing more complex and interesting queries to be constructed. Subqueries can be placed in the `where` clause, greatly enhancing the filtering capabilities of the `select` statement, as the following query demonstrates.

```
select *
from sales
where sales.region in
(select unique region
 from    sales_tmp
 where   region_type = 'E')
```

In this example, the query selects the sales records for all sales where the region occurs in the query that is returned by the subquery. The subquery is select-ing unique or distinct regions from the `sales_tmp` table. (We can assume that the processing that populated the `sales_tmp` table did so with some meaningful business logic, such as finding sales regions that had a high growth rate or sales regions that exceeded sales predictions.)

Subqueries can be used to construct more complex queries that express more than one level of processing logic, as the following example shows.

```
select *
from sales
where sales.region in
(select unique region
 from    sales_tmp
 where   region_type = 'E' and
         sales_amount > (   select min( sales_amount )
                            from    sales )
   )  and
   sales_amount > ( select avg( sales_amount)
                    from sales )
```

In this example, sales are filtered based on the occurrence of the region in the `sales_tmp` table, and the `sales_amount` figure in the `sales_tmp` table is greater than the minimum sales amount from sales.

Additionally, these records are filtered based on the `sales_amount` for the `sales` record being greater than the average sales amount from that same table. This type of filtering allows us to effectively make multiple filtering passes at the same table in a single SQL statement. Furthermore, in what is known as a *correlated subquery*, we can relate record filtering in an inner query with records in the table in the outer query, as shown in the following example.

```
select *
from sales so
where sales.region in
(select unique region
 from    sales_tmp
 where   region_type = 'E'  and
         sales_amount > (  select min( sales_amount )
                            from    sales )
 )   and
 sales_amount > ( select avg( sales_amount)
                     from sales si
                     where si.sale_code = so.sale_code )
```

In this example, the outermost query selects from the `sales` table and creates a table alias named `so` for the table. The last two lines of the query, which are in fact a subquery, use an alias name of `si` for the sales table in the inner query and, in the `where` clause of the query statement on the last line of the query, matches the `sale_code` of the inner `sales` table (`si`) with the `sale_code` of the outer `sales` table (`so`).

Recursive Queries

There are often relationships in tables that are more succinctly designed as *recursive*. That is, the data in these tables is best modeled as a hierarchical relationship of related records in the *same table*. A common example of this is the `parts` table (Table 2–1).

This parts table has three columns: the `part_id`, the `sub_part`, and the name. The `part_id` is the part number for the part, and the `sub_part` is a constituent `part_id` of which the part is composed. Any given part can be composed of one or more other parts. So in this hypothetical example, a car door is part number 10 and is composed of a door handle, part 11.

In turn, the door has a `sub_part` of 11 which we see in the table is the `part_id` for the door handle. The door handle in turn has a `sub_part` of 15, which is the `part_id` for the lock. The relationships for this table are relation-

Table 2–1	Recursive Table Design	
part_id	**sub_part**	**name**
10	11	Door
11	15	Door handle
15	18	Lock
18	0	Lock tumbler

ships to itself. Querying the data in this table requires what is sometimes referred to as a self-join. A query to retrieve this information could be written as follows.

```
select pa.* , pb.*
from   parts pa, parts pb
where  pa.part_id = pb.sub_part
```

This query would retrieve the rows in the table recursively, tracing all of the parts relationships two levels deep in the output.

The downside of this approach is that it limits the depth of the recursion to the number of times the table name is repeated. The database engine will scan the table for the relationship shown for each occurrence of the table name, so to scan the table four times to retrieve recursion to a depth of four would require a tedious query that repeated and aliased the table name four times in the `from` clause of the query. (Some database engines support a very powerful `connect by` clause in the `select`' statement, which will recurse to however many depths are required to reach the end of the recursive relationship.)

Outer Joins

An equal join, or equi-join, represents the intersection of two relations and is sometimes referred to as a *natural join* or *inner join*. This is the default join for a relational database. It returns a row from table A joined to a row from table B. A resulting joined row is only returned if a row in table B satisfies the join condition and can therefore be joined to a row in a table A.

There may be times when you want to return a row from a table even if it does not have corresponding joined rows in another table. The following query provides an example.

```
select sales_id, sales_amount, promo_description
from   sales, special_promotions
where  sales.promotion_id = special_promotions.promotion_id
```

This query, written as an inner join, will return `sales` table records only if there is a corresponding `special_promotion` table record (meaning that a `special_promotion` table record satisfies the join condition to the `sales` table). Since it is logical to assume that not all sales records will have associated special promotion records (they wouldn't be so special if everyone had them). Writing the query as a natural join would eliminate records from the results that we did not want eliminated. We would like to write a query that retrieved the `sales` table records even though there are no corresponding `sales_promotions` table records. As it happens, an *outer join* on the `special_promotions` table would produce the results we want. We can phrase an outer join query as follows.

```
select sales_id, sales_amount, promo_description
from    sales, outer special_promotions
where   sales.promotion_id = special_promotions.promotion_id
```

Executing this query would return results as follows.

sales_id	sales_amount	promo_description
1	100.00	half-price sale
2	80.00	null
3	50.00	one-third off
4	30.00	null

The records that were returned by the natural join have values in the `promo_description` field. But the records that were joined using the outer join returned a null value for the `sales` table rows that could not be joined with `special_promotion` rows. Developers writing queries that are outer joins need to be aware that null values are potentially going to be returned in the results.

Unions

A `union` clause in an SQL `select` statement represents the union of two sets that have been specified by `select` statements. By default, the `union` statement will eliminate duplicate rows; using the `all` keyword as part of the `union` statement will change this behavior and bring back all rows in the union operation, including the duplicate rows.

The `union` clause allows similar data from different tables to be retrieved in a single result. The following query demonstrates the use of the `union` clause to join data in separate tables.

```
  select *
  from    sales
  where   sales_code = 20
union
  select *
  from    sales_tmp
```

```
   where   sales_code = 30
union
   select  *
   from    db1@srv1:sales
   where   sales_code = 30
```

This query selects data from three different tables and brings back the results as a single result with duplicates eliminated. Had the union all clause been used in the query, the results would have included duplicates.

A union query can often be rewritten as a single select, which simply joins the tables identified in the separate select statements. In many cases, the union clause is just used to add clarity to the SQL statement and reduce the complexity of the query.

The Update Statement

The update statement updates rows in a table. Updates can only be performed on one table at a time. Filter criteria may be specified with a where clause using the same format as when this clause is used with other SQL statements with some minor restrictions. The where clause is optional, though without a where clause, all rows in the table will be updated; this is not usually the desired behavior for an update statement. The format for the update statement is as follows:

```
update <table name>
set    <column list>
where  <filter criteria>
```

An example of this statement follows.

```
update items
set    price = price * 1.1
where  cost > 10
```

This example updates the items in the items table where the price is greater than $10. It updates each record by increasing the price column by 10 percent.

The Delete Statement

The delete statement deletes rows from a table. The delete statement can only be performed on one table at a time. The where clause can be used to indicate the specific rows to be deleted. As with the update statement, the where clause is optional, though without the where clause, the delete statement will delete all rows in the specified table. If this is not the desired result and database logging is not in place, then there is most likely no means of undoing the delete statement without resorting to a backup. The format for the delete statement is as follows:

```
delete
from          <table name>
where         <filter criteria>
```

The following is an example of this statement.

```
delete
from    items
where order_num = 123456
```

This example deletes rows from the `items` table. The `where` clause provides a filter and indicates that only those `items` table records where the `order_num` is equal to 123456 will be deleted.

TRANSACTIONS, DATABASE LOGGING AND ISOLATION LEVELS, AND CONCURRENCY

When working with a relational database, a series of updates may be made to a set of related tables. In order for database integrity to remain intact, all of these updates must succeed together. Should one of the update statements fail, a master record could exist without all corresponding detail records, and the integrity of the database would be compromised.

This is the case when a customer order record is inserted into two tables: an order master table containing the order date, the amount of the order, the customer number, and due date, and a series of order detail records containing the items the customer has ordered. This is illustrated in Figure 2–4.

With this example, an order master record is inserted and three corresponding order detail table records are inserted. Because transaction logging is in place, should one of the updates to the detail table fail, the entire transaction would be rolled back and the database would remain in a consistent state. But should one of the updates to the order detail table fail and transaction logging is not in place, then the order amount column in the order master record will not balance with the constituent detail records. This will leave the database in a corrupt state.

Using transaction logging can help eliminate this problem. With transaction logging, a series of updates can be treated as a single transaction; should one of the updates fail, all updates will fail. Thus the database integrity is preserved.

Transaction logging requires that the programmer identify what statements comprise the transaction. In the case of the order updates, the order master record update and the order items record updates are one transaction.

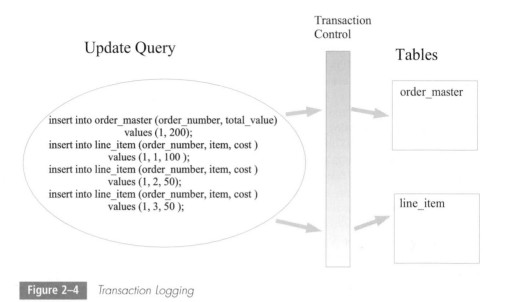

Figure 2–4   *Transaction Logging*

Isolation Levels and Concurrency

When using transaction logging, there are concurrency issues to be considered. Concurrency involves the use of a database by multiple users, by far the most common use of relational databases. When using transaction logging, there are situations where a record may have been updated in a SQL statement but the transaction has not been committed. This would be the case in the previous example where the first `order_detail` record had been inserted but not the second or third; a user reading the order at this point in time would be reading uncommitted records (if that was allowed) and would read an incomplete order.

Transaction isolation levels take such issues into account. Using isolation levels, programmers and database administrators can restrict the user's view into the database. A programmer can set an isolation level to a very unrestrictive level that allows any record to be read regardless of whether or not it has been committed. Or, an isolation level can be set that allows only committed records to be read. Isolation levels are implementation-dependent—a number of different flavors of isolation levels are available from various database vendors. The code below demonstrates the call necessary to set the isolation level for a database using JDBC `Connection` class method `setTransactionIsolation`.

```
...
con.setAutoCommit( false );
 con.setTransactionIsolation( Connection.TRANSACTION_READ_COMMITTED  );
...
```

The choice of isolation levels is not a trivial issue. The isolation level in effect during database updates can create serious problems in an application. If an application is not tested with concurrent access, these problems may not appear until an application is live and accepting multiple user requests.

Should an unrestrictive isolation level be in effect that allows incomplete transactions to be read, an application generating a report of active orders could produce an unbalanced report by reading incomplete transactions. Conversely, an application using a restrictive isolation level could be prohibited from reading critical records being accessed by a user who has not yet committed his or her transaction. (This could be an even more serious problem if the user fails to commit the record before taking a two-hour lunch.)

The issue is further complicated when developing applications that can potentially be run against different databases over the Internet. The application programmer must be aware of isolation levels and different flavors of transaction logging on the databases to be accessed. Different isolation levels and logging procedures could have an impact on the application.

To provide an example, consider a database server that supports four levels of transaction isolation: dirty-read, committed-read, cursor stability, and repeatable-read. These isolation levels provide varying degrees of concurrency isolation from virtually unrestricted concurrency with dirty-read to very restrictive concurrency with repeatable-read. These isolation levels are explained in more detail in the following sections. Different vendors have different variations and terms for isolation levels, but the functionality and restrictions are similar. JDBC supports four levels of isolation mode. These modes and their correspondence to Informix database isolation modes are shown in Table 2–2.

Committed-Read Isolation

This isolation level guarantees that every row retrieved has been committed to the database at the time of retrieval. Rows that are being updated by a user and have not been committed to the database cannot be read. No exclusive locks are acquired; one user can process a row while another user modifies the row.

Cursor-Stability Isolation

This isolation level acquires a shared lock on each row being examined, thus eliminating the possibility that another user can update the row being processed. A first user can read and update a row and second user can read and acquire a shared lock on the same row, but the exclusive lock needed for an update by the second user cannot be acquired until the first user releases the lock. When the first user moves to the next row, the lock is released.

| Table 2–2 | *Four Levels of Isolation Mode* |

JDBC Isolation Mode	Informix Mode	Description
TRANSACTION_NONE	n/a	Transactions are not supported.(Informix does allow a database to be created with no logging, but once logging is in place, it cannot simply be turned off.)
TRANSACTION_READ_COMMITTED	Committed -Read	Only reads on the current row are repeatable.
TRANSACTION_READ_UNCOMMITTED	Dirty -Read	Rows being used by a transaction can be read even if the rows have not been committed.
TRANSACTION_REPEATABLE_READ	Repeatable-Read	Reads on all rows of a results are repeatable.
TRANSACTION_SERIALIZABLE	Repeatable-Read	Reads on all rows of a transaction are repeatable in the order in which they were executed.

Repeatable-Read Isolation

This isolation level acquires a shared lock on every row selected during the transaction. Any row touched by a user in repeatable-read isolation will be locked using a shared lock. Another user can read the row but will not be granted the exclusive lock needed to perform an update. The shared locks are released only when the row is committed or rolled back. This differs from committed-read in that the entire selected set, not just the current row, is locked by the user.

Dirty-Read Isolation

The dirty-read isolation level allows rows being used in a transaction to be read by other database users even though the rows have not yet been committed. While this may seem like a poor way to run a database, this isolation mode does have the benefit of allowing fast, unfettered access to data for reports or quick queries of current status. Since it is possible that a row or set of rows may be used in a transaction that will not commit for some time, it doesn't make sense to have reports or quick status queries wait for these commits. In many databases, this is the default isolation mode.

Choosing Isolation Levels

Generally, it is the purpose of the application that drives the decision on which isolation level to use. For report applications, a dirty-read or committed-read isolation level may be adequate. A report does not perform updates and would not need to acquire an exclusive lock on a row. The committed-read isolation level would access only committed data and would therefore give only a consistent view of the database.

For an application that has to perform groups of updates, such as the data-entry application for an order-entry system, a cursor-stability or repeatable-read isolation level would be needed. The application would need to know that no other user has updated a row while the application was holding the row; otherwise, the other users's update would be invalid. With an isolation level of cursor-stability, a lock would be acquired as soon as the row to be modified is read. When the application was finished modifying the row, the update would be made, the next row accessed, and the lock would be released using the cursor-stability isolation level. If a number of rows must be updated together, as is the case with most master–detail relationships, then the repeatable-read isolation level may be desirable.

There are tradeoffs in these choices. With the repeatable-read isolation level, the application programmer can be confident that the transaction maintained database consistency. But there will be a corresponding loss of concurrency required to maintain this integrity. Other applications that need to update rows already updated by the repeatable-read process will not be able to acquire the locks needed to update the row, even though their update may not affect the process using the repeatable-read isolation level. For example, if a process started a transaction at the repeatable-read isolation level, then updated a status record and proceeded to begin updating various rows, another application needing to update the same status record would not be able to proceed because it could not acquire the shared lock needed.

Some tables allow and default to page-level locking, which means that rather than locking a single row in shared mode, the entire page (with multiple rows) is locked, which can severely limit concurrency. There are times when the database administrator may choose to use page locking to reduce the number of locks required in a database and reduce the amount of overhead involved in locking the row. The type of locking being used on a table can affect the decisions as to what type of isolation mode to use for a transaction.

SQL QUERY OPTIMIZATION

Modern relational databases provide the capability to determine the data access path at runtime. While most vendors provide some ability to store the access paths in the database, the most common mode of access determines the optimal access path at runtime using an optimizer (see Figure 2–5).

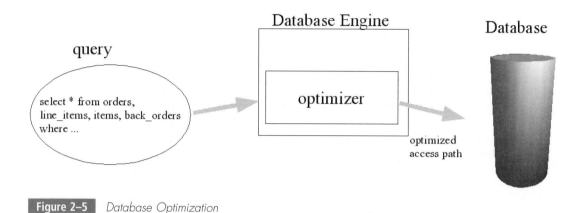

Figure 2–5 *Database Optimization*

When a SQL statement is presented to the database, the database engine must first evaluate the statement for correct syntax. The statement is first parsed, and the parameters in the statement are evaluated. For instance, a `select` statement must be evaluated to determine if the required clauses are present (the `select column list` and the `from` clause) and the parameters or objects of those clauses are valid database objects.

Once the statement has been parsed, the access path is then determined by the optimizer. There has been a great deal of study done on SQL optimizers and how to determine the most efficient query access paths. Some of the factors that are considered by the optimizer are the numbers of rows in the tables, the presence of indexes, the uniqueness of the indexed data, statistical skew of data, and the efficiency of a sort or a hash-merge-join operation.

DYNAMIC SQL EXECUTION

Most relational databases allow execution of dynamic SQL statements. These are SQL statements where some portion of the query is unknown until runtime. This could require the substitution of parameters or the complete construction of the query statement at runtime.

An example of this would be an ad-hoc report where the user chooses the columns to be returned in the report and the filter and sort criteria. In order for an application to process this report, it must be able to build the `select` statement at runtime. This can be accomplished fairly easily using JDBC; because the query to be executed is a string parameter, the application must merely concatenate an SQL `select` statement into the string parameter for the query and then execute it.

Or better yet, the statement could be reviewed, optimized and *prepared* by the database before it is executed. Parameters used to provide filter criteria for the dynamic statement could be identified and then the prepared statement could be saved by the program. When the parameters for the query are known at runtime, the prepared statement could be retrieved and executed using the runtime parameters. Presumably the database engine, having reviewed and optimized the query previously, would be able to execute the query quicker. Techniques for creating dynamic queries using the various techniques available to JDBC developers will be shown in Chapter 10.

SUMMARY

Programming using JDBC implies working with a database—most likely a relational database. This chapter covered some of the basics of the relational database, providing background information and common terminology.

Relational databases are grounded in mathematics and have succeeded in large part because of their flexibility over other alternatives. (To change the table structure on many network databases requires the entire database to be unloaded and then reloaded.)

The SQL query language is the most widely adopted language for manipulating relational databases and the subject of various international standards. This nonprocedural language allows complex queries to be phrased succinctly. Though powerful, it does have its limitations. This has led database vendors to extend the language and in the process has diluted the benefit of a standard query language.

Transactions, the ability to group multiple database updates together as a single update, is an important and widely used feature of relational databases. Combined with isolation levels, these are very important considerations for developers, a topic that will be discussed again in Chapter 9 and demonstrated in various code examples throughout the text.

COMING UP NEXT

Chapter 3 begins the detailed coverage of the JDBC API. This discussion will focus on the API: the actual interfaces and class definitions that comprise the JDBC API.

Code examples in the first few chapters will be short and concise. They will be used to illustrate how to use the API, focusing on specific method calls and how they are used. Later chapters will use longer, more extensive examples to demonstrate how JDBC is used in complete applications.

The JDBC API Explained

INTRODUCTION

To write a database application, certain events need to take place: You must load a database driver, you must create a connection to the database, you must execute a query, and if the query has results, you must receive the results and process them. It is precisely this sequence of events that has driven the design of the JDBC API.

The JDBC specification provides Java interfaces that reflect database interaction in a Java program. These are `DataSource`, `Driver`, `DriverManager`, `Connection`, `Statement`, `PreparedStatement`, and `ResultSet`. These are the interfaces that are defined as part of the JDBC specification and must be implemented by driver providers.

This chapter will cover the basics of the JDBC API, including the origin of the API and the goals of those who developed the specification. To introduce some of the basic concepts of using JDBC, a short example program will show how to connect to a database, execute a query, and retrieve and examine the results.

PURPOSE

The purpose of the JDBC API is to provide vendor-neutral access to relational databases. The implementation differences of the various databases used are *abstracted* from the user through the use of the JDBC API. Though the specification does not indicate that the API is to be used solely for relational databases (in fact, it can be used to access any tabular data including a spreadsheet or flat file), historically it has been used primarily for relational database access.

The developers of the JDBC API specification have tried to keep the API as simple as possible so that it can be a foundation upon which other APIs are built. For instance, the `Connector` API could be implemented on top of an existing JDBC API using appropriate resource adapters.

THE STRUCTURE OF JDBC

JDBC is composed of a number of interfaces and classes that are implemented by driver developers. As mentioned in Chapter 1, there are four different types of JDBC drivers that have been implemented, as listed in Table 3–1.

Part of the delineation between these types of drivers is what software is required by the client application, the application that will be using JDBC to communicate with the database.

Table 3–1   *JDBC Driver Types*

Driver	Description
Type 1	Implements JDBC by mapping JDBC calls to other CLI calls. Communicates with a binary library written in another language, using some form of inter-process communication. Requires software, such as the JDBC-ODBC bridge driver, on the client machine.
Type 2	Driver is composed partially of Java code and partially of native code using another CLI. Requires some client-side binary code. Native code runs in the Java VM.
Type 3	Pure Java driver; uses middleware to convert JDBC calls to vendor-specific calls.
Type 4	Pure Java driver; implements the native protocol. Does not require middleware or any client-side binary. Can be downloaded to a client if necessary.

Both the type 1 and type 2 drivers require a binary file on the client machine. A client application, however, could use a type 3 or type 4 driver to communicate with a database using JDBC and would not require any client-side binaries.

The type 4 JDBC driver is considered the best driver to use for two reasons. One reason is that since the driver has been written completely in Java, it is extremely portable. Another reason is that the driver is not required to map JDBC calls to corresponding native CLI calls. This avoids the overhead of mapping logic required by the type 1 or type 2 driver, or the overhead of communicating with middleware required by the type 3 driver. Such improvements in efficiency should allow the driver to execute faster than the other types of JDBC drivers.

HISTORY OF JDBC REVISIONS

The initial version of JDBC included the ability to connect to a database, create an SQL statement, execute the statement, and if there were results, retrieve the results and iterate serially through them. The process of reading the results of a query was done with a `ResultSet`, which is synonymous to a database cursor (a pointer into the results). While many database vendors at the time provided cursors that could be read both forwards and backwards, the initial version of JDBC could read the cursors only in one direction: serially.

Early versions of JDBC had process of connecting to the database using a connection string or URL, which provided details about the connection. While this connection process worked and was somewhat flexible, it was nevertheless problematic, since each program that needed to connect to the database needed the connection details. For large, complex applications communicating with a number of database servers, this connection process could become tedious. Also, the process of connecting to the database was expensive and time consuming and created problems for applications that needed to manage a large number of connections.

In JDBC 2.0, a set of optional extensions in JDBC (meaning driver developers did not need to provide these features for compliance) enhanced the connection process. A `DataSource` object was defined, which abstracted the details of the connection. This object could be obtained from an object server, a naming service that could receive a request for an object using an object name, a string that relates to the object (for example, `accountingDB`), and return a `DataSource` object, an instance of the implemented `javax.sql.DataSource` interface, containing the details of connecting to the database.

The Java Naming and Directory Interface (JNDI) provides a simple interface to various name servers and allows the `DataSource` object to be obtained through a simple call. Since the application doesn't carry around the details of connecting to the `DataSource`, changing the location of the actual database (it is not uncommon for a database to be moved from one server to another) allows the details to be changed in a single location and then broadcast to any application wishing to connect to the `DataSource`.

Additional features were added in the JDBC 2.0 extensions including support for *scroll cursors* and updateable ResultSet objects. These `ResultSet` objects can be read both forwards and backwards using both relative and absolute positioning within the set. Though not required for JDBC compliance, most major database vendors have provided these features in their JDBC driver.

SQL ESCAPE SYNTAX

While SQL provides a somewhat standardized query language, there are some areas of syntax in the standard that are not clearly defined. Syntax for these areas of the language can vary from database to database. JDBC provides an escape syntax that lets the driver map the values provided into the correct syntax.

JDBC provides the escape syntax for stored procedures, dates, times, scalar functions, and outer joins. This syntax is then mapped to database-specific syntax by the driver and is provided via an escape clause denoted by curly brackets, as follows:

```
{keyword ... parameters }
```

Stored Procedures, Time and Date Literals, and Scalar Functions

The syntax used to call a stored procedure uses the SQL escape sequence, as follows:

```
{call this_proc( arg1, arg2 ...) }
```

If the stored procedure returns a value, it is called as follows:

```
{? = call this_proc( arg1, arg2 ...) }
```

Databases use slightly different syntax for their representation of date and time. An escape clause is used by the driver to format this representation in such a way that the current database understands it. The following is an example of a date and time literal:

```
// datetime literal

 { d 'yyyy-mm-dd' }
```

```
// timestamp literal

{ ts 'hh:mm:ss' }
```

Scalar Functions

Scalar functions are also available through the JDBC escape clause syntax. JDBC supports numeric, string, date, time, system, and conversion functions on scalar values. These functions are denoted by the keyword fn followed by the name of the function.

Some drivers may not support all of these functions. The metadata method getNumericFunctions returns a comma-separated list of the names of numeric functions, and getStringFunctions returns a comma-separated list of string functions. The functions potentially supported are listed in Appendix B of this book.

THE JDBC CODE STRUCTURE

The JDBC package is divided into two packages: java.sql and javax.sql. The java.sql is the core package initially created circa 1997 for the JDBC 1.0 release. The JDBC 2.0 release included a set of extensions to the JDBC package that were separated into the javax.sql package. The contents of these two packages are listed in Table 3–2.

Table 3–2   *java.sql Package Classes/Interfaces*

Class/Interface	Description
java.sql.Array	Used for storage of a database array type.
java.sql.BatchUpdateException	Java exception for batch updates.
java.sql.Blob	Used for storage of Blob data types. .
java.sql.CallableStatement	Used to create and execute stored procedures.
java.sql.Clob	Used for storage of the Clob data type.
java.sql.Connection	Used to create and manage a connection to the database.
java.sql.DataTruncation	An exception thrown for data truncation errors.
java.sql.DatabaseMetaData	Used to gather information about the underlying data source
java.sql.Date	Used to store a database Date data type. Subclasses java.util.Date.

Table 3–2   *java.sql Package Classes/Interfaces (cont.)*

Class/Interface	Description
java.sql.Driver	The database driver for a specific database.
java.sql.DriverManager	Automatically loads the drivers used by a JDBC instance. Provides access to the drivers loaded using a number of static methods.
java.sql.DriverPropertyInfo	Provides information on the properties of a driver.
java.sql.ParameterMetaData	Provides information on parameters for PreparedStatement objects as part of the JDBC 3.0 specification.
java.sql.PreparedStatement	Used to create and execute prepared statements, statements that have been registered and stored within the database before the statement is executed.
java.sql.Ref	Represents the Ref (reference) type.
java.sql.ResultSet	Used to iterate through a set of rows retrieved from the database.
java.sql.ResultSetMetaData	Used to gather information about a ResultSet.
java.sql.Savepoint	Used to create a transactional savepoint as part of the JDBC 3.0 specification.
java.sql.SQLData	Used for the custom mapping of SQL types;. not expected to be called by the programmer;. intended for use internally by vendor tools.
java.sql.SQLException	Standard Java exception for the JDBC class.
java.sql.SQLInput	An SQL input stream.
java.sql.SQLOutput	An SQL output stream.
java.sql.SQLPermission	Used with the Java SecurityManager to provide security for JDBC applications running in restricted environment.
java.sql.SQLWarning	Contains information about the SQL Warning generated by the last statement executed.
java.sql.Statement	Used to create and execute an SQL statement.
java.sql.Struct	Used to represent the database Struct data type.
java.sql.Time	Used to represent the database Time data type.
java.sql.Timestamp	Used to represent the database TimeStamp data type.
java.sql.Types	Defines constants used to define custom SQL types.

These various interfaces and classes are implemented to create JDBC drivers. Some are more obscure than others so that not all those listed are commonly used. Those more commonly used are as follows:

* `DriverManager`
* `Connection`
* `Statement`
* `PreparedStatement`
* `ResultSet`

The following sections provide a brief introduction to how these classes are used in a JDBC application.

The DriverManager Class

The `DriverManager` class is responsible for managing access to the drivers that have been loaded by the JDBC application. Since more than one driver can be loaded at any particular time, the `DriverManager` must select among the drivers to determine which driver will be used. It makes this determination based on a call to its `getConnection` method. The `getConnection` method is passed a string that provides the URL of the database to be used for the connection. Based on the contents of this database URL, the `DriverManager` selects a driver to manage the connection and then returns a `Connection` object to be used by the application.

The Connection Class

The `Connection` class is used primarily to create `Statement` objects, which are used to execute SQL statements against the database. An object of the `Connection` class type is returned by the `DriverManager` (as a return value from the `getConnection` method). At that point, the `Connection` object represents the connection to the database specified in the URL passed to the `getConnection` method.

The `Connection` class also provides a number of methods to determine the properties of and the state of the connection to the database. Transactions are managed through this class, which contains a method for committing data to the database and for altering the auto-commit behavior of the connection. (By default, JDBC drivers will commit the results of each single SQL statement to the database, which means that you must make an explicit call on the `Connection` object to begin using transactions.)

Since there is significant overhead to creating connections to a database (this is due to resources that must be allocated in the database server and is not an issue with the JDBC driver or the Java language), it is useful to create a pool of connections with physical database connections on application startup and then use connections from this pool. The `javax.sql.PooledConnection` class is an optional though widely implemented interface that provides this capability. (Pooled connections are virtually transparent to the developer; they require no special coding on the part of the developer.)

The Statement Class

The `Statement` class is used to execute SQL statements against a database. The statements can be SQL `select` statements or some type of `update` statement (`insert`, `update`, `delete`) or a Data Definition Language statement(`create table`, `create index`). The result of the execution of a `select` statement is stored in a `ResultSet` object. The result of the execution of an `update` statement returns an integer value indicating the number of rows updated by the statement.

Batch update capabilities are an optional though widely supported set of features. These features allow multiple `update` statements to be grouped together and sent to the database for processing at the same time.

The PreparedStatement Class

The `PreparedStatement` class is similar to the `Statement` class in that it allows a SQL statement to be executed against the database. But unlike the `Statement` class, the `PreparedStatement` class presents the query to the database before it is executed. The database engine then processes the query which includes parsing the statement, setting aside storage for any parameters that may be passed at runtime, and determining the most efficient method of executing the statement. The database engine stores a reference to the processed or *prepared* statement. When a call against the `PreparedStatement` object is made to execute the statement, the prepared statement in the database is used to perform the operation. For statements that must be executed multiple times, using the `PreparedStatement` can potentially provide improved performance.

The ResultSet Class

The `ResultSet` class is used to iterate through a set of rows (or tuples) returned from the execution of a SQL `select` statement. This class provides methods to iterate serially through the set, or if the JDBC driver and database support it, to iterate backwards and forwards through the `ResultSet`. In order to use a scroll cursor capability, the underlying data store must support the capability. A method is available to determine the type of the `ResultSet` object that indicates whether or not the cursor is scrollable.

The javax.sql Package

The `javax.sql` package was originally introduced as part of the JDBC 2.0 Standard Extensions, an optional package that was not part of the JDBC core package. In JDBC 3.0, it is considered part of the core JDBC API though drivers are not required to support all of the features to be compliant. The `java.sql` package includes the classes and interfaces listed in Table 3–3.

The `javax.sql` package does not replace the JDBC API but instead supplements the API. For the `javax.sql` package to be used, an existing JDBC implementation must be in place.

Table 3–3   *The javax.sql Package Classes/Interfaces*

Class/Interface	Description
`javax.sql.ConnectionEvent` `javax.sql.ConnectionEventListener`	Used to create event listeners for database connections.
`javax.sql.ConnectionPoolDataSource`	Used to create event listeners for database connections.
`javax.sql.DataSource`	Used to create a connection to a data source that supports connection pooling.
`javax.sql.PooledConnection`	A data source that represents an underlying data store and manages connections to the data store.
`javax.sql.RowSet`	A connection that interfaces with an underlying pool of connections.
`javax.sql.RowSetEvent`	Extends the `ResultSet` class and adds support for JavaBeans; a `RowSet` can be used as a JavaBean.
`javax.sql.RowSetInternal`	Used to manage events on a `RowSet`.
`javax.sql.RowSetListener`	Manages `RowSetObjects`.
`javax.sql.RowSetMetaData`	Provides an event listener for a `RowSet`.
`javax.sql.RowSetReader`	Used to gather information on a `RowSet`.
`javax.sql.RowSetWriter`	Provides a `Reader` for `RowSet`.
`javax.sql.XAConnection`	Provides a `Writer` for a `RowSet`.
`javax.sql.XADataSource`	A connection that supports distributed transactions.
	A connection to an `XADataSource` used to provide distributed transactions.

The DataSource Class

The `DataSource` class, the implementation of `javax.sql.DataSource`, provides an abstraction for a connection to a database. The `DataSource` encapsulates the details of the database connection, thus removing from the application the responsibility of managing these details.

The `DataSource` object is usually retrieved using JNDI. This allows the configuration and location of the database to be controlled at a central location and broadcast to the applications that require access to the database.

The `DataSource` class allows additional features to be added to the connection process. For instance, connection pooling and distributed transaction support are both implemented through data sources.

Using Connection Pooling

Connection pooling provides for the efficient management of connections to the database being supported. The process of connecting to a database is time consuming and needs to be avoided for any application that must create and then drop a large number of connections.

Connection pooling is implemented through a `DataSource` object, so a client application would need to obtain an appropriate data source object to use connection pooling. A JDBC driver is not required to support connection pooling, though many do.

Connection pooling is transparent to the application code. An application coded for a nonpooled connection should not require code changes to begin using a pooled connection.

Distributed Transactions with XADataSource

Distributed transaction support allows database transactions to span multiple databases from different vendors on multiple servers. This requires the support of a *transaction manager* that is in communication with the various participants in the transaction.

An implementation of the `XADataSource` interface provides access to distributed transactions. This interface is usually implemented by the JDBC driver provider or as required by the J2EE specification, a J2EE application server provider.

JavaBean Wrapper Support (Rowsets)

The `RowSet` class effectively wraps the `ResultSet` class with JavaBean event functionality. This class makes it easier for the developers of visual programming environments to create JDBC objects for integration into those environments.

JDBC EXAMPLE

Often the best method for learning a new API is to look at a basic, minimal implementation of the classes and methods. The following code provides just such a demonstration using only four JDBC classes—implementations of the JDBC interfaces shown in Table 3–4.

Table 3–4   *Core JDBC Classes/Interfaces*

Interface/Class	Purpose
`java.sql.DriverManager`	Loads the JDBC driver and manages the connection.
`java.sql.Connection`	Connects to the database and allows the creation of `Statement` objects.
`java.sql.Statement`	Allows the execution of SQL statements and returns results, either integer values for the number of rows updated or `ResultSet` objects representing the rows returned by the execution of a SQL `select` statement.
`java.sql.ResultSet`	Allows access to individual rows in the set of rows returned by a SQL `select` statement query.

The basic process for a single data retrieval operation using JDBC would be as follows.

- a JDBC driver would be loaded;
- a database `Connection` object would be created from using the `DriverManager` (using the database driver loaded in the first step);
- a `Statement` object would be created using the `Connection` object;
- a SQL `select` statement would be executed using the `Statement` object, and a `ResultSet` would be returned;
- the `ResultSet` would be used to step through (or iterate through) the rows returned and examine the data.

The following code sample demonstrates this sequence of calls.

JDBCExample1.java

```
1.import java.sql.*;
2.
3.public class JDBCExample1 {
```

```
4.
5.public static void main( String args[] ) {
6.
7.String connectionURL =
8.  "jdbc:postgresql://localhost:5432/movies;user=puser;password=puser";
9.
10.try {
11.
12.      // load the Driver class
13.      Class.forName("org.postgresql.Driver");
14.
15.      // create the connection using the static getConnection method
16.      Connection con = DriverManager.getConnection( connectionURL );
17.
18.      // create a Statement class to execute the SQL statement
19.      Statement stmt = con.createStatement();
20.
21.      // execute the SQL statement and get the results in a ResultSet
22.      ResultSet rs   =
23.      stmt.executeQuery(
24.              "select movie_name, release_date from movies" );
25.
26.      // iterate through the ResultSet, displaying two values
27.      // for each row using the getString method
28.      //
29.      while ( rs.next() )
30.              System.out.println( "******************" + "\n" +
31.                              "movie_name: " + "\t" +
32.                                      rs.getString("movie_name") + "\n" +
33.                              "release_date: " + "\t" +
34.                                      rs.getString("release_date")   );
35.
36.}
37.catch (SQLException e) {
38.      e.printStackTrace();
39.}
40.catch (Exception e) {
41.      e.printStackTrace();
42.}
43.finally {
44.      // should always close the connection when done
45.      //
46.      con.close();
47.}
48.
49.}
50.
51.}
```

This example provides a simple, straightforward sample of JDBC code. In an effort to be succinct and keep the sample easy, the JDBC calls to create the load the driver, create the connection, and create the statement are all located in one block of code (the Java `main` programming block, no less). In production code, this code, which is responsible for locating the loading the driver, should be placed elsewhere. It is generally considered good practice to encapsulate the process of locating and loading the database driver in a set of database utility classes.

This code sample also shows the original JDBC process for loading the database driver: using the `class.forName` call to load the `Driver` class and then passing a connection URL to the static `DriverManager getConnection` method to obtain a connection to the database.

Now the preferred method for connecting using JDBC is to use a `DataSource` object. This involves locating and retrieving a `DataSource` object and then using the object to create a connection to the database. The steps involved in this process will be shown in Chapter 4.

Though the `DataSource` method is the better approach to performing these tasks, the actual difference in the code for the two approaches is not significant. And demonstrating the older method in this example will help highlight the benefits of using the `DataSource` for connections.

Since only the core JDBC classes will be used in this example, an `import` statement on line 1 only imports `java.sql`. On lines 7 and 8, a string is created and initialized to store the connection URL for the database. The connection URL contains the details of the database connection in a format that tends to vary for each database vendor. To find the correct format for a connection URL it is necessary to consult the vendor's documentation. The URL specified in this example is as follows:

```
jdbc:postgresql://localhost:5432/movies;user=puser;password=puser
```

The basic structure of the connection URL is that of the character constant `jdbc` followed by a colon (:) and a subprotocol then followed by a colon and a subname, as follows:

```
jdbc:<subprotocol>:<subname>
```

The subprotocol identifies a database connectivity mechanism that the driver may support. In this example, the subprotocol of `postgresql` is specified, indicating the protocol of the underlying database will be used by the JDBC driver.

The URL then contains the subname for the connection. The subname is dependent on the subprotocol. If a network address is to be used as part of the subname, then the naming convention should follow that of standard URL server names as follows:

```
//hostname:port/
```

Using this scheme, the URL for the PostgreSQL database would be as shown below (and in the code example).

```
//localhost:5432/movies;user=puser;password=puser
```

The server name and port is then followed by the name of the database to connect to and the user name and password for the connection. This information is optional, and the format is specific to the database vendor.

Continuing with our example, on line 13 the database driver is loaded using the `Class.forName` call to dynamically load the class when the program is executed. In this example, the string `org.postgresql.Driver` is used to indicate the fully qualified class name of the `Driver` class. The content of this string is also vendor-specific.

Once the driver has been loaded, a connection is obtained using the static `getConnection` method of the `DriverManager`. As shown on line 16 in the code sample, the call to the `getConnection` method takes the connection URL string shown above. Using the information in the connection URL, the `DriverManager` determines which database driver to use (since multiple drivers may be loaded) and then makes the internal calls to connect to the database. It returns a `Connection` object representing a connection to the database, as specified in the connection URL.

The `Connection` object is used to create `Statement` objects to use to execute SQL statements against the database. This is done on line 19 in the example.

The `Statement` object uses different methods to execute a query depending on whether the query is an `update` statement (`executeUpdate`) or a `select` statement (`executeQuery`). In this example, the `executeQuery` method is called on line 23. This method will execute an SQL `select` statement and return its results in a `ResultSet` object.

On line 29, a Java `while` loop is used to iterate through the results returned. The `ResultSet` class has a `next` method and the first call to this method will position the underlying cursor before the first row returned in the `ResultSet`. The `next` method returns a boolean value indicating whether or not there is a current row. (So a `select` query that returned no rows would return `false` on the first call to the `next` method.) As long as the `next` method returns `true`, then there is a row that can be examined and the `while` loop will continue.

The `ResultSet` class includes a set of `getXXXX` methods that can be used to examine the results in the current row. There is a `getXXXX` method for the various data types that can be returned from a database query. Most current relational database implementations are flexible about allowing nonstring data types to be converted to strings. In this example, both columns are retrieved using the `getString` method, but the `release_date` column retrieved on line 34 is not a string: It is a SQL `Date` data type. The call to the `getString` method will do the conversion for us.

All of the work with JDBC calls requires an enclosing Java `try/catch` block to catch the `SQLException` that may be thrown. On line 46 in the `try/catch`, the `Connection` is closed within the `finally` block of the `try/catch` block. Since Java guarantees that the `finally` block will always be executed (even in the event an exception has been thrown), we can be assured that the call to the `close` method will always occur. (It is always a good policy to close the database connection when it is no longer being used in an application or component.)

SUMMARY

This chapter began the discussion of the main topic of this book: the JDBC API. We examined the basis of the API, specifically what the developers were trying to accomplish when the API was designed. We also examined the core classes of the API and reviewed the popular extensions that were introduced in the JDBC 2.0.

To conclude the chapter, we examined a small example of the JDBC API in action. This example demonstrated the main steps in using JDBC: loading a database driver, opening a connection, obtaining a statement object, executing a query, and examining the results.

COMING UP NEXT

In Chapter 4, we will take a closer look at the process of obtaining a connection to the database. As we discovered in this chapter, there are two approaches to obtaining a connection with JDBC. The first approach, using a `DriverManager` class, was shown in this chapter. In the next chapter we will look at using a `DataSource` object to obtain a connection, and we will review what is needed to do that.

Getting Connected

INTRODUCTION

Before we can do anything significant with JDBC, we must get connected to the database. As we will find in this chapter, we will not connect directly to the database; we will connect with one or more layers of software, which will control our connection to the database. The reasons for using these layers of software will be explained in this chapter.

As we discussed in Chapter 3, there are two distinct approaches for connecting to a database using JDBC: using a `DriverManager` directly or using a `DataSource` connection. This chapter will present both approaches.

LOADING THE DATABASE DRIVER

There is, unfortunately, no standard protocol for direct communication with relational databases. Each relational database vendor has created a proprietary low-level protocol for communicating with its database engine.

In the intensely competitive world of database software, there is a continuous effort to make database operations fast, efficient, and accurate. Part of the effort to create fast and accurate communication has involved tweaking the communication protocol and the APIs that use that protocol. For this reason, database vendors regard their low-level communication protocols as trade secrets. This competition led to the creation of different database APIs and different communication protocols for each vendor's product.

In order for the standardized API to work, a driver must be created to map the standard JDBC calls to the vendor's proprietary communication protocol. And since each database vendor has a different communication protocol, a different driver is needed for each vendor.

Prior to the JDBC 2.0 API, the only method available for loading a JDBC driver was to use a *driver manager* by calling static members of the `DriverManager` class. Using this approach, the JDBC driver would be loaded by the static initializers when the class was loaded using the `Class.forName` call, as shown below.

```
...
Class.forName( "org.postgresql.driver");
...
```

This call will lead to the class identified by the fully qualified class name provided as a parameter to the `forName` call to be loaded. When coded as shown, with a string constant for the class name, it tends to tie the source code to the particular driver and reduces the portability of the code. Following this call, a call must be made to connect to the database. That call must address the specifics of the connection as shown in the following code snippet.

```
...
Connection con = DriverManager.getConnection(
   "jdbc:postgresql://localhost:5432/movies;user=puser;password=puser");
...
```

This connection URL reveals a number of details about the database connection (including in this example the user name and password for the connection). Placing this in the application further reduces the portability of the code.

One solution to this problem of binding the source code to the database vendor is to take the connection details out of the application and place them in a properties file. The application will then read the properties file at startup. A Java properties file can contain lines for the connection URL and the driver manager class, as follows.

Properties File with JDBC DB Connection Information

```
connectionURL: jdbc:postgresql://localhost:5432/movies;user=puser;password=puser
driverManager: org.postgresql.driver
```

The properties file is then read when the application is started. The calls to load the driver manager (`Class.forName`) and connect to the database (`DriverManager.getConnection`) will use the properties from the properties file, as shown in the following code snippet:

```
1.import java.sql.*;
2.import java.util.*;
3.import java.io.*;
4....
5.try {
6.
7.      Properties prop = new Properties();
8.      prop.load( new FileInputStream( "basic.properties" ) );
9.
10.     // load the Driver class
11.     Class.forName(
12.            prop.getProperty( "driverManagerClass" ) );
13.
14.     // create the connection using the static getConnection method
15.     Connection con = DriverManager.getConnection(
16.                   prop.getProperty( "connectionURL") );
17....
```

In this example, the appropriate package names are imported on lines 1 through 3 to allow the use of the `Properties` class (part of the `java.util` package), the `FileInputStream` class (the `java.io` package), and the JDBC API (the `java.sql` package). On line 7 a `Properties` object is created and loaded on line 8 with a call to the `load` method. The `load` method requires an `InputStream` object argument, which is returned by the `FileInputStream` constructor.

Once the `Properties` class `load` method has been called, the properties can be accessed using the `get` method. The end result of these efforts is that on lines 12 and 16 the details of loading the database driver and the connection to the database are not written into the application. The details are retrieved from a properties file (`basic.properties`). Should these details change because a database has been moved or a server name has been changed, then the change would only need to be made in the properties file. The application code could remain untouched.

This does provide a solution to the problem of binding database specifics to application code. But this solution generally requires a file to be present on the machine where the application is run. This means that if the application is moved from one machine to another, the file must follow and must be placed in the correct directory. Should the application be deployed across several machines, each of the machines would require a copy of the file. Should some of the database details change and the application is deployed across several machines, the file would need to be changed on each of the machines.

A more robust and increasingly popular solution available through the JDBC 2.0 standard extension (and part of JDBC 3.0) is the use of `DataSources` with JNDI. Using JNDI, a `DataSource` is looked up through a service, which returns an appropriate `DataSource` object reference. Using the `DataSource` object reference, a connection that corresponds to the `DataSource` can be established with the database. To understand the benefits of this approach, it is important to understand the functionality provided by JNDI.

JNDI and Name Spaces

JNDI provides a uniform, standard method of accessing resources over a network. It builds on the existing technology of naming services, and creates a standardized Java API for accessing the resources provided by these servers. Using JNDI, a Java application can create a *federated* or combined space for existing name spaces provided by multiple servers.

Naming services have been in existence for some time. These servers are referred to by various names, including directory servers (LDAP, NDIS), registries (RMI registry, Windows/NT registry), and name servers (DNS).

A *name server* maps a name, an arbitrary string, to an IP address. A *directory server* maps a key to a value. Directory servers have generally been used to store information about users on the network, information such as the user name, phone number, email, and password. Directory servers primarily use the standard LDAP (Lightweight Directory Access Protocol) for communications, but some vendors offer extensions to this protocol.

Directory servers are used to store more than just user profile information. Because of their speed and low cost, they are used to store any *query-intensive* data that must be globally accessible. This query-intensive data are entities that are not updated on a constant basis and remain relatively static over a period of time, such as employee information or corporate building addresses.

It is possible to make all of these servers available under JNDI using a Service Provider Interface (SPI) developed for the specific server. Where JNDI really offers value is in providing a common interface to the various disparate servers it is used to access.

JNDI works with one or more *context*. A context is effectively a *name space,* and within a name space are resources that are identified by a key. A resource is an object that is stored or bound into the name space using a key and can be retrieved by the key. Name spaces can optionally form a hierarchy much like a directory hierarchy, so that a series of entries relating to computer servers could be organized as follows.

```
/regional
      /corporate_it
```

```
        /corporate_backup
/national
        /north
                /local
                        /departmental
                                /accounting
                                /finance
                                /human_resources
        /south
                /local
                        /departmental
                                /accounting
                                /finance
                                /human_resources
```

Using this example, a fully qualified path name for a server in the national north region would be
`/national/north/local/departmental/human_resources`.

Not all name spaces will support hierarchies. Some name spaces are *flat* and only allow binding for key (name) and corresponding values.

The JNDI API requires a Service Provider Interface (SPI) implementation in order to work with the various name servers and directory servers. The SPI implementation is defined in a set of Java interfaces that must be implemented. At runtime, the JNDI application must have the implementing classes for the SPI in its CLASSPATH.

The JNDI API implements the factory design pattern for the management of contexts. This factory pattern implementation is responsible for the creation of objects to manage contexts. Since the behavior of a context may vary depending upon the type of underlying server, we must identify the context factory, the class that will be responsible for managing the context, before we begin working with JNDI.

This can be done in one of several ways. In the following example, a `Hashtable` is created, and entries are added for the `INITIAL_CONTEXT_FACTORY` (the class to manage the initial context or name space). We must also be able to communicate with a directory or naming service in order to use the service, so we need a URL for accessing the service. In this example, the `PROVIDER_URL` (where JNDI will connect to access the service) is also placed in the `Hashtable`.

```
. . .
    Hashtable env = new Hashtable();
    env.put(Context.INITIAL_CONTEXT_FACTORY,
     "com.sun.jndi.rmi.registry.RegistryContextFactory" );
    env.put(Context.PROVIDER_URL, "rmi://localhost:1099");
    // get the initial context
    InitialContext ctx = new InitialContext( env );
. . .
```

But this approach to obtaining the initial context inserts details about the directory server into the code and would require the code to change should the location or vendor of the directory server change. An alternative approach is to place the details of the JNDI service into a properties file named `jndi.proper-ties`. If this properties file is in the CLASSPATH for the application, it will be read, and if the appropriate properties for the initial context are provided, they will be used to obtain the initial context. If a JNDI properties file is available, then the `no-arg` constructor for the `InitialContext` can be used as shown in the following code snippet.

```
...
// initial context is retrieved from the "jndi.properties" file.
InitialContext ctx = new InitialContext(  );
...
```

At a minimum, in order to obtain the initial context, the `jndi.properties` file must contain the following lines:

```
java.naming.factory.initial=com.sun.jndi.rmi.registry.RegistryContextFactory
java.naming.provider.url=rmi://localhost:1099
```

If the directory server is not a local resource (for instance, it is a server on the network), then a security manager must be provided. The `jndi.properties` file could optionally contain an entry for the `java.naming.rmi.security.man-ager` property, or a default security manager for the SPI will be used. Appropriate security manager entries must be made, granting the applications that will be using the SPI permission to connect and dynamically download classes.

Once the initial context is obtained, we can begin using JNDI. The resources available through the JNDI server can be any arbitrary type supported by the SPI being used for the context. The `lookup` method is used to retrieve the resource (the value) stored using the key (or name). The `lookup` method returns an `Object` reference and requires a cast to convert the `Object` reference to the correct reference for the stored value, as shown in the following example:

```
...
    // get the DataSource from the JNDI name server
    DataSource ds = (DataSource) ctx.lookup("movies");
...
```

Now that we know about JNDI and the ability to load resources using this API, we can connect this to our discussion of JDBC. Using JNDI, we can conveniently load a JDBC `DataSource`. Using data sources allows us to transparently use some of the various features of the JDBC 2.0 Standard Extensions. The next section will examine the loading and use of data sources.

JNDI AND DATASOURCES

The JNDI API is integral to the use of `DataSources`. JNDI and `DataSource` objects have the potential to make the life of the Java developer and the application deployer easier. The following code snippet provides an example of using JNDI to obtain a JDBC connection.

BasicExample5.java

```
1.import java.sql .*;
2.import javax.sql.*;
3.import javax.naming.*;
4.import java.util.*;
5.import com.codestudio.sql.PoolMan;
6.
7.public class BasicExample5 {
8.
9.
10.public static void main( String args[] ) {
11.
12.Connection con=null;
13.try {
14.
15.     // Can set these here, or in a "jndi.properties"
16.     // properties file in the classpath
17.     //
18.     Hashtable env = new Hashtable();
19.     env.put(Context.INITIAL_CONTEXT_FACTORY,
20.      "com.sun.jndi.rmi.registry.RegistryContextFactory" );
21.     env.put(Context.PROVIDER_URL, "rmi://localhost:1099");
22.
23.     // get the initial context
24.     InitialContext ctx = new InitialContext( env );
25.
26.     // get the DataSource from the JNDI name server
27.     DataSource ds = (DataSource) ctx.lookup("movies");
28.
29.     // get the connection from the DataSource
30.     con = ds.getConnection( );
```

In this code example, a number of packages are imported on lines 1 through 5. The `java.sql` package is imported for the JDBC API, and the `javax.sql` package is imported for the JDBC 2.0 standard extensions. Additionally, the `java.util` package is imported for the `Hashtable` created on line 19. On line 5, the `Poolman` package is imported and used to provide the various JDBC capabilities that the current PostgreSQL driver does not support (`DataSource`, JNDI lookup, connection pooling, and scroll cursors).

On line 18, a `Hashtable` is created and two entries are added to the `Hashtable`. These entries are needed to create the JNDI `InitialContext` that will be used to find the `DataSource`. Two key/value entries are added into the `Hashtable` on lines 19 and 21: the initial context factory, used for creating the initial or topmost context for the directory server, and the provider URL for making the connection to the directory server provider are set. For local resources, which this example demonstrates, these two entries are required to create the `InitialContext`. Some operating environments such as application servers place these properties in the program's environment and they do not need to be set explicitly in the code.

On line 24, a call is made to the constructor for the `InitialContext`. This call is passed the `Hashtable` created and loaded on lines 18 and 21. Using the `Context` object returned by the constructor, a call is made to the `Context` `lookup` method on line 27. The `lookup` method looks for bindings in the name space of the service provider here and, if it finds a match, returns an appropriate object reference. Since the `lookup` method returns an `Object` reference, it must be cast up to the correct object type that has been returned. In our case, we know we have returned a `DataSource` reference and we cast the object to that type on line 27.

Once we have a `DataSource` object, we can call the `getConnection` method to make a connection to the underlying database which is done on line 30. Since the `DataSource` object encapsulates the connection details, we do not need to specify the database connection specifics in our `getConnection` call.

LOADING JDBC DRIVERS WITH THE DRIVERMANAGER

As shown in the previous example, the JDBC driver can be explicitly loaded using the `Class forName` method. But the `DriverManager` can also load JDBC drivers implicitly. When the `DriverManager` class is loaded, static initializers in the class definitions are executed and look for entries in the `jdbc.drivers` System property. If there are entries in this property, then each of the entries is treated as a driver class and is loaded by the driver manager. For example, the system `jdbc.drivers` property could be set using the following command line:

```
java -Djdbc.drivers=org.postgresql.Driver BasicExample1
```

This command line would set the `System` property as instructed, have the `DriverManager` load the `org.postgresql.Driver` class, the driver for the PostgreSQL database, and execute the program `BasicExample1`. (The `-D` argument to the Java runtime indicates the next string on the command line is to be used to set a `System` property.) The program `BasicExample1` would not need to explicitly load the PostgreSQL database driver; the `DriverManager` would load it based on the `System` property setting.

Alternatively, as shown in the example in the previous chapter, the database driver could be loaded explicitly using the `Class.forName` call, as shown in the following code snippet:

```
// load the Driver class
Class.forName("org.postgresql.Driver");
```

This code would explicitly load the class `org.postgresql.Driver`, the driver for the PostgreSQL database. (The `Class.forName` method returns a reference to an object of the class loaded, but the return value is ignored in these examples.)

The `DriverManager` is responsible for managing the connections for the database. The static `getConnection` method of the `DriverManager` class is used to create JDBC `Connection` objects. The `DriverManager` can load more than one `Driver`, and the `Driver` can create one or more `Connection` objects (see Figure 4–1).

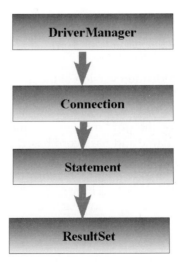

Figure 4–1   *Relationship between DriverManager and Managed Objects*

Since more than one database driver could be loaded in a particular application you may think there should be some way to direct the DriverManager to use the correct driver. But the DriverManager takes the responsibility for finding the correct driver to manage a connection. It determines which driver to use by checking the URL argument passed to the getConnection method. The getConnection method (and all overloaded versions) in the DriverManager class requires a URL parameter, as shown in the following code snippet:

```
...
    // create the connection using the static getConnection method
    Connection con = DriverManager.getConnection(
"jdbc:postgresql://localhost:5432/movies;user=puser;password=puser");
...
```

The database connection URL carries a great deal of information about the database connection, including the server and TCP/IP port where the database can be found and the database name. In the previous example, the user name and password were also part of the database connection URL, though they can also be passed as separate arguments to the getConnection method, as shown in the following code snippet:

```
...
    // create the connection using the static getConnection method
    Connection con = DriverManager.getConnection(
        "jdbc:postgresql://localhost:5432/movies",  // connection URL
        "puser",                                     // user name
        "puser");                                    // user password
...
```

With this overloaded version of the getConnection method, the first argument is the database connection URL (minus the user name and password), the next argument is the user name, and the final argument is the password for the user. (This form of the getConnection method is useful for applications that must set the user name and password based on some information passed into the application.)

The following code sample demonstrates the use of the DriverManager class to create database connections:

BasicExample1.java

```
1.import java.sql.*;
2.
3.public class BasicExample1 {
4.
5.
6.public static void main( String args[] ) {
```

```
7.
8.String connectionURL =
9.  "jdbc:postgresql://localhost:5432/movies;user=puser;password=puser";
10.
11.try {
12.
13.
14.      // load the Driver class
15.      Class.forName("org.postgresql.Driver");
16.
17.      // create the connection using the static getConnection method
18.      Connection con = DriverManager.getConnection( connectionURL );
19.
20.      // create a Statement class to execute the SQL statement
21.      Statement stmt = con.createStatement();
22.
23.      // execute the SQL statement and get the results in a ResultSet
24.      ResultSet rs   = stmt.executeQuery(
25.                     "select movie_name, release_date from movies" );
26.
27.      // iterate through the ResultSet, displaying two values
28.      // for each row using the getString method
29.      //
30.      while ( rs.next() )
31.              System.out.println( "*****************" + "\n" +
32.                              "movie_name: " + "\t" +
33.                              rs.getString("movie_name") + "\n" +
34.                              "release_date: " + "\t" +
35.                              rs.getString("release_date")  );
36.
37.    // close the connection
38.    con.close();
39.
40.}
41.catch (SQLException e) {
42.      // display SQL specific exception information
43.      System.out.println("**************************" );
44.      System.out.println("SQLException in main: " + e.getMessage() );
45.      System.out.println("** SQLState: " + e.getSQLState());
46.      System.out.println("** SQL Error Code: " + e.getErrorCode());
47.      System.out.println("**************************" );
48.      e.printStackTrace();
49.}
50.catch (Exception e) {
51.      e.printStackTrace();
52.}
53.
54.}
55.
56.}
57.
```

The code sample uses a single `import` statement on line 1 to provide access to the JDBC package. On lines 8 and 9 a string is used to load the database connection URL for the "movies" database used in this example. On line 15, the appropriate `Driver` class implementation is loaded explicitly, using a `Class.forName` call with a string argument containing the name of the class to load.

At this point in the application, a `DriverManager` is available and an appropriate JDBC driver has been loaded for the PostgreSQL database. All that must be done is to request a connection to the database, which is done on line 18, using a call to the static `getConnection` method in the `DriverManager` class. The call to the `getConnection` method passes the following connection URL:

```
jdbc:postgresql://localhost:5432/movies;user=puser;password=puser
```

The first part of this connection URL indicates the protocol, the subprotocol, and the server host, using the following format.

```
<protocol>:<subprotocol>:<serverhost:serverport>
```

In this example, the protocol is `jdbc`, the subprotocol is `postgresql`, the server host is the `localhost`, and the server port is `5432`.

The remainder of the URL string is proprietary. In this example, the server name and port is followed by a forward slash and the name of the database to be accessed by the connection. A semicolon follows the database, and a parameter for the user name and the user password are supplied, separated by a semicolon.

The call to the `getConnection` method of the `DriverManager` class returns a `Connection` object, which now represents the connection to the database. On line 21 of this example, the `Connection` object is used to create a `Statement` object. The purpose of the `Statement` object, as explained previously, is to execute SQL statements against the database.

The `executeQuery` method of the `Statement` object is used to execute a simple SQL statement on line 24. The `executeQuery` method returns a `ResultSet` object, an object that represents the set of rows returned by the execution of the SQL statement. The `ResultSet` object will be explained in detail in Chapter 8, but suffice to say at this point the `ResultSet` object must be used to access the results of the query. In this example, this is done in a simple fashion on line 30. A Java `while` loop is executed based on the results of the `ResultSet` `next` method. The `next` method will return a boolean `true` if there are rows remaining in the `ResultSet`. If there is a row to output, the code on lines 31 through 35 will be executed to output the values of the columns in the rows. The `getString` method of the `ResultSet` class is passed a string argument that corresponds to the column in the `ResultSet` to be retrieved. The `getString` method expects the column to be either a `String` data type or a data type that can easily be converted to a Java `String`.

At the conclusion of the execution of the `while` loop, all of the rows in the `ResultSet` have been output and the connection can be closed. This is done on line 38. Closing the connection will close all corresponding `Statement` objects and will also terminate any database activity on the part of the `Connection`. Since this example is not using a pooled connection, the *true* database connection will be closed, and communication between this application and the database server will be terminated.

TIP

Pooled Connections

With a *pooled connection,* calling the `close` method on the `Connection` object will not execute a true close, since the database connection is part of a pool of connections. Instead, the pool manager will just set a flag indicating the connection is no longer being used and can be distributed to another user requesting a connection. In most cases, any open transactions on the connection will be rolled back, but this is not a requirement of the JDBC specification and could change depending on the database, the database configuration, and the configuration of the JDBC driver.

The output of this application for a small set of sample rows is as follows:

```
jdbc.drivers: org.postgresql.Driver
*******************
movie_name:    Gone with the Java
release_date:  2002-01-01
*******************
movie_name:    Here in the Code
release_date:  2002-02-01
*******************
movie_name:    The Adventures of Major Tom
release_date:  2002-03-01
*******************
movie_name:    Java in the City
release_date:  2001-01-01
*******************
movie_name:    Summer in the Code
release_date:  2001-09-01
*******************
movie_name:    More Trouble than Recursion
release_date:  2002-10-01
```

CREATING A CONNECTION USING A DATASOURCE

The recommended method for getting a database connection is to use a `DataSource`. One of the most significant advantages of this approach is that the details of the database connection (the URL, the user name, and password, if any) do not need to be known by the application. All the application needs to know is the name of the `DataSource`. Should the details of the `DataSource` change, they only need to be changed in one location, in the `DataSource` which is then bound into JNDI naming service.

The `DataSource` represents a layer of software above the database driver. The `DataSource` uses the database driver to add features to the database communication process. For instance, the `DataSource` can be configured to use a connection pool, a pool of database connections that are created and made available at runtime. Using a connection pool can make the process of gaining connection to the underlying database faster and more efficient. The following example shows how a connection can be accessed using a `DataSource` lookup using JNDI.

BasicExample3.java

```java
import java.sql.*;
import javax.sql.*;
import javax.naming.*;
import com.codestudio.sql.PoolMan;

public class BasicExample3 {
public static void main( String args[] ) {

Connection con=null;

try {
    //
    // the initialization properties for the
    // InitialContext constructor will be read from
    // the jndi.properties file in the CLASSPATH

    //
    // Create the initial naming context
    //
    InitialContext ctx = new InitialContext( );

    //
    // get the DataSource from the JNDI name server.
    // ('movies' name has been defined in poolman.xml and
    // bound to the naming service by Poolman).
    //
    DataSource ds = (DataSource) ctx.lookup("movies");

    //
```

```
    // get a connection from the DataSource
    //
    con = ds.getConnection( );

    //
    // create a Statement class to execute the SQL statement
    //
    Statement stmt = con.createStatement();

    //
    // execute the SQL statement and get the results in a ResultSet
    //
    ResultSet rs   = stmt.executeQuery(
            "select movie_name, release_date from movies" );

    //
    // iterate through the ResultSet, displaying two values
    // for each row using the getString method
    //
    while ( rs.next() ) {
        System.out.println( "******************" + "\n" +
                        "movie_name: " + "\t" +
                        rs.getString("movie_name") + "\n" +
                        "release_date: " + "\t" +
                        rs.getString("release_date")  );
    }


}
catch (SQLException e) {


    // display SQL specific exception information
    System.out.println("*************************" );
    System.out.println("SQLException in main: " + e.getMessage() );
    System.out.println("** SQLState: " + e.getSQLState());
    System.out.println("** SQL Error Code: " + e.getErrorCode());
    System.out.println("*************************" );
    e.printStackTrace();
}
catch (NamingException e) {
    System.out.println( "NamingException in main: " +
                        e.getMessage() );
}
catch (Exception e) {
    System.out.println("Exception in main: " + e.getMessage() );
    e.printStackTrace();
}
finally {
    try {
        // close the connection
        if ( con != null )
            con.close();
```

```
      }
    catch (SQLException e) {
          e.printStackTrace();
  }
 }
}

}
```

As explained previously in this chapter, in order to use JNDI, a SPI is required. This means that a server must be running to provide the lookups and return the appropriate objects requested. For this example, the reference implementation of the JNDI SPI for the `rmiregistry` (`http://java. sun.com/products/jndi/`) was used. This required that an appropriate set of JAR files be placed in the CLASSPATH for the application. The JNDI `InitialContext` class needs information on what SPI is being used (what `ContextFactory` needs to be accessed and other pertinent information). This information can be provided in one of several ways, but for this example a `jndi.properties` file in the current CLASSPATH is used. The `jndi.properties` file has the following entries:

```
java.naming.factory.initial= com.sun.jndi.rmi.registry.RegistryContextFactory
java.naming.provider.url= rmi://localhost:1099
```

Since the initialization properties for the `InitialContext` will be read from the properties file, there is no need to load a `Hashtable` with this information, as shown in the previous example, and the `InitialContext` constructor can be called with no arguments.

The `InitialContext` returns a `Context` object, which provides the utilitarian `lookup` call. As shown in this example, this call can take a string parameter with the name of the object to look up, and then will return a Java `Object` reference. Since in this example we know the type of the object reference being returned, we can cast it to the `DataSource` type. So, with no more knowledge than a string for the name of the `DataSource`, the application is able to obtain an object for the `DataSource`.

Once the data source has been obtained, it can be used to return a `Connection` object that represents a connection to the database. This `Connection` object can be used just as if the `DriverManager` class had returned it. As shown in this example, a `Statement` is created from the `Connection` object.

The `Statement` object is used to execute a query, which returns a `ResultSet`. The `ResultSet` is then iterated through to the end of the set, using the Java `while` loop. This `while` loop will print out a set of columns for each row returned.

The code example also includes a `try/catch` block, which catches a `SQLException` and a generic Java Exception. These exceptions will be covered in more detail in Chapter 6.

THE JAVAX.SQL.DATASOURCE CLASS

The `DataSource` class, the implementation of the `DataSource` interface, contains a number of methods that are worth mentioning at this point. These methods allow information about the `DataSource` to be obtained and allow some of the configuration parameters for the `DataSource` to be adjusted at runtime. Table 4–1 details the methods for the `DataSource` class.

The `getConnection` method returns a `Connection` object representing a connection to the underlying database. Since no connection URL is provided to this method (as is done when using a `DriverManager` to obtain a connection), the specific database to use for the connection is implied in the selection of the `DataSource` object. This means that the `DataSource` object has an underlying definition (as shown previously in this chapter for the PoolMan data source driver), which provides a connection URL, so a connection URL is not needed (and not allowed) for the call to the `getConnection` method for the `DataSource`.

Table 4–1   *DataSource Methods*

Method	Description
`Connection` `getConnection()`	Returns a `Connection` object representing a connection to the database defined for the `DataSource`.

`Connection`
`getConnection( String username,`
`String user_password)`
	Returns a `Connection` object representing a connection to the database defined for the `DataSource`. Uses the user name and password passed as parameters for authentication.

`int` `getLoginTimeout()`	Returns an integer indicating the maximum time that the `DataSource` will wait for a database connection.
`PrintWriter getLogWriter()`	Returns a `PrintWriter` object that represents the logging facility (writer) for the `DataSource`.
`void setLoginTimeout(int seconds)`	Sets the time for the login timeout, the maximum time the `DataSource` will wait for a database connection.
`void setLogWriter(PrintWriter out)`	Sets the log writer for the `DataSource` to the `PrintWriter` object passed as an argument.

The `getConnection` does allow an optional set of parameters for user name and password. If this overloaded version of the method is used, then the user name and password provided are used to authenticate that connection to the database.

The `getLoginTimeout` method is used to determine the current timeout setting for the database. This method returns an integer value indicating the amount of time the database driver will wait for a connection to the database. The default for login timeout for the `DataSource` is zero, indicating that the system timeout is used. The system timeout usually reflects the network timeout for a TCP/IP socket connection and is on the order of between 3 and 5 minutes, or 180 to 300 seconds. A `setLoginTimeout` method is also available to set the login timeout for the `DataSource`.

Usually, the setting for connection timeout is not an issue. For high performance systems where a database is always expected to be available, the 180 to 300 seconds system default is more than enough. If a database connection is taking anywhere near 180 seconds to complete, then other database issues must be resolved.

It is possible on a system where the database may not always be online that the connection timeout parameter may need to be adjusted. If there is the possibility that a database will only periodically be available, then it may be advisable to set the connection timeout value to a smaller interval, perhaps 30 seconds to 1 minute.

The `getLogWriter` method returns a `PrintWriter` object that represents the log output device for the `DataSource`. The `setLogWriter` method allows an application to set the log output device by accepting a `PrintWriter` object parameter to be used as the new log output.

Adding Functionality through the DataSource

The JDBC 2.0 Standard Extension API introduced the `DataSource` interface and provided two additional interfaces that could optionally be used to create a `DataSource` with more specific capabilities: the `ConnectionPoolDataSource` and `XADataSource` interfaces.

The `ConnectionPoolDataSource` and the `XADataSource` interfaces are expected to be implemented by a class in addition to the `DataSource` interface. This means that casting the `XADataSource` reference returned by the `lookup` call as a `DataSource` would work, since the underlying class would have implemented both the `DataSource XADataSource` interfaces. For this reason, the JNDI lookup for a `ConnectionPoolDataSource` would be the same as for a standard `DataSource` interface, as shown in the following code snippet:

```
...
    InitialContext ctx = new InitialContext();
    // lookup the data source to be used for connection pooling
    DataSource ds = (DataSource) ctx.lookup("MoviesDBConnPool");
...
```

The `ConnectionPoolDataSource`, as the name implies, provides a data source with an underlying connection pool. The `XADataSource` adds transaction management capabilities to the data source, allowing a transaction to span multiple databases, potentially from different vendors. The following sections will explain these two interfaces.

The javax.sql.ConnectionPoolDataSource Interface

The `ConnectionPoolDataSource` interface is implemented as a factor for `PooledConnection` objects, which can be retrieved with the `getPooledConnection` method. The `getPooledConnection` method returns a `PooledConnection` representing a connection from the connection pool that will be returned to the calling program. Table 4–2 details all of the methods in the `ConnectionPoolDataSource` interface.

Table 4–2   *ConnectionPoolDataSource Method*

Method	Description
`int getLoginTimeout()`	Returns an integer representing the maximum time out in seconds to wait while connecting to a database.
`PrintWriter getLogWriter()`	Returns the log writer for the `DataSource` as a `PrintWriter` object.
`PooledConnection getPooledConnection()`	Returns a `PooledConnection` object representing a connection to the `DataSource`.
`PooledConnection getPooledConnection(String user, String password)`	Returns a `PooledConnection` object representing a connection to the `DataSource`. Uses the user name and password passed as parameters for authentication.
`void setLoginTimeout(int seconds)`	Sets the maximum number of seconds to wait while connecting to a database.
`void setLogWriter(PrintWriter out)`	Sets the log writer for the `DataSource`. The parameter passed is the `PrintWriter` to use for the log writer.

As with the `DataSource` interface, methods are provided to get and set the connection login time-out value and to get and set the log output device. A method is also defined to get the physical pooled connection from the pool, though when implemented by the pool manager/application server, this method will not be visible to the application client.

HOW CONNECTION POOLING WORKS

Connection pooling has become the standard for middleware database drivers. The process of creating a connection, always an expensive, time-consuming operation, is multiplied in these environments where a large number of users are accessing the database in short, unconnected operations. Creating connections over and over in these environments is simply too expensive.

The transaction profile for Web applications, probably the most common application in use today, is that of a large number of users performing short, discrete database operations. These applications usually perform work centered around creating a Web page that will be sent back to the user's browser. Transactions are generally short-lived, and user sessions are often limited in time.

A connection pool operates by performing the work of creating connections ahead of time. In the case of a JDBC connection pool, a pool of `Connection` objects is created at the time the application server (or some other server) starts. These objects are then managed by a *pool manager* that disperses connections as they are requested by clients and returns them to the pool when it determines the client is finished with the `Connection` object. A great deal of housekeeping is involved in managing these connections (see Figure 4–2).

When the connection pool server starts, it creates a predefined number of `Connection` objects. A client application would then perform a JNDI lookup to retrieve a reference to a `DataSource` object that implements the `ConnectionPoolDataSource` interface. The client application would not need to make any special provisions to use the pooled data source; the code would be no different from code written for a nonpooled `DataSource`.

When the client application requests a connection from the `ConnectionPoolDataSource`, the data source implementation would retrieve a physical connection from the preexisting pool, perform some housekeeping, and return the connection to the client application. The `ConnectionPoolDataSource` would return a `Connection` object that implemented the `PooledConnection` interface (which is detailed in the next section).

The `PooledConnection` interface dictates the use of *event listeners*. These event listeners allow the connection pool manager to capture important connection

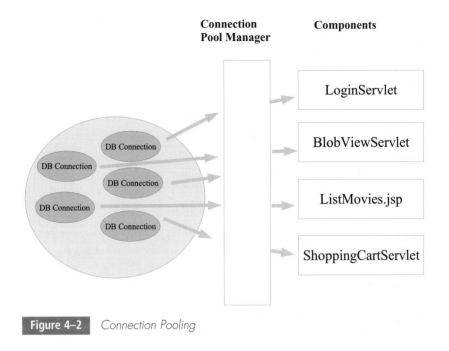

Figure 4–2 *Connection Pooling*

events, such as attempts by the client application to close the connection. When the driver traps a close-connection event, it intercedes and performs a pseudo-close operation that merely takes the `Connection` object, returns it to the pool of available connections, and performs any housekeeping that is necessary.

The operation of the connection pool should be completely transparent to the client application. The triggering of connection events, the manipulation of the object pool, and the creation and destruction of physical connections are all managed by the pool manager. The activities of the connection pool are, however, configurable by the application developer or the application deployer.

THE XADATASOURCE INTERFACE

The `XADataSource` provides the ability to encapsulate the properties of a transaction manager using a `DataSource`. The resulting `XADataSource` will provide management of distributed transactions, transactions which involve connections with one or more data sources. Table 4–3 identifies the methods in the `XADataSource` interface.

Table 4–3   *XADataSource Methods*

Method	Description
`int getLoginTimeout()`	Returns an integer indicating the maximum time in seconds the driver will wait for a connection to the database.
`PrintWriter getLogWriter()`	Returns a `PrintWriter` object for the log writer for the `DataSource`.
`XAConnection getXAConnection()`	Returns an `XAConnection` representing a connection to the `XADataSource`.
`XAConnection getXAConnection(` `java.lang.String user,` `java.lang.String password)`	Returns an `XAConnection` representing a connection to the `XADataSource`. Uses the user name and password for authentication to the `DataSource`.
`void setLoginTimeout(int seconds)`	Sets the maximum time that the driver will wait for a connection to the `XADataSource`.
`void setLogWriter(java.io.PrintWriter out)`	Sets the log writer for the `XADataSource` to the `PrintWriter` object passed into the method.

As with the `DataSource` interface, the `getLoginTimeout` and `setLoginTimeout` methods are provided to get or set the connection login time-out, the time the driver will wait for a connection to the underlying data source. The `getLogWriter` and `setLogWriter` methods are also provided to get or set the log output device for the data source. In addition to these methods, an internal method that will not be visible to the public is provided to get the `XAConnection` representing the connection to the underlying transaction manager.

Using an `XADataSource` is virtually transparent to the client application, with some minor exceptions. There are some restrictions on the methods that can be called when an `XADataSource` connection is used to control transactions. The `XADataSource` will be discussed along with conventional transactions in Chapter 9.

SUMMARY

This chapter covered the first step in using JDBC: loading a driver and getting connected to the database. As we've seen from the contents of this chapter, JDBC makes this process simple and provides the tools to reduce the coupling between the database, the database driver, and the application.

By using JNDI and a `DataSource` to obtain a connection, the specifics of the database connection and the driver are not hardcoded into the application. Using this technique, when and if the database name, or the server, or the password, or the driver class name changes, only the configuration parameters for the `DataSource` need to be changed, not the application code.

The JDBC API also provides for connection pooling. If the JDBC driver supports this, it is virtually transparent to the application code. An `XADataSource` is also available to provide connections for distributed transactions.

COMING UP NEXT

Once we've obtained a connection from whichever source we choose to use, the `DataSource` or the `DriverManager`, we must put it to good use. Chapter 5 covers the `Connection` interface and the various methods available in it. Sample applications will also be used to demonstrate how to use the `Connection` class to create `Statement` objects and `PreparedStatement` objects.

Using the Connection

INTRODUCTION

Chapter 4 covered the process of obtaining a connection with JDBC. This chapter focuses on what to do once you've obtained that connection.

The `java.sql.Connection` object is a required part of any database interaction with JDBC. The `Connection` object represents the physical connection to the database, usually using an underlying network connection, and is responsible for maintaining and managing the connection.

Though the `Connection` represents a physical connection, the process of obtaining a connection may not represent the creation of a physical connection to the database. The JDBC API provides hooks for driver developers to use *connection pooling* to distribute database connections in the `javax.sql.PooledConnection` interface. This can provide significant performance improvements for many applications and is implemented in a way that is transparent to the developer.

Some applications are required to interact with more than one database from more than one database vendor. These applications must often create *distributed transactions*, transactions that span multiple databases. These transactions must be able to ensure the integrity of the work being performed in each of the databases and across all of the databases as one unit of work. The JDBC API provides the `javax.sql.XAConnection` interface to provide transaction managers access to the JDBC driver's transaction resources. This chapter discusses these various interfaces and their class implementations in JDBC.

THE JAVA.SQL.CONNECTION CLASS

The JDBC driver you will use provides an implementation of the `java.sql.Connection` interface. For the purposes of this discussion, we will refer to this as the `Connection` class. The `Connection` class represents a connection to the underlying database. The `Connection` object is returned by either the `DriverManager` object or the `DataSource` object, depending on the driver being used in the JDBC application. Regardless of the method being used, the `Connection` object will behave the same with the exception of connections obtained from an `XADataSource`.

A `Connection` object can also provide information about the tables in the database, the supported SQL grammar, the stored procedures available, and the general capabilities of the database connection by using the `DatabaseMetaData` object returned by the `getMetaData` method. (Chapters 11 and 12 cover the `DatabaseMetaData` class in detail.)

A JDBC connection is in *auto-commit* mode by default. With auto-commit set, each SQL `update` statement (`insert`, `update`, `delete`) executed is automatically committed to the database separately on successful execution of the statement. In order to group a set of database updates together, the auto-commit mode must be set off (using the `setAutoCommit` method). Once the auto-commit behavior has been turned off, every SQL statement is part of a transaction and must be explicitly committed, using the `Connection commit` method, to become a permanent part of the database. Failure to commit with auto-commit turned off will generally cause an implicit rollback by the database and any updates will be lost. Transactions are covered in more detail in Chapter 9.

Table 5–1 provides a description of the methods in the `Connection` class. All methods throw an `SQLException`.

Given the importance and the prevalence of the `Connection` class in JDBC, it is worthwhile to review the various methods that are available in this class. The following sections will cover these methods.

Table 5-1   *java.sql.Connection Class Methods*

Method	Description
`void clearWarnings()`	Clears the various warnings that may have accumulated for this `Connection` object.
`void close()`	Closes the database connection. Terminates the relationship of this object to the underlying data store. (With pooled connections, retains the connection and returns it to the pool of available connections.)
`void commit()`	Places all updates in a permanent state in the underlying data store. A transactional commit operation. Releases any locks currently held by the connection.
`Statement createStatement()`	Creates a `Statement` object for the execution of SQL statements.
`Statement createStatement(int resultSetType, int resultSetConcurrency)`	Creates a `Statement` object for the execution of SQL statements. Parameters are provided to indicate that the `ResultSet` generated by the statement should be of the `ResultSet` type specified and should provide the concurrency specified.
`boolean getAutoCommit()`	Returns a boolean value for the auto-commit state of the `Connection`. If true, auto-commit is on. If false is returned, auto-commit is not on.
`String getCatalog()`	Returns a string with the catalog name for the current catalog of the connection.
`DatabaseMetaData getMetaData()`	Returns a `DatabaseMetaData` object for the underlying database for the current connection.
`int getTransactionIsolation()`	Returns an integer value representing the transaction isolation mode for the current database connection. Integer value returned relates to the integer constants in the `Connection` class.
`Map getTypeMap()`	Returns a `java.util.Map` object to be used for the custom type mapping of User Defined Types (UDT) in the current database.
`SQLWarning getWarnings()`	Returns an `SQLWarning` object containing the warnings for the current connection.
`boolean isClosed()`	Returns a boolean value indicating true if the database connection has been closed with a call to the close method, and false if the database connection is open. (If the connection has been invalidated for some other reason, the client may need to catch an exception and react accordingly.)

Table 5–1 *java.sql.Connection Class Methods (cont.)*

Method	Description
`boolean isReadOnly()`	Returns a boolean true if the database is a read-only database, and a boolean false if the database can be updated.
`String nativeSQL(String sql)`	Converts an SQL statement into the native SQL of the underlying database. Returns a string containing the converted SQL statement.
`CallableStatement prepareCall(String sql)`	Creates and returns a `CallableStatement` object using the SQL statement passed as a parameter to be used with the current database connection. (An object to be used for calling database stored procedures.)
`CallableStatement prepareCall(String sql, int resultSetType, int resultSetConcurrency)`	Creates and returns a `CallableStatement` object for use with the current connection. (An object to be used for calling database stored procedures.) Indicates that the `ResultSet` returned will be of the defined type and will use the specified concurrency. Usually throws an `SQLException` if the `ResultSet` type is not supported by the database or the driver.
`PreparedStatement prepareStatement(String sql)`	Creates a *prepared* SQL statement, a parsed, pre-compiled, reusable statement for use with the current database connection. Returns a `PreparedStatement` object.
`PreparedStatement prepareStatement(String sql, int resultSetType, int resultSetConcurrency)`	Creates and returns a `PreparedStatement` object for use with the current database connection. The `ResultSet` returned will have the specified `ResultSet` type and will use the specified `ResultSet` concurrency mode.
`void rollback()`	Will roll-back or undo the changes (updates) made in the current transaction. (The auto-commit mode must be turned off.) Will release any database locks held by the connection.
`void setAutoCommit(boolean autoCommit)`	Will set the auto-commit mode based on the boolean parameter passed to the method. If the boolean value is true, the auto-commit mode is set on, meaning each SQL statement represents a transaction. If the parameter is false, then auto-commit is turned off and it is possible to create multi-statement database transactions.
`void setCatalog(String catalog)`	Sets the database catalog to the string catalog name passed into the method.

Table 5–1	*java.sql.Connection Class Methods (cont.)*

Method	Description
`void setReadOnly(boolean readOnly)`	Sets the current database connection to read-only mode as a hint for database optimizations.
`void setTransactionIsolation(int level)`	Sets the transaction isolation mode to the specified value.
`void setTypeMap(Map map)`	Sets the type map for the database connection based on the `Map` object passed as a parameter. The Map object will provide mapping between the UDTs and corresponding Java classes.

THE CLOSE METHOD

The `close` method closes the connection to the database. This effectively terminates the relationship between the client application and the database, and releases all resources held in the database. Resources released include any transactions that were open and any locks held implicitly or explicitly by the connection. This means that any transaction that was open and uncommitted would be rolled back by calling the `Connection close` method. This rollback would be performed quietly, without any exception being thrown. The following code snippet demonstrates this.

```
1.//
2.      // get the initial context
3.      //
4.      InitialContext ctx = new InitialContext(  );
5.
6.      //
7.      // get the DataSource from the JNDI name server
8.      //
9.      DataSource ds = (DataSource) ctx.lookup("movies");
10.
11.      //
12.      // get the connection from the DataSource
13.      //
14.      con = ds.getConnection( );
15.
```

```
16.     //
17.     // create a Statement class to execute the SQL statement
18.     //
19.     Statement stmt = con.createStatement();
20.
21.     //
22.     // turn auto-commit off and start the transaction
23.     //
24.     con.setAutoCommit( false );
25.
26.     //
27.     // we are now in a transaction ... perform a series of updates
28.     //
29.     updateResult = stmt.executeUpdate(
30."insert into users (user_id, first_name, last_name, address1," +
31." city, state_province, postal_code, country)   " +
32." values ( 0, 'Fred', 'Smith', '2020 Nowhere Lane', 'Newark', 'NJ', '09090',
'US');" );
33.
34.     updateResult = stmt.executeUpdate(
35."insert into users (user_id, first_name, last_name, address1," +
36." city, state_province, postal_code, country)   " +
37." values ( 0, 'Sally', 'Smith', '2020 Nowhere Lane', 'Newark', 'NJ', '09090',
'US');" );
38.
39.     updateResult = stmt.executeUpdate(
40."insert into users (user_id, first_name, last_name, address1," +
41." city, state_province, postal_code, country)   " +
42." values ( 0, 'Harry', 'Henderson', '3030 Milbourne', 'Tuckamarin', 'NJ',
'08090', 'US');" );
43.
44.
45.     // oops ... forgot to commit !
46.     // con.close() call will cause all of the updates above
47.     // to be lost !
48.     //
49.      con.close();
50....
```

In this example, a `DataSource` is obtained using a JNDI lookup, and a `Statement` object is obtained via the `Connection`. (The `Statement` object and updates will be covered in more detail in Chapter 6.) The auto-commit feature is then turned off, effectively starting a database transaction.

A series of database updates is performed on lines 29 through 42, but because there is not a call to commit the transactions, all of the updates will be lost when the `Connection close` method call is executed on line 49. A call to the `Connection commit` method (`con.commit()`) on the previous line would have saved the work to the database.

THE GETAUTOCOMMIT AND SETAUTOCOMMIT METHODS

The auto-commit state of the database driver indicates how the driver will manage transaction logging with the database. The default value for auto-commit is on (a setting of `true`), which means that every SQL statement executed is a separate transaction and is committed to the database separately; there is no active transaction processing spanning multiple database updates.

The `getAutoCommit` method returns a boolean value that indicates the current auto-commit state of the database. A boolean value of `true` indicates that auto-commit is turned on (the default), and a boolean value of `false` indicates that auto-commit has been turned off. In order to create a transaction and group a set of SQL statements together, the auto-commit behavior must be turned off, as shown in this code snippet.

```
1....
2.      // get the initial context
3.      //
4.      InitialContext ctx = new InitialContext(  );
5.
6.      //
7.      // get the DataSource from the JNDI name server
8.      //
9.      DataSource ds = (DataSource) ctx.lookup("movies");
10.
11.      //
12.      // get the connection from the DataSource
13.      //
14.      con = ds.getConnection( );
15.
16.      //
17.      // create a Statement class to execute the SQL statement
18.      //
19.      Statement stmt = con.createStatement();
20.
21.      //
22.      // turn auto-commit off
23.      //
24.      con.setAutoCommit( false );
25.
26.
27.      //
28.      // we are now in a transaction ... perform a series of updates
29.      //
30.
31.      updateResult = stmt.executeUpdate(
32."insert into users (user_id, first_name, last_name, address1," +
33." city, state_province, postal_code, country)  " +
34." values ( nextval('user_id'), 'Fred', 'Smith', '2020 Nowhere Lane', 'Newark',
'NJ', '09090', 'US');" );
```

```
35.
36.       updateResult = stmt.executeUpdate(
37."insert into users (user_id, first_name, last_name, address1," +
38." city, state_province, postal_code, country)   " +
39." values ( nextval('user_id'), 'Sally', 'Smith', '2020 Nowhere Lane', 'Newark',
'NJ', '09090', 'US');" );
40.
41.       updateResult = stmt.executeUpdate(
42."insert into users (user_id, first_name, last_name, address1," +
43." city, state_province, postal_code, country)   " +
44." values ( nextval('user_id'), 'Harry', 'Henderson', '3030 Milbourne',
'Tuckamarin', 'NJ', '08090', 'US');" );
45.
46.
47.       // user_id = 2 is renting a movie
48.       updateResult = stmt.executeUpdate(
49.           "insert into user_rentals (user_id, rental_date, movie_id) " +
50.           " values ( 2, current_date, 1 ); " );
51.       // user_id = 3 is renting a movie
52.       updateResult = stmt.executeUpdate(
53.           "insert into user_rentals (user_id, rental_date, movie_id) " +
54.           " values ( 2, current_date, 3 ); " );
55.
56.
57.       //
58.       // need to perform a commit to save the work
59.       //
60.       con.commit();
61.
62.       // 'finally' block will close the connection
63....
```

This example obtains a `DataSource` from JNDI, and then obtains a `Connection`. Using the connection, a `Statement` object is created. Before the actual database update statements are executed, a call is made to the `setAutoCommit` method on line 24 to turn auto-commit off. This is done by passing the `setAutoCommit` method a boolean value of false. Following the `setAutoCommit` call, a series of database `update` statements are executed on lines 31 through 52. Since auto-commit mode is not on, these statements will not be committed to the database until the `Connection` commit method is executed at line 60.

THE COMMIT AND ROLLBACK METHODS

The `commit` and `rollback` methods provide for direct programmatic control over transaction logging in the client application. The `commit` method commits all database update activity in the current transaction to the database. The `rollback` method rolls back or ensures that all update activity in the current transaction will not be committed to the database. If the auto-commit state is on, then each statement executed is automatically committed to the database, leaving nothing for the `commit` or `rollback` method to work with. The auto-commit state of the database driver must be set off (`false`) in order for these methods to work correctly. The following code snippet demonstrates the use of these methods:

```
1....
2.//
3.      // get the initial context
4.      //
5.      InitialContext ctx = new InitialContext(  );
6.
7.      //
8.      // get the DataSource from the JNDI name server
9.      //
10.      DataSource ds = (DataSource) ctx.lookup("movies");
11.
12.      //
13.      // get the connection from the DataSource
14.      //
15.      con = ds.getConnection( );
16.
17.      //
18.      // create a Statement class to execute the SQL statement
19.      //
20.      Statement stmt = con.createStatement();
21.
22.      //
23.      // turn auto-commit off
24.      //
25.      con.setAutoCommit( false );
26.
27.      //
28.      // we are now in a transaction ... perform a series of updates
29.      //
30.      updateResult = stmt.executeUpdate(
31.      "insert into users (user_id, first_name, last_name, address1," +
32.      " city, state_province, postal_code, country)   " +
33.      " values ( nextval('user_id'), 'Fred', 'Smith', '2020 Nowhere Lane',
'Newark', 'NJ', '09090', 'US');" );
34.
35.      updateResult = stmt.executeUpdate(
36.      "insert into users (user_id, first_name, last_name, address1," +
37.      " city, state_province, postal_code, country)   " +
38.      " values ( nextval('user_id'), 'Sally', 'Smith', '2020 Nowhere Lane',
'Newark', 'NJ', '09090', 'US');" );
39.
40.      updateResult = stmt.executeUpdate(
41.      "insert into users (user_id, first_name, last_name, address1," +
```

```
42.      " city, state_province, postal_code, country)   " +
43.      " values ( nextval('user_id'), 'Harry', 'Henderson', '3030 Milbourne',
'Tuckamarin', 'NJ', '08090', 'US');" );
44.
45.      // user_id = 2 is renting a movie
46.      updateResult = stmt.executeUpdate(
47.      "insert into user_rentals (user_id, rental_date, movie_id) " +
48.                     " values ( 2, current_date, 1 ); " );
49.      // user_id = 3 is renting a movie
50.      updateResult = stmt.executeUpdate(
51.      "insert into user_rentals (user_id, rental_date, movie_id) " +
52.                     " values ( 2, current_date, 3 ); " );
53.
54.      // need to perform a commit to save the work
55.      // this expression tests true about half the time
56.      //
57.      if ( ( (int)(Math.random() * 10) % 2) > 0 ) {
58.          con.commit();
59.            System.out.println("Transactions have been committed.");
60.      }
61.      else {
62.          con.rollback();
63.            System.out.println("Transactions have been rolled back.");
64.      }
65.
66.      //
67.      // 'finally' block will close the connection
68.      //
69.
70.
71....
```

This example gets a `DataSource` from the `InitialContext` and then creates the `Connection` from the `DataSource`. The database driver auto-commit is turned off at line 25, and a series of database updates are performed on lines 30 through 52. At line 57, a random value (the expression will randomly generate a 0 or 1) is generated to make a decision whether to commit or roll back the transaction. The `Connection` `commit` method is called at line 58 to commit the transaction, or the `Connection` `rollback` method is called at line 62 to roll back the transaction.

THE CLEARWARNINGS AND GETWARNINGS METHODS

When a connection is made to a relational database, a series of warnings may be generated by the database. These warnings potentially, but not necessarily, provide information about the level of ANSI SQL support, how NULL values are handled, and other pertinent information. (Whether or not warnings are used at all is dependent on the database being used; developers should review the documentation for the driver to determine what information is relayed in warnings.)

Other JDBC objects return SQLWarnings for the database operations they represent (Statement, ResultSet). These warnings are returned by the underlying database and are represented as *chains* of warnings, with each SQLWarning object retrieved potentially containing a reference to an additional SQLWarning object.

The getWarnings method returns a SQLWarning object (java.sql.SQLWarning), which is an exception (a subclass of java.sql.SQLException). The SQLWarning class contains a getNextWarning method, which returns a SQLWarning object if another warning exists in the chain, or a null reference if no more warnings exist. The following code snippet provides an example of using the getWarnings and clearWarnings methods:

```
...
DataSource ds;
...
Connection con  = ds.getConnection();

//
// check for warnings from the database connection
//
SQLWarning sqlw = con.getWarnings();

//
// warning may be null reference
//
if (sqlw != null) {

    //
    // iterate through the chain of warnings
    //
    while ( sqlw != null )
        System.out.println("Warning: " + sqlw );
         sqlw = sqlw.getNextWarning();
    }
else
    System.out.println("There are no warnings.");

//
// clear all warnings on the connection
//
con.clearWarnings();

...
```

In this example, a connection is made to a database using a `DataSource`, and a `Connection` object is returned. The `Connection` object will potentially have a series of warnings (`SQLWarning` objects) attached to it as a result of the database connection operation. Since the `getWarnings` method may have returned a null object reference, a conditional statement is first used to test for this condition. If the `SQLWarning` object is not null, then a `while` loop is used to extract the entire chain of objects.

For an application that must connect to various databases with varying levels of support that may not be known when the application is developed, the `SQLWarning` may provide useful information. As shown in the previous code snippet, warnings are not thrown like exceptions; the programmer must make the `getWarnings` call on the `Connection` object to obtain the first warning (if any), and then iterate through the warnings to examine all warnings.

Though warnings may warrant examination if the database uses them, in practice, the `DatabaseMetaData` class provides more finely grained and useful information on database support than the `SQLWarning` object. (The `DatabaseMetaData` class is covered in detail in Chapters 11 and 12.)

THE createStatement METHOD

The `createStatement` method is used to create SQL statements for execution. Both database `select` and `update` statements are created using this method. The `createStatement` method has been overloaded to take two sets of arguments, as shown below.

```
Statement createStatement()

Statement createStatement(int resultSetType,
                          int resultSetConcurrency)

Statement createStatement( int resultSetType,
                           int resultSetConcurrency,
                           int resultSetHoldability)
```

One version takes no arguments and returns a `Statement` object. The other version takes arguments for the type of result set to be returned and the type of result set concurrency to use. The JDBC 3.0 API overloads this method and adds a *cursor holdability* parameter indicating whether or not a cursor will be held open after a commit.

The `ResultSet` class contains the constants that can be used for these calls. The possible values are listed in Table 5–2.

Table 5–2   *ResultSet Constants*

Constant	Type/Concurrency	Description
CONCUR_READ_ONLY	Concurrency	Indicates that read-only concurrency will be used. The ResultSet object will not be updated.
CONCUR_UPDATABLE	Concurrency	Indicates that the ResultSet created may be updated.
HOLD_CURSORS_OVER_COMMIT	Cursor	Cursors remain open after database commit
CLOSE_CURSORS_AT_COMMIT	Cursor	Cursors close after database commit

There are two concurrency types that impact how the ResultSet (cursor) created by the Statement object will manage updates. The type of concurrency selected must be supported by the underlying database and driver.

Using the CONCUR_READ_ONLY parameter value will create a regular cursor—a ResultSet without update capabilities. Using the CONCUR_UPDATABLE parameter will create a ResultSet with update capabilities. The second argument to the createStatement method takes an integer value corresponding to the scrolling and concurrency type, which would take one of the values shown in Table 5–3. This method will usually throw an exception if a ResultSet type requested is not supported by the database or the driver.

Table 5–3   *ResultSet Constants*

Constant	Type	Description
TYPE_FORWARD_ONLY	Scroll	Indicates that the ResultSet will be processed only in a forward direction; it is not a scroll cursor.
TYPE_SCROLL_INSENSITIVE	Scrolling	Indicates that the cursor is scrollable, but is not sensitive to changes made in the database while the cursor is being moved.
TYPE_SCROLL_SENSITIVE	Scrolling	Indicates that the cursor is scrollable and is sensitive to changes made in the database while the cursor is being used.

The `ResultSet` created by the `Statement` object is implemented with a database cursor. A database cursor can be either a *serial cursor,* meaning that it will be traversed in one direction only, from the beginning of the cursor to the end of the cursor. The other type of cursor is the *scroll cursor.* This type of cursor allows the entire result set to be traversed in an arbitrary fashion. Cursor evaluation can start at the first row, jump to the fifth row, and then move to the second row. The database may also provide options for managing concurrency (simultaneous database updates to the rows being evaluated by the cursor). The cursor may optionally be sensitive to changes in the rows being evaluated and refresh the rows from the database if needed.

The type parameters passed to the `createStatement` method indicate the type of cursor to be created for the `ResultSet` that will be produced by the execution of the SQL statement. The `TYPE_FORWARD_ONLY` will create a normal cursor that does not provide scroll capability. The `TYPE_SCROLL_INSENSITIVE` scroll cursor is not sensitive to changes in the database; changes in the database are effectively ignored by the cursor. The `TYPE_SCROLL_SENSITIVE` scroll cursor is sensitive to changes in the database, potentially re-reading database rows if they have changed.

The following code snippet reads rows from the a database, using a `ResultSet` to iterate through the results. This demonstrates the use of the `createStatement` method.

```
1....
2.
3.      // get the DataSource from the JNDI name server
4.      DataSource ds = (DataSource) ctx.lookup("movies");
5.
6.      // get the connection from the DataSource
7.      con = ds.getConnection( );
8.
9.      // create a Statement class to execute the SQL statement
10.      Statement stmt = con.createStatement();
11.
12.      // execute the SQL statement and get the results in a ResultSet
13.      ResultSet rs   = stmt.executeQuery(
14.          "select movie_name, release_date from movies" );
15.
16.      // iterate serially through the ResultSet, displaying two values
17.      // for each row using the getString method
18.      //
19.      while ( rs.next() ) {
20.          System.out.println( "*******************" + "\n" +
21.                          "movie_name: " + "\t" +
22.                              rs.getString("movie_name") + "\n" +
23.                          "release_date: " + "\t" +
24.                              rs.getString("release_date")   );
25....
26.
```

The `Connection` object obtained on line 7 is used to create a `Statement` object, using the `createStatement` method on line 10. This form of the method takes no arguments and creates a `Statement` object, which will return a `ResultSet` using the default cursor type, a serial cursor. The `ResultSet` is created on line 13 and then used to step through the results serially, using a `while` loop on line 19.

Alternatively, a scroll cursor can be used to move through a `ResultSet` in an arbitrary manner. This requires the `createStatement` method to identify the cursor to be created as a scroll cursor. The following code snippet demonstrates this approach:

```
1....
2.      //
3.      // load the DataSource
4.      //
5.      DataSource   ds    = PoolMan.findDataSource("movies");
6.
7.      //
8.      // create the connection using the static getConnection method
9.      //
10.      Connection con = ds.getConnection( );
11.
12.      //
13.      // create a Statement object to execute the SQL statement
14.      // define the cursor type to get a scroll cursor
15.      //
16.      Statement stmt = con.createStatement(
17.                            ResultSet.TYPE_SCROLL_INSENSITIVE,
18.                            ResultSet.CONCUR_UPDATABLE );
19.
20.      // execute the SQL statement and get the results in a ResultSet
21.      ResultSet rs    = stmt.executeQuery(
22.          "select movie_name, movie_id, release_date from movies" );
23....
```

In this example, a `DataSource` is obtained from the `InitialContext` and a connection is created from the `DataSource` on line 10. On line 16 a `createStatement` method is executed using the optional arguments to define concurrency and cursor type. In this example, a scroll-insensitive cursor is declared, meaning the cursor will be a scroll cursor but will not be sensitive to changes made in the database while the cursor is being used by the client application. The `createStatement` method also accepts a parameter for the concurrency and in this case defines concurrency to be *updatable,* meaning that updates may be performed using the `ResultSet`.

THE getCATALOG AND setCATALOG METHODS

The getCatalog and setCatalog methods are used to get the current catalog for the database connection. A catalog represents a portion of a database that is visible to a client application. The getCatalog method returns a string, and the setCatalog method takes a string argument, as demonstrated in the following code snippet:

. . .
```
//
// load the DataSource
//
DataSource  ds   = PoolMan.findDataSource("movies");

//
// create the connection using the static getConnection method
//
Connection con = ds.getConnection( );

System.out.println("Using catalog: " + con.getCatalog() );
//
// set the catalog for this connection
//
con.setCatalog("sales_north_region");
```
. . .

THE getMETADATA METHOD

The getMetData method returns a DatabaseMetaData object. Every relational database has metadata—data about data. Metadata can provide a wealth of information about a database and is useful to developers who write applications that must work with many different databases. Metadata information is useful not only when working with databases from different vendors, but can also help when working with different versions of the same database.

While much of the information delivered by the DatabaseMetaData class is available through database system catalogs or database functions, JDBC provides a consistent API to access this information regardless of the database vendor. The ability to access and use this information is one of the more significant benefits of JDBC. The following code snippet demonstrates the use of the getMetaData method:

. . .
```
//
// load the DataSource
//
DataSource  ds   = (DataSource) ctx.lookup("movies");
```

```
//
// create the connection using the static
// getConnection method
//
Connection con = ds.getConnection( );

 // create a meta-data object for the connection
//
 DatabaseMetaData dmd = con.getMetaData();

    // get a list of System functions
    //

 String sysFuncts = dmd.getSystemFunctions();
 System.out.println("System functions: " +
                    sysFuncts );

    //
    // get a list of tables in the database
    //
ResultSet tables = dmd.getTables("","","",null);

while ( tables.next() )
      System.out.println( "tables: " +
      tables.getString("TABLE_NAME")  );
```

...

In the code snippet above, a `DataSource` is retrieved using a JNDI lookup, and a `Connection` is obtained from the `DataSource`. The `getMetadata` method is then called on the `Connection` object to retrieve a `DatabaseMetaData` object on line 14. One of the more common operations to perform on a `DatabaseMetaData` object is to list the tables available in the database. This is done on line 25 using the `getTables` method of the `DatabaseMetaData` class. This method returns a `ResultSet`, which is then used to iterate over the results, listing the tables in the database using the `while` loop on line 27.

THE GETTYPEMAP AND SETTYPEMAP METHODS

The `getTypeMap` and `setTypeMap` methods are used to manage UDTS (SQL `DISTINCT` data types) in the database. The `getTypeMap` method returns a `java.util.Map` object that contains a map of the UDTs in the database. The `Map` relates UDTs to Java classes that can be used to store the data in the UDT column. The Java class must implement the `java.sql.SQLData` interface.

There is no default type map in a database. For this reason, a call to the getTypeMap method without a previous call to the setTypeMap method will result in an empty map. The type map must be configured, a Map object prepared and then passed to a setTypeMap method to inform the database of the mappings.

THE GETTRANSACTIONISOLATION AND SETTRANSACTIONISOLATION METHODS

The getTransactionIsolation method returns the isolation mode of the current database connection in the form of an integer. (Transaction isolation modes were explained in Chapter 2.) The integer value must then be evaluated against the integer constants in the Connection class to determine what the current isolation mode is.

The isolation mode can optionally be changed using the setTransactionIsolation method and passing a valid integer value for the isolation mode to which the connection should be changed. If the database does not support the isolation mode requested, then a SQLException will be thrown. The following code snippet demonstrates the use of this method:

```
...
// get the initial context
    InitialContext ctx = new InitialContext( );

    // get the DataSource from the JNDI name server
    DataSource ds = (DataSource) ctx.lookup("movies");

    // get the connection from the DataSource
    con = ds.getConnection( );


    // examine the isolation mode
    //
    System.out.println("Transaction isolation mode is: " +
            formatIsolationMode( con.getTransactionIsolation()) );
    //
    // let's set the isolation mode to allow dirty reads since
    // we are just creating a simple report
    //
    con.setTransactionIsolation(
            Connection.TRANSACTION_READ_UNCOMMITTED );
...
```

```
static String formatIsolationMode( int isolationMode ) {
//
// Translate integer value for Transaction Isolation Mode
// into an appropriate string and return string value
//
switch (isolationMode) {
    case Connection.TRANSACTION_NONE:
                return "No Transaction Isolation Mode" ;
    case Connection.TRANSACTION_READ_COMMITTED:
                return "Read Committed Isolation Mode" ;
    case Connection.TRANSACTION_READ_UNCOMMITTED:
                return "Read Uncommitted  Isolation Mode" ;
    case Connection.TRANSACTION_REPEATABLE_READ:
                return "Repeatable Read Isolation Mode" ;
    case Connection.TRANSACTION_SERIALIZABLE:
                return "Serializable Isolation Mode" ;
}

// if at this point, then this is an invalid value
// so return a null reference
//
return null;


}
...
```

This code snippet examines the isolation mode and displays the output. A formatting routine is used to convert the integer value constant to a meaningful string. The isolation mode is then explicitly set to the *read uncommitted* isolation mode (a dirty-read). This is an isolation mode that requires fewer locks be held in the database engine. Using a less restrictive isolation mode should improve performance for database operations that do not require locking.

THE isCLOSED METHOD

The isClosed method is used to determine whether or not a connection is open. In a complex application performing a number of operations, it may not be readily clear whether or not a connection is open. When using connection pooling, a JDBC driver will close a connection if it has been opened and unused for a certain period of time. If a connection is closed, the DriverManager or the DataSource must be used to create a new connection for the Connection object reference. The following code snippet demonstrates the use of this method:

```
...
    // get the initial context
    InitialContext ctx = new InitialContext( );

    // get the DataSource from the JNDI name server
    DataSource ds = (DataSource) ctx.lookup("movies");

    // get the connection from the DataSource
    con = ds.getConnection( );


    //
    // demonstrate how to manage a closed connection
    //
    con.close();

    if ( con.isClosed() ) {

        System.out.println("The connection is closed.");

        //
        // open a new connection
        //
        con = ds.getConnection();

}
...
```

This example uses a `DataSource` to open a connection, then for purposes of this example, the connection is closed. The `isClosed` method is then used to test the connection, and if it is closed, the `DataSource getConnection` method is used to reestablish a connection to the database. Alternatively, if a `DriverManager` had been used to create the connection, the `DriverManager getConnection` method could be used to reestablish the connection.

THE isREADONLY AND setREADONLY METHODS

The `isReadOnly` method checks the read-only status of the database connection (through the database driver). The `setReadOnly` method can be used to set the read-only status to `true` and thus **suggest** to the driver that the database connection is read-only. But the `setReadOnly` method just provides a suggestion to the driver; it does not affect other database connections and does not guarantee that the connection is a true read-only database connection. (For many databases, the database administrator must make changes to internal database engine parameters to create a read-only database.)

THE PREPARECALL METHOD

The `prepareCall` method is used to prepare a database stored-procedure statement for processing. This method is similar to the `prepareStatement` method except that it should only be used for stored procedures. The following code snippet demonstrates:

```
// get the initial context
   InitialContext ctx = new InitialContext( );

   // get the DataSource from the JNDI name server
   DataSource ds = (DataSource) ctx.lookup("movies");

   // get the connection from the DataSource
   con = ds.getConnection( );

   CallableStatement stmt =
               conn.prepareCall(
                   "{call CheckReferences(?, ?)}");
    stmt.setString(1, "EmailAccount");
    stmt.setObject(2, new Integer(8));

   if (stmt.execute()) {
       ResultSet rs = stmt.getResultSet();
       while (rs.next()) {
           System.out.println("Referenced by " + rs.getString(1) +
                           "." + rs.getString(2) +
                           " " + rs.getObject(3) + " times.");

...
```

In this example, the `CheckReferences` stored procedure is called and passed two parameters. Note that the stored procedure is called using JDBC *escape processing*. The syntax for calling stored procedures varies from database to database. The curly braces ({) in the query string indicates that the specific database syntax for the following query will be provided by the JDBC driver. This provides a convenient method of calling stored procedures without having to be concerned about which database is being used on the current connection.

The question marks in the query string represent parameters to be substituted in the query. The values of these parameters are set, and then the statement is executed and the results are reviewed. (Chapter 7 will cover the setting of prepared statement parameters in more detail.)

THE PREPARESTATEMENT METHOD

The prepareStatement method is used to prepare a SQL statement for processing. Most relational databases support this capability to preprocess a SQL statement before it is actually used and optimize the processing of the query.

While this may sound like a trivial process, determining the best way to process a complex SQL statement with 10 table joins and 20 lines of where clause filters is not trivial. Being able to preprocess a SQL statement that will be executed multiple times can lead to a significant performance improvement. The following code snippet demonstrates the use of these methods.

```
1....
2.// get the DataSource from the JNDI name server
3.     DataSource ds = (DataSource) ctx.lookup("movies");
4.
5.     // get the connection from the DataSource
6.     con = ds.getConnection( );
7.
8.     // create a Statement class to execute the SQL statement
9.     PreparedStatement pstmt = con.prepareStatement(
10.    " select distinct first_name, last_name, state_province, " +
11.    " movie_name, rental_date "                     +
12.    " from users, movies, user_rentals "            +
13.    " where (users.user_id    = user_rentals.user_id and " +
14.    "        movies.movie_id  = user_rentals.movie_id) and " +
15.    "        user_rentals.user_id = ? " );
16.
17.    // set the PreparedStatement parameters
18.    pstmt.setInt(1, 2); // set to user_id = 2
19.
20.    // execute the SQL statement and get the results in a ResultSet
21.    ResultSet rs  = pstmt.executeQuery();
22.
23.    // iterate through the ResultSet, displaying two values
24.    // for each row using the getString method
25.    //
26.    while ( rs.next() ) {
27.           System.out.println( "Name: " + "\t" +
28.                      rs.getString("first_name").trim() + "\t" +
29.                      " " + "\t" + rs.getString("last_name").trim() +
30.                      "\t" + " Movie: " + "\t" +
31.                      rs.getString("movie_name") + "\t" +
32.                      " Rental Date: " + "\t" +
33.                      rs.getString("rental_date") );
34....
```

In this example, the prepareStatement method of the Connection class is called and returns a PreparedStatement object on line 9. The call to the prepareStatement method is passed a query string, which joins several tables to list the movie rental transactions in the database for a specific user ID. The PreparedStatement uses the '?' as a placeholder to indicate where a parameter value will be substituted when the statement is executed. As the code on line 19 shows, the values of parameters are set with setXXXX calls before the statement is executed with the executeQuery method of the PreparedStatement class on line 21.

THE NATIVESQL METHOD

The nativeSQL method is used to return a string displaying the SQL that will be executed in the database, which may differ from the SQL that is passed as a parameter. Escape characters are replaced with appropriate values for the database. This method is generally used by those creating or debugging a JDBC driver, not by database application developers.

THE POOLEDCONNECTION INTERFACE

The PooledConnection is an interface defined in the javax.sql package for pooled database connections. It provides for a number of methods to set and unset event handlers for the various events that are generated by the application server for connections. The methods in this interface are generally used by the driver developers to manage connection pools. These would not usually be used by JDBC developers. The methods in this interface are shown in Table 5–4.

Table 5–4   *PooledConnection*

Method	Description
void addConnectionEventListener(ConnectionEventListener listener)	Adds an event listener to the connection.
void close()	Closes the physical connection.
Connection getConnection()	Returns a Connection object for the physical connection.
void removeConnectionEventListener(ConnectionEventListener listener)	Removes an event listener from the list of listeners for this connection.

Using a pooled connection is transparent to the developer. While some decisions may be made about the configuration of the pool and how connections should behave, the runtime usage of the connection is the same as with a non-pooled connection.

The behavior of the `Connection close` method with pooled connections is different from that of non-pooled connections. The close of a pooled connection is a *logical* close; the physical connection may or may not remain open after the call. If transactions are being used, explicit commits or rollbacks should be called before the `Connection close` method is called. Calling a `Connection close` on a connection with open transactions generally initiates a rollback on the transactions, but this is not guaranteed behavior, and the developer should provide explicit code controlling transactions when they are used.

The XAConnection Interface

The `XAConnection` interface is used by vendors to create an interface for an XA distributed transaction manager. This allows transactions to be managed between different databases from different vendors. This interface inherits from the `PooledConnection` interface, which provides for a number of event callback methods. The interface provides for a method that returns the XA resource for the connection, which allows transaction managers to coordinate the transactions for this connection with other connections. As with the `PooledConnection` interface, this interface and the method it exposes is generally intended for use by JDBC driver developers or transaction manager developers adding support for a specific JDBC driver. See Table 5–5.

Table 5–5	*XAConnection*	

Method	Description
`javax.transaction.xa.XAResource getXAResource()`	Return an `XAResource` object representing the underlying data resource.

Summary

There really isn't much that can be done in JDBC without a connection. This chapter dove into the details of creating and maintaining connections using JDBC.

A JDBC connection to a database is represented by the `java.sql.Connection` interface, which provides an abstraction for the process of connecting to and maintaining a connection to a database.

The process of connecting to a database has further been abstracted with the `javax.sql.DataSource` interface. This interface abstracts and encapsulates much of the functionality of obtaining and managing database connections.

COMING UP NEXT

Chapter 6 takes a look at the next logical step in working with JDBC: retrieving and manipulating data from the database. It will examine the use of the `Statement` class to create and execute SQL statements using JDBC.

Retrieving and Manipulating Data: The Statement Class and JDBC Exceptions

INTRODUCTION

The previous chapter covered the process of getting connected to the database. The next logical step after getting connected to the database is to execute a query and process the results. This chapter examines that process with a focus on the `Statement` class, the class that encapsulates the processing of a SQL statement.

The `Statement` class allows a SQL statement to be presented to the database for execution. As part of that process, the `Statement` class allows suggestions to be sent to the database on how to process the query and how to return the results.

Extensions to the `Statement` class allow batches of updates to be sent to the database and processed together. This can improve performance for applications where a large number of updates must be performed.

Since SQL syntax can vary slightly from database to database, the JDBC API provides for escape processing to allow the JDBC driver to manage the database-specific syntax (such as stored procedure calls). The JDBC driver is then responsible for providing the correct syntax for these statements before presenting them to the database server.

This chapter begins with a program example that demonstrates the process of connecting to the database and using a `Statement` object to execute queries.

PROCESSING DATA

As detailed in Chapter 5, a JDBC application must load the appropriate driver and connect to a database. In practice, this involves very few method calls. The bulk of the work takes place in a database application in the processing of the database data. That involves using primarily three JDBC classes: the `Statement` class, the `PreparedStatement` class, and the `ResultSet` class.

The designers of the JDBC API made a distinction between the execution of a SQL statement and the processing of results from a statement. For this reason there are distinct classes designed for executing SQL statements (`Statement`, `PreparedStatement`) and examining the results (`ResultSet`).

The `Statement` class encapsulates the calls used to create and execute SQL statements. Where the `Statement` class expects to receive and execute a SQL statement once, the `PreparedStatement` class allows a SQL statement to be processed before it is used and then executed multiple times with potentially different parameters. A `Statement` object can execute both SQL Data Manipulation Language (DML) statements, including `select`, `insert`, `update`, and `delete`. The `Statement` class can also be used to execute Data Definition Language (DDL) statements, including `create table`, `alter table`, `create schema`, and `drop table`.

Both the `Statement` and the `PreparedStatement` classes provide methods that can return results. The results returned by these methods are encapsulated in the `ResultSet` class. The `ResultSet` allows database results to be extracted either serially, in the arbitrary order in which they are received from the database, or using a scroll cursor capability where the data set returned can be reviewed in random order if the database server and the JDBC driver support it. A `ResultSet` may also provide the ability to update the database using the `ResultSet` object. (The `ResultSet` is covered in Chapter 8.)

A Program Example

A good place to start is with a complete working example that shows all of the parts necessary to complete the puzzle. The following code example demonstrates the retrieval and processing of data from a data source. It is similar to examples shown in Chapter 5, with a few new twists.

StatementExampleX.java

```
1.import java.sql.*;
2.import javax.sql.*;
3.import javax.naming.*;
4.
5.public class StatementExampleX {
6.
```

```
7.public static void main( String args[] ) {
8.
9.ResultSet rs    = null;
10.Connection con  = null;
11.
12.try {
13.
14.     //
15.     // Either connect to an existing poolman instance
16.     // or start poolman here. This will register JNDI name
17.     // with the JNDI service provider and initialize pools
18.     //
19.
20.     //
21.     // JNDI startup parameters are stored in
22.     // the "jndi.properties" file in the classpath.
23.     //
24.        InitialContext ctx = new InitialContext( );
25.
26.     // get the DataSource from the JNDI name server
27.      DataSource ds = (DataSource) ctx.lookup("moviesmysql");
28.
29.     // get the connection from the DataSource
30.     con =  ds.getConnection( );
31.
32.     // create a Statement class to execute the SQL statement
33.     // create two statements from the same connection
34.     Statement stmt = con.createStatement();
35.
36.     //
37.     // execute a query. can be an update or a select will still
38.     // use the same code to process the query
39.     //
40.     String[] queries = {"select * from users",
41.                            "select * from movies",
42.    "update users set country = 'USA'", // perform update
43.    "select * from users"};             // view update results
44.
45.for ( int n = 0; n < queries.length; n++ ) {
46.
47.     //
48.     // execute the query
49.     //
50.     System.out.println("\n** Executing query: " + n + " : " +
51.                         queries[n] );
52.     boolean isResultSet = stmt.execute( queries[n] );
53.
54.     //
55.     // if we were successful, get a ResultSet
56.     //
57.     if ( isResultSet ) {
58.         rs = stmt.getResultSet();
```

```
59.     }
60.
61.     //
62.     // print the results whether this is an update or a select
63.     //
64.     if ( isResultSet ) {  // it's a ResultSet
65.         System.out.println( "\nSelect Performed - Results: " );
66.
67.         while ( rs.next() ) {
68.             //
69.             //
70.             //
71.             System.out.println("** Table: " +
72.                         rs.getMetaData().getTableName(1) );
73.
74.
75.                     //
76.                 // loop through all columns in the ResultSet
77.                 //
78.             for ( int i = 1;
79.                     i < rs.getMetaData().getColumnCount();
80.                     i++ ) {
81.                 System.out.println( "\tColumn: "   +
82.                             rs.getMetaData().getColumnName(i) +
83.                   " - value :\t" +
84.                             rs.getObject(i) ); // value
85.             }
86.         }
87.
88.      }
89.     else {            // it's an update
90.         System.out.println("\n Update Performed - Rows updated: " +
91.                         stmt.getUpdateCount() );
92.      }
93.
94.rs =  null; // reset this for the next loop
95.
96.} // end for loop
97.
98.}
99.catch (SQLException e) {
100.
101.     // display SQL specific exception information
102.     System.out.println("**************************" );
103.     System.out.println("SQLException in main: " + e.getMessage() );
104.     System.out.println("** SQLState: " + e.getSQLState());
105.     System.out.println("** SQL Error Code: " + e.getErrorCode());
106.     System.out.println("**************************" );
107.     e.printStackTrace();
108.}
109.catch (Exception e) {
110.     System.out.println("Exception in main: " + e.getMessage() );
```

```
111.      e.printStackTrace();
112.}
113.finally {
114.
115.     try {
116.
117.    if ( con != null )
118.             con.close();
119.     }
120.     catch (SQLException e) {
121.             e.printStackTrace();
122.     }
123.}
124.
125.
126.
127.}
128.
129.}
130.}
```

This code example builds on the code examples of Chapter 5 and adds some new twists by focusing on some additional data manipulation features that will be examined in more detail in this chapter. In short, the program connects to a data source, executes several SQL statements, and examines the results of the statement execution. Though for convenience and simplicity, the SQL statements are hard-coded into program, they are treated in a generic way by the code. This means that once the program code begins processing the query, it assumes that it doesn't know what type of database query it is. The program does not know whether or not the query is a select query or an update query. An expansion of this approach to query processing allows queries to be processed dynamically and provides some unique benefits that will be examined in more detail later in this chapter and in Chapters 10 and 11.

The program code begins by identifying the package names for import on lines 1 through 4. Several variables that will be used in the program are declared on lines 9 through 11. An initial JNDI context is obtained on line 24 and used to look up a DataSource reference for the moviesmysql data source on line 27. The DataSource object is then used to obtain a Connection object on line 30.

The Connection object is used to obtain a single Statement object on line 33. This statement object is used to process all of the queries to be executed by the program. A String array is used to store the queries that will be processed in this example. This array is declared and populated on lines 41 through 43.

A for loop starting at line 45 is used to process the array of queries. All processing within the for loop makes no assumption about the nature of the query being processed. The queries are effectively treated as dynamic queries within this loop.

The loop iterates for the length of the queries array (`< queries.length`), as indicated on line 45. For reach iteration of the loop, it will execute the query and examine the results. The `Statement` class `execute` method is used to execute the query on line 52. It takes a string argument representing the query to be executed. The query can be either a database update or a `select` statement. The `execute` method returns a boolean `true` indicating that a `ResultSet` was returned. This boolean value is stored in the `isResultSet` program variable.

The `if` conditional statement on line 57 tests the result `isResultSet` boolean variable, and if it is set `true`, will continue processing the query results. If the method returns `true`, then the `ResultSet` is retrieved using a call to the `Statement` class `getResultSet` method on line 58.

The next section of the code processes the `ResultSet`, if in fact there is a `ResultSet`; otherwise, it processes the update count for the update operation that was performed. This is done with the `if` conditional statement that extends from line 64 to line 92. At line 64 the boolean value `isResultSet` is tested. If the value is a boolean true, then a `ResultSet` has been retrieved and a `while` loop is executed on lines 67 through 86 to process the results in the `ResultSet`.

This processing of the `ResultSet` makes few assumptions about the contents of the `ResultSet`. It is intended to demonstrate some of the features available for managing dynamic queries. Within the processing on line 72, a `ResultSetMetaData` object is obtained for the `ResultSet`. This object can be used to gather information about the contents of the `ResultSet`. In this example, the `ResultSetMetaData` object is used to determine the name of the table for the column being output and the name of the column. Later in the program on line 81, the `ResultSetMetaData` object is used to determine the number of columns in the `ResultSet` allowing the loop on line 81 to iterate through all of the columns in the current `ResultSet` row.

If the `else` condition on line 89 is executed, then the `ResultSet` reference was null and the query is assumed (and the program logic would ensure it) to have been an update query. The update count is obtained on line 91 with a call to the `Statement` class `getUpdateCount` method.

Lines 94 through 122 are used to catch the various exceptions that may be thrown in the main program block. As a result of executing this program, the following output would be produced.

Output from StatementExampleX.java

```
** Executing query: 0 : select * from users

Select Performed - Results:
** Table: users
        Column: user_id - value :      101
        Column: first_name - value :  Cal
        Column: last_name - value :    Coder
        Column: address1 - value :      12 Joe Dimaggio Rd.
```

```
        Column: address2 - value :      null
        Column: city - value :West Amwell
        Column: state_province - value :       NY
        Column: postal_code - value : 12134
        Column: country - value :      UK
** Table: users
        Column: user_id - value :      201
        Column: first_name - value :  Carrie
        Column: last_name - value :   Coder
        Column: address1 - value :      25 Norma Jean La.
        Column: address2 - value :      null
        Column: city - value :East Amwell
        Column: state_province - value :       NY
        Column: postal_code - value : 21393
        Column: country - value :      UK

** Executing query: 1 : select * from movies

Select Performed - Results:
** Table: movies
        Column: movie_id - value :    3
        Column: movie_name - value : Stamping Out the Evil Null Reference
        Column: release_date - value :        2001-01-01
        Column: movie_desc - value : ** not provided **
        Column: special_promotion - value :  1
        Column: update_date - value : 2002-01-14
        Column: category - value :    Comedy
** Table: movies
        Column: movie_id - value :    4
        Column: movie_name - value : The Last Compile
        Column: release_date - value :        2000-01-11
        Column: movie_desc - value : ** not provided **
        Column: special_promotion - value :  2
        Column: update_date - value : 2002-01-14
        Column: category - value :    Comedy
** Table: movies
        Column: movie_id - value :    902
        Column: movie_name - value : Another Dog Day
        Column: release_date - value :        2002-05-22
        Column: movie_desc - value : ** not provided **
        Column: special_promotion - value :  1
        Column: update_date - value : 2001-10-20
        Column: category - value :    Documentary

** Executing query: 2 : update users set country = 'USA'

 Update Performed - Rows updated: 2

** Executing query: 3 : select * from users

Select Performed - Results:
** Table: users
```

```
    Column: user_id - value :      101
    Column: first_name - value :   Cal
    Column: last_name - value :    Coder
    Column: address1 - value :     12 Joe Dimaggio Rd.
    Column: address2 - value :     null
    Column: city - value :West Amwell
    Column: state_province - value :      NY
    Column: postal_code - value : 12134
    Column: country - value :      USA
** Table: users
    Column: user_id - value :      201
    Column: first_name - value :   Carrie
    Column: last_name - value :    Coder
    Column: address1 - value :     25 Norma Jean La.
    Column: address2 - value :     null
    Column: city - value :East Amwell
    Column: state_province - value :      NY
    Column: postal_code - value : 21393
    Column: country - value :      USA
```

This example provided an introduction to using JDBC to retrieve rows and review them. But it did not use all of the methods available in the Statement class—that would have made for a very long and tedious example. To be thorough, the following sections will cover the Statement class in more detail, using code snippets to demonstrate many of the methods within the class.

THE STATEMENT CLASS

In any JDBC application, a Connection object is obtained either from the DriverManager or from the DataSource. This object is an instance of the Connection class, which encapsulates the functionality of the data source connection and acts as a factory (effectively implementing a Factory design pattern) for the creation of Statement and PreparedStatement objects.

A SQL select statement that is expected to return results should be executed using the executeQuery method of the Statement class. This method will return a ResultSet object, which will contain the results of the query. A SQL update statement should be executed using the executeUpdate method, which will return an integer representing the number of rows affected by the update. If the type of SQL statement is unknown, then the execute method should be used to execute either type of statement.

The Statement class is best used when a query is going to be executed only once and return results. If a query is going to be executed repeatedly, then the PreparedStatement class will provide better performance. (The PreparedStatement class is described in the following section of this chapter.)

The methods for the `Statement` class are listed in Table 6–1. As with the other methods described previously, all throw a `SQLException` when errors are encountered.

> If a statement is to be executed multiple times, it is better for performance reasons to use the `PreparedStatement` class to execute the SQL statement. A prepared statement is sent to the database engine to be parsed and optimized before being used. Therefore, each time the statement is executed, the overhead of parsing and optimization is eliminated.

Table 6–1   *Statement Class Methods*

Method	Description
`void addBatch(String sql)`	Inserts an SQLa SQL command at the end of the current batch of commands for the `Statement` object.
`void cancel()`	This command allows a statement to be canceled. (Not all drivers will support this operation, and those that do will still not allow all statements to be canceled.)
`void clearBatch()`	Clears the current batch of SQL update statements.
`void clearWarnings()`	Clears warnings on the current object.
`void close()`	Closes and releases any data source resources associated with this object.
`boolean execute(String sql)`	Executes the SQL statement passed as a parameter. This alternative form of query execution can be used for either `'select'` or `'update'` queries and is therefore useful when the type of SQL statement is not known. This method can also be used for queries which that return multiple results (for example, stored procedures supported by some database vendors).
`int[] executeBatch()`	Executes a batch of SQL updates and returns an array of update counts on successful execution.
`ResultSet executeQuery(String sql)`	Executes a SQL `'select'` statement and returns a single ResultSet object.
`int executeUpdate(String sql)`	Executes an SQLa SQL `'update'` statement. Returns an integer count of the rows updated.
`Connection getConnection()`	Returns the `Connection` object that created this object.
`int getFetchDirection()`	Returns the *'fetch direction'* for the results returned by this object. (The fetch direction is a suggestion to the data base for the creation of cursors. The integer value returned relates to integer constants in the `ResultSet` class.)

Table 6–1 *Statement Class Methods (cont.)*

Method	Description
`int getFetchSize()`	Returns the default fetch size for `ResultSet` objects returned by this object.
`int getMaxFieldSize()`	Returns the maximum number of bytes allowed for any column value returned by this object.
`int getMaxRows()`	Returns the maximum number of rows that a `ResultSet` object can contain.
`boolean getMoreResults()`	When the `Statement` object contains multiple ResultSet objects, this method moves to the next ResultSet.
`int getQueryTimeout()`	Returns the number of seconds the driver will wait for an SQLa SQL statement to execute.
`ResultSet getResultSet()`	Returns the current `ResultSet` object.
`int getResultSetConcurrency()`	Returns the concurrency for `ResultSet` objects created by this object. (The integer value returned relates to integer constants in the ResultSet class.)
`int getResultSetType()`	Returns the type for `ResultSet` objects created by this object. The integer value returned relates to constants in the `ResultSet` class.
`int getUpdateCount()`	Returns the current update count for the last statement executed by this object. If the last statement executed was not an update (it was a 'select' query), then −1 is returned. If there are no current results, then an −1 is returned.
`SQLWarning getWarnings()`	Returns the first warning reported on this object. Additional warnings will be chained to the first warning.
`void setCursorName(String name)`	Is used to set the cursor name to be used by 'select' query execution by this object.
`void setEscapeProcessing(boolean enable)`	Sets *'escape'* processing for the current `Statement` object. Passing a boolean `true` will turn escape processing on; passing a boolean `false` will turn it off.
`void setFetchDirection(int direction)`	Sets the 'fetch direction' for this object. This is a hint to the database on the direction cursors will be used. The integer value provided is a constant from the `ResultSet` interface.
`void setFetchSize(int rows)`	Provides a hint to the JDBC driver on the fetch size to be returned by this object.
`void setMaxFieldSize(int max)`	Sets the maximum number of bytes for a column returned by this object.

Table 6–1	*Statement Class Methods (cont.)*

Method	Description
`void setMaxRows(int max)`	Sets the limit for the maximum number of rows that any `select` query can return.
`void setQueryTimeout(int seconds)`	Sets the number of seconds the driver will wait for a query to execute using the current `Statement` object.

The following sections provide additional detail on these methods and provide examples on how they might be used in applications. The methods are grouped based on their purpose and usage.

EXECUTING THE QUERY

The `Statement` class provides a number of methods for executing queries. Which method is used depends on the nature of the application. The methods available are called using the following signatures:

- `boolean execute(String sql)`
- `ResultSet executeQuery(String sql)`
- `int executeUpdate(String sql)`
- `int[] executeBatch()`
- `void addBatch(String sql)`
- `void clearBatch()`

The `execute` method in the `Statement` class takes a string argument that contains the SQL statement to execute. The SQL statement can be any type of SQL statement—an `insert` or `update` statement, a `select` query, a `create table` statement, or a stored procedure that returns multiple results. The `execute` method returns a boolean value indicating `true` if the statement executed was a `ResultSet`, or `false` if it was an `update` statement or if no results were returned. If the SQL statement executed using the `execute` method returns multiple `ResultSet` objects, then the `getMoreResults` method can be called to determine if there are more results to retrieve, and the `getResultSet` method can be called to retrieve the next `ResultSet`. The previous example demonstrated the use of this method but did not call `getMoreResults`, since only one `ResultSet` was returned by the executed statement. Generally speaking, the `execute` method is a convenient method to use if the specific type of SQL statement being executed is not known.

The executeQuery method is used to execute queries against the database. The intention of the name is to imply that only queries or select operations are to be executed with this method. Unfortunately, the term database query is often applied to database update operations as well as to database select operations. This method, however, should only be used to execute database select queries that are expected to return a ResultSet. It is allowed that the ResultSet returned may be empty (and that is not an error).

The executeQuery method accepts a string that contains a valid SQL query. If escape processing is turned on for the driver, then the string may have valid JDBC escape sequences in the SQL statement. Only one SQL statement should be passed in the string.

The executeQuery method will return a ResultSet. As with most Java methods, this return value could be ignored, but this is not common practice with JDBC. (The execute method provides more coherent syntax for select operations where results will be ignored.) The following code snippet provides an example of the executeQuery method:

```
...
// get the DataSource from the JNDI name server
    DataSource ds = (DataSource) ctx.lookup("movies");

    // get the connection from the DataSource
    con = ds.getConnection( );

    // create a Statement class to execute the SQL statement
    Statement stmt = con.createStatement();

    // execute the SQL statement and get the results in a ResultSet
    ResultSet rs   = stmt.executeQuery
                ("select movie_name, release_date from movies" );

...
```

In this code snippet, a Connection object is obtained from the DataSource and is used to create a Statement object. The executeQuery method is used to execute a SQL select statement to retrieve specific columns for all rows in the movies table.

The executeUpdate method is used to execute queries that perform database update operations. This method returns an integer count for the number of records updated by the update operation. While it appears to be common practice to ignore the return value from this method, this is not recommended. The following code snippet provides an example of the executeUpdate method.

```
...
DataSource ds = (DataSource) ctx.lookup("movies");
```

```
    //
    // get the connection from the DataSource
    //
    con = ds.getConnection( );

    //
    // create a Statement class to execute the SQL statement
    //
    Statement stmt = con.createStatement();

    //
    // turn auto-commit off
    //
    con.setAutoCommit( false );

    //
    // we are now in a transaction ... perform a series of updates
    //
    int updateResult = stmt.executeUpdate(
 "insert into users (user_id, first_name, last_name, address1," +
 " city, state_province, postal_code, country)   " +
 " values ( 0, 'Fred', 'Smith', '2020 Nowhere Lane', " +
 " 'Newark', 'NJ', '09090', 'US');" );
...
```

In this example, a `DataSource` is obtained for the movies data source and then used to create a `Statement` object. Then, as is common with database `update` operations, a transaction boundary must be established to span multiple database update operations. Since the auto-commit facility of JDBC is turned on by default, it must be set off before a multistatement transaction can be created. The `executeUpdate` method is then called, and the results of the update operation, how many rows were updated by the `update` statement, are returned as an integer value and stored in the `updateResult` variable. At some later point in the code (not shown), the transaction will either be committed or rolled back based on the success or failure of the individual SQL statements being executed.

WORKING WITH BATCHES

As of JDBC 2.1, the JDBC API supports batch operations for updates if the underlying driver and database support it. Batch `update` operations allow multiple updates to be directed at the database at one time, thus providing the potential of improved update performance. Batches are supported using the following methods.

- `int[] executeBatch()`
- `void addBatch(String sql)`
- `void clearBatch()`

The `addBatch` method takes a string argument that contains the SQL `update` operation to be added to the batch. This method is called repeatedly with each separate SQL statement to be added to the batch. Alternatively, the `clearBatch` method could be called to clear the batch of any existing entries; this method should be called in any code that may reuse a `Statement` object for batch operations.

Once all SQL entries have been added to a batch statement, the batch can be executed using the `executeBatch` method. The `executeBatch` method will return an integer array containing corresponding integer values for each update operation performed in the batch. The integer entries will correspond in sequence to the `update` operations, so the first `update` operation results would be stored in the result array element zero, the second in the result array element one, and so on. The following code snippet provides an example of the batch `update` operations in JDBC:

```
...
//
// get the DataSource from the JNDI name server
//
DataSource ds = (DataSource) ctx.lookup("movies");

//
// get the connection from the DataSource
//
con = ds.getConnection( );

//
// create a Statement class to execute the SQL statement
//
Statement stmt = con.createStatement();

//
// add a batch of SQL statements
//
stmt.addBatch(
        "insert into users (user_id, first_name, last_name) " +
                " values ( 101, 'Sam', 'Snape')" );
stmt.addBatch(
        "insert into users (user_id, first_name, last_name) " +
                " values ( 102, 'Sal', 'Snake')" );
stmt.addBatch("insert into movies (movie_id, movie_name) " +
                " values ( 201, 'The Evil Null Reference')" );
stmt.addBatch("update movies  " +
                " set movie_desc = '** not provided **' " );

// execute the batch and get the results
//
int results[] = stmt.executeBatch();
```

```
//
// print the results. integer values represents rows updated
//
for (int n=0;n<results.length;n++)
    System.out.println("Result from query " + n +
                        " = " + results[n] );
```
. . .

In this code snippet, the `DataSource` is obtained for the `movies` data source. The `DataSource` object obtained is used to create a `Statement` object, and the `addBatch` method of the `Statement` class is then called repeatedly to add SQL update statements to the `Statement` object. Once all appropriate update statements have been added to the batch, the `executeBatch` method is called, and the results are stored in an integer array. This integer array is then examined in a `for` loop to determine the results of the batch update operation.

Examining Query Results

Once a SQL statement has been executed, the program needs to examine the results. If the SQL statement was a `select` query, then a `ResultSet` will be returned, and the results of the query will be examined using `ResultSet` class methods (covered later in this chapter). If the query was an `update` query, then results of the statement execution can be examined with the `Statement` class methods listed below.

- `int getUpdateCount()`
- `boolean getMoreResults()`
- `ResultSet getResultSet()`

The `getUpdateCount` method returns the number of records updated by the last executed `update` statement. If the last statement executed was a `select` query, then this method should return a –1.

The `getMoreResults` method returns a boolean value indicating whether or not there are more `ResultSet` objects available from the last executed query. This method will close any currently open `ResultSet` objects returned by the `Statement` object and requires a call to the `getResultSet` method to obtain the next `ResultSet`. The following code snippet provides an example:

. . .
```
//
// get the DataSource from the JNDI name server
//
DataSource ds = (DataSource) ctx.lookup("movies-mysql");

//
```

```
  // get the connection from the DataSource
  //
  con = ds.getConnection( );

  //
  // create a Statement class to execute the SQL statement
  //
  Statement stmt = con.createStatement();

  //
  // execute a query that returns multiple ResultSet objects
  //
  isResultSet = stmt.execute( query );

  if ( isResultSet )   {

      //
      // loop through all returned results
      //
      while( stmt.getMoreResults() ) {
          //
      // if true, then we have a result set
      //
          rs = stmt.getResultSet();

          //
          // process the ResultSet
          //
          processResults( rs ) ;
      }
  }
  else {              // it's an update
       System.out.println("\n Update Performed - Rows updated: " +
                          stmt.getUpdateCount() );
  }
. . .
```

In this code snippet, the `DataSource` is used to obtain a `Connection` object, which is then used to create a `Statement` object. A query that will return multiple `ResultSet` objects is executed using the `Statement execute` method.

The return value from the `execute` method is a boolean value that indicates whether or not the execute method has returned results. If the method returns a `true` value, then a `ResultSet` has been returned. In this code snippet, the return value from the `execute` method (`isResultSet`) is used in an `if` statement; if the value is `true`, then a `while` loop is executed using the `getMoreResults` method. As long as the `getMoreResult` method returns `true`, then there is a `ResultSet` that can be retrieved using the `getResultSet` method.

If, however, the return value from the `execute` method is `false`, then the `execute` method executed an update, and the `getUpdateCount` method is called to return the number of rows that have been updated.

Controlling and Tuning Results Processing

When a `select` query is executed, results are provided in the form of a `ResultSet` object as returned by the `Statement` object. The behavior of this `ResultSet` object is partly controlled by the `Statement` object. (This is largely because the database system should be informed of how the results will be processed when the statement is executed.) A number of methods are available that may optionally be used by the driver to control the processing of database queries. These methods are as follows.

- `int getFetchSize()`
- `int getMaxFieldSize()`
- `int getMaxRows()`
- `void setFetchSize(int rows)`
- `void setMaxRows(int max)`
- `void setMaxFieldSize(int max)`

These methods allow examination and manipulation of the size of the *fetch* buffer. The process of retrieving rows from the database is often referred to as a `fetch` operation. The integer value returned by the `getFetchSize` method is the number of rows that will be retrieved in increments during the processing of a `ResultSet`. The default value for the fetch size is dependent on the database vendor. The `setFetchSize` method can be used to set the size of the fetch buffer for the database driver by passing an integer value for the size of the fetch buffer in rows.

Performance can be improved by tuning the fetch buffer size to an appropriate size for the operation being performed. For example, if the application component being developed will probably work with only 50 rows from a `select` query, then setting the fetch buffer size to 50 would improve performance. If in this example, you consider the alternative of setting the fetch buffer size to 200, then the component would be required to wait for 150 rows to be placed in the fetch buffer (instead of the 50 that the client is ready to use), rows that may never be used by the application. Additionally, in this hypothetical example, the 200 rows would require allocation of additional memory that is not really needed by the application.

The fetch buffer size is an internal buffer size that provides a hint or some advice to the database driver. The database driver and the database are not required to use this information. If the fetch buffer size is set to zero, then the hint for the fetch buffer size is explicitly ignored by the database driver and an internal default value is used; this is the default value for this parameter.

The getMaxRows method can be used to determine the maximum number of rows that a driver can return for select query processing. This method returns an integer indicating the current setting for the maximum number of rows to be returned by a ResultSet. A return value of zero indicates that there is no fixed limit to the number of rows returned (a common default setting). The default value returned is vendor-specific. Per the JDBC specification, if this limit is exceeded, then additional rows are silently dropped; that is, no exception is thrown. Setting and using this limit should therefore be used with caution.

The getMaxFieldSize method returns an integer representing the maximum number of bytes that certain fields should have. The setMaxFieldSize method takes an integer argument representing the number of bytes that certain fields can contain before being returned by the driver. These methods apply only to the JDBC data types of BINARY, VARBINARY, LONGVARBINARY, CHAR, and VARCHAR. These fields are quietly truncated if the size is exceeded; this means that no exception will be thrown. The following code snippet provides an example of these methods.

```
// get the DataSource from the JNDI name server
DataSource ds = (DataSource) ctx.lookup("movies");

// get the connection from the DataSource
con = ds.getConnection( );

// create a Statement class to execute the SQL statement
Statement stmt = con.createStatement();

//
// get some information about the fetch limits
//
System.out.println( "Fetch size: " + stmt.getFetchSize() );
System.out.println( "Field size: " + stmt.getMaxFieldSize() );
System.out.println( "Max rows: " + stmt.getMaxRows() );

//
// tune these parameters
//
stmt.setMaxRows( 500 );
stmt.setFetchSize( 100 );
```

In this code snippet, the Connection object returns a Statement object, which is used to obtain the current settings (the default settings) for the fetch buffer size, the maximum field size, and the maximum number of rows to be retrieved using a ResultSet. Running this portion of the application against a

`MySql` database returns the following output:

```
Fetch size: 0
Field size: 1048576
Max rows: 0
```

This indicates that the fetch buffer size for the data source is set to zero, indicating the fetch buffer size hint has not been set to any particular value (this is the default), the field size for the data types affected by `setMaxFieldSize` is 1,048,576 bytes, and there is no limit on the number of rows returned by a `ResultSet`. The settings for the fetch buffer size and the maximum number of rows are then changed to suit the application.

CONTROLLING QUERY PROCESSING

Several aspects of query processing are dictated by the `Statement` object. The amount of time the driver will wait for a query to execute and the type of concurrency to be used by the database can be controlled using `Statement` object methods. The direction in which a `ResultSet` will be processed can also be passed to the database as a hint for execution of the query. The methods used to control this behavior are as follows.

- `int getQueryTimeout()`
- `int getResultSetConcurrency()`
- `int getResultSetType()`
- `int getFetchDirection()`
- `void setFetchDirection(int direction)`
- `void setQueryTimeout(int seconds)`

The `getResultSetConcurrency` method returns the concurrency type (as specified by integer constants in the `ResultSet` class) defined for `ResultSet` objects created by the `Statement`. The `getResultSetType` returns an integer that indicates the type of `ResultSet` created by this `Statement` as defined by the integer constants in the `ResultSet` class. There are no corresponding `set` methods for these methods in the `Statement` class because the `ResultSet` behavior is set when the `Statement` object is created. The `ResultSet` behavior for `ResultSet` objects created by a `Statement` object is dictated when the `Statement` object is created using an overloaded version of the `Connection` `createStatement` method as follows:

```
Statement createStatement(int resultSetType,
                          int resultSetConcurrency)
```

The `ResultSet` type and `ResultSet` concurrency values passed into this method are integer constants from the `ResultSet` class. Possible for concurrency are `ResultSet.CONCUR_READ_ONLY` and `ResultSet.CONCUR_UPDATABLE`. Possible values for type are `ResultSet.TYPE_FORWARD_ONLY`, `ResultSet.TYPE_SCROLL_INSENSITIVE`, and `ResultSet.TYPE_SCROLL_SENSITIVE`.

The time the driver will wait for a query to execute can be set using the `setQueryTimeout` method. This method is passed an integer indicating the number of seconds to wait for a query to execute. If the value specified is exceeded, then an exception is thrown. The `getQueryTimeout` method returns an integer indicating the current setting of this parameter. The default value is vendor-specific. A value of zero indicates an unlimited timeout and is a common vendor setting. (Note that even with an unlimited setting for a query timeout parameter, network socket timeout values could potentially cancel a long-running query.) Many database vendors will also allow query timeout parameters to be set, which can be used to timeout a query initiated by a client irrespective of the client timeout setting.

The `setFetchDirection` method takes an integer argument representing a hint to the database driver on the direction in which query processing will proceed. The `getFetchDirection` method returns an integer argument representing the fetch direction. The integer value is one of the integer constants in the `ResultSet` as follows.

- `ResultSet.FETCH_FORWARD`
- `ResultSet.FETCH_REVERSE`
- `ResultSet.FETCH_UNKNOWN`

The default value is `ResultSet.FETCH_FORWARD`. Corresponding methods for getting and setting the fetch direction also exist in the `ResultSet` class. Since many databases provide optimizations based on how a `select` query will be processed, it may be best to set these parameters in the `Statement` object before the query is executed.

MISCELLANEOUS AND UTILITY

A number of miscellaneous methods are available to control processing and retrieve useful information about the `Statement`. These methods are as follows.

- `void setCursorName(String name)`
- `void setEscapeProcessing(boolean enable)`
- `Connection getConnection()`
- `void clearWarnings()`
- `SQLWarning getWarnings()`

- void cancel()
- void close()

The `setCursorName` method can be passed a string argument for the cursor name to set the cursor name for all cursors to be created by the `Statement` object. This name can then be used in positioned `update` and `delete` statements. This method will work only on databases and JDBC drivers that support positioned update as indicated by the `DatabaseMetaData supportsPositionedUpdate` method; otherwise this method will quietly fail.

As of JDBC 2.0, drivers may optionally support updates through `ResultSets`. This provides a vendor-neutral facility for positioned updates. While it is assumed that JDBC drivers will map this capability to the vendor-specific syntax, this is not required.

Controlling JDBC Escape Processing

The `setEscapeProcessing` method can be used to turn escape processing in the driver on or off. By default, escape processing is turned on in the JDBC driver.

JDBC escape processing allows the JDBC driver to intervene in the processing of SQL queries. Since some SQL features are not implemented by all databases, and some features are implemented differently, the escape processing feature of the JDBC driver allows a standard JDBC "escape syntax" to be used to access these features and leaves it to the JDBC driver to implement the database-specific syntax. This enhances the portability across databases of the JDBC application. JDBC escape processing uses special characters in the SQL string to inform the driver that it must preprocess that portion of the query.

The escape processing feature is implemented for scalar functions, date and time literals, outer joins, stored procedures, and `where` clause matching. For instance, escape processing can be used to provide a standard syntax for date literals and timestamp literals, as the following code snippet shows:

```
ResultSet rs = stmt.executeQuery(
               "select *  from movies " +
       "where movie_date = {d '2001-01-12'} and   "
       " return_timestamp = {d '2002-01-28' 12:00:00' ");
```

Virtually every database vendor provides a unique syntax for processing outer joins. JDBC provides a standard escape processing syntax using the following format:

```
{oj <table_name> [LEFT|RIGHT|FULL] OUTER JOIN
        <table_name> | <outer_join>
        on <search_condition> }
```

Using this syntax, a left outer join could be used to join the `user_rentals` and `movies` table, thus returning all movies whether or not they have been rented. The following code snippet demonstrates this join using JDBC escape syntax:

```
...
Statement stmt;
DatabaseMetaData dmd;
...
  System.out.println( "supportsFullOuterJoins: " +
                     dmd.supportsLimitedOuterJoins() );
  ResultSet rs = stmt.executeQuery(
          "select user_id, movies.movie_id, movie_name, rental_date " +
        " from {oj movies LEFT OUTER JOIN user_rentals " +
        " on movies.movie_id=user_rentals.movie_id} " );
...
```

Stored procedures can also be called using escape syntax, as the following code demonstrates:

```
...

  //
  // execute the processMovieTransfers stored procedure
  //
  CallableStatement stmt2 = conn.prepareCall(
              "{?= call   processMovieTransfers(?)}");

    stmt.registerOutParameter(0, Types.VARCHAR);

    stmt.setObject(2, new Integer(43));

    if (stmt.execute()) {
      ResultSet rs = stmt.getResultSet();

...
```

The getConnection Method

The `getConnection` is a convenience method that retrieves the database connection that was used to create this `Statement` object. This method provides access to the methods of the `Connection` object, methods that allow transactions to be managed and metadata information about the database to be retrieved (through a `DatabaseMetaData` object).

Processing Statement Warnings

The `clearWarnings` method clears all warnings from the `Statement` object. The `getWarnings` method retrieves the warnings for the `Statement` object. Warnings are received in a chain, one warning chained to the next in the chain, so that all warnings must be iterated through to determine the full extent of the warnings retrieved. The following code snippet demonstrates:

```
1....
2.//
3.// check for warnings on the Statement
4.//
5.SQLWarning sqlw = statement.getWarnings();
6.
7.//
8.// warning may be null reference
9.//
10.if (sqlw != null) {
11.
12.    //
13.    // iterate through the chain of warnings
14.    //
15.    while ( sqlw != null ) {
16.            System.out.println("Warning: " + sqlw );
17.      sqlw = sqlw.getNextWarning();
18.    }
19.else
20.    System.out.println("There are no warnings.");
21....
```

This code retrieves a `SQLWarning` object reference for the `Statement` on line 5. The code then checks to determine whether or not the warning object is null (which is common). If the `SQLWarning` object is not null, then the warnings are iterated through using a `while` loop. Each warning message is displayed using the `toString` method of the `SQLWarning` interface on line 16. The next warning in the chain is retrieved on line 17.

The cancel Method and the close Method

The `cancel` method allows a database query to be canceled through the statement that executed the query. Since the various `execute` methods (`executeQuery`, `execute`, and others) block while an `execute` method is processing, some other processing thread must be used to cancel the current processing thread (the thread that executed the query with the `Statement` object).

The `close` method closes the database connection associated with the `Statement` object. If the `Statement` object had a `ResultSet` object, it is also closed. (Closing a `Connection` object also closes any associated objects and is the most common approach for releasing database resources.)

EXCEPTIONS AND ERRORS AND WARNINGS

The JDBC API provides a number of exceptions and warnings that capture error information useful to database programmers.

The SQLException Class

A `SQLException` is thrown by a large number of the JDBC methods. This exception inherits from `java.lang.Exception` and provides the usual exception reason or message through the inherited `getMessage` method. But this exception also provides information specific to databases, such as the SQL code of the error and the SQLState—standardized database error-reporting facilities.

The `SQLException` class contains a string, which is the reason given by the database server or JDBC driver for the exception, the SQL state, which is a standardized string containing information about the state of SQL processing for the exception, and an integer error code containing an error code specific to the database vendor or provider. Table 6–2 contains the constructors for this exception class.

The `SQLException` contains a small number of methods to provide access to its internal data about the exception that was thrown. Table 6–3 provides a listing of these methods.

Table 6–2   *The Constructors for the SQLException Class*

Constructor	Description
SQLException()	Creates a new SQLException with null values for the reason, SQLState, and vendor error code.
SQLException(String reason)	Creates a new SQLException with the reason provided as a parameter. Substitutes a null value for the SQLState and vendor error code.
SQLException(String reason, String SQLState)	Creates a new SQLException with the reason provided as a parameter and the SQLState provided as a parameter. Substitutes a zero for the vendor error code.
SQLException(String reason, String SQLState, int vendorCode)	Creates a new SQLException with the reason provided, the SQLState provided, and the vendor error code provided as a parameter.

Table 6–3	*Methods for the SQLException Class*

Method	Description
`int getErrorCode()`	Returns the vendor error code for the exception that was thrown to create the exception.
`SQLException getNextException()`	Retrieves the next exception in the chain, if there is another exception.
`String setNextException(SQLException e)`	Sets the next exception in the chain of exceptions attached to the current object.

The SQLWarning Class

The `SQLWarning` is similar in use and functionality to the `SQLException` class except that warnings are, by definition, some event or occurrence that the application can possibly overcome. A `SQLWarning` is not thrown by the application like an exception, so declaring a catch block for `SQLWarning` will have no effect (and would generate a compile time error). Instead, the `SQLWarning` is returned by the `getWarnings` methods of the `Connection` and `Statement` class. Table 6–4 lists the constructors for the `SQLWarning` class.

Table 6–4	*Constructors for the SQLWarning Class*

Constructor	Description
`SQLWarning()`	Creates a new `SQLWarning` with null values for the reason, SQLState, and vendor error code.
`SQLWarning(String reason)`	Creates a new `SQLWarning` with the reason provided as a parameter. Substitutes a null value for the SQLState and vendor error code.
`SQLWarning(String reason, String SQLState)`	Creates a new `SQLWarning` with the reason provided as a parameter and the `SQLState` provided as a parameter. Substitutes a zero for the vendor error code.
`SQLWarning(String reason, String SQLState, int vendorCode)`	Creates a new `SQLWarning` with the reason provided, the `SQLState` provided and the vendor error code provided as a parameter.

The SQLWarning class is a subclass of SQLException, and so inherits the methods of that class, making those methods available to call if needed. Table 6–5 lists the methods in this class.

Table 6–5   *Methods for the SQLWarning Class*

Method	Description
SQLException getNextWarning()	Retrieves the next warning in the chain if there is another exception.
String setNextWarning(SQLWarning w)	Sets the next warning in the chain of warnings attached to the current object.

The DataTruncation Class

The DataTruncation class is a subclass of SQLException and provides a warning or exception that specifically reports on errors of data truncation.

On SQL select operations, a DataTruncation warning would be placed on the Statement object and could be retrieved using the getWarnings method. On write operations or database updates, a DataTruncation exception would be thrown. The following constructor is available for this class.

Table 6–6   *DataTruncation Class Constructor*

Constructor	Description
DataTruncation(int index, boolean parameter, boolean read, int dataSize int transferSize)	Creates a DataTruncation object using the specified parameters.

The DataTruncation class is a subclass of SQLWarning and the SQLException class, and so has access to the inherited methods of that class. The class contains a number of methods to reveal information about truncation that took place, as shown in Table 6–7.

Table 6–7 *Methods for the SQLWarning Class*

Method	Description
`int getDataSize()`	Returns an integer indicating the size of the number of bytes that should have been written.
`int getIndex()`	Returns an index to the column or parameter that was truncated.
`Boolean getParameter()`	Returns a boolean indicating whether or not the value truncated.
`Boolean getRead()`	Returns a boolean true if the truncation occurred on a database read operation.
`int GetTransferSize()`	Returns an integer representing the number of bytes actually transferred.

The BatchUpdateException Class

The `BatchUpdateException` is a class that is thrown by the batch update methods in the `Statement` class. This class is a subclass of `SQLException` and simply augments the behaviors of that class to include a method that returns the update counts for the batch just executed. Table 6–8 contains the constructors for this method.

Table 6–8 *Constructors for the BatchUpdateException Class*

Constructor	Description
`BatchUpdateException()`	Creates a new `BatchUpdateException` with null values for the reason, zero for the update counts, and the SQL state.
`BatchUpdateException( int[] UpdateCounts)`	Creates a new `BatchUpdaeException` with null values for the reason, and the update counts.
`BatchUpdateException( String reason, int[] updateCounts)`	Creates a new `BatchUpdateException` with the designated parameters.
`BatchUpdateException( String reason, String SQLState, int updateCounts)`	Creates a new `BatchUpdateException` with the designated parameters.

The `BatchUpdateException` class inherits the methods of its superclass, the `SQLException` class, which is itself a subclass of the `Exception` class. This leaves a number of methods available to `BatchUpdateException` instances. The `BatchUpdateException` class adds a single method, as shown in Table 6–9.

Table 6–9   *Method for the BatchUpdateException Class*

Method	Description
`Int[] getUpdateCounts()`	Returns an integer array of the update count for the updates executed by the batch before the exception was thrown.

The `getUpdateCounts` method returns an integer array. The integer array contains the update counts, the number of records updated for each of the update statements in the batch that generated the exception.

SUMMARY

Once connected to a database, SQL statements can be executed using the `Statement` class. Using this class, SQL statements, whether they are `select` statements or the various SQL update statements (`insert`, `delete`, `update` statements) can be executed.

As we saw in this chapter, the `Statement` class not only allows SQL statements to be executed, but provides methods and parameters that can be used to control the type of `ResultSet` returned by the `Statement` class for a statement execution. The `Statement` class can also be used to tune the `ResultSet`, setting the size of the buffer to be used to retrieve the results.

Exceptions can be thrown by most JDBC methods. As shown in this chapter, specialized exceptions are thrown by JDBC methods which provide the specific information needed to track and respond to the errors encountered when working with databases.

Coming Up Next

The SQL prepared statement is a type of SQL statement that is preprocessed by the database engine. This provides performance improvements and other benefits for SQL statements that must be executed repeatedly within an application.

The `PreparedStatement` interface models the process of managing SQL prepared statement. The `PreparedStatement` interface also extends the `Statement` interface and so implements all `Statement` class methods. Chapter 7 examines this class in detail.

The PreparedStatement and CallableStatement Classes

INTRODUCTION

As we saw in Chapter 6, the `Statement` class processes a query by taking a string parameter that contains a SQL statement. The `Statement` class instance takes the SQL statement, presents it to the database for execution, and then returns the results to the client. Any attempt to execute the query a second time would require the entire process to be repeated. As part of this process, the SQL statement would need to be formulated again (the string created) and if any `where` clause parameters had changed, the query string would need to reflect those changes. The second execution of the query string would need to perform the same processing as the first execution: The query would be presented to the database, and the database server would parse, optimize, and execute the query and return the results.

The `PreparedStatement` class, the implementation of the `PreparedStatement` interface, provides for some optimization of this process. Using this class, a *prepared* SQL statement is created with placeholders for any parameters in the SQL statement. Parameters can be values in the `where` clause for a `select` or `update` statement, or the `values` clause of an `insert` statement, or

133

the `set` clause of an `update` statement. The SQL statement and any parameters are then presented to the database to be *preprocessed*. When the database receives the query, it parses, optimizes, and then retains the query for processing again. Repeated calls to the prepared statement are more efficient, since they do not require the database server to parse and optimize the query.

The `PreparedStatement` class also provides a certain amount of object-oriented convenience for the Java database developer. Once a SQL statement has been prepared, its object representation then becomes the `PreparedStatement` object. The parameters of the query can be changed not by restating the query, but by making method calls on the `PreparedStatement` object.

If the full range of queries to be presented to an application are known when the application is being developed, and the range of queries is limited and manageable, then it may make very good sense to use the `PreparedStatement` class to develop the application.

If all of the queries an application may need to run are known beforehand, and the number of queries is limited, then it probably makes sense to use the `PreparedStatement` class over the `Statement` class. This chapter presents an example of just such a JDBC application.

THE PREPAREDSTATEMENT CLASS

Like the `Statement` class, the `PreparedStatement` class encapsulates the processing of a SQL statement. But unlike the `Statement` class, the `PreparedStatement` class allows a statement to be presented to the database for *pre-processing*, creating *prepared* statement.

A large portion of the `PreparedStatement` class is devoted to setting the values for the prepared statement. The methods to perform these operations make up the bulk of the API.

There are several advantages to using the `PreparedStatement` class over the `Statement` class. As stated previously, the most notable advantage is the improved performance gained by preparing the query before using it. In today's large, complex, intelligent databases, there is a certain degree of effort involved in processing a query. Decisions must be made about access paths, memory must be set aside in the database server for the fetch buffer, control blocks must be created to control query processing and manage any threads that may be used, and various other activities must be performed. While this may seem trivial for small queries, for larger, more complex queries (which are not uncommon), this processing could require over a second. For a query that must be executed repeatedly by thousands of users, this would represent a significant drag on performance.

Another advantage of using `PreparedStatement` objects is that they help modularize the database processing. Each `PreparedStatement` object can represent a specific database query and be managed accordingly. The alternative, to continually create query strings by appending or inserting query text, as shown in previous code snippets and examples, can quickly become tedious and cumbersome. For these reasons, the more common approach to query processing with JDBC, when the query is known at development time, is to use the `PreparedStatement` class. The following code snippet demonstrates the use of this class:

. . .

```
//
// initial context information is in jndi.properties file
// get the initial context
//
InitialContext ctx = new InitialContext( );

// get the DataSource from the JNDI name server
DataSource ds = (DataSource) ctx.lookup("movies-mysql");

//
// get the connection from the DataSource
//
con = ds.getConnection( );

//
// create a Statement class to execute the SQL statement
//
PreparedStatement pstmt = con.prepareStatement(
   " select distinct first_name, last_name, state_province, " +
   " movie_name, rental_date "                               +
   " from users, movies, user_rentals "                      +
   " where (users.user_id    = user_rentals.user_id and " +
   "        movies.movie_id   = user_rentals.movie_id) and " +
   "        user_rentals.user_id = ? " );

//
// set the PreparedStatement parameters
//
pstmt.setInt(1, 2); // set to user_id = 2

//
// execute the SQL statement and get the results in a ResultSet
//
ResultSet rs   = pstmt.executeQuery();

//
// iterate through the ResultSet, displaying two values
// for each row using the getString method
//
while ( rs.next() ) {
      System.out.println( "Name: " + "\t" +
         rs.getString("first_name").trim() + "\t" +
            " " + "\t" +
```

```
rs.getString("last_name").trim() + "\t" +
    " Movie: " +        "\t" +
rs.getString("movie_name") +
    "\t" +
    " Rental Date: " + "\t" +
rs.getString("rental_date") );

}
...
```

In this example, a `DataSource` object for the `movies-mysql` data source is obtained from the JNDI name server and used to create a `Connection` object. The `Connection` object is then used to create the `PreparedStatement`. This is done using the `prepareStatement` method, which takes a string argument for the SQL statement to prepare.

The SQL query string passed to this method performs a join between the `users`, `movies`, and the `user_rentals` table. The `where` clause of this query performs a filter operation using the `user_id`; the query will only select movies rented by the `user_id` specified in the `where` clause. The value for the `user_id` is not supplied in the string passed to the `prepareStatement` method. Instead, a '`?`' *placeholder* is placed in the `where` clause where the value should go.

The values for the placeholders in the prepared statement are supplied using various `setXXXX` methods with a separate `setXXXX` method for each JDBC data type. The `setXXXX` methods take two parameters: an integer representing the ordinal position of the parameter moving in a left to right direction in the query statement and *starting at one* (not zero, as Java indexes and almost everything else in Java does) and the value to be set. In this example, the first placeholder element to appear in the query string (and the only one) is an integer at position one. The `PreparedStatement` `setInt` call is used to set this integer parameter value to two. This will have the query execute with a filter clause to retrieve only the movies rented by the user with the user ID of two (`user_id = 2`).

The `PreparedStatement` query is then executed using the `executeQuery` method. As with the `Statement` class, this method returns a `ResultSet` representing the rows returned by the query execution.

The processing of the `ResultSet` is the same as with the `Statement` class. The values of the `ResultSet` are examined using a `while` loop, which will continue to loop as long as the `ResultSet` `next` method returns `true`.

Per the JDBC specification, the `PreparedStatement` interface extends the `Statement` interface so that any class which implements the `PreparedStatement` interface will also provide implementations for all of the `Statement` interface methods.

Table 7–1 describes all of the methods of the `PreparedStatement` class (exclusive of the methods inherited from the `Statement` class).

The most important and obvious aspect of using the `PreparedStatement` class is the setting of parameters. The developers of the JDBC driver specification

One Not Zero

Arrays, string indexing, and collections all have something in common in Java: They use zero-based ordinal positions. That is, they begin counting positions starting at position zero, so a substring of the string "0123" from position zero through position three inclusive (in Java syntax: `"0123".substring(0,3)`) would be "012."

But JDBC is a different beast. The positions in a `select` string list of columns start at one (1), not zero (0). For example,

```
select first_name, last_name, age
from customers
```

In this query, any reference to the `first_name` would be as column one, `last_name` would be column two, and so on. Similarly, if we are setting parameters in the `where` clause, positional parameters are also referenced starting from position one, as shown below.

```
select first_name, last_name, age, status_code
from customers
where age > ? and
      status_code in (?, ?, ?)
```

In this example, the first parameter to be referenced, the parameter being compared to the age column, is parameter one (1); the next parameter would be the first item in the `status_code` list, which would be parameter two (2).

This same one-based strategy persists throughout the JDBC API. For the database developer, it can be a source of frustration, but as shown throughout the code examples in this book, by making minor adjustments in loop control logic, it is easily managed.

(The origin of this seeming inconsistency may be that relational databases and SQL syntax have often referred to these parameters in the same fashion. Thus, to more easily reconcile the JDBC API with existing relational database CLIs, the JDBC API uses the same approach.)

have elected to create separate `set` methods for each data type. All of these methods take an initial (first) method argument that is an integer indicating the ordinal position of the parameter (or placeholder) in the SQL statement. This parameter position is from left to right as the parameters appear in the statement, starting with the number one and progressing up to however many parameters exist in the statement. The second method argument is the value to substitute for the parameter. In several cases, additional arguments are used with the `set` method signature to clarify the data value (for example, a `Calendar` object with the `setDate` method).

Table 7–1   *PreparedStatement Methods*

Method	Description
`void addBatch()`	When using batch statements, adds the current set of parameters to the object's batch. (The underlying JDBC driver and database must support batch processing.)
`void clearParameters()`	Clears the current value settings for the object's parameters.
`boolean execute()`	Executes the object's SQL statement, regardless of the statement type (`'update'`update or `'select'`select query).
`ResultSet executeQuery()`	Executes the current SQL query and returns the results as a ResultSet.
`int executeUpdate()`	Executes the `'update'`update query in the object and returns an integer representing the number of rows updated by the statement.
`ResultSetMetaData getMetaData()`	Returns the `ResultSetMetaData` for the implicit `ResultSet` of the `Statement` object.
`void setArray(int i, Array x)`	Sets the index parameter identified by `i`, the first argument, to the Array (`java.sql.Array`) object identified by `x`, the second argument.
`void setAsciiStream(int parameterIndex, InputStream x, int length)`	Sets the index parameter for the placeholder identified by `i`, the first parameter, to the value of the second parameter `x`. The placeholder value will be set to the `InputStream` with the specified number of bytes. Asserts the data is convertible to characters.
`void setBigDecimal(int parameterIndex, BigDecimal x)`	Sets the index parameter for the placeholder identified by `i`, the first parameter, to the value of the second parameter `x`. The placeholder value will be set to the `java.math.BigDecimal` value specified.
`void setBinaryStream(int parameterIndex, InputStream x, int length)`	Sets the index parameter for the placeholder identified by `i`, the first parameter, to the value of the second parameter x. The placeholder value will be set to the `BinaryStream` value with the number of bytes specified by the third argument.
`void setBlob(int i, Blob x)`	Sets the index parameter for the placeholder identified by `i`, the first parameter, to the value of the second parameter x. The placeholder value will be set to the value of the binary large object, or BLOB`Blob` (`java.sql.Blob`), object provided by the second argument.

Table 7–1	*PreparedStatement Methods (cont.)*

Method	Description
void setBoolean(int parameterIndex, boolean x)	Sets the index parameter for the placeholder identified by i, the first parameter, to the value of the second parameter x. The placeholder value will be set to the value of the boolean variable provided by the second argument.
void setByte(int parameterIndex, byte x)	Sets the index parameter for the placeholder identified by i, the first parameter, to the value of the second parameter x. The placeholder value will be set to the value of the byte variable provided by the second argument.
void setBytes(int parameterIndex, byte[] x)	Sets the index parameter for the placeholder identified by i, the first parameter, to the value of the second parameter x. The placeholder value will be set to the value of the byte array variable provided by the second argument.
void setCharacterStream(int parameterIndex, Reader reader, int length)	Sets the index parameter for the placeholder identified by i, the first parameter, to the value of the second parameter x. The placeholder value will be set to the value of the Reader (java.io.Reader) object provided by the second argument using the length specified by the third argument.
void setClob(int i, Clob x)	Sets the index parameter for the placeholder identified by i, the first parameter, to the value of the second parameter x. The placeholder value will be set to the value of the character large object, or Clob CLOB (java.sql.Clob), object provided by the second argument.
void setDate(int parameterIndex, Date x)	Sets the index parameter for the placeholder identified by i, the first parameter, to the value of the second parameter x. The placeholder value will be set to the value of the Date (java.sql.Date) object provided by the second argument.
void setDate(int parameterIndex, Date x, Calendar cal)	Sets the index parameter for the placeholder identified by i, the first parameter, to the value of the second parameter x. The placeholder value will be set to the value of the Date (java.sql.Date) object provided by the second argument using the Calendar (java.util.Calendar) object provided by the third argument.

| **Table 7–1** | *PreparedStatement Methods (cont.)* |

Method	Description
`void setDouble(int parameterIndex, double x)`	Sets the index parameter for the placeholder identified by `i`, the first parameter, to the value of the second parameter `x`. The placeholder value will be set to the value of the double variable provided by the second argument.
`void setFloat(int parameterIndex, float x)`	Sets the index parameter for the placeholder identified by `i`, the first parameter, to the value of the second parameter `x`. The placeholder value will be set to the value of the `float` variable provided by the second argument.
`void setInt(int parameterIndex, int x)`	Sets the index parameter for the placeholder identified by `i`, the first parameter, to the value of the second parameter `x`. The placeholder value will be set to the value of the `int` variable provided by the second argument.
`void setLong(int parameterIndex, long x)`	Sets the index parameter for the placeholder identified by `i`, the first parameter, to the value of the second parameter `x`. The placeholder value will be set to the value of the `long` variable provided by the second argument.
`void setNull(int parameterIndex, int sqlType)`	Sets the index parameter for the placeholder identified by `i`, to a null value for the JDBC SQL type specified by the second argument.
`setNull(int paramIndex, int sqlType, String typeName)`	Sets the index parameter for the placeholder identified by `i`, to a null value for the JDBC SQL type specified by the second argument and the type name specified by the third argument.
`void setObject(int parameterIndex, Object x)`	Sets the index parameter for the placeholder identified by `i`, the first parameter, to the value of the second parameter `x`. The placeholder value will be set to the value of the `Object` variable provided by the second argument.
`void setObject(int parameterIndex, Object x, int targetSqlType)`	Sets the index parameter for the placeholder identified by `i`, the first parameter, to the value of the second parameter `x`. The placeholder value will be set to the value of the `Object` variable provided by the second argument converting it to the SQL type specified by the third argument.

Table 7–1   *PreparedStatement Methods (cont.)*

Method	Description
`void setObject(int parameterIndex, Object x, int targetSqlType, int scale)`	Sets the index parameter for the placeholder identified by i, the first parameter, to the value of the second parameter x. The placeholder value will be set to the value of the `Object` variable provided by the second argument converting it to the SQL type specified by the third argument using the scale specified by the fourth argument.
`void setRef(int i, Ref x)`	Sets the index parameter for the placeholder identified by i, the first parameter, to the value of the second parameter x. The placeholder value will be set to the value of the `Ref` (`java.sql.Ref`) variable (a structured type) provided by the second argument.
`void setShort(int parameterIndex, short x)`	Sets the index parameter for the placeholder identified b i, the first parameter, to the value of the second parameter x. The placeholder value will be set to the value of the `short` variable provided by the second argument.
`void setString(int parameterIndex, String x)`	Sets the index parameter for the placeholder identified by i, the first parameter, to the value of the second parameter x. The placeholder value will be set to the value of the `String` variable provided by the second argument.
`void setTime(int parameterIndex, Time x)`	Sets the index parameter for the placeholder identified by i, the first parameter, to the value of the second parameter x. Sets the designated parameter to a `java.sql.Time` value.
`void setTime(int parameterIndex, Time x, Calendar cal)`	Sets the index parameter for the placeholder identified by i, the first parameter, to the value of the second parameter x. The placeholder value will be set to the value of the `Time` (`java.sql.Time`) variable provided by the second argument using the `Calendar` (`java.util.Calendar`) provided by the third argument.
`void setTimestamp(int parameterIndex, Timestamp x)`	Sets the index parameter for the placeholder identified by i, the first parameter, to the value of the second parameter x. The placeholder value will be set to the value of the `Timestamp` (`java.sql.Timestamp`) variable provided by the second argument.

| Table 7–1 | PreparedStatement Methods (cont.) |

Method	Description
`void setTimestamp(int parameterIndex, Timestamp x, Calendar cal)`	Sets the index parameter for the placeholder identified by `i`, the first parameter, to the value of the second parameter `x`. The placeholder value will be set to the value of the `Timestamp` (`java.sql.Timestamp`) variable provided by the second argument using the `Calendar` (`java.sql.Calendar`) provided by the third argument.
`void setUnicodeStream(int parameterIndex, InputStream x, int length)`	This method has been deprecated. Should use `setReader` or `setCharacterStream` instead.

Since this class is a subclass of the `Statement` class (the `PreparedStatement` interface extends the `Statement` interface), the various 'get' methods of the Statement class are available. Several methods are provided to manage the parameter substitution mechanism for prepared statements. The following sections will explain these methods and provide some code examples where appropriate.

Setting Parameters

As mentioned previously and as will be shown in the following example, the `PreparedStatement` class allows substitution parameters to be identified in the SQL statement to be executed. These parameters can then be set using the various `set` methods shown in the previous table. This approach allows SQL statement parameters to be changed easily, using a simple method call. It also avoids the problems associated with placing large and unwieldy parameter values in SQL statement strings. For very large character strings such as large blocks of text or large binary strings (a CLOB or BLOB column, for example), creating SQL statements as a string becomes difficult if not impossible.

The `clearParameters` method is used to clear all existing parameter values from the `Statement` object. `Statement` objects are generally used to execute a query numerous times with different parameters each time the query is executed. Setting a parameter automatically clears a previous value and substitutes the new value for the parameter. But in cases where not all parameters may be set by the application, the `clearParameters` method is convenient, since it will ensure that all parameters are set to default values.

A PreparedStatement Example

The following code example demonstrates the use of the PreparedStatement class to repeatedly execute queries. The application creates a report, a common usage for the PreparedStatement. The program design was to create a PreparedStatement that reflects the data to be retrieved for each query in the report. These queries are prepared at the start of the program. Then, when the reports are run, the PreparedStatement objects are executed using the parameters provided for the report.

Each report is generated by executing a separate method that accepts parameters for the report and returns a ResultSet. The report is generated by a generic method that accepts a ResultSet and a label for the report. The complete code for this example follows:

PreparedExample2.java

```
1.import java.sql.*;
2.import javax.sql.*;
3.import javax.naming.*;
4.import java.util.*;
5.import java.text.*;
6.import java.io.*;
7.
8.
9.
10.public class PreparedExample2 {
11.
12.PreparedStatement rentalsbyDate;
13.PreparedStatement rentalsbyUserID;
14.PreparedStatement rentalsbyCustName;
15.
16.public static void main( String args[] ) {
17.
18.ResultSet rs;
19.
20.Connection con=null;
21.try {
22.
23.     PreparedExample2 pe = new PreparedExample2();
24.
25.     // get the initial context
26.     InitialContext ctx = new InitialContext(  );
27.
28.     // get the DataSource from the JNDI name server
29.     DataSource ds = (DataSource) ctx.lookup("movies");
30.
31.     // get the connection from the DataSource
32.     con = ds.getConnection( );
33.
```

```
34.       // prepare statements
35.       pe.doPrepares( con );
36.
37.       // execute a report
38.       // get all records for customer id = 2
39.       rs = pe.getRentalsbyCustName( "Smith" );
40.
41.       // print results
42.       if ( rs != null )
43.           pe.printResults( "Rentals by Customer Name: Smith", rs );
44.
45.       // execute another report
46.       // greater all records greater than or equal to this date
47.       rs = pe.getRentalsbyDate( "2001-01-01" );
48.
49.       // print results
50.       if ( rs != null )
51.           pe.printResults( "Rentals by Date: > 1/1/2001", rs );
52.
53.       // execute another report
54.       // get all records for customer id = 2
55.       rs = pe.getRentalsbyUserID( 2 );
56.
57.       // print results
58.       if ( rs != null )
59.           pe.printResults( "Rentals by Customer ID: 2", rs );
60.
61.}
62.catch (SQLException e) {
63.
64.      // display SQL specific exception information
65.      System.out.println("*************************" );
66.      System.out.println("SQLException in main: " + e.getMessage() );
67.      System.out.println("** SQLState: " + e.getSQLState());
68.      System.out.println("** SQL Error Code: " + e.getErrorCode());
69.      System.out.println("*************************" );
70.      e.printStackTrace();
71.}
72.catch (Exception e) {
73.      System.out.println("Exception in main: " + e.getMessage() );
74.      e.printStackTrace();
75.}
76.finally {
77.
78.      try {
79.          // close the connection if it exists
80.      if ( con != null )
81.              con.close();
82.      }
83.    catch (SQLException e) {
84.          e.printStackTrace();
85.      }
```

```
86.}
87.
88.} // end main
89.
90.void doPrepares( Connection con) {
91.
92.// use instance members to store PreparedStatements
93.try {
94.    rentalsbyDate = con.prepareStatement(
95.       " select distinct first_name, last_name, state_province, " +
96.       " movie_name, rental_date "                          +
97.       " from users, movies, user_rentals "                 +
98.       " where (users.user_id    = user_rentals.user_id and " +
99.       "         movies.movie_id  = user_rentals.movie_id) and " +
100.      "         user_rentals.rental_date >= ? " );
101.
102.
103.   rentalsbyUserID = con.prepareStatement(
104.        " select first_name, last_name, state_province, " +
105.        " movie_name, rental_date "                       +
106.     " from users, movies, user_rentals "                 +
107.     " where (users.user_id    = user_rentals.user_id and " +
108.     "         movies.movie_id  = user_rentals.movie_id ) and " +
109.     "         user_rentals.user_id = ? " );
110.
111.   rentalsbyCustName = con.prepareStatement(
112.        " select distinct first_name, last_name, state_province, " +
113.        " movie_name, rental_date "                       +
114.     " from users, movies, user_rentals "                 +
115.     " where ( users.user_id    = user_rentals.user_id and " +
116.     "          movies.movie_id = user_rentals.movie_id ) and " +
117.     "          users.last_name like ? " );
118.
119.}
120.catch (SQLException e) {
121.
122.     // display SQL specific exception information
123.     System.out.println("**************************" );
124.     System.out.println("SQLException in doPrepares(): " +
125.                         e.getMessage() );
126.     System.out.println("** SQLState: " + e.getSQLState());
127.     System.out.println("** SQL Error Code: " + e.getErrorCode());
128.     System.out.println("**************************" );
129.     e.printStackTrace();
130.}
131.
132.}
133.// *************************************************************
134.ResultSet getRentalsbyUserID ( int custID ) {
135.
136.ResultSet rs = null;
137.
```

```
138.try {
139.
140.// set the customer ID parameter as an integer
141.rentalsbyUserID.setInt(1, custID);
142.
143.// execute the query using the PreparedStatement object
144.rs = rentalsbyUserID.executeQuery();
145.
146.}
147.catch (SQLException e) {
148.
149.    // display SQL specific exception information
150.    System.out.println("*************************" );
151.    System.out.println("SQLException in getRentalsbyUserID(): " +
152.                       e.getMessage() );
153.    System.out.println("** SQLState: " + e.getSQLState());
154.    System.out.println("** SQL Error Code: " + e.getErrorCode());
155.    System.out.println("*************************" );
156.    e.printStackTrace();
157.
158.}
159.finally {
160.    // return the ResultSet object reference
161.    return rs;
162.}
163.}
164.
165.// ********************************************************************
166.ResultSet getRentalsbyDate( String rentalDate ) {
167.
168.ResultSet rs = null;
169.
170.try {
171.
172.// convert rentalDate string to java.sql.Date and pass
173.rentalsbyDate.setDate(1,  java.sql.Date.valueOf( rentalDate ) );
174.
175.// execute the query using the PreparedStatement object
176.rs = rentalsbyDate.executeQuery();
177.
178.}
179.
180.catch (SQLException e) {
181.
182.    // display SQL specific exception information
183.    System.out.println("*************************" );
184.    System.out.println("SQLException in getRentalsbyDate(): " +
185.                       e.getMessage() );
186.    System.out.println("** SQLState: " + e.getSQLState());
187.    System.out.println("** SQL Error Code: " + e.getErrorCode());
188.    System.out.println("*************************" );
189.    e.printStackTrace();
```

```
190.
191.}
192.finally {
193.// return the ResultSet object reference
194.    return rs;
195.}
196.
197.}
198.// ****************************************************************
199.ResultSet getRentalsbyCustName( String custName ) {
200.
201.ResultSet rs = null;
202.
203.try {
204.// set the custName parameter
205.rentalsbyCustName.setString( 1, custName );
206.
207.// execute the query using the PreparedStatement object
208.rs = rentalsbyCustName.executeQuery();
209.
210.}
211.catch (SQLException e) {
212.
213.    // display SQL specific exception information
214.    System.out.println("*************************" );
215.    System.out.println("SQLException in getRentalsbyCustName(): " +
216.                        e.getMessage() );
217.    System.out.println("** SQLState: " + e.getSQLState());
218.    System.out.println("** SQL Error Code: " + e.getErrorCode());
219.    System.out.println("*************************" );
220.    e.printStackTrace();
221.}
222.finally {
223.    return rs;
224.}
225.
226.}
227.
228.// ****************************************************************
229.void printResults( String header, ResultSet rs) {
230.
231.try {
232.
233.// output a report header
234.System.out.println("********************************************");
235.System.out.println("\n******** " + header.trim() + " ********" );
236.System.out.println("********************************************");
237.System.out.println(
238.        "First \tLast \t State \t Movie \t\t\t\tRental Date ");
239.System.out.println(
240.        "----- \t---- \t ----- \t ----- \t\t\t\t---------- ");
241.
```

```
242.// output results
243.while ( rs.next() ) {
244.   System.out.println( rs.getString( "first_name") + "\t" +
245.                        rs.getString( "last_name" ) + "\t" +
246.                        rs.getString( "state_province" ) + "\t" +
247.                        formatString( rs.getString( "movie_name" ),
248.                              22) +
249.                           "\t\t" +
250.                        rs.getString( "rental_date" )  ) ;
251.}
252.System.out.println("*********************************************");
253.
254.
255.
256.}
257.
258.catch (SQLException e) {
259.
260.      // display SQL specific exception information
261.      System.out.println("*************************" );
262.      System.out.println("SQLException in printResults(): " +
263.                         e.getMessage() );
264.      System.out.println("** SQLState: " + e.getSQLState());
265.      System.out.println("** SQL Error Code: " + e.getErrorCode());
266.      System.out.println("*************************" );
267.      e.printStackTrace();
268.
269.}
270.finally {
271.}
272.
273.}
274.// ********************************************************
275.
276.String formatString( String s, int size ) {
277.
278.// declare local work buffers
279.String blanks = "                          ";
280.String retString = null;
281.
282.// pad or trim the string to be exactly 'size' in length
283.
284.if ( s.length() < size )    // need to pad string
285.   retString = s + blanks.substring( 0, size - s.length()) ;
286.else                        // need to trim (substring) string
287.   retString = s.substring( 0, size );
288.
289.return retString;
290.
291.}
292.void clearAllParams() {
293.
```

```
294.try {
295.//
296.// call clearParameters on each PreparedStatement object
297.// this will clear all existing parameter settings
298.//
299.rentalsbyDate.clearParameters();
300.rentalsbyUserID.clearParameters();
301.rentalsbyCustName.clearParameters();
302.}
303.catch (SQLException e) {
304.       // display SQL specific exception information
305.       System.out.println("*************************" );
306.       System.out.println("SQLException in clearAllParams(): " +
307.                          e.getMessage() );
308.       System.out.println("** SQLState: " + e.getSQLState());
309.       System.out.println("** SQL Error Code: " + e.getErrorCode());
310.       System.out.println("*************************" );
311.       e.printStackTrace();
312.
313.}
314.
315.}
```

PreparedExample.java: main Program Block

This code example performs a number of imports on lines 1 through 7, and then declares the `PreparedStatement` instance members on lines 12 through 14; these are declared as instance members to avoid the overhead of passing them as parameters throughout the program.

Since the work performed in this code example is not static and requires an object instance, an instance of the `PreparedExample2` class is created on line 23. Next, the usual JDBC startup operations are performed. The JNDI initial context is obtained on line 26 and used to obtain a `DataSource` object reference on line 29. A `Connection` object is then obtained from the `DataSource` object on line 32.

The remainder of the `main` program block is then devoted to calling the methods that will perform the work for the application. The methods will create the `PreparedStatement` objects, execute the prepared statements and return the results, and then output the results.

Before the prepared statements can be used, they must be declared and the parameter values must be set. A single method is used to prepare all of the statements. This has the advantage of placing the SQL query strings for the statements in a single location in the code. Since there is a distinct possibility that these statements could change over time, this consistency makes code maintenance easier. The prepared statements are created with a call to the `doPrepares` method on line 35.

The application is now ready to generate a report. To generate a report, a method must be called to execute the appropriate prepared statement and return the results. The method must also be passed the parameters to use to run the report. In this code example, the execution of the prepared statements is contained in several `getXXXX` methods, the first of which is called on line 39. This method, named `getRentalsbyCustName`, is called with a string that is the customer name. The method will use the string argument to the method, the customer name, assign it to a parameter (placeholder) in the prepared statement, and then execute the prepared statement. The method will return the results of the execution of the query in the form of a `ResultSet`.

Once the `getRentalsbyCustName` method is called, the `ResultSet` returned is passed to the `printResults` method. The job of the `printResultsMethod` is to take the `ResultSet` returned by any of the `getXXXX` methods (which all return the same column values in a `ResultSet`) and a string argument that represents the header for the report. These argument values are used to output a simple character-based report. According to the logic in the `main` program block, the `printResults` method is called only if the `ResultSet` object reference returned by the `getXXXX` methods is not null. A null `ResultSet` returned by a `getXXXX` method would indicate an error condition.

Next, in the `main` program block, the `getRentalsbyDate` method is called. This method is passed a date in the format of a string (not a `java.sql.Date` object) and returns a `ResultSet`. As was done previously in the application, the `printResults` method is called to output the results.

Finally, the `getRentalsbyUserID` method is called. This method is passed an integer value for the user ID and returns a `ResultSet`, which is then output using the `printResults` method.

Now that we see the control logic of the `main` program block, we can move on to examine the various methods that perform the work for this application. These are covered in the following sections.

The doPrepares Method

The `doPrepares` method on lines 90 through 132 is used to create the `PreparedStatement` objects used in the application. This method is passed the `Connection` object created in the `main` program block; this is needed to execute the `createPreparedStatement` method called on lines 94, 103, and 111. The `createPreparedStatement` method calls that are executed in this method are passed strings that contain the SQL statement and appropriate placeholders for the prepared statement. The `createPreparedStatement` method will return a `PreparedStatement` object reference, which is stored in the instance members declared on lines 12 through 14 in the application. The `rentalsbyName` `PreparedStatement` reference is created on line 94, the `rentalsbyUserID` reference is created on line 103, and the `rentalsbyCustName` reference is created on line 111. These instance members will be used by the `getXXXX` methods to execute the prepared statements and return results.

The getRentalsbyUserID Method

The body for the `getRentalsbyUserID` method is started on line 134 and completed on line 162. This method will search the database for movie rentals for a given user ID, using the `rentalsbyUserID PreparedStatement`, and will return the results.

Before the `rentalsbyUserID` prepared statement can be executed, the parameter or placeholder for the user ID value must be set to the integer value for the user ID that was passed into the method as an argument. This is done with a call to the `PreparedStatement setInt` method on line 141. The prepared statement is executed on line 144, using the `PreparedStatement executeQuery` method. This overloaded version of the `executeQuery` method takes no arguments (since the query string is actually part of the `PreparedStatement` object, the arguments do not need to be passed as they do with a `Statement executeQuery` method). The method returns a `ResultSet` reference. A `try/catch` block is used to catch exceptions locally so that specific error messages can be returned, a strategy that makes the debugging process easier.

The `ResultSet` reference is returned in the `finally` block, which allows for the possibility of an exception being thrown by the `executeQuery` method. Since the `ResultSet` reference has been set to null on line 136, if the `executeQuery` method throws an exception, it will not return a `ResultSet` reference, and a null value reference will be returned on line 161 in the `finally` block. This is okay, since the code in the `main` program block quietly treats a null `ResultSet` reference as an error and does not attempt to manipulate it.

TIP   Failures of specific queries directed at specific database tables are not uncommon in database programming, since database administrators may sometimes change tables without informing developers. Being able to trap and specifically identify queries against which tables are failing within an application helps to isolate the problem. Catching the `SQLException` in the local program block where the exception was thrown makes it easier to identify the query that failed. If the `SQLException` is merely thrown to the calling method (declaring the method block with `throws SQLException`), the process of identifying where the exception was thrown and why becomes more difficult.

The getRentalsbyDate Method

The `getRentalsbyDate` method begins on line 166 and runs through line 195. This method will use the `rentalsbyDate PreparedStatement` to search the database for movie rentals greater than or equal to a given date. The rental date is passed to the method as an argument but the argument is not the same data type as the database column with which it will be used. The corresponding column for the rental date in the `user_rentals` table is the `rental_date` column, which is a `Date` data type (in the PostgreSQL database). The `Date` data type maps to the `java.sql.Date`. Though most databases will freely convert data types from string representations, the conversions are in many cases vendor-specific. Since we would like to limit our dependence on vendor-specific features and behavior as much as possible, we will try to provide specific code to convert to the appropriate data types wherever possible.

The conversion of the date string takes place in the call to `PreparedStatement setDate` on line 173. The version of the `setDate` method called on this line takes an integer argument for the parameter (placeholder) index in the SQL statement and a second argument for the value of the parameter. The second argument for this version of the `setDate` method is a `java.sql.Date` data type. (The `java.util.*` package also contains a `Date` class, and since that package name space is included in this program, we must clarify the `Date` class name with the fully qualified class name: `java.sql.Date`.)

The static `valueOf` method in the `java.sql.Date` class takes a string in the correct format and returns a `java.sql.Date` object having the date value passed into the method. This object is then passed to the `setDate` method on line 173.

The `PreparedStatement executeQuery` method is then called on line 176 for the `rentalsbyDate PreparedStatement` object. This call will return a `ResultSet` object reference, which is returned on line 194.

The getRentalsbyCustName Method

The `getRentalsbyCustName` method body begins on line 199 and extends to line 226. This method will scan the database for rentals made by a customer of the specified name supplied as a method argument. It will search the database using the `rentalsbyCustName PreparedStatement` object.

The customer name is set with a call to the `PreparedStatement setString` method on line 208, which is used to set the value of the customer name parameter in the `rentalsbyCustName PreparedStatement` object.

The `executeQuery` method of the `rentalsbyCustName` object is called on line 208. This method will execute the `rentalsbyCustName` query declared in the `prepareStatements` method and will return its results as a `ResultSet` reference. The `ResultSet` reference is returned on line 223.

The printResults Method

The `printResults` method declared on line 229 is used to print the contents of the `ResultSet` object reference passed as the second argument, using the first argument string as a header for the report.

The `while` loop on line 243 prints the contents of the `ResultSet`. The columns in the `ResultSet` are printed as unformatted strings with the exception of the `movie_name` column on line 247, which is passed to the internal `formatString` method (explained below) for formatting. Also note that the `rental_date` column retrieved on line 250 is retrieved as a string when the data type for the column (as identified earlier) is `date`. This is allowed because the database and the JDBC driver (as required by the specification) will freely convert to string data types in most cases. In this case, the default format for the `java.sql.Date` data type is in the JDBC date escape format, as follows:

```
yyyy-mm-dd
```

where `yyyy` is the year in four-digit format, `mm` is the two-digit month, and `dd` is the two-digit day.

Since the `java.util.Date` class is the superclass of `java.sql.Date`, all of the robust formatting facilities available to format `java.util.Date` objects are available for `java.sql.Date`. Using this knowledge, the `rental_date` column could have been formatted as follows:

```
//
// create a date formatter which uses the LONG format by default
//

DateFormat df = DateFormat.getDateInstance( DateFormat.LONG );

. . .

//
// format the rental_date field using the LONG date format
//
System.out.println( "Rental Date: " +
                    df.format( rs.getDate( "rental_date" ) ) );

. . .
```

This would produce dates formatted using the *long* date format: January 1, 2000. Substituted in this application, this would produce the following results:

```
. . .
******* Rentals by Customer Name: Smith *******
***********************************************
First  Last   State  Movie                Rental Date
---    ---    ---    ---                  ---
Fred   Smith  NJ     Gone with the Java   January 1, 2000
Fred   Smith  NJ     Gone with the Java   February 1, 2001
Fred   Smith  NJ     Here in the Code     January 1, 2000
. . .
```

The formatString Method

The formatString method is declared on line 276. The purpose of this method is just to improve the output of the report by forcing the string passed into the method to be a consistent, specified length. The method will either pad or trim the string to get the specified length and will return the formatted result as a Java String.

The clearAllParams Method

The clearAllParams method is declared on line 292 and is used to ensure that all existing parameters on the PreparedStatement have been cleared. The PreparedStatement clearParameters method clears all existing parameter settings for a PreparedStatement object. This type of method is useful in an application where the PreparedStatement object is being used repeatedly.

The various setXXXX methods used to set parameter values implicitly reset the parameter before inserting the new value. In an application where each parameter is set every time the PreparedStatement object is used, it is not necessary to use this method (and doing so merely adds overhead to the application). But in large, complex applications where it may not be possible to ensure that parameter values have not been touched by other objects, using this method could provide a useful insurance policy for statement execution. (Given the design of this example, it is technically not necessary to call this method; it is shown here to provide an example of its usage.)

PreparedExample2.java: Program Output

The PreparedExample2.java application prints a few simple reports using a set of PreparedStatement objects. The output of this sample application will produce the following results:

Output of PreparedExample2.java

```
************************************************

******** Rentals by Customer Name: Smith ********
************************************************
First   Last    State   Movie               Rental Date
--      --      --      --                  --
Fred    Smith   NJ      Gone with the Java  2000-01-01
Fred    Smith   NJ      Gone with the Java  2001-02-01
Fred    Smith   NJ      Here in the Code    2000-01-01
Fred    Smith   NJ      Major Tom           2000-01-01
Fred    Smith   NJ      Major Tom           2001-02-01
Sally   Smith   NJ      Gone with the Java  2001-01-01
Sally   Smith   NJ      Gone with the Java  2002-01-01
Sally   Smith   NJ      Here in the Code    2001-01-01
Sally   Smith   NJ      Major Tom           2001-01-01
```

```
*************************************************
*************************************************

******** Rentals by Date: > 1/1/2001 ********
*************************************************
First   Last    State  Movie                Rental Date
--      --      ---     ---                  ------
Fred    Smith   NJ     Gone with the Java    2001-02-01
Fred    Smith   NJ     Major Tom             2001-02-01
Sally   Smith   NJ     Gone with the Java    2001-01-01
Sally   Smith   NJ     Gone with the Java    2002-01-01
Sally   Smith   NJ     Here in the Code      2001-01-01
Sally   Smith   NJ     Major Tom             2001-01-01
*************************************************
*************************************************

******** Rentals by Customer ID: 2 ********
*************************************************
First   Last    State  Movie                Rental Date
--      --      ---     ---                  ------
Fred    Smith   NJ     Gone with the Java    2000-01-01
Fred    Smith   NJ     Gone with the Java    2001-02-01
Fred    Smith   NJ     Here in the Code      2000-01-01
Fred    Smith   NJ     Major Tom             2000-01-01
Fred    Smith   NJ     Major Tom             2001-02-01

*************************************************
```

Executing Queries with the PreparedStatement Class

The `PreparedStatement` class provides several overloaded methods to perform statement execution. These methods overload the corresponding methods in the `Statement` class to account for the parameter-driven nature of `PreparedStatements`. These methods are as follows.

- `boolean execute()`
- `ResultSet executeQuery()`
- `int executeUpdate()`

The `PreparedStatement execute` method is called with no arguments; it takes the existing parameters and executes the query regardless of the type of SQL query.

As shown in the code example in Chapter 6 using the `Statement` class and shown again in the code snippet below, the execution of this method returns a boolean value, which is an indication of whether a SQL `select` or `update` query was executed. If the value is `true`, then the execute method executed a `select` query and there are one or more `ResultSet` objects available. The getMoreResults method returns `true` if there are more than one `ResultSet` objects and the `getResultSet` method is used to return the `ResultSet`.

```
...
PreparedStatement pe;
...

// execute either a 'select' or 'update'
boolean isResultSet = pe.execute();
if ( isResultSet) {                    // if true, it was a 'select'
    while ( rs.getMoreResults() ) {
           ResultSet rs = pe.getResultSet();
           processResults( rs );
    }
}
else {                                 // false, it was an 'update'
    int updateCount = pe.getUpdateCount();
}
...
```

Like the `execute` method, the `PreparedStatement executeUpdate` method is called with no arguments. The method takes existing parameter value substitutions and executes the prepared `update` query, returning an integer representing the number of rows updated by the execution of the statement.

The `PreparedStatement executeQuery` method takes no arguments, takes the existing parameter value substitutions and executes the prepared SQL `select` statement and returns a `ResultSet` representing the results of the statement execution.

Working with Batches and PreparedStatements

The `PreparedStatement` class can also work with batch updates if the driver supports it. Batch updates are used as they are with the `Statement` class, the difference being the manner in which the individual updates are added to the batch. The following code example demonstrates this:

PreparedExample5.java

```
1.import java.sql.*;1.import java.sql.*;
2.import javax.sql.*;
3.
4.
5.
6.public class PreparedExample5 {
7.
8.public static void main( String args[] ) {
9.
10.ResultSet rs    = null;
```

```
11.Connection con  = null;
12.try {
13.
14.      // load the driver
15.      //
16.      Class.forName("org.gjt.mm.mysql.Driver");
17.      con = DriverManager.getConnection(
18.              "jdbc:mysql://localhost/movies?user=art&password=YES");
19.
20.      //
21.      // add a batch of SQL statements
22.      //
23.      PreparedStatement ps = con.prepareStatement(
24.          "insert into users (user_id, first_name, last_name) " +
25.          " values ( ?, ?, ?)" );
26.      ps.setInt( 1, 101);              // user_id
27.      ps.setString( 2, "Cal" );        // first_name
28.      ps.setString( 3, "Coder" );      // last_name
29.
30.      // add the first batch update
31.      ps.addBatch();
32.
33.      ps.setInt( 1, 201);                    // user_id
34.      ps.setString( 2, "Carrie" );           // first_name
35.      ps.setString( 3, "Coder" );            // last_name
36.
37.      // add the second batch update
38.      ps.addBatch();
39.
40.      ps.setInt( 1, 401);                    // user_id
41.      ps.setString( 2, "Sal" );              // first_name
42.      ps.setString( 3, "Snake" );            // last_name
43.
44.      // add the third batch update
45.      ps.addBatch();
46.
47.      //
48.      // use the inherited Statement class addBatch
49.      // these queries can't contain parameter placeholders
50.      //
51.      ps.addBatch("insert into movies (movie_id, movie_name) " +
52.                              " values ( 501, 'Trying Again')" );
53.      ps.addBatch("update movies   " +
54.                  " set movie_desc = '** not provided **' " );
55.
56.      //
57.      // execute the batch and examine the results
58.      //
59.      int results[] = ps.executeBatch();
60.
61.      //
62.      // print the results. integer values represents rows updated
```

```
63.      //
64.      for (int n=0;n<results.length;n++)
65.          System.out.println("Result from query " + (n+1) + " = " +
66.                              results[n] );
67.
68.}
69.catch (SQLException e) {
70.
71.      // display SQL specific exception information
72.      System.out.println("**************************" );
73.      System.out.println("SQLException in main: " + e.getMessage() );
74.      System.out.println("** SQLState: " + e.getSQLState());
75.      System.out.println("** SQL Error Code: " + e.getErrorCode());
76.      System.out.println("**************************" );
77.      e.printStackTrace();
78.}
79.catch (Exception e) {
80.      System.out.println("Exception in main: " + e.getMessage() );
81.      e.printStackTrace();
82.}
83.finally {
84.
85.      try {
86.
87.      if ( con != null )
88.              con.close();
89.      }
90.      catch (SQLException e) {
91.              e.printStackTrace();
92.      }
93.}
94.
95.}
96.
97.}
```

In this example, the JDBC driver is loaded using a `Class.forName` call, and the `Connection` object is obtained using a `DriverManager getConnection` call on line 17. The `PreparedStatement` is created on lines 23 through 25. This statement will be used to insert users into the users table. Placeholders are provided for the `user_id`, the `first_name`, and the `last_name` columns in the SQL `insert` statement.

On lines 26 and 27, several calls are made to `setXXXX` methods to set the values for the `user_id`, `first_name`, and `last_name` placeholders. On line 31, the `PreparedStatement addBatch` method is called with no arguments. This version of the method will use the current values of the parameters to create the SQL `insert` statement to be used in the batch update operation.

On lines 33 through 36, the `setXXXX` methods are called again with a different set of values for a different user. The `PreparedStatement addBatch` method is called once again on line 38, this time adding an `insert` statement with the values specified on lines 33 through 36. The operation is repeated for a third time with the values set on lines 40 through 42 and added with a call to the `addBatch` method on line 45.

On line 51 a demonstration of the use of the inherited `Statement` methods is provided with a call to the `addBatch` method using a string argument. The string argument contains a SQL `update` statement, which performs an insert into the `movies` table. The SQL `update` statements added using `addBatch` cannot contain any placeholders (`?`); only standard SQL statements can be added. On line 53, an additional query is added using the `addBatch` method with a string parameter, this time adding an `update` statement to the batch instead of an `insert` statement.

Finally, on line 59, the `executeBatch` method is called. This method will return an integer array with the update counts for each of the SQL `update` statements contained in the `PreparedStatement` batch. On lines 64 through 66, a `for` loop is used to iterate through the results integer array and output the result count for each update performed. This program provides output as follows.

```
Result from query 1 = 1
Result from query 2 = 1
Result from query 3 = 1
Result from query 4 = 1
Result from query 5 = 5
```

Miscellaneous and Informational Methods

The `PreparedStatement` class provides a method for retrieving the `ResultSetMetaData` information. This allows metadata information to be retrieved without actually creating the `ResultSet`. Alternatively, the `ResultSetMetaData` object can be retrieved from the `ResultSet`, a common approach. The `ResultSetMetaData` class is covered in more detail in Chapter 8.

THE CALLABLESTATEMENT CLASS

The `CallableStatement` class is used to execute stored procedure statements in a nonproprietary, more portable fashion. Substitutable value parameters can be used with the `CallableStatement`. These value parameters can be set with methods contained in this class.

Most stored procedure language implementations have both input parameters (which can be set with the `set` methods inherited from the `PreparedStatement` class) and output parameters—values that will be returned from stored procedure. The output parameters, also referred to as OUT parameters, must be managed with special methods in the `CallableStatement` class, methods used to *register* the parameters. The following code snippet provides an example of `CallableStatement` usage:

```
...
   try {

     //
     // get the InitialContext
     //
     Context ctx = new InitialContext();

     //
     // get the DataSource
     //
      DataSource ds = (DataSource) ctx.lookup( "moviesmysql" );

     //
     // create a CallableStatement
     //
     CallableStatement stmt = conn.prepareCall(
             "{?= call reconcileTransfers(?, ?)}");

     //
     // set IN parameters
     //
     stmt.setString(1, "Main");
     stmt.setInt(2, 5);

     //
     // register the OUT parameter
     //
     stmt.registerOutParameter(1, Types.VARCHAR );

     //
     // execute the statement
     //
     if (stmt.execute()) {

         //
         // get the ResultSet
         //
         ResultSet rs = stmt.getResultSet();

         //
         // output VARCHAR maps to Java String
         //
         while ( rs.next() ) {
                 System.out.println( "Transfer Results: "
                 rs.getString(1) );        // VARCHAR to String
...
```

In this example, a `CallableStatement` is created to call the `reconcileTransfers` stored procedure. This stored procedure takes two parameters, which we set as a `String` and a Java `int` value.

The `CallableStatement` also has an `OUT` parameter, which is set as a Java `VARCHAR` (a variable length character string). When the statement is executed, a `ResultSet` is made available through the `getResultSet` method (inherited from the `Statement` class, the superclass of our superclass, `PreparedStatement`). The `ResultSet` is used to retrieve the contents of the `VARCHAR` column using the `getString` method.

The `CallableStatement` interface extends the `PreparedStatement` interface and adds specific methods needed to work with stored procedures. The methods for the `CallableStatement` class are shown in Table 7–2. All methods throw a `SQLException` on error.

Table 7–2 *CallableStatement Methods*

Method	Description
`Array getArray(int i)`	Returns the value of the parameter identified by the integer argument as a `java.sql.Array` type.
`BigDecimal getBigDecimal(int parameterIndex)`	Returns the value of the parameter identified by the integer argument as a `java.math.BigDecimal` type.
`BigDecimal getBigDecimal(int parameterIndex, int scale)`	This method has been deprecated. (Should use the version of the method without the `'scale'` parameter, and then execute setScale on the `BigDecimal` object.)
`Blob getBlob(int i)`	Returns the value of the parameter identified by the integer argument as a `java.sql.Blob` type.
`boolean getBoolean(int parameterIndex)`	Returns the value of the parameter identified by the integer argument as a Java `boolean` primitive type.
`byte getByte(int parameterIndex)`	Returns the value of the parameter identified by the integer argument as a Java byte primitive type.
`byte[] getBytes(int parameterIndex)`	Returns the value of the parameter identified by the integer argument (`BINARY` or `VARBINARY`) as a Java primitive byte array.
`Clob getClob(int i)`	Returns the value of the parameter identified by the integer argument as a `java.sql.Clob` type.
`Date getDate(int parameterIndex)`	Returns the value of the parameter identified by the integer argument as a `javsjava.sql.Date` class reference.

Table 7–2 *CallableStatement Methods (cont.)*

Method	Description
Date getDate(int parameterIndex, Calendar cal)	Returns the value of the parameter identified by the integer argument as a java.sql.Date type, using the Calendar parameter to create the date.
Double getDouble(int parameterIndex)	Returns the value of the parameter identified by the integer argument as a Java language double primitive type.
float getFloat(int parameterIndex)	Returns the value of the parameter identified by the integer argument as a Java language float primitive type.
int getInt(int parameterIndex)	Returns the value of the parameter identified by the integer argument as a Java int primitive type.
long getLong(int parameterIndex)	Returns the value of the parameter identified by the integer argument as a Java long primitive type.
Object getObject(int parameterIndex)	Returns the value of the parameter identified by the integer argument as a Java Object type.
Object getObject(int i, Map map)	Returns the value of the parameter identified by the integer argument as a Java Object type, using the Map object to provide type mapping. (Usually used for custom data types.)
Ref getRef(int i)	Returns the value of the parameter identified by the integer argument as a java.sql.Ref type.
Short getShort(int parameterIndex)	Returns the value of the parameter identified by the integer argument as a Java language short type.
String getString(int parameterIndex)	Returns the value of the parameter identified by the integer argument as a Java language String.
Time getTime(int parameterIndex)	Returns the value of the parameter identified by the integer argument as a java.sql.Time type.
Time getTime(int parameterIndex, Calendar cal)	Returns the value of the parameter identified by the integer argument as a javas.sql.Time type, using the Calendar object to create the time.
Timestamp getTimestamp(int parameterIndex)	Returns the value of the parameter identified by the integer argument as a java.sql.Timestamp type.
Timestamp getTimestamp(int parameterIndex, Calendar cal)	Returns the value of the parameter identified by the integer argument as a java.sql.Timestamp type.
void registerOutParameter(int parameterIndex, int sqlType)	Registers the OUT parameter value identified by the parameter index as the type identified by the second parameter. Types are of java.sql.Types.

Method	Description
void registerOutParameter(int parameterIndex, int sqlType, int scale)	Registers the OUT parameter value identified by the parameter index as the type identified by the second parameter. Types are of java.sql.Types with the scale identified by the third argument.
void registerOutParameter(int paramIndex, int sqlType, String typeName)	Registers the OUT parameter value identified by the parameter index as the type identified by the second parameter. This version of the method is usually used for User Defined Types (UDTs) that require explicit type mapping by the UDT and a Java type.
boolean wasNull()	Returns a boolean value indicating whether or not the last OUT parameter read was a null value.

Note that it may be possible to execute stored procedures using vendor-specific SQL to execute the procedure and return results. What the CallableStatement class offers is a vendor-neutral method for using this feature.

Summary

The use of prepared statements, SQL statements that have been presented to the database prior to being used, can provide a potential performance improvement and added convenience for the developer who takes advantage of them. This chapter covered the PreparedStatement class and demonstrated how parameters can be identified in the SQL statement and values can later be substituted for the parameters.

The CallableStatement interface extends the PreparedStatement interface and identifies those behaviors that are required to specifically prepare and execute stored procedures.

Coming Up Next

Chapter 8 covers a class we've already seen in use: the ResultSet class. This implementation of the JDBC ResultSet interface provides the means to retrieve the results of the query. This chapter provides detailed coverage of the extensive set of methods in the ResultSet class. A number of examples demonstrate some of the more interesting features of the class, including a scrollable ResultSet and performing updates through ResultSet objects.

The ResultSet Class

INTRODUCTION

Once a database connection has been made and a SQL statement is executed, any results from the execution of a SQL statement that returns results are represented with a `ResultSet` object. As we've seen in previous code examples, this class allows programmatic loops to be written to review the results.

The `ResultSet` class encapsulates the rows or tuples resulting from the execution of a SQL `select` query. Originally, in the early releases of the JDBC API, the `ResultSet` class only allowed for the serial progression through a set of results, from the first to the last. Random movement through the results was not allowed. Additionally, data in the `ResultSet` could only be read; updates through the `ResultSet` were not allowed.

With the JDBC 2.0 optional extensions, additional capabilities were added to the `ResultSet` specification that allow results to be reviewed in a random order. This is referred to as a *scrollable* `ResultSet` or *scrollable cursor*. Later JDBC releases also added the capability to perform updates through `ResultSets`.

Though these additional features are provided in the current API, it is up to the JDBC driver provider to provide them—they are not required for compliance. Fortunately, partly because of the demand, a large number of JDBC drivers provide these features.

This chapter provides several ResultSet examples. The best place to start with the ResultSet class is with an example that shows serial progression through a ResultSet, moving from the first row to the last row. An example of random access or scroll cursor ResultSets will also be shown together with a description of the methods used with this type of ResultSet. Finally, a demonstration of *updateable* ResultSets will be provided along with the methods used with these ResultSets.

USING A RESULTSET FOR SERIAL ACCESS

The default behavior for a ResultSet object and the behavior required for JDBC compliance is serial access, accessing the rows or tuples returned from the first row to the last in a serial fashion. Using this type of access, once a row has been read, it cannot be read again. For many applications, such as producing reports or informational pages for a Web site, this is a perfectly acceptable form of access. The following code sample uses this type of access.

ResultSetExample1.java

```
1.import java.sql.*;
2.import javax.sql.*;
3.import javax.naming.*;
4.import com.codestudio.sql.PoolMan;
5.
6.public class ResultSetExample1 {
7.
8.
9.public static void main( String args[] ) {
10.
11.Connection con=null;
12.try {
13.      //
14.      // JNDI startup parameters are stored in
15.      // the "jndi.properties" file in the classpath.
16.      //
17.      InitialContext ctx = new InitialContext( );
18.
19.      // get the DataSource from the JNDI name server
20.      DataSource ds = (DataSource) ctx.lookup("movies-mysql");
21.
22.      // get the connection from the DataSource
23.      con = ds.getConnection( );
```

```
24.
25.      // create a Statement class to execute the SQL statement
26.      Statement stmt = con.createStatement();
27.
28.      // execute the SQL statement and get the results in a ResultSet
29.      ResultSet rs    = stmt.executeQuery(
30.          "select movie_name, release_date from movies" );
31.
32.      // display the ResultSet type
33.      System.out.println(
34.              "\nResultSet type: " +
35.              getCursorTypeString( rs.getType()) +
36.              "\n" );
37.
38.      // iterate through the ResultSet, displaying two values
39.      // for each row using the getString method
40.      //
41.      while ( rs.next() ) {
42.              System.out.println(
43.                      "******************" + "\n" +
44.                  "movie_name: " + "\t" +
45.                      rs.getString("movie_name") + "\n" +
46.                  "release_date: " + "\t" +
47.                      rs.getString("release_date")   );
48.      }
49.
50.}
51.catch (SQLException e) {
52.
53.      // display SQL specific exception information
54.      System.out.println("**************************" );
55.      System.out.println("SQLException in main: " + e.getMessage() );
56.      System.out.println("** SQLState: " + e.getSQLState());
57.      System.out.println("** SQL Error Code: " + e.getErrorCode());
58.      System.out.println("**************************" );
59.      e.printStackTrace();
60.}
61.catch (Exception e) {
62.      System.out.println("Exception in main: " + e.getMessage() );
63.      e.printStackTrace();
64.}
65.finally {
66.
67.      try {
68.          // close the connection
69.      if ( con != null )
70.              con.close();
71.      }
72.      catch (SQLException e) {
73.              e.printStackTrace();
74.      }
75.}
```

```
76.
77.
78.} // end main
79.
80.static String getCursorTypeString( int type ) {
81.
82.if ( type == ResultSet.TYPE_FORWARD_ONLY )
83.     return "Forward Only ResultSet.";
84.
85.if ( type == ResultSet.TYPE_SCROLL_INSENSITIVE )
86.     return "Scroll Insensitive ResultSet.";
87.
88.if ( type == ResultSet.TYPE_SCROLL_SENSITIVE )
89.     return "Scroll Sensitive ResultSet.";
90.
91.return "Unknown";
92.
93.}
94.
95.}
```

In this example, rows are retrieved from the `movies` table in the `movies` database to produce a listing of the movies available. In code that is no doubt familiar at this point, the application obtains an initial JNDI context on line 17, obtains a `DataSource` reference on line 20 for the `movies-mysql` data source, and then creates a `Statement` object on line 26.

On line 27, a SQL `select` statement query is executed using the `Statement` `executeQuery` method. This statement merely selects the `movie_name` and `release_date` column from the `movies` table.

On line 33, the `getType` method of the `ResultSet` class is called to retrieve the type of `ResultSet` we have obtained by executing the query. The `getType` method will return an integer, which is matched with the integer constants from the `ResultSet` interface in the `getCursorTypeString` method, which is declared on line 80. The `getCursorTypeString` method will convert the value of the integer argument into an appropriate string for display.

The loop that is started on line 44 demonstrates a typical loop used to output the contents of a normal serial `ResultSet`. The `ResultSet next` method is called as the controlling argument to the `while` loop. The first call to the `ResultSet next` method after the `ResultSet` has been created will position the cursor or pointer for the `ResultSet` before the first record in the result set and return `true` if there are records to be retrieved. If the query has failed to return records, then the call to the `ResultSet next` method will return `false`. As this program loop is designed, a failure to return any records will cause it to quietly fail.

TIP   **Checking for Returned Rows**

Since it is not uncommon for a query that worked fine during programmer testing to fail to return rows in production, it is a good practice to create code that will manage this situation correctly. Note that a `select` query that fails to return rows will not necessarily throw an exception; the programmer must test for this condition. When we examine the `ResultSetMetaData` class, we will find other methods for determining the contents of a `ResultSet`. Still, testing for rows using the `ResultSet` `next` method is a common and simple approach for determining whether or not there are rows to process.

A `catch` block on line 51 catches the `SQLException` that may be thrown by the various JDBC calls being made. This catch block displays information on the SQL state and SQL error code. These methods can provide additional information on a SQL error when they occur (though not all JDBC drivers will provide this information).

The `finally` block on line 65 will close the `Connection` object if it is non-null. Closing the connection in this block insures that the connection will be closed even in the event an exception is thrown (since the `finally` block is always executed).

On line 80, the `getCursorTypeString` method is declared. This method takes the integer argument and maps it to the appropriate `ResultSet` integer constant. It returns a meaningful string for the type of cursor that the `ResultSet` implements. The output of this program is as follows:

Output of the ResultSetExample1.java

```
ResultSet type: Forward Only ResultSet.

* * * * * * * * * * * * * * * * * *
movie_name:     The Evil Null Reference
release_date:   2001-01-01
* * * * * * * * * * * * * * * * * *
movie_name:     The Last Reference
release_date:   2001-01-01
* * * * * * * * * * * * * * * * * *
movie_name:     Just One More Compile
release_date:   2001-01-01
* * * * * * * * * * * * * * * * * *
movie_name:     One More Lonely Harley
release_date:   2001-01-01
* * * * * * * * * * * * * * * * * *
movie_name:     One Last Try Before the Lights Go Down
release_date:   2002-01-11
```

General Purpose ResultSet Methods

There are a number of basic `ResultSet` methods that are used regardless of the specific `ResultSet type` being used. These methods perform such operations as closing the `ResultSet` or retrieving the SQL warnings from the object. Table 8–1 lists these methods.

Table 8–1   *General-Purpose ResultSet Methods*

Method	Description
`void clearWarnings()`	Clears all current warnings (`SQLWarning`) on the `ResultSet`.
`void close()`	Closes the current `ResultSet` object and releases the database driver and related database resources for the `ResultSet`. Does not close the connection.
`int findColumn(String columnName)`	Returns the column position in the current `ResultSet` for the column name string passed.
`SQLWarning getWarnings()`	Returns the first SQLWarning for this `ResultSet`.
`void refreshRow()`	Refreshes the current row contents from the database. (This will overwrite any current `ResultSet` row updates not committed to the database.)
`void setFetchDirection(int direction)`	Uses the integer argument to provide a hint to the JDBC driver on the direction in which the `ResultSet` will be processed.
`void setFetchSize(int rows)`	Uses the integer argument to set the fetch buffer size for the `ResultSet`. The size represents the number of rows the JDBC driver will place in the buffer on each retrieval operation from the database.
`int getType()`	Returns the type of the `ResultSet` object. The integer value returned references one of the integer constants in the `java.sql.ResultSet`, one of `TYPE_FORWARD_ONLY`, `TYPE_SCROLL_INSENSI-TIVE`, or `TYPE_SCROLL_SENSITIVE`.
`String getCursorName()`	Returns the name of the cursor used by the `ResultSet`.
`Statement getStatement()`	Returns the `Statement` that was used to create this `ResultSet`.
`boolean next()`	Moves the `ResultSet` pointer from the current row to the next row in the `ResultSet`.

Table 8–1	*General-Purpose ResultSet Methods (cont.)*

Method	Description
`int getConcurrency()`	Returns the concurrency of this `ResultSet`. The concurrency is one of the integer constants defined in `java.sql.ResultSet`. The concurrency of the `ResultSet` is set in the `createStatement` or `prepareStatement` call when the `Statement` or `PreparedStatement` object is created.
`int getRow()`	Returns the current row number as an integer. Row numbers begin at 1. A returned row number of 0 indicates there are no more rows available in the `ResultSet`.

The `setFetchSize` method sets the size of the *fetch buffer,* the buffer used by the driver to retrieve data from the database server. It takes an integer argument for the number of rows to be retrieved. The `setFetchDirection` method takes an integer argument that relates to the `ResultSet` integer constants. The fetch direction is a hint to the driver that can possibly improve the performance of the `ResultSet`.

TIP

Setting Fetch Direction

The `setFetchDirection` and `setFetchSize` methods are also available in the `Statement` and `PreparedStatement` classes. On database queries where the data will be retrieved when the statement is executed—for example, `select` queries—it is a good idea to set these to optimal settings in the `Statement` or `PreparedStatement` class so that the data retrieval operations can be optimized before the creation of the `ResultSet`.

The `getWarnings` and `clearWarnings` methods are used to retrieve or clear the SQL warnings on the `ResultSet`. There may be one or more SQL warnings generated by each database operation the driver performs. Multiple warnings are chained one to another, so that retrieving the first warning would provide access to the second warning, the second warning would provide access to the third warning, and so on.

The `findColumn` method is used to find the ordinal position of the column in the `ResultSet`. This integer value can then be used for the `getXXXX` methods, which require an integer argument. (There are some who feel that use of the getXXXX methods with integer arguments provides better performance than using their alternative string column name versions because expensive string matches do not need to be performed on each iteration.)

The getType method returns an integer value that corresponds to the ResultSet types as defined in the ResultSet interface. This is a useful method to determine the type of ResultSet that has been provided and what its capabilities are. For example, a call to getType could indicate that a specific ResultSet does not support dynamic access (scroll cursor) capabilities; therefore, the calls to the positioning ResultSet methods for positioning should not be made.

The getCursorName method returns the name of the underlying cursor in the database as a string. This string could then be used to build a string for creating a SQL statement that supports positioned updates or for using other database-specific syntax for manipulating the cursor. (This obviously has the effect of binding the application to the database and limiting portability.)

The getStatement method returns the Statement object that has created the ResultSet. This allows the ResultSet reference to be used to make calls against the corresponding Statement object—for example, where rs is a ResultSet object: rs.getStatement().getConnection().commit().

The refreshRow method is used to refresh the row being examined from the database. This has utility when using ResultSet updates and we want to be sure no one has interfered with the data while we've been examining it.

As we've seen, the next method is used for iterating or stepping through the contents of a ResultSet. This method returns true if there are rows in the ResultSet that can be processed. The method also moves the cursor to the next available row or record in the ResultSet. When the ResultSet is first created the cursor or pointer for the ResultSet is *before* the first row. If there are records in the ResultSet, the first call to the next method will set the cursor or pointer at the first row in the ResultSet.

The getConcurrency method returns an integer which indicates the concurrency mode of the current ResultSet (and underlying database cursor). The integer value relates to one of the integer constants in the ResultSet class and is one of CONCUR_READONLY or CONCUR_UPDATABLE.

The getRow method returns an integer, which is the current row position in the ResultSet. Row numbers start at one (1). A return value of zero (0) indicates that there is no current row; this would occur if the ResultSet pointer was positioned before the first row (before the first call to the next method) or after the last row (after all rows have been read or the pointer has been moved to this position).

The ResultSet getXXXX Methods

There are a number of getXXXX methods in the ResultSet class, one set for each JDBC data type defined in java.sql.Types. Each getXXXX method references a column in the select list. The column can be referenced in two ways. One common process for addressing the column is through the identification of the offset or ordinal position of the column in the select list, starting at the far left with the number one (1) and moving to the right through the number of columns in the select list.

The other process for addressing the column in the select list is to provide a string name for the column in the list (for example, `movie_name`). For each data type, there are two versions of the `getXXXX` method, one for each type of access. Table 8–2 provides a complete listing of all of the `getXXXX` methods in the `ResultSet` class.

The process of using the `getXXXX` methods is as shown in the various examples in this and other chapters. The rear portion of the method name represents the type such that the naming formats are as follows.

```
get<type_name>(integer <column_index>);
get<type_name>(String <column_name>);
```

The return type from these methods is the return type that is being retrieved, whether that be a Java primitive data type or an object reference of the specified type. There are a few cases of variation from this standard format where a third argument is added to indicate precision or length of the data type being retrieved from the `ResultSet`.

Table 8–2   *ResultSet getXXXX Methods*

Method	Description
`Array getArray(int i)`	Returns the value of the column identified by the integer index argument as a `java.sql.Array`.
`Array getArray(String colName)`	Returns the value of the column identified by the string name parameter as a `java.sql.Array`.
`InputStream getAsciiStream(int columnIndex)`	Returns the value of the column identified by the integer index argument as an `InputStream`.
`InputStream getAsciiStream(String columnName)`	Returns the value of the column identified by the string column name argument as an `InputStream`.
`BigDecimal getBigDecimal(int columnIndex)`	Returns the value of the column identified by the integer index argument as a `java.math.BigDecimal` with full precision.
`BigDecimal getBigDecimal(int columnIndex, int scale)`	Deprecated. (Should use `getBigDecimal` method without scale argument.)
`BigDecimal getBigDecimal(String columnName)`	Returns the value of the column identified by the string name argument as a `java.math.BigDecimal` with full precision.

Table 8–2   *ResultSet getXXXX Methods (cont.)*

Method	Description
`BigDecimal getBigDecimal(String columnName, int scale)`	Deprecated. (Should use `getBigDecimal method` without `scale` argument.)
`InputStream getBinaryStream(int columnIndex)`	Returns the value of the column identified by the integer index argument as a `BinaryStream`.
`InputStream getBinaryStream(String columnName)`	Returns the value of the column identified by the string name argument as a `BinaryStream`.
`Blob getBlob(int i)`	Returns the value of the column identified by the integer index argument as a `java.sql.Blob`.
`Blob getBlob(String colName)`	Returns the value of the column identified by the string column name argument as a `java.sql.Blob`.
`boolean getBoolean(int columnIndex)`	Returns the value of the column identified by the integer index argument as a Java `boolean` primitive data type.
`boolean getBoolean(String columnName)`	Returns the value of the column identified by the string column name argument as a Java `boolean` primitive data type.
`byte getByte(int columnIndex)`	Returns the value of the column identified by the integer index argument as a Java `byte` primitive data type.
`byte getByte(String columnName)`	Returns the value of the column identified by the string column name argument as a Java `byte` primitive data type.
`byte[] getBytes(int columnIndex)`	Returns the value of the column identified by the integer index argument as a Java `byte` array primitive data type.
`byte[] getBytes(String columnName)`	Returns the value of the column identified by the string column name argument as a Java `byte` array primitive data type.
`Reader getCharacterStream(int columnIndex)`	Returns the value of the column identified by the integer index argument as a Java `Reader` object reference.
`Reader getCharacterStream(String columnName)`	Returns the value of the column identified by the string column name argument as a Java `Reader` object reference.
`Clob getClob(int i)`	Returns the value of the `ResultSet` column referenced by the integer argument as a `java.sql.Clob` object reference
`Clob getClob(String colName)`	Returns the value of the `ResultSet` column referenced by the string column name argument as a java.sql.Clob reference.

| Table 8–2 | *ResultSet getXXXX Methods (cont.)* |

Method	Description
`Date getDate(int columnIndex)`	Returns the value of the `ResultSet` column referenced by the integer index argument as a `java.sql.Date` reference.
`Date getDate(int columnIndex, Calendar cal)`	Returns the value of the `ResultSet` column referenced by the integer index argument as a `java.sql.Date` reference. Uses the `java.util.Calendar` object to create the `Date` object if the underlying database does not contain time zone information.
`Date getDate(String columnName)`	Returns the value of the `ResultSet` column referenced by the string column name argument as a `java.sql.Date` reference.
`Date getDate(String columnName, Calendar cal)`	Returns the value of the `ResultSet` column referenced by the integer index argument as a `java.sql.Date` reference. Uses the `java.util.Calendar` object to create the `Date` object if the underlying database does not contain time zone information.
`double getDouble(int columnIndex)`	Returns the value of the `ResultSet` column referenced by the integer index argument as a Java `double` primitive data type.
`double getDouble(String columnName)`	Returns the value of the `ResultSet` column referenced by the string column name argument as a Java `double` primitive data type.
`int getFetchDirection()`	Returns the fetch direction hint that was provided to the database driver for the creation of the `ResultSet`. The integer value relates to the integer constants in the `java.sql.ResultSet` interface.
`int getFetchSize()`	Returns the fetch buffer size for this ResultSet as an integer value.
`float getFloat(int columnIndex)`	Returns the value of the `ResultSet` column referenced by the string column name argument as a Java float primitive data type.
`float getFloat(String columnName)`	Returns the value of the `ResultSet` column referenced by the string column name argument as a Java `float` primitive data type.
`int getInt(int columnIndex)`	Returns the value of the `ResultSet` column referenced by the integer index argument as a Java `int` primitive data type.
`int getInt(String columnName)`	Returns the value of the `ResultSet` column referenced by the string column name argument as a Java `int` primitive data type.

Table 8–2   *ResultSet getXXXX Methods (cont.)*

Method	Description
`long getLong(int columnIndex)`	Returns the value of the `ResultSet` column referenced by the integer index argument as a Java `long` primitive data type.
`long getLong(String columnName)`	Returns the value of the `ResultSet` column referenced by the string column name argument as a Java `long` primitive data type.
`ResultSetMetaData getMetaData()`	Returns the `ResultSetMetaData` object for the `ResultSet`. (See Chapter 10 for ResultSetMetaData)
`Object getObject(int columnIndex)`	Returns the value of the `ResultSet` column referenced by the integer index argument as an `Object` reference.
`Object getObject(int i, Map map)`	Returns the value of the `ResultSet` column referenced by the integer index argument as an `Object` reference. Uses the `Map` argument to perform mapping of SQL type names to Java classes.
`Object getObject(String columnName)`	Returns the value of the `ResultSet` column referenced by the string column name argument as an `Object` reference.
`Object getObject(String colName, Map map)`	Returns the value of the `ResultSet` column referenced by the string column name argument as an `Object` reference. Uses the `Map` argument to perform mapping of SQL type names to Java classes.
`Ref getRef(int i)`	Returns the value of the `ResultSet` column referenced by the integer index argument as a `java.sql.Ref` object reference.
`Ref getRef(String colName)`	Returns the value of the `ResultSet` column referenced by the string column name argument as a `java.sql.Ref` object reference.
`short getShort(int columnIndex)`	Returns the value of the `ResultSet` column referenced by the integer index argument as a Java `short` primitive data type.
`short getShort(String columnName)`	Returns the value of the `ResultSet` column referenced by the string column name argument as a Java `short` primitive data type.
`String getString(int columnIndex)`	Returns the value of the `ResultSet` column referenced by the integer index argument as a Java `String` data type.

Table 8–2	*ResultSet getXXXX Methods (cont.)*

Method	Description
`String getString(String columnName)`	Returns the value of the `ResultSet` column referenced by the string column name argument as a Java `String` data type.
`Time getTime(int columnIndex)`	Returns the value of the `ResultSet` column referenced by the integer index argument as a `java.sql.Time` object reference.
`Time getTime(int columnIndex, Calendar cal)`	Returns the value of the `ResultSet` column referenced by the integer index argument as a `java.sql.Time` object reference.
`Time getTime(String columnName)`	Returns the value of the `ResultSet` column referenced by the string column name argument as a `java.sql.Time` object reference.
`Time getTime(String columnName, Calendar cal)`	Returns the value of the `ResultSet` column referenced by the string column name argument as a `java.sql.Time` object reference. The `Calendar` object argument is used to obtain the time zone information if the underlying database does not provide that information.
`Timestamp getTimestamp(int columnIndex)`	Returns the value of the `ResultSet` column referenced by the integer index argument as a `java.sql.Timestamp` object reference.
`Timestamp getTimestamp(int columnIndex, Calendar cal)`	Returns the value of the `ResultSet` column referenced by the integer index argument as a `java.sql.Timestamp` object reference. The `Calendar` object argument is used to obtain the time zone information if the underlying database does not provide that information.
`Timestamp getTimestamp(String columnName)`	Returns the value of the `ResultSet` column referenced by the string column name argument as a `java.sql.Timestamp` object reference.
`Timestamp getTimestamp(String columnName, Calendar cal)`	Returns the value of the `ResultSet` column referenced by the string column name argument as a `java.sql.Timestamp` object reference. The `Calendar` object argument is used to obtain the time zone information if the underlying database does not provide that information.
`InputStream getUnicodeStream(int columnIndex)`	Deprecated. Recommend using `getCharacterStream` in place of `getUnicodeStream`.
`InputStream getUnicodeStream(String columnName)`	Deprecated.

Moving in the ResultSet

One of the more notable omissions in the early releases of the JDBC API was the ability to position the `ResultSet` pointer or cursor within the result set. The `ResultSet` could only be read in a serial fashion, from the first record to last record. Once a row was read and the `ResultSet` pointer was moved to the next row in the set, the previous row could not be read again. But relational databases generally provided more robust access facilities through their proprietary APIs (referred to as Call Level Interfaces, or CLIs).

Fairly early in the history of relational databases, relational database vendors provided proprietary APIs to access database data. These APIs have for some time supported *cursors*, the ability to execute a SQL `select` statement and review the results in some native language, such as C or C++, or using a database stored procedure language. These vendor APIs have generally supported *scroll cursors*, cursors that allow `select` results to be reviewed serially and randomly. Using a scroll cursor, a completely random access order could be used. For example, the first, second, and third rows of a result set could be read, then the second row could be read again, then the third, and then the fifth row could be read.

The `ResultSet` class contains a number of methods that provide for this random access or scroll cursor capability. These methods allow positioning within the results serially, by absolute record number from the start of the result set, or by a relative record number from the current position in the result set. The major database vendors all provide this capability in their JDBC driver, as do many of the open source databases. But technically, a scroll cursor or random access `ResultSet` capability is not required in the JDBC driver for JDBC compliance. The following code example demonstrates the use of scroll cursors using JDBC.

ScrollExample2.java

```
1.import java.sql.*;
2.import javax.sql.*;
3.
4.
5.public class ScrollExample2 {
6.
7.public static void main( String args[] ) {
8.
9.try {
10.     // get the initial context
11.     InitialContext ctx = new InitialContext(  );
12.
13.     // get the DataSource from the JNDI name server
14.     DataSource ds = (DataSource) ctx.lookup("movies-mysql");
15.
16.     // create the connection using the static getConnection method
17.     Connection con = ds.getConnection( );
```

```
18.
19.      // create a Statement class to execute the SQL statement
20.      Statement stmt = con.createStatement(
21.                       ResultSet.TYPE_SCROLL_INSENSITIVE,
22.                       ResultSet.CONCUR_UPDATABLE );
23.
24.      // execute the SQL statement and get the results in a ResultSet
25.      ResultSet rs   = stmt.executeQuery(
26.           "select movie_name, movie_id, release_date from movies" );
27.
28.      // show the cursor type
29.      System.out.println("Cursor Type: " +
30.                getCursorTypeString( rs.getType() ) );
31.
32.      // iterate through the ResultSet, displaying two values
33.      // for each row using the getString method
34.       System.out.println("Cursor has the following rows.");
35.       while ( rs.next() )
36.              System.out.println( "*****************" + "\n" +
37.                          "movie_id: " + "\t" +
38.                    rs.getString("movie_id") + "\n" +
39.                          "movie_name: " + "\t" +
40.                    rs.getString("movie_name") + "\n" +
41.                          "release_date: " + "\t" +
42.                    rs.getString("release_date")   );
43.
44.      // jump to the first record
45.      if ( rs.first() {
46.         System.out.println("\n\nThis is the first record.");
47.         System.out.println( "*****************" + "\n" +
48.                     "movie_id: " + "\t" +
49.                 rs.getString("movie_id") + "\n" +
50.                     "movie_name: " + "\t" +
51.                 rs.getString("movie_name") + "\n" +
52.                     "release_date: " + "\t" +
53.                 rs.getString("release_date")   );
54.      }
55.      // jump to the last record
56.       if ( rs.last() ) {
57.         System.out.println("\n\nThis is the last record.");
58.         System.out.println( "*****************" + "\n" +
59.                          "movie_id: " + "\t" +
60.                    rs.getString("movie_id") + "\n" +
61.                          "movie_name: " + "\t" +
62.                    rs.getString("movie_name") + "\n" +
63.                          "release_date: " + "\t" +
64.                    rs.getString("release_date")   );
65.       }
66.      // jump to the third record - absolute
67.      if ( rs.absolute(3) ) {
68.         System.out.println("\n\nThis is the third record.");
69.         System.out.println( "*****************" + "\n" +
```

```
70.                                "movie_id: " + "\t" +
71.                       rs.getString("movie_id") + "\n" +
72.                           "movie_name: " + "\t" +
73.                       rs.getString("movie_name") + "\n" +
74.                          "release_date: " + "\t" +
75.                       rs.getString("release_date")  );
76.      }
77.
78.     // jump to the last record - 2
79.     if ( rs.absolute(-2) ) {
80.         System.out.println("\n\nThis is the second to last record.");
81.         System.out.println( "*******************" + "\n" +
82.                              "movie_id: " + "\t" +
83.                     rs.getString("movie_id") + "\n" +
84.                          "movie_name: " + "\t" +
85.                     rs.getString("movie_name") + "\n" +
86.                          "release_date: " + "\t" +
87.                     rs.getString("release_date")  );
88.      }
89.     // jump to the last record
90.     if ( rs.relative(1) ) {
91.         System.out.println("\n\nThis is the last record - again.");
92.         System.out.println( "*******************" + "\n" +
93.                              "movie_id: " + "\t" +
94.                     rs.getString("movie_id") + "\n" +
95.                              "movie_name: " + "\t" +
96.                     rs.getString("movie_name") + "\n" +
97.                              "release_date: " + "\t" +
98.                     rs.getString("release_date")  );
99.      }
100.    // close the connection
101.    con.close();
102.
103.}
104.catch (SQLException e) {
105.
106.     // display SQL specific exception information
107.     System.out.println("*************************" );
108.     System.out.println("SQLException in main: " + e.getMessage() );
109.     System.out.println("** SQLState: " + e.getSQLState());
110.     System.out.println("** SQL Error Code: " + e.getErrorCode());
111.     System.out.println("*************************" );
112.     e.printStackTrace();
113.}
114.catch (Exception e) {
115.     System.out.println("Exception in main: " + e.getMessage() );
116.     e.printStackTrace();
117.}
118.finally {
119.
120.     try {
121.
```

```
122.    if ( con != null )
123.            con.close();
124.    }
125.    catch (SQLException e) {
126.            e.printStackTrace();
127.    }
128.}
129.}
130.
131.static String getCursorTypeString( int ctype ) {
132.
133.if ( ctype == ResultSet.TYPE_FORWARD_ONLY )
134.    return "Forward Scrolling Only";
135.
136.if ( ctype == ResultSet.TYPE_SCROLL_INSENSITIVE )
137.    return "Scrolling Insensitive";
138.
139.if ( ctype == ResultSet.TYPE_SCROLL_SENSITIVE )
140.    return "Scrolling Sensitive";
141.
142.return "Unknown";
143.
144.}
145.}
```

None of this code looks much different from that shown in the previous examples. It is the `Connection` class `createStatement` method on line 20 that looks different. This overloaded version of the `createStatement` method contains arguments for the cursor type (`ResultSet.TYPE_SCROLL_INSENSITIVE`) and the concurrency type (`ResultSet.CONCUR_UPDATABLE`). This indicates to the JDBC driver that we will be using scroll cursor functionality and we will allow concurrent updates to the data we will be reading in our `ResultSet`, thus we are *sharing* the data with other database users.

Though the specification does not require it, requesting a `ResultSet` type that is not supported usually throws an exception. If a `ResultSet` type is `TYPE_FORWARD_ONLY`, then any attempt to try to position the `ResultSet` pointer (absolute, relative, first, last) will throw an exception. (Note that the `createStatement` method in the `Connection` class, which requests the `ResultSet` type, may not throw an exception.)

On line 25, we call the `executeQuery` method, passing in a SQL statement that selects a number of columns from the movie table. The `executeQuery` method returns a `ResultSet`, which is used throughout the remainder of the program.

On line 30, a call is made to the `getCursorTypeString` method (declared as part of this class—not part of the JDBC API) to display the type of cursor implemented by the `ResultSet`. The `getCursorTypeString` method is passed an integer that relates to one of the integer constants in the `ResultSet` class. The `getCursorString` maps the integer parameter to a string that indicates the cursor type. This string is returned by the method.

The remainder of the program iterates through the `ResultSet`, moving in various directions to demonstrate the use of the scroll cursor functionality. A `while` loop on line 35 demonstrates that simple serial iteration is available by making successive calls to the `ResultSet next` method to move the `ResultSet` pointer to the next record in the results. This `while` loop will iterate through all of the results, from the first record to the last record in the `ResultSet`.

Once the `while` loop has completed, the `ResultSet` first method is called on line 45 to move iteration back to the first record in the `ResultSet`. On lines 47 through 53, the value of the columns in the first record are displayed.

On line 56, the `ResultSet last` method is called to move the `ResultSet` pointer to the last record in the `ResultSet`. On lines 58 through 63, the values of the columns in the last record are displayed.

The next positioning call is made on line 67, where a call is made to the `absolute` method. This method takes an integer argument that indicates the absolute position within the `ResultSet` for the move. In this example, the integer 3 is passed into the method, indicating that the third record in the `ResultSet` should be retrieved.

The `ResultSet absolute` method is called again on line 79, where a negative two (–2) is passed as an argument to the method. A negative number passed to the absolute method indicates that the positioning is relative to the last record, so an argument of negative two will move the cursor to the second to last record.

The negative numbers passed into the `absolute` method can be confusing. The call on line 79 of `absolute(-2)` has moved us to the record before the last record in the `ResultSet`. A call of `absolute(-1)` would have moved the `ResultSet` pointer to the last record. This makes sense when you consider we are working from a base of 1, not 0, so that 1 is the first record, 2 is the second record, and so on. Using this logic, –1 should be the last record, –2 the record before last, and so on.

Since the `ResultSet` pointer is on the second to last record, moving one position from where we are currently would place us on the last record. This is exactly what is done on line 90 with a call to the `ResultSet relative` method. The method call on line 90 passes a value of positive one into the method (`relative(1)`), thus placing the `ResultSet` pointer on the last record. The value of the records columns are displayed on lines 92 through 98.

A number of `catch` blocks are used on lines 115 through 128 to catch the various exceptions that may be thrown by the JDBC calls. In the `finally` block started on line 129, the connection is closed (if it has been created). As usual, it is good practice to close the connection and release resources in the `finally` block, which we know will be executed even in the event an exception is thrown by one of the many JDBC method calls being made.

On line 131, the body of the `getCursorTypeString` method is declared. This method simply maps the integer value passed into the method to one of the `ResultSet` constant values. It returns the name of the cursor type being used. The output from the execution of this program would be as follows.

```
Cursor Type: Scrolling Insensitive
Cursor has the following rows.
*******************
movie_id:      1
movie_name:    Stamping Out the Evil Null Reference
release_date:  2001-01-01
*******************
movie_id:      2
movie_name:    The Last Compile
release_date:  2000-01-11
*******************
movie_id:      3
movie_name:    The Final Test
release_date:  1997-01-22
*******************
movie_id:      4
movie_name:    One Last Try Before the Lights Go Down
release_date:  1998-01-11
*******************
movie_id:      5
movie_name:    Another Dog Day
release_date:  2002-05-22
*******************
movie_id:      6
movie_name:    Trying Again
release_date:  2001-01-28


This is the first record.
*******************
movie_id:      1
movie_name:    Stamping Out the Evil Null Reference
release_date:  2001-01-01


This is the last record.
*******************
movie_id:      6
movie_name:    Trying Again
release_date:  2001-01-28
```

```
This is the third record.
*******************
movie_id:      3
movie_name:    The Final Test
release_date:  1997-01-22


This is the second to last record.
*******************
movie_id:      5
movie_name:    Another Dog Day
release_date:  2002-05-22


This is the last record - again.
*******************
movie_id:      6
movie_name:    Trying Again
release_date:  2001-01-28
```

This illustrative example demonstrated the use of the versatile scroll cursor `ResultSet`. While this example demonstrated a number of the methods available, to thoroughly understand what a scroll cursor `ResultSet` can do for you, you should be aware of all the methods in the `ResultSet` class that pertain to this capability. The following section details these methods.

Methods for the Scroll Cursor ResultSet

As mentioned previously, the underlying database and the JDBC driver must support scrollable `ResultSets` for these methods to be usable. (If they have not been implemented, the driver will usually throw an exception indicating the method has not been implemented.) The `DatabaseMetaData` method `supportsResultSetType` can be called to determine whether or not the underlying database supports the scrollable `ResultSet`. An example of this call follows:

```
...
//
// get the DatabaseMetaData object from the Connection
//
DatabaseMetaData dmd = con.getMetaData();

//
// test for scrolling
//
if ( dmd.supportsResultSetType(ResultSet.TYPE_SCROLL_INSENSITIVE) ) {
    // it's ok to create and use scroll cursor ResultSet
...
```

Table 8–3   *Scroll Cursor ResultSet Methods*

Method	Description
`boolean previous()`	Moves the `ResultSet` pointer from the current row to the previous row.
`boolean isBeforeFirst()`	Returns `true` if the `ResultSet` pointer is currently before the first row in the `ResultSet`.
`boolean isFirst()`	Returns `true` if the `ResultSet` pointer is currently at the first row of the `ResultSet`.
`boolean isLast()`	Returns `true` if the `ResultSet` pointer is currently at the last row of the `ResultSet`.
`boolean last()`	Moves the `ResultSet` pointer to the last row in the `ResultSet`.
`void afterLast()`	Moves the `ResultSet` pointer to after the last row.
`void beforeFirst()`	Moves the `ResultSet` pointer to before the first row. tThe cursor to the front of this `ResultSet` object, just before the first row.
`boolean isAfterLast()`	Returns `true` if the `ResultSet` pointer is currently after the last row in the `ResultSet`.
`boolean first()`	Moves the `ResultSet` pointer to the first row in the `ResultSet`.
`Boolean relative(int rows)`	Moves the `ResultSet` pointer to the row specified by the integer argument. This movement is relative to the current `ResultSet` pointer position. A positive number argument moves forward. A negative number argument moves back.
`boolean absolute(int row)`	Moves the `ResultSet` pointer to the first row in the `ResultSet`.

Table 8–3 lists the methods which are available for scrollable `ResultSets`.

All of these methods will throw a `SQLException` if the cursor is not a scrollable cursor, a cursor created as one of `ResultSet.TYPE_SCROLL_SENSITIVE` or `ResultSet.TYPE_SCROLL_INSENSITIVE`.

These methods will not throw an exception if an invalid request is made to move to a nonexistent row (for example, making an `rs.absolute(20)` call when only 10 rows are in the `ResultSet`). What they will do on an invalid call is return a boolean value `false`. Applications should test for a value of `true` before proceeding to work with the `ResultSet` row (this was the technique shown in the previous example).

The `previous` method moves the cursor or pointer to the record before the current record. This method returns a boolean value `true` if there is a record at the requested position, or it returns `false` if there is no previous record.

The `isBeforeFirst` method returns a boolean `true` if the cursor is before the first record in the `ResultSet`. The `beforeFirst` method will move the cursor to before the first record in the `ResultSet`; this is where the cursor (`ResultSet` pointer) should be before the first call to the `ResultSet next` method.

The `isAfterLast` method returns `true` if the cursor or pointer is after the last record in the `ResultSet`. The `afterLast` method will move the cursor to after the last record in the `ResultSet`.

The `first` method will move the cursor or pointer to the first record in the `ResultSet`. The `isFirst` method will return `true` if the cursor is on the first record of the `ResultSet`. Alternatively, the `last` method will move the cursor to the last record in the `ResultSet` and the `isLast` method will return `true` if the cursor is at the last record in the `ResultSet`. (A call to the `last` method followed by a call to the `getRows` method will return the number of rows in the `ResultSet`.)

The `relative` method takes an integer argument that represents the number of positions the cursor will move in the `ResultSet` *relative* to the current position in the `ResultSet`. A positive value integer argument indicates the cursor should move forward in the `ResultSet`, and a negative number indicates the cursor should move back in the `ResultSet`. This method will throw an exception if there is no current row in the `ResultSet` (the cursor is before the first row or after the last row). This method can be called with a zero integer argument (`relative(0)`) but the cursor will not be moved (which is exactly what was requested by the call).

The `absolute` method takes an integer argument that represents the number of positions to move relative to the *absolute* start or end of the `ResultSet`. A positive value provided as an argument indicates the position being requested is relative to the beginning of the `ResultSet`. A negative value provided as an argument requests a position relative to the end of the `ResultSet`. Calling the method with an argument of zero (`absolute(0)`) will throw an exception. Calling the method with positional value beyond the beginning of the `ResultSet` will position the cursor before the first record. Calling the method with a positional value beyond the end of the `ResultSet` will position the cursor after the last record.

USING UPDATEABLE RESULTSETS

As of JDBC 2.0 it is possible to update the database using a `ResultSet`. This provides a convenient mechanism for browsing and updating a database using the same object. Though most major relational database vendors and open source relational database organizations provide a JDBC driver that supports this feature, it is not required for JDBC compliance.

Using `ResultSet` updates may place some requirements on the type of query used to create the `ResultSet`. The JDBC driver must be able to locate the row in the database table that corresponds to the row being updated. This requires either a unique row ID for the current row or knowledge of the primary key for the current row. The driver must be able to effectively create an `update` statement to update the columns of the current record to the appropriate database row. The following code example demonstrates `ResultSet` updates.

ResultSetExample2.java

```
1.import java.sql.*;
2.import java.util.*;
3.import javax.sql.*;
4.import javax.naming.*;
5.//import com.codestudio.sql.PoolMan;
6.
7.public class ResultSetExample2 {
8.
9.
10.// demonstrate updatable resultsets
11.
12.
13.public static void main( String args[] ) {
14.
15.// set ourDate to the current date
16.java.sql.Date ourDate =  new java.sql.Date(
17.                   Calendar.getInstance().getTime().getTime() );
18.
19.Connection con = null;
20.ResultSet  rs  = null;
21.try {
22.
23.        // load the database driver
24.        Class.forName("org.gjt.mm.mysql.Driver");
25.        // create the connection
26.        con= DriverManager.getConnection(
27.           "jdbc:mysql://localhost/movies?user=art&password=YES");
28.
29.        // create a Statement class to execute the SQL statement
30.        Statement stmt = con.createStatement();
31.
32.        // ** with this driver: must use a table with
33.        // ** a primary key defined; must select the pk and
34.        // ** must only use one table; must select the columns
35.        // ** we are going to update
36.        //
37.        // execute the SQL statement and get the results in a ResultSet
38.        rs    = stmt.executeQuery("select movie_id, update_date, " +
39.                                " movie_name, release_date, " +
40.                                " category, special_promotion" +
```

```
41.                                    " from movies" +
42.                         " where category='Comedy'" +
43.                         " order by movie_id" );
44.
45.       // display the ResultSet type
46.       System.out.println(
47.             "\nResultSet type: " +
48.             getCursorTypeString( rs.getType())  +   "\n" );
49.
50.       // iterate through the ResultSet, displaying two values
51.       // for each row using the getString method
52.       while ( rs.next() ) {
53.             System.out.println( "*******************" + "\n" +
54.                     "movie_name: "    + "\t" +
55.                      rs.getString("movie_name") + "\n" +
56.                     "special_promotion: "   + "\t" +
57.                      rs.getString("special_promotion") + "\n" +
58.                        "update_date: "   + "\t" +
59.                      rs.getDate("update_date") +   "\n" +
60.                     "release_date: " + "\t" +
61.                      rs.getString("release_date")   );
62.
63.             // change the update date to today
64.          rs.updateDate( "update_date", ourDate );
65.
66.          // change the special_promotion to 5
67.          rs.updateInt( "special_promotion", 5 );
68.
69.          // update the database row
70.          rs.updateRow();
71.       }
72.
73.       // perform an insert
74.       //
75.       // first, set the values
76.       rs.moveToInsertRow();
77.       rs.updateInt( "movie_id", 601 );
78.       rs.updateDate( "update_date", ourDate );
79.       rs.updateString( "movie_name",
80.             "One Last Try" );
81.       rs.updateDate( "release_date", ourDate );
82.       rs.updateString( "category", "Comedy" );
83.       rs.updateInt( "special_promotion", 0 );
84.
85.       // perform the insert
86.       rs.insertRow();
87.
88.       // let's examine the results
89.       rs   = stmt.executeQuery("select movie_id, movie_name, "  +
90.                " update_date, release_date, special_promotion " +
91.                " from movies" +
92.                " where category = 'Comedy'" );
```

```
93.
94.      System.out.println( "\n ** After updates: \n" );
95.
96.      while ( rs.next() ) {
97.             System.out.println( "******************" + "\n" +
98.                "movie_name: "     +           "\t" +
99.                 rs.getString("movie_name") + "\n" +
100.                "special_promotion: "   + "\t" +
101.                 rs.getString("special_promotion") + "\n" +
102.             "update_date: "   +          "\t" +
103.                rs.getDate("update_date") +  "\n" +
104.                 "release_date: " +           "\t" +
105.                rs.getString("release_date")   );
106.      }
107.
108.}
109.catch (SQLException e) {
110.
111.     // display SQL specific exception information
112.     System.out.println("**************************" );
113.     System.out.println("SQLException in main: " + e.getMessage() );
114.     System.out.println("** SQLState: " + e.getSQLState());
115.     System.out.println("** SQL Error Code: " + e.getErrorCode());
116.     System.out.println("**************************" );
117.     e.printStackTrace();
118.}
119.catch (Exception e) {
120.     System.out.println("Exception in main: " + e.getMessage() );
121.     e.printStackTrace();
122.}
123.finally {
124.
125.    try {
126.         // close the connection
127.    if ( con != null )
128.              con.close();
129.      }
130.       catch (SQLException e) {
131.             e.printStackTrace();
132.      }
133.   }
134.
135.} // end main
136.
137.static String getCursorTypeString( int type ) {
138.
139.if ( type == ResultSet.TYPE_FORWARD_ONLY )
140.     return "Forward Only ResultSet.";
141.
142.if ( type == ResultSet.TYPE_SCROLL_INSENSITIVE )
143.     return "Scroll Insensitive ResultSet.";
144.
```

```
145.if ( type == ResultSet.TYPE_SCROLL_SENSITIVE )
146.     return "Scroll Sensitive ResultSet.";
147.
148.return "Unknown";
149.
150.}
151.
152.}
```

This example begins by performing a number of imports on lines 1 through 4. On line 16, a local variable is declared as a `java.sql.Date` type variable and set to an initial value of the current date.

`Connection` and `ResultSet` objects are declared on lines 19 and 20. The JDBC driver is loaded on line 24, and a `Connection` is obtained from the database driver at line 26, using a URL database connection string. On line 30, a `Statement` object is created from the connection, using the `createStatement` method with no arguments. (The default database concurrency for this database supports updates. A call to the `getConcurrency` method at this point would return a value of `ResultSet.CONCUR_UPDATABLE`.)

The `Statement executeQuery` method is called on line 38 with a SQL `select` query. On line 45, the `getCursorTypeString` method is called and is passed the value returned by the `ResultSet getType` call. The `getCursorTypeString` will simply map the `ResultSet` integer value to a string representing the name of the concurrency type.

Next, on line 52, to demonstrate the versatility of the `ResultSet`, a `while` loop is started to iterate through the results of the query. This block of code should look familiar, since it has been used several times already in this book. The `ResultSet next` method is used to move from record to record in the `ResultSet`, from the beginning to end of the result set.

But within this `while` loop, a number of updates are performed on the database, using the `ResultSet`. The `update_date` field for the current record is changed on line 64 and is set to the value of the `ourDate` variable (which has been assigned the value of today's date on line 16). The value for the `special_promotion` field is set to the value of five. The `ResultSet updateRow` method is called on line 70 to update the current row to the underlying data store. These updates are performed for each record examined by the `ResultSet` within the loop, which is terminated on line 71.

The next portion of this program performs a SQL `insert` operation. Before an insert can be done, the cursor must be positioned over the insert row. This is done with a call to the `moveToInsertRow` method on line 76. (If this were not done, then the values of the current row would simply be overwritten by the updates to the insert row.) A series of `updateXXXX` methods are then called on lines 77 through 83. These methods are called for database updates just as they are called for database insert operations. On line 86, the `insertRow` method is called to insert the row into the underlying database.

On line 89, a query is executed to review the results of the update operation. This `ResultSet` is used to control the loop that is executed on line 96. The columns within the `ResultSet` are displayed using the `println` method call on line 97.

The remainder of this program contains code that was explained in the previous program example and is shown again for completeness. The `finally` block for the main program on line 123 contains the method call to close the connection, and the `getCursorTypeString` method on line 137 is used to map the cursor type integer constant to a corresponding string value. The output of this program is as follows:

Output of ResultSetExample2.java

```
ResultSet type: Scroll Insensitive ResultSet.

******************
movie_name:    The Evil Null Reference
special_promotion:    0
update_date:   2001-01-22
release_date:  2001-01-01
******************
movie_name:    Just One More Compile
special_promotion:    1
update_date:   2001-10-22
release_date:  2001-01-01
******************
movie_name:    Another Funny Story
special_promotion:    1
update_date:   2001-10-22
release_date:  2001-01-01

  ** After updates:

******************
movie_name:    The Evil Null Reference
special_promotion:    5
update_date:   2002-01-11
release_date:  2001-01-01
******************
movie_name:    Just One More Compile
special_promotion:    5
update_date:   2002-01-11
release_date:  2001-01-01
******************
movie_name:    One Last Try Before the Lights Go Down
special_promotion:    0
update_date:   2002-01-11
release_date:  2002-01-11
```

```
******************
movie_name:    Another Funny Story
special_promotion:      5
update_date:   2002-01-11
release_date:  2001-01-01
```

The updateXXXX Methods of the ResultSet Class

The ResultSet class contains a number of methods used to provide updateable ResultSets. As with the getXXXX methods used to retrieve ResultSet data, the ResultSet class has been designed to contain a group of updateXXXX methods with a method for each data type used in JDBC. The naming convention used for these methods is as follows.

```
update<type_name>( integer <column_index>,
                   <data_type_value>);
update<type_name>( String <column_name>,
                   <data_type_value>);
```

Given this naming convention, the method name for updating a String column would be as follows.

```
void updateString(int columnIndex, String value);
```

Table 8–4 lists the various update methods for the updateable result sets.

Table 8–4   *Methods for Updating a ResultSet*

Method	Description
void updateAsciiStream(int columnIndex, InputStream x, int length)	Updates the ResultSet column identified by the integer index argument as an InputStream using the InputStream argument. Will set the InputStream to the length specified by the third argument.
void updateAsciiStream(String columnName, InputStream x, int length)	Updates the ResultSet column identified by the string column name argument as an InputStream using the InputStream argument. Will set the InputStream to the length specified by the third argument.
void updateBigDecimal(int columnIndex, BigDecimal x)	Updates the column identified by the integer index argument with the java.math.BigDecimal value provided by the second argument.

| **Table 8–4** | *Methods for Updating a ResultSet (cont.)* |

Method	Description
`void insertRow()`	Inserts the current contents of the `ResultSet` into the database.
`void moveToInsertRow()`	Moves the `ResultSet` pointer to the insert row.
`void updateBigDecimal(String columnName, BigDecimal x)`	Updates the column identified by the string column name argument with the `java.math.BigDecimal` value provided by the second argument.
`void updateBinaryStream(int columnIndex, InputStream x, int length)`	Updates the column identified by the integer index argument with the `java.io.InputStream` value provided by the second argument. The third argument indicates the length of the `InputStream`.
`void updateBinaryStream(String columnName, InputStream x, int length)`	Updates the column identified by the string column name argument with the java.io.`InputStream` value provided by the second argument. The third argument indicates the length of the `InputStream`.
`void updateBoolean(int columnIndex, boolean x)`	Updates the column identified by the integer index argument with the Java `boolean` value provided by the second argument.
`void updateBoolean(String columnName, boolean x)`	Updates the column identified by the string column name argument with the Java `boolean` value provided by the second argument.
`void updateByte(int columnIndex, byte x)`	Updates the column identified by the integer index argument with the Java `byte` value provided by the second argument.
`void updateByte(String columnName, byte x)`	Updates the column identified by the string column name argument with the Java `byte` value provided by the second argument.
`void updateBytes(int columnIndex, byte[] x)`	Updates the column identified by the integer index argument with the Java `byte` array value provided by the second argument.
`void updateBytes(String columnName, byte[] x)`	Updates the column identified by the string column name argument with the Java `byte` array value provided by the second argument.
`void updateCharacterStream(int columnIndex, Reader x, int length)`	Updates the column identified by the integer index argument with the `java.io.Reader` value provided by the second argument. The third argument indicates the length the character stream to be read by the `Reader`.

Table 8–4 *Methods for Updating a ResultSet (cont.)*

Method	Description
`void updateCharacterStream(String columnName, Reader reader, int length)`	Updates the column identified by the string column name argument with the `java.io.Reader` value provided by the second argument. The third argument indicates the length the character stream to be read by the `Reader`.
`void updateDate(int columnIndex, Date x)`	Updates the column identified by the integer index argument with the `java.sql.Date` value provided by the second argument.
`void updateDate(String columnName, Date x)`	Updates the column identified by the string column name argument with the `java.sql.Date` value provided by the second argument.
`void updateDouble(int columnIndex, double x)`	Updates the column identified by the integer index argument with the Java `double` value provided by the second argument.
`void updateDouble(String columnName, double x)`	Updates the column identified by the string column name argument with the Java `double` value provided by the second argument.
`void updateFloat(int columnIndex, float x)`	Updates the column identified by the integer index argument with the Java `float` value provided by the second argument.
`void updateFloat(String columnName, float x)`	Updates the column identified by the string column name argument with the Java `float` value provided by the second argument.
`void updateInt(int columnIndex, int x)`	Updates the column identified by the string column name argument with the Java `int` value provided by the second argument.
`void updateInt(String columnName, int x)`	Updates the column identified by the string column name argument with the Java `int` value provided by the second argument.
`void updateLong(int columnIndex, long x)`	Updates the column identified by the integer index argument with the Java `long` value provided by the second argument.
`void updateLong(String columnName, long x)`	Updates the column identified by the string column name argument with the Java `long` value provided by the second argument.
`void updateNull(int columnIndex)`	Updates the column identified by the integer index argument to an appropriate `null` value.

Table 8–4   *Methods for Updating a ResultSet (cont.)*

Method	Description
void updateNull(String columnName)	Updates the column identified by the string column name argument to an appropriate null value.
void updateObject(int columnIndex, Object x, int scale)	Updates the column identified by the integer index argument with the Object reference value provided by the second argument.
void updateObject(int columnIndex, Object x)	Updates the column identified by the integer index argument with the Object reference value provided by the second argument. The scale of the Object, if appropriate, is provided by the third argument. (The scale will be ignored for types other than Decimal or Numeric types.)
void updateObject(String columnName, Object x, int scale)	Updates the column identified by the string column name argument with the Object reference value provided by the second argument.
void updateObject(String columnName, Object x)	Updates the column identified by the string column name argument with the Object reference value provided by the second argument. The scale of the Object, if appropriate, is provided by the third argument. (The scale will be ignored for types other than Decimal or Numeric types.)
void updateRow()	Updates the row in the underlying database with the current row of the ResultSet.
void updateShort(int columnIndex, short x)	Updates the column identified by the integer index argument with the Java short value provided by the second argument.
void updateShort(String columnName, short x)	Updates the column identified by the string column name argument with the Java short value provided by the second argument.
void updateString(int columnIndex, String x)	Updates the column identified by the integer index argument with the Java String value provided by the second argument.
void updateString(String columnName, String x)	Updates the column identified by the string column name argument with the Java String value provided by the second argument.
void updateTime(int columnIndex, Time x)	Updates the column identified by the integer index argument with the java.sql.Time value provided by the second argument.
void updateTime(String columnName, Time x)	Updates the column identified by the integer index argument with the java.sql.Timestamp value provided by the second argument.

Table 8–4   *Methods for Updating a ResultSet (cont.)*

Method	Description
`void updateTimestamp(int columnIndex, Timestamp x)`	Updates the column identified by the string column name argument with the `java.sql.Timestamp` value provided by the second argument.
`void updateTimestamp(String columnName, Timestamp x)`	Returns `true` if the last column read is an SQLa SQL null value. (A `getXXXX` method call must precede this call.)
`void updateTime(int i, Time x)`	Updates the column identified by the string column name argument with the `java.sql.Time` value provided by the second argument.
`void deleteRow()`	When working with updateable `ResultSet` objects, this deletes the current row from the `ResultSet` and the underlying database.
`boolean rowDeleted()`	Returns `true` if the row has been deleted, or `false` if the row has not been deleted or the `ResultSet` cannot detect deletions.
`boolean rowInserted()`	Returns `true` if the row has been inserted into the database. Returns `false` if the row has not been inserted or the `ResultSet` cannot detect inserts.
`boolean rowUpdated()`	Returns `true` if the row has been updated. Returns `false` if the row has not been updated or the `ResultSet` cannot detect updates.
`void cancelRowUpdates()`	Cancels all of the previously entered updates to the current row.

In addition to the methods for updating the column values in the `ResultSet`, methods are provided to perform the database update operations. The `updateRow` method updates the database with the values of the updated columns which have been previously updated with the appropriate `updateXXXX` methods.

The `updateRow` method does not return a status value. The `rowUpdated` method must be called to determine the status of the update operation. This method will return `true` if the update succeeded *and* the JDBC driver can detect deletions. But since not all database drivers can detect udpates, it is possible that this method will return `false` even if the update succeeded.

The `insertRow` method sends the updated values of the inserts on the `ResultSet` to the database. As shown in the previous code example, inserting using a `ResultSet` for SQL `insert` updates requires moving to the *insert row* using the `moveToInsertRow` method and then using the appropriate `updateXXXX` methods to update the column values in the insert row. Then, once the updates have been performed, the `insertRow` method is called to apply the updates (in this case, a database insert) to the database.

As with the `updateRow` method, the `insertRow` method does not return a status value. The `rowInserted` method must be called to determine the status of the insert operation. This method will return a boolean `true` if the insert succeeded and the driver can detect database updates. It will return `false` if the insert failed **or** if the driver simply cannot determine the status of the update.

The `deleteRow` method is used to delete the current row. Naturally, as with any delete operation, this should be used with caution. The code should include various checks using `getXXXX` methods to determine that the correct row is being deleted.

As with the `updateRow` and `insertRow` methods, the `deleteRow` method does not return a value. The `rowDeleted` method must be called to determine the status of the operation. This method will return a boolean `true` if the JDBC driver can detect deletes and the delete succeeded. The method will return a `false` value if the delete operation failed or if the JDBC driver cannot determine the status of the operation.

Obviously, a return value of `false` from `rowDeleted` or `rowUpdated` creates red flags for using an updateable `ResultSet`. If the JDBC driver admits it cannot determine whether or not an update or delete has succeeded, it is probably best not to make use of the updateable `ResultSet` with that driver.

RESULTSET CONSTANTS

A number of integer constants, or `static   int` values, are declared in the `ResultSet` interface. These values are used not only in `ResultSet` methods but in various other classes as well. Table 8–5 lists these `ResultSet` constants.

DATA TYPE MAPPING

As you might expect, the data types of the Java language do not have the same names as the data types of the various relational databases. In fact, relational databases do not have consistent naming among all of the data types they use. Though most relational databases implement some or all of the ANSI SQL 92 data types, most have added additional data types. Part of the reason for this was an effort to distinguish database products and provide additional functionality that users desired, functionality such as a more robust set of data types to serve users' needs.

Table 8–5	ResultSet Constants

Data Type	Name	Description
static int	CONCUR_READ_ONLY	Indicates that the ResultSet concurrency does not support updates through the ResultSet.
static int	CONCUR_UPDATABLE	Indicates that the ResultSet concurrency supports updates through the ResultSet.
static int	FETCH_FORWARD	Indicates that the rows in the ResultSet will be processed serially, in a forward direction, from first to last.
static int	FETCH_REVERSE	Indicates that the rows in the ResultSet will be processed in reverse order, last to first.
static int	FETCH_UNKNOWN	Indicates that the direction of processing for the ResultSet is unknown.
static int	TYPE_FORWARD_ONLY	Indicates that the ResultSet may only be processed serially, in a forward direction.
static int	TYPE_SCROLL_INSENSITIVE	Indicates that the ResultSet is scrollable, supporting random access, but is not sensitive to changes in the underlying database for the rows in the ResultSet.
static int	TYPE_SCROLL_SENSITIVE	Indicates that the ResultSet is scrollable, supporting random access, and is sensitive to changes to ResultSet data in the underlying database.

The data type picture becomes more interesting when the ANSI SQL 99 data types are added to the mix. The ANSI SQL 99 specification includes distinct data types, the ability of the database user to create types as they see fit. This powerful capability adds significant extensibility to a database, which is no longer limited to the set of data types that have been with us virtually since the dawn of the computer (integers, strings, decimals). But adding this extensibility in the database server requires that drivers using the server also support the same extensibility. The JDBC 3.0 specification does provide support for distinct data types and provides a flexible mechanism for driver developers to extend data types as needed.

Since relational databases do not use Java data types, the database data type must be mapped to a Java data type. The mapping operations are fairly logical and are listed in Table 8–6.

These data type mappings are discussed in more detail in the following sections.

Table 8–6	JDBC SQL Data Type Mappings

SQL Type	Java Type
CHAR	String
VARCHAR	String
LONGVARCHAR	String
NUMERIC	java.math.BigDecimal
DECIMAL	java.math.BigDecimal
BIT	boolean
TINYINT	byte
SMALLINT	short
INTEGER	int
BIGINT	long
REAL	float
FLOAT	double
DOUBLE	double
BINARY	byte[]
VARBINARY	byte[]
LONGVARBINARY	byte[]
DATE	java.sql.Date
TIME	java.sql.Time
TIMESTAMP	java.sql.Timestamp

SQL char Data Type

The SQL CHAR data types all map into the Java String data type. Java has no fixed-length character string arrays; character string arrays in Java should be treated as String data types that can assume a variable length. There is therefore no need to distinguish between variable-length and fixed-length character strings with Java. The SQL data types of CHAR, VARCHAR, and LONGVARCHAR all can be stored in a Java String data type.

SQL DECIMAL and NUMERIC

The SQL DECIMAL and NUMERIC data types are used to represent fixed-point numbers. These two data types are represented using a java.math.BigDecimal data type. This data type is a subtype of the java.lang.Number type. This type provides math operations for `Numeric` data types to be added, subtracted, multiplied, and divided with `Numeric` types and other data types.

SQL BINARY, VARBINARY, and LONGVARBINARY Data Types

These three data types all can be expressed as `byte` arrays in Java. Because the `LONGVARBINARY` data type can be very large, JDBC allows the programmer to set the return value of a `LONGVARBINARY` to be a Java input stream.

BIT Data Types

The SQL `BIT` type can be mapped to the Java `boolean` type. A call to the `ResultSet getObject` method will return `java.lang.Boolean` reference for a `BIT` column.

TINYINT, SMALLINT, INTEGER and BIGINT Data Types

The SQL `TINYINT`, `SMALLINT`, `INTEGER` and `BIGINT` types can be mapped to the Java `byte`, `short`, `int`, and `long` data types, respectively. A call to the `ResultSet getObject` method will return a subclass of `java.lang.Number` for an integer column. The `TINYINT`, `SMALLINT`, and `INTEGER` will map to `java.lang.Integer`. The `BIGINT` will map to `java.lang.Long`.

REAL, FLOAT, and DOUBLE Data Types

The SQL floating-point data types of `REAL`, `FLOAT`, and `DOUBLE` can be mapped as follows. The `REAL` data type can be stored in a Java `float` data type, and the `REAL` and `DOUBLE` can be stored in a Java `double`.

DATE, TIME, and TIMESTAMP Data Types

SQL provides three date- and time-related data types: `DATE`, `TIME`, and `TIMESTAMP`. The `java.util.Date` class provides date and time information, but this class does not directly support any of the three SQL date and time data types. To accommodate these SQL data types, three subclasses were declared from `java.util.Date`: `java.sql.Date`, `java.sql.Time`, and `java.sql.TimeStamp`.

The `java.util.Date` class can be used to store SQL `DATE` data. The `java.util.Time` class can be used to store SQL `TIME` information. And the `java.sql.Timestamp` can be used to store SQL `TIMESTAMP` data.

SUMMARY

In JDBC, the `ResultSet` represents the results of a `select` query; it represents a group of records retrieved from the database. The execution of a SQL `select` statement with the `Statement executeQuery` method will return a `ResultSet`, and the execution of a stored procedure using `CallableStatement executeQuery` (inherited from `PreparedStatement`) may also return a `ResultSet`.

The `ResultSet` class provided by the driver, the implementation of the `ResultSet` interface defined in the JDBC specification, provides the ability to move serially through the database results. Also specified is the ability to move randomly through the results, forward and backward, and to absolute or relative positions. But these features are not a requirement of JDBC compliance and are available only if the JDBC driver and the underlying database support the features. The `ResultSet` may also support positioned updates using the `ResultSet`, but once again, only if the JDBC driver supports the feature. Various `DatabaseMetaData` methods (Chapter 11) can be called to determine exactly what it is that the database and driver support.

COMING UP NEXT

Transactions are an important part of any business-critical application. They are managed in a simple, straightforward manner in JDBC using the `Connection` object. Chapter 9 covers transactions and provides examples of how they are used with the JDBC API.

Transactions in JDBC

INTRODUCTION

A database transaction is a series of database updates that are grouped together as a single atomic update transaction (see Chapter 2). In the event any single update in the transaction fails, the remaining updates are rolled back; that is, their effect on the database is removed and any records they may have deleted or updated are restored to the state they were in before the transaction was started. This chapter examines the relatively simple process of using transactions in JDBC.

THE ACID PRINCIPAL

The ACID principal is the foundation which has guided the implementation of transactions in relational databases. This acronym stands for the following:

- Atomicity
- Consistency

- Isolation
- Durability

These terms are explained in the following sections.

Atomicity

The term atomicity applies to the ability to group multiple database updates into a single transaction that can be treated as an atomic update. The term atomic is derived from the Greek word for the smallest indivisible element. An atomic transaction is indivisible, since the failure of one of the updates in the group is considered a failure for the entire group of updates. Either all of the updates will be completed or none will be completed, and the transaction will be rolled back, leaving the database in the state it was in before the transaction started.

Consistency

The term consistency applies to the various rules associated with the data in the transactions. These rules may apply to relationships between the tables in the update or to rules concerning the primary key for a table. These rules may be broken during the transaction, but the inconsistent data will not be visible to other users. Once the transaction is complete, the rules must be valid and the database must be in a consistent state.

Isolation

A given transaction should appear as though it is running alone in the database. The work of other users must be coordinated with other transactions to maintain this isolated view. The work of other transactions is invisible to the user in a transaction.

Durability

The work of a committed transaction is guaranteed to persist and remain in the database even in the event of various system failures. A transaction is not considered durable until it commits. A system failure entails a database recovery, which includes a rollback procedure for all uncommitted transactions, ultimately leaving the database in a consistent state.

USING TRANSACTIONS IN JDBC

By default, JDBC classes operate in *auto-commit* mode. This means that each SQL statement executed is considered a separate transaction (a singleton transaction), and a commit is made at the completion of the statement. In order to group a set of transactions together, this autocommit mode must be disabled using the `Connection` class `setAutoCommit` method and passing the method a boolean `false` value.

With autocommit disabled, there is always an implicit transaction in place. To commit a series of previously executed SQL statements to the database, an explicit commit can be made by calling the `Connection` method `commit`. Alternatively, a rollback can be made by calling the `Connection` method `rollback`. This rolls back the current transaction and restores the database to the state it was in before the start of the current transaction. Failure to commit a transaction before closing the corresponding `Connection` object will lead to an automatic rollback of the database updates; all work will be lost. Developers should be sure that all work is committed to the database before closing the `Connection`.

Various database-dependent isolation levels can be set. There are methods in the `DatabaseMetaData` class to learn the existing defaults in place in the current session and methods in the `Connection` class to change the current isolation level.

The isolation levels provided by JDBC are listed in Table 9–1.

These isolation modes and how they impact database reads and updates are covered in more detail in Chapter 2. The remainder of this chapter examines an example of transaction management with JDBC.

Table 9–1   *JDBC Isolation Modes*

JDBC Isolation Mode	Description
TRANSACTION_NONE	Transactions are not supported. Not all databases support this mode; most require some level of transactions to be in place.
TRANSACTION_READ_COMMITTED	Only reads on the current row are repeatable.
TRANSACTION_READ_UNCOMMITTED	Rows being used by a transaction can be read even if the rows have not been committed.
TRANSACTION_REPEATABLE_READ	Reads on all rows of a result are repeatable.
TRANSACTION_SERIALIZABLE	Reads on all rows of a transaction are repeatable in the order in which they were executed.

A Transaction Example

The following code example demonstrates the use of transactions with JDBC. The application performs an insert of several users to the `users` table and a corresponding insert of user rentals to the `user_rentals` table. The inserts to the `user_rentals` table contain a `user_id` column that references the entry in the user table. We can assume, then, that we should not be inserting into the user_rentals table if we don't have a corresponding entry in the users table. We should therefore perform all of this work within a transaction, and if any of the database updates fail, we should roll back all of the work.

TransExample3.java

```
1.import java.sql.*;
2.import javax.sql.*;
3.import javax.naming.*;
4.import java.util.*;
5.import java.io.*;
6.import com.codestudio.sql.PoolMan;
7.
8.public class TransExample3 {
9.
10.
11.public static void main( String args[] ) {
12.
13.Connection con=null;
14.int updateResult = 0;
15.try {
16.
17.
18.      //
19.      // get the initial context
20.      //
21.      InitialContext ctx = new InitialContext(  );
22.
23.      //
24.      // get the DataSource from the JNDI name server
25.      //
26.      DataSource ds = (DataSource) ctx.lookup("movies");
27.
28.      //
29.      // get the connection from the DataSource
30.      //
31.      con = ds.getConnection( );
32.
33.      //
34.      // create a Statement class to execute the SQL statement
35.      //
36.      Statement stmt = con.createStatement();
37.
38.      //
39.      // turn auto-commit off
40.      //
41.      con.setAutoCommit( false );
42.
43.      //
44.      // we are now in a transaction ... perform a series of updates
```

```
45.      //
46.
47.
48.      // let's count updates to ensure transaction integrity
49.      int updateCount = 0;
50.
51.
52.      updateResult = stmt.executeUpdate(
53.        "insert into users (user_id, first_name, last_name, " +
54.        " address1, city, state_province, postal_code, country)   " +
55.        " values ( nextval('user_id'), 'Fred', 'Smith', " +
56.        " '2020 Nowhere Lane', 'Newark', 'NJ', '09090', 'US');" );
57.
58.      // increment update count
59.      updateCount += updateResult;
60.
61.      updateResult = stmt.executeUpdate(
62.      "insert into users (user_id, first_name, last_name, address1," +
63.      " city, state_province, postal_code, country)   " +
64.      " values ( nextval('user_id'), 'Sally', 'Smith', " +
65.      " '2020 Nowhere Lane', 'Newark', 'NJ', '09090', 'US');" );
66.
67.      // increment update count
68.      updateCount += updateResult;
69.
70.      updateResult = stmt.executeUpdate(
71.        "insert into users (user_id, first_name, last_name, " +
72.        "address1, city, state_province, postal_code, country)   " +
73.        " values ( nextval('user_id'), 'Harry', 'Henderson', " +
74.        " '3030 Milbourne', 'Tuckamarin', 'NJ', '08090', 'US');" );
75.
76.      // increment update count
77.      updateCount += updateResult;
78.
79.
80.      // user_id = 2 is renting a movie
81.      updateResult = stmt.executeUpdate(
82.        "insert into user_rentals (user_id, rental_date, movie_id) " +
83.        " values ( 2, current_date, 1 ); " );
84.      // increment update count
85.      updateCount += updateResult;
86.
87.      // user_id = 3 is renting a movie
88.      updateResult = stmt.executeUpdate(
89.        "insert into user_rentals (user_id, rental_date, movie_id) " +
90.        " values ( 2, current_date, 3 ); " );
91.
92.      // increment update count
93.      updateCount += updateResult;
94.
95.      //
96.      // need to perform a commit to save the work
```

```
97.     //
98.     if ( updateCount == 5  ) {
99.         con.commit();
100.    System.out.println("Transactions have been committed.");
101.     }
102.     else {
103.         con.rollback();
104.    System.out.println(
105.            "Transactions have been rolled back. Update count: " +
106.            updateCount);
107.     }
108.
109.    //
110.    // 'finally' block will close the connection
111.    //
112.
113.}
114.catch (SQLException e) {
115.
116.    // display SQL specific exception information
117.    System.out.println("*************************" );
118.    System.out.println("SQLException in main: " + e.getMessage() );
119.    System.out.println("** SQLState: " + e.getSQLState());
120.    System.out.println("** SQL Error Code: " + e.getErrorCode());
121.    System.out.println("*************************" );
122.    e.printStackTrace();
123.
124.    //
125.    // if we are in this block, then an error occurred and
126.    // our transaction should not continue
127.    //
128.    try {
129.        con.rollback();
130.    }
131.    catch (SQLException se) {
132.
133.        // display SQL specific exception information
134.        System.out.println("*************************" );
135.        System.out.println(
136.            "SQLException in main. COULD NOT ROLLBACK: " +
137.            se.getMessage() );
138.        System.out.println("** SQLState: " + se.getSQLState());
139.        System.out.println("** SQL Error Code: " +
140.                        se.getErrorCode());
141.        System.out.println("*************************" );
142.        se.printStackTrace();
143.    }
144.
145.}
146.catch (Exception e) {
147.    System.out.println("Exception in main: " + e.getMessage() );
148.    e.printStackTrace();
```

```
149.}
150.finally {
151.
152.     try {
153.         // close the connection
154.     if ( con != null )
155.             con.close();
156.     System.exit(1);
157.     }
158.     catch (SQLException e) {
159.             e.printStackTrace();
160.     }
161.}
162.}
163.}
```

This application begins with a number of import statements on lines 1 through 6. The initial JNDI context is obtained on line 21, and the context is used to obtain the DataSource for the movies database on line 26. The DataSource is then used to obtain a Connection object, and the Connection object is used to create a Statement object on line 36.

Up to this point, this example does not look much different than the previous examples. On line 41, however, we have a method call that has not yet appeared in any of the code examples thus far. This call is to the Connection class setAutoCommit method and passes a boolean value of false to the method. This has the effect of turning off the autocommit feature of the JDBC driver and requiring explicit database commits to commit updates to the database. As discussed previously, this call is required to create a transaction that spans more than one SQL statement. With autocommit turned off, we are automatically in a transaction. (We have executed an implicit "begin work" statement in the database.)

On line 49, an integer variable named updateCount is declared to keep a count of the updates to the database. This variable will be evaluated at the end of the update statements to determine if the number of updates performed by the database (as returned by the executeUpdate method) are what we expect. Since five updates will be performed, we will expect the updateCount variable to have a value of 5 when the updates are complete.

On line 52, a SQL update statement is executed using the Statement class executeUpdate method. This insert operation inserts a record into the users table and the executeUpdate method should return a value of 1, which will be stored in the updateResult variable and then added to the current total in the updateCount variable on line 59.

On line 61, another record is inserted into the users table, using the executeUpdate method, and the corresponding update count is added to the updateCount variable on line 68. On line 70, the final user is added to the users table, and the update count is ultimately added to the updateCount variable on line 77.

At this point, we are still in a transaction and we have updated three database records but have not committed those records to the database. We now insert corresponding records for the users into the `user_rentals` table. We add a record to the `user_rentals` table for `user_id = 2` on line 81 and store the update count result in the `updateCount` variable on line 85. We then add a similar `user_rentals` record for `user_id = 3` on line 88 and store the update count for that update into the `updateCount` variable on line 93.

At this point, we expect our `updateCount` to contain a value of 5 if all updates succeeded. If an update had failed and an exception was thrown, then the `catch` block for the `SQLException` would have been executed. (As we will see shortly, this `catch` block contains a call to the `rollback` method, which would roll back the transaction.) But if an exception had not been thrown and we had quietly failed to update all five records, we would expect the update count to be less than 5 (`updateCount < 5`), and that would indicate a condition that would require a rollback. We test for that condition on line 98, and if the value of `updateCount` is not equal to 5, the `Connection rollback` method is called on line 103, forcing a rollback of the database work.

On line 114, the `catch` block for the `SQLException` begins. Unlike the previous examples, this `catch` block must do more than just report an error. On line 128, we begin a `try` block (the `commit` method throws a `SQLException` that must be caught or thrown) that executes the `Connection rollback` method on line 129. This method will roll back all database work that has been done up to that point.

As in the previous examples, the `finally` block is used to close the connection. Note that closing the connection when in a transaction without having executed a commit (`Connection commit`) will lead to an automatic rollback of any updates that had been done in the transaction.

DISTRIBUTED TRANSACTIONS IN J2EE

Distributed transactions involve transactions which span multiple data resources. Unlike a database transaction which usually occurs within the context of a single database server, a distributed transaction can span multiple database database servers and with J2EE, could span multiple servers from different database vendors.

Providing this feature is a very useful service for enterprise applications which must often access and update data across numerous legacy databases. In fact, the Enterprise Java Beans (EJB) specification requires an EJB compliant application server to provide this functionality.

Providing for distributed transactions requires the inclusion of a transaction manager service. The transaction manager provides the coordination between the multiple data resources involved in the transaction. The transaction manager, most likely an implementation of the Java JTA package, does not perform the transactions with the individual data resources. The transaction manager provides these transaction coordination services through the participants in the form of implementations of `javax.transaction.xa.XAResource`. These participants in turn interact with `XADataSource` components which represent the data resource which will perform the database updates and transactions.

The goal of J2EE is to make the process of a client using a distributed transaction a simple and natural process. For this reason, the J2EE client program for a distributed transaction does not differ from any other program using transactions with the exception of some limitations on calls that can be made by the client. The application server exposes a `DataSource` object reference to the client. The client extracts a `Connection` object from the `DataSource` object and uses it to programmatically create transaction boundaries.

The client for a distributed transaction would simply access both `DataSources` through the application server using the database resource components provided by the application server; it would not load JDBC drivers directly since this would bypass the transaction manager.

This is done using a JNDI lookup as shown in the following code.

Distributed Transactions Client

```
...
Context ctx  = new InitialContext();
DataSource moviesDS = (DataSource) ctx.lookup("jdbc/moviesdb");
DataSource stockDS  = (DataSource) ctx.lookup("jdbc/stockdb");

// get a connection
Connection moviesCon = moviesDS.getConnection();
Connection stockCon  = stockDS.getConection();

// get the transaction manager resource from the app server (container)

//
// sessionContext implements javax.ejb.EJBContext
// provides access to the container's services, including trans manager
//
UserTransaction txMgr = sessionContext.getUserTransaction();


//
// begin our transaction
//
txMgr.begin();

Statement moviesStmt = moviesCon.createStatement();
Statement stockStmt = stockCon.createStatement();
```

```
//
// update movies with the sale
//
moviesStmt.executeQuery(
    "insert into sales (movie_id, quantity) values (101,10) ");

//
// update stock on hand
//
stockStmt.executeQuery(
    "update stock " +
    " set quantity = quantity - 10");

//
// commit if ok - exception causes rollback
//
txMgr.commit();


...
catch( SQLException e ) {
      // rollback and log error
      txMgr.rollback();
}
...
```

In the example above, a data source object is retrieved and cast as a DataSource type. The object retrieved implements the DataSource interface and the XADataSource interface. The DataSource objects are used to retrieve a java.sql.Connection object which implements java.sql.Connection and java.sql.XAConnection.

Once the connection objects are retrieved, a call is made to the SessionContext object of the J2EE application server. The getUserTransaction method returns an object that allows transaction boundaries to be demarcated. The application server accomplishes this by effectively forwarding the calls to the userTransaction object to the transaction manager. JDBC driver transaction calls are not used.

The getUserTransaction method returns a javax.transaction. UserTransaction reference. The UserTransaction interface provides methods that provide some control over the transaction manager and, more importantly, allows the client application to indicate the boundaries of the transaction (to demarcate the transaction boundaries). These boundaries are set with begin method calls to begin the transaction, and commit method calls to commit the work to the database, or a rollback call to rollback the transaction.

Note that programmatic transaction management with J2EE requires an explicit commit method call. This differs from the JDBC transaction control where the application is always in a transaction until an explicit commit call is made.

JDBC also operates in a default auto-commit mode where each database operation is processed as a singleton transaction - a transaction of one. Auto-commit must be turned off so that explicit transaction boundaries can be used; this is not the case with distributed transactions.

Distributed transactions do not require the auto-commit mode be turned off (though it is good policy and creates clearer code to do so). If the auto-commit mode is set, it will be ignored. In addition to `setAutoCommit` method calls, the transaction manager does not allow the following `Connection` class methods to be called.

- setAutoCommit(true)
- commit
- rollback
- setSavePoint
- setTransactionIsolation

Is is considered an error to call any of these methods if a distributed transacation is in effect and an exception should be thrown by the controlling transaction manager on any attempt to do so. The call to `setTransactionIsolation` may not throw an error; the behavior of this method within a distributed transaction is implementation dependent.

DECLARATIVE TRANSACTIONS WITH J2EE

Optionally, J2EE application servers allow transactions to be managed implicitly by nature of the way the components interact. These servers offer what is referred to as *declarative transactions*. The complete implementation of declarative security is beyond the scope of this book, but a short description is worthwhile.

J2EE declarative transactions allows transactions to be declared relative to the components. The interaction between the components (the methods) represents the transaction boundary. Transactions can be inherited from the calling method, or the method being called can create it's own transaction. Alternatively, the method being called could be declared not to use transactions at all.

Figure 9–2 shows the use of declarative transactions between a check-out bean and two client components. The checkout bean creates a transaction and then, using declarative transactions, can simply call the appropriate methods in the customer bean and the account bean. By calling these methods and using the appropriate declarations, the customer bean operations and the account bean operations will run under the same transactions (Transaction A).

DISTRIBUTED TRANSACTIONS UNDER THE COVERS

As shown in the previous sections, the process of coordinating a two phase commit is transparent to the client program. Under the covers, there is coordination and management of the various resources as managed by the transaction manager. As shown in Figure 9–1, a number of object instances are used to coordinate the transaction. These object instances are `XAResource`, `XAConnection` and `XADataSource`. The sequence of events in the operation of an `XAResource` are as follows.

1. Access XAResource object for participants
2. Start the transaction
3. Clients perform updates which are applied to participants
4. Notify participants that they need to *prepare* to commit
5. If any resources throw an exception, rollback work
6. Commit work

The transaction manager is first made aware of the connections that will be participating in the transaction session. Since all connections are made through the J2EE container, it can track the connections for a session. These connections will provide implementations of the `javax.sql.XAConnection` interface which will require them to provide a `getXAResource` method to return an `XAResource` implementation for their connection. The transaction manager will not access the `XAConnection` objects directly but will work through the `XAResource` instance to manage the transaction.

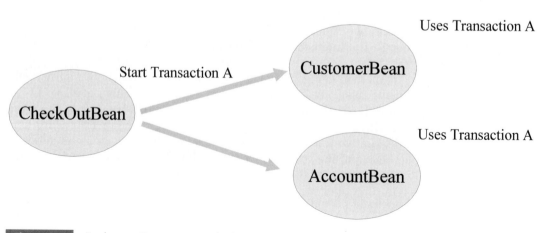

Figure 9–1   *Declarative Transactions with J2EE Components*

The transaction manager will then start a transaction using the XAResource start method. Following the start, various database update operations will take place across the two or more resources within the transaction.

When the update work is completed, the XAResource prepare method is called informing the resources that they must *prepare* to commit their work. If any of the resources throws an exception at this point, then the transaction will be rolled back on all the resources currently associated with the transaction. If none of the resources throws an exception (XAException), then the transactions are committed using the XAResource commit method.

Table 9–2 contains the complete list of methods which are implemented to provide the XAResource object provided to the transaction manager. These are methods used by developers of drivers and transaction managers, and are not usually used by database developers. They are shown here for informational purposes.

Table 9–2   *XAResource Methods*

Method	Description
void commit(Xid xid, boolean onePhase)	Requests a commit of the global transaction. If the one phase flag is passed with with a boolean true, then a one phase commit protocol will be used.
void end(Xid xid, int flags)	Ends the work performed for the current transaction branch. Any existing transactions are committed. Flags may be passed to indicate how to manage the current set of transactions.
void forget(Xid xid)	Instructs the resource manager to forget about a completed transaction.
int getTransactionTimeout()	Returns the current transaction timeout parameter.
boolean isSameRM(XAResource xares)	Compares the current XAResource object with the object reference passed to determine whether or not the two are the same.
int prepare(Xid xid)	Instructs the resource to prepare for a transactional commit for the transaction specified by xid.
Xid[] recover(int flag)	Returns an integer array of transactions from the resource manager.
void rollback(Xid xid)	Instructs the resource manager to perform a rollback for the xid transaction.
boolean setTransactionTimeout(int seconds)	Establishes a transaction timeout value for the XAResource instance.
void start(Xid xid, int flags)	Used to start a new transaction or to re-start an existing transaction. Depending on the flag passed, may join a transaction or resume an existing transaction.

SUMMARY

This chapter provided information on transactions using JDBC. The fundamental principals of transactions, the ACID principal, was covered and a code sample was provided showing what is required to use transactions with JDBC. What we found was that while the implementation of transactions by database vendors may be complex, using this feature in application code is not difficult.

Distributed transactions extend the notion of transactions to multiple databases (data sources). Once again, though the underlying functionality provided by distributed transactions may be complex, their usage is a relatively simple task and requires basically the same code as a normal transaction.

COMING UP NEXT

The next chapter begins the coverage of an interesting and extremely useful feature of JDBC: dynamic queries. This is a feature that could be a complex task using native database CLIs, but is a fairly simple process with JDBC.

JDBC and Dynamic Queries

INTRODUCTION

There are times when, for various reasons, it is simply not possible to determine which queries an application will be executing when it is run. One solution to manage this problem is to code all possible queries that may be executed and then allow the application to choose which one to run based on user input or some other criteria. But for a large number of queries, this could prove to be a tedious and error-prone solution that is difficult to maintain.

Another possible solution to this problem is to develop an application that can process *dynamic queries:* queries that can be developed and executed dynamically when the application runs. Thus, one relatively small block of code can be used to service a large number of queries.

JDBC provides a number of classes that aid in managing dynamic queries. The `ResultSetMetaData` class provides metadata, or information about data, for the result set (or executed query) that it represents. In addition to this, the `DatabaseMetaData` class provides detailed information about the underlying database.

This chapter begins coverage of dynamic queries, demonstrating how to manage queries in a general fashion using `ResultSet` and `ResultMeta` objects. Chapters that follow will cover the `DatabaseMetaData` class and demonstrate its capabilities.

USING DYNAMIC QUERIES

When you consider the design for an end-user application that must present an interface for the user, it is not uncommon for some portion of the application to allow the user to ask questions of, or query, the underlying database for information. While in some cases, these queries may be very well defined and static, it is much more likely for them to be highly variable and inconsistent.

An attractive alternative to managing multiple and variable database queries in an application is to create a mechanism for processing *dynamic queries*. As described previously, these are queries that are not known until runtime, until the point at which they are presented to the application component that must process the query.

With JDBC, the execution of an unknown query is not a problem; it is the return of the data from the `select` queries that presents a problem. If the application developer does not know about the composition of a query when the application is being written, then he or she cannot write specific code to manage the results of the query. So with dynamic queries, the composition of the `ResultSet` is unknown. It is with the `ResultSetMetaData` class that we can discover and process the contents of the `ResultSet`, as we will see in the following example.

A SAMPLE DYNAMIC QUERY APPLICATION: DYNAMICQUERY.JAVA

The `DynamicQuery.java` application demonstrates the process of creating and executing queries dynamically. This application reads a file containing a single SQL `select` statement, executes the query, and returns a `ResultSet`. The `ResultSet` is then processed using the `ResultSetMetaData` class to produce text output.

This application demonstrates two approaches to processing the data in the `ResultSet`. One approach simply uses the `ResultSet` to perform output. The other approach, which provides some additional flexibility, converts `ResultSet` data into the Java language wrapper objects for the data types in the `ResultSet` and loads the data into `java.util.Vector` objects.

Since this is a relatively large portion of example code, the explanation will be done by code block, beginning with the `main` program block and then proceeding with explanations of each of the method program blocks.

The DynamicQuery.java Program: Class Declaration and the main Program Block

The `DynamicQuery.java` program as shown below begins, as you would expect, with a series of import statements on lines 1 through 5. These statements import the `java.sql` package, which includes the core JDBC API; the `javax.sql` package, which is needed for the use of the `DataSource` connection facility; and the `javax.naming` package, which is needed to use the JNDI naming facility to retrieve the `DataSource` object. Additionally, the `java.util` package is imported to use the `Vector` class, and the `java.io` package is imported and used to perform file I/O.

A `Connection` object is declared as an instance member on line 9, and on lines 13 through 15, several variables are declared to be local to the `main` program block, including a reference to an instance of the `DynamicQuery` class.

On line 22, an instance of the `DynamicQuery` class is created and stored in one of the reference variables that are local to the `main` program block. This object reference will be used to invoke the various methods of the `DynamicQuery` class, which will be used to process the query.

The program allows the name of the file containing the query to process to be passed into the program on the command line. On line 28, the command-line arguments for the program are examined. Since the application allows a single command-line argument to be passed, the argument array for the `main` program block is simply checked to determine whether or not a single (1) argument has been given to the program. If an argument has been passed, the value of the argument is stored in the `fileName` variable by assigning the argument's reference address to the `fileName` variable on line 29. If no argument has been passed, the default file name of `query.sql` is assigned to the variable.

The next step in the `main` block is to retrieve the SQL query from the file whose name is stored in the `fileName` variable. This is accomplished using the `getQuery` method, which will open the file and concatenate all lines of the file into a single string. If the `getQuery` method cannot find the file or cannot read the contents of the file, it will return a null `String` reference. This contingency is tested on line 37 in this case, and since there is no query to process, the application will terminate at this point.

If a query string has successfully been read from the file, the application will continue and a series of informational messages will be output on lines 45 through 48. Then, on line 54, the `processQuery` method is called. This method will perform all of the work necessary to execute the query and will return the results in a

ResultSet object. The processQuery method is passed the connection object and the query string reference for the query to execute.

On line 55, the result returned from the processQuery method is tested for a null reference. The null reference would indicate that the processQuery method could not process the query or that the query returned no rows. Since there is no data to process, the program will stop execution at this point with a call to the System class exit method.

On line 59, the convertResultSet method is called. This method is passed a ResultSet and converts the contents of the ResultSet into a Vector object. The Vector returned by this method is actually a Vector of Vector objects, with each row of the ResultSet represented by a Vector of object references for the column data and the entire ResultSet represented by a Vector of row Vector objects. This aggregation of the ResultSet data creates an object that can be accessed randomly in the manner of scrollable ResultSets (not all drivers will support scrollable result sets) and is also useful in caching data in multitiered applications, as will be demonstrated in a later example. (A Vector collection is used in these examples over some other java.util collection because it retains the order of the contents, which is required if we want to emulate cursor behavior.)

The data Vector that stores the converted column and row data from the ResultSet (created on line 59) does not store the names of the columns that we will use to produce meaningful output. These column names are retrieved on line 60 and stored in a Vector object. The getColumnNames method is passed the ResultSet on line 60 and returns a Vector of column names for the ResultSet.

For demonstration purposes, two different output methods are shown. The outputResultSet method is called on line 69 and uses ResultSetMetaData methods to produce output of the contents of the ResultSet. But before this method can be called, the ResultSet cursor must be repositioned to before the first row. This is because the position of the cursor has been moved by the convertResult method, which iterated through the contents of the ResultSet from first to last. Because of the manner in which the outputResultSet method uses the ResultSet cursor, the cursor must be repositioned to before the first row, which is accomplished with a call to the ResultSet beforeFirst method on line 68.

The outputData method is called on line 74 and is passed the Vector object containing the rows of the ResultSet (data) and the Vector containing the column names for the columns in the ResultSet (colNames).

On lines 78 through 84, two catch blocks are used to capture exceptions thrown by the JDBC calls made in the main block. On line 86, the finally block is used to close the JDBC connection to the database. The code for the main program block follows:

DynamicQuery.java: main Program Block

```
1.import java.sql.*;
2.import javax.sql.*;
3.import javax.naming.*;
4.import java.util.*;
5.import java.io.*;
6.
7.public class DynamicQuery {
8.
9.Connection con      = null;
10.
11.public static void main( String args[] ) {
12.
13.String     fileName = null;
14.String     query    = null;
15.DynamicQuery dq      = null;
16.
17.try {
18.
19.    //
20.    // get a local object reference
21.    //
22.    dq = new DynamicQuery();
23.
24.    //
25.    // if we didn't get a command line argument, just use
26.    // the default file name
27.    //
28.    if ( args.length == 1 )
29.        fileName = args[0];
30.    else
31.        fileName = "query.sql";
32.
33.    //
34.    // get the query
35.    //
36.    query = dq.getQuery( fileName );
37.    if ( query == null ) {
38.        System.out.println( "No query found. Exiting ... " );
39.        System.exit( -1 );
40.    }
41.
42.    //
43.    // process the query
44.    //
45.    System.out.println("****************************");
46.    System.out.println("Processing file: " + fileName );
47.    System.out.println("Processing Query: " + query );
48.    System.out.println("****************************");
```

```
49.
50.       //
51.       // pass the connection into the processQuery method.
52.       // it is responsible for executing the query
53.       //
54.       ResultSet rs = dq.processQuery( dq.con,  query );
55.       if ( rs == null )
56.                   System.exit( -1 );
57.       //
58.       // convert ResultSet data to Java types
59.       Vector data      = dq.convertResultSet( rs );
60.       Vector colNames = dq.getColumnNames( rs );
61.
62.       //
63.       // output ResultSet
64.       //
65.       // reset the ResultSet pointer moved by the
66.       // convertResultSet method
67.       //
68.       rs.beforeFirst();
69.       dq.outputResultSet( rs );
70.
71.       //
72.       // output converted data
73.       //
74.       dq.outputData( data, colNames );
75.
76.
77.}
78.catch (SQLException e) {
79.    System.out.println("SQLException in main: " + e.getMessage() );
80.}
81.catch (Exception e) {
82.     System.out.println("Exception in main: " + e.getMessage() );
83.     e.printStackTrace();
84.}
85.
86.finally {
87.
88.     try {
89.          // close the connection
90.     if ( dq.con != null )
91.               dq.con.close();
92.     }
93.     catch (SQLException e) {
94.            e.printStackTrace();
95.     }
96.}
97.
98.}
```

The DynamicQuery.java Application: The Constructor

As you might expect, the constructor is used to obtain a connection to acquire the `DataSource` object and create a `Connection` object for the database. This is the only constructor for the `DynamicQuery` class. The code for this constructor is shown next.

DynamicQuery Constructor

```
// ──────────────────────────────────────
public DynamicQuery() {
try {
     //
     // JNDI startup parameters are stored in
     // the "jndi.properties" file in the classpath.
     //
     InitialContext ctx = new InitialContext( );

     //
     // get the DataSource from the JNDI name server
     //
     DataSource ds = (DataSource) ctx.lookup("moviesmysql");

     //
     // get the connection from the DataSource
     //
     con = ds.getConnection( );
}
catch (NamingException e ) {
     System.out.println( "NamingException in DynamicQuery: " +
                         e.getMessage() );
}
catch (SQLException e) {
     System.out.println( "SQLException in DynamicQuery: " +
                         e.getMessage() );
}

}
```

The DynamicQuery.java Application: The processQuery Method

The `processQuery` method is used, as the name implies, to process the query and return the results. The method is overloaded and takes two forms: one that takes a single `String` argument for the query to process and another that takes a

String query argument and a Connection to use to process the query. The form that takes the single String argument simply calls the second form, using the Connection object instance member as the connection.

The method takes the query, calls the Connection createStatement method to execute the query, and returns a ResultSet, which is then returned by the method.

DynamicQuery.java: processQuery Method

```
// ──────────────────────────────
public ResultSet processQuery( String query ) {

    return processQuery( con, query );

}

// ──────────────────────────────
public ResultSet  processQuery( Connection con, String query ) {

ResultSet rs = null;
try {

Statement stmt = con.createStatement();

rs = stmt.executeQuery( query );

}

catch (SQLException e ) {
    // display SQL specific exception information
    System.out.println("**************************" );
    System.out.println("SQLException in processQuery: " +
            e.getMessage() );
    System.out.println("** SQLState: " + e.getSQLState());
    System.out.println("** SQL Error Code: " + e.getErrorCode());
    System.out.println("**************************" );
    e.printStackTrace();
}
finally {
  return rs;
}


}
```

DynamicQuery.java: The outputResultSet Method

The `outputResult` method accepts a `ResultSet` argument and then, using methods in the `ResultSetMetaData` class, processes the query and produces text format results. This method begins by retrieving the `ResultSetMetaData` object for the `ResultSet` to be processed.

Since we don't know how many columns are in the `ResultSet`, we need to use the metadata object to discover this crucial piece of information. On line 8, the `ResultSetMetaData getColumnCount` method is called to return the integer value for the number of columns in the `ResultSet`. The method then uses a `while` loop to process the results in the `ResultSet`. For each row in the `ResultSet`, a `for` loop is used to iterate through each of the columns in the row being processed. For each column in the row, the `ResultSetMetaData getColumnLabel` method is called on line 16 to retrieve the appropriate label for the column data to be printed. (If the database does not store a column label, the column name from the schema is usually substituted and returned by this method.)

The column data is then printed using the `ResultSet getString` method called on line 18. This method will return an appropriate string representation for virtually any data type stored in the database, as this code demonstrates. So, even if the column is an integer column, a string representing the integer value will be returned by this method. The code for this method is shown next.

DynamicQuery.java: The outputResultSet Method

```
1.// -------------------------------------------------------
2.void outputResultSet( ResultSet rs ) {
3.
4.try {
5.
6.      ResultSetMetaData resMetaData = rs.getMetaData();
7.
8.     int colCount = resMetaData.getColumnCount();
9.     while ( rs.next() ) {
10.
11.         //
12.         //      System.out.println(
13.                 "*********************************" );
14.        for (int n = 1; n <= colCount; n++ ) {
15.             System.out.println(
16.                     resMetaData.getColumnLabel( n )   +
17.                 ": " + "\t\t" +
18.                         rs.getString( n ) );
19.
20.            }
21.        System.out.println( "*********************************" );
22.
```

```
23.        }
24.}
25.catch (SQLException e ) {
26.      // display SQL specific exception information
27.      System.out.println("*************************" );
28.      System.out.println("SQLException in outputResultSet: " +
29.                          e.getMessage() );
30.      System.out.println("** SQLState: " + e.getSQLState());
31.      System.out.println("** SQL Error Code: " + e.getErrorCode());
32.      System.out.println("*************************" );
33.      e.printStackTrace();
34.}
35.
36.}
37.
```

The DynamicQuery.java Application:
The getQuery Method

The getQuery method is responsible for retrieving the query string from the file designated by the file name passed into the method. The method will open the file, read the contents, and concatenate the contents onto a string, which will then be returned by the method.

The method begins by defining local variables for a StringBuffer and a string reference for the return value for the method, declared on lines 3 and 4. A java.io.BufferedReader method is then created on line 10, and the BufferedReader readLine method is called on line 16. The readLine method reads a line of input from the file up to the line terminator (a newline or carriage return). The method will return a null if there is no line to retrieve. The while loop on line 17 will continue until a null is encountered, indicating that there are no more lines to read. Within the while loop, the string returned by the readLine method is appended onto the string variable, which will be returned by the getQuery method. This loop makes an exception for the first pass through the loop (indicated by a null value for the buffer variable) and sets the return value variable (retVal) to that of the buffer on lines 19 and 20. (If this were not done, then the start of the query string would contain a null character, which would most likely cause the database to reject the query.) If it is not the first pass, then on line 23, the value of the buffer variable (returned by the readLine method) is appended to the return value string (retVal). On line 28, the next line of the file is read using the readLine method.

On line 34, the file that was opened on line 10 is closed. A number of catch statement blocks are included on lines 36 through 43 to catch I/O exceptions that may be thrown by the `BufferedReader` methods and the `FileReader` constructor (called on line 11). On line 45, within the `finally` block, the string that has been concatenated with the contents of the file is returned. If an I/O error has occurred during the file open process, then a null value is returned. If an I/O error has occurred during the file read operation (within the `while` loop), then a partial string is returned. (This will generally not lead to a problem, since the query will be rejected by the database and the application will recognize this by returning a null `ResultSet` from the `processQuery` method.) The code for this method is shown next.

DynamicQuery.java: getQuery Method

```
1.// --------------------------------------------------------------------
2.public String getQuery( String fn ) {
3.String buffer   = null; // data buffer
4.String retVal   = null; // query string to return
5.
6.try {
7.      //
8.      // create a file reader for the file containing the query
9.      //
10.      BufferedReader reader = new BufferedReader (
11.                                  new FileReader( fn ));
12.
13.      //
14.      // start reading the file
15.      //
16.      buffer = reader.readLine();
17.      while ( buffer != null ) {
18.
19.          if ( retVal == null ) {    // this is the first pass
20.              retVal = buffer;
21.          }
22.          else {
23.              retVal += buffer;      // append
24.          }
25.      //
26.      // continue reading the file
27.      //
28.      buffer = reader.readLine();
29.      }
30.
31.      //
32.      // close the file reader
33.      //
34.      reader.close();
```

```
35.}
36.catch (FileNotFoundException e) {
37.     System.out.println("FileNotFoundException in getQuery: " +
38.                         e.getMessage() );
39.}
40.catch (IOException e) {
41.     System.out.println(
42.             "IOException in getQuery: " + e.getMessage() );
43.}
44.finally {
45.     return retVal;
46.}
47.
48.}
```

The DynamicQuery.java Application: The getRows Method

The `getRows` method simply gets a count of the number of rows in the `ResultSet`. It creates a local integer variable and iterates through the `ResultSet`, incrementing the `ResultSet` pointer and the integer variable with each iteration. All work is performed within a `try/catch` block, and the `finally` block is used to return the value of the integer variable. The code listing for this method follows:

DynamicQuery.java: getRows Method

```
// ─────────────────────────────────────

public int getRows( ResultSet rs ) {
int rows = 0;
try {

    while ( rs.next() ) {
            rows++;
    }

}
catch (SQLException e) {
      System.out.println("SQLException in getRows: " + e.getMessage() );
}
finally {
    return rows;
}

}
```

The DynamicQuery.java Application:
The convertResultSet Method

The `convertResultSet` method takes the contents of the `ResultSet` and loads it into a `Vector` collection. The `Vector` returned is actually a collection of a `Vector` for each row in the `ResultSet`. Using these common collections expands the capabilities of the `ResultSet` class, which, depending on the driver used, may or may not support random positioning (a scrollable `ResultSet`). This conversion to a Java collection also provides easier integration with other programmatic structures that were developed for collections or arrays. (One of the more helpful aspects of using these collections is that they are zero-based rather than one-based, as with the `ResultSet`, making them a more natural collection type for Java, where collections and arrays begin at zero.)

The `convertResultSet` method accepts a single argument: the `ResultSet` to convert. The method begins by creating a `Vector` to be used for the storage of rows on line 4. A `while` loop is started on line 8, which will iterate through all of the rows in the `ResultSet`.

On line 10, for each row in the `ResultSet`, a `Vector` is created to represent the row. This `Vector` will be used to store the column data for the row. On lines 11 through 13, a `for` loop is executed, which iterates through the columns in the `ResultSet`. The `ResultSetMetaData getColumnCount` method is executed on line 12 and returns the count of columns in the `ResultSet`. This column count value is used to step through the contents of the `ResultSet` row. Note that since the `ResultSet` is one-based, we loop for less than or equal to (<=) the total count of columns in the `ResultSet`.

On line 16, within the `for` loop used to process the contents of the row, the `JDBCTypeMapper getColumnData` method is called to retrieve the contents of the `ResultSet` column (`JDBCTypeMapper` is a class developed for this demonstration—not part of JDBC). This method (shown later in this chapter) will map the JDBC data type to an appropriate Java wrapper class data type (`Integer`, `Boolean`, etc.) and return an `Object` reference. (The underlying object is the defined type, and the reference can be cast down to the class if needed.) Each column is converted in this manner, and when row processing is complete on line 19, the completed `row Vector` is added to the data vector representing the result set.

The `catch` statement block on line 19 catches any `SQLException` that may be thrown, and the `finally` block on line 26 is used to return the data `Vector`, which, as mentioned previously, is a `Vector` containing a collection of separate `Vector` objects for each row in the `ResultSet`. The code for this method is shown next.

DynamicQuery.java: convertResultSet Method

```
1.public Vector convertResultSet( ResultSet rs ) {
2.// convert the ResultSet data into an array of Objects
3.// and store in a Vector
4.Vector data = new Vector();
5.
6.try {
7.
8. while ( rs.next() ) {
9.
10.       Vector row  = new Vector();
11.       for ( int n = 1;
12.              n <= rs.getMetaData().getColumnCount();
13.              n++ ) {
14.
15.            // return an Object reference for Java wrapper types
16.            row.add( JDBCTypeMapper.getColumnData( n, rs ) );
17.       }
18.
19.       data.add( row );
20. }
21.}
22.catch (SQLException e) {
23.      System.out.println(
24.            "SQLException in getRows: " + e.getMessage() );
25.}
26.finally {
27.   return data;
28.}
29.
30.}
```

The DynamicQuery.java Application: The getColumnNames Method

The getColumnNames method, true to its title, retrieves the column names for the ResultSet and returns them in a Vector. The method begins by creating a new Vector object on line 2 and then creates a ResultSetMetaData object using the ResultSet getMetaData method on line 7.

The ResultSetMetaData object is used to return the column count for the ResultSet (the number of columns in the ResultSet). This column count is used to control a for loop on line nine which uses the ResultSetMetaData getColumnName method to extract the column name for a given column index. Note that since the ResultSet is one-based, we loop for less than or equal to (<=) the total count of columns in the ResultSet. Within the loop on line 10, the column name for each column is added to the column name Vector (colNames).

The `catch` statement block on line 14 traps any `SQLException` that may be thrown and the `finally` block on line 18 returns reference for the column name `Vector` for the columns (`colName`). The code listing for this reference follows:

DynamicQuery.java: getColumnNames Method

```
1.public Vector getColumnNames( ResultSet rs ) {
2.Vector colNames          = new Vector();
3.
4.
5.try {
6.
7.  ResultSetMetaData rsmd = rs.getMetaData();
8.
9.  for ( int n = 1; n <= rsmd.getColumnCount(); n++ ) {
10.        colNames.add( rsmd.getColumnName( n ) );
11.  }
12.
13.}
14.catch (SQLException e) {
15.    System.out.println(
16.        "SQLException in getColumnNames: " + e.getMessage() );
17.}
18.finally {
19.  return colNames;
20.}
21.
22.}
23.
```

The DynamicQuery.java Application: The outputData Method

The `outputData` method is used to take the contents of two `Vector` objects, contents that represent the results of a SQL query, and produce text output of the contents. The method takes two arguments: the data `Vector`, which contains the contents of the rows in the result set, and the `colNames Vector`, which contains the names of the columns in the result set.

The method begins by creating an `Iterator` for the data `Vector`. The `Iterator` is used to control a loop started on line 5. Within this loop, the contents of each row of the data `Vector` are extracted using the `Iterator` next method. For each of these row `Vector` objects, the `Vector size` method is called to determine the number of elements (the number of columns) in the row.

On line 17, a `for` loop is started to move through the elements in the row. For each of these elements, the `Vector get` method is called on line 18 to retrieve the contents of the `Vector`. The class name of the object being output is printed on line 20. The code for this method is shown next.

DynamicQuery.java: outputData Method

```
1.void outputData( Vector data, Vector colNames ) {
2.Iterator i = data.iterator();
3.
4.     while ( i.hasNext() ) {
5.
6.        //
7.        // use the iterator to move through the rows
8.        //
9.        Vector   row = (Vector) i.next();
10.            int colCount = row.size();
11.        System.out.println( "**********************************" );
12.
13.        //
14.        // print the column data for the row
15.        //
16.        for (int n = 0; n < colCount; n++ ) {
17.            System.out.println( colNames.get( n )   +
18.                            " - (" +
19.               row.get( n ).getClass().getName() + "): " +
20.               "\t\t" + row.get( n ) );
21.            }
22.        System.out.println(
23.            "**********************************" );
24.
25.     }
26.
27.}
```

THE JDBCTYPEMAPPER CLASS: JDBC TO JAVA TYPE MAPPING

One of the more common tasks when using dynamic queries and working with JDBC and its underlying database is the process of converting data from the database types and the corresponding JDBC data types to Java data types and formatting the data into strings. With this example, a class that exposes several static methods is used to perform the conversion.

The `JDBCTypeMapper` class contains a single method to perform conversion of a JDBC type to a `String` data type. Note that JDBC drivers will perform much of this conversion by default. Virtually all SQL data types can be converted into Java `String` using the `ResultSet getString` method. The `ResultSet getObject` method will freely retrieve any SQL data type into an appropriate

Java language wrapper class. What the JDBCTypeMapper class provides is the ability to intervene in this process within an efficient Java switch statement and apply specific formatting to the conversion process. This is demonstrated in the code in the following section.

As with many of the Java wrapper class conversion methods, these methods are exposed as Java static methods—they are loaded with the class and do not require an object to be instantiated. This avoids the need (and the overhead) of instantiating and managing an object to perform type mapping. In large, robust applications which must process a large number of database rows, the process of extracting and converting data can potentially become a bottleneck. For this reason, this process should be kept as streamlined as possible.

As with the previous code example, this discussion will be divided into the sections of the application. The complete, continuous code listing is provided in the Appendix.

The JDBCTypeMapper.java Application: The getColumnDataString Method

The JDBCTypeMapper class performs a number of imports on lines 1 through 3. The java.text package is used to provide access to some of the formatting routines used to convert JDBC data types (which primarily correspond to ANSI SQL types) to Java Strings, and the java.math package is used to provide access to the BigDecimal class for retrieval and manipulation of large decimal numbers from the database.

The first method shown is the getColumnDataString method on line 10. This method will retrieve a column from a ResultSet and convert the column data to a Java String. It takes an integer argument for the column position in the current ResultSet row and the ResultSet reference to use for column retrieval.

On line 11, an Object reference is declared to be used for the return value from the method and an integer variable to be used for the storage of the column data type. On line 15, the ResultSetMetaData object is retrieved from the ResultSet and used (by way of an anonymous object) to call the getColumnType method, which is passed the column number of the ResultSet column to use. This returns the column type (from java.sql.Types), which is used in the switch statement started on line 17. The switch statement maps the type integer value to the cases listed in the switch statement block.

The remainder of the method just uses the case statement blocks (which "fall through" in Java just as they do in the C language) to the conversion necessary to convert the JDBC type to a Java String. With the integer types on line 22, we count on the underlying toString method for the JDBC type (which is ultimately called via Java's polymorphic method execution) to provide the correct conversion. Since mapping an integer to a string is generally pretty straightforward, this conversion should not present a problem.

The conversion of decimal numbers, however, can present issues. The rounding of the fractional part, the number of decimal points to display, and how to display them are all issues that must be managed by the developer. In this example on line 29 through 37, we perform some conversion to limit the number of decimal digits to three in the resulting string. A `NumberFormat` object had been created, and on line 35, the `setMaximumFractionDigits` method is called to limit the fractional portion of the resulting string to three decimal places. Now that the number formatter is ready, we call the `ResultSet getDouble` method to retrieve the value of the column (which could be a `Decimal`, `Numeric`, or `Float` type) and pass the Java `double` primitive type to the format method for our number formatter. The `NumberFormat format` method will return a string formatted using the specified internal format. This `String` object reference is effectively cast up to an `Object` reference on line 36, which will be used as the return value for the method.

On line 39, the SQL `Bit` data type is retrieved from the database as a `boolean` data type and is mapped to a string value of 1 for true or 0 for false.

On line 43, the SQL `Date` data type is mapped to a string. Formatting dates can vary not only by locale but by the requirements of the user community using the application. The Java JDK provides a `DateFormat` class to output various date format strings. The factory method for creating the `DateFormat` object can be created to produce default formats specified in the constructor. In this example, the formatter has been created as an instance variable and is set to use the long date format. The date column is then retrieved using the `ResultSet getDate` method on line 48 and passed to the `DateFormat` format method (where the argument is cast up to the `java.util.Date`, the super class of `javs.sql.Date`). The result of this code is that date fields displayed using this method will be displayed in the long date format: January 14, 2002, for example.

On lines 52 through 54, character fields from the database (SQL `CHAR`, `VARCHAR`, and `LONGVARCHAR` types) are mapped, as would be expected, to the Java `String` type, using the `toString` method of the underlying object. Given that these data types are essentially character strings, this conversion does not present a problem.

On lines 58 and 59, the default for this method, for any data type that has not fulfilled one of the cases, is to attempt a conversion to `String`.

JDBCTypeMapper.java: The getColumnDataString Method

```
1.import java.sql.*;
2.import java.text.*;
3.import java.math.*;
4.
5.public class JDBCTypeMapper {
```

```
6.
7.NumberFormat nf = (DecimalFormat) NumberFormat.getInstance();
8.DateFormat   df =  DateFormat.getDateInstance( DateFormat.LONG );
9.
10.public static Object getColumnDataString( int col, ResultSet rs ) {
11.   Object obj  = null;
12.   int    type = 0;
13.
14.   try {
15.        type = rs.getMetaData().getColumnType( col );
16.
17.        switch(type) {
18.
19.              case Types.INTEGER:
20.              case Types.SMALLINT:
21.              case Types.TINYINT:
22.                  obj =  rs.getObject( col ).toString();
23.                  break;
24.
25.              case Types.DOUBLE:
26.              case Types.DECIMAL:
27.              case Types.NUMERIC:
28.              case Types.FLOAT:
29.                  //
30.                // Perform some formatting - limit to 3
31.                  // decimal digits on output
32.                  //
33.
34.
35.               nf.setMaximumFractionDigits( 3 );
36.               obj = nf.format( rs.getDouble( col ));
37.                  break;
38.
39.              case Types.BIT:
40.                  obj = rs.getBoolean( col) ? "1" : "0";
41.                   break;
42.
43.              case Types.DATE:
44.                  //
45.                // use the long date format
46.                  //
47.
48.                   obj = df.format( rs.getDate( col ) );
49.
50.            break;
51.
52.               case Types.CHAR:
53.               case Types.VARCHAR:
54.               case Types.LONGVARCHAR:
55.                   obj = rs.getObject( col ).toString();
56.            break;
57.
```

```
58.                    case Types.BLOB:
59.                    case Types.CLOB:
60.                            obj = "<BLOB>";
61.                            break;
62.
63.                    case Types.NULL:
64.                            obj = " "; // map to blank string
65.
66.                default:
67.                        obj = rs.getObject( col ).toString();
68.                        break;
69.            }
70.
71.      }
72.    catch (SQLException e) {
73.            System.out.println(
74.                "SQLException in getColumnData: " + e.getMessage() );
75.      }
76.
77.    finally {
78.          return obj;
79.      }
80.
81.}
```

THE RESULTSETMETADATA CLASS

The previous code sample demonstrated a dynamic query. This is a process that would not have been possible without methods like the `ResultSetMetaData` `getColumnCount` method to return the number of columns in the result set or the `ResultSetMetaData getColumnType` to determine the data type of the column.

The various methods in the `ResultSetMetaData` class allow the type and status of a database column in the `ResultSet` to be interrogated. These methods allow not only the data type to be determined, but also whether or not the column can be written to in the database, what the precision of the column is (if it is a decimal type), whether or not the column is case-sensitive, as well as other details.

With the exception of one method (`getColumnCount`), all methods take an integer argument that represents the column index in the `ResultSet` starting from one. (There are no corresponding "column name" versions of the methods as there are in the `ResultSet` class.) As this implies, the focus of this class is on providing very specific information about the columns in the `ResultSet`. The information provided by this class is directly related to the query that generated the `ResultSet` and the database where the query was executed. But the `ResultSetMetaData` class provides very limited, focused information about the query. For information about the database in general, the `DatabaseMetaData` class is available and provides a prolific number of methods. This class is covered in chapters 11 and 12.

The complete listing of the `ResultSetMetaData` is shown in Table 10–1.

Table 10–1 *ResultSetMetaData Methods*

Method	Description
`String getCatalogName(int column)`	Retrieves the catalog name of the table from which the column was retrieved. The column is identified by the integer argument, which is an index to the corresponding field in the select list.
`String getColumnClassName(int column)`	Returns a string which is the fully-qualified name of the Java class for the column (the SQL data type will be mapped to this Java class). The `ResultSet getObject` method will retrieve an instance of an object of this class.
`int getColumnCount()`	Returns an integer representing the number of columns in the `ResultSet`.
`int getColumnDisplaySize(int column)`	Indicates the maximum width of the column in characters.
`String getColumnLabel(int column)`	Returns a string that is the recommended label for the column. (Most drivers will return the column name from the table schema if the database does not have a specific column label facility.) Takes an integer argument for the column that references the corresponding field in the query select list.
`String getColumnName(int column)`	Returns a string that is the name of the column as identified in the table schema. Takes an integer argument for the column that references the corresponding field in the query 'select' list.
`int getColumnType(int column)`	Returns an integer that identifies the SQL type of the column referenced by the integer argument. The type is one of `java.sql.Types`. Takes an integer argument for the column that references the corresponding field in the query 'select' list.
`String getColumnTypeName(int column)`	Returns a string that is the specific type name as defined in the database schema. Takes an integer argument for the column that references the corresponding field in the query 'select' list.

| **Table 10–1** | *ResultSetMetaData Methods (cont.)* |

Method	Description
`int getPrecision(int column)`	Returns an integer that represents the total number of decimal digits in the column (the precision). Takes an integer argument for the column that references the corresponding field in the query `'select'` list. May return a −1 or 0 if the column is not a decimal column.
`int getScale(int column)`	Returns an integer that represents the total number of digits to the right of the decimal point in the column, also known as the scale. Takes an integer argument for the column that references the corresponding field in the query `'select'` list.
`String getSchemaName(int column)`	Returns a string that is the name of the schema for the table from which the column was retrieved. Takes an integer argument for the column that references the corresponding field in the query `'select'` list.
`String getTableName(int column)`	Returns a string that represents the table name from which the column was retrieved. Takes an integer argument for the column that references the corresponding field in the query `'select'` list.
`boolean isAutoIncrement(int column)`	Returns a boolean value of `true` if the column is an auto-increment column, a column that will set its own value and guarantee it to be unique. If a boolean `false` is returned, the column is not an auto-increment column. Takes an integer argument for the column that references the corresponding field in the query `'select'` list.
`boolean isCaseSensitive(int column)`	Returns a boolean value of `true` if the column is case sensitive, and returns a boolean value of `false` if the column is not case sensitive. Takes an integer argument for the column that references the corresponding field in the query `'select'` list.
`boolean isCurrency(int column)`	Returns a boolean value of `true` if the column is a currency column (used to represent money values), and returns a boolean value of `false` if the column is not a currency field. Takes an integer argument for the column that references the corresponding field in the query `'select'` list.

Table 10–1   *ResultSetMetaData Methods (cont.)*

Method	Description
boolean isDefinitelyWritable(int column)	Returns a boolean value of true if the column is writable, and returns a boolean value of false if the column is not writable (read-only) or the driver can't determine if the column is writable. Takes an integer argument for the column that references the corresponding field in the query 'select' list.
int isNullable(int column)	Returns an integer value that indicates whether or not the column can be set to a null value. Value returned will be equal to either columnNoNulls, columnNullable, or columnNullableUnknown integer values from the ResultSetMetaData class. Takes an integer argument for the column that references the corresponding field in the query 'select' list.
boolean isReadOnly(int column)	Returns a boolean value of true if the column is read-only, and returns a boolean value of false if the column is writeable. Takes an integer argument for the column that references the corresponding field in the query 'select' list.
boolean isSearchable(int column)	Returns a boolean value of true if the column can be used in a set of search criteria (a SQL where clause), or returns false. Takes an integer argument for the column that references the corresponding field in the query select list.
boolean isSigned(int column)	Returns a boolean value of true if the column carries a mathematical sign, or returns false. Takes an integer argument for the column that references the corresponding field in the query select list.
boolean isWritable(int column)	Returns a boolean value of true if the column is writable, and returns a boolean value of false if the column is not writable (read-only). This method allows that it may still be possible for the write operation for the column data to fail even though the user has permission to write to the column. Takes an integer argument for the column that references the corresponding field in the query select list.

These methods are explained in more detail in the following sections, where they are grouped in a relatively logical fashion.

The ResultSetMetaData Class Methods: General Information about the Column

The `ResultSetMetaData` class provides a number of methods that are useful for providing some general information about the query that generated the `ResultSet`. These methods are as follows:

- `String getCatalogName(int column)`
- `String getSchemaName(int column)`
- `String getTableName(int column)`
- `int getColumnCount()`

The `getCatalogName` and `getSchemaName` methods provide the catalog and schema names for the designated column in the `ResultSet`. These methods take an integer argument representing the column position in the `ResultSet`. Not all databases make use of schemas and catalogs. If there is no catalog or schema in the database for the column, these methods return a blank (not a null).

The `getTableName` method returns the name of the table for the column. Unlike the `getCatalogName` and `getSchemaName` methods, which may not return values for all databases, the `getTableName` will work with all relational databases, since by definition a relational database is a collection of tables.

The Column Type Methods

A number of methods are available to determine the type of the column and information about the column that is specific to certain data types. These methods are as follows.

- `String getColumnClassName(int column)`
- `String getColumnTypeName(int column)`
- `int getColumnType(int column)`
- `int getPrecision(int column)`
- `int getScale(int column)`
- `boolean isSigned(int column)`

The `getColumnClassName` returns the fully qualified class name of the underlying JDBC class. This is the name the `ResultSet` `getObject` method will map to.

The `getColumnType` method returns the column type as defined in `java.sql.Types` in integer format. The `getColumnTypeName` returns a string that relates to the JDBC type, as defined in `java.sql.types`, providing the same information as the `getColumnType` method but in a string format. These methods are useful for discovering the type of the column and using that information to determine how to convert it, and for debugging purposes.

The `getPrecision` method returns the precision of the column if it is a decimal column, or it returns zero (0) if the column is not a decimal type. Likewise, the `getScale` method returns the scale of the column if it is a decimal type, or it returns a zero if the column is not a decimal column.

The `isSigned` method indicates whether or not a column stores a signed value, returning a boolean `true` if the column is signed, and a `false` otherwise.

Column Name and Display Size Methods

The `ResultSetMetaData` class provides several methods useful for the formatting and output of data in a `ResultSet`. These methods are as follows.

- `int getColumnDisplaySize(int column)`
- `String getColumnLabel(int column)`
- `String getColumnName(int column)`

The `getColumnDisplaySize` method can be used to determine the display size, the maximum size of the column in characters. The `getColumnLabel` method can be used to display the column label, which may differ from the column name if the database supports the storage of such labels; otherwise, the column name may be supplied by this method. The `getColumnName` returns a string, which is the name of the column as provided in the table schema.

Methods to Evaluate Writing to a Column

Several methods provide information about the process of writing to a particular column in the `ResultSet`. These methods are as follows.

- `boolean isAutoIncrement(int column)`
- `boolean isCaseSensitive(int column)`
- `boolean isCurrency(int column)`
- `int isNullable(int column)`
- `boolean isDefinitelyWritable(int column)`
- `boolean isReadOnly(int column)`
- `boolean isWritable(int column)`

An auto-increment column is a column that automatically increments its value as rows are inserted into the table. The incrementing process is automatic and is provided by the database server. The database server guarantees a unique value for a column in a table. The implementation of auto-increment columns varies among databases. The `ResultSetMetaData` class provides methods for evaluating whether or not a column is an auto-increment column with the `isAutoIncrement` method.

The `isAutoIncrement` method takes an integer argument, which is the `ResultSet` column to evaluate. The method returns a boolean value of `true` if the column is an auto-increment (sometimes referred to as a `serial` or `AutoNumber`) column, or a value of `false` if the column is not. Since many databases do not allow writes to an auto-increment column, or expect a special value for the column when it is being inserted, having some knowledge of the column's auto-increment status is useful.

The `isCaseSensitve` method can be used to determine whether or not a column is case-sensitive. If a column is not case sensitive, then the case of the value being placed into the column does not need to be managed. If a character string column is going to be used in searches, then it is often useful to make the column insensitive to case, since this will make indexing and searching easier.

The `isCurrency` method can be used to determine if a column contains a currency value. A currency value is a decimal number that should be formatted correctly for the currency of the locale where the output is going to be used. The `isCurrency` method would be called, therefore, to determine whether or not to do currency formatting for a column.

Though given the name, it may appear that the `isNullable` method would return a `boolean` value; it does not. The `isNullable` method returns an integer value indicating the behavior of the column with null values. The integer value returned corresponds to one of the integer constants in the `ResultMetaData` class, one of either `columnNoNulls`, `columnNullable`, or `columnNullableUnknown`. A return value of `columnNoNulls` indicates the column will not accept nulls and any attempt to update the column to a null value will fail. A return of the `columnNullable` value indicates the column will accept null values, and a return value of `columnNullableUnknown` indicates the JDBC driver could not determine whether or not the column can be set to a null value.

Since SQL `insert` operations do not require that all columns in the database be identified, many databases will simply substitute null values for any columns that have not been addressed in the `insert` column list. This commonly leads to `insert` failures for what the database server sees as attempts to insert a null into a column that does not allow nulls. Since the `isNullable` method is available in the JDBC API, it makes good sense to test for the ability to set a column to null before it is attempted.

The `isDefinitelyWritable` method can be used to determine whether or not a column can be written at the time the method is called. This method returns a boolean `true` if the driver can determine that the update on the column will succeed. The `isWritable` method indicates that writes are allowed to the column specified, but does not evaluate whether or not the current update will succeed or fail. This method returns a boolean `true` if the column was created to allow writes. The `isReadOnly` method indicates that the database definition of the column is read-only. This method returns a boolean `true` if the designated column is a read-only column.

Searching on a Column

There are some columns that cannot be used in a search (for example, a BLOB column). This is because it is simply too expensive or too difficult to retrieve the contents of the column for each row to be searched. These columns can be identified with the `isSearchable` method as shown below.

```
boolean isSearchable(int column)
```

The `isSearchable` method returns a boolean value of `true` if the column is searchable and can be used in a SQL `select` statement `where` clause. It returns a boolean `false` if the column cannot be used in a `where` clause.

ResultSet Constants

There are a small number of constants in the `ResultSetMetaData` class. These are values returned by some methods to indicate whether or not the column can accept null values (some databases allow the null value to be optional for a field). These constants are shown in Table 10–2.

Table 10–2 *ResultSetMetaData Constants*

Method	Description
`static int columnNoNulls`	Indicates that a column does not allow NULL values.
`static int columnNullable`	Indicates that a column allows NULL values.
`static int columnNullableUnknown`	Indicates that it is not known whether or not a column can be set to a null value.

SUMMARY

This chapter demonstrated some of the more flexible features of the JDBC API—the processing of dynamic queries, queries whose contents are not known until the application is run. Using dynamic queries can reduce the amount of code that needs to be written for an application and can add a great deal of flexibility to the user interface. A code sample was used to demonstrate the processing queries dynamically.

As shown in this chapter, the `ResultSetMetaData` class provides a great deal of information about a `ResultSet`, including the number of columns in the results, the column names of the columns, and the data types of the columns. This is information that can be used to process queries dynamically.

COMING UP NEXT

The JDBC API has been designed to be database-independent. One of the goals in designing the API was to allow developers to write applications that could work with a number of databases with little or no code changes. The `DatabaseMetaData` class provides a wealth of information about a database. Using this extensive class, an application can dynamically react to the database connection and adjust accordingly.

CHAPTER 11

The DatabaseMetaData Interface

INTRODUCTION

At one time there were hopes that through well-defined standards, relational databases would be easily interchangeable. A set of SQL statements written for one database would execute and run in another database without any changes. But the reality of a capitalistic software industry intruded on this dream. In pursuit of the goal to differentiate their product, database vendors took what standards existed and extended them in various ways. Unfortunately (or fortunately, depending on your point of view), many of these extensions were very good and timely, and were used by developers. Consequently, most applications written to work with the *standard* SQL relational database (conforming to some degree to the ANSI 92 SQL specification) intentionally or unwittingly made use of features that were not part of ANSI standard SQL and thus precluded having the application run against another relational database without some changes.

So in the harsh light of this reality, unless some effort is made to use only ANSI SQL, database applications are developed with some dependence on the underlying database. Database developers write SQL statements that manipulate

245

the database, often working with database administrators to create efficient and accurate SQL statements. Additional development iterations may be used to tweak the SQL statements to improve performance or provide the correct level of transaction control.

For the vast majority of applications, this development process is perfectly acceptable. Developers and managers are aware of database dependence issues and think long and hard before moving an application from one database to another. There are many ANSI-SQL extensions that can provide significant savings in development time if used correctly (for example, Oracle's `connect by` clause to support recursive queries). But there are some applications that do not meet this development profile.

Value-added resellers (VARs) often create applications such as code generators and database management tools that must support multiple databases. These applications must either be ported to specific database vendor products and versions or must contain code that evaluates the version and capabilities of the database being used and responds accordingly. There are business applications that also fit this profile having to interact with different database products installed throughout the business entity. These applications can be written and maintained more easily using the classes and methods defined in the `DatabaseMetaData` interface.

The `DatabaseMetaData` interface, as implemented by the JDBC driver developer, provides access to information about a database and its contents. The information ranges from the general to the specific. The following sections cover this interface, starting with a demonstration application that uses the implementation of `DatabaseMetaData` interface to gather a subset of the database information available and display it in a Swing GUI window with tabbed panes. The remaining sections of this chapter break this large interface definition down into manageable pieces for discussion.

DATABASEMETADATA INTERFACE: DEMONSTRATION APPLICATION

The `DatabaseMetaData` is a large interface with over 150 methods. In practice, however, it is usually only a small number of these methods that are used to determine how to build a SQL statement or how to manage a transaction. Used in this manner, a small number of statements may appear in an application, most likely in decision statements to determine which SQL statement to execute or which SQL statement clause to append to a particular query.

To show the extent of information available in the `DatabaseMetaData` interface, the following `DBInfoGUI` example executes a subset of the methods available and stores them in Java `Collection` objects. These ordered collections contain label/value pairs of information on the database. For instance, Database Vendor and Oracle would represent a label/value pair.

These collections of database information are then used to create a series of GUI panes that are used to display the information in a Swing tabbed window (JTabbedPane), as shown in Figure 11–1.

As with other long examples, this discussion will be divided into sections that cover each significant code block.

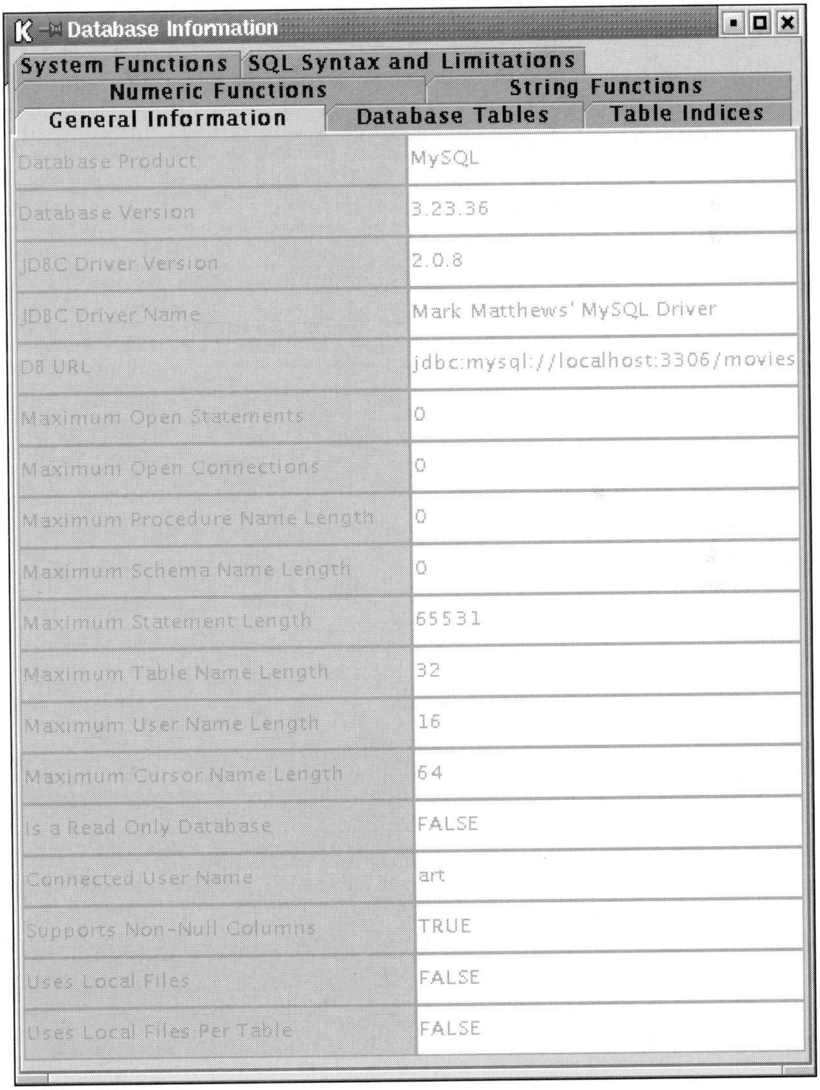

K ─ Database Information	▪ ☐ ✖
System Functions	**SQL Syntax and Limitations**
Numeric Functions	**String Functions**
General Information	**Database Tables** **Table Indices**
Database Product	MySQL
Database Version	3.23.36
JDBC Driver Version	2.0.8
JDBC Driver Name	Mark Matthews' MySQL Driver
DB URL	jdbc:mysql://localhost:3306/movies
Maximum Open Statements	0
Maximum Open Connections	0
Maximum Procedure Name Length	0
Maximum Schema Name Length	0
Maximum Statement Length	65531
Maximum Table Name Length	32
Maximum User Name Length	16
Maximum Cursor Name Length	64
Is a Read Only Database	FALSE
Connected User Name	art
Supports Non-Null Columns	TRUE
Uses Local Files	FALSE
Uses Local Files Per Table	FALSE

Figure 11–1 *DBInfoGUI Application*

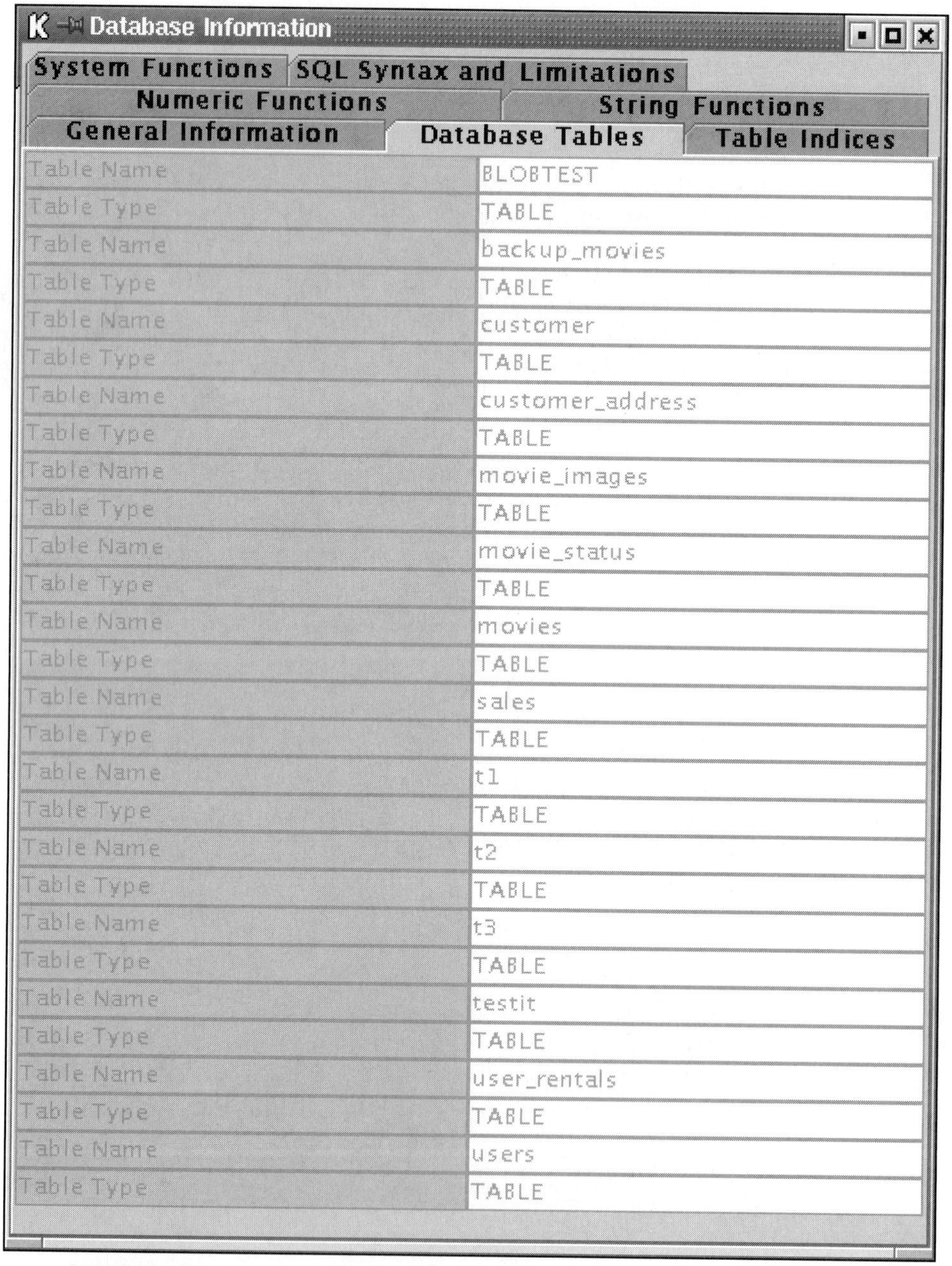

Figure 11–1   *DBInfoGUI Application (cont.)*

The DBInfoGUI Application: main Program Block

The `DBInfoGUI` class requires a number of imports, which appear on lines 1 through 7. These are required to display the Swing GUI and to aggregate the database information extracted using the `DatabaseMetaData interface` into Java collections.

Within the `main` program block, a string is declared to store the `DataSource` name for the application to use. The application uses a default `DataSource` and allows a `DataSource` name to be passed into the application. An `ArrayList` collection is declared on line 17 to store the database information (for the GUI panel) to be collected in a single program structure. (The application assumes the contents of the various collections are ordered, so a `set` collection would not be compatible.)

On line 19, the application checks to determine whether or not a command-line argument has been passed in with a `DataSource` name. If no command-line argument is provided, the default `DataSource` name is used on line 23.

The application code then calls the constructor for the `DBInfoGUI` class on line 27 and passes in the `DataSource` name. The constructor is responsible for creating the connection to the `DataSource`.

The `main` program block then contains a number of calls that gather information about the database (using the `DatabaseMetaData interface`) and return the information in a `Collection` object (an instance of `ArrayList`). In turn, this information is gathered or aggregated into another `ArrayList` object, the `panelInfo` object. This takes place on lines 31 through 47. These calls to add objects to the `panelInfo` collection include calls to the methods of the `DBInfoGUI` class to collect the database information. For example, on line 32, a call is made to the `getGeneralInfo` method to obtain general database information and return an `ArrayList` object, which is then added to the `panelInfo` collection (using the anonymous object reference returned). The same activity takes place on line 35 with a call to the `getTables` method and on lines 38, 41, 44, and 47 with other `DBInfoGUI` methods.

When all of the data has been loaded, a call is made to the `buildGUI` method, which passes the `panelInfo` collection. This call will be used to build the GUI for the application, using the information that has been collected in the `panelInfo ArrayList`. The code listing for this program block follows:

The DBInfoGUI.java: main Program Block

```
1.import java.sql.*;
2.import javax.sql.*;
3.import java.util.*;
4.import javax.naming.*;
```

```
5.import javax.swing.*;
6.import java.awt.*;
7.import java.awt.event.*;
8.
9.
10.public class DBInfoGUI {
11.
12.private DatabaseMetaData dbMetaData;
13.
14.public static void main( String[] args )   {
15.
16.String dataSourceName = null;
17.ArrayList panelInfo = new ArrayList();
18.
19.if ( args.length == 1 ) { // DataSourceName on the command line
20.    dataSourceName = args[0];
21.}
22.else {
23.    dataSourceName = "moviesmysql";
24.}
25.
26.// create object and get connected
27.DBInfoGUI dbinfo = new DBInfoGUI( dataSourceName );
28.
29.// general db info
30.System.out.println( "Loading database metadata ... " );
31.panelInfo.add( "General Information");
32.panelInfo.add( dbinfo.getGeneralInfo() );
33.
34.panelInfo.add( "Database Tables" );
35.panelInfo.add( dbinfo.getTables() );
36.
37.panelInfo.add( "Table Indices" );
38.panelInfo.add( dbinfo.getIndices( (ArrayList) dbinfo.getTables() ) );
39.
40.panelInfo.add( "Numeric Functions" );
41.panelInfo.add( dbinfo.getNumFunctions() );
42.
43.panelInfo.add( "String Functions" );
44.panelInfo.add( dbinfo.getStrFunctions() );
45.
46.panelInfo.add( "System Functions" );
47.panelInfo.add( dbinfo.getSysFunctions() );
48.
49.// build the GUI and display
50.System.out.println( "Building and displaying GUI ... " );
51.dbinfo.buildGUI( panelInfo );
52.
53.}
```

THE DBINFOGUI APPLICATION: CONSTRUCTOR AND BUILDGUI METHOD

The constructor for the DBInfoGUI class uses the DataSource name passed in and calls the getConnected method to obtain a connection to the database and create a DatabaseMetaData object.

The buildGUI method performs the various Swing API calisthenics required to render the GUI window used to display the database information. On lines 9 through 11, the Frame for the window and the content panel used to add components is created. A tabbed window is created on line 13 and instructed to place the window tabs on the top of the windows.

The next section of this method loops through the contents of the panelInfo ArrayList (which contains the database information) and will load the database information into separate panels, creating a tabbed window for each panel. The loop begins at line 18 and loops through the panelInfo ArrayList. The panelInfo is loaded with pairs of entries that include a description entry, which describes the information, and an ArrayList object reference entry, which contains the information.

The DBInfoGUI loadPanel method is called at line 23. This method returns a JPanel that has been populated with a series of fields containing the database information. The panel is loaded into the tabbed pane on line 24 using the description contained in the panelInfo ArrayList at the designated position. On line 26, the position variable is incremented two positions to move past the current pair of panelInfo entries (the entries that have just been processed).

On line 34, the window-closing event is managed using an anonymous class to map the window-closing event to a System exit method call.

On line 41, the tabbed pane that now contains all of the panes containing database information is added to the content panel. On lines 44 and 45, the window is prepared for display by calling the pack method, and then displayed by calling setVisible with a parameter of a boolean true. The code listings for these program blocks follows.

Constructor and buildGUI Method

```
1.public DBInfoGUI( String dataSourceName ) {
2.
3.getConnected( dataSourceName );
4.
5.}
6.
7.private void buildGUI( ArrayList panelInfo ) {
8.
9.JFrame frame = new JFrame("Database Information");
10.JPanel  contentPanel = new JPanel(new BorderLayout());
```

```
11.frame.setContentPane(contentPanel);
12.
13.JTabbedPane tabbedPane = new JTabbedPane( JTabbedPane.TOP );
14.
15.int position = 1;
16.
17.// load the panels with the information we've collected
18.while ( position < panelInfo.size() ) {
19.
20.    // every 1st element is the name of the info stored
21.    // every 2nd element is the ArrayList with info
22.
23.    JPanel panel = loadPanel( (ArrayList) panelInfo.get( position ) );
24.    tabbedPane.add( panel, (String) panelInfo.get( (position - 1) ) );
25.
26.    position += 2;
27.
28.}
29.
30.
31.//
32.// set the window closing event
33.//
34.frame.addWindowListener(new WindowAdapter() {
35.        public void windowClosing(WindowEvent e) {
36.                System.exit(0);
37.        }
38.    });
39.
40.// add the tabbed pane to the frame's content panel
41.contentPanel.add( tabbedPane );
42.
43.// turn it on
44.frame.pack();
45.frame.setVisible(true);
46.
47.
48.}
```

The DBInfoGUI Application: The getConnected Method

The getConnected method performs the task of connecting to the DataSource and creating a DatabaseMetaData instance for the DBInfoGUI object to work with. This method is passed a string that contains the name of the DataSource for the application to use. The initial context is obtained at line 6, and the DataSource is obtained through an InitialContext lookup call on line 8. The DataSource getConnection method obtains the Connection object, and then the Connection object is used to obtain the DatabaseMetaData object through a call to the `Connection getMetaData` method on line 12. The code for this method is shown next.

The getConnected Method

```
1.private void getConnected( String DataSourceName ) {
2.
3.Connection con;
4.try {
5.
6.InitialContext ctx = new InitialContext();
7.
8.DataSource ds = (DataSource) ctx.lookup( DataSourceName );
9.
10.con = ds.getConnection();
11.
12.dbMetaData = con.getMetaData();
13.
14.}
15.catch (NamingException e) {
16.        System.out.println("NamingException in getConnected: " +
17.                              e.getMessage() );
18.}
19.catch (SQLException e) {
20.        System.out.println("SQLException in getConnected: " +
21.                              e.getMessage() );
22.}
23.
24.
25.}
```

The DBInfoGUI Application: The getTables Method

The `getTables` method performs the job of retrieving a listing of tables from the database, loading them into an `ArrayList`, and returning the list. This method makes a call to the `DatabaseMetaData getTables` method on line 6. The method takes a number of arguments, which are commonly set to null values. Arguments allow filtering on catalog, schema, table name, and table types. For this example (and this is a common call to this method), we want to retrieve all tables in the database, so all arguments provided are set to null values.

The `getTables` method returns its results in a `ResultSet`. In this example, the table name ("TABLE_NAME") and table type ("TABLE_TYPE") columns are retrieved from the `ResultSet` on lines 14 and 16. Labels for these respective columns are added to the `ArrayList` on lines 13 and 15. The `ArrayList` that is created in this `while` loop is returned in the `finally` block on line 24. The listing for this method is shown next.

DBInfoGUI getTables Method

```
1.public Collection getTables() {
2.ArrayList retList = new ArrayList();
3.
4.try {
5.
6.ResultSet rs = dbMetaData.getTables(
7.                              null,   // catalog
8.                              null,   // schema
9.                    null,   // table name pattern
10.                   null ); // table types to include
11.
12.while ( rs.next() ) {
13.   retList.add( "Table Name");
14.      retList.add( rs.getString( "TABLE_NAME" ));
15.      retList.add( "Table Type" );
16.      retList.add( rs.getString( "TABLE_TYPE" ));
17.}
18.
19.}
20.catch (SQLException e) {
21.      System.out.println("SQLException in getTables: " +
22.                      e.getMessage() );
23.}
24.finally {
25.   return retList;
26.}
27.
28.}
```

The DBInfoGUI Application: The getIndices Method

The `getIndices` method retrieves a list of indices from the database. This method requires a table name. Since we want to list all of the tables in the database, an `ArrayList` of all the tables is passed into the method on line 1.

The method then creates a string to hold the table name, which is retrieved from the `tables ArrayList` on line 3, and an `ArrayList` to hold the results accumulated in the method.

The tables `ArrayList` has been populated by the `getTables` method and contains pairs of entries. These entries include a *label* and a *value entry*, where the label indicates what the value entry contains (for example, `Table Name` is the label, and the value entry is `movies`).

The `position` variable created on line 6 is used to control the `while` loop on line 12. Within the body of the loop, the table name is extracted from the tables `ArrayList` on line 14 and placed in the `tableName` string, which is in turn used as a parameter to the `getIndexInfo` method call on line 21 (passed on line 24).

The process of incrementing the position variable must take into account the nature of the entries in the `ArrayList`. By incrementing the position counter four positions on line 19, the various other information in the tables `ArrayList` (which is not of interest to us here) is bypassed.

The `DatabaseMetaData` `getIndexInfo` method call on line 21 returns a `ResultSet` containing the information on indices in the database. This `ResultSet` must be iterated through and results stored in the `retList` `ArrayList` to be returned by the method. This is done on lines 31 through 38. The populated `ArrayList` is returned in the `finally` block on line 48. The code for this method follows:

The getIndices Method

```
1.public Collection getIndices( ArrayList tables ) {
2.
3.String tableName    = null;
4.ArrayList retList   = new ArrayList();
5.
6.int position = 1;       // start at 1 and skip the first label
7.int size      = tables.size();
8.
9.try {
10.
11.// for each table
12.while ( position < size ) {
13.
14.    tableName = (String) tables.get( position );
15.
16.    //
17.    // move past the table type info and labels
18.    //
19.    position += 4;
20.
21.    ResultSet rs = dbMetaData.getIndexInfo(
22.                            null,      // catalog
23.                            null,      // schema
24.                      tableName, // table name pattern
25.                      false,     // unique index
26.                        true);     // approximate stats
27.        //
28.        // add each index info entry in the ResultSet to
29.        // our return list
30.        //
31.      while ( rs.next() ) {
32.            retList.add( "Table Name" );
33.            retList.add( rs.getString( "TABLE_NAME" ));
34.            retList.add( "Index Name" );
35.            retList.add( rs.getString( "INDEX_NAME" ));
```

```
36.                retList.add( "Column Name" );
37.                retList.add( rs.getString( "COLUMN_NAME" ));
38.     }
39.
40.}
41.
42.}
43.catch (SQLException e) {
44.      System.out.println("SQLException in getIndices: " +
45.                        e.getMessage() );
46.}
47.finally {
48.    return retList;
49.}
50.
51.}
```

The DBInfoGUI Application: The getGeneralInfo Method

The getGeneralInfo method performs the task of retrieving the general database information using the DatabaseMetaData object, storing the information in an ArrayList collection object, and returning the object reference. This method begins by creating the ArrayList to return on line 3. Then, on lines 8 through 58, calls are made to various DatabaseMetaData methods to retrieve what is considered to be general information about the database (the product name, the product version, the maximum number of open statements, etc.).

Information is stored in the ArrayList in pairs. For example, on line 8, the *label* for the information is added to the retList ArrayList (Database Product). Then, on line 9, the corresponding information for the preceding label is inserted into the list. In this case, the value is the output of the DatabaseMetaData getDatabaseProductName method, which returns a string that is inserted into the retList ArrayList.

Some of the DatabaseMetaData methods return Java primitive data types (integer, boolean). These primitive data types cannot be added directly to the ArrayList, since the ArrayList add method requires an Object reference argument. For this reason, the primitive data types are either wrapped with Java language wrapper classes (as is done with the integers returned on lines 21 and 24) and then added to the ArrayList or the primitive data type is mapped to a meaningful string and then added, as is done with the boolean returned using the Java tertiary operator on lines 45 and 52.

When all the methods have been executed, the retList ArrayList is returned in the finally block on line 65.

The getGeneralInfo Method

```
1.public Collection getGeneralInfo() {
2.
3.ArrayList retList = new ArrayList();
4.
5.try {
6.
7.// info goes into the set in pairs - label-value
8.retList.add( "Database Product" );
9.retList.add( dbMetaData.getDatabaseProductName() );
10.
11.retList.add( "Database Version" );
12.retList.add( dbMetaData.getDatabaseProductVersion() );
13.
14.retList.add( "JDBC Driver" );
15.retList.add( dbMetaData.getDriverVersion() );
16.
17.retList.add( "DB URL" );
18.retList.add( dbMetaData.getURL() );
19.
20.retList.add( "Maximum Open Statements" );
21.retList.add( new Integer( dbMetaData.getMaxStatements())  );
22.
23.retList.add( "Maximum Open Connections" );
24.retList.add( new Integer( dbMetaData.getMaxConnections()) );
25.
26.retList.add( "Maximum Procedure Name Length" );
27.retList.add( new Integer( dbMetaData.getMaxProcedureNameLength())  );
28.
29.retList.add( "Maximum Schema Name Length" );
30.retList.add( new Integer( dbMetaData.getMaxSchemaNameLength()) );
31.
32.retList.add( "Maximum Statement Length" );
33.retList.add( new Integer( dbMetaData.getMaxStatementLength()) );
34.
35.retList.add( "Maximum Table Name Length" );
36.retList.add( new Integer( dbMetaData.getMaxTableNameLength()) );
37.
38.retList.add( "Maximum User Name Length" );
39.retList.add( new Integer( dbMetaData.getMaxUserNameLength()) );
40.
41.retList.add( "Maximum Cursor Name Length" );
42.retList.add( new Integer( dbMetaData.getMaxCursorNameLength()) );
43.
44.retList.add( "Is a Read Only Database" );
45.retList.add( (dbMetaData.isReadOnly() ? "TRUE" : "FALSE") );
46.
47.retList.add( "Connected User Name" );
48.retList.add( dbMetaData.getUserName() );
49.
50.retList.add( "Supports Non-Null Columns" );
```

```
51.retList.add(
52.      (dbMetaData.supportsNonNullableColumns() ? "TRUE" : "FALSE") );
53.
54.retList.add( "Uses Local Files" );
55.retList.add( (dbMetaData.usesLocalFiles() ? "TRUE" : "FALSE") );
56.
57.retList.add( "Uses Local Files Per Table" );
58.retList.add( (dbMetaData.usesLocalFilePerTable() ? "TRUE" : "FALSE") );
59.
60.}
61.catch (SQLException e) {
62.      System.out.println( "SQLException in getGeneralInfo: " + e.getMessage() );
63.}
64.finally {
65.      return retList;
66.}
67.
68.
69.}
```

The DBInfoGUI Application:
The parseFunctionsFromString Method

The parseFunctionsFromString method takes a comma-delimited string and maps the contents into an ArrayList object. The contents of the comma-delimited string are assumed to be a list of one of the database functions supported by JDBC. These comma-delimited lists are returned by the getNumFunctions, getStrFunctions, getSysFunctions, and getSQLSyntax, as defined in the DatabaseMetaData interface.

In order to map or convert the information in the comma-separated list, the Java StringTokenizer class is used to parse the contents of the string. The method begins by creating an ArrayList to process the results, and then on lines 5, 6, 7, and 8, the StringTokenizer is created to process the comma-delimited string. The constructor for the StringTokenizer is passed the comma-delimited string to parse.

The StringTokenizer is created with parameters that indicate that the delimiter for the string is a comma (,) character and that the delimiter should not be returned with the token (the strings returned by parsing the comma-separated list).

One benefit of using a StringTokenizer instance is that the StringTokenizer implements the Enumeration interface, and the returned value can be used to iterate through the contents of the Enumeration. A method is available to call to determine whether or not there are more elements to extract, and a method to extract and return the element is also available.

The `hasMoreTokens` method determines whether or not there are string tokens to be extracted. If this method returns a boolean `true`, then the label for the element ("Function Name") is added to the `retList ArrayList`, and the actual value of the function name is extracted from the comma-separated list with a call to the `StringTokenizer nextToken` method and added to the `retList ArrayList`.

When the processing loop is complete, the `retList ArrayList` is returned on line 16. The listing for this method is shown next.

The parseFunctionsFromString Method

```
1.public Collection parseFunctionsFromString( String functionList ) {
2.
3.ArrayList retList = new ArrayList();
4.
5.StringTokenizer stringParser =
6.        new StringTokenizer( functionList, // String to parse
7.                        ",",            // token delimiter
8.                    false );       // don't return the token
9.
10.// parse the string into a collection
11.while ( stringParser.hasMoreTokens() ) {
12.        retList.add( "Function Name" );
13.        retList.add( stringParser.nextToken() );
14.}
15.
16.   return retList;
17.
18.}
```

The DBInfoGUI Application: The getNumFunctions Method

The `getNumFunctions` returns a `Collection` with the label/value pairs of the numeric functions available in the current database. It uses the `parseFunctionsFromString` method to parse the string and return the `ArrayList` results. The code for this method follows:

The getNumFunctions Method

```
public Collection getNumFunctions() {
Collection coll = null;

try {

    coll =  parseFunctionsFromString( dbMetaData.getNumericFunctions() );
```

```
}
catch (SQLException e) {
      System.out.println( "SQLException in getGeneralInfo: " +
                              e.getMessage() );
}
finally {
    return coll;
}


}
```

The DBInfoGUI Application: The getSysFunctions Method

The getSysFunctions method returns an ArrayList containing the system functions available in the current database. It uses the parseFunctionsFromString method to parse the string and return the ArrayList results. The code for this method follows:

The getSysFunctions Method

```
public Collection getSysFunctions() {
Collection coll = null;

try {
     coll = parseFunctionsFromString(
                   dbMetaData.getSystemFunctions() );
}
catch (SQLException e) {
   System.out.println("SQLException caught in getSysFunctions: " +
                        e.getMessage() );
}
finally {
        return coll;
}


}
```

The DBInfoGUI Application: The getStrFunctions Method

The getSysFunctions method returns an ArrayList containing the system functions available in the current database. It uses the parseFunctionsFromString method to parse the string and return the ArrayList results. The code for this method follows:

```
catch (SQLException e) {
public Collection getStrFunctions() {
Collection coll = null;
try {
    coll = parseFunctionsFromString(
                dbMetaData.getStringFunctions() );
}
catch (SQLException e) {
    System.out.println("SQLException caught in getStrFunctions: " +
                        e.getMessage() );
}
finally {
        return coll;
}

}
```

The DBInfoGUI Application: The loadPanel Method

The loadPanel method performs the job of taking the contents of an ArrayList and creating a panel to place in the GUI. (If you are not familiar with GUIs or with the Swing API, just think of the panel as a whiteboard with useful information, and we are going to take a stack of these whiteboards and make them all accessible in the same window, using tab buttons on the top of the window.)

The loadPanel method begins by creating a JPanel, a Swing API GUI panel, on line 10. The layout manager (the facility that decides which GUI components will go where) is set to the GridLayout manager. The GridLayout manager will lay out a specified grid and allow GUI components to be placed in the grid in a left-to-right fashion, from top to bottom, in the order in which they are added to the panel. This provides a fairly simple method of processing the data in our ArrayList objects and loading it into a simple grid.

The JPanel component is created on line 10. The GridLayout manager constructor is invoked with two arguments: the rows and the columns in the grid, in that order. Since the row parameter tends to be ignored, it is set to zero in this example, and the column parameter is set to two. This creates a table with two columns and however many rows we choose to add—a convenient display structure for our data, which has been loaded with pairs of elements.

An ArrayList (info) object has been passed into the method. The loop on line 12 continues processing until the number of elements (info.size()) in the ArrayList (info) have been read. For each element in the info ArrayList, a JTextField is created and passed the element for the table cell. Since the data in a text field should be a string, the toString method is called on line 14 for each object reference retrieved from the ArrayList.

If an even-numbered element is being processed from the `ArrayList`, then the element is going to be used as a label for the display and will be set with a background color that makes the text field easier to see on the display.

On line 23, the field editing is turned off, and on line 24, the `JTextField` component is added to the panel. On line 28, the panel is returned. The listing for this method is shown next.

The loadPanel Method

```
1.public JPanel loadPanel( ArrayList info ) {
2.//
3.// create a JPanel and load it with the 'info' data
4.//
5.
6.//
7.// create grid of 2 columns for the data
8.// GridLayout tends to ignore the row parameter, so we use 0
9.//
10.JPanel panel = new JPanel( new GridLayout( 0, 2 ) );
11.
12.for ( int n  = 0; n < info.size(); n++ ) {
13.
14.    JTextField field = new JTextField( info.get( n ).toString() );
15.
16.    if ( ( n % 2 ) == 0 ) {              // even numbers are labels
17.        //
18.        // set the background to make this column standout
19.        //
20.         field.setBackground( new Color( 0x70E0E0 ) );
21.    }
22.
23.    field.setEnabled( false );           // don't edit anything
24.    panel.add( field );
25.
26.}
27.
28.return panel;
29.
30.}
```

The DBInfoGUI Application: The output Method

The `output` method was created for debug purposes, but nevertheless demonstrates another alternative to processing these collections of data. The `output` method takes the collection passed into the method, along with the title for the output, and creates formatted text output. The method creates an `iterator` on line 3, and then uses the `iterator hasNext` method to control a loop. For each pass through the loop, a pair of elements will be output. When there are no more elements, the loop will be terminated. The complete code listing for this method follows:

The output Method

```
1.public void output( String title, Collection outputCollection ) {
2.
3.Iterator i = outputCollection.iterator();
4.
5.System.out.println( "*********************************" );
6.System.out.println( "<<<< " + title + ">>>>" );
7.System.out.println( "*********************************" );
8.while ( i.hasNext() ) {
9.        System.out.println( i.next() + "\t" +   // the label
10.                            i.next()  );         // the value
11.}
12.System.out.println( "*********************************" );
13.
14.}
```

The partial output from this method is as follows.

Partial Output of DBInfo output Method

```
*********************************
<<<< General Database Information>>>>
*********************************
Database Product       MySQL
Database Version       3.23.36
JDBC Driver     2.0.8
DB URL jdbc:mysql://localhost:3306/movies
Maximum Open Statements      0
Maximum Open Connections     0
Maximum Procedure Name Length 0
Maximum Schema Name Length   0
Maximum Statement Length     65531
Maximum Table Name Length    32
Maximum User Name Length     16
Maximum Cursor Name Length   64
Is a Read Only Database      FALSE
Connected User Name    art
Supports Non-Null Columns    TRUE
Uses Local Files       FALSE
Uses Local Files Per Table   FALSE
*********************************
*********************************
<<<< Database Tables>>>>
*********************************
Table Name     BLOBTEST
Table Type     TABLE
```

```
Table Name      backup_movies
Table Type      TABLE
Table Name      movie_images
Table Type      TABLE
Table Name      movies
Table Type      TABLE
Table Name      user_rentals
Table Type      TABLE
Table Name      users
Table Type      TABLE
********************************
********************************
<<<< Table Indices>>>>
********************************
Table Name      BLOBTEST
Index Name      PRIMARY
Column Name     pos
Table Name      movies
Index Name      PRIMARY
Column Name     movie_id
Table Name      user_rentals
Index Name      PRIMARY
Column Name     user_id
Table Name      user_rentals
Index Name      PRIMARY
Column Name     rental_date
Table Name      users
Index Name      PRIMARY
Column Name     user_id
********************************
********************************
<<<< Numeric Functions>>>>
********************************
Function Name   ABS
Function Name   ACOS
Function Name   ASIN
Function Name   ATAN
Function Name   ATAN2
Function Name   BIT_COUNT
Function Name   CEILING
Function Name   COS
Function Name   COT
Function Name   DEGREES
Function Name   EXP
Function Name   FLOOR
Function Name   LOG
Function Name   LOG10
Function Name   MAX
Function Name   MIN
Function Name   MOD
Function Name   PI
Function Name   POW
```

```
Function Name    POWER
Function Name    RADIANS
Function Name    RAND
Function Name    ROUND
Function Name    SIN
Function Name    SQRT
Function Name    TAN
Function Name    TRUNCATE
```

Summary

Relational databases have many similarities and many differences. While they all share in being relational databases based on the relational model for data storage, and they all use a standard version of SQL, the differences in the implementation and SQL versions are sometimes subtle—but nevertheless common. These subtle differences can mean the difference between an application working and not working.

The JDBC API was designed to allow an application to be written to be vendor-neutral. Applications could be written with one database and then easily moved with little or no code changes to another database.

Unfortunately, the variations in SQL compliance and the implementation of nonstandard features makes this difficult. The `DatabaseMetaData` interface implementation allows an application to discover the capabilities of a database and react accordingly by changing SQL syntax or performing database work in a different sequence.

This chapter provided a demonstration application: a graphical application that gathered information on database features and content and displayed the information in a Swing tabbed window.

Coming Up Next

Chapter 12 takes an even closer look at the `DatabaseMetaData interface`, examining the many methods available and discussing how these methods could be used to discern database capabilities.

DatabaseMetaData Methods

INTRODUCTION

The `ResultMetaData` class has a large number of methods, over 150 in fact. Though it is most likely that you will only ever use a handful of these, knowing that they exist and what they can provide may be helpful.

This large and sometimes unwieldy collection must be reviewed using the old adage of divide and conquer. A good, logical breakdown of these methods based on their purpose yields the following groupings.

- Driver Product and General Database Information
- Database Table Lists and General Table and Index Information
- Stored Procedure Information
- Table Column Information
- Data Type Information
- Identifier Name Support and Limitations
- Catalog and Schema Information
- Keywords, Extensions, and Functions Available

- Behavior and Support of Null Values
- Behavior and Visibility of Updates
- Transaction Behavior
- SQL Statement Syntax and Support
- ResultSet Behavior

The following sections list the methods in each group and then provide a discussion of how the methods work and where using them they might be useful.

Driver Product and Database General Information

The `DatabaseMetadata` class provides a number of methods that are best grouped as providing detailed information about the database itself. Product and general database information include such details as the database vendor, the database product version, and the system functions available in the database. These methods are listed in Table 12–1.

Methods such as `getDatabaseProductName` and `getDatabaseProductVersion` return a string that indicates the name of the database product and the version. These methods are probably some of the more commonly used methods for applications that must connect to databases from various vendors and use different product versions. It is common for these applications to be developed to work specifically with a database product/version combination. By calling these methods and matching the resulting strings, the application can quickly determine if it is connecting to a supported database, as shown in the code snippet below.

. . .

```
Connection con = dataSource.getConnection();

// get the meta data for this connection
DatabaseMetaData dmd = con.getMetaData();

 // get the database product and version
 String dbProduct = dmd.getDatabaseProductName();
 String dbVersion = dmd.getDatabaseProductVersion();

 // is this the correct product and version ?
 if ( dbProduct.equals("Oracle") ) {
     if ( dbVersion.equals("9i") )   {
         // continue processing
         . . .
     }
 }
 else {        // indicate error and exit
        System.out.println( "Invalid database product or version. Exiting ..."
);
 . . .
```

Table 12–1   *Driver Product and General Database Information*

Method	Description
String getDatabaseProductName()	Returns the name of the database product.
String getDatabaseProductVersion()	Returns the version of the database product.
int getDriverMajorVersion()	Returns an integer that is the driver's major version number.
int getDriverMinorVersion()	Returns an integer that is the driver's minor version number.
String getDriverName()	Returns a string name of the JDBC driver. (Not necessarily the fully qualified class name of the driver.).
String getDriverVersion()	Returns the version of the JDBC driver.
String getURL()	Returns a string containing the URL for the database. This will return a null reference if the driver cannot determine the URL for the database.
int getMaxStatements()	Returns an integer which represents the maximum number of active statements that can be open at one time.
int getMaxConnections()	Returns an integer representing the maximum number of connections this driver can have active with the database.
boolean isReadOnly()	Returns true if the database is in read-only mode and no updates are allowed by the current connection.
String getUserName()	Returns a string containing the current user name for the current database connection.
int getMaxStatementLength()	Returns an integer representing the maximum length of a statement in bytes. A result of zero (0) indicates the length is either unlimited or unknown.
boolean usesLocalFilePerTable()	Returns a boolean true if the database uses a local file for each table in the database.
boolean usesLocalFiles()	Returns a boolean true if the database uses the local file system to store data.
Connection getConnection()	Returns the JDBC Connection object that was used to create this metadata object.

In this code snippet, if the application determines that it is not connected to the correct database product or version, it quits running. This is a common and useful approach to managing the database compatibility problem. The application will run only with the correct product and version. By not running with other products or versions, the potential incompatibility problems, which can often be subtle and not quickly detected, are completely avoided. (This approach also avoids the need to perform additional, detailed checking of the database capabilities using the `DatabaseMetaData` class, since all compatibility is based on the database product version.)

The `getDriverMajorVersion` and `getDriverMinorVersion` methods return integers relating to the specific JDBC driver version (unlike the `getDatabaseProductVersion` method, which returns a string). The `getDriverName` method returns a string that indicates the name of the driver that has been used to obtain the connection (not the class name, just an informational name), and the `getDriverVersion` returns a string that indicates the version of the driver. These methods are used like the `getDatabaseProduct` and `getDatabaseProductVersion` methods in testing compatibility up front, in a coarse-grained fashion, rather than checking detailed database or driver capabilities.

The `getURL` method returns the database connection URL that was used to connect to the database. This could be useful for debugging purposes or for potentially creating an additional connection to the database.

A number of methods are available to detect the limitations of the database and driver. The `getMaxConnections` and `getMaxStatement` methods return an integer indicating the maximum number of `Connection` and `Statement` objects respectively that can be created with the current database/driver combination. The `isReadOnly` method returns a boolean value indicating `true` if the database is read-only; that is, no database updates are allowed on the current connection.

The `getUserName` method can be used to detect the user name for the connection. This is the name or *user identity* of the user that created the database connection, not necessarily the name of the user who created the client connection. While the user name may be significant for two-tier client-server applications, this has become less significant for multitiered applications that may have a number of users sharing the same database identity (and managing security through some other means).

The `useLocalFiles` and `usesLocalFilePerTable` methods return boolean values that essentially indicate whether or not the database is using local files. Most relational databases do not.

Database Table Lists and General Table Information

Some of the more commonly used methods in the `DatabaseMetaData` class list the tables available in a database in a non-proprietary fashion. This is useful because while almost all relational databases store information on the tables in a database, they do so in a proprietary fashion, each using a different set of database tables or catalogs to store the information. The `DatabaseMetaData` methods provide an open, generally easy to use facility for gathering this database table information. These methods are listed in Table 12–2.

Table 12–2   *Database Table Lists and General Table Information*

Method	Description
`boolean allTablesAreSelectable()`	Returns a boolean `true` if a select query can be run against all of the tables in the current database.

`ResultSet getImportedKeys(`
`String catalog,`
`String schema,`
`String table)`
	Returns a `ResultSet` list of the primary key columns (from other tables) that are referenced by a table's foreign keys, i.e., —the primary keys imported by a table.

`ResultSet getIndexInfo(`
`String catalog,`
`String schema,`
`String table,`
`boolean unique,`
`boolean approximate)`
	Returns a list of a table's indices and statistics about the indices. Accepts parameters for the catalog name to search for, the schema name to search for, and the table name to search for. Additional parameters are provided to optionally return only unique indices and approximate information (not necessarily current).

`ResultSet getPrimaryKeys(`
`String catalog,`
`String schema,`
`String table)`
	Returns a `ResultSet` which describes a table's primary key columns.

`ResultSet getTablePrivileges(`
`String catalog,`
`String schemaPattern,`
`String tableNamePattern)`
	Returns a `ResultSet` describing the access privileges for each table in the database or catalog. This method is passed parameters for catalog name, schema pattern, and table name pattern. The catalog name and schema pattern parameters can be set to null, but the table name (or pattern) must be supplied.

`ResultSet getTables(`
`String catalog,`
`String schemaPattern, String`
`tableNamePattern, String[] types)`
	Returns a `ResultSet` describing the tables in the database. Parameters are provided for the catalog, the schema, table name, and types of tables to retrieve. For the catalog parameter, a null would indicate that it is not used. A blank string for the catalog matches all. For the `SchemaPattern`, `tableNamePattern`, – null matches null names only and a blank string matches all. A null passed for the `Types` parameter matches all table types.

Table 12–2   *Database Table Lists and General Table Information (cont.)*

Method	Description
ResultSet getTableTypes()	Returns a ResultSet containing the types of tables available in the current database. Table types are returned in a string column in the ResultSet and are usually one of TABLE", "VIEW", "SYSTEM TABLE", "GLOBAL TEMPORARY", "LOCAL TEMPORARY", "ALIAS", or "SYNONYM". Table types could take on different values depending on the database connection and the JDBC driver.
ResultSet getVersionColumns(String catalog, String schema, String table)	Returns a ResultSet containing the columns in a table that are automatically updated when the row is updated.
boolean isCatalogAtStart()	Returns a boolean true if the catalog name will appear at the start of a qualified table name. If this returns false, then the catalog name will appear at the end of the table name.
int getMaxIndexLength()	Returns an integer representing the maximum length of an index in bytes.

All of these methods provide varying degrees of details about the tables in a database. Probably the most commonly used method is the getTables method, which can be passed null values to retrieve a list of all tables in the database, or it can be passed a table name pattern to return information on a single table or a group of tables with names that match that pattern. (The pattern is matched using the SQL-like regular expression matching.)

Applications that must connect to a database and then potentially create a set of tables may need to know if the tables are currently in place. This would allow the application to avoid the overhead of creating the tables and the potential issues with destroying any existing data. The application could call the getTables method with the table name patterns for the tables as follows:

```
...
//
// call getTables and scan for our production tables
//
ResultSet rs = dbMetaData.getTables(
                null,           // catalog
                null,           // schema
            "ProdTable%",   // table name pattern
```

```
                 null );        // table types to include
while ( rs.next() ) {
     if ( rs.getString( "TABLE_NAME" ).equals( "ProdTable1")) {
         // table is already there, let's use it
         ...
     }
     else {   // table is not there, let's create it
         ...
     }
...


     //
     // did we find the other production table
     //
     if ( rs.getString( "TABLE_NAME" ).equals( "ProdTable2")) {
             // table is already there, let's use it
         ...
     }
     else {   // table is not there, let's create it
         ...
     }
...
```

(Unfortunately, there are not overloaded versions of the getTables and getIndexInfo methods that leave out the parameters that are not needed, which is the more common object-oriented development approach.) The getPrimaryKeys method is useful to determine the primary keys of a table.

Most applications, however, are created by developers already aware of this information. But applications that may need to work with different versions of tables (from different versions of the application), may need to make this determination.

Stored Procedure Information

A number of methods are available to provide detailed information on the stored procedures within a database. These methods are listed in Table 12–3.

These methods are similar in signature to the methods available for gathering table information. They accept various parameters, some of which can be set to null if they do not apply to the current database. The method allProceduresAreCallable can be used to determine if all procedures in the database can be called by the current user.

The method getProcedures can be used to determine whether or not a particular procedure is available in the database. Like the getTables method, the getProcedures method can be passed a procedure name pattern to return results for a single stored procedure.

Table 12–3   *DatabaseMetaData Stored Procedure Methods*

Method	Description
`boolean allProceduresAreCallable()`	Returns a boolean `true` if all stored procedures can be called by the current user. This is effectively the list returned by `getProcedures` filtered for the procedures this user is allowed to call.

`ResultSet getProcedureColumns(`
`String catalog,`
`String schemaPattern,`
`String procedureNamePattern,`
`String columnNamePattern)`
	Returns a `ResultSet` which describes the columns for stored procedures in a catalog or database. Returns information on the stored procedure parameters and return values.

`ResultSet getProcedures(`
`String catalog,`
`String schemaPattern, String`
`procedureNamePattern)`
	Returns a `ResultSet` describing the stored procedures in a catalog or database, providing information such as the procedure name and the procedure type.

`String getProcedureTerm()`	Returns a string representing the term used for stored procedures by the database vendor.
`boolean supportsStoredProcedures()`	Returns a boolean `true` if the database supports stored procedures using the escape syntax. (Stored procedures may still be callable using `ResultSet executeQuery` with database-specific syntax.)

Table Column Information

The `DatabaseMetaData` class provides methods to gather information on the columns within a table. These methods are listed in Table 12–4.

Table 12–4   *Table Column Information Methods*

Method	Description

`ResultSet getColumnPrivileges(`
`String catalog,`
`String schema,`
`String table, String`
`columnNamePattern)`
	Returns a `ResultSet` which describes the access rights for one or more columns in a table.

`ResultSet getExportedKeys(`
`String catalog,`
`String schema,`
`String table)`
	Returns `ResultSet` that lists the foreign key columns (columns in other tables) that reference this table's primary key, i.e.,—the foreign keys exported to other tables.

| Table 12–4 | *Table Column Information Methods (cont.)* |

Method	Description

`ResultSet getColumns(`
`String catalog,`
`String schemaPattern, String`
`tableNamePattern, String`
`columnNamePattern)`
	Returns a `ResultSet` which describes the table columns available in a catalog.

`ResultSet getCrossReference(`
`String primaryCatalog, String`
`primarySchema, String primaryTable,`
`String foreignCatalog, String`
`foreignSchema, String foreignTable)`
	Returns a description of the foreign key columns in the table and how they relate to the primary key.

`boolean doesMaxRowSizeIncludeBlobs()`	Returns a boolean `true` if the maximum row size value returned by `getMaxRowSize` includes the size of any BLOBlob columns within the row.

`ResultSet getBestRowIdentifier(`
`String catalog,`
`String schema,`
`String table,`
`int scope,`
`boolean nullable)`
	Returns a `ResultSet` that identifies the optimal set of columns that uniquely identifies a row (the primary key).

`int getMaxColumnsInTable()`	Returns an integer representing the maximum number of columns that can be in a table.
`int getMaxRowSize()`	Returns an integer that represents the maximum length of a table row in bytes. If the method returns zero (0), then the maximum row length is unlimited or unknown.

These methods provide information on the columns in a table and on the relationships of those columns to other tables. Most applications will be written by developers who have this knowledge.

The process of gathering information on table columns and relationships is difficult and complex. The use of these methods is probably limited only to those applications that are to be used for database modeling or analysis of existing databases.

Data Type Information

Two methods have been grouped as being used to gather database data type information. These methods are listed in Table 12–5.

Table 12–5 *Database Data Type Information*

Method	Description
`ResultSet getTypeInfo()`	Returns a ResultSet containing information on the SQL types available in the database.
`ResultSet getUDTs( String catalog, String schemaPattern, String typeNamePattern, int[] types)`	Returns a ResultSet with the user-defined types (UDTs) available in the database. Can optionally filter on the schema and the type name or an integer array of types from java.sql.Types.

The `getTypeInfo` method returns a `ResultSet` that identifies which SQL types are available in the database. The `getUDTs` method returns a `ResultSet` that lists the UDTs in the database.

Part of the information in the row returned from the `getTypeInfo` method includes the `java.sql.Types` data type of the column and precision and scale information for decimal columns. This is information that can be used to prepare the processing of a row from the table.

Identifier Name Support and Limitations

For applications that must create identifiers in the database and may have to work with multiple databases, it may be prudent to verify the naming limitations of the database before creating database objects. The `DatabaseMetaData` class contains several methods that provide this information, as shown in Table 12–6.

Table 12–6   *Identifier Name Support and Limitations Methods*

Method	Description
`boolean storesLowerCaseIdentifiers()`	Returns a boolean `true` if the database will treat unquoted SQL identifiers (table names, column names) as case-insensitive and will store them in lower case.
`boolean storesLowerCaseQuotedIdentifiers()`	Returns a boolean `true` if the database will treat quoted SQL identifiers (table names, column names) as case-insensitive and will store them in lower case.
`boolean storesMixedCaseIdentifiers()`	Returns a boolean `true` if the database will treat unquoted SQL identifiers (table names, column names) as case-insensitive and will store them in mixed case.

Table 12-6   *Identifier Name Support and Limitations Methods (cont.)*

Method	Description
`boolean storesMixedCaseQuotedIdentifiers()`	Returns a boolean `true` if the database treats mixed-case quoted identifiers as case-insensitive and stores them in mixed case.
`int getMaxProcedureNameLength()`	Returns an integer representing the maximum length of a procedure name in bytes.
`int getMaxSchemaNameLength()`	Returns an integer which represents the maximum length of a schema name.
`int getMaxTableNameLength()`	Returns an integer representing the maximum length of a table name. A return value of zero (0) indicates the length is unlimited or cannot be determined by the JDBC driver.
`int getMaxUserNameLength()`	Returns an integer representing the maximum length of a user name. A return value of zero (0) indicates the maximum is unknown or cannot be determined.
`int getMaxCursorNameLength()`	Returns an integer representing the maximum length of a cursor name.
`boolean storesUpperCaseIdentifiers()`	Returns a boolean `true` if the database treats mixed-case unquoted identifiers as case-insensitive and stores them in upper case.
`boolean storesUpperCaseQuotedIdentifiers()`	Returns a boolean `true` if the database treats mixed-case quoted identifiers as case-sensitive and stores them in upper case.
`boolean supportsMixedCaseIdentifiers()`	Returns a boolean `true` if the database treats mixed case identifiers that are not quoted as case-sensitive and stores the identifiers in mixed case. A JDBC-compliant driver will always return false.
`boolean supportsMixedCaseQuotedIdentifiers()`	Returns a boolean `true` if quoted identifiers are treated as case-sensitive and stored in mixed case. A JDBC-compliant driver should always return true.
`int getMaxColumnNameLength()`	Returns an integer representing the maximum length of a column name.

The maximum length of name identifiers varies from database to database. Applications that must work with multiple databases need to know the limitations of the current database and adjust their behavior accordingly.

Methods such as `getMaxProcedureNameLength`, `getMaxStatement Length`, and others allow the naming limitations of the database to be examined. These methods return an integer value indicating the length in characters.

Catalog and Schema Information

A number of databases support catalogs and schemas, further delineation of the data stored in the database. For these databases, a set of `DatabaseMetaData` methods are available to gather information about the catalogs and schemas available. These methods are listed in Table 12–7.

Keywords, Extensions, and Functions Available

For those applications that must connect to different databases and different versions of the same database, the `DatabaseMetaData` class has some methods that are useful in determining specifically what SQL functionality is supported in the database. Most databases also provide a number of useful string, numeric, and

Table 12–7   *Catalog and Schema Information Methods*

Method	Description
ResultSet getCatalogs()	Returns a ResultSet with the names of the catalogs available in this database.
String getCatalogSeparator()	Returns the string used as a separator between the catalog and the table name.
String getCatalogTerm()	Returns a string for the term used by the vendor for the database catalog.
ResultSet getSchemas()	Returns a ResultSet with the names of the schemas available in the database.
String getSchemaTerm()	Returns a string which represents the term used for database schema by the database vendor or provider.
boolean supportsSchemasInDataManipulation()	Returns a boolean true if the schema name can be used in data manipulation statements.
boolean supportsSchemasInIndexDefinitions()	Returns a boolean true if the schema name can be used in an index create statement.
boolean supportsSchemasInPrivilegeDefinitions()	Returns a boolean true if the schema name can be used in a statement granting access privileges to users.
boolean supportsSchemasInProcedureCalls()	Returns a boolean true if the schema name can be used in a stored procedure call.
boolean supportsSchemasInTableDefinitions()	Returns a boolean true if the schema name can be used in a table definition statement.

system functions that are above and beyond what the SQL standards define. The `DatabaseMetaData` class also provides methods to discover which of these functions are available. The methods that provide this information are listed in Table 12–8.

Table 12–8 *Keywords, Extensions, and Functions Available Methods*

Method	Description
`String getNumericFunctions()`	Returns a string containing a comma-separated list of the math functions available in the database.
`String getSQLKeywords()`	Returns a string that is a comma-separated list of SQL keywords used in the database. These are keywords exclusive of ANSI SQL92 keywords.
`String getStringFunctions()`	Returns a string containing a comma-separated list of string functions available in the database.
`String getSystemFunctions()`	Returns a string containing a comma-separated list of system functions available in the database.
`String getTimeDateFunctions()`	Returns a string with a comma-separated list of time and date functions in the database.

Being able to determine which functions are available can have a practical benefit of making code more concise and durable. But just knowing that the function is available does not guarantee that it can be used. Testing must be done with all potential databases to determine the correct order of parameters and the number and type of return values to be assured that the call will succeed at runtime. The following code snippet provides an example of optionally using the modulo (MOD) function in a query (if the MOD function is available).

```
...

//
// select sales that occurred on odd numbered days
// will use modulo function (MOD) if available
//
if ( dbMetaData.getNumericFunctions().indexOf( "MOD" ) >= 0 )  {
    query = "select * " +
                " from sales "  +
                " where mod( weekday, 2 ) > 0 ";
}
else {
```

```
//
// re-state query
//
query = "select * " +
             " from sales "   +
             " where weekday = 1 or weekday = 3 " +
             " or weekday = 5 or weekday = 7";
}
...
```

This code will use the MOD function, if it is available, under the assumption that it provides a more concise and potentially faster running query than the alternative.

Behavior and Support of Null Values

The null data value implies the absence of data. It is not to be confused with 0, which is a valid numeric value, or a blank character, which is a valid character value, but instead implies an absence of value, a *null set*.

Database support for null values is a requirement of ANSI SQL compatibility, so virtually all relational databases support this. While the support for a null data value is common, the behavior of these data values in database operations can vary. The following methods in the DatabaseMetaData class can be used to reveal the behavior of nulls.

Table 12–9   *Behavior of Null Values Methods*

Method	Description
boolean nullPlusNonNullIsNull()	Returns true if a null value plus any other value will return a null. For SQL-92 support, a JDBC driver should always return true.
boolean nullsAreSortedAtEnd()	Returns a boolean value of true if nulls are stored at the end of a sorted list.
boolean nullsAreSortedAtStart()	Returns a boolean value of true if nulls are stored at the start of a sorted list.
boolean nullsAreSortedHigh()	Returns a boolean true if nulls are sorted high in the result set order.
boolean nullsAreSortedLow()	Returns a boolean true if nulls are sorted low in the result set order .
boolean supportsNonNullableColumns()	Returns a boolean true if the database supports the creation of columns that cannot be set to a null value. A JDBC-compliant driver will always return true.

Technically speaking, a null plus any other data value is a null. While this may seem obvious when stated, this can lead to unlikely results when running database queries. Consider a table that contains a unit column and a unit price column, as follows:

Column	Data Type	Description
stock_number	integer	stock number
units	integer	number of units on hand
unit_price	decimal(5,2)	unit price of stock item

Consider that this hypothetical stock table contained the following values:

Rows	Stock_number	units	unit_price
1	1001	10	10.22
2	1002	20	20.33
3	1003	null	20.33

If the following query were run against this table, the results might not be what was expected.

```
select *
from stock
where units*unit_price > 100;
```

The results of running this query against a database where the nullPlusNonNullIsNull returns a boolean true would be that row 3 would not be returned, since the units * unit_price calculation would return null. Knowing that this type of behavior exists and preparing for it can help avoid problems. (Scanning a database table for any unexpected null values is one solution, and writing a query that filters or converts these values before performing the calculation is another.)

Behavior and Visibility of Updates

With the addition of updatable cursors in JDBC 2.0, the issue of update visibility becomes even more important to the users of JDBC. Updates by the JDBC database user and by other users are often important issues that must be managed by an application. Understanding how the database handles updates is central to managing this issue. The `DatabaseMetaData` class provides the methods listed in Table 12–10 to determine the capabilities of the underlying database.

Table 12–10   *Behavior and Visibility of Updates*

Method	Description
`boolean deletesAreDetected(int type)`	Returns a boolean `true` if deletes can be detected by the JDBC driver. If `true`, then the `ResultSet` `rowDeleted` method can be used to detect deletes.
`boolean othersDeletesAreVisible(int type)`	Returns a boolean `true` if delete operations performed by others are visible to the current user on the current connection. The type parameter is one of `ResultSet.TYPE_FORWARD_ONLY`, `ResultSet.TYPE_SCROLL_INSENSITIVE`, `ResultSet.TYPE_SCROLL_SENSITIVE`.
`boolean othersInsertsAreVisible(int type)`	Returns a boolean `true` if insert operations by others are visible by the current user on the current connection.
`boolean othersUpdatesAreVisible(int type)`	Returns a boolean `true` if update operations (SQL 'update') by other users are visible by the current user on the current connection. The type parameter is one of `ResultSet.TYPE_FORWARD_ONLY`, `ResultSet.TYPE_SCROLL_INSENSITIVE`, `ResultSet.TYPE_SCROLL_SENSITIVE`.
`boolean ownDeletesAreVisible(int type)`	Returns a boolean `true` if the delete operations by other users (SQL 'delete') are visible by the current user on the current connection. The type parameter is one of `ResultSet.TYPE_FORWARD_ONLY`, `ResultSet.TYPE_SCROLL_INSENSITIVE`, `ResultSet.TYPE_SCROLL_SENSITIVE`.
`boolean ownInsertsAreVisible(int type)`	Returns a boolean `true` if the insert operations by this user are visible by the current user on the current database connection. The type parameter is one of `ResultSet.TYPE_FORWARD_ONLY`, `ResultSet.TYPE_SCROLL_INSENSITIVE`, `ResultSet.TYPE_SCROLL_SENSITIVE`.

Table 12–10	*Behavior and Visibility of Updates (cont.)*

Method	Description
`boolean ownUpdatesAreVisible(int type)`	Returns a boolean `true` if the update operations by this user are visible by the current user on the current database connection. The type parameter is one of `ResultSet.TYPE_FORWARD_ONLY`, `ResultSet.TYPE_SCROLL_INSENSITIVE`, `ResultSet.TYPE_SCROLL_SENSITIVE`.
`boolean insertsAreDetected(int type)`	Returns a boolean value indicating whether or not a row insert can be detected by the database driver. If this returns true, then the `ResultSet` `rowInserted` can be called to determine if a row has been inserted for a `ResultSet`. The type parameter is one of `ResultSet.TYPE_FORWARD_ONLY`, `ResultSet.TYPE_SCROLL_INSENSITIVE`, `ResultSet.TYPE_SCROLL_SENSITIVE`.
`boolean updatesAreDetected(int type)`	Returns a boolean `true` if the database update can be detected using the `ResultSet` `rowUpdated` method. The type parameter is one of `ResultSet.TYPE_FORWARD_ONLY`, `ResultSet.TYPE_SCROLL_INSENSITIVE`, `ResultSet.TYPE_SCROLL_SENSITIVE`.

Any application that must connection to multiple databases should understand the capabilities of the underlying database either through thorough testing during the development process, if the database connections are to a consistent set of known databases, or by calling one of these methods to determine the database behavior. For instance, to determine whether or not updates can be detected by an updatable `ResultSet`, the approach shown in the following code snippet could be used.

```
...
ResultSet rs = stmt.executeQuery();

if ( dbMetaData.updatesAreDetected( ResultSet.TYPE_SCROLL_SENSITIVE ) )  {

   // the row has *not* been updated, so we will apply our changes
   if ( !(rs.rowUpdated()) ) {
      rs.updateRow();
   }
   else {  // need to refresh the row and check for changes
...
```

In this example, the `DatabaseMetaData updatesAreDetected` method is called and passed a parameter of `ResultSet.TYPE_SCROLL_SENSITIVE`. This call will determine whether or not the scroll cursor (random positioning) `ResultSet`, which is sensitive to database updates, is supported with the current database. If the result of this call is `true`, then updates are visible and the `ResultSet rowUpdated` call can be made. The `rowUpdated` call should return `false`, indicating that the row has not been updated and the `ResultSet updateRow` call can be made without any concurrency issues intruding. If the `rowUpdated` call returns `true`, then the row has been updated (by this user or another user) and that contingency has to be managed, either by refreshing the row and checking for changes or by simply allowing this update to overwrite the update that occurred previously.

Transaction Behavior

While most databases support transactions, the ability to group multiple SQL `update` statements together conceptually as a single statement, there are differences in the way transactions are supported and in how transactional activity affects API objects (`Statement`, `ResultSet`). The `DatabaseMetaData` class provides a number of methods that can be used to discern transaction behavior. These methods are listed in Table 12–11.

Table 12–11   *ResultSetMetaData Transaction Behavior Methods*

Method	Description
`boolean dataDefinitionCausesTransactionCommit()`	Returns `true` if a SQL dData dDefinition Language statement (DDL) statement causes a transaction to commit. (Examples of DDL statements are `create table`, and `create view`.)
`boolean dataDefinitionIgnoredInTransactions()`	Returns a boolean `true` if the DDL statements within a transaction will not be rolled back.
`int getDefaultTransactionIsolation()`	Returns the default transaction isolation level for the database connection.
`boolean supportsDataDefinitionAndDataManipulation Transactions()`	Returns a boolean `true` if both dData mManipulation Language statements (DML) statements and data definitionDDL statements (DDL) are included in transactions.
`boolean supportsDataManipulationTransactions Only()`	Returns a boolean `true` if only DML statements are included in transactions.

Table 12–11	*ResultSetMetaData Transaction Behavior Methods (cont.)*

Method	Description
`boolean supportsOpenCursorsAcrossCommit()`	Returns a boolean `true` if the database supports cursors (`ResultSet`) remaining open after transactional commit has taken place. If this method returns `false`, the developer should not count on this behavior.
`boolean supportsOpenCursorsAcrossRollback()`	Returns a boolean `true` if the database supports cursors (and their `ResultSet` objects) remaining open after transaction rollback operations.
`boolean supportsOpenStatementsAcrossCommit()`	Returns a boolean `true` if the database supports `Statement` objects remaining open after a transaction commit has taken place.
`boolean supportsOpenStatementsAcrossRollback( )`	Returns a boolean `true` if the database supports `Statement` objects remaining open after a transaction rollback has been executed.
`boolean supportsMultipleTransactions()`	Returns a boolean `true` if the database and JDBC driver supports having multiple transactions on different connections open at the same time.
`boolean supportsTransactionIsolationLevel(int level)`	Returns a boolean `true` if the database supports the specified transaction isolation level. The isolation level is specified using an integer argument that is one of the isolation levels identified in the `ResultSet` class.
`boolean supportsTransactions()`	Returns a boolean `true` if the database supports transactions.

Understanding the transactional capabilities of the database and the JDBC driver are an important part of using JDBC effectively. It is not uncommon for a moderately complex application to perform a series of updates, perform a database commit, and then attempt to traverse a cursor using a `ResultSet`. Depending on how the JDBC driver and the database manage transactions, these actions may or may not succeed. The following code snippet illustrates.

```
...
    Connection con;
    Statement stmt;
...


//
// can our driver manage this ?
//
if ( dbinfo.dbMetaData.supportsOpenCursorsAcrossCommit() ) {
```

```
//
// auto-commit is off - transactions are on
// effective begin work
//
con.setAutoCommit( false );
ResultSet rs = stmt.executeQuery("select * from movies");


stmt.executeUpdate( "update movies set special_promotion = 5 " +
                    " where movie_id in (901,902,903) ");
stmt.executeUpdate( "update movie_status set status_code = 20 " +
                    " where movie_id in (901,902,903) " );

//
// commit work
//
con.commit();

//
// if cursors are closed after commit,
// then using this ResultSet would fail
//
while ( rs.next() )
      System.out.println(
         "movie_id: " + rs1.getString( "movie_id" ) +
         " - movie_name: " + rs1.getString( "movie_name" ) );
}
...
```

In the code above, if the database supports maintaining cursors across commits, then the JDBC calls can be executed as shown within the body of the if statement. What is of primary concern here is the sequence of the operations. In this example, the transaction begins, then the query statement is executed and returns a ResultSet with an underlying cursor, so at this point a cursor is open. Two update statements are then executed against separate tables: the movie table and the movie_status table. Theoretically, these are updates that must succeed or fail together for the database to maintain a consistent state. Then, when the updates have completed, the transaction is committed to the database. On the next line of the example, the ResultSet is used to begin reading through the rows of the movie table. Even though a transaction commit has occurred on the previous line, the ResultSet can still be used, since the database and the JDBC driver allow cursors (the ResultSet) to remain open across commits.

If, however, the JDBC driver and the database cannot support this type of operation, then the database activity would have to be coded differently, performing the database commit, and then executing the select query to create the ResultSet, as shown in the following.

```
...
//
//   if driver can't handle open cursors across commit operations
//   we process differently
//
if ( !(dbinfo.dbMetaData.supportsOpenCursorsAcrossCommit()) ) {


        //
        // auto-commit is off - transactions are on
        // effective begin work
        //
        con.setAutoCommit( false );



        stmt.executeUpdate( "update movies set special_promotion = 5 " +
                            " where movie_id in (901,902,903) ");
        stmt.executeUpdate( "update movie_status set status_code = 20 " +
                            " where movie_id in (901,902,903) " );

        //
        // commit work
        //
        con.commit();

        //
        // ** now open cursor **
        //
        ResultSet rs = stmt.executeQuery("select * from movies");
        while ( rs.next() )
              System.out.println(
                 "movie_id: " + rs1.getString( "movie_id" ) +
                 " - movie_name: " + rs1.getString( "movie_name" ) );
}
...
```

Some JDBC drivers and their underlying databases do not support open cursors across rollback operations. The supportsOpenCursorsAcrossRollback method returns a boolean true if the driver and database do support this type of operation; otherwise, it returns a value of false.

Some JDBC drivers will close statement objects when a commit is executed. If the driver supports keeping the Statement object open after a commit, then the supportsOpenStatementsAcrossCommit method will return true; if not, then the method will return a boolean false. Similar methods test for the ability to maintain the Statement objects across rollback operations.

Not all databases and JDBC drivers will support multiple transactions across the same connection. The supportsMultipleTransactions method will return a boolean true if the driver does support multiple transactions on the connection; otherwise, a false value is returned.

The supportsTransactions method returns a boolean true if the database and driver support transactions at all; this is a method that generally returns true, but is not required for JDBC compliance. In fact, if transactions are not supported, then the Connection commit method fails quietly without throwing an exception.

SQL Statement Syntax and Support

The specifics of SQL syntax and limitations are usually discovered in sometimes excruciating detail during the development process. So to a large number of developers, these DatabaseMetaData methods that provide information on SQL syntax and support may never be needed. But as stated previously, there are applications that must connect to a number of different databases, and developers for these applications must therefore write code that can react to these subtle differences and limitations in SQL support. For these developers these methods are important. These DatabaseMetaData methods are listed in Table 12–12.

Table 12–12   *SQL Statement Syntax and Support*

Method	Description
String getExtraNameCharacters()	Returns a string with the characters that can be used in identifier names without being quoted.
String getSearchStringEscape()	Returns the string used in the database to escape wildcard characters.
String getIdentifierQuoteString()	Returns the string used to quote SQL identifiers. Will return a blank if identifier quoting isn't supported.
int getMaxBinaryLiteralLength()	Returns an integer value that represents the maximum length of a literal character string. These are hexadecimal representations of binary characters.
int getMaxCatalogNameLength()	Returns an integer representing the maximum length of a catalog name.
int getMaxCharLiteralLength()	Returns an integer representing the maximum length of a literal character string in an SQL statement.
int getMaxColumnsInGroupBy()	Returns an integer representing the maximum number of columns allowed in a 'group by' clause in a 'select' statement.
int getMaxColumnsInIndex()	Returns an integer representing the maximum number of columns allowed in an index.

Table 12–12 *SQL Statement Syntax and Support (cont.)*

Method	Description
`int getMaxColumnsInOrderBy()`	Returns an integer representing the maximum number of columns in an `'order by'` clause in an SQL `'select'` statement.
`int getMaxColumnsInSelect()`	Returns an integer representing the maximum number of columns allowed in a `'select'` statement list.
`int getMaxTablesInSelect()`	Returns an integer representing the number maximum number of tables that can be listed in a `'select'` statement. A return value of zero (0) indicates the number is unknown or cannot be determined.
`boolean supportsColumnAliasing()`	Returns a boolean `true` if column aliasing is allowed in a `'select'` statement. A JDBC -compliant driver should always return `true`.
`boolean supportsConvert()`	Returns a boolean `true` if the database supports the `'convert'` function used to convert between SQL types.
`boolean supportsConvert(int fromType, int toType)`	Returns a boolean `true` if the database supports conversion between the types specified in the argument list. Integer types are from `java.sql.Types`.
`boolean supportsCoreSQLGrammar()`	Returns a boolean `true` if the ODBC core SQL grammar is supported.
`Boolean supportsCorrelatedSubqueries()`	Returns a boolean `true` if the database supports correlated subqueries in SQL `'select'` statements. A JDBC- compliant driver should always return `true`.
`boolean supportsANSI92EntryLevelSQL()`	Returns a boolean `true` if the ANSI 92 Entry Level SQL grammar is supported.
`boolean supportsANSI92FullSQL()`	Returns a boolean `true` if the ANSI 92 full SQL grammar is supported.
`boolean supportsANSI92IntermediateSQL()`	Returns a boolean `true` if the ANSI 92 intermediate SQL grammar is supported.
`boolean supportsBatchUpdates()`	Returns a boolean `true` if batch updates are supported by the JDBC driver.
`boolean supportsCatalogsInDataManipulation()`	Returns a boolean `true` if the catalog name can be used in a data manipulationDML statement. (DML).
`boolean supportsCatalogsInIndexDefinitions()`	Returns a boolean `true` if the catalog name can be used in an index create statement.
`boolean supportsCatalogsInPrivilegeDefinitions()`	Returns a boolean `true` if the catalog name can be used in a privilege statement.

Table 12–12   *SQL Statement Syntax and Support (cont.)*

Method	Description
boolean supportsCatalogsInProcedureCalls()	Returns a boolean true if the catalog name can be used in stored procedure calls.
boolean supportsCatalogsInTableDefinitions()	Returns a boolean true if t the catalog name can be used in a 'create table' or 'alter table' statement.
boolean supportsDifferentTableCorrelationNames()	Returns a boolean true if the database supports correlated query names but requires them to be named differently than regular database tables.
boolean supportsExpressionsInOrderBy()	Returns a boolean true if the database supports expressions in SQL 'select' statement 'order by' lists.
boolean supportsExtendedSQLGrammar()	Returns a boolean true if the database supports the ODBC Extended SQL grammar.
boolean supportsFullOuterJoins()	Returns a boolean true if the database supports full outer joins.
boolean supportsGroupBy()	Returns a boolean true if the database supports the SQL 'select' statement 'group by' clause.
boolean supportsGroupByBeyondSelect()	Returns a boolean true if the database supports the SQL 'select' statement 'group by' clause with columns not listed in the select.
boolean supportsGroupByUnrelated()	Returns a boolean true if the database supports a SQL 'select' statement 'group by' clause with columns that are not in the 'select' statement list.
boolean supportsIntegrityEnhancementFacility()	Returns a boolean true if the database supports the SQL Integrity enhancement.
boolean supportsLikeEscapeClause()	Returns a boolean true if the database supports the SQL 'select' statement 'like' escape clause. A JDBC- compliant driver should always return true.
boolean supportsLimitedOuterJoins()	Returns a boolean true if the database provides only limited outer join support. (If the supportsFullOuterJoins method returns true, this method should also return true.)
boolean supportsMinimumSQLGrammar()	Returns a boolean true if the minimum SQL grammar is supported. All JDBC- compliant drivers should return true.

Table 12–12   *SQL Statement Syntax and Support (cont.)*

Method	Description
`boolean supportsOrderByUnrelated()`	Returns a boolean `true` if the SQL `'select'` statement `'order by'` clause can use columns that are not in the `'select'` list.
`boolean supportsOuterJoins()`	Returns a boolean `true` if the database supports outer joins in the SQL `'select'` statement.
`boolean supportsSelectForUpdate()`	Returns a boolean `true` if the database supports a `'select'` statement with a `'for update'` clause.
`boolean supportsSubqueriesInExists()`	Returns a boolean `true` if the database supports subqueries in SQL `'select'` statement `'exist'` clauses. A JDBC- compliant driver should always return `true`.
`boolean supportsSubqueriesInIns()`	Returns a boolean `true` if the database supports subqueries in SQL `'select'` statement `'in'` clauses. A JDBC- compliant driver should always return `true`.
`boolean supportsSubqueriesInQuantifieds()`	Returns a boolean `true` if the database supports subqueries in quantified expression. A JDBC -compliant driver should always return `true`.
`boolean supportsTableCorrelationNames()`	Returns a boolean `true` if the database supports table correlation names in SQL `'select'` statement correlated subqueries. A JDBC- compliant driver should always return `true`.
`boolean supportsSubqueriesInComparisons()`	Returns a boolean `true` if the database supports subqueries in a comparison expression. A JDBC - compliant driver should always return `true`.
`boolean supportsUnion()`	Returns a boolean `true` if the database supports the SQL `'select'` statement `'union'` clause.
`boolean supportsUnionAll()`	Returns a boolean `true` if the database supports the SQL `select` statement `union all` clause.
`boolean supportsAlterTableWithAddColumn()`	Returns a boolean indicating whether or not the `alter table` statement supports an `add column` clause.
`boolean supportsAlterTableWithDropColumn()`	Returns a boolean `true` if the `alter table` statement supports a `drop column` clause.

Methods such as `getSearchStringEscape` and `getIdentifierQuote String` return characters that reveal important information about how to construct queries. In practice, these characters don't vary much from database to database.

A number of methods are available to determine some of the limits the database places on SQL processing. The `getMaxCharLiteral` and `getMaxBinaryLiteral` methods determine just how large certain literals can be in an SQL expression, a number generally on the order of several thousand to over a million characters, probably larger than would be practical to manage.

A series of methods provide information on the maximum number of columns that can be used in SQL statements. The `getMaxColumnsInGroupBy`, `getMaxColumnsInOrderBy` indicate the maximum number of columns that can be placed in their respective SQL `select` statement clauses. These limitations can be worth checking, since in some databases they may come short of what is needed (mySQL places the limit at 16).

The `getMaxTablesInSelect` method indicates the maximum number of tables that can be placed in a `select` statement. In some complex databases, large queries can join across ten or more tables. This method can indicate whether or not such a query will succeed.

The remainder of the methods in this group provide a boolean result indicating whether or not a particular feature is supported. These methods use the naming syntax as follows:

```
supports<feature_name>
```

The ANSI-92 specification indicates level of compliance: Entry Level, Intermediate, and Full. Most popular databases vendors comply.

It is worth noting that in this group are the methods that indicate the level of SQL support: `supportsANSI92EntryLevelSQL`, `supportsANSI92FullSQL`, and `supportsANSI92IntermediateSQL`. For applications that are coded to use only ANSI-level functionality (which may be a good direction to take if a large number of databases are going to be used), these may be important methods.

Other important SQL features that can be revealed using these methods are column aliasing (`DatabaseMetaData supportsColumnAliasing`), the ability to create alias names for columns, as shown below.

```
select stock_num,
       ( unit_price * units ) extended_price,
       units
from stock
```

In this query, the `unit_price * units` expression is given the alias name of `extended_price`. If this were not done, then the database would assign a default name to the expression pseudo-column that would make it more difficult to use the column. Using a column alias, the column can be retrieved using the name with a `ResultSet getXXXX` method using the column name of `extended_price`.

Database *outer joins* are now an important and widely supported feature of relational databases. They allow the rows from joined tables to be returned even though related rows joined by primary key–foreign key relationships may not exist in all joined tables (thus the term outer join). There are various levels of joins and, unfortunately, inconsistent syntax across databases. Fortunately, JDBC supports escape processing, a common syntax for accessing these database features.

The `DatabaseMetaData supportsOuterJoins` method can be used to indicate whether or not the query feature is even supported (it usually is), and the `supportsFullOuter` joins can be used to indicate the level of support (indicating full outer joins are supported).

The term *correlated subqueries* applies to the ability to place queries within queries and have an internal subquery refer to tables in the external query. Once again, this is a common and widely supported feature in relational databases. The `supportsCorrelatedSubqueries` method can be used to indicate whether or not this feature is supported.

Grouping updates together in a single update query to be applied against the database can provide performance gains for large, complex updates. The `supportsBatchUpdates` method reveals whether or not this feature is supported in the currently connected database.

Union queries an alternative to expressing joins and in some cases are the better SQL syntax to express a query. The `supportsUnion` method reveals whether or not the SQL `select` statement `union` clause is supported. By default, a `union  select` will eliminate duplicate row entries; the `union  all` clause overrides that behavior and returns all rows. The `supportsUnionAll` method indicates whether or not the `union  all` clause can be used in the currently connected database.

The `select` statement group by clause allows results to be grouped or aggregated, thus providing some ability to *roll- up* or subtotal data in the database by writing a query. The `supportsGroupBy` method indicates whether or not this SQL `select` statement clause will work in the currently connected database.

ResultSet Behavior

The `ResultSet` does manage to make data selection and manipulation open and relatively nonproprietary. The `ResultSet` will consistently work the same from database to database. But there are some `ResultSet` features that can vary depending on the database and the JDBC driver. These methods are shown in Table 12–13.

Some databases allow a stored procedure to return multiple `ResultSet` objects. With JDBC, this stored procedure would be run using the `Statement`

Table 12–13   *DataBaseMetaData ResultSet Behavior Methods*

Method	Description
`boolean supportsMultipleResultSets()`	Returns a boolean `true` if the database and JDBC driver support the return from multiple `ResultSet` objects from a single `ResultSet` execute call. (Some databases allow stored procedures to return multiple result sets.)
`boolean supportsResultSetType(int type)`	Returns a boolean `true` if the database supports the specific `ResultSet` type. The `ResultSet` type parameter is one of the integer constants from the `ResultSet` interface.
`boolean supportsPositionedDelete()`	Returns a boolean `true` if the database supports positioned delete operations through the `ResultSet`.
`boolean supportsPositionedUpdate()`	Returns a boolean `true` if the database and JDBC driver support positioned update operations through the `ResultSet`.
`boolean supportsResultSetConcurrency( int type, int concurrency)`	Returns a boolean `true` if the database supports the concurrency type for a given `ResultSet` type. Two integer parameters are supplied using values provided from the `ResultSet` interface.

class `execute` method, and then the multiple `ResultSet` objects would be retrieved using the `getResultSet` method of the `Statement` class. The `supportsMultipleResultSets` method returns a boolean value indicating whether or not this capability is available with the current database and JDBC driver.

There are three types of `ResultSet` objects that can be created by the database: The `ResultSet.TYPE_FORWARD_ONLY` is a `ResultSet` that does not allow positional methods (such `absolute`, `relative`, `first`, and `last`) to be executed. The `ResultSet.TYPE_SCROLL_INSENSITIVE` `ResultSet` allows scrolling or positional methods to be executed, but is not sensitive to database changes made by other users. The `ResultSet.TYPE_SCROLL_SENSITIVE` `ResultSet` allows scrolling methods to be executed and is sensitive to database changes made by other users.

Database concurrency affects how data is shared among the users of the database. The two types of concurrency supported directly by JDBC are `ResultSet.CONCUR_READ_ONLY`, which indicates that updates will not be performed through the `ResultSet`, and `ResultSet.CONCUR_UPDATABLE`, which indicates that updates will be performed through the `ResultSet`. Indicating that updating will be done through the `ResultSet` requires additional resources in the database, since a shared locking mechanism must be used to manage concurrency. Consequently, this could slow performance over a read-only approach to retrieving the data from the database. For this reason, `CONCUR_READ_ONLY` should be used if database updates will not be performed using the `ResultSet`. The `supportsResultSetConcurrency` method can be called to determine whether or not a particular type of concurrency is available using the driver and the underlying database.

DatabaseMetaData Constants

The constants provided in the `DatabaseMetaData` class are shown in Table 12–14.

Table 12–14   *ResultSetMetaData Constants*

Constant	Description
`static int bestRowNotPseudo`	A value which indicates that the best row identifier is not a pseudo-column—it is a true column.
`static int bestRowPseudo`	A value which indicates that best row identifier is a pseudo-column.
`static int bestRowSession`	A value which indicates that the scope of the best row identifier will only be used for the remainder of the current session.
`static int bestRowTemporary`	A value which indicates that the scope of the best row identifier is temporary and will only be in effect for the current session.
`static int bestRowTransaction`	A value which indicates that the scope of the best row identifier will be for the duration of the current transaction.
`static int bestRowUnknown`	A value which indicates that the JDBC driver cannot determine whether or not the best row identifier is a pseudo-column.
`static int columnNoNulls`	A value which indicates that the column may not allow null values.
`static int columnNullable`	A value which indicates that the column will allow null values.
`static int columnNullableUnknown`	A value which indicates that the JDBC driver cannot determine whether or not the column will allow null values.

Table 12–14   *ResultSetMetaData Constants (cont.)*

Method	Description
static int importedKeyCascade	A value which indicates that the foreign key relationships may support cascading updates and deletes.
static int importedKeyInitiallyDeferred	A value which indicates that the imported key behavior of the database supports deferred key imports. (Sometimes it is useful to build a schema of multiple tables with complex primary key, –foreign key relationships and defer the activity of integrity constraints until all tables in the schema have been built and data has been loaded. These are sometimes referred to as *'deferred constraints'*.)
static int importedKeyInitiallyImmediate	A value which indicates that the imported key relationships are initially immediate and are not deferred.
static int importedKeyNoAction	A value which indicates that the imported keys for a table will not trigger any action in the database.
static int importedKeyNotDeferrable	A value which indicates that the imported keys for a table cannot be deferred and become active when the table is created.
static int importedKeyRestrict	A value that describes the update and delete rule behavior for table constraints.
static int importedKeySetDefault	A value that describes the update and delete rule behavior of the imported keys and integrity constraints for a table.
static int importedKeySetNull	A value that describes the behavior of imported keys in the database.
static int procedureColumnIn	A value which indicates that a column stores 'in' parameters. (Used for stored procedure parameter description.)
static int procedureColumnInOut	A value which indicates that a column stores 'inout' parameters. (Used for stored procedure parameter description.)
static int procedureColumnOut	A value which indicates that a column stores 'out' parameters. (Used for stored procedure parameter description.)
static int procedureColumnResult	A value which indicates that a column stores results.
static int procedureColumnReturn	A value which indicates that a column stores return values.

Table 12–14   *ResultSetMetaData Constants (cont.)*

Method	Description
`static int procedureColumnUnknown`	A value which indicates that a column stores unknown values.
`static int procedureNoNulls`	A value which indicates that null values are not allowed in the column in the stored procedure.
`static int procedureNoResult`	A value which indicates that the stored procedure does not return a value.
`static int procedureNullable`	A value which indicates that null values are allowed as parameter values.
`static int procedureNullableUnknown`	A value which indicates that the JDBC driver cannot determine whether or not the stored procedure parameter can be a null value.
`static int procedureResultUnknown`	A value which indicates that the JDBC driver cannot determine whether or not the stored procedure returns a result.
`static int procedureReturnsResult`	A value which indicates that a stored procedure does return a result.
`static short tableIndexClustered`	A value which indicates that the table has a clustered index.
`static short tableIndexHashed`	A value which indicates that the table index is using a hashing algorithm.
`static short tableIndexOther`	A value which indicates that the table index is using some other type of indexing method.
`static short tableIndexStatistic`	A value that indicates that the index uses probability rules based on past retrieval.
`static int typeNoNulls`	A value which indicates that data type does not allow null values.
`static int typeNullable`	A value which indicates that the data type does allow null values.
`static int typeNullableUnknown`	A value which indicates that the JDBC driver cannot determine whether or not the type allows null values.
`static int typePredBasic`	A value which indicates that only basic searches can be performed.
`static int typePredChar`	A value which indicates that character searches can be performed.
`static int typePredNone`	A value which indicates that the column can't be searched.
`static int typeSearchable`	A value which indicates that the data type is searchable.

Table 12–14	*ResultSetMetaData Constants (cont.)*

Constant	Description
static int versionColumnNotPseudo	A value indicating that the version information is not a pseudo-column.
static int versionColumnPseudo	A value indicating that the version column is a pseudo-column.
static int versionColumnUnknown	A value indicating that the JDBC driver cannot determine whether or not the version column is a pseudo-column.

SUMMARY

The DatabaseMetaData class allows us to discern a great deal of information about a database. While most users may not need access to this information, for those who do, there is quite a bit available. This chapter examined the DatabaseMetaData class in detail.

COMING UP NEXT

The next chapter begins a discussion of using JDBC with J2EE applications. This includes JDBC with client-server applications, servlets and Java Server Pages, and Enterprise Java Beans. These chapters will discuss various J2EE packages and demonstrate the use of Java design patterns and JDBC with the package.

Advanced Topics JDBC in Action: Introduction to JDBC Design Patterns

INTRODUCTION

The previous chapters focused on specific portions of the JDBC package. This chapter begins the study of how to use JDBC in a full-scale application. Space and clarity naturally limit the size of the application we will examine; it would be easy to become lost in 5,000 lines of Java code. Nevertheless, it is useful and instructive to examine how JDBC and database-centric applications should be written in Java.

A common and proven approach to any Java development effort is to apply what are known as *design patterns*. This chapter examines several design patterns that have been known to work well with database programming with Java.

Teaching through examples is always a good instructional technique for complex technology and we will use that approach here. To show what happens when "the rubber meets the road," we will take a look at design patterns in action.

Our first sample application will be a database *table browser* developed using the Java Swing API. This application allows the user to enter a query in a text window and then execute the query and see the results displayed in a grid format. The user can then edit the data returned from the database and then apply the updates to the database. Before we take a detailed look at that example however, we will first be sure we completely understand the design patterns that will be applied. This chapter will review Java design patterns which apply to database development and see how they drive the class design process.

USING JAVA DESIGN PATTERNS WITH JDBC

The development of J2EE applications requires a *multitiered* approach to application development. Unlike the *fat-client* approach, where a single application included presentation logic, business logic, and data access (resources) logic, the Web application takes this functionality and places it in various components across multiple tiers.

The use of multiple tiers requires a different development approach, one that takes into account the capabilities of the components that will reside on each tier and the developers who will create the components (see Figure 13–1). This is referred to as providing a *division of responsibilities* for the components of the application.

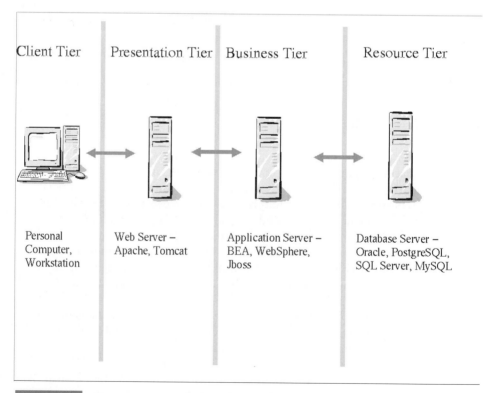

Client Tier	Presentation Tier	Business Tier	Resource Tier
Personal Computer, Workstation	Web Server – Apache, Tomcat	Application Server – BEA, WebSphere, Jboss	Database Server – Oracle, PostgreSQL, SQL Server, MySQL

Figure 13–1   *Components on multiple architectural tiers.*

As discussed previously, the distributed tiers of an multitiered application are *logical* divisions and do not necessarily relate to physically separate divisions. Though the diagram shows separate servers components that are distributed across two or three tiers could reside on a single server. The multiple tiers of our Web application are listed in Table 13–1 and described in the following sections.

Table 13–1   *Multiple Tiers of Web Application*

Tier	Description
Client	The client -side of the application. This should be a thin client with the responsibility to render the application's visual components, accept user interaction, and relay to the results of any interaction to the presentation tier.
Presentation	The responsibility of this tier is to control the presentation of the application and to relay user interactions to the business tier. For our examples, this tier is synonymous with the Web tier, comprising HTTP servers, JSP (Java Server Pages) environments, and servlet containers.
Business	Components in this tier encapsulate the business logic of the application. Development in this tier will primarily be in Java using Java Beans, though other components could be used (for instance, Enterprise Java Beans).
Resource	The resource tier represents the persistent data store for the site, most commonly a relational database. Integration tier components communicate with this tier.

Client Tier

The client tier, logically enough, represents the client application. The purpose of this tier is to render the presentation prepared by the presentation tier and to react to the input from the user. The client tier must also communicate with the presentation tier and relay the user's input to that tier.

The client tier can be a Web browser or a Swing applet. Using a thin-client architecture, the component should have a minimal footprint. The goal is to avoid the problems of fat-client architectures where deploying to the client tier was difficult and expensive.

In order to keep this client a thin client, the responsibilities of this tier must be minimized. By minimizing and focusing the responsibilities of this tier, the amount of information that must be sent to the tier will be minimized. If we determine that this tier should only render the display and respond to the user's input, then decisions on what to display and how to display it should be left to another tier.

Presentation Tier

The presentation tier is responsible for the preparation of the output to the client tier. This tier encapsulates the logic required to create the presentation. Since we are usually preparing these pages dynamically, this tier must be able to store and retain information between calls, either in memory or in a data store.

If we are using a Web browser as our client, then the protocol between the client tier and the presentation tier is HTTP. The most logical server for the presentation tier is a server that can perform the HTTP protocol. A server such as Apache can perform this function. Additionally, we would like the server to be able to manage dynamic content using a robust language such as Java. The Tomcat server provides this capability using servlets and JSP pages.

The components used most often on this tier are either Java servlets, JSPs, Java Beans, or Tag libraries. But the component could also be an applet running in a Web browser. The question we need to answer at the design stage is which type of component should be used. If we want to create components on this tier that require minimal support from Java developers, then JSP should be used to provide the bulk of the presentation logic. Java Beans and Tag libraries could be used to isolate more complex logic, leaving a JSP page that would be familiar and maintainable by most Web page developers.

By maintaining this separation of roles, staff with more specialized skill sets can maintain the presentation tier components. If these components are primarily HTML, then developers familiar with HTML can be used to maintain these pages. Java provides a number of tools that make this approach even more attractive: Tag libraries and Java Bean integration into the JSP. Using these tools, presentation tier logic can be isolated in the JSP and any additional logic can be moved to backend components like Java Beans and Tag libraries. The resulting JSP, composed primarily of HTML elements, can be maintained by an HTML developer.

Business Tier

The business tier isolates and encapsulates business logic for the application. Logic that could have resided in the presentation tier in Web components, such as JSPs or servlets, is effectively pushed off and encapsulated in this tier.

The components on this tier can be created using a variety of Java tools: Java Beans, Tag libraries, and Enterprise Java Beans (EJB) or remote components delivered using the Remote Method Invocation (RMI). (Though Java scriptlets in Web pages could be used to manage business logic, this is generally not recommended.)

Business tier components should provide for the retrieval of data from the database and the application of business rules against this data. This is where JDBC most commonly fits into this architecture. This data retrieval is accomplished by communicating with integration tier components, which will provide the data retrieval.

Resource Tier

The resource tier is represented by the data store, most commonly the relational database to be used. For our purposes, the resource tier is represented by the PostgreSQL database.

The resource tier is responsible for storing the persistent data and maintaining the consistency of the data. Communication with the resource tier is accomplished with a standard API such as JDBC for relational databases.

The Integration Tier

Some design patterns include the discussion of an *integration tier*. The job of this integration tier is to perform complex data conversions and to interact with legacy database systems. This tier is often eliminated from multitier architecture discussions, and since integration with legacy systems is not a common usage of JDBC, we will eliminate the integration tier from this discussion as well.

DESIGN PATTERNS

A *design pattern* is a reusable solution to a recurring problem in the software development process. Originally, design patterns were applied to physical building architecture, but several prescient individuals felt that these same principles could be applied to the design of object-oriented software.

Design patterns can be used to promote consistency in the software development process. They provide a common means of communicating tried and proven solutions to frequently encountered problems.

While design patterns have been applied to object-oriented software development, including the development of Java applications, for a number of years, in recent years Sun Microsystems has increased the emphasis on design patterns with Java applications, more specifically on J2EE design patterns.

Design patterns are applied to the design of the software components. For the presentation tier, the components would be either JSP pages or servlets. For the business tier, the components would be either Java Beans, Tag libraries, or EJBs. Applying a pattern to these components would involve the application of a specified pattern to the design of the components for that tier. Several of the more important patterns for these tiers are identified in the sections below.

Business Tier Patterns

The job of business tier components is to isolate and encapsulate the business logic of the application. Logic that could have resided in the presentation tier in Web components, such as JSPs or servlets, is effectively encapsulated in this tier.

For any database application, the business logic would most certainly involve retrieving and filtering data from the database and validating and performing updates of the data from the database. Several useful design patterns for this tier are as follows.

Value Object Pattern

The `ValueObject` pattern (see Figure 13–2) encapsulates the data elements of a business domain object (a business object) and provides a means of transporting that information from the business tier to the presentation tier, where it can be cached. The `BusinessObject` and `ValueObject` therefore have an association. The `ValueObject` contains members that represent the elements of the business domain object and methods to retrieve those members.

The `ValueObject` is generally intended to be immutable, meaning that it is a *read-only* object and the members should not be changed. A `ValueObject` may however contain `setXXXX` methods that allow instance members to be changed, but calling these methods alone will not change the persistent data *behind* the `ValueObject`; instead they will only change data in the `ValueObject` on the presentation tier. It is the responsibility of the `BusinessObject` to manage the persistent data store, and it is therefore the `BusinessObject` that must be called to update the persistent data store by exposing an `update` method to the presentation tier client.

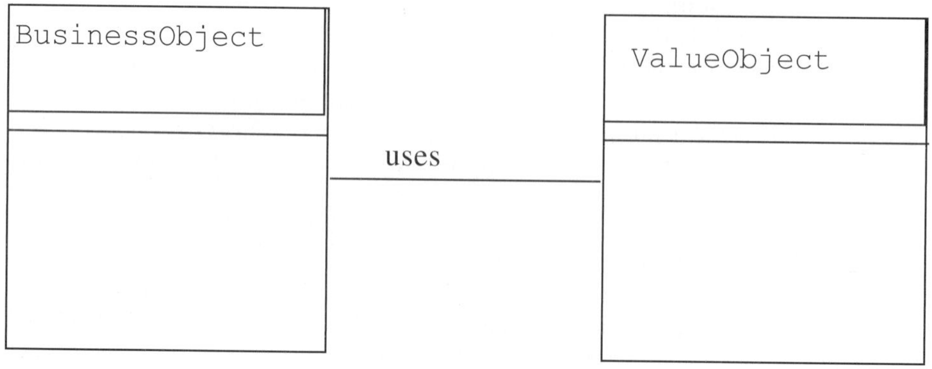

Figure 13–2   *ValueObject - BusinessObject Association*

The use of this pattern has the practical benefit of reducing the amount of communication between the presentation tier and the business tier, since only one method call must be made to retrieve all the data required, as opposed to making numerous method calls to the business tier to populate an object on the presentation tier. (Note that the performance benefits of this approach are more significant when using EJBs than when using Java Bean components, but the practical benefits derived during the development process from the reduced coupling and exposure of the presentation tier to the business tier still apply.) (See Figure 13–3.)

The `ValueObject` is created and loaded via a `BusinessObject` component. The responsibility of this `BusinessObject` component is to instantiate the `ValueObject` and then load the attributes of the `ValueObject` with the correct values. This is performed using a `create` method that the `BusinessObject` component exposes to the presentation tier.

Aggregate Value Object

Sometimes referred to as a *value list,* the *aggregate value object* takes on the role of a value object but represents an aggregation of value objects, so for a value object that represents a movie record, an aggregate value object models an aggregation of those movie records.

The functionality of this design pattern closely tracks that of the `ResultSet`, but as we will see in the implementations shown here, these objects can be designed to provide additional functionality and flexibility to record manipulation.

One of the major benefits of the aggregate value object is the ability to use this object as a data cache on the client tier. An aggregate value object can be serialized and sent to the client tier, where it can be used independently of the database. A mutable version of the aggregate value object can even be designed to support and cache updates, which are then sent to the database as a cached set, avoiding the

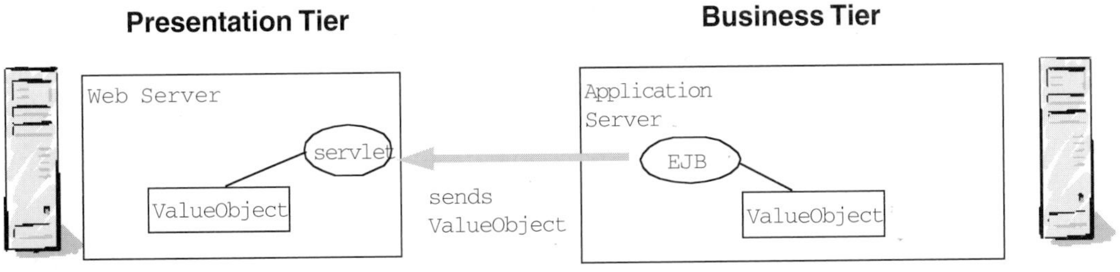

Figure 13–3

overhead of individual database updates for each row. In fact, the implementation shown in the example in this text is a mutable aggregate value object that is closely integrated with a data access object to provide consistent database updating.

Data Access Object (DAO) Pattern

The `DataAccessObject` pattern provides encapsulation of the data access process. The `DataAccessObject` provides the specifics of data access and exposes a simplified API to allow business tier components to access resource tier data.

The component created by this pattern will be accessed from the business tier by the business object. The component will request data in the data store using an API method call, which will conceal the details of the request. The `DataAccessObject` will manage the details of the data access operation, which may involve requesting access to the data source as a specific user, connecting to the data source, performing transactional logic, and preparing and executing a query and retrieving data. The `DataAccessObject` may use a `ValueObject` to provide operation results to client objects. In turn, the `BusinssObject` may use the `DataAccessObject` to manage database operations and receive `ValueObject` references that reflect the results of those database operations. Those `ValueObject` references would then be passed on to presentation tier components as needed.

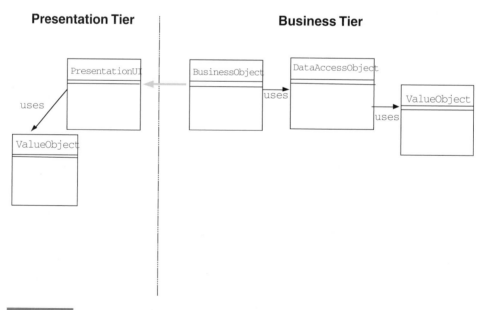

Figure 13–4 *DataAccessObject Associations*

Presentation Tier   **Business Tier**

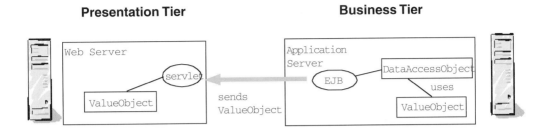

Figure 13–5

Two-Tiered Example: The Table Browser Application

The following example demonstrates the use of JDBC in an application. This is an example of a *database table browser* application – an application that reads the contents of a database table and allows the user to browse the contents. The table contents can be updated, rows can be inserted, deleted or modified.

The application takes any query, executes the query and then renders the results of the query in a table (spreadsheet) format displayed in a scrollable GUI window. When the application starts, it reads a query from a file in the local directory (query.sql) and then executes that query. Once the application is running and the window is displayed, a text field in the lower portion of the window allows the user to enter and execute a new query. Thus allowing other tables to be browsed by the application.

The application uses an updatable ResultSet to allow the table to be updated. If for some reason the query executed cannot be updated through the ResultSet, the updates will fail and an error message will be displayed back to the user. Generally, if a query selects from more than one table, then the ResultSet returned by the query is not updatable. Additionally, many databases require a primary key to be declared for a table before it can be updated using a ResultSet, so the lack of a primary key on a table could lead to failed ResultSet updates.

This example demonstrates the application of several design patterns. The value object pattern is used to provide an abstraction of data records. But this example uses a specialized version of a value object—an *aggregate value object*. This pattern provides for an aggregation of value objects, an array of multiple value objects that essentially represents the results of a query. This is ultimately a data structure that mimics the capabilities of the ResultSet but does so without requiring any knowledge of the database. This is beneficial when using multitiered development, since the client tier should not need any knowledge of the resource tier.

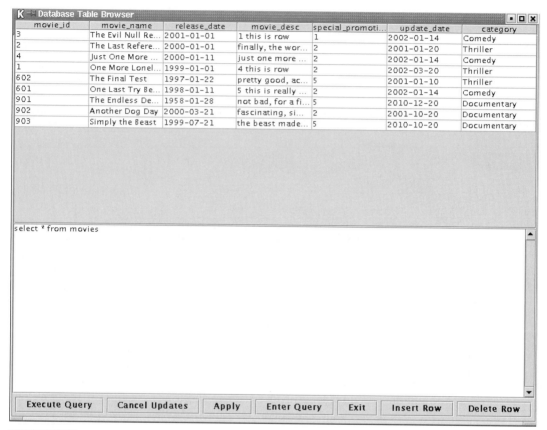

movie_id	movie_name	release_date	movie_desc	special_promoti...	update_date	category
3	The Evil Null Re...	2001-01-01	1 this is row	1	2002-01-14	Comedy
2	The Last Refere...	2000-01-01	finally, the wor...	2	2001-01-20	Thriller
4	Just One More ...	2000-01-11	just one more ...	2	2002-01-14	Comedy
1	One More Lonel...	1999-01-01	4 this is row	2	2002-03-20	Thriller
602	The Final Test	1997-01-22	pretty good, ac...	5	2001-01-10	Thriller
601	One Last Try Be...	1998-01-11	5 this is really ...	2	2002-01-14	Comedy
901	The Endless De...	1958-01-28	not bad, for a fi...	5	2010-12-20	Documentary
902	Another Dog Day	2000-03-21	fascinating, si...	2	2001-10-20	Documentary
903	Simply the Beast	1999-07-21	the beast made...	5	2010-10-20	Documentary

select * from movies

| Execute Query | Cancel Updates | Apply | Enter Query | Exit | Insert Row | Delete Row |

Figure 13–6 *Table Browser Application*

Additionally, and more importantly, the aggregate value object presented here allows caching of updates. This becomes very important for multitiered programming, where updates usually involve communication over a network connection and can easily become a performance bottleneck. By caching updates, the frequency of communication can be limited and controlled.

This example also demonstrates the use of a *data access object*. In this case, it is a data access object that returns an aggregate value object. The data access object provides a coarse-grained approach to data access, executing a query and returning the aggregated results or executing an update and returning results. Since this data access object is working with an aggregate value object, it is responsible for both populating the aggregate object and applying updates contained in the aggregate object.

Table Browser Application: Design Approach

To demonstrate the use of these objects and to focus on the manipulation of data (and the use of the JDBC API), this demonstration application does not include a business tier. In a larger, more complex application, the data access object would not be used by the client application (as is done in this example) but would instead be contained and used by some other component (perhaps a session facade object). Close examination of this code, however, will show that the amount of binding between this client and the data access object is minimal and the process of removing the data access object and substituting a facade object to manage updates would not be difficult.

This example is presented first as a two-tier application, which applies the design patterns discussed previously. Then, in an example that highlights some of the benefits of using this approach, the same example is shown using a multitiered approach using RMI to provide access to the data access object. Such an RMI-based application is better suited to client database access across a network, since the client does not need to communicate directly to the database, but communicates indirectly to the database through the RMI object (in this case, the data access object).

The approach in developing this application was to keep it as streamlined as possible and reduce the complexity. When programming GUI applications in Java, it is easy to create large complex code blocks that perform the bulk of the application processing. This application tries to avoid that as much as possible.

It was also important to reduce the binding between the data and the application, since this is the client and we would prefer that decisions about the data (and about the business logic for the data) be handled by another tier. By applying the data access object design pattern, virtually all knowledge about the data is managed by the data access object. (Since we are treating the data in a very general way, this data knowledge is primarily data type manipulation and decisions on when and how to update the database.)

This example will be explained in the following sections based on code blocks and the responsibility of the methods.

THE DATA ACCESS OBJECT: THE GeneralDAO CLASS

The data access object encapsulates the specifics of data access in a class design. It is intended to be a coarse-grained object, meaning that the details of the data being accessed (the columns, the data types) are not necessarily understood or managed by the class.

Note that a design pattern is a recommended solution, a desirable approach. A design pattern is not a template, though a template for a class or an interface for a class could result from the implementation of a design pattern. For that reason, there is no template for a data access object; there is just a set of recommendations.

This data access object presents a *generalized* approach to retrieving data. It has not been written to access a single table or a set of tables (which is a common approach to creating DAOs). Instead, it treats data access in a general manner, executing a query and returning a `ResultSet`, then taking the `ResultSet` and loading it into an aggregate value object, an aggregation of data rows similar to the `ResultSet`. The contents of the `ResultSet`, the specific columns in the rows returned by the `ResultSet`, are not known, so the data access object is written to read each column in the row as an `Object` reference and place the reference into the aggregate value object (which will store the reference internally in a Java `Vector` collection). This will work with virtually all standard SQL data types. More complex types (`Blobs`, distinct types) are not managed by this implementation. (There are several optional ways to manage this query-result loading operation that allow additional formatting and manipulation of the data and will be discussed when the `loadResults` method is shown.)

Since this approach treats data in a general manner, the presentation of this example revisits some of the concepts of using dynamic queries with JDBC. A more specific treatment of data, one where our application is written with the intention of accessing a known set of database tables and columns, is shown in chapter 16. The examples in that chapter show DAOs and value objects written to be used with a specific database and a specific set of tables.

The GeneralDAO Class: The Class Declaration and the executeQuery Method

The `GeneralDAO` class is shown in the sections below. Since this is a large example, the discussion will be presented by code block in the sequence in which the code blocks appear in the source file.

The source file begins with declarations that you would expect, `import` statements to include the JDBC API in the class name space for the application (`java.sql` and `javax.sql` package) in addition to the `javax.naming` package for using JNDI. The `java.util` package is included to provide access to the Java collections classes, and the `java.io` package is included for file I/O used in the method that reads a database query from a file.

A number of instance members are declared on lines 9 through 12. Since they must be used constantly throughout the life of the `GeneralDAO` object, we delcare them as instance members. Note that since we are defining a `Connection` object as an instance member, we expect to have a single connection per data access object. This is also true of the `Statement` and `ResultSet` objects, where we also define a one-to-one relationship between these objects and our class.

An aggregate value object is declared as an instance member of the class on line 14 (`gvo`). Once the `loadResults` method of this class has been called, this member will contain the results of the query that has been executed for the data access object.

The declaration for the executeQuery method starts on line 16. This method must be called before the GeneralDAO object can be used. The method begins with a call on line 19 to the clear method of the GeneralAggregateVO object. This will clear the various internal flags of the GeneralAggregateVO object and avoid any confusion when the object is loaded as a result of the executeQuery method call.

The method calls prepareStatement on line 20 on the connection object, then executes the prepared statement. (The statement is prepared for performance reasons; the overloaded executeQuery method with no arguments will simply execute this prepared statement.) The prepared statement is then executed using the executeQuery method on line 21, and a ResultSet is returned. The ResultSet is then passed to the loadResults method on line 26, which will load the contents of the ResultSet into the internal aggregate value object.

An overloaded version of the executeQuery method for the GeneralDAO object is shown on line 31. This version of the method asserts that executeQuery method for the GeneralDAO object has been called previously with a query argument and that the internal prepared statement (preparedQuery) has a valid, active prepared statement associated with it.

GeneralDAO.java: The executeQuery Method

```
1.import java.sql.*;
2.import javax.sql.*;
3.import javax.naming.*;
4.import java.util.*;
5.import java.io.*;
6.
7.public class GeneralDAO   {
8.
9.Connection                    con;
10.PreparedStatement preparedQuery;
11.ResultSet              resultSet;
12.ResultSetMetaData      resultMD;
13.
14.GeneralAggregateVO       gvo = new GeneralAggregateVO();
15.
16.public void executeQuery( String query ) throws SQLException {
17.
18.    // execute the query and store in our local ResultSet
19.    System.out.println("Preparing and executing query ... ");
20.    preparedQuery = con.prepareStatement( query );
21.    resultSet     = preparedQuery.executeQuery();
22.    resultMD      = resultSet.getMetaData();
23.
24.    // store the resultSet in our GeneralVO object
```

```
25.    System.out.println( "Loading results ... " );
26.    loadResults();
27.
28.}
29.// ------------------------------------------------
30.
31.public void executeQuery() {
32.
33.    resultSet      = preparedQuery.executeQuery();
34.    resultMD       = resultSet.getMetaData();
35.
36.    // store the resultSet in our GeneralVO object
37.    System.out.println( "Loading results ... " );
38.    loadResults();
39.
40.}
41.
```

The GeneralDAO Class: The Constructor

The constructor for the `GeneralDAO` class performs the task of obtaining a `DataSource` object and connecting to the database. Called with no arguments, it constructs a `GeneralDAO` object with the default `DataSource`, which for purposes of this example is `moviesmysql`. If the overloaded version of the constructor is called with a string parameter, the string parameter is used as a `DataSource` name and the various methods and constructors called to create a `DataSource` and connection are used to ultimately create a connection to the `DataSource`.

```
public GeneralDAO() {

    //
    // construct with the default DataSourceName
    //
     this( "moviesmysql" );

}
// ————————————————————————————


public GeneralDAO( String dataSourceName ) {

try {
    //
    // JNDI startup parameters are stored in the
    // "jndi.properties" file in the classpath.
    //
    InitialContext ctx = new InitialContext( );

    //
    // get the DataSource from the JNDI name server
```

```
      //
      DataSource ds = (DataSource) ctx.lookup( dataSourceName );

      //
      // get the connection from the DataSource
      //
      con = ds.getConnection( );
}
catch (NamingException e ) {
      System.out.println( "NamingException in GeneralDAO: " +
                          e.getMessage() );
}
catch (SQLException e) {
      System.out.println( "SQLException in GeneralDAO: " + e.getMessage() );
}

}
```

The GeneralDAO Class: The getQuery Method

The getQuery method reads a query string from the file name passed as a parameter and returns the string containing the query. This method simply wraps the file access work needed to read the query string from a file.

The method begins by declaring a data buffer for reading the file on line 2 and a string reference for the return value on line 3. On line 9, the named file is opened and a buffered file reader is associated with the file.

Since we assume we are reading new text with new line delimiters from this file, the readLine method is used on line 15 to read the first line of text. The readLine method returns a null if it fails to read a line of text, so the controlling while loop on line 16 tests for a null value.

If the String reference return value (retVal) is null, then we have yet to set this string to a value. This condition is tested on line 18, and if the value is null, then the string is assigned to the first row read from the file. If not, on line 22, the return value buffer (retVal) is appended with the current content of the current line. On line 27, the readLine method is used to read the next line from the file.

When the file read operation is complete and there are no more rows to read, the file is closed on line 33, and in the finally block on line 44, the return value string (retVal) is returned by the method.

The GeneralDAO Class: The getQuery Method

```
1.public String getQuery( String fn ) {
2.String buffer  = null; // data buffer
3.String retVal  = null; // query string to return
4.
5.try {
```

```
6.      //
7.      // create a file reader for the file containing the query
8.      //
9.      BufferedReader reader = new BufferedReader (
10.                     new FileReader( fn ));
11.
12.     //
13.     // start reading the file
14.     //
15.     buffer = reader.readLine();
16.     while ( buffer != null ) {
17.
18.         if ( retVal == null ) {    // this is the first pass
19.             retVal = buffer;
20.           }
21.         else {
22.             retVal += buffer;      // append
23.           }
24.     //
25.     // continue reading the file
26.     //
27.      buffer = reader.readLine();
28.      }
29.
30.    //
31.    // close the file reader
32.    //
33.    reader.close();
34.}
35.catch (FileNotFoundException e) {
36.     System.out.println("FileNotFoundException in getQuery: " +
37.                          e.getMessage() );
38.}
39.catch (IOException e) {
40.     System.out.println( "IOException in getQuery: " +
41.                          e.getMessage() );
42.}
43.finally {
44.     return retVal;
45.}
46.}
```

The GeneralDAO Class: The setAggregateVO Methods

The setAggregateVO method is used to set the internal ResultSet (resultSet) to the values of the internal aggregate value object (gvo). Since the strategy in this implementation of the data access object is to use the aggregate value object as a data cache, at various points during processing we would expect to have updates applied to the aggregate value object that must be applied to the internal ResultSet so that the two objects are synchronized. (Ultimately the

ResultSet will be used to update the database, so we want the updates that have been applied to the aggregate value object to be applied to the ResultSet before we perform our database update using the ResultSet.)

The method begins with a for loop on line 8 that iterates through all of the rows in the internal aggregate value object. For each row, it performs a series of checks to determine whether or not updates are needed, first for the row and then for the column in the row. Whether or not the aggregate value object has been updated can be determined using various flags within the general aggregate value object (gvo).

Before checking the update flags, the general aggregate value object is positioned with a call to its absolute method on line 13. This method behaves as does the absolute method within the ResultSet class–it moves to the requested absolute position, the position from the first record in the contents of the aggregate value object. (Note that unlike the ResultSet class that uses one-based positioning, the aggregate value object shown here uses zero-based positioning.)

On line 16, the getUpdateStatus method is called to determine the update status of the currently positioned row. If this method returns true, then there are updates in the current row in the aggregate value object, and the corresponding row in the internal ResultSet must be updated. At line 20, the internal ResultSet is positioned to the current row, and then at line 27, a loop is executed to loop through all of the columns in the current row. Within this loop, on line 32, the ResultSet updateObject method is called for the current column as controlled by the loop started at line 27. The updateObject method is called with parameters for the column and an object reference to use to update the column. In this case, the object reference must come from the internal aggregate value object, the source of our update value. The GeneralAggregateVO method getObject is called on line 33 and is passed an integer value for the column value to retrieve. This method will retrieve an object reference, which will be passed to the ResultSet updateObject method to update the designated object. The code for this method follows:

The GeneralDAO Class: The setAggregateVO Method

```
1.public void setAggregateVO( ) throws SQLException {
2.//
3.// Sets the internal ResultSet (resultSet) to the values of the
4.// the internal aggregate value object (gvo).
5.// Effectively synchronizes the two objects.
6.//
7.
8.    for ( int n = 0; n < gvo.getRowCount(); n++ ) {
9.
10.            //
11.            // move to the row in our aggregate value object
12.            //
```

```
13.        gvo.absolute( n );
14.
15.      // if true, there are updates in this row
16.      if ( gvo.getUpdateStatus( n ) ) {
17.                                      //
18.              // move to the row
19.              //
20.              resultSet.absolute( n + 1 );
21.
22.        //
23.        // set all columns for the row to values stored
24.        // in the value object
25.        //
26.
27.        for ( int z = 0; z < gvo.getColumnCount(); z++ ) {
28.
29.            //
30.        // update the object in the resultset
31.            //
32.            resultSet.updateObject( (z + 1),
33.                                    gvo.getObject( z ) );
34.
35.      }
36.
37.      }
38.  }
39.
40.}
```

The GeneralDAO Class: The loadAggregateVO and deleteRow Methods

The loadAggregateVO method is used to set the current GeneralDAO to the value of the GeneralAggregateVO object being passed into the method. This method effectively synchronizes the data access object to the value of the aggregate value object passed as a parameter.

The method is passed a parameter for the GeneralAggregateVO object to use for the synchronization. On line 4, it sets the internal aggregate value object (gvo) to the object reference passed into the method. The setAggregateVO method is then called to synchronize the internal ResultSet to the values of the internal aggregate value object.

The deleteRow method deletes a specified row from the internal ResultSet. It first positions to the row to delete (and assumes the parameter being passed in is zero-based) and then calls ResultSet deleteRow to delete the row from the ResultSet. The code for these methods is shown next.

The GeneralDAO Class: The loadAggregateVO and deleteRow Methods

```
1.public void loadAggregateVO( GeneralAggregateVO   gvo )
2.                         throws SQLException {
3.
4.    this.gvo = gvo;
5.    setAggregateVO();    // set our resultset to look like the gvo
6.
7.}
8.
9.public void deleteRow( int row ) throws SQLException {
10.
11.    // delete our current row
12.    resultSet.absolute( row + 1 );
13.    resultSet.deleteRow();
14.
15.}
```

The GeneralDAO Class: The applyUpdates Method

The `applyUpdates` method takes the cached updates in the internal aggregate value object and applies them to the database, using the `updateable ResultSet` features of the internal `ResultSet`.

The method will loop through all of the rows in the internal aggregate value object (`gvo`) and will check the update flags of the aggregate value object. If updates need to be performed, the `ResultSet` will be updated and then, through the `ResultSet`, the updates will be applied to the database.

On line 7, the loop, which will move through the aggregate value object, is started. For each iteration of the loop, the internal aggregate value object is moved to the current row at line 11, and the internal `ResultSet` is moved to the same position so that both structures are now synchronized.

Since `insert` operations are treated differently than `update` operations: The current aggregate value object row is tested to determine if an `insert` update operation must be done on this row at line 17. The `GeneralAggregateVO getInsertStatus` method is called on line 17 and passed the row number of the current row. If this method returns a `true`, then the current aggregate value object row must be inserted into the database, and the `ResultSet moveToInsertRow` method is called on line 18.

On line 21, the `GeneralAggregateVO getUpdateStatus` method is called to determine whether or not the current aggregate value object row must be updated. Note that the update in this case can be either a SQL `update` of an existing row or a SQL `insert` of a new row—both are considered to be updates and will lead to the update flag being set. If this test for updates tests `true`, then a loop is started on line 25 that is used to determine specifically which columns need to be updated. On line 29, the `GeneralAggregateVO getUpdateStatus` method is called with an additional parameter (it is an overloaded version of the method used on line 21) to test the update status for a row and column combination. If this method tests `true`, then the current column (as controlled by the loop on line 25) is updated using the `ResultSet updateObject` method on line 30. This method is passed the column to update and the object reference to update the column with. The object reference to use for the update is the object reference returned by a call to the `GeneralAggregateVO getObject` method on line 31.

At the conclusion of the loop, which iterates for each of the columns in the row, the `ResultSet` is ready to be applied to the database. The internal `ResultSet` has either an update or an insert to apply. The code on line 35 tests to determine if the row contains an inset row. If this tests `true`, then the `ResultSet insertRow` method is called on line 36 to insert the row. If the call on line 35 tests `false`, then the row must be updated, which is done on line 39 with a call to the `ResultSet updateRow` method.

The GeneralDAO Class: The applyUpdates Method

```
1.public void applyUpdates() throws SQLException {
2.//
3.// apply updates from the generalAggregateVO
4.// asserts that setAggregateVO() has been called previously
5.//
6.
7.    for ( int n = 0; n < gvo.getRowCount(); n++ ) {
8.
9.           // move to the row
10.       gvo.absolute( n );           // our aggregate VO data
11.         resultSet.absolute( n + 1 ); // the underlying resultset
12.
13.        //
14.        // if this is an insert update then
15.        // we need to move to an 'insert' row
16.        //
17.        if ( gvo.getInsertStatus( n ) ) {    // is this an insert row
18.        resultSet.moveToInsertRow();
19.          }
20.
21.        if ( gvo.getUpdateStatus( n ) ) { // any update in this row ?
22.          //
23.          // update only those columns that need updating
24.          //
25.        for ( int z = 0; z < gvo.getColumnCount(); z++ ) {
26.              //
27.              // get update status for the row & column combination
28.              //
29.          if ( gvo.getUpdateStatus( n, z ) ) {
30.              resultSet.updateObject( (z + 1),
31.                                      gvo.getObject( z ));
32.                }
33.        }
```

```
34.
35.     if ( gvo.getInsertStatus( n ) ) {    // this an insert row
36.         resultSet.insertRow();            // insert the row
37.     }
38.       else {                                   // this is an update
39.         resultSet.updateRow();           // update the row
40.     }
41.   }
42.  }
43.
44.}
```

The GeneralDAO Class: The loadResults Method

The `loadResults` method is used to load results from the internal `ResultSet` into the internal general aggregate value object (`GeneralAggregateVO`), where it will most likely be delivered to a client program to use. The method is overloaded to allow the use of a no-argument version, which calls the version with a single `ResultSet` argument on line 4.

The `loadResults` method that actually does the work starts with a call to the internal aggregate value object to clear its contents. This call will not only clear some of the internal collections in the aggregated value object of values, but will clear the various flags in the value object that are used to track updates to the value object.

The method begins by gathering the column labels of the columns in the `ResultSet`. A loop is started at line 20, which uses the internal `ResultSetMetaData` object (`resultMD`) to return the column count used in the `for` loop and to return the column label on line 22. For each column in the `ResultSet`, the column label and the corresponding column number are stored in the aggregate value object using the `GeneralAggregateVO` method `setColKey`. (This method stores the information needed to associate a column name with a column number in the value object.)

Next, on line 28, a loop is started for each of the rows in the `ResultSet`. (This asserts that the internal `ResultSet` is positioned before the first row.) For each row in the `ResultSet`, a loop is conducted over each of the columns in the `ResultSet` on line 30. For each of the columns, the type of the column is mapped to a Java String type with a call to the `JDBCTypeMapper` `getColumnDataString` method. The `getColumnDataString` method will perform some type-mapping operations and apply data formatting. (The `JDBCTypeMapper` class is used to perform customized data type transformations and was explained in Chapter 9.)

The output of the `JDBCTypeMapper` `getColumnDataString` method will be passed to the `addObject` method of the aggregate value object. This will add the object to the current row in the aggregate value object. When all columns have been iterated over, the `GeneralAggregateVO` `addRow` method is called on line

43 to add the current row to the aggregate value object and prepare the value object for the next row to add. The listing for this method is shown next.

The GeneralDAO Class: The loadResults Method

```
1.public void loadResults() throws SQLException {
2.
3.       // by default we use the internal resultset
4.       loadResults( resultSet );
5.}
6.
7.// ------------------------------------------------------------
8.//
9.// load results from the resultset into the GeneralAggregateVO
10.//
11.public void loadResults( ResultSet rs ) throws SQLException {
12.       //
13.       // clear GeneralAggregateVO
14.       //
15.       gvo.clear();
16.
17.       //
18.       // set the columns in the gvo
19.       //
20.       for ( int c = 1; c <= resultMD.getColumnCount(); c++) {
21.
22.             gvo.setColKey( resultMD.getColumnLabel( c ), (c-1) );
23.       }
24.
25.       //
26.       // for each row
27.       //
28.       while ( rs.next() ) {
29.
30.         for ( int n = 1; n <= resultMD.getColumnCount(); n++ )   {
31.
32.               //
33.           // apply some general conversion
34.               //
35.           gvo.addObject( JDBCTypeMapper.getColumnDataString(
36.                            n,
37.                            rs ) );
38.         }
39.
40.         //
41.         // add the row to our aggregate object
42.         //
43.         gvo.addRow();
44.
45.     }
46.
47.}
```

The GeneralDAO Class: The clearUpdates and getGeneralAggregateVO Methods

The `clearUpdates` and `getGeneralAggregateVO` methods perform simple operations on the instance members of the `GeneralDAO` class. The `clearUpdates` method simply maps to the internal aggregate value object to call the `clearUpdates` method on that object; this will clear the update flags in the general aggregate value object but will *not* do anything to the database, nor does it reload the general aggregate value with data from before the update.

The `getGeneralAggregateVO` method returns the internal reference to the aggregate value object of the `GeneralDAO` instance. This allows client applications to use the value object to examine the data and potentially update the data without requiring interaction with the `GeneralDAO` object. The code listing for these methods is shown next.

The GeneralDAO Class: The clearUpdates and getGeneralAggregateVO Methods

```
public void clearUpdates() {

    // reset update flags
    // does NOT reload data to pre-updates state
    gvo.clearUpdates();
}
// ————————————————————————————-

public GeneralAggregateVO getGeneralAggregateVO() {

        return gvo;
}

}
```

THE GENERALAGGREGATEVO CLASS

The `GeneralAggregateVO` class demonstrates one possible implementation of the aggregate value object pattern. As discussed previously, this design pattern encapsulates fine-grained access to the data in an aggregated form. While the value object pattern is sometimes referred to as *immutable* and unchanging, this pattern is specifically designed for updates, since one of the main goals of the object is to cache update operations at the client level.

The `GeneralAggregateVO` class makes heavy use of object-oriented "has a" type of object associations. A great deal of the code in this class is devoted to the process of keeping these various objects synchronized.

The Java Development Kit provides a number of very useful collections for the aggregation of objects. These collections are heavily used by this class. Since the aggregate value object represents the results of a query operation, results that can often be ordered; the `Vector` is the Java collection of choice for this operation since it is an ordered collection.

The following sections present the `GeneralAggregateVO` class. The discussion is divided into sections on each code block, starting with the class declaration.

The GeneralAggregateVO Class: Instance Members

A number of instance members are declared for the `GeneralAggregateVO` class. These instance members contain either data or flags that indicate the update status of the data. A combination of `java.util.Vector` and `java.util.Hashtable` are used.

A `Vector` object is declared for the rows. This `Vector` will contain a set of objects; each of the objects will represent a row, which itself will be a `Vector` object for each of the columns in the row.

A `Vector` object is declared for the current row. During an `insert` operation, the various objects that represent the data for the current row will be added to the current row `Vector`, then the current row `Vector` will be added to the `rowsVector` and a new current row `Vector` will be created.

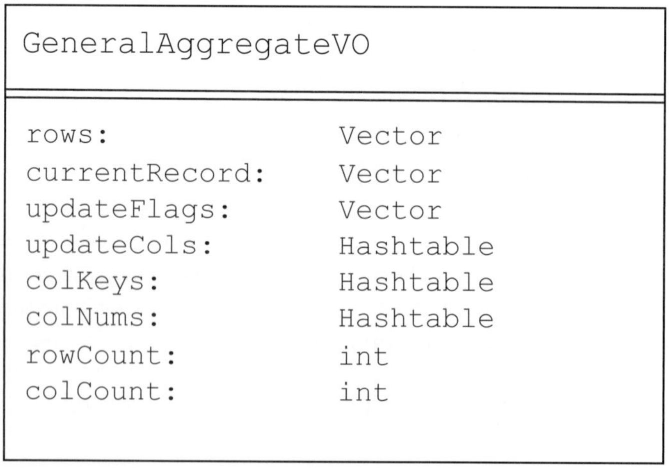

```
GeneralAggregateVO


rows:              Vector
currentRecord:     Vector
updateFlags:       Vector
updateCols:        Hashtable
colKeys:           Hashtable
colNums:           Hashtable
rowCount:          int
colCount:          int
```

Figure 13–7   *The GeneralAggregateVO Class*

Adding and viewing the data stored in the aggregate value object is fairly straightforward. The process of updating the value object is more difficult. Various flags must be set for each row that has been updated and for each column. Since we do not assume that each and every row in the aggregate value object will be updated, we do not need to create some type of array to track the updates on each row. Instead, it makes more sense to just store the rows and columns that have been changed and use a mechanism that allows it to be easily searched for updated rows and columns. For this reason, a `Hashtable` is used for the process of tracking updates.

The names of the columns must also be stored and a mechanism provided to allow them to be retrieved easily. Two `Hashtable` instance members are created for this purpose. One stores the column number as a key and maps to the column name. The other stores the column name as a key and maps to the column number. The code listing for these declarations follows:

The GeneralAggregateVO Class: Declaration and Instance Members

```
import java.util.*;
import java.io.*;


public class GeneralAggregateVO implements GenericVO, Serializable {

// internal vectors


//
 // stores and array of currentRecord vectors - one for each row
//
private Vector     rows       = new Vector();

//
 // an update flag for each row - indicates update status
//
private Vector     updateFlags  = new Vector();

//
// the column values (object references) for the current record
//
private Vector      currentRecord = new Vector();

//
// stores a HashSet for each row containing the columns
// updated in that row
//
private Hashtable updateCols    = new Hashtable();

//
// for column name mapping
```

```
//
private Hashtable colKeys        = new Hashtable();
private Hashtable colNums         = new Hashtable();

//
// current position
//
private int        currentRow    = 0;

//
// maintain counts
//
private int        rowCount      = 0;
private int        columnCount   = 0;
```

The GeneralAggregateVO Class: The setXXXX Methods

Various methods are used to set values of the aggregate value object. The setColKey method is used to update the column name and column number Hashtable objects with the column name and number. The colKeys Hashtable stores the column name and maps it to the column number. The colNums Hashtable stores the reverse—the column number mapped to the column name. The Hashtable put method stores these values in the appropriate Hashtable on lines 7 and 10.

The setObject method on line 16 takes two arguments: the integer column for the object to set and the object reference for the column value. The Vector set method is then called on the current record Vector to set the object reference at the designated position to the value of the object reference passed into the method.

An alternative version of the setObject method is shown on line 20. This overloaded version of the method is passed the String name of the column to set and the object reference value. The method performs a lookup in the column name Hashtable (colKeys) and retrieves the object reference. The object reference in the colKeys Hashtable is an Integer class reference, the wrapper class for Java integers. The object reference returned by the Vector get method on line 21 is cast as an Integer, and then the intValue method is used to retrieve the value of the entry as an integer. This position value is then used to set the value of the reference at the designated position (as retrieved from the colKeys Hashtable). The code for these methods is shown next.

The GeneralAggregateVO Class: The setXXXX Methods

```
1.//
2.// set keys for colname to positional mapping
3.//
4.public void setColKey( String name, int pos ) {
5.
```

```
6.    // map column name to position
7.    colKeys.put( name, new Integer( pos ) );
8.
9.    // reverse map. for lookup position and match to name
10.   colNums.put( new Integer( pos ), name );
11.
12.   columnCount++;
13.
14.}
15.
16.public void setObject( int col, Object obj ) {
17.    currentRecord.set( col, obj );
18.}
19.
20.public void setObject( String keyName, Object obj ) {
21.    int pos  = ((Integer) colKeys.get( keyName )).intValue();
22.    setObject( pos, obj );
23.}
```

The GeneralAggregateVO Class: The addObject and addRow Methods

The `GeneralAggregateVO addObject` method adds an object to the value object, and the `addRow` method adds the completed row to the internal list of rows.

This method takes a single object reference argument. It then makes a quick check to see if adding the current column will not exceed the number of columns in the current record (as set by the `setColKey` method, which we assert has been called before this method is called).

If the object being added does not exceed the column count limit, then the object reference is added to the internal current record `Vector` using the `add` method. If the current record does exceed the number of columns, an error message is displayed.

The `addRow` method is used to add the current row `Vector` to our internal `Vector` used to store all of the rows in the table. The `add` method is called on the rows `Vector` and then the `updateFlags Vector` gets a new row, a blank string indicating nothing has been updated yet.

Next, a new `Vector` object is created and assigned to the current record `Vector` reference.

The `currentRow` counter and the `rowCount` integer variables are incremented to track the size of the current row and the number of rows.

The GeneralAggregateVO Class: The addObject and addRow Methods

```
public void addObject( Object obj ) {
```

```
      // will fail if we attempt to go beyond columnCount
      if ( currentRecord.size() <= columnCount ) {

          // add the object
          currentRecord.add( obj );
      }
      else
          System.out.println(
              "Attempt to get beyond number of columns in VO.");
}
// ─────────────────────────────────────

// add the current VO to our rows
public void addRow() {
      rows.add( (Object) currentRecord );
      //
      // create a new row
      updateFlags.add( new String( "" ) );      // null for 'no updates'
      currentRecord = new Vector();
      currentRow++;
      rowCount++;

}
```

The GeneralAggregateVO Class: Row Action Methods

The `GeneralAggregateVO` object allows rows to be cleared, deleted, and appended. The `clearCurrentRow` method simply clears the contents of the current row by calling the `removeAllElements` method of the `Vector` class (which is the data type of the `currentRecord` object).

The `deleteRow` method calls the `remove` method of the `Vector` class on the current row. It then decrements the current row pointer (`currentRow`) and decrements the internal row count (`rowCount`).

The `appendRow` method adds a row onto the end of the current row list. This requires that the various flags that track updates also be appended with new objects, which is done on line 33. On line 34, a new `Vector` object is created for the new row to be appended.

A loop is then started on line 40 to create a set of objects for the new row by calling the `addObject` method for each column. This allows `updateObject` to be called successfully to update the contents of the new row. If this were not done, then the `updateObject` calls would fail.

The record for the new row is then added onto the end of the internal list of rows on line 44. The row count (`rowCount`) is then incremented, and the current row pointer (`currentRow`) is set to point to the newly added row on line 46 (which is the total count of rows less one). The code for these methods follows:

The GeneralAggregateVO Class: The deleteRow, clearCurrentRow, and appendRow Methods

```
1.// clear our current row
2.public void clearCurrentRow() {
3.
4.      currentRecord.removeAllElements();
5.
6.}
7.
8.// ----------------------------------------------------------------
9.// delete our current row
10.public void deleteRow() {
11.
12.      rows.remove( currentRow );
13.      currentRow--;
14.      rowCount--;
15.
16.}
17.// ----------------------------------------------------------------
18.
19.//
20.// append a row onto the end of our data set
21.//
22.public void appendRow() {
23.
24.// This is considered an 'insert' row.
25.// It will need to be placed into the underlying database
26.// with an 'insert' operation.
27.// Will append a blank row onto the current set. The new row
28.// becomes the current record
29.
30.      //
31.      // this is an insert row
32.      //
33.      updateFlags.add( new String( "" ) );
34.      currentRecord = new Vector();
35.
36.      //
37.      // create empty object references. Assert they will be updated
38.      // by updateObject calls.
39.      //
40.      for ( int n = 0; n < getColumnCount(); n++ ) {
41.          addObject( "" );
42.      }
43.
44.      rows.add( (Object) currentRecord );
45.      rowCount++;
46.      currentRow = rowCount - 1;        // we are at the last row
47.
48.      //
49.      // set the update flag for this row. This is an
50.      // 'insert' row.
```

```
51.     //
52.     updateFlags.set( getRowPos(), new String( "I" ) );
53.
54.}
```

The GeneralAggregateVO Class: The updateObject Method

The `updateObject` method is used to update a column member of the current row of the aggregate value object to the value of the object reference supplied. It is passed two parameters: the column to update in the current row and the object reference to use for the update. The process of updating or setting an internal object reference to a reference passed in is a straightforward matter. It is the process of maintaining the update flags correctly that involves some additional effort.

A `Hashset` reference is created on line 5, and a variable which stores the current row position as an `Integer` object is created on line 6. These variables will be used to maintain the update flags of the aggregate value object.

An update is either a SQL `update` operation or a SQL `insert` operation. If a row has been inserted into the aggregate value object, both the update and insert flags will be set.

On line 11, the insert status of the row is checked with a call to the `getInsertStatus` method and passes in a parameter for the current row position. Note that this call, which returns a boolean `true` if the insert status flag has been set, is negated so that the body of the conditional statement will be executed only if the method returns `false`, that is, only if the insert flag has *not* been set will the call on line 15 be made.

On line 15, the update flag is set for the row with a call to the `set` method of the `updateFlags Vector`. (For purposes of this class, and this is behavior that is reflected in the `updatable ResultSet`, the SQL `insert` operation is treated differently than a SQL `update` operation, which is why we make an effort here to indicate with the update flag whether this is a SQL `insert` or an `update`.)

Update flags are maintained not only for the row but for each of the columns in the row. But column update flags are stored only if they are needed because a column has been updated in a row, so not every row will have a set of column update flags. We must therefore check for the incidence of column flags for this row. On line 19, a call is made to determine if a set of column update flags exists for this row. The update flags for the columns are stored in a `Hashset` for each row; only columns that have been updated are added to the `Hashset`. The call on line 19 will return `true` if there is an entry in the `updateCols Hashtable` for the current row position (`rowPos`). If this call returns `true`, then the `Hashset` for the column list of updated columns is retrieved from the `updateCols Hashtable` on line 23, and the integer value of the column being updated is added to the `Hashset` on line 27 (as an `Integer` object). (Since we are working with a reference to the `colSet` object, we have updated the `Hashset` that is stored in the `updateCols Hashtable`.)

On line 29, we deal with the contingency that there is currently no column update flags `Hashset` stored in the `updateCols Hashtable` for the current row. If that is the case, then the code at line 32 will be executed to create a new `Hashset`. An entry is then added to the `Hashset` for the column being updated, and the `Hashset` is added to the `updateCols Hashtable` on line 41.

At this point, we have finished setting the appropriate update flags. On line 47, we finally call the `setObject` method to set the value of the designated column to the designated value. The code for this method is shown next.

The GeneralAggregateVO Class: The udpateObject Method

```
1.//
2.// update an Object - set flags to indicate update status
3.//
4.public void updateObject( int col, Object value ) {
5.HashSet colSet = null;
6.Integer rowPos = new Integer( getRowPos() ); // current row position
7.
8.      // set the update flags
9.      // only set this if the 'insert' flag has NOT been set
10.     //
11.     if  ( !( getInsertStatus( getRowPos() )) )    {
12.         //
13.         // set the update flag for this row
14.         //
15.         updateFlags.set( getRowPos(), new String( "U" ) );
16.
17.     }
18.
19.     if ( updateCols.containsKey( rowPos ) ) {
20.         //
21.         // get the cols hashtable for this row
22.         //
23.         colSet = (HashSet) updateCols.get( rowPos );
24.         //
25.         // add this column to the list of updated cols
26.         //
27.         colSet.add( new Integer( col ));
28.     }
29.     else {
30.         // create the cols hashtable for this row
31.
32.         colSet = new HashSet();
33.          //
34.         // add this column to the list of updated cols
35.         //
36.         colSet.add( new Integer( col ));
```

```
37.
38.         //
39.         // add to the updateCols Hashtable
40.         //
41.         updateCols.put( rowPos, colSet );
42.      }
43.
44.      //
45.      // set the object with designated value (update the object)
46.      //
47.      setObject( col, value );
48.
49. }
```

The GeneralAggregateVO Class: Get Status Information

A number of methods are used to return status information for the aggregate value object. This is information on the insert and update status of certain rows and row and column combinations, information needed when it comes time to synchronize the aggregate value object with a database.

The `getInsertStatus` method on line 2 returns the insert status for the specified row. This method retrieves the object in the `updateFlags` `Vector` at the designated row position, casts the `Object` as a `String`, and calls the `equals` method for the `String` to determine whether or not the flag is set to a value of "I". This setting indicates an insert; any other value would indicate another type of update. The method returns a boolean `true` if the flag is an insert value; otherwise, it returns a value of boolean `false`.

The `getupdateStatus` method on line 11 tests for an update status at a specified row and column position. The method first tests to see if the update flag is set to an value of "I" for inserts, and if it is, it sets the return value for the method to a boolean `true`, since for inserts we want all columns in the internal aggregate value object row to be updated in the database.

If the row is an update row, then the test on line 24 will return `true`. This code indicates the update status flag for the row is "U", indicating that updates have been performed on the row. If this is an update row, then the `Hashset` for the update column flags is retrieved on lines 27 and 28, and on line 31, the `Hashset` (`colSet`) is tested to see if it contains an entry for the column that is being tested. The `Hashset` `contains` method called on line 31 performs a lookup based on a key value passed as a parameter. This method will return a boolean `true` if the `Hashset` contains an entry for the column; otherwise, it will return a boolean `false`. The return value (`retVal`) is set to the value returned by the `contains` method on line 31. On line 34, the return value (`retVal`) is returned by the method.

On line 39, an overloaded version of the `getUpdateStatus` method is declared to take no arguments. This method assumes that the update status of the current row is required and simply tests the udpateFlags Hashtable to determine if there is an entry for the current row (as returned by the getCurrentRow method).

On line 54, the getUpdateStatus method is overloaded again to accept a single integer argument, which is considered to be the row to test for update flags. The method makes a call to the updateFlags Hashtable to determine the update status. As with the previous method, if the Hashtable contains an entry for the row, the method assumes (correctly) that the update flag has been set and returns a boolean true; otherwise, it returns a boolean false. The code for these methods follows:

The GeneralAggregateVO Class: The Get Status Information Methods

```
1.// ------------------------------------------------------------------
2.public boolean getInsertStatus( int row ) {
3.       if ( ( (String) updateFlags.get( row ) ).equals( "I" ) )
4.            return true;
5.       else
6.            return false;
7.}
8.// ----------------------------------------------------------------
9.
10.// get the update status for a specific row and column
11.public boolean getUpdateStatus( int row, int col ) {
12.boolean retVal = false;
13.
14.    // is this an 'insert' column ?
15.    If   ((
16.            (String) updateFlags.get( row )).toString().equals("I") ) {
17.          retVal = true;    // all columns need 'updating' for inserts
18.    }
19.
20.    //
21.    // is this an 'update' column ?
22.    // if so, then check the column for updates
23.    //
24.    if ( ((String) updateFlags.get( row )).toString().equals("U") ) {
25.
26.         // get the Hashset for this row
27.         HashSet colSet = (HashSet)
28.                              updateCols.get( new Integer( row ));
29.
30.    // is this column in the HashSet ?
31.    retVal = colSet.contains( new Integer( col ) );
32.    }
33.
34.   return retVal;
35.}
36.// ----------------------------------------------------
```

```
37.
38.// get the update status for the current row
39.public boolean getUpdateStatus() {
40.
41.     //
42.     // if non-null, then the 'update' flag has been set
43.     //
44.     if ( ((String) updateFlags.get( getRowPos() )) != null ) {
45.         return true;
46.     }
47.     else {
48.         return false;
49.     }
50.
51.}
52.// ----------------------------------------------------
53.
54.public boolean getUpdateStatus(int row ) {
55.//
56.// get the update status for a specific row
57.//
58.
59.     //
60.     // if not null,then the some 'update' flag has been set
61.     //
62.     if ( ((String) updateFlags.get( row )) != null ) {
63.         return true;
64.     }
65.     else {
66.       return false;
67.     }
68.
69.}
```

The GeneralAggregateVO Class: Get Internal Counts and getObject Methods

A number of methods are provided to return the values from internal flags. The getRowCount method returns the value of the internal row count variable (rowCount). The getColumnName method is passed an integer value and returns a column name string for the column in the aggregate value object. The getRowPos method returns an integer value of the current row position (currentRow).

The overloaded getObject method returns an object reference for the object at the integer column value passed into the method. The first version of this method takes an integer argument and retrieves the object from the internal Vector for the current row (currentRow) using the Vector get method.

The second version of the `getObject` method takes a string argument that is assumed to be the name of the column to retrieve. The `colKeys Hashtable` contains key/value pairs of column names and corresponding integer values for the column position. This `Hashtable` is searched for the column name value using the `get` method, which returns an object reference that is cast as a `java.lang.Integer` value, and then the `intValue` method is called to return the integer value. This returns the integer position of the column being requested, and this position is then passed to the `getObject` method (the first version of the method) to retrieve the object at that column position. The code for these methods is shown next.

The GeneralAggregateVO Class: The Get Internal Counts and getObject Methods

```
public int getRowCount() {
    return rowCount;
}
public int getColumnCount() {
    return columnCount;
}
public String getColumnName( int col ) {
    //
    // column name must be String
    //
    return (String) colNums.get( new Integer( col ) );
}

public int getRowPos() {
    return currentRow;
}

// get the String value at the column offset
public Object getObject( int col )   {
    return currentRecord.get( col );
}

// ----------------------------------------------------------------
 // get the String value at the column name position
public Object getObject( String colName ) {

    int pos = ((Integer) colKeys.get( colName )).intValue();
    return getObject( pos ) ;

}
```

The GeneralAggregateVO Class: Positioning Methods

A number of methods are used to provide positioning for the internal pointers in the aggregate value object. The `absolute` method is used to position the aggregate value object to the absolute position of the row that has been designated by the parameter. This is the absolute position from the start of the internal set of rows. Within the rows `Vector` there is a `Vector` that corresponds to the column values of the designated row. This `Vector` is retrieved and is used to set the value of the `currentRecord Vector`.

The relative method takes an integer parameter for the relative position to move, relative to the current row. The internal `currentRow` pointer is incremented based on the position parameter, and then the Vector for the specified row is retrieved from the rows Vector and used to set the value of the currentRecord Vector. The code for these methods follows:

The GeneralAggregateVO Class: The Positioning Methods

```
// move to the absolute position
public void absolute( int pos ) {

    currentRow = pos;
    currentRecord = (Vector) rows.get( currentRow );

}

// move to the relative position
public void relative( int pos ) {

    currentRow += pos;
    currentRecord = (Vector) rows.get( currentRow );

}
```

Positioning Methods and Negative Values

Note that the current version of the GeneralAggregateVO class does not support negative positioning values and does not test for out of bounds positions. This could obviously be added to these methods, but for the sake of clarity and brevity, it has been eliminated from this presentation.

The GeneralAggregateVO Class: Output Contents

The dumpContents method is used primarily for debugging. The code demonstrates how to iterate through the contents of the aggregate value object, using a few of the public methods of the GeneralAggregateVO class.

The method starts a loop on line 7, which iterates from zero (since this is a zero-based list) through the total number of rows in the aggregate value object. For each row in the aggregate value object, the internal pointer is moved to the row position on line 8, and a loop on line 11 is used to iterate over the contents of the current record, using the getColumnCount method to return the number of columns in the record. For each column in the record, the column name is output using the getColumnName method, and the value of the column is output using the getObject method. The code for this method is shown next.

The GeneralAggregateVO Class: The dumpContents Method

```
1.public void dumpContents() {
2.
3.System.out.println( "*********************************" );
4.System.out.println("Column Count: " + this.getColumnCount() );
5.System.out.println("Row Count: " + this.getRowCount() );
6.
7.    for ( int n = 0; n < this.getRowCount(); n++ ) {
8.          this.absolute( n );
9.          System.out.println( "*********************************" );
10.         System.out.println( "Row: " + n );
11.         for ( int z = 0; z < this.getColumnCount(); z++ ) {
12.              System.out.println( "Column Name: " +
13.                      this.getColumnName( z ) +
14.                      " - Column Value: " + this.getObject( z ) );
15.
16.    }
17.   }
18.
19.}
```

The GeneralAggregateVO Class: Clear Contents

Two methods are available to clear the update flags and values of the aggregate value object: the clearUpdates method and the clear method. The clearUpdates method clears the update flags for the current set of updates; it does not set the value of the aggregate value object to the values that existed before the updates were made. (If the database had not been updated by the controlling program, then this could be done by simply executing a refresh operation from the database and then reloading the aggregate value object.)

The `clear` method clears all internal objects and pointers and allows the aggregate value object to be reused. This method clears the rows Vector, the `updateFlags Vector`, and the `currentRecord Vector` by calling the removeAllElements method. New Hashtables are then created for the objects that store column names (`colKeys` and `colNums`) and the columns that have been updated (`updateCols`). The internal pointers for the current row (currentRow), the number of rows stored (`rowCount`), and the number of columns in each row (`columnCount`) are set to zero. At this point the aggregate value object is ready to receive the contents of a new query. The code for these methods is shown next.

The GeneralAggregateVO Class: The clearUpdates and clear Methods

```
//
// clears update flags ... does NOT reset data to
// pre-update state
//
public void clearUpdates() {

for ( int n = 0; n < getRowCount(); n++ )
    //
    // set the update flag for this row
    //
    updateFlags.set( n, new String( "" ) );

}

// -------------------------------------------------------------
//
// clear internal counters and vectors and
// allow this object to be reused
//
public void clear() {

//
// clear the vectors
//
rows.removeAllElements();
updateFlags.removeAllElements();
currentRecord.removeAllElements();

//
// need a new object reference for the Hashtables
//
colKeys    = new Hashtable();
colNums    = new Hashtable();
updateCols = new Hashtable();

//
// clear the counters
//
```

```
currentRow    = 0;
rowCount      = 0;
columnCount   = 0;

}

}
```

EXTENDING GENERALDAO AND GENERALAGGREGATEVO TO CREATE SPECIFIC IMPLEMENTATIONS

Though the presentation of the aggregate value object and data access object shown here is generalized, they could both be converted into more specific versions.

The `GeneralAggregateVO` class stores the column data from the `ResultSet` as object references to the appropriate Java language wrapper classes. If this approach to storing data is acceptable, then the only change required to make this design specific would be to change the `GeneralDataAccessObject` to execute specific queries to load the `GeneralAggregateVO` class.

Alternatively, the `GeneralAggregateVO` could be extended and specific methods could be added for each of the columns to be retrieved from the database. For example, the `movies` table would have `getMovieName` and `getMovieID` methods, and the users table value object would have `getFirstName` and `getLastName` methods. The `GeneralDAO` could also be extended to perform operations on only a specific set of tables.

Though not a subclass of these classes, examples in chapter 16 show specific implementations of value objects and DAOs.

SUMMARY

This chapter provided an example of a set of design patterns applied to the manipulation of data using JDBC. Two design data manipulation design patterns were shown: the value object and the data access object. We extended the design for the value object to support aggregation—the aggregate value object.

We used an approach here that combined the work done in supporting dynamic queries with the use of design patterns. The design patterns shown here managed the data in a generic fashion, providing some additional flexibility. They could, however, be extended easily to support specific database operations.

COMING UP NEXT

In Chapter 14, we apply these design patterns to a specific application: a database table browser application. The program shown accepts and executes a query and then displays the query in a GUI window using a tabular (spreadsheet) format.

Table Browser Application

INTRODUCTION

In this chapter, we let "the rubber meet the road" in a full-scale example of a JDBC application. Here the focus shifts from the specifics of the JDBC API to using the JDBC in a fashion that applies good Java design principles. In this chapter we apply the Java design patterns discussed in Chapter 13 to the development of a GUI application which allows database contents to be browsed and updated.

THE TABLE BROWSER APPLICATION

The application demonstrated here uses the Swing API to create a GUI window that displays the results of a query in a tabular format and allows the user to modify those results and apply updates to the database (see Figure 14–1). The user can delete rows from the table display and have those deletes applied to the database table. The user can also insert rows into the table display and have those inserts applied along with other updates directly to the database table.

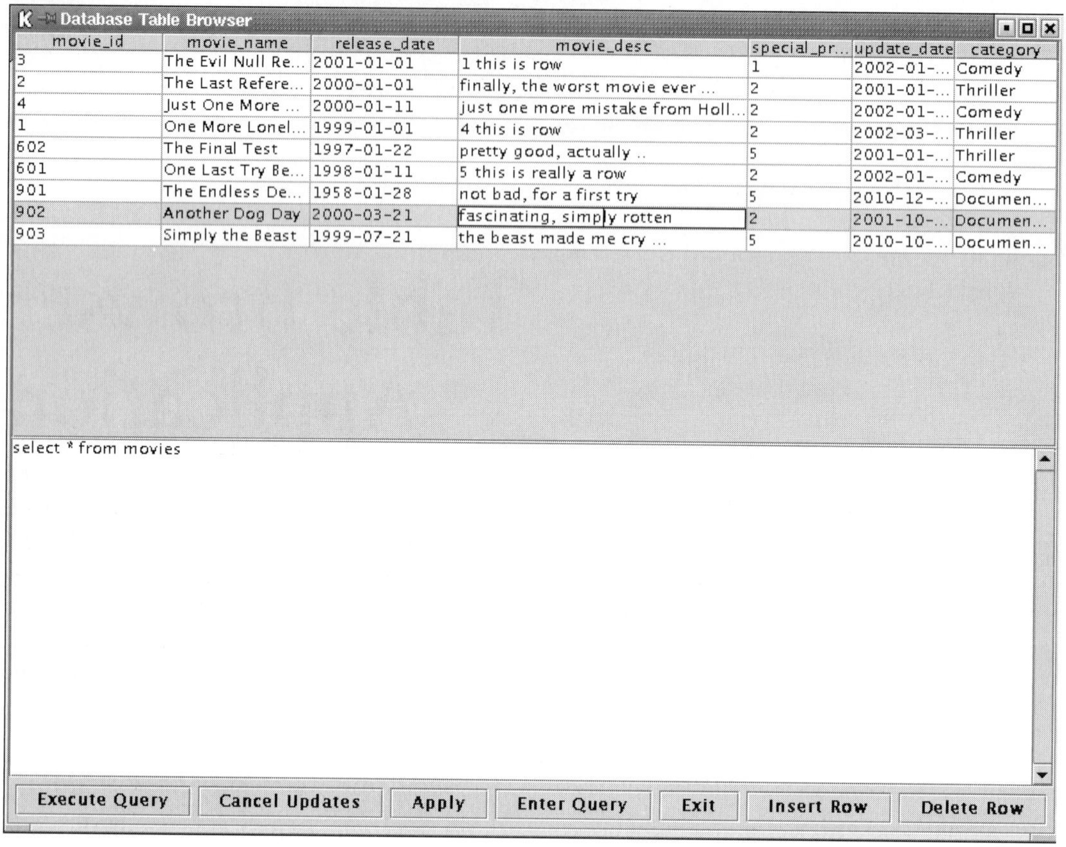

movie_id	movie_name	release_date	movie_desc	special_pr...	update_date	category
3	The Evil Null Re...	2001-01-01	1 this is row	1	2002-01-...	Comedy
2	The Last Refere...	2000-01-01	finally, the worst movie ever ...	2	2001-01-...	Thriller
4	Just One More ...	2000-01-11	just one more mistake from Holl...	2	2002-01-...	Comedy
1	One More Lonel...	1999-01-01	4 this is row	2	2002-03-...	Thriller
602	The Final Test	1997-01-22	pretty good, actually ..	5	2001-01-...	Thriller
601	One Last Try Be...	1998-01-11	5 this is really a row	2	2002-01-...	Comedy
901	The Endless De...	1958-01-28	not bad, for a first try	5	2010-12-...	Documen...
902	Another Dog Day	2000-03-21	fascinating, simply rotten	2	2001-10-...	Documen...
903	Simply the Beast	1999-07-21	the beast made me cry ...	5	2010-10-...	Documen...

select * from movies

| Execute Query | Cancel Updates | Apply | Enter Query | Exit | Insert Row | Delete Row |

Figure 14-1   *Table Browser Database Application*

This application will first be shown as a client-server application, where the client works with the data and updates directly to the database using a *data access object*, an application of a design pattern which will be described in more detail in chapter 16. We will then trace through the process of converting it to a Remote Method Invocation (RMI)-based application, where the client will retrieve the data access object through RMI and interact with the database through remote calls to the data access object.

Because of the design of the objects we are using here, the application is amenable to conversion to an RMI application. The results of the query are aggregated in an object that is passed to the client in one call, thus avoiding network traffic in trying to access the database a row at a time. Updates are then applied to the aggregate value object and applied to the database (through the data access object) all at once, thereby reducing the network traffic of trying to access the database a row at a time.

The general data access object (`GeneralDAO`) is used to execute the query and access the database, and the aggregate value object (`GeneralAggregateVO`) is used to cache the results and updates to the results on the client.

Technical Approach

The table browser application, for simplicity in presentation and because it is a Swing application, implements both the client and presentation tiers in a single class: the `TableBrowser` class. This class contains all of the component references needed to display the GUI and to manage the user interaction. This means that all event handlers are contained in this class as inner classes. (At 400 lines, this is not an unmanageable class, but in the development of a production system, you could argue to refactor the inner classes for the event handlers and table data model to external classes.)

Looking at the screen grab in Figure 14–1, you can see the major functions that need to be performed by the application: enter a query, execute a query, insert data, update data, delete data, apply changes to the database, cancel any pending updates, and exit the application. The advantages of having flexible and robust business objects become clear when you examine the implementation of this demonstration application. Before we begin looking at the code, let's first examine the operation of the application.

Enter Query and Execute Query

The *enter query* option clears any text in the text field in the lower part of the GUI window and allows the user to enter a new query. The *'execute query* option reads the text in the lower portion of the window and attempts to execute it as a query using the general data access object (a `GeneralDAO` instance). If the query is successful, then the general data access object will load its internal aggregate value object (a `GeneralAggregateVO` instance) with the values from the query. The event handler that is managing the execute query option will retrieve the aggregate value object from the data access object and use it to display the GUI tabular window used to display the data.

Insert, Update, and Delete Functions

The insert and update operations are mapped directly to general aggregate value object operations, so they are effectively cached in the aggregate value object until the user decides to apply them to the database (using the apply updates operation). As you will see when you examine the code, the event handlers for the buttons that allow the user to execute these operations simply map to one or two calls in the general aggregate value object.

The delete operation is handled differently. Because of the potential headaches involved in caching delete operations (managing an internal phantom row), deletes are handled immediately when the user requests the operation. The user is first prompted whether or not he or she really wants to delete, as seen in Figure 14–2 (we give them a second chance), and if they do elect to delete, the delete is performed immediately against the database, using the data access object to perform the operation.

Apply Changes

Once the user chooses the apply changes option, the event handler simply maps the call to a single data access object method to apply the updates in the general aggregate value object to the database. This option does not make any decisions concerning concurrency but simply applies the updates that have been done (they are flagged in the general aggregate value object) to the database.

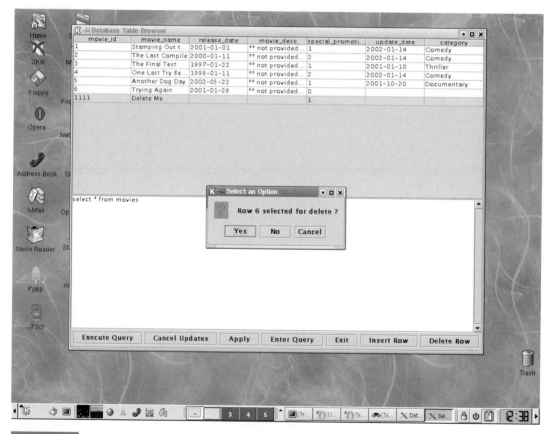

Figure 14–2 *The delete operation prompts the user for confirmation before performing the delete.*

Clear Updates and Exit

The clear updates option allows the user to clear any updates that have been done in the GUI (and have been automatically reflected in the internal general aggregate value object). The event handler maps this call to the general aggregate value object method to clear its internal flags. This method does not refresh the aggregate value object from the database.

The exit option does as the name implies, exits the application. It does not attempt to apply (nor does it check for) any existing updates.

The following sections will review the code for the table browser application in detail.

The TableBrowser Class: Class Declaration and Instance Members

Various object references for the GUI components are declared at the start of the `TableBrowser` class definition. Declaring them here as instance members with visibility throughout the class allows them to be accessed easily. Buttons are declared to allow the user to initiate processing. Buttons are provided for executing the query currently loaded into the table browser, for canceling any updates the user may have entered, for deleting the current row, for inserting a new row, and for exiting the program.

A text area is created and will be placed at the bottom of the window. A table (`JTable`) is created and will be placed at the top of the window. A data table model object (`dtModel`) reference is declared on line 57 and will be used to map the program data (as stored in the aggregate value object) to the GUI table (a `JTable` instance). The code for this program block follows:

The TableBrowser Class: Declaration and Instance Members

```
1.import javax.swing.*;
2.import javax.swing.table.*;
3.import java.sql.*;
4.import java.awt.event.*;
5.import java.awt.*;
6.
7.public class TableBrowser {
8.
9.//
10.// store internal data
11.//
12.private GeneralAggregateVO gvo;
13.private GeneralDO         gdo;
14.
15.
16.//
```

```
17.// query string set to default value
18.//
19.private String         query = "select * from movies";
20.
21.//
22.// GUI components
23.//
24.private JFrame     frame;
25.
26.//
27.// buttons
28.//
29.private JButton    enterQuery;
30.private JButton    executeQuery;
31.private JButton    cancelUpdates;
32.private JButton    executeUpdate;
33.private JButton    executeInsert;
34.private JButton    executeDelete;
35.private JButton    exitButton;
36.private JButton    deleteButton;
37.
38.//
39.// panels
40.//
41.private JPanel     buttonPanel;
42.private JPanel     contentPanel;
43.
44.//
45.// text area for entering a query
46.//
47.private JTextArea queryText;
48.
49.//
50.// table for data display and update
51.//
52.private JTable     table;
53.
54.//
55.// store data for JTable
56.//
57.dataTableModel dtModel=null;
```

TableBrowser.java: main Program Block

The main program block contains a small number of method calls that are used to start the application. The methods retrieve data and load it into the instance members of the TableBrowser class instance, and then start the GUI.

A `TableBrowser` instance is created first on line 6. This instance is then used to invoke the `getData` method, which will do as the name implies: get data to be used in the program.

Once the data has been loaded, the GUI can be created and used to display the data. This is done through a call to the `buildGUI` method on line 19. The code for this program block is shown next.

The TableBrowser Class: The main Program Block

```
1.public static void main( String args[] ) {
2.
3.      //
4.      // create table browser
5.      //
6.      TableBrowser tablebrowser = new TableBrowser();
7.
8.      //
9.      // get data from database
10.     //
11.     System.out.println("Loading data ... ");
12.     tablebrowser.getData();
13.
14.     //
15.     // build the GUI, display the data
16.     // and allow user edits
17.     //
18.     System.out.println("Starting GUI ... ");
19.     tablebrowser.buildGUI();
20.
21.} // end main
```

The TableBrowser Class: The getData Method

The `getData` method performs the steps necessary to execute the default query used by the program and use the results to display the GUI window. This could be a complex process, but fortunately for us, we have a data access object to manage most of the details of this operation.

The method begins by creating a data access object on line 6. This is an instance of the `GeneralDAO` class shown previously. The `GeneralDAO` instance is then used to execute the query on line 11. The `executeQuery` method of the `GeneralDAO` will execute the query and load the results of the query into the internal data members of the `GeneralDAO` instance.

Internally, the `GeneralDAO` instance is using an aggregate value object to store the retrieved data. In this application, we will use that aggregate value object, an instance of `GeneralAggregateVO`, within the application to provide for the display of the data and allow updates of the displayed data without having to perform expensive database interaction. For that reason, the internal aggregate value object of the data access object is retrieved and stored in the TableBrowser program on line 30 in the internal instance member gvo. The code for this example follows:

The TableBrowser Class: The getData Method

```
1.protected void getData() {
2.
3.      //
4.      // create general Data Access Object for dynamic queries
5.      //
6.      gdo = new GeneralDAO();
7.
8.      try {
9.          // execute the query and store results
10.          System.out.println("Executing query: " + query );
11.          gdo.executeQuery( query );
12.      }
13.      catch (SQLException e) {
14.
15.              System.out.println(
16.                "SQLException in TableExample1. Message: " +
17.                e.getMessage());
18.          JOptionPane.showMessageDialog( null,
19.                  "Database error on load. Message: " +
20.                          e.getMessage(),
21.                          "Error",
22.                          JOptionPane.ERROR_MESSAGE);
23.      }
24.
25.      //
26.      // get the GeneralAggregateVO - aggregate
27.      // Value Object with data and access methods
28.      //
29.      System.out.println( "Retrieving VO ... " );
30.      gvo = gdo.getGeneralAggregateVO();
31.
32.
33.      //
34.      // display dialog box about rows loaded
35.      //
36.      JOptionPane.showMessageDialog( null,
37.                      "Loaded " +
38.                              gvo.getRowCount() + " rows.",
39.                      "Message",
40.                  JOptionPane.INFORMATION_MESSAGE);
41.
42.}
```

The TableBrowser Class: The buildGUI Method

The `buildGUI` method does as you might expect: It builds the GUI. This method makes heavy use of Swing classes. If you are not familiar with Swing, this may seem confusing, but understanding the basic concepts and approach will help you understand how JDBC and database access fits into all of this.

The first few lines of the method on lines 6 through 8 are used to create the frame (an instance of `JFrame`), which will be used for the window of the GUI. The `contentPanel` object will be used to place the various GUI components that will be used in this window.

On line 13, the data table model is created. This object is used by `JTable` to gather and display the contents (the data) for the `JTable`. This object, which will be shown later, essentially just wraps the aggregate value object returned by the data access object. The table for the display of the data is created on line 16 and passed this same data table model (created on line 13).

The scroll pane is created on line 21. This is a GUI component that allows another component, in our case the `JTable`, to scroll within a region of the window.

On line 27, a window listener is added. This is used to allow the window to close gracefully if the user clicks on the close window button for the window. (Neither Swing nor AWT provide this by default.)

On line 36, a text area is created to provide for the display of the default query string and to allow the user to enter a new query string. Lines 36 through 38 describe the dimensions of the area and the behavior of the component. On lines 43 through 46, a scrolling region is created for the text area.

On line 51, a method is called to create the buttons and button handlers for the various buttons that will populate the bottom of the window.

Finally, starting on line 62, the components are added to the window. Using the layering approach of Swing, components are added to scroll panes or panels, and it is the underlying pane or panel that is added to the window. The window (or `JFrame` instance) is using a default layout manager to display the components. This layout manager is known as the `BorderLayout` layout manager and will control the placement of the components based partly on compass locations (north, south, east, west, and center). Since we have three basic components to add, we can just place them in north, center, and south and let the layout manager stretch the component to fit the window. This will give us the desired effect shown in Figure 14–1. We place the data output table in the north, the query text input field in the center, and the buttons in the south.

When all of this work is complete, the calls on lines 77 and 78 will display the window. The code listing for this method is next.

The TableBrowser Class: The buildGUI Method

```
1.protected void buildGUI() {
2.
3.        //
4.        // create the frame and content pane
5.        //
6.        frame = new JFrame("Database Table Browser");
7.        contentPanel = new JPanel(new BorderLayout());
8.        frame.setContentPane(contentPanel);
9.
10.       //
11.       // load our table model with the data using our object instance
12.       //
13.       dtModel = this.new dataTableModel(   );
14.
15.       // create GUI table
16.       table = new JTable( dtModel );
17.
18.       //
19.       // add the table to the scrollpane
20.       //
21.       JScrollPane scrollpane = new JScrollPane( table );
22.       scrollpane.setPreferredSize( new Dimension( 700, 300 ) );
23.
24.       //
25.       // set the window closing event
26.       //
27.       frame.addWindowListener(new WindowAdapter() {
28.             public void windowClosing(WindowEvent e) {
29.                   System.exit(0);
30.             }
31.       });
32.
33.       //
34.       // text area for query input
35.       //
36.       queryText = new JTextArea( query, 5, 80 );
37.       queryText.setLineWrap( true );
38.       queryText.setWrapStyleWord( true );
39.
40.       //
41.       // create a scrollpane for the text area
42.       //
43.       JScrollPane queryPane = new JScrollPane( queryText );
44.       queryPane.setVerticalScrollBarPolicy(
45.                         JScrollPane.VERTICAL_SCROLLBAR_ALWAYS);
46.       queryPane.setPreferredSize(new Dimension(250, 250));
47.
```

```
48.     //
49.     // create buttons and handlers
50.     //
51.     createButtonsHandlers();
52.
53.     //
54.     // add all constituent panels and panes to the contentPanel
55.     //
56.
57.     // ** add the components to the window **
58.
59.     //
60.     // data output
61.     //
62.     contentPanel.add( scrollpane, BorderLayout.NORTH );
63.
64.     //
65.     // query
66.     //
67.     contentPanel.add( queryPane, BorderLayout.CENTER );
68.
69.     //
70.     // buttons
71.     //
72.     contentPanel.add( buttonPanel, BorderLayout.SOUTH ); // buttons
73.
74.     //
75.     // now let's roll ...
76.     //
77.     frame.pack();
78.     frame.setVisible(true);
79.
80.}
```

The TableBrowser Class:
The createButtonsHandlers Method

The `createButtonHandlers` method creates the action event handlers for the button click events; this is the code that will be executed when the user presses the button. All of the buttons that appear in the bottom panel of the window are created and then added to the panel in this method. (Not all handlers for the button are handled; this method creates listeners for the most common event, the button click, which will cause the GUI to fire the `actionPerformed` event.)

Since this represents a significant portion of the processing 4 done in the program, it is worth covering each of these button handlers separately. The following sections discuss each of the button handlers in this method.

The createButtonsHandlers Method: Button Declarations

The `createButtonHandlers` method begins by creating the button components to be used in the application. These button components are `JButton` objects, which are declared in sequence in the following code:

The TableBrowser Class: The createButtonHandlers Method Button Declarations

```
// ————————————————————————-
protected void createButtonsHandlers() {

     //
     // create some buttons and corresponding listeners
     //
     enterQuery     = new JButton ( "Enter Query" );
     executeQuery   = new JButton ( "Execute Query" );
     cancelUpdates  = new JButton ( "Cancel Updates" );
     executeUpdate  = new JButton ( "Apply" );
     executeInsert  = new JButton ( "Insert Row" );
     executeDelete  = new JButton ( "Delete Row" );
     exitButton     = new JButton ( "Exit" );

  // button listener/handlers
  exitButton.addActionListener( new ActionListener() {
        public void actionPerformed( ActionEvent e) {
              System.exit(0);
        }
   } );
   // ————————————————————————-
```

The executeInsert Button Handler

The `executeInsert` button is pressed by the user to insert a new blank row into the table in the GUI window. This method makes use of the aggregate value object (`gvo`) by calling the `appendRow` method. This will append a blank row onto the end of the current aggregate value object (which is controlling the display of the table). Once the row has been appended to the aggregate value object, the `fireTableStructureChanged` method is called to inform the GUI that the table (and the data that supports the table) has changed. This will force the GUI to update the table, which it will do by re-reading each row of the underlying data object, the `GeneralAggregateVO` object instance. Since the aggregate value object now has an additional row with a row of blank columns, that will be displayed by the GUI window. This method is as follows.

The TableBrowser Class: The executeInsert Event Handler

```
// button listener/handlers
executeInsert.addActionListener( new ActionListener() {
     public void actionPerformed( ActionEvent e) {

          gvo.appendRow(); // append a new row
          dtModel.fireTableStructureChanged();

     }
 } );
```

The executeDelete Button Handler

The executeDelete button is used by the user to delete the current row (the row where the cursor is currently located). To avoid much of the confusion that would stem from trying to track deleted rows before performing an update, this method will perform delete operations by deleting the row directly from the database, refreshing the aggregate value object by calling the executeQuery method, and then informing the GUI table that the data has changed. The end result is that the table will be displayed with the deleted row removed from the table view.

It is always good policy to prompt users before allowing them to actually delete something, and that policy is followed in this example. First, the method obtains the currently selected row by calling the getSelectedRow method of the JTable class on line 14. This method returns an integer, which is assumed to be the row the user wishes to delete. If the method returns a value of –1, that means that for some reason, there is no current row.

If the getSelectedRow method did return a valid value, then just to be sure, the user is prompted on lines 23 through 25 to confirm the delete of the row.

If the user has confirmed that yes, he or she would really like to delete the row, then the row is deleted using the calls on line 30 and line 31. Note that the general data access object is used to call the deleteRow method. So, unlike the other operations, which operate on the aggregate value object (gvo) and then apply their updates to the database at some later time, the TableBrowser class will apply delete operations immediately and then refresh the TableBrowser class data by executing the query again with a call to the executeQuery method.

At this point, the data in the aggregate value object has been refreshed and can be used for the application. The call to getGeneralAggregateVO on line 32 is used to set the internal GeneralAggregateVO method to the new value provided by the GeneralDAO.

After the successful conclusion of the updates, a message is displayed to the user indicating that the row selected has been deleted. Finally, on line 60, the fireTableDataChanged method is called. This will force the GUI to redisplay the table with the new data. The complete code for this example is shown next.

The TableBrowser Class: The executeDelete Action Listener

```
1.      // button listener/handlers
2.      executeDelete.addActionListener( new ActionListener() {
3.            public void actionPerformed( ActionEvent e) {
4.
5.                  // this method will go directly to the database and
6.                  // delete the row and then execute the query again
7.                  // to refresh the data
8.
9.
10.                 //
11.                 // determine which row to delete
12.                 //
13.         int confirm  = 0;
14.                 int row = table.getSelectedRow();
15.         if ( row == -1 ) {
16.                 JOptionPane.showMessageDialog(
17.                                     null,
18.                             "No row selected for delete.",
19.                                 "Error",
20.                         JOptionPane.ERROR_MESSAGE);
21.         }
22.         else {      // we have a row to delete. get confirmation
23.                     confirm = JOptionPane.showConfirmDialog(
24.                             null,
25.                     "Row " + row + " selected for delete ?");
26.         }
27.
28.             if ( confirm == JOptionPane.YES_OPTION ) {
29.             try {
30.                     gdo.deleteRow( row );
31.                     gdo.executeQuery( query );
32.                     gvo = gdo.getGeneralAggregateVO();
33.
34.         // if at this point, success
35.             JOptionPane.showMessageDialog( null,
36.                     "Row " + row + " has been deleted.",
37.                     "Message",
38.                 JOptionPane.INFORMATION_MESSAGE);
39.             }
40.             catch (SQLException ex) {
41.                     System.out.println(
42.                         SQLException on query execution. Message: " +
43.                                     ex.getMessage() );
44.             JOptionPane.showMessageDialog( null,
45.                     "Error on query execution. Message: " +
46.                             ex.getMessage(),
47.                             "Error",
48.                         JOptionPane.ERROR_MESSAGE);
49.             }
50.             }
```

```
51.        else {                    // user chose not to delete
52.
53.              JOptionPane.showMessageDialog( null,
54.                              "No rows deleted.",
55.                              "Message",
56.                          JOptionPane.INFORMATION_MESSAGE);
57.        }
58.
59.        // this will redraw the table
60.        dtModel.fireTableStructureChanged();
61.
62.     }
63.   } );
```

The executeQuery Button Handler

The executeQuery button is used to execute the query currently defined for the application. The action listener uses calls on executeQuery in the general data access object to execute the current query. The listener first calls the queryText textfield to retrieve any query that may be there and passes the resulting query string to the executeQuery method.

Once the executeQuery method has been called, a popup window is displayed with a message indicating the query has been executed. The prompt also displays the number of rows returned by the query, as returned by the getRowCount method of the aggregate value object.

When the user prompt has been completed, the getGeneralAggregateVO method is called on the general data access object. This returns the new aggregate value object for the query that has just been executed by the general data access object. Since the table structure has changed (the underlying data has changed), the fireTableStructureChanged method is called to redraw the GUI table. The code listing for this handler is shown next.

The TableBrowser Class: The executeQuery Button Action Listener

```
executeQuery.addActionListener( new ActionListener() {
    public void actionPerformed( ActionEvent e) {
        // use DynamicQuery object to execute the query
        // and process the results
        try {
            gdo.executeQuery( queryText.getText() );
            JOptionPane.showMessageDialog(
                        null,
                        "Loaded " + gvo.getRowCount() +
                        " rows.",
                    "Message",
                JoptionPane.INFORMATION_MESSAGE);
```

```
                              //
                              // get the new GeneralAggregateVO
                              //
                              gvo = gdo.getGeneralAggregateVO();
                              dtModel.fireTableStructureChanged();
                              dtModel.fireTableDataChanged();
                          }
                    catch (SQLException ex) {
                              System.out.println(
                                "SQLException on query execution. Message: "   +
                                   ex.getMessage() );

                          JOptionPane.showMessageDialog(
                                        null,
                                        "Error on query execution. Message: " +
                                         ex.getMessage(),
                                        "Error",
                                        JOptionPane.ERROR_MESSAGE);
                    }
             }
        } );
```

The enterQuery Button Handler

The job of the `enterQuery` button is to allow the user to begin entering a new query in a blank text field. It does this by calling the `setText` method in the `JTextField` class; this clears the text and makes the field ready for input. The code listing for this example follows:**??insert code listing reference??**

The TableBrowser Class: The enterQuery Button

```
enterQuery.addActionListener( new ActionListener() {
     public void actionPerformed( ActionEvent e) {
            queryText.setText( "" );
      }
} );

executeUpdate.addActionListener( new ActionListener() {
      public void actionPerformed( ActionEvent e) {
            //
            // execute all pending updates
          //
        try {
            gdo.applyUpdates( );
           JOptionPane.showMessageDialog( null,
             "Updates applied to database.",
```

```
                    "Message",
              JOptionPane.INFORMATION_MESSAGE);
       }
    catch (SQLException ex) {
            System.out.println(
         "SQLException on query execution. Message: " +
         ex.getMessage() );
      JOptionPane.showMessageDialog(
                null,
             "Error on query execution. Message: " +
                ex.getMessage(),
             "Error",
           JOptionPane.ERROR_MESSAGE);
       }
    }
} );
```

The cancelUpdates Button Handler and Adding to Panel

The `cancelUpdates` button allows the user to cancel any updates that have been applied to the `GeneralAggregateVO` object. This `actionHanlder` simply calls the `clearUpdates` method of the `GeneralAggregateVO` object instance (`gvo`). This will clear all update flags in the current object instance.

The final lines of this method are used to add the buttons that have been created to the `buttonPanel`, a blank panel. Button handlers will be displayed in the sequence in which they are added to the panel. The code for this listing follows:

The TableBrowser Class: The cancelUpdates button

```
cancelUpdates.addActionListener( new ActionListener() {
    public void actionPerformed( ActionEvent e) {
          gvo.clearUpdates();
          JOptionPane.showMessageDialog( null,
                        "Updates were cleared.",
                        "Message",
                JOptionPane.INFORMATION_MESSAGE);
     }
} );

//
// create a panel for the buttons and add them
//
buttonPanel = new JPanel();
buttonPanel.add( executeQuery );
buttonPanel.add( cancelUpdates );
```

```
        buttonPanel.add( executeUpdate );
        buttonPanel.add( enterQuery );
        buttonPanel.add( exitButton );
        buttonPanel.add( executeInsert );
        buttonPanel.add( executeDelete );
```

}

THE TABLEBROWSER.JAVA APPLICATION: THE DATATABLEMODEL INNER CLASS

Inner classes in Java provide a very useful syntax to obtain the concise encapsulation of the business logic while still maintaining class scope for the contents of the class. The inner class in this example is used to control the table displayed by the GUI. In this case, the class extends the `AbstractTableModel` class and overrides certain methods so that they return sensible values for this data model.

The `getColumnCount` and `getRowCount` methods return a count of the current number of the rows and columns in the model. These methods just map directly to the `GeneralAggregateVO` object (`gvo`) stored as an instance member of the application.

The `getValueAt` method takes an integer row and column argument and uses the internal general aggregate value object to position to the designated row. The `gvo` `getObject` method is then used to retrieve an object reference for the designated column. The code for this example is shown next.

The `getColumnName` method simply returns the column name for the designated integer column. This implementation maps to the general aggregate value object method to return the column name.

The `isCellEditable` method returns a boolean `false` if the cell is not editable. In this example, the value is set to return `true` to facilitate the processing of the example.

The `getColumnClass` method returns the class of the column in the cell. In this example, the class is set to return the class of an `Object` with each call.

The TableBrowser Class: The dataTableModel Inner Class

```
class dataTableModel extends AbstractTableModel {

boolean updateFlag = false;  // set true if we have pending updates

    public int getColumnCount() {
        return gvo.getColumnCount();
    }
// ────────────────────────────
```

```
   public int getRowCount() {
        return gvo.getRowCount();
   }
// ——————————————
   public Object getValueAt(int row, int col) {
           gvo.absolute( row );
           return  gvo.getObject( col );
   }

// ——————————————
   public String getColumnName( int col ) {
        return gvo.getColumnName( col );
   }

// ——————————————


   public boolean isCellEditable( int row, int col ) {
        return true;
}
// ——————————————
   public Class getColumnClass( int col ) {
        return new Object().getClass();
   }
```

The dataTableModel Inner Class: The setValueAt Method

The setValueAt method is called by the GUI event loop when a cell is edited. It receives arguments for the value, the row, and the column. These values are passed into the method which then sets the values of the internal objects to the appropriate values.

The method takes the updateFlag and sets its value to true. This is a flag used by the application to track updates in the dataModel.

The generalAggregateValue object is then moved to the current rows with a call to its absolute method, using the row value passed into the method. Next, the updateObject method is called and passed the column to update and the corresponding value. Finally, the GUI table is updated using the fireTableCellUpdated method call.

The code for this method follows:

The dataTableModel Inner Class: The setValueAt Method

```
// called when data has changed for a column
public void setValueAt(Object value, int row, int col) {

        // set the update flag
        updateFlag = true;

        // update the gvo
        gvo.absolute( row );
        gvo.updateObject( col, value );
        fireTableCellUpdated( row, col ); // update just this row

    }

    }
}
```

Three-Tiered RMI Example: The Table Browser Remote Application

Our previous example demonstrated a two-tiered client-server approach. This example demonstrates how JDBC code could be used in a multitiered application using RMI. Because the data access design patterns have been used effectively, and data access and data containership is neatly encapsulated into DAOs and aggregate value objects, the process of converting the application to a multitiered RMI application is relatively simple. We need only identify a small set of methods that will perform database access (on a server) and will return our aggregate value object.

To provide a clear example, this demonstration uses a separate set of classes to implement RMI, but the existing classes could easily have been used. For the sake of brevity, only those methods and declarations that have changed are shown.

The first step in this conversion process is to make the class that will be delivered using RMI extend `UnicastRemoteObject` and identify it as implementing an interface that contains the methods that will be called remotely. The code for this follows:

RMI Changes in DAO Class Declaration

```
import java.sql.*;
import javax.sql.*;
import javax.naming.*;
import java.util.*;
import java.io.*;
```

```
//
// for RMI
//
import java.rmi.*;
import java.rmi.server.*;

public class RemoteGeneralDAO extends UnicastRemoteObject implements RemoteDAO {

...
```

The `RemoteDAO` interface identifies the methods to be used remotely. It is not necessary to expose all the methods of the data access object remotely; only those that need to be used in the client (the table browser application) need to be identified in the interface. The following code listing shows the interface declaration:

The RemoteDAO Class Declaration

```
import java.rmi.*;
import java.sql.*;

public interface RemoteDAO extends Remote {

public void executeQuery( String query ) throws RemoteException, SQLException;

public void applyUpdates( GeneralAggregateVO gvo ) throws RemoteException,
SQLException;

public GeneralAggregateVO getGeneralAggregateVO() throws RemoteException;

public void deleteRow( int row ) throws RemoteException, SQLException;

}
```

All remotely accessed methods must throw a `RemoteException`. All parameters passed and values returned must implement the `Serializable` or `Remote` interface. For our purposes, we need only execute the query using the execute query method, apply any updates that the table browser performs using the `applyUpdates` method, return the aggregate value object using the `getGeneralAggregateValue` object method, and delete a row using the `deleteRow` method. The `applyUpdates` version used in this remote access example is different; this version takes an aggregate value object as an argument. The reason for that will be explained shortly.

The code for the table browser client application requires minor modifications. The changes need to be made in the portion of the application that retrieves the data access object. Since this data access object is going to be a remote object, we need to provide the code to retrieve the object correctly. The following code demonstrates this process. The boldfaced portion of the code shows what has changed in the `getData` method. The instance of the `GeneralDataAccessObject`, the object that neatly encapsulates all of our data access, is retrieved using the JNDI name server with a call to the `lookup` method. This returns a reference that we've identified as a reference that implements the `RemoteDAO` interface (not the `GeneralDAO` object used in the client server example). (When using RMI, the object returned from the `lookup` call will always be treated as an implementation of an interface, not a class.) Once the reference is retrieved from the `lookup` call, the code for accessing and using the data access object is unchanged, with the minor exception of the `applyUpdates` call, shown next.

The RemoteTableBrowser Class: The getData Method

```
protected void getData() {

    try {
    //
    // create general Data Object for dynamic queries
    // do a lookup to retrieve the remote object
    //
    System.out.println("Getting RemoteDAO ... " );
    gdo = ( RemoteDAO ) Naming.lookup( "remote_general_dao" );

        //
        // execute the query and store results
        //
    System.out.println("Executing Query ... " );
        gdo.executeQuery( query );

        //
        // get the GeneralAggregateVO -
        // aggregate Value Object with data and access methods
        //
    System.out.println("Retrieving gvo ... " );
        gvo = gdo.getGeneralAggregateVO();

    }
    catch (SQLException e) {

            System.out.println(
        "SQLException in TableExample1. Message: " +
        e.getMessage());
            e.printStackTrace();
            JOptionPane.showMessageDialog( null,
                    "Database error on load. Message: " +
                    e.getMessage(),
                    "Error",
                    JOptionPane.ERROR_MESSAGE);
    }
```

```
catch (Exception ex) {
      System.out.println(
         "RemoteException in TableExample1. Message: " +
          ex.getMessage());
      ex.printStackTrace();
}
finally {

// print message about rows loaded
 if ( gvo != null ) {
    JOptionPane.showMessageDialog( null,
                    "Loaded " +
                       gvo.getRowCount() + " rows.",
                    "Message",
              JOptionPane.INFORMATION_MESSAGE);
  }
}

}
```

The RemoteTableBrowser Class: The applyUpdates Method

The `applyUpdates` method is responsible for applying the updates that have been cached in the aggregate value object to the database, using the internal updatable `ResultSet` of the data access object. When using a remote object server such as RMI, the remote object is running in a separate Java virtual machine (VM), quite possibly on a completely different server. This requires consideration when using object references.

In the previous table browser example, the client application executed a query using the data access object. The data access object loaded the results of the query into an aggregate value object and returned the object reference to the client application, the table browser. The table browser then applied updates to the aggregate value object and then called the `applyUpdates` method to apply the updates to the database. The call to apply the updates did not include an argument. No argument was needed because the data access object contained a reference to an aggregate value object, the same aggregate value object being used by the client application with the same object reference.

When using remote object servers, any data passed using method invocations is *passed by value*. This means that a new object reference is being created in the client code to receive the object from the server. For this reason, with the RMI version, the table browser client is working with a *different* aggregate value object reference than the data access object running on the RMI server. So, to apply the updates from the client application, the `applyUpdates` method must be changed to accept an aggregate value object reference and then that object reference must be used to apply the updates. The following code shows how this was done.

The `applyUpdates` method for the RMI version of the table browser (`RemoteTableBrowser`) takes the aggregate value object argument (a `GeneralAggregateVO` instance) and calls the `loadAggregateVO` method with the same argument. After making that call, it calls the `applyUpdates` method with no argument; this method will use the internal aggregate value object (which has just been set to the value of the argument passed in) to apply the updates. The `loadAggregateVO` method, as shown below, simply takes the aggregate value object reference passed in and assigns the internal reference to that value.

The RemoteGeneralDAO Class: The applyUpdates Method

```
public void applyUpdates ( GeneralAggregateVO gvo ) throws SQLException,
RemoteException {
//
// apply the gvo before applying the updates, to get the two in synch
// this is needed for RMI access of the gdao
//

try {

    //
    // load the general aggregate value object passed in
    //
    this.loadAggregateVO( gvo );

    //
    // apply updates
    //
    this.applyUpdates();
}
catch (Exception e)  {
      System.out.println( "Exception in applyUpdates: " + e.getMessage() );
      throw new RemoteException( e.getMessage() );
}

}


public void loadAggregateVO( GeneralAggregateVO  gvo ) throws SQLException,
Exception {

   this.gvo = gvo;

}
```

RMI Binding

Before the remote object can be used, it must be bound into an RMI registry. Though the nitty-gritty details of RMI are beyond this discussion, the process of binding the object into the RMI registry provided by Sun Microsystems with the JDK involves the following code. This code instantiates an object reference, which implements the `java.rmi.Remote` interface and the interface with the remotely invoked methods for the data access object we are using. The object is then bound into the RMI namespace using the `naming.rebind` method.

Together, JNDI and RMI provide a number of options for providing access to remote objects; using the RMI registry is only one option. Other options allow objects to be bound into LDAP or other directory servers and the namespaces for those servers integrated into the RMI accessible namespace. These other servers and registries provide additional features and performance benefits that may make them a better choice for RMI than the default registry provided by Sun.

bindRemoteGeneralDAO.java

```
import java.rmi.*;
import javax.naming.*;

public class bindRemoteGeneralDAO {


public static void main( String args[] ) {

try {

//
// this object should implement the Remote interface
//
RemoteGeneralDAO rgdao = new RemoteGeneralDAO();

//
// bind the object into a namespace
//
System.out.println( "Binding RemoteGeneralDAO ... " );
Naming.rebind( "remote_general_dao", rgdao );

}
catch (Exception e) {
  System.out.println( "Exception in main: " + e.getMessage() );
}


} // end main


}
```

SUMMARY

This chapter demonstrated how using the appropriate Java design patterns with JDBC can simplify the development process. We implemented a GUI first with a two-tiered, client-server approach, connecting to the database, collecting data and returning the data all in one program. We used various Java design patterns to encapsulate the database access. Because we used this approach, moving the application from a two-tiered client-server design to a multi-tiered, distributed application was not difficult.

Our move to a multitiered approach was accomplished by using RMI to deliver the single object we used to manage the data. Since we have applied our data access object design pattern, all our data access is encapsulated in a single object: our data access object. We can easily create a multi-tiered, distributed application by serving this data access object using RMI.

COMING UP NEXT

Our next chapter covers a well-worn topic in object-oriented programming: how to persist our object state. This chapter presents an example which takes a Java object and using a Blob data column in the database, persists a Java object to the database. Though certainly not appropriate for all object persistence, this approach does have some practical application which will be discussed in the next chapter.

Persisting Data Objects with JDBC

INTRODUCTION

One of the more common coding tasks encountered when working with JDBC is the conversion of relational data into a format that is usable by the Java application. Java applications are invariably object-oriented and so are written to work with objects. Relational data must therefore be converted into a form appropriate for use in a Java program.

Up to this point we have demonstrated various techniques for making that conversion process easier using generic and specific *data access objects* (see Chapter 13). We will revisit the data access object design pattern later in this book, but in this chapter we will look at the capability to store Java objects directly into the database. Using this capability, we can create and manipulate our Java objects, then store them in the database when we are finished using them, thus precluding the need to convert relational data into Java object form and vice versa. This is a technique that, though not appropriate for all application data, does have a number of useful applications in JDBC programming.

Why Persist Standard Java Objects

The process of converting relational data into the members of Java objects is often straightforward and efficient. There are advantages to storing this data in a relational format, not the least of which is the ability to quickly and easily search the data for specific elements. The data integrity features of mature relational databases, if used correctly, can also keep the database in a consistent state regardless of the various failures that may befall the system where the database is running.

But where relational databases begin to suffer some performance limitations is in the process of joining and aggregating across a number of tables. Though database vendors have expended a great deal of effort into making this process more efficient, there is still a performance hit to be incurred for large, multi-table joins and aggregations.

In cases where the data being retrieved does not need to be up to the minute, it may be feasible to place complex joined and aggregated data into special tables within the database. This is data that is no longer part of a normalized relational model; it represents a denormalized *snapshot* of existing data in the database that has been prepared on some regular basis, perhaps once a week. To be useful, users must be aware that the data is a snapshot.

Since we are using the object-oriented Java language, it would be convenient to create such consolidated data as an object and then simply persist this object into the database. The following example demonstrates this process.

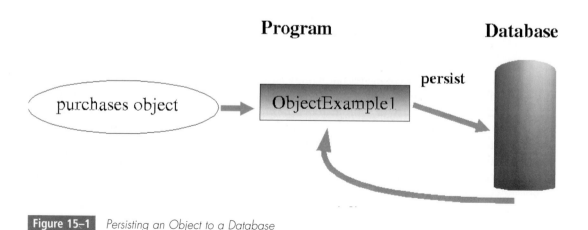

Program   **Database**

persist

purchases object → ObjectExample1

Figure 15–1   *Persisting an Object to a Database*

THE OBJECT PERSISTENCE EXAMPLE

This example demonstrates the creation of a *customer purchases* object, an object that stores a record of one or more customer purchases for a given period of time. It aggregates this purchase history in an object (representing an aggregation relationship between the objects). See Figure 15–1.

Once this object has been created, it is stored (persisted) in the database using a Blob column. After this object has been saved, the example program then demonstrates the process of materializing the object from the database by reading the object back from the database.

The class definition for the customer purchase object effectively represents a purchase record for the customer and is shown next.

CustomerPurchases.java

```java
import java.util.*;
import java.text.*;


public class CustomerPurchase implements java.io.Serializable {

private String title;
private String stockNumber;
private Date date;
private double amount;

DateFormat df = DateFormat.getDateInstance(DateFormat.SHORT);

//
// setters
//
public void setDate( String date ) {
try {
  this.date = df.parse( date );
}
catch (ParseException e) {
   System.out.println(
         "ParseException in CustomerPurchase.setDate: " +
         e.getMessage() );
}
}

public void setTitle( String title ) {
  this.title = title;
}

public void setStockNumber( String stockNumber ) {
   this.stockNumber = stockNumber;
}
```

```
public void setAmount( double amount ) {
    this.amount = amount;
}

// getters

public String getTitle() {
    return this.title;
}

public String getStockNumber() {
    return this.stockNumber;
}

public Date getDate() {
    return this.date;
}

public double getAmount() {
    return this.amount;
}

}
```

This class definition simply uses a set of `get` and `set` methods to provide for the storage of the customer purchase information. Unlike previous examples, where we sometimes stored dates as strings and allowed the database to perform the conversion for us, this example stores the date as a `java.util.Date` type and performs the conversion using the `java.text.DateFormat` parse method.

THE OBJECTEXAMPLE1 CLASS

The `CustomerPurchase` class represents a single customer purchase. What we would like to do is store an aggregation of these purchases, using a collection. In the following example, a `java.util.Vector` is used to store a list of customer purchase objects. It is this list, stored in a `Vector` object, that is then stored to the database.

This program takes advantage of the flexible Java I/O streams design. Since any `Blob` can be represented as a *stream*, we can read and write a variety of data to these streams, including Java objects, using the `java.io.ObjectOutputStream` class.

But we cannot simply output our object directly to the `Blob` column. The `PreparedStatement` interface allows an `InputStream` (`java.io.InputStream`) to be associated with a `Blob` column using the `setBinaryStream` method. We must provide an object to this method that can be used as an `InputStream`. We do this by writing our object to an internal byte array and converting the byte array to an `InputStream` object. The following code demonstrates this process.

The ObjectExample1 Class: The main Program Block

```
import java.sql.*;
import javax.sql.*;
import javax.naming.*;

import java.util.*;
import java.io.*;

public class ObjectExample1 {

public static void main( String args[] ) {

Connection con=null;
ResultSet rs = null;

try {


    ObjectExample1 objectExample = new ObjectExample1();

    //
    // obtain a connection
    //
    con = objectExample.getConnected();

    //
    // create a prepared statement
    //
    PreparedStatement pstmt = con.prepareStatement(
                "insert into objects values ( ?, ? )" );

    //
    // set the 'name' of the object
    //
    pstmt.setString( 1, "customer_purchases-4" );

    //
    // gather customer purchases in a collection
    //
    Vector purchases = objectExample.getCustomerPurchases();

    //
    // Output the collection to an internal bytestream
    //
    ByteArrayOutputStream byteArrayStream =
```

```
                   new ByteArrayOutputStream();
ObjectOutputStream     out    = new ObjectOutputStream(
                                     byteArrayStream );
out.writeObject( (Object) purchases );

//
// Create an InputStream on the bytearray
// (created from the byte array stream)
// set the Input for the PreparedStatement to the
//   ByteArrayInputStream
//
ByteArrayInputStream input =
     new ByteArrayInputStream(
                     byteArrayStream.toByteArray() );
pstmt.setBinaryStream( 2, input, 0 );

//
// update the database
//
int recCount = pstmt.executeUpdate();

//
// ** read the stored object data **
//
Statement stmt = con.createStatement();
rs = stmt.executeQuery(
"select * from objects where obj_name like 'customer_purchase%'" );

//
// get the record and output the object
//
while ( rs.next() ) {

   ObjectInputStream objInput = new ObjectInputStream(
                  rs.getBinaryStream( "obj_ref" ));

   System.out.println( "Found object. Contents: " );

   //
   // records were stored in Vector objects
   //
   Vector retrievedPurchases =
          (Vector) objInput.readObject();
   for (int n = 0;
       n < retrievedPurchases.size();
       n++ ) {


     //
     // cast each element of Vector to our object type
     //
   CustomerPurchase custPurch = (CustomerPurchase)
```

```
                    retrievedPurchases.get( n );

            System.out.println(
                 "***************************" );
              System.out.println("title: " + custPurch.getTitle() );
              System.out.println("stockNumber: " +
                            custPurch.getStockNumber() );
              System.out.println("Date: " + custPurch.getDate() );
              System.out.println("Amount: " + custPurch.getAmount() );


          }
       }


}
catch (SQLException e) {

      // display SQL specific exception information
      System.out.println("*************************" );
      System.out.println("SQLException in main: " + e.getMessage() );
      System.out.println("** SQLState: " + e.getSQLState());
      System.out.println("** SQL Error Code: " + e.getErrorCode());
      System.out.println("*************************" );
      e.printStackTrace();
  }
  catch (Exception e) {
      System.out.println("Exception in main: " + e.getMessage() );
      e.printStackTrace();
  }
  finally {

      try {
          // close the connection
        if ( con != null )
            con.close();
        System.exit(1);
      }
      catch (SQLException e) {
            e.printStackTrace();
      }
  }
}
```

The ObjectExample1 Class: The main Program Block

In this example, within the `main` program block, the `getConnected` method is called to obtain the database connection. The `getCustomerPurchases` method is then called to obtain a collection of `CustomerPurchase` objects stored in a `java.util.Vector` object.

A `java.io.ByteArrayOutputStream` is then created; this object wraps an internal byte array with an `OutputStream`. This object is then wrapped with an `ObjectOutputStream`, which will allow us to write objects to the stream. We then use this `ObjectOutputStream` to write the collection of `CustomerPurchase` objects to the internal byte array.

At this point we have an internal byte array containing our object. We have written to an `OutputStream`, but in order to write this data to a `Blob` column, we need an `InputStream`. We can obtain this by converting our `ByteArrayOutputStream` to a byte array using the `toByteArray` method, and then wrapping the byte array obtained with a `ByteArrayInputStream`. This is done by calling the `toByteArray` method for our `ByteArrayOutputStream` and passing the results (a byte array) to the constructor for the `ByteArrayInputStream` class.

Once we have the `ByteArrayInputStream`, we can associate or bind this stream to the `Blob` column. This is done with a call to the `PreparedStatement` `setBinaryStream` method, which takes an `InputStream` argument (the `ByteArrayInputStream` class extends the `InputStream` class and thus is an *'instance* of that class).

Once we have associated our `Blob` column with the `InputStream` containing our object, we can call the `executeUpdate` method for the `PreparedStatement`. This will update the database with the contents of the `PreparedStatement`, which in this example includes the `Blob` column (`obj_ref`) and the string name we associate with the object (`obj_ref`).

The next step in this program is to demonstrate the process of reading the objects back into the application. A `select` statement is executed to read from the objects table, which has been used to store the `Blob` containing the object. A `while` loop is then executed to read the results of the query.

Within the `while` loop that is reading the data, the `getBinaryStream` method is called for the `Blob` column (`obj_ref`). This method returns an `InputStream` object which is wrapped with an `ObjectInputStream` object (`objInput`) to provide the ability to read our object.

We then execute the `getObject` method on the `ObjectInputStream` (`objInput`). which retrieves an `Object` reference. This reference is then cast as the type of object we have stored in the `Blob` column, a `Vector`, and stored in the `retrievedPurchases` variable. This effectively materializes the object we have stored (persisted) in the database.

A `while` loop is then executed to retrieve the contents of the `retrievedPurchases` variable to extract the contents of the `Vector`, which is a collection of `CustomerPurchase` objects. By calling the `Vector` `get` method for each element in the `Vector`, we retrieve the `Object` references stored in the `Vector`. We know that each of these references stored is an instance of a `CustomerPurchase` object, so they are cast accordingly. We then call the various `get` methods on each element of the object to display the contents. The output from the execution of this `main` program block is as follows.

ObjectExample1 Output

```
Found object. Contents:
***************************
title: The Evil Null Reference
stockNumber: X334334
Date: Tue Jan 02 00:00:00 EST 2001
Amount: 29.22
***************************
title: Another Lonely One
stockNumber: X333484
Date: Wed Jan 02 00:00:00 EST 2002
Amount: 59.22
***************************
title: The Last Compile
stockNumber: X333434
Date: Thu Jan 02 00:00:00 EST 2003
Amount: 59.22
***************************
title: The Last Compile: The Sequel: 0
stockNumber: X32113434
Date: Thu Jan 02 00:00:00 EST 2003
Amount: 109.22
***************************
title: The Last Compile: The Sequel: 1
stockNumber: X32113434
Date: Thu Jan 02 00:00:00 EST 2003
Amount: 109.22
***************************
title: The Last Compile: The Sequel: 2
stockNumber: X32113434
Date: Thu Jan 02 00:00:00 EST 2003
Amount: 109.22
***************************
title: The Last Compile: The Sequel: 3
stockNumber: X32113434
Date: Thu Jan 02 00:00:00 EST 2003
Amount: 109.22
***************************
title: The Last Compile: The Sequel: 4
stockNumber: X32113434
Date: Thu Jan 02 00:00:00 EST 2003
Amount: 109.22
***************************
title: The Last Compile: The Sequel: 5
stockNumber: X32113434
Date: Thu Jan 02 00:00:00 EST 2003
Amount: 109.22
***************************
```

```
title: The Last Compile: The Sequel: 6
stockNumber: X32113434
Date: Thu Jan 02 00:00:00 EST 2003
Amount: 109.22
**************************
title: The Last Compile: The Sequel: 7
stockNumber: X32113434
Date: Thu Jan 02 00:00:00 EST 2003
Amount: 109.22
**************************
title: The Last Compile: The Sequel: 8
stockNumber: X32113434
Date: Thu Jan 02 00:00:00 EST 2003
Amount: 109.22
**************************
title: The Last Compile: The Sequel: 9
stockNumber: X32113434
Date: Thu Jan 02 00:00:00 EST 2003
Amount: 109.22
```

The ObjectExample1 Class: The getConnected Method

The `ObjectExample1` classes uses the `getConnected` method to obtain the connection for the object. This method simply obtains the `InitialContext`, then obtains a specific `DataSource` using the context. A `Connection` object is obtained from the `DataSource` and is ultimately returned by the method. The code for this method is shown next.

The ObjectExample1 Class: The getConnected Method

```
public Connection getConnected() {

Connection con = null;

try {

    //
    // get the InitialContext
    //
    InitialContext ctx = new InitialContext(  );

    //
    // obtain a DataSource to our 'test' database
    //
    DataSource  ds  = (DataSource) ctx.lookup("test");


    //
    // get a connection
```

```
    //
    con = ds.getConnection();

}
catch (SQLException e) {
    System.out.println( "SQLException caught in getConnected: " + e.getMessage() );
     e.printStackTrace();
}
catch (NamingException e) {
    System.out.println( "NamingException caught in getConnected: " +  e.getMessage()
);
}
catch (IOException e) {
    System.out.println( "IOException caught in getConnected: " +  e.getMessage() );
}
finally {

    //
    // return the connection
    //
    return con;
}


}
```

The ObjectExample1 Class: The getCustomerPurchases Method

The `getCustomerPurchases` method creates an aggregation of the `CustomerPurchases` objects, stores them in a `Vector` object, and returns the object. The objects stored in the `Vector` are instances of the `CustomerPurchases` class shown previously.

This is certainly not how data would be captured and stored in a production program; this merely generates test data for this demonstration application. A more likely implementation in production would execute queries that scan multiple tables, capture various sales records, and then store the results in a collection object. The end result would be the same, a `Vector` or some other collection object that would then be persisted into the database.

The ObjectExample1 Class: The getCustomerPurchases Method

```
public Vector getCustomerPurchases() {

//
// create a new CustomerPurchase object
//
```

```
CustomerPurchase custPurch = new CustomerPurchase();

//
// create a new Vector
//
Vector purchases = new Vector();

//
// set the object members
//
custPurch.setTitle( "The Evil Null Reference" );
custPurch.setDate( "01/02/2001" );
custPurch.setAmount( 29.22 );
custPurch.setStockNumber( "X334334" );

//
// add to the Vector
//
purchases.add( custPurch );

//
// add a new object
//
custPurch = new CustomerPurchase();
custPurch.setTitle( "Another Lonely One" );
custPurch.setDate( "01/02/2002" );
custPurch.setAmount( 59.22 );
custPurch.setStockNumber( "X333484" );

purchases.add( custPurch );

//
// add a new object
//
custPurch = new CustomerPurchase();
custPurch.setTitle( "The Last Compile" );
custPurch.setDate( "01/02/2003" );
custPurch.setAmount( 59.22 );
custPurch.setStockNumber( "X333434" );

purchases.add( custPurch );

//
// add a series of objects
//
for ( int n = 0;n < 10;n++) {
    custPurch = new CustomerPurchase();
    custPurch.setTitle( "The Last Compile: The Sequel: " + n);
    custPurch.setDate( "01/02/2003" );
    custPurch.setAmount( 109.22 );
    custPurch.setStockNumber( "X32113434" );
    purchases.add( custPurch );
```

```
}


//
// return the collection (Vector) of objects
//
return purchases;


}


}
```

ALTERNATIVE TECHNIQUES

Persistent Java objects have been of interest to developers since the inception of the Java language. The Java language provides the object streams (`ObjectInputStream` and `ObjectOutputStream`), as shown in the application demonstrated in this chapter. These object streams allow Java objects to be written to flat files for persistence or to be transferred over a network connection. Persisting objects to a database instead of an operating system file, however, allows a number of the benefits of using a relational database to be realized as part of the object persistence solution.

Object-relational mapping tools provide transparent object persistence over relational databases. Independent software vendors such as TopLink *(http://www.webgain.com/products/toplink)* and CocoBase *(http://www.thoughtinc.com/cber_index.html)* and PrismTech *(http://ww.prismtechnologies.com)* have provided the OR-mapping tools and stand behind the Java Data Objects (JDO) specification. Additionally, CastorJDO *(http://castor.exolab.org/jdo.html)* represents an open source persistence solution that deviates from the JDO specification.

JDO is a nascent Java standard that will provide a standardized API for object persistence mechanisms in Java. When complete, this should provide a consistent standard for developers who do not want to be locked into a proprietary OR-mapping/object persistence solution.

SUMMARY

This chapter demonstrated a very useful technique for persisting Java objects into any database that supports a `Blob` column. This provides a convenient, widely supported method for using JDBC to provide object persistence.

While useful and relatively easy to implement, this is not a technique for storing all application data. The cottage industry of data warehousing is built on the creation of large databases storing aggregated, consolidated data. Once stored, various tools are then provided to allow fast searching and analysis of this data. Persistent Java objects cannot currently compete with the functionality or speed of these tools.

Additionally, data stored in these objects is not searchable and is not subject to the data integrity features of relational constraints. Common relational database tables still represent a convenient storage mechanism for many types of data.

But as this chapter demonstrated, the process of storing objects in `Blob` columns is not difficult and provides a convenient mechanism for storing aggregate objects. This mechanism could also be a useful technique for storing any complex object that an application must persist. If there is no compelling reason to search the contents of the object, and the underlying classes for the object provide appropriate data integrity validations, and the object must be persistent, storage in a `Blob` column could represent a useful mechanism for persistence.

COMING UP NEXT

Chapter 16 takes a closer look at Data Access Objects and value object design patterns using specific implementations of these design patterns as examples.

JDBC Design Patterns: Data Access Objects and Value Objects

INTRODUCTION

Data Access Objects (DAOs) encapsulate the details of database access, providing *coarse-grained*, or record-at-a-time, access to the database tables. Value objects encapsulate the structure of the data being accessed and effectively represent the records being used. Both types of objects were used consistently throughout the application to model access to the database tables and the data records within those tables; they are shown and explained in detail in this chapter.

To provide further modularity, a database utility class was used to isolate the low-level database access activity and remove the responsibility for these operations from the business methods that must retrieve and update data. This allows the specifics of database activity to be left to the utility class and effectively shared among the various objects that use the class.

This chapter provides samples of the database access code used in the sample application. Note that not all DAO and value object classes will be shown, since the same basic pattern is repeated throughout.

DAOs Description

The DAO is intended to encapsulate database access and provide a means of shielding the business object from the details of this access. As stated previously, such an approach provides code sharing, and since the DAO is shared among various business objects, it also helps to localize any changes that may be required to the database access code.

These DAOs are tightly coupled with corresponding value objects for the tables with which they interact. In one set of examples, the class members to store values from the table are stored in a value object that is a class member. In another example, data values from the table are stored in primitive data types within the class.

To optimize performance, the database queries are prepared before being used by the business methods that call these methods. These prepared queries are retained and are used when the business methods accessing the DAOs request data. Each DAO retains its own connection to the database through a reference to a `DBUtil` object that is a private instance member of the DAO. (The `DBUtil` object, not the DAO, actually contains the JDBC `Connection` reference.)

All DAOs contain methods to set the DAO to the values within a value object or to return the values of the DAO in a value object. This structure provides an easy to use, efficient means of using the DAO and interacting with the database. The use of a single method to set a DAO or retrieve values from the DAO simplifies the interface between the business methods using the DAO and reduces the amount of communication required (the friction) between the objects.

The methods used in the DAO are listed in Table 16–1. These methods will be shown and explained in the following sections.

Code Example: The Simple DAO—CategoryDAO

The `CategoryDAO.java` code sample provides an example of a simple DAO to perform the database access for the category table. Using the methods shown in Table 16–1 in conjunction with calls to the database utility class, this DAO will encapsulate the details of the database access for the category table and effectively shield the business methods from these details.

The following sections cover this code sample in detail, describing each method, its parameters, the code it executes, and return values and exceptions. This example provides an understanding of the basic structure of a DAO and the methods it should contain. Following this example, a more complex DAO will be shown.

Table 16–1   *Standard DAO Methods*

Method	Description
`Get<propertyName>()`	Retrieve the class property (member) with the name `<propertyName>`.
`Set<propertyName>()`	Set the value of the class property (member) variable of the name `<propertyName>`.
`public void createPreparedStatements()`	Create the prepared SQL statements used to provide the low-level database access.
`public void insertDAO() throws SQLException`	Execute the prepared SQL statement to perform the `insert` operation in the database. This requires setting the correct parameter values in the SQL statement from the class attribute values (the current state of the DAO).
`public void deleteDAO()`	Execute the prepared statement to perform the delete operation. This requires setting the correct prepared statement parameters from the class attribute values (the current state of the DAO).
`public void loadDAO( String category )`	Used to load the DAO from the database. The parameter passed is the primary key and will be used to select the row from the database.
`public void loadDAO( CategoriesVO vo )`	Used to load the DAO from the database. This method is overloaded to receive a value object as a parameter. The value object is assumed to contain the primary key of the database row to load.
`public void setVO( CategoriesVO vo )`	Used to set the DAO to the values contained in the value object. Note that this method is not intended to perform the database update; an update DAO will need to be called to perform the database update. Updates the database using the current values of the DAO attributes.

Import Statements and Declarations

As shown in the code example, the DAO class contains a number of `import` statements to make a small number of packages available to the local namespace. Following these `import` statements, class attributes are declared. Two members, the category and the description, are declared on lines 12 and 13 to hold the values or state of the DAO. (An alternative approach is to declare a corresponding value object, for example a `CategoryVO` instance, to carry the value of the DAO.)

A number of Java `String` types are then declared on lines 16 and 20 to hold the the SQL statements that will be used to create the prepared statements. JDBC prepared statements are then declared on lines 23 through 27 to hold the prepared SQL statements that will be used to provide database access. These class attributes will be used in the `createPreparedStatements` method to prepare the SQL statements used by the DAO.

CategoryDAO.java

```
1.package knowledgebase ;
2.
3.import javax.servlet.*;
4.import java.util.*;
5.import java.sql.*;
6.
7.import db.*;
8.
9.public class CategoriesDAO {
10.
11.// private members
12.private String category;
13.private String description;
14.
15.// hold query strings
16.private String insertStmtStr;
17.private String updateStmtStr;
18.private String deleteStmtStr;
19.private String selectStmtStr;
20.private String selectCategoryListStr;
21.
22.// hold prepared statements
23.private PreparedStatement insertStmt;
24.private PreparedStatement updateStmt;
25.private PreparedStatement deleteStmt;
26.private PreparedStatement selectStmt;
27.private PreparedStatement selectCategoryListStmt;
28.
29.DBUtil dbutil;
```

DAO Example: CategoryDAO get and set Methods

As shown in the next code sample, a number of `get` and `set` methods are then declared to retrieve and set the class members of the DAO. As would be expected, the `get` methods retrieve the requested data element, and the `set` method sets the requested element.

CategoryDAO (Continued)

```
...
// getXXXX methods
public String getCategory() {
    return this.category;
}

public String getDescription() {
    return this.description;
}

// setXXXX methods
public void setCategory( String category ) {
    this.category = category;
}

public void setDescription( String description ) {
    this.description = description;
}
...
```

DAO Example: CategoryDAO—Preparing the Statements

The DAO must perform a number of standard functions: load, update, insert, and delete data in the database. A set of standard methods is declared to perform these functions, as shown in the next code sample. These methods should use a consistent naming convention to improve readability and understanding.

The first of these standard methods presented, and one of the most important, is the createPreparedStatements method. This method will create corresponding prepared statements for each of the SQL statements that must be executed for the DAO. Within this method the DBUtil class method createPreparedStatement is called. This method (shown later in this chapter) executes a JDBC prepareStatment method and returns the results as a JDBC PreparedStatement. This PreparedStatement reference is stored as a member variable of the DAO class. This process of setting the SQL statement string and using this string to create the prepared statement is repeated for each of the database operations the DAO must execute. This includes the expected select, insert, update, and delete operations, which operate on a single row. But this particular DAO also includes a set of statements on lines 18 and 19 to retrieve multiple rows, which are returned as a Collection object containing a list of categories. A getCategoryList method in this class is used to execute this query and capture the results.

All calls to the dbutil object (a reference to an instance of the DBUtil class) throw an SQLException, and all calls within the createPreparedStatements method are performed within a `try/catch` block, which catches and reports any exceptions thrown.

createPreparedStatements Method

```
...
// standard DAO methods
public void createPreparedStatements() {

try {
insertStmtStr = "insert into categories( category, description) values (?,?)";
insertStmt = dbutil.createPreparedStatement( insertStmtStr );

updateStmtStr = "update categories set description = ? where category = ? ";
updateStmt = dbutil.createPreparedStatement( updateStmtStr );

deleteStmtStr = "delete from categories where category = ?";
deleteStmt = dbutil.createPreparedStatement( deleteStmtStr );

selectStmtStr = "select category, description from categories where category = ?";
selectStmt = dbutil.createPreparedStatement( selectStmtStr );

selectCategoryListStr = "select category, description from categories";
selectCategoryListStmt = dbutil.createPreparedStatement( selectCategoryListStr );

}
catch( Exception e) {

  System.out.println("Exception in categoriesDAO.CreatePreparedStatement(): " +
e.getMessage() );

}

}
...
```

DAO Example: CategoryDAO—Update, Insert, Delete, and Select Operations

The following methods are used to perform the update, insert, delete and select operations for the DAO. Each of these methods sets parameter values needed to execute one of the prepared statements that was created in the `createPreparedStatements` method, then executes the prepared statement and stores results in the internal members (attributes) for the DAO class. Since the methods use the values of the internal members of the DAO (the class attributes/parameters), they do not need to receive method parameters to perform their function.

CategoryDAO: The updateDAO Method

The `updateDAO` method shown next is used to perform update operations for the DAO. This method will execute the SQL statement that was prepared in the `createPreparedStatments` method, as follows:

```
...
updateStmtStr = "update categories set description = ? where category = ? ";
...
```

This statement requires two parameters to be set: the `description` column and the `category` column in the SQL `where` clause. The `PreparedStatement` that contains this statement is used to set these parameters using the `PreparedStatement.setString` calls on lines 3 and 4. Then the `executeUpdate` call on line 5 is used to perform the update operation. Should any of these operations throw an exception, the exception would be thrown by the `updateDAO` method to the calling method.

updateDAO Method

```
1.      public void updateDAO() throws SQLException {
2.
3.              updateStmt.setString(1, getDescription() );
4.              updateStmt.setString(2, getCategory() );
5.              updateStmt.executeUpdate();
6.
7.      }
```

CategoryDAO: The insertDAO Method

The next method shown is the `insertDAO` method used to insert a new row into the database. This method must set the parameters—the category and the description—shown in the following statement:

```
insertStmtStr = "insert into categories( category, description) values (?,?)";
```

As shown in the method listing, on lines 3 and 4, the `PreparedStatement.setString` method is used to set the parameters corresponding to the category and description parameters. Then on line 5, the `PreparedStatement.executeUpdate` method is called to perform the update operation. Should the update operation fail, a `SQLException` would be thrown by the `PreparedStatement` operation, and the `insertDAO` method would throw the exception to the calling method.

The insertDAO Method

```
1.      public void insertDAO() throws SQLException {
2.
3.              insertStmt.setString(1, getCategory() );
4.              insertStmt.setString(2, getDescription() );
5.              insertStmt.executeUpdate();
6.      }
7.  ...
```

CategoryDAO: The deleteDAO Method

The next method shown is the `deleteDAO` method used to delete a row from the database. The row deleted is the row that corresponds to the value of the internal class members of the DAO, specifically the row that matches the primary key of the DAO class. In this case, the primary key is the category field, and the value of the internal category member is used to set the category parameter for the `PreparedStatement` update operation, as shown on line 4. On line 5, the `executeUpdate` method of the `PreparedStatement` class is called to perform the delete operation. Should the delete operation fail for any reason and throw a SQLException, the `deleteDAO` method would throw an exception to the calling method.

The deleteDAO Method

```
1.
2.      public void deleteDAO() throws SQLException {
3.
4.              deleteStmt.setString(1, getCategory() );
5.              deleteStmt.executeUpdate();
6.
7.      }
```

CategoryDAO: The loadDAO Method

The `loadDAO` method is used to load the DAO with values from the database. The method is overloaded to accept either a string representing the category record to load or a category value object. The method shown below accepts the a string representing the category. The prepared `select` statement used to perform the select accepts a single parameter, the category to select.

```
...
selectStmtStr = "select category, description from categories where category = ?";
...
```

Once the category has been set with the `setString` method, the `PreparedStatement.executeQuery` method is called to retrieve the row and return the results in a `ResultSet`.

The first call to the `ResultSet.next` method will return `false` if no rows have been found. If rows have been returned, then the first call to this method will return `true` and set the pointer to the first row where the results can then be retrieved using the `getXXXX` methods

The `ResultSet.next` method is called in a conditional statement on line 6. If the statement tests `true` (indicating there are rows), then the `setCategory` and `setDescription` methods are called on lines 7 and 8 to retrieve the column values from retrieved by the select statement. If no rows were found, then the internal values are not set (and retain their previous values or the default class member values).

The loadDAO Method

```
1.      public void loadDAO( String category )  throws SQLException {
2.
3.        selectStmt.setString(1, category );
4.        ResultSet rs = selectStmt.executeQuery();
5.
6.      if ( rs.next() ) {
7.        setCategory( rs.getString(1) );
8.        setDescription( rs.getString(2) );
9.      }
10.
11.     }
12.
```

The overloaded version of the `loadDAO` method shown below takes a value object as a parameter and sets the DAO members to the corresponding values stored in the value object. The calls to `setCategory` and `setDescription` on lines 3 and 4 retrieve the values from the value object and set the internal members of the DAO to those values.

The loadDAO Method

```
1.      public void loadDAO( CategoriesVO vo ) {
2.
3.        setCategory( vo.getCategory() );
4.        setDescription( vo.getDescription() );
5.
6.      }
```

Using these methods, the database could be updated to values stored in a value object by executing a series of calls. The `loadDAO` method for the DAO could be called passing the value object to use as a parameter, thus setting the DAO to the values stored in the value object. The `updateDAO` method for the DAO could then be called to update the database with those current values.

CategoryDAO: Using Value Objects—The setVO Method

The `setVO` method shown in the listing below is used to set a value object passed as a parameter to the current values stored in the DAO. The `set` methods of the value object are used on lines 3 and 4 to set the members of the value object to the members of the DAO.

Division of Responsibilities Revisited

Having the DAO return an entire record rather than making a large number of calls to retrieve each element of the data record individually represents a *coarse-grained* approach to data retrieval. This approach further defines the division of responsibilities for these data objects, making the DAO responsible for manipulating the database and leaving the responsibility for the fine-grained retrieval of data fields to the value object.

This approach provides even better performance improvements when using application servers with Enterprise JavaBeans (EJB), where the DAO would be an EJB (running on the business tier) and would require network communication via RMI to access any method in the EJB.

The `setVO` Method

```
1.
2.    public void setVO( CategoriesVO vo ) {
3.
4.    vo.setCategory( this.getCategory() );
5.    vo.setDescription( this.getDescription() );
6.
7.    }
```

CategoryDAO: Producing a List of Records— The getCategoryList Method

The next method is used to populate a drop-down list box of categories on the `inputKB.jsp` page. The code in this method demonstrates the retrieval of a set of records by a DAO.

The `getCategoryList` method retrieves a list of categories based on the execution of the SQL statement that has been prepared in `createPreparedStatements` (`selectCategoryListStmt`). The SQL statement for this operation does not contain a filter statement and retrieves all categories in the database, as shown below.

Where is the getRecord Method ?

Note that there is no explicit `getRecord` method in this DAO implementation. Since the client is expected to hold a reference to a value object, a combination of a call to the `loadDAO` method followed by a call to the `setVO` method would provide the same results as a `getRecord` method. The code sample below provides an example.

```
. . .
CategoryDAO categoryDAO = new CategoryDAO();
CategoryVO categoryVO = new CategoryVO();
. . .

// load the DAO from the database for the "System" category
categoryDAO.loadDAO( "System");
// set our Value Object from the DAO
categoryDAO.setVO( categoryVO );
// use our Value Object
System.out.println( "Category: " + categoryVO.getCategory() + " - "
+
                              "Description: " +
catgoryVO.getDescription() );
. . .
```

While these calls could be combined into a single `getRecord` method, this separation of responsibilities provides more flexibility and a clearer approach.

```
. . .
selectCategoryListStr = "select category, description from categories";
. . .
```

This method begins by creating a local `Vector` object and a reference to a `CategoryVO` object. The `PreparedStatement.executeQuery` method is then executed and a `ResultSet` is returned. A `while` loop is used to iterate through this `ResultSet`. For each iteration of the loop, a category value object (`CategoryVO`) is created and populated with the contents of the `ResultSet` iteration. The value object is then added to the `Vector`. At the conclusion of the loop, the reference to the `Vector` is returned by the method (where it is implicitly cast as a `Collection` reference).

The getCategoryList Method

```
...
public Collection getCategoryList() throws SQLException {
Vector v = new Vector();
CategoriesVO vo = null;

ResultSet rs = selectCategoryListStmt.executeQuery();

while ( rs.next() ) {
      vo = new CategoriesVO();
      vo.setCategory( rs.getString(1) );
      vo.setDescription( rs.getString(2) );
      v.add( vo );
}

return v;

}
...
```

CategoryDAO: The DAO Constructor

The constructor for the DAO needs to instantiate and initialize the class members. These class members include a DBUtil class member, which is created at line 5. The createPreparedStatements method is called at line 8. Calling this statement on object creation provides some performance benefits, since the queries will be prepared and ready before the methods requiring them are called.

There is no need to load database drivers or create database connections within this code; that housekeeping is localized and performed in the DBUtil class methods, which will be discussed later in this chapter.

If the DAO were using a value object internally (an approach not used in this example), then that value object would instantiated here.

CategoriesDAO Constructor

```
1.      ...
2.      public CategoriesDAO() {
3.
4.            // create db wrapper
5.            dbutil = new DBUtil();
6.
7.            // create SQL prepared statements
8.            createPreparedStatements();
9.
10.     }
```

```
11.
12.     }
13.
```

VALUE OBJECT EXAMPLES

The value object design pattern encapsulates the data record, containing class members or attributes that reflect the fields of the data record. A set of `get` and `set` methods are declared in the class to get values from the class members and set the class members to specific values. Though technically the value object is intended to be immutable (i.e., its value should not change), in a system design where these objects are going to be used to send a record to be inserted or updated in a database, then `set` methods are virtually a requirement. (The alternative would be declaring a constructor that received parameters for all of the fields in the record, which could become tedious for large records.)

Though this object design corresponds to a single table in a relational database, there is no requirement that that be the case. In fact, its design should represent the business domain being modeled and not the normalized or denormalized relational structure of the database.

The following example shows the category value object declared as the `CategoryVO` class. The class declaration declares several local members with private protection.

CategoryVO.java

```
1.      package knowledgebase;
2.
3.      // categories table value object
4.      public class CategoriesVO {
5.
6.      private String category;
7.      private String description;
8.      ...
```

In the code listing below, the `get` and `set` methods for the value object are declared. The `get` methods are used to retrieve the corresponding class members, and the `set` methods are used to set the values of the class members. In this example, no special treatment of the class members is required. In other cases, it may be necessary to validate the data being used to set a class member by a `set` method, or to manipulate or massage the data being returned by a `get` method.

CategoryVO.java *(Continued)*

```
...
// getXXXX
public String getCategory() {
   return this.category;
}

public String getDescription() {
   return this.description;
}

public void setCategory( String category ) {

  this.category = category;

}

public void setDescription( String description ) {

   this.description = description;

}

}
```

A DATABASE UTILITY CLASS: DBUTIL

All of the DAOs in the sample application, including the `CategoryDAO` shown previously, make use of a database utility class, `DBUtil`. This utility class is used to encapsulate the specifics of database access and provide a set of convenience methods for database interaction.

In the code used for this sample application, the standard JDBC driver for PostgreSQL provides access to the database resource, but this could be easily modified to use some other database driver, a `DataSource` connection, or a database pooling access class such as `PoolMan`.

The `DBUtil` class contains a number of methods to perform the housekeeping needed to access a database, such as loading a database driver and creating the connection needed to access the database. These methods are intended to simplify the process of interacting with the database by localizing these decisions and lowering the coupling of the client code (the DAOs) to the actual database being used. Should it become necessary to change the database location, use a different database driver, or change the process of managing connections, then this could be changed in a single location rather than in each DAO used in the system.

Table 16–2 identifies the methods used in this class and provides a description of each method.

Table 16–2 *DBUtil Class Methods*

Method	Description
`public void loadDriver()`	Loads the database driver for the class. The driver is currently retrieved from a local class member.
`public void getConnected()`	Creates a connection to the database (as identified in the driver URL).
`public void createDBStatement()`	Creates the internal JDBC `Statement` object used by the class.
`public PreparedStatement createPreparedStatement( String stmt )`	Creates a prepared SQL statement using the string parameter.
`public ResultSet executePreparedStatement( PreparedStatement pstmt )`	Executes the prepared statement passed as a parameter. This is executed with the expectation that the statement being executed will return results.
`public int executePreparedStmtUpd( PreparedStatement pstmt )`	Executes a prepared statement that is passed as a parameter. The statement is expected to be an `update` statement, and an integer value of the number of rows updated will be returned.
`public ResultSet executeDBQuery( String query )`	Executes a query as contained in the string parameter and returns the results in a `ResultSet`.
`public ResultSet getdbResultSet()`	Returns the internal `ResultSet` currently being used.
`public String getdbDriverName()`	Returns the name of the driver currently being used.
`public Connection getdbConnection()`	Returns the current connection being used.
`public String getDbURL()`	Returns the database connection URL currently being used.
`public Statement getdbStatement()`	Returns the internal JDBC Statement currently used.
`public void setdbDriverName ( String dbDN )`	Sets the database driver to be used to by the object. (Should then call `loadDriver` and `getConnected` to establish the new connection.)
`public void setOutputStream( PrintStream Out )`	Sets the output `PrintStream` for the class.
`public void setdbURL ( String dbURL )`	Sets the database connection URL based on the string parameter passed.

DBUtil Class Code Description: Imports and Class Member Declarations

This class imports a number of packages to provide namespace access to collections, JDBC methods, and `java.io` facilities. Following these `import` statements, a number of class members are declared. A database connection URL and a database driver name string are declared on lines 9 and 11 respectively and are then initialized to the values needed for this application.

Required JDBC class references are declared on lines 13, 14, and 15, and will be used throughout the class. Following these declarations, several boolean flags are declared on lines 17, 18, and 19. These flags will be used to determine whether or not the driver is currently loaded and whether or not the database connection has been established. The use of these flags in this convenience class are intended to provide some flexibility in the use of the class. As the code will demonstrate, if the value of a particular flag is `false`, for example, the database connection is not currently established, then the `getConnection` method will be called to create the connection.

DBUtil Class

```
1.      package db;
2.
3.      import java.sql.*;
4.      import java.io.*;
5.      import java.util.*;
6.
7.      public class DBUtil {
8.
9.      String dbURL =
10.      "jdbc:postgresql://localhost:5432/knowledgebase;user=puser;password=puser";
11.     String      dbDriverName = "org.postgresql.Driver";
12.
13.     Connection dbConnection = null;
14.     ResultSet  dbResultSet  = null;
15.     Statement  dbStatement  = null;
16.
17.     boolean driverLoaded      = false;
18.     boolean Connected         = false;
19.     boolean StatementCreated  = false;
20.
```

DBUtil Class Code Description: loadDriver and getConnected Methods

The `loadDriver` method shown below simply encapsulates the `Class.forName` call used to load the database driver. The driver name parameter provided to the `forName` method is the `dbDriverName` class member, which has been initialized to the name of the database driver to load, in this example to the value `org.postgresql.Driver`.

The `getConnected` method that follows is used to obtain a database connection if one does not already exist. The code in this method first examines the `driverLoaded` flag. If the driver has not been loaded, then the `loadDriver` method is called to load the driver and the `driverLoaded` flag is set to `true`. Once we are certain the database driver has been loaded, we can create the database connection, which is done on line 13. On line 14, the `Connected` flag is set to `true`.

DBUtil Class *(Continued)*

```
1.      public void loadDriver()   throws Exception {
2.                  Class.forName( dbDriverName);
3.          }
4.
5.
6.      public void getConnected()   throws Exception {
7.
8.          if ( !driverLoaded ) {
9.              loadDriver();
10.             driverLoaded = true;
11.         }
12.
13.         dbConnection = DriverManager.getConnection( dbURL );
14.         Connected = true;
15.
16.     }
17.
```

The `createDBStatement` method is used to create the JDBC `Statement` object used internally. The method first checks to determine whether or not a connection has been established. If there is no connection, then the `getConnected` method is called.

Once we are sure the connection has been created, the `createStatement` method is called using the `dbConnection` member (a JDBC `Connection` reference) to create the statement (a JDBC `Statement` reference).

DBUtil Class *(Continued)*

```
public void createDBStatement() throws Exception {

    if ( !Connected )
        getConnected();

    dbStatement   = dbConnection.createStatement();

}
```

DBUtil Class Code Description: createPreparedStatement Method

The `createPreparedStatement` method is used to build a JDBC `PreparedStatement` from a string passed into the method. As with other methods in this class, it is tolerant of the lack of database connection and will create a connection if one does not exist (shown on lines 3 and 4). Once the connection has been made, the `prepareStatement` method of the JDBC `Connection` class is called to create the `PreparedStatement` object, which is then returned from the method. If this process throws a `SQLException`, it is in turn thrown to the calling method.

The DBUtil Class: createPreparedStatement Method

```
1.      public PreparedStatement createPreparedStatement( String stmt ) throws
Exception {
2.
3.          if ( !Connected )
4.              getConnected();
5.          return dbConnection.prepareStatement( stmt );
6.
7.      }
8.
```

DBUtil Class Code Description: The executePreparedStatement and executePreparedStmtUpd Methods

The `executePreparedStatement` method shown next executes the `PreparedStatement` passed as a parameter. This method first checks to see if a database connection exists and, if it does not, it calls the `getConnected` method to create the database connection. Once the method code is sure that a connection exists, it calls the `PreparedStatement.executeQuery` method to execute the statement and returns the `ResultSet` as a return parameter.

The `executePreparedStmtUpd` performs a similar operation except that it expects the query being executed to be an `update` statement. Like the `executePreparedStatement` method, it takes a single parameter, which is a `PreparedStatement`. If a connection to the database does not exist, it creates one and then executes the `PreparedStatement` update statement using the `PreparedStatement.executeUpdate` method and returns the integer result.

DBUtil Class: The executePreparedStatement and executePreparedStmtUpd Methods

```
public ResultSet executePreparedStatement( PreparedStatement pstmt ) throws
Exception {
```

```
    if ( !Connected )
        getConnected();
    return pstmt.executeQuery();

}

public int executePreparedStmtUpd( PreparedStatement pstmt )  throws Exception{

    if ( !Connected )
        getConnected();
    return pstmt.executeUpdate();

}
```

DBUtil Class Code Description: executeQuery Method

The `executeQuery` method shown below executes a query string passed as a parameter and returns a `ResultSet` for the string executed. As with the other convenience methods, this method first checks to see that a connection exists, and if it does not, it calls `getConnected` to obtain a connection.

The method then checks to determine whether or not the JDBC statement has been created for the instance. If the statement has not been created, it calls `createDBStatement` at line 9 to create the `Statement` object and then sets the `statementCreated` flag to `true` on line 10.

At this point the method is ready to execute the query, and at line 14, it executes the JDBC `Statement.executeQuery` method and stores the `ResultSet` reference returned in the `dbResultSet` class member. At line 16, it returns this same reference to the calling method.

The executeDBQuery Method

```
1.     public ResultSet executeDBQuery( String query ) throws Exception {
2.
3.         // make sure we are ready to do this
4.
5.         if ( !Connected )
6.             getConnected();
7.
8.         if ( !StatementCreated ) {
9.             createDBStatement();
10.                 StatementCreated = true;
11.         }
12.
13.         // execute query
14.         dbResultSet    = dbStatement.executeQuery( query );
15.
```

```
16.           return dbResultSet;
17.
18.     }
19.
```

DBUtil Class Code Description: The executeUpdDBQuery Method

The `executeUpdDBQuery` method executes a database query passed in as a string parameter and returns an integer corresponding to the number of rows that have been updated by the method. This method also checks to determine whether or not we are connected to the database and, if not, calls `getConnected` to obtain the connection on line 5. It performs the same function with the `createDBStatement` method, checking to see if the statement exists and, if not, creating the DB statement.

Once everything is ready, the method calls the JDBC `Statement.executeUpdate` method to perform the update contained in the query that has been passed in. The integer result of this operation, which indicates the number of rows updated, is returned by the method.

The executeUpdDbQuery Method

```
1.      public int executeUpdDBQuery( String query ) throws Exception {
2.
3.          // make sure we are ready to do this
4.          if ( !Connected )
5.              getConnected();
6.
7.          if ( !StatementCreated ) {
8.              createDBStatement();
9.              StatementCreated = true;
10.         }
11.
12.         // execute query
13.         int retVal    = dbStatement.executeUpdate( query );
14.
15.          // return number of rows updated
16.          return retVal;
17.
18.     }
19.
```

DBUtil Class Code Description: get and set Methods

A number of `get` methods are used in the `DBUtil` class to return the values of class members, essentially information about how the `DBUtil` object is being used, and to allow usage of the JDBC `Connection` or JDBC `Statement` independent of the `DBUtil` class. These methods are shown next.

The getdbResultSet Method

```
// Bean methods
public ResultSet getdbResultSet() {
       return dbResultSet;
}

public String getdbDriverName() {
       return dbDriverName;
}

public Connection getdbConnection() {
       return dbConnection;
}

public String getDbURL() {
       return dbURL;
}

public Statement getdbStatement() {
       return dbStatement;
}
```

Two set methods are used to set various members of the DBUtil class. A setdbDriver method is a public method available to set the database driver name. This method takes a string parameter for the name of the database driver and sets the internal member dbDriverName to this value on line 2. On line 3, the driverLoaded flag is set to false, which will force the driver to be loaded the next time a database operation is performed.

The setdbURL method can be used to set the URL or the connection string for the database connection. This method takes a string parameter for the database URL, as shown on line 6. On line 7, the local member dbURL is set to the value of the parameter, and on line 8, the Connected flag is set to false to force the database connection to be remade the next time a database operation is attempted.

The setdbDriverName Method

```
1.     public void setdbDriverName ( String dbDN ) {
2.            this.dbDriverName = dbDN;
3.            driverLoaded = false; // force new driver load
4.     }
5.
6.     public void setdbURL ( String dbURL ) {
7.            this.dbURL = dbURL;
8.            Connected = false; // force new connection
9.     }
10.
11.    } // end class
12.
```

A COMPLEX DAO: THE KNOWLEDGE_BASEDAO CLASS

The `CategoryDAO` class shown previously was a simple, direct example of a DAO. The category table contains only two columns, and inserts, updates, and deletes are simple database operations. The `knowledge_base` table, however, is more complex, containing a larger number of columns and additional queries to support filtered `select` statements (for the `pickKB.jsp` page).

A number of the methods in this class are very similar to the methods within the `CategoryDAO` class, so they won't be covered in detail in these sections, but they will be shown for completeness (and to avoid viewing fragmented pieces of code that don't seem to go together).

The `Knowledge_baseDAO` class is responsible for managing the database operations for the `knowledge_base` table. This involves not only simple `select`, `insert`, `update`, and `delete` operations with the table, but also handling queries filtered on keywords that have been stored with the message entries (in the `base_keys` table). These filtered operations require the passing of collections for the filter criteria and returning iterators or collections containing the results of the query. The `getAll` and `getFiltered` methods provide examples of this type of operation. We will examine the `Knowledge_baseDAO` class in the following sections.

Complex DAO Example: The Knowledge_baseDAO Class

The `Knowledge_baseDAO` class performs the same imports as the `CategoryDAO` class, providing the local namespace for a number of packages used in the class. These imports are followed by the declaration of class members on lines 12 through 21 to hold the elements of the `knowledge_base` table. And on lines 27 through 40, class members are declared to hold the prepared statements used to provide the database operations for the DAO.

The Knowledge_baseDAO Class

```
1.      package knowledgebase;
2.
3.      import javax.servlet.*;
4.      import java.util.*;
5.      import java.sql.*;
6.
7.      import db.*;
8.
9.      public class Knowledge_baseDAO {
10.
11.     // private members
12.     private int doc_key;
13.     private String doc_name;
```

```
14.      private String doc_location;
15.      private String post_user;
16.      private int link_doc;
17.      private int level;
18.      private String entry_date; // date
19.      private String date_submitted; // date
20.      private String category;
21.      private int base_doc_key;
22.
23.      // wraps JDBC methods
24.      DBUtil dbutil;
25.
26.      // string to hold SQL statements
27.      private String insertStmtStr;
28.      private String updateStmtStr;
29.      private String deleteStmtStr;
30.      private String selectStmtStr;
31.      private String selectAllStmtStr;
32.      private String selectFilterStmtStr;
33.
34.      // Prepared SQL statements
35.      PreparedStatement insertStmt;
36.      PreparedStatement updateStmt;
37.      PreparedStatement deleteStmt;
38.      PreparedStatement selectStmt;
39.      PreparedStatement selectAllStmt;
40.      PreparedStatement selectFilterStmt;
41.
```

Complex DAO Example: The Knowledge_baseDAO Class—get Methods

The next code listing shows the `get` methods for the `Knowledge_baseDAO` class on lines 2 through 40. These methods do little more than return the DAO member, as their names imply.

(Though these members are declared public, they are primarily used by local methods. Whenever possible, value objects are passed to and returned from the DAO, resulting in a cleaner, more convenient approach to managing these objects.)

The Knowledge_baseDAO Class *(Continued)*

```
1.      // getXXXX methods
2.      public int getDoc_key() {
3.        return doc_key;
4.      }
5.
6.      public String getDoc_name(){
7.        return doc_name;
8.      }
```

```
9.
10.
11.    public int getBase_doc_key() {
12.          return this.base_doc_key;
13.    }
14.
15.    public int getLink_doc() {
16.        return this.link_doc;
17.    }
18.
19.    public String getDoc_location() {
20.      return doc_location;
21.    }
22.
23.    public String getPost_user() {
24.      return post_user;
25.    }
26.    public int getLevel() {
27.        return level;
28.    }
29.
30.    public String getEntry_date() {
31.        return entry_date;
32.    }
33.
34.    public String getDate_submitted() {
35.        return this.date_submitted;
36.    }
37.
38.    public String getCategory() {
39.        return category;
40.    }
41.
```

Complex DAO Example: The Knowledge_baseDAO Class—set Methods

The code listing below shows the set methods for the DAO on lines 2 through 42. These methods are responsible for, as the names imply, setting the values of the internal class members of the Knowledge_baseDAO class. Though they are declared public, they are primarily used by the local methods of the class to work with value objects corresponding to the schema of the knowledge_base table.

The Knowledge_baseDAO Class *(Continued)*

```
1.
2.      // set methods
3.      public void setDoc_name( String doc_name ) {
4.          this.doc_name = doc_name;
```

```
5.        }
6.
7.        public void setDoc_key( int doc_key ) {
8.            this.doc_key = doc_key;
9.        }
10.
11.       public void setDoc_location( String doc_location ) {
12.           this.doc_location = doc_location;
13.       }
14.
15.       public void setPost_user( String post_user ) {
16.           this.post_user = post_user;
17.       }
18.
19.       public void setLevel( int level ) {
20.           this.level = level;
21.       }
22.
23.       public void setLink_doc( int link_doc ) {
24.           this.link_doc = link_doc;
25.       }
26.
27.       public void setBase_doc_key( int base_doc_key ) {
28.           this.base_doc_key = base_doc_key;
29.       }
30.
31.       public void setEntry_date( String entry_date ) {
32.           this.entry_date = entry_date;
33.       }
34.
35.       public void setDate_submitted( String date_submitted ) {
36.           this.date_submitted = date_submitted;
37.       }
38.
39.       public void setCategory( String category ) {
40.           this.category = category;
41.       }
42.
```

Complex DAO Example: The Knowledge_baseDAO Class—createPreparedStatement Method

Following the get and set methods in the Knowledge_baseDAO class file, we encounter a number of the general-purpose methods of the class that are used to perform the database update operations the DAO must perform.

The first of these we will examine is the createPreparedStatement method. This method is responsible for creating the prepared statements that will be used to execute the queries for the DAO. The structure of the method is to create the query string (storing the string in a local class member in case it needs to

be used again) and then calling `DBUtil.createPreparedStatement` to prepare the statement and return the result, a JDBC `PreparedStatement` object reference, which will be stored in a class member and used by the other methods.

   In the belief that a well-phrased nonprocedural SQL statement can replace a
significant portion of procedural Java language code, a complex query is phrased
on lines 41 through 57. The purpose of this query is to return the results that filter on a SQL `select` statement for the `base_keys` table to get records with the
correct keywords and join those results with corresponding rows from the
`knowledge_base` table.

   This query is a SQL `union` of two queries. One query retrieves all base document keys for the keywords being used, and a second query retrieves all document keys for documents that match the keywords being used. This resulting
`union` query is sorted by document key, base document key, date submitted, and
date last modified. Because a `union` query is used, duplicates will be filtered out
of the query. This query is used to produce the filtered listing produced by the
`pickKB.jsp` page.

The Knowledge_baseDAO.createPreparedStatements Method

```
1.      public void createPreparedStatements( ) throws Exception {
2.
3.      try {
4.          insertStmtStr = "insert into knowledge_base " +
5.                          "
(doc_key,doc_name,category,post_user,doc_location,link_doc, level, base_doc_key,
entry_date, date_submitted) values " +
6.                          " ( ?,      ?,         ?,         ?,          ?,
?,        ?,       ?,              ? ) "  ;
7.
8.          insertStmt = dbutil.createPreparedStatement( insertStmtStr );
9.
10.         updateStmtStr = "update knowledge_base " +
11.                 " set doc_name = ?, " +
12.              "   doc_location = ?, " +
13.              "   category = ?, "   +
14.              "   post_user = ?, "  +
15.              "   level = ?, "  +
16.              "   link_doc = ?, "   +
17.              "   entry_date = ? "  +
18.                 "  where doc_key = ? "  ;
19.
20.         updateStmt = dbutil.createPreparedStatement( updateStmtStr );
21.
22.         deleteStmtStr = "delete from knowledge_base " +
23.                 "          where doc_key = ?" ;
24.
25.         deleteStmt = dbutil.createPreparedStatement( deleteStmtStr );
26.
```

```
27.         selectStmtStr = "select doc_key,doc_name,category,post_user,doc_loca-
tion,link_doc, " +
28.                         " base_doc_key,entry_date, date_submitted,level " +
29.                         " from knowledge_base " +
30.                         " where doc_key = ? ";
31.
32.         selectStmt = dbutil.createPreparedStatement( selectStmtStr );
33.
34.         selectAllStmtStr = "select doc_key,doc_name,category,post_user,doc_loca-
tion,link_doc, " +
35.                         " base_doc_key,entry_date, date_submitted,level " +
36.                         " from knowledge_base " +
37.                         " order by doc_key, base_doc_key, date_submitted,
entry_date";
38.
39.         selectAllStmt = dbutil.createPreparedStatement( selectAllStmtStr );
40.
41.         selectFilterStmtStr = " select " +
42.         " doc_key, doc_name,category, post_user, doc_location, link_doc, " +
43.         " base_doc_key,entry_date, date_submitted, level " +
44.         " from knowledge_base " +
45.         " where base_doc_key in (" +
46.         " select knowledge_base.doc_key " +
47.         " from knowledge_base, base_keys   " +
48.         " where keyword in (?,?,?,?) and "   +
49.         " knowledge_base.doc_key = base_keys.doc_key ) " +
50.         " union "   +   // union query
51.
52.         " select "   +
53.         " knowledge_base.doc_key, doc_name,category, post_user, doc_location,
link_doc, " +
54.         " base_doc_key,entry_date, date_submitted, level " +
55.         " from knowledge_base, base_keys   " +
56.         " where keyword in (?,?,?,?) and " +
57.         " knowledge_base.doc_key = base_keys.doc_key " +
58.         " order by knowledge_base.doc_key, base_doc_key, date_submitted,
entry_date ";
59.
60.         selectFilterStmt = dbutil.createPreparedStatement( selectFilterStmtStr );
61.
62.     }
63.
64.     catch (SQLException e) {
65.
66.         throw new Exception("SQLException thrown in createPreparedStatements(): "
+ e.getMessage() );
67.
68.     }
69.     catch (Exception e)   {
70.
71.         throw new Exception("Exception thrown in createPreparedStatements(): " +
```

```
e.getMessage() );
72.
73.      }
74.
75.      }
76.
```

Managing Self-Incrementing Keys:
The Knowledge_baseDAO insertDAO Method

The next method we encounter in the `Knowledge_baseDAO` class is the `insertDAO` method as shown next. This listing performs an insert into the `knowledge_base` table, but unlike the previous insert operation into the categories table, this insert operation must manage a self-incrementing primary key—an integer column that is guaranteed to be a unique identifier for the table. Using the PostgreSQL database, a database sequence is used to produce this number. This `sequence` is a database object that retains an integer counter that can be queried and incremented to return a distinct integer number.

Since the `knowledge_base` table represents a parent table for a number of child tables (related records should not appear in these tables unless there is a corresponding record in this table), the primary key of this table, the `doc_key`, must be communicated to the method controlling the insert operation, the `insertKBRecs` method in the `KnowledgeBaseFacade` class, and then used to perform the insert of those records.

Therefore, the `insertDAO` method not only must retrieve this unique integer and use it for the database insert operation, but it must return this number to the calling method controlling the insert of the parent and child tables for the message.

This method begins by creating a local integer variable for the `doc_key` and initializing it to zero on line 4. A call is then made to the `Knowledge_baseDAO.generateDoc_key` method to generate the integer by reading from the sequence. This key is then used to provide the values for the `insert` statement query shown below.

```
. . .
    insertStmtStr = "insert into knowledge_base " +
 " (doc_key,doc_name,category,post_user,doc_location,link_doc, level, base_doc_key,
entry_date, date_submitted) values " +
 " ( ?, ?, ?, ?, ?, ?, ?, ?, ?, ? ) "  ;
. . .
```

On line 9 of the listing, the document key (`doc_key`) that has been returned by the `generateDoc_key` method is used to set the document key parameter to be inserted into the table using the prepared insert statement (`insertStmt`). The remaining `set` statements on lines 10 through 18 are used to set the other parameters in the prepared insert statement.

Once all of the parameters in the prepared statement have been set, the `PreparedStatement.executeUpdate` method is called at line 20. This method returns an integer value for the number of rows updated, which is ignored by this method. On line 22, the value of the document key used for the insert is returned by the method (to be used for the insert of values into the child tables of the `knowledge_base` table).

The knowledge_baseDAO.insertDAO Method

```
1.      ...
2.      public int insertDAO( ) throws SQLException, Exception {
3.
4.      int doc_key = 0;
5.
6.      // set elements
7.      // set with 'sequence' on insert
8.      doc_key = generateDoc_key();
9.      insertStmt.setInt(1, doc_key );
10.     insertStmt.setString(2, getDoc_name() );
11.     insertStmt.setString(3, getCategory() );
12.     insertStmt.setString(4, getPost_user() );
13.     insertStmt.setString(5, getDoc_location() );
14.     insertStmt.setInt(6, getLink_doc() );
15.     insertStmt.setInt(7, getLevel() );
16.     insertStmt.setInt(8, getBase_doc_key() );
17.     insertStmt.setString(9, getEntry_date() );
18.     insertStmt.setString(10, getDate_submitted() );
19.
20.     int retval = insertStmt.executeUpdate();
21.
22.     return doc_key;
23.
24.     }
25.     ...
26.
```

Complex DAO Example: The Knowledge_baseDAO Class—updateDAO Method

The `updateDAO` method is used to perform updates on the `knowledge_base` table. This method uses the prepared statement shown below to update the database.

```
...
updateStmtStr = "update knowledge_base " +
            " set doc_name = ?, " +
        "   doc_location = ?, " +
        "   category = ?, "   +
        "   post_user = ?, "   +
```

```
"   level = ?,  "   +
"   link_doc = ?,  "   +
"   entry_date = ?  "   +
     "   where doc_key = ?  "   ;
```

. . .

All columns except the primary key column (doc_key) can be be updated and must be set using the PreparedStatement set methods. These set methods are used on lines 4 through 11 to set the parameters using the internal values of the DAO, as returned by the various get methods in the Knowledge_baseDAO class we are reviewing. On line 13, the PreparedStatement.executeUpdate method is called to perform the update operation. This method returns an integer for the number of rows updated, which is ignored by the updateDAO method. Any exception returned by the updateDAO method is thrown to the calling method.

The updateDAO Method

```
1.      . . .
2.      public void updateDAO( ) throws SQLException {
3.      // set elements
4.      updateStmt.setString(1, getDoc_name() );
5.      updateStmt.setString(2, getDoc_location() );
6.      updateStmt.setString(3, getCategory() );
7.      updateStmt.setString(4, getPost_user() );
8.      updateStmt.setInt(5, getLevel() );
9.      updateStmt.setInt(6, getLink_doc() );
10.     updateStmt.setString(7, getEntry_date() );
11.     updateStmt.setInt(8, getDoc_key() );
12.
13.     int retval = updateStmt.executeUpdate();
14.
15.     }
16.
```

Complex DAO Example: The Knowledge_baseDAO Class—deleteDAO Method

The next method in our journey through the Knowledge_baseDAO class is the deleteDAO method. As the name implies, this method is responsible for the deletion of a knowledge base record and uses the query statement shown below.

. . .

```
deleteStmtStr = "delete from knowledge_base "  +
            "            where doc_key = ?" ;
```

. . .

This prepared statement requires only one parameter to be set, which is set in the code listing below. Once the parameter has been set, the `PreparedStatement.executeUpdate` method is called and returns an integer value representing the number of rows updated. As with the previous update examples, the value returned from the `executeUpdate` method is ignored and any exception thrown by the method is in turn thrown to the calling method, where it must be handled or thrown to yet another method.

The deleteDAO Method

```
public void deleteDAO( ) throws SQLException {

deleteStmt.setInt(1, getDoc_key() );

int retval = deleteStmt.executeUpdate();

}
```

Complex DAO Example: The Knowledge_baseDAO Class—loadDAO Method

The next method in the `Knowledge_baseDAO` class is the `loadDAO` method, a method responsible for loading the DAO, using the value of the parameter passed into the method.

This method is overloaded in this class. One version loads the DAO from the database, using the primary key parameter passed into the method, an integer representing the document key. The other version loads the DAO based on a value object passed into the method.

The version of the `loadDAO` method shown in listing loads the DAO from the database, using the integer value passed into the method, a value representing a primary key for the `knowledge_base` table. This value is used to set the single parameter in the prepared statement shown below.

```
. . .
    selectStmtStr = "select
doc_key,doc_name,category,post_user,doc_location,link_doc, " +
                " base_doc_key,entry_date, date_submitted,level " +
                " from knowledge_base " +
                " where doc_key = ? ";
. . .
```

In the code listing below, this parameter is set on line 6, using the `PreparedStatement.setInt` method, and the prepared statement is executed on the line 7, returning a `ResultSet` response.

The call to `ResultSet.next` on line 9 will return a boolean `true` if there are rows to be traversed in the `ResultSet`, and `false` if there are none, so the body of the `if` statement will be executed only if there is in fact a row to be processed. Since this method asserts there is only one row to be found for the primary key passed (as should be the case), this assertion should not be a problem. A series of `set` methods for the `Knowledge_baseDAO` class are called on lines 11 through 20, which use calls to appropriate `ResultSet` `get` methods for the `ResultSet` returned by the `executeQuery` call on line 7.

Should the query fail to return any rows, the body of the `if` statement would not be executed and the DAO members would not be set. While this may appear to be a problem, the manner in which this method is used precludes the failure of a select. This method is called from the `inputKB.jsp` page, which is in turn called from the `pickKB.jsp`. The `pickKB.jsp` page lists either all available messages or messages that have been filtered. In either case, the page lists only messages currently in the database, and the links that are provided with the listing contain references to the primary key for the listed item, so only valid primary keys are listed. This means that when this method is called within the message system application, we can assert that only valid primary keys will be used, and we should never have a case where the query execution returns no rows.

In the case that an attempt to execute the query generates an exception, a `catch` statement traps the exception, displays an error message, and then throws an exception to the calling method.

The loadDAO Method

```
1.
2.      public void loadDAO( int doc_key ) throws Exception {
3.
4.      try {
5.
6.      selectStmt.setInt(1, doc_key );
7.      ResultSet rs = selectStmt.executeQuery();
8.
9.      if ( rs.next() )   {
10.
11.          setDoc_key( rs.getInt(1) );
12.          setDoc_name( rs.getString(2) );
13.          setCategory( rs.getString(3) );
14.          setPost_user( rs.getString(4) );
15.          setDoc_location( rs.getString(5) );
16.          setLink_doc( rs.getInt(6) );
17.          setBase_doc_key( rs.getInt(7) );
18.          setEntry_date( rs.getString(8) );
19.          setDate_submitted( rs.getString(9) );
```

```
20.          setLevel( rs.getInt(10) );
21.
22.      }
23.
24.      }
25.      catch (SQLException e) {
26.          System.out.println("SQLException thrown in Knowlege_baseDAO.loadDAO(): "
+ e.getMessage() );
27.          throw new Exception( "Exception in Knowlege_baseDAO.loadDAO(): " +
e.getMessage() );
28.      }
29.
30.      }
```

Complex DAO Example: The Knowledge_baseDAO Class—The Overloaded loadDAO Method

Since our design goal is to have the DAOs work with value objects, we would like the DAO to be able to accept a value object as a parameter and to set the internal parameters using the values in these value objects.

The `loadDAO` method accepts a value object as a parameter and then sets the class members of the DAO to those values. The operation of this method is fairly straightforward, with a series of `set` methods on lines 4 through 13 being used to set the values of the local members to the values of the value object members for the value object passed in as a parameter. The value object `get` methods are used to retrieve the values of that object.

The Overloaded loadDAO Method

```
1.
2.      public void loadDAO( Knowledge_baseVO knowledge_base ) {
3.
4.      setDoc_key( knowledge_base.getDoc_key() );
5.      setDoc_name( knowledge_base.getDoc_name() );
6.      setCategory( knowledge_base.getCategory() );
7.      setPost_user( knowledge_base.getPost_user() );
8.      setDoc_location( knowledge_base.getDoc_location() );
9.      setLink_doc( knowledge_base.getLink_doc() );
10.     setBase_doc_key( knowledge_base.getBase_doc_key() );
11.     setLevel( knowledge_base.getLevel() );
12.     setEntry_date( knowledge_base.getEntry_date() );
13.     setDate_submitted( knowledge_base.getDate_submitted() );
14.
15.     }
```

Complex DAO Example: The Knowledge_baseDAO Class—setVO Method

In continuing with our goal to use value objects and DAOs together, the next method we examine, the `setVO` method, is used to set the value of a value object to the internal values (the values of the class members) of the DAO, as shown next.

This method receives a value object parameter for a `Knowledge_baseVO`, a value object that reflects the elements of the `knowledge_base` table. A series of `set` methods are called for the value object using arguments that make calls to the `get` methods of the DAO to retrieve the values of the internal members of the DAO.

The setVO Method

```
// set ValueObject members from DAO
      public void setVO( Knowledge_baseVO vo ) throws Exception {

      vo.setDoc_key( this.getDoc_key() );
      vo.setDoc_name( this.getDoc_name() );
      vo.setCategory( this.getCategory() );
      vo.setPost_user( this.getPost_user() );
      vo.setDoc_location( this.getDoc_location() );
      vo.setLink_doc( this.getLink_doc() );
      vo.setLevel( this.getLevel() );
      vo.setBase_doc_key( this.getBase_doc_key() );
      vo.setEntry_date( this.getEntry_date() );
      vo.setDate_submitted( this.getDate_submitted() );

      }
```

Database Access: Retrieving Multiple Rows with the getAll Method

The next method we will examine is the `getAll` method used to retrieve all `knowledge_base` records currently in the database. This method demonstrates a technique for retrieving multiple rows from the database and returning the results, and is shown next.

The `getAll` method will return an `Iterator`, a convenient Java object for moving through a set of object references. The object references to be returned will be references to `Knowledge_baseVO` objects, value objects that reflect the columns of the `knowledge_base` table.

The method first creates a `Vector` to be used to store the results and then executes a `PreparedStatement` query on line 9 that contains no filter clause and will retrieve all rows from the database. The query executed on this line is shown below.

```
. . .
selectAllStmtStr = "select
doc_key,doc_name,category,post_user,doc_location,link_doc, " +
                    " base_doc_key,entry_date, date_submitted,level " +
                    " from knowledge_base " +
                    " order by doc_key, base_doc_key, date_submitted, entry_date";
. . .
```

A `while` loop is started at line 11 to step through the results of the query. This loop creates a new `Knowledge_baseVO` value object on each iteration and then stores the values of the current row into this value object, using the statements executed on lines 15 through 24. On line 26, a reference to the value object that has just been created and populated is added to the `Vector` object.

A `catch` clause on line 31 catches any exceptions that may be thrown and throws an exception to the calling method, providing a message that describes where the error occurred.

The `Iterator` for the `Vector` that contains the value object references is generated on line 36 with a call to the `iterator` method of the `Vector` class and is returned to the calling method.

The getAll Method

```
1.
2.      // retrieve a collection of all knowledge_base record ValueObjects
3.
4.      Iterator getAll() throws Exception {
5.      Vector v = new Vector();
6.
7.      try {
8.
9.      ResultSet rs = selectAllStmt.executeQuery();
10.
11.     while ( rs.next() ) {
12.
13.         Knowledge_baseVO vo = new Knowledge_baseVO();
14.
15.         vo.setDoc_key( rs.getInt(1) );
16.         vo.setDoc_name( rs.getString(2) );
17.         vo.setCategory( rs.getString(3) );
18.         vo.setPost_user( rs.getString(4) );
19.         vo.setDoc_location( rs.getString(5) );
20.         vo.setLink_doc( rs.getInt(6) );
21.         vo.setBase_doc_key( rs.getInt(7) );
22.         vo.setEntry_date( rs.getString(8) );
23.         vo.setDate_submitted( rs.getString(9) );
24.         vo.setLevel( rs.getInt(10) );
25.
26.         v.add( vo ) ;
27.
```

```
28.      }
29.
30.    }
31.    catch (SQLException e) {
32.       throw new Exception("SQLException caught in knowledge_baseDAO.getAll(): "
+ e.getMessage() );
33.    }
34.
35.    // return the iterator for this collection
36.    return v.iterator();
37.
38.    }
39.
```

Complex DAO Example: The Knowledge_baseDAO Class—generateDoc_key Method

Database Access: Generating a Unique Key

The `generateDoc_key` method shown below is used to generate the unique integer value used to generate the document key (`doc_key`) for the `knowledge_message` table. This method uses the `DBUtil.executeDBQuery` method to execute a query string passed to the method. The query string used is hardcoded in this method to retrieve the output of the database function `nextval` for the argument `doc_key` on line 6. In the PostgreSQL database used with this application, this instructs the database engine to retrieve the next value from the `doc_key` sequence and to increment the sequence by one at the same time. Since this will be treated as a singleton transaction by the database, no other user will be able to retrieve that sequence value at the same time, and we can be assured that we are retrieving a unique value.

The execution of the query will return a `ResultSet`, which we assert will retrieve only a single row. The `if` statement on line 7 tests the `ResultSet` for rows, and if the `ResultSet` has rows, the value of the first and only column in that row, the unique integer value, is returned. If the `ResultSet` has not returned any rows, a 0 is returned, indicating that an error has occurred.

The generateDoc_key Method

```
1.
2.     private int generateDoc_key() throws Exception {
3.
4.     try {
5.
6.     ResultSet rs = dbutil.executeDBQuery( "select nextval('doc_key')" );
7.     if ( rs.next() )
8.        return rs.getInt(1);
```

```
9.      else
10.        return 0;
11.     }
12.     catch (SQLException e) {
13.
14.        throw new Exception( "Error in doc_key generation: " + e );
15.
16.     }
17.
18.     }
19.
```

Note that the SQL statement to retrieve the self-incrementing value would need to be changed in the event another database were used. Isolating this platform-specific code as much as possible, as was done in this example, makes the process of managing this code that much easier.

Complex DAO Example: The Knowledge_baseDAO Class—getFilteredList Method

Database Access: Using a Filtered List

We will now look at the getFilteredList method, which accepts a collection that contains the query criteria for the filtered list. This filtered list uses a set of keywords associated with the message to create and execute a query against the database for messages that use those keywords. Currently, this application is limited to four keywords per search.

This method begins by creating a new Vector, which will be used within the method to accumulate the list of rows that match the filter criteria. The criteria parameter passed into the method is a Collection, so the iterator method is available to create an iterator at line 7 and to use this object to step through the criteria values. Since a union query is used to produce the filtered list and the criteria values appear in the where clause for both queries, the iterators must be traversed twice, once at line 11 and again at line 17.

Once the query has been prepared, it is executed at line 21, and the ResultSet obtained is used to control a loop on line 23. Within this loop a value object is created on each iteration (on line 25) of type Knowledge_baseVO, and the values that are returned in the ResultSet row are stored in the value object. The value object reference is then stored in the Vector that was created at the start of the method (on line 3).

This loop is used to capture the results for each row and store them in the value object on lines 27 through 36. On line 38, the value object itself is added to the Vector.

Several `catch` blocks are placed on lines 47 through 50 to catch any existing exceptions and throw new exceptions. If all is well and no exceptions have been thrown, then the `Vector` we have populated is used to produce an `Iterator`, which is returned by the method at line 53.

The getFilteredList Method

```
1.
2.      Iterator getFilteredList( Collection criteria ) throws Exception {
3.      Vector v = new Vector();
4.
5.      try {
6.
7.      Iterator i = criteria.iterator();
8.      int n = 1;
9.      // currently, only store four search keywords
10.     // since using a Union statement with two queries we need to set these key-
words twice
11.     for ( n = 1; n < 5 && i.hasNext(); n++ )  {
12.         selectFilterStmt.setString( n, (String) i.next() );
13.         }
14.
15.     // set the next 4
16.     i = criteria.iterator();
17.     for ( n = 1; n < 5 && i.hasNext(); n++ )  {
18.         selectFilterStmt.setString( n + 4, (String) i.next() );
19.         }
20.
21.     ResultSet rs = selectFilterStmt.executeQuery();
22.
23.     while ( rs.next() ) {
24.
25.         Knowledge_baseVO vo = new Knowledge_baseVO();
26.
27.         vo.setDoc_key( rs.getInt(1) );
28.         vo.setDoc_name( rs.getString(2) );
29.         vo.setCategory( rs.getString(3) );
30.         vo.setPost_user( rs.getString(4) );
31.         vo.setDoc_location( rs.getString(5) );
32.         vo.setLink_doc( rs.getInt(6) );
33.         vo.setBase_doc_key( rs.getInt(7) );
34.         vo.setEntry_date( rs.getString(8) );
35.         vo.setDate_submitted( rs.getString(9) );
36.         vo.setLevel( rs.getInt(10) );
37.
38.         v.add( vo ) ;
39.
40.      }
41.
42.     }
43.     catch (SQLException e) {
```

```
44.        System.out.println("SQLException caught in
knowledge_baseDAO.getFilteredList): " + e );
45.        throw new Exception("SQLException caught in
knowledge_baseDAO.getFilteredList(): " + e );
46.    }
47.    catch (Exception e ) {
48.        System.out.println("Exception caught in
knowledge_baseDAO.getFilteredList(): " + e );
49.        throw new Exception( "Exception caught in
knowledge_baseDAO.getFilteredList(): " + e );
50.    }
51.
52.    // return the iterator for this collection
53.    return v.iterator();
54.
55.    }
56.
```

Complex DAO Example: The Knowledge_baseDAO Class—Constructor

Finally, we see the constructor for the `Knowledge_baseDAO` class. This constructor needs to perform some minor housekeeping to get the object ready for use. It needs to create an instance of the database utility class `DBUtil`, which it does at line 5. It then needs to see that all of the SQL statements to be used are prepared, which it does at line 8.

The Knowledge_baseDAO Constructor
```
1.
2.    public Knowledge_baseDAO() throws Exception {
3.
4.        // create our database helper
5.        dbutil = new DBUtil();
6.
7.        // prepare SQL statements
8.        createPreparedStatements();
9.
10.    }
11.
12.    }
13.
```

The Value Object in the DAO

An alternative approach to having a DAO use class members for retention of data values is to simply have the DAO carry an internal reference to a value object, what is effectively a *compositional* object-oriented relationship. This approach provides the ability to leverage the design of the value object within the DAO and thus gain access to any data validation logic that may already be in place in the value object. Additionally, since the DAO will be returning a value object, in many cases a reference to the internal value object could be returned, providing better performance than would creating and passing a new value object instance as a return value.

The following code example demonstrates this approach. The `message_user` table is managed with the `Message_userDAO`, which, as it happens, contains an internal reference to a `Message_userVO` value object.

The Value Object in the DAO: The Message_userDAO Example

The following DAO example is used to manage the `message_user` table, which is stores information on the users of the message system. As with the previous value object examples, the class performs a number of import operations and then, on lines 12 through 21, declares class members that will be used to store SQL statements to prepare and execute. On line 24, a reference to the database utility class `DBUtil` object is declared, and on line 27, a reference to a `message_user` table value object, the `Message_userVO` class, is declared. Since this will encapsulate the current state of the DAO, there is no need to declare internal class members to hold the current DAO state.

The Message_userVO Class

```
1.
2.        package knowledgebase;
3.
4.        import java.util.*;
5.        import java.sql.*;
6.
7.        import db.*;
8.
9.        public class Message_userDAO {
10.
11.       // hold SQL statements
12.       private String insertStmtStr;
13.       private String updateStmtStr;
14.       private String deleteStmtStr;
15.       private String selectStmtStr;
16.
17.       // hold prepared statements
18.       private PreparedStatement   insertStmt;
19.       private PreparedStatement   updateStmt;
20.       private PreparedStatement   deleteStmt;
21.       private PreparedStatement   selectStmt;
22.
```

```
23.     // DB utility class
24.     DBUtil dbutil;
25.
26.     // internal Value Object
27.     Message_userVO message_userVO;
28.
```

The Value Object in the DAO: The Message_userDAO Example—createPreparedStatements

Since this DAO is being manipulated using a value object, specific `get` and `set` methods for the DAO members (as encapsulated in the value object) are not used. If the `message_user` table is being updated, a value object with the updated values would be passed to the `setVO` method and then the `updateDAO` method would be called.

The `createPreparedStatements` method creates the statements that will be used to perform the database updates for this class. This method is functionally similar to the `createPreparedStatements` method shown for the `Knowledge_baseDAO` DAO class, creating a separate JDBC `PreparedStatement` for each database `select`, `update`, `delete`, and `insert` statement used.

The Message_userDAO.createPreparedStatements Method

```
// getXX methods

// setXX methods

// convenience methods
public void createPreparedStatements() {

try {

insertStmtStr = "insert into message_user( login, first_name, last_name, location,
date_submitted, last_login, pwd ) " +
            " values (?,?,?,?,?,?,?)";

insertStmt = dbutil.createPreparedStatement( insertStmtStr );

updateStmtStr = "update message_user set " +
            " first_name    = ?, " +
            " last_name     = ?, " +
            " location      = ?, " +
            " date_submitted = ?, " +
            " last_login    = ?, " +
            " pwd           = ? " +
            " where login = ? ";
```

```
updateStmt = dbutil.createPreparedStatement( updateStmtStr );

deleteStmtStr = "delete from message_user where login = ?";

deleteStmt = dbutil.createPreparedStatement( deleteStmtStr );

selectStmtStr = "select login,   " +
                " first_name," +
                " last_name," +
                " location,  " +
                " date_submitted," +
                " last_login," +
                " pwd " +
                " from message_user where login = ?";

selectStmt = dbutil.createPreparedStatement( selectStmtStr );


}
catch (Exception e ) {

 System.out.println("Exception in Message_userDAO.createPreparedStatements(): " + e
);


}
```

The Value Object in the DAO: The Message_userDAO Example—updateDAO Method

The updateDAO method uses the update statement that has been prepared in the createPreparedStatement method. The method makes a series of setString methods to set the prepared statement parameters on lines 4 through 10, but unlike the previous examples that used class members (attributes) to provide these values, this method makes calls to the get methods of the message_userVO value object that belongs to the class (it is a member of the DAO). On line 12, the executeUpdate method is called to update the database, using the parameters that have been set on the previous lines. The executeUpdate method returns an integer value, but this value is ignored by this method.

The Message_userDOA.updateDAO Method

```
1.
2.      public void updateDAO() throws SQLException{
3.
4.      updateStmt.setString(1, message_userVO.getFirst_name() );
5.      updateStmt.setString(2, message_userVO.getLast_name() );
6.      updateStmt.setString(3, message_userVO.getLocation() );
7.      updateStmt.setString(4, message_userVO.getDate_submitted() );
8.      updateStmt.setString(5, message_userVO.getLast_login() );
9.      updateStmt.setString(6, message_userVO.getPwd() );
```

```
10.        updateStmt.setString(7, message_userVO.getLogin() );
11.
12.        updateStmt.executeUpdate();
13.
14.      }
```

The Value Object in the DAO: The Message_userDAO Example—insertDAO Method

The `insertDAO` method is used to perform insert operations for the DAO. As with the previous method, a series of `PreparedStatement.setString` methods are used to set the insert statement parameters on lines 4 through 10, using calls to the internal value object. On line 12, the `executeUpdate` method is called to perform the insert operation.

The insertDAO Method

```
1.
2.        public void insertDAO() throws SQLException {
3.
4.        insertStmt.setString(1, message_userVO.getLogin() );
5.        insertStmt.setString(2, message_userVO.getFirst_name() );
6.        insertStmt.setString(3, message_userVO.getLast_name() );
7.        insertStmt.setString(4, message_userVO.getLocation() );
8.        insertStmt.setString(5, message_userVO.getDate_submitted() );
9.        insertStmt.setString(6, message_userVO.getLast_login() );
10.       insertStmt.setString(7, message_userVO.getPwd() );
11.
12.       insertStmt.executeUpdate();
13.
14.      }
```

The Value Object in the DAO: The Message_userDAO Example—deleteDAO Method

The `deleteDAO` method sets a single parameter for the login field, using the `setString` method. The method then executes the `executeUpdate` method to perform the delete operation for the login that has been used as the parameter for the prepared statement.

The deleteDAO method

```
public void deleteDAO() throws SQLException {

deleteStmt.setString(1, message_userVO.getLogin() );
```

```
deleteStmt.executeUpdate();


}
```

The Value Object in the DAO: The Message_userDAO Example—loadDAO Method

The loadDAO method is used to load the DAO with the appropriate values. This method is passed a single string parameter corresponding to the login. The select statement shown below uses this login value as its parameter.

```
. . .
selectStmtStr = "select login,    " +
                " first_name," +
                " last_name," +
                " location,  " +
                " date_submitted," +
                " last_login," +
                " pwd " +
                " from message_user where login = ?";


. . .
```

A setString method is used to set this value on line 6, and the executeQuery method of the PreparedStatement class is used to execute the select statement and returns a ResultSet. On lines 12 through 18, the values returned by the ResultSet are used to set the values of the internal value object, the message_userVO object.

If no records are found, an error message is printed on line 21. Any exceptions thrown by any of the statements in the method are caught on line 25, and an error message is printed and then a new exception is thrown.

The loadDAO Method

```
1.
2.      public void loadDAO( String login ) throws Exception {
3.
4.      try {
5.
6.      selectStmt.setString(1, login );
7.
8.      ResultSet rs = selectStmt.executeQuery();
9.
10.     if ( rs.next() ) {
11.
```

```
12.          message_userVO.setLogin( rs.getString(1) );
13.          message_userVO.setFirst_name( rs.getString(2) );
14.          message_userVO.setLast_name( rs.getString(3) );
15.          message_userVO.setLocation( rs.getString(4) );
16.          message_userVO.setDate_submitted( rs.getString(5) );
17.          message_userVO.setLast_login( rs.getString(6) );
18.          message_userVO.setPwd( rs.getString(7) );
19.      }
20.    else {   // no records found
21.          System.out.println("Message_userDAO.loadDAO(): no records found.");
22.      }
23.
24.      }
25.    catch (SQLException e) {
26.          System.out.println("SQLException caught in Message_userDAO.loadDAO() " +
e );
27.          throw new Exception("Exception caught in Message_userDAO.loadDAO() " + e
);
28.      }
29.
30.      }
31.
```

The Value Object in the DAO: The Message_userDAO Example—setVO and getVO Methods

The `setVO` method is used to set the internal value object equal to the value object reference being passed into the method. This method merely sets the internal reference to the object reference being passed into the method.

The setVO Method

```
// set internal ValueObject
public void setVO( Message_userVO vo ) {

    this.message_userVO = vo;

}
```

The `getVO` method returns the reference for the internal value object. This simply returns the reference to the internal value object member.

The getVO Method

```
...
// return the internal value object
public Message_userVO getVO() {
```

```
  return this.message_userVO;
}
...
```

The Value Object in the DAO: The Message_userDAO Example—Constructor

The constructor for the `Message_userDAO` class performs some of the house-keeping chores that need to be performed before a `Message_userDAO` object can be created. It creates the internal `Message_userVO` object to be used by the class, and then creates the `DBUtil` utility class used to interact with the database. Finally, it calls `createPreparedstatements` to create the prepared statements to be used to perform the database `select`, `insert`, `update`, and `delete` operations.

Message_userDAO Constructor

```
...
// constructor
public Message_userDAO() {

    // create our value object
    message_userVO = new Message_userVO();

    // create dbutil
    dbutil = new DBUtil();

    // create prepared statements
    createPreparedStatements();

}

}
...
```

SUMMARY

In this chapter, several DAOs were shown, from a fairly simple DAO to a more complicated DAO. In each case, the responsibility of the DAO was to perform the low-level database access, the `select`, `insert`, `update`, and `delete` operations, using complete records. The role of the value object was to reflect the data record for the table being operated on by the DAO. In practice, this meant the DAO would manipulate value objects as database records. Value objects would be used to set the internal values of DAOs, and value objects would be returned by DAOs.

The DAOs did not access the database directly using JDBC. Database access was further abstracted into a database utility class named `DBUtil`. The `DBUtil` class, as shown in this chapter, managed the specifics of loading the database driver, connecting to the database, and wrapping the JDBC method to create prepared statements and execute queries.

COMING UP NEXT

Chapter 17 will begin the review of JSP, the presentation tier technology that will be used in later chapters to create a sample application using JDBC.

JSP Basics

INTRODUCTION

The previous chapters introduced many of the basics of building an application with Java. The syntax of the JSP language, the tags, directives, and scriptlets that make up the language, were all explained. This chapter builds on the work of the previous chapter by using a series of examples to explain how to develop Web applications using JSP with JavaBeans and custom tag libraries.

Since it is not uncommon for Web applications to require the display of a one-month calendar on a Web page, this chapter provides an example of a JavaBean that does just that providing a useful demonstration of both JSP/script-let development as well as the use of custom tags. The conversion of the JavaBean into a custom tag highlights the differences between tag libraries and JavaBeans and demonstrates the relative ease of performing this conversion.

SOME JSP EXAMPLES

As discussed in Chapter 16, the JSP page includes HTML tags interspersed with special tags that are interpreted by the JSP compiler.

These tags can contain attributes, or a body, which is interpreted by the compiler. The <% tag is used to indicate that Java code follows. The Java code contained within a block of these tags is not a formal Java class declaration with data members and method declarations; instead it is a fragment of Java code that will be executed when the page is accessed. For this reason, this inserted Java is considered to be a *script*, often referred to as a *scriptlet*, and is not considered to be a complete Java program. The following fragment contains an example of a JSP script.

```
1. <HTML>
2. <BODY bgcolor="#FFFFFF">

3. <%@ page errorPage="ErrorPage.jsp" %>

4. <% for (int n = 0; n < 10; n++ ) { %>

5. <p> This text will be displayed 10 times.

6. <% } %>

7. </BODY>
8. </HTML>
```

In this example, a directive is used to identify an error page to be used in the event an error is triggered within the page. A Java `for` loop is started and runs for 10 iterations. An opening brace appears on the same line. Note that the declaration of the `for` loop, and a starting brace, are enclosed in a single scriptlet block, which is terminated.

On line 8, HTML paragraph text appears. On line 10, a scriptlet block is used to enclose a closing brace. This closing brace is matched with the opening brace on line 6, and for that reason all HTML text that appears between line 8 and line 10 is subject to the control of the loop. With this technique, HTML in a JSP page can enjoy the benefits of Java flow-of-control loops. The output of this page is shown in Figure 17–1.

JSP also provides convenient access to Java code (or classes) external to the page. This is provided through either an import directive, which works like the Java language import statement, or the useBean tag.

The useBean tag includes JavaBeans in the JSP page and provides a mechanism for associating the JavaBean with a tag within the JSP page. The syntax for the useBean tag is shown below.

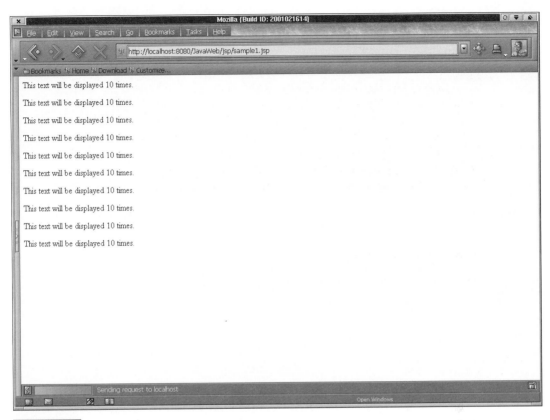

Figure 17–1 JSP sample1.jsp output.

```
...
<jsp:useBean id="dbutil" class="db.dbUtil" scope="session" />
<jsp:useBean id="kbutil" class="knowledgebase.kbUtil" scope="session" /> ...
```

These tags provide for the inclusion of JavaBeans modules in the JSP, providing for modularized code and code re-use throughout the JSP application. Specifically, these tags include modules that will be referenced on the JSP page, using the names dbutil and kbutil. The class files for the modules are also specified.

```
...
<!- table for ResultSet output ->
<table border=0 cellpadding=2 bgcolor="white">

<tr>
<td bgcolor="#C0D9D9"><b>Problem Description<b></td>
```

```
<td bgcolor="#C0D9D9"><b>Message<b></td>
<td bgcolor="#C0D9D9"><b>Category<b></td>
<td bgcolor="#C0D9D9"><b>Action<b></td>
</tr>

<!— // print each column —>
<%
    while ( more ) {
%>

<tr>
<td bgcolor="#E0E0E0"> <%= rs.getString( "doc_name" ) %> </td>
<td bgcolor="#E0E0E0"> <%= rs.getString( "message_txt" ) %> </td>
<td bgcolor="#E0E0E0"> <%= rs.getString( "category" ) %> </td>

<td bgcolor="#C0C0C0"> <a href="viewKB.jsp?pdoc_key=<%= doc_key %>" >View Entry</a>
</td>

<% if ( !request.getParameter( "action" ).equals( "showthread" ) ) { %>
<td bgcolor="#C0C0C0"> <a href="listKB.jsp?pdoc_key=<%= doc_key
%>&action=showthread" >Show Thread</a> </td>
<% } %>

</tr>

<%
    more = rs.next();
    } // end while
%>
</table>
```

In this example, an HTML table is created to display the output of a database query, which is returned in a JDBC `ResultSet` object. In order to place the contents of the `ResultSet` object into the HTML table, a Java `while` loop is executed for each row returned in the `ResultSet` object.

Note that the `while` loop is not completed in the first Java code block in the HTML page. Instead, a great deal of HTML is inserted between the sections of the `while` loop. This is allowed in JSP scriptlets.

At the end of the `while` loop, a call is made to the `ResultSet next()` method to retrieve the next row in the `ResultSet`. If this call succeeds, the script variable `more` is set to the boolean value of `true`. If the call fails, the script variable is set to `false`. The boolean value of the script variable `more` is tested at the start of the `while` loop, and if it tests `false`, the `while` loop will not be executed.

Note that this code demonstrates a direct approach to JSP script programming. In this example, a portion of the underlying business logic is exposed to the JSP page. Since it is exposed, it is visible and can be changed by the same developer who will develop the HTML code within the page. Using the *separation of roles* concept, this HTML page developer will most likely know nothing of JSP and could easily become confused and, worse yet, may change some of the Java code.

The preferred development model for JSP is to make every effort to limit the amount of Java code that appears on the JSP page. While it may be necessary to have some Java code on the page (for example, to perform decision logic or to execute a loop), this code should be limited, and the majority of the business logic should be handled within the Java code behind the page, not in the scriptlet code on the page.

JAVA SOFTWARE COMPONENTS: JAVABEANS AND EJBS

To hide the business logic of the application and thus reduce the complexity of the Java code on the JSP page, we need a facility to encapsulate the business logic of the application. This business logic should be encapsulated in the form of software components. The use of these software components fits into what is known as a *software component architecture,* and Java provides two forms of software components: *Java Beans* and *Enterprise Java Beans (EJBs)*as shown in the figure below.

JavaBeans are a coding facility in Java that allows for the creation of a local component that provides some degree of encapsulation. These components are not as complex as EJBs, and for applications that do not need the features of EJBs, they are more than suitable. Most notably, they do not explicitly support a distributed environment, an environment where the location of the component is not defined; that is, the component could be on the local machine, or the component could be on a machine elsewhere on the network.

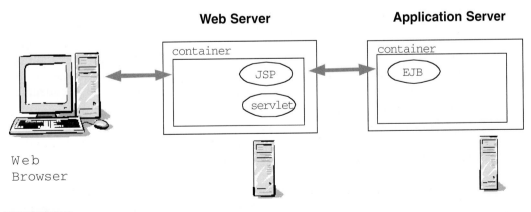

Figure 17–2 *Tomcat server: application server comparison.*

EJBs provide a number of features that are suitable for a more intensive, robust production environment. EJBs are designed with a notion of *containership*. Just as servlets and JSPs have containers that implicitly provide many of the services needed by those components, so too an EJB has a container that provides a number of services. EJB containers and their servers provide persistence, location transparency, failure fall-back capabilities, and scalability features that heavily used, business-critical applications require.

But this robust feature set comes with a price. EJBs can be difficult to develop and even more difficult to deploy. The servers they use are complex, can be expensive (though there are some interesting open-source EJB servers available) and can require some level of system maintenance. This is not to say that EJBs should not be used; they have significant value with the right application. But there are simpler, more direct approaches to development that are appropriate for a large number of small to medium-sized applications.

EJBs are generally used on applications that will have a heavy user load, require integration with legacy applications on disparate systems (e.g., a UNIX-based system must use mainframe data), or require a high degree of failover capabilities. For these applications, EJBs provide significant value and are easier to use and more flexible than many of the alternatives available on the market today.

USING JAVABEANS WITH JSPS

JavaBeans are Java classes coded using a set of methods with a standard naming convention. With these classes it is assumed that class data members (or attributes) will be declared with `private` accessibility and will only be manipulated using `get` and `set` methods; the `get` and `set` methods are named with the naming standard `get<attribute_name>` and `set<attribute_name>`, where the attribute name is the name of the attribute or private data member that is to be set.

These `getXX` and `setXX` methods are sometimes referred to as *accessor* and *mutator* methods of the class. JavaBeans do not require the implementation of a Java interface and do not need to be a subclass of any particular class; they are just another Java class with appropriate methods written to manage their attributes. The following provides an example.

```
1.package samples;
2.
3.public class myBean {
4.private int counter;
5.private String name = "MyBean"; // default name
6.
7.public void setCounter( int count ) {
8.this.counter = count;
9.}
10.public void setName( String name ) {
```

```
11.this.name = name;
12.}
13.
14.public String getName() {
15.    return name;
16.}
17.
18.public int getCounter() {
19.    return counter;
20.}
21.
22.public void incrementCounter() {
23.    counter++;
24.}
25.}
```

In this example, a JavaBean named `myBean` is created as a Java class. The JavaBean class has two private data members (or properties): `counter` and `name`, as declared on lines 4 and 5. The four public methods used to access these private members are declared on lines 7 through 20. The `set` methods are used to set the values of these members, and the `get` methods are used to access the value of the member. The `setCounter` method on line 7 is written to set the value of the `counter`, and the `setName` method on line 10 is used to set the value of the `name` member. Likewise, the `getName` method on line 14 is available to retrieve the value of the `name` member. The `getCounter` method on line 18 is available to retrieve the value of the `counter` member.

The `incrementCounter` method on line 22 is an example of how a simple method could be part of a JavaBean. This method increments a counter variable and then returns. The following example demonstrates the use of this JavaBean in a JSP page.

```
1.<HTML>
2.<BODY>
3.<jsp:useBean id="myBean" class="samples.myBean" scope="page" />
4.<jsp:setProperty name="myBean" property="counter" value="1" />
5.
6.<H1>JSP Samples<H1>
7.<p>
8.
9.<% myBean.incrementCounter(); %>
10.
11.<p>Name: <jsp:getProperty name="myBean" property="name" />
12.
13.<p>Counter: <jsp:getProperty name="myBean" property="counter" />
14.
15.</BODY>
16.</HTML>
```

In this sample page, the `useBean` tag on line 3 is identifies the bean to be used and associates the bean with an `id` name in the page. The `useBean` tag uses the `id` attribute to identify the name of the class to load for the bean and the scope attribute to identify the scope of the JavaBean within the JSP page.

The scriptlet on line 9 is used to invoke a method within one of the JavaBeans loaded on the current page or potentially one of the classes available to the servlet built from the page. This scriptlet invokes the `incrementCounter` method to increment the internal counter variable for the JavaBean.

The `getProperty` tags on lines 11 and 13 retrieve the value of the members of the JavaBean class (`counter` and `name`). The values of these members are retrieved and inserted into the HTML page at line 11 after the `Name:` string and at line 13 after the `Counter:` string.

Note that it is not required to write public `get` and `set` methods for all members. Should you wish to hide certain details of the JavaBean, the `get` and `set` methods could be either eliminated or declared private methods, thus restricting access to the methods.

The process of *introspection* is the capability of a Java application to dynamically examine the members of a class and then access the members of that class. This is the facility used by runtime JavaBeans activation and by the JSP container when it implements the `getProperty` or `setProperty` tags on the JSP page.

When a JavaBean is used in a JSP page, the `useBean` tag is used to identify the JavaBean class to load for the bean. The JSP container will then find and load the class. When a `getProperty` tag is encountered for the JavaBean, the container will use *introspection* to determine whether an appropriate `get<PropertyName>` method is available to call and, if it is available, will make the method call and return the value. If a `setProperty` tag is encountered, then introspection is once again used to determine whether or not an appropriate `set<PropertyName>` method is available to call. If an appropriate `set<PropertyName>` method is found, it is called and passed the correct value for the call. Note that the property name in the `set<PropertyName>` method must match the `property` attribute of the `jsp:getProperty` tag.

A JSP/JavaBeans Example

A common problem that must be tackled when developing a Web site is to dynamically create Web pages based on the contents of some subset of database tables. Since it is safe to assume we will be retrieving multiples rows of data from the database, we must be able to iterate through these rows. In this situation, a simple set of `getXX` and `setXX` methods that simply retrieve the values of properties contained in the JavaBean will not be adequate.

The JDBC API provides methods that, among other things, execute a query and return an object representing the set of results (a `ResultSet` object). Methods within the `ResultSet` class can then be used to iterate through the results. While we could place this code directly into the JSP page, it would involve placing some portion of business logic into the page where it would be visible (and subject to change) for anyone with access to the page.

It is preferable to encapsulate as much business logic for the application into JavaBeans. In order to accomplish this hiding with JDBC operations, principal JDBC methods must be wrapped with Java code and combined into a small, manageable set of methods.

The process of iterating through the `ResultSet` must include the populating of private members of the `CustBean` class with internal calls to its `set` methods. The `next()` method of the class will provide this functionality.

Once this method has been called in the JSP script, the properties of the bean will contain the appropriate value and can be rendered on the page using the `getProperty` tag. The following contains an example of this approach.

The sample1.jsp Page

```
1.<HTML>
2.<BODY>
3.
4.<jsp:useBean id="custBean" class="/classes/custBean" scope="page" />
5.<jsp:setProperty name="custBean" property="userID" value="<%
request.getParameter("userID") %>" />
6.<jsp:setProperty name="pageID" property="pageID" value="P2023" />
7....
8.<%
9.while ( custBean.getNext() ) {
10.%>
11.
12.<tr>
13.<td bgcolor="#E0E0E0"> <jsp:getProperty name="custBean" property="doc_name" />
</td>
14.<td bgcolor="#E0E0E0"> <jsp:getProperty name="custBean" property="message_text"
/> </td>
15.<td bgcolor="#E0E0E0"> <jsp:getProperty name="custBean" property="category" />
</td>
16.<td bgcolor="#C0C0C0"> <a href="viewKB.jsp?pdoc_key=<jsp:getProperty
name="custBean" property="doc_key" />" >View Entry</a> </td>
17.
18.<% if ( !request.getParameter( "action" ).equals( "showthread" ) ) { %>
19.<td bgcolor="#C0C0C0"> <a href="listKB.jsp?pdoc_key=<jsp:getProperty
name="custBean" property="doc_key" />&action=showthread" >Show Thread</a> </td>
20.<% } %>
21.</tr>
22.<%    } // end while %>
23.</BODY>
24.</HTML>
```

In this example, the JSP page needs to read the contents of a database table and then, based on the results of this iterative read operation, create an HTML table using the contents. Our goal is to limit the amount of Java code that we must expose in the JSP page and to use HTML/JSP tags as much as possible.

On line 4 of this example, the JavaBean that is to be used for this page is identified in a JSP `useBean` tag. This tag directs the JSP container to load the bean. On lines 5 and 6, parameters required to perform the retrieval of customer records from the database are set.

By the time the `next` method is called on line 9, the information needed to retrieve the data has been loaded into the JavaBean. The call to the `next` method will position the data retrieval to the first row of the data set returned and internally set the properties of the `CustBean` object to the appropriate values for the first row retrieved.

Within the `<td>` tags in the table on lines 13 through 15, a series of `<jsp:getProperty/>` tags are then used to retrieve the data and insert it into the output stream for the HTML table that will be created from this JSP page.

The terminating tag for the `while` loop on line 19 forces execution to branch back to line 9, where the `while` loop will call the `CustBean.next` method again. If there are no rows available, the method will return `false` and the `while` loop will terminate. If there are rows available, the method will once again internally load the properties (set the local data members) for the object.

JSP Example: The Calendar Java Bean

Many business applications work with calendars, requiring presentation controls that display both a calendar and the current date. While many GUI APIs provide controls (or widgets) to display this information, basic HTML does not provide this capability.

Since static HTML cannot provide this capability, JSP/Java is uniquely suited to this task, providing a calendar API that can retrieve the current date and time for the current time zone of the computer and return information about specific dates that can be used to create a calendar display. Since the purpose of this class is to provide a display *widget*, producing the calendar output at a specified point on the page, it should be invoked with a small number of JSP tags and produce the output necessary.

The Java code that generates the output for these tags will be required to send output to the response stream `JspWriter`. While on the surface this may appear to break our rule of having separation of presentation logic appearing only on the JSP page and not in the Java code, given our requirements for this widget, this development approach makes sense. A JSP page that uses a calendar JavaBean to display a calendar is shown below.

The cal1.jsp JSP Page

```
1.<HTML>
2.<HEAD><TITLE>
3.     Calendar
4.</TITLE></HEAD>
5.
6.<%@ page errorPage="ErrorPage.jsp" %>
7.<BODY BGCOLOR="white">
8.
9.<h1> JSP Calendar  </h1>
10.<jsp:useBean id="Cal" scope="page" class="JSPCal.Cal" />
11.<b>Current Date:</b> <jsp:getProperty name="Cal"
12.                      property="currentDate" />
13.<%
14.Cal.printCal( out );
15.%>
16.
17.</BODY>
18.</HTML>
```

This sample JSP page uses a JavaBean to display the contents of a calendar. A `jsp:useBean` tag on line 10 locates and loads the `JSPCal.Cal` class and associates the class with the name `Cal` to be used within this JSP page. The bean is given page scope, since it will only be used for the current page.

Once the bean is loaded, the `getProperty` tag on line 11 is used to request the `currentDate` from the bean. As shown in the code below, the `currentDate` property will have the JSP/servlet engine call the `getCurrentDate` method, which will retrieve the current date from the calendar and display the date in a text string.

Finally, the `printCal` method is called on line 14 and is passed the `out` object, which in a JSP page relates to the `JspWriter` for the output stream (the response) for the page. The results of this operation is a page that appears as shown in Figure 17–3.

Alternatively, custom tags could be used to display the calendar. Though very similar to the JavaBean approach, the JSP custom tag library provides a cleaner, simpler set of tags to be used in the JSP page, as shown below.

The cal2.jsp Page

```
<html>
<body bgcolor="#FFFFFF">

<%@ taglib uri="/WEB-INF/jsp/TagCal.tld" prefix="tagcal" %>

<H1>A Birthday</H1>
<tagcal:Calendar year="1991" month="6" day="6" highLightColor="pink" />
```

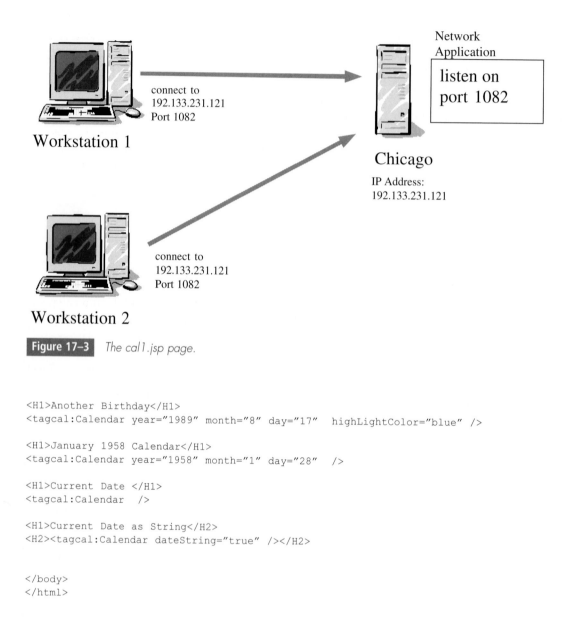

Figure 17–3   *The call.jsp page.*

```
<H1>Another Birthday</H1>
<tagcal:Calendar year="1989" month="8" day="17"   highLightColor="blue" />

<H1>January 1958 Calendar</H1>
<tagcal:Calendar year="1958" month="1" day="28"   />

<H1>Current Date </H1>
<tagcal:Calendar   />

<H1>Current Date as String</H2>
<H2><tagcal:Calendar dateString="true" /></H2>


</body>
</html>
```

This page loads the tag library using the `taglib` directive, which instructs the JSP/servlet engine to read the `TagCal.tld` to obtain information about how to load the custom tag library class and how to identify the tags. The prefix attribute identifies the prefix to be used to identify the tags on the page.

This tag library uses one tag, the `Calendar` tag, but allows most of the attributes for the tag to be optional. The first use of the tag is to display a specific date (a birthday) specifying a highlight color for the date. The second use of the tag performs the same operation, but this time uses a different highlight color. In the third example, the highlight color is not passed as a parameter (which will cause the tag library to use the default value).

The final use of the `Calendar` tag on this page sets the `dateString` flag to true and does not specify the date for the calendar. The result of using these attributes to invoke the `Calendar` tag (which results in distinct execution of the code) is that the current date will be output in text string format. This page produces output as shown in Figure 17-4.

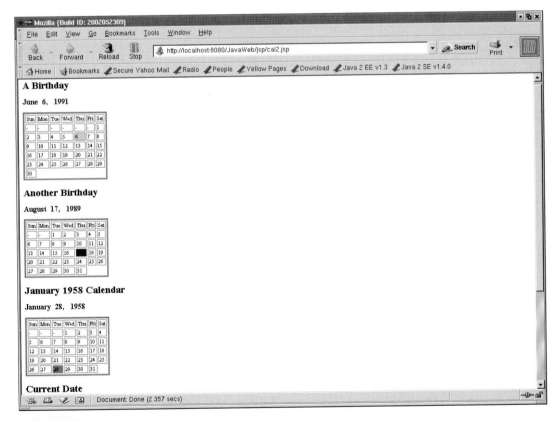

Figure 17–4 JSP cal2.jsp page output

JavaBeans Versus Custom Tag Libraries

As we can see from these examples, we have two different approaches available to placing content on the JSP page: using JSP scriptlets and tags (getProperty, setProperty) or using custom tags. The differences between the implementation of these two approaches will become more apparent as we examine the code behind these JSP pages in more detail. While the two approaches share many similarities, there are distinct differences between the structure of the Java code required for each, and later in this chapter we will discuss both solutions and provide recommendations on where each is considered appropriate.

The following sections present both approaches, using both the calendar JavaBean and the custom tag library. The first code example uses the JavaBean solution to provide the calendar, and the second example modifies this JavaBean code to create a custom tag to provide the same calendar output.

JSP Calendar: JavaBean Code

The Java code for the calendar bean defines a class named Cal, which contains data members and methods to implement the calendar. A series of getXX and setXX methods within the class are used to access the class methods from JSP getProperty and setProperty flags.

The Cal class uses the GregorianCalendar class to create the calendar requested. The GregorianCalendar class contains a number of convenience methods to create calendars, including a number of methods to perform date arithmetic and determine the day of the month and day of the week, essential information needed to display a calendar.

A number of packages are included into the class, as shown below.

```
package JSPCal;
import java.text.*;
import java.util.*;
import java.io.*;
import javax.servlet.*;
import javax.servlet.jsp.*;
```

Within the body of the Cal class, Java final static members are created to store the names of the months and the names of the days of the week as well as the abbreviations for the days of the week.

The Cal.java Class

```
...
public class Cal {

// array for months
```

```
private static final String[] months = new DateFormatSymbols().getMonths();

// array for days of week in string format
private static String days[] = new DateFormatSymbols().getWeekDays();

// array for day abbreviations
private static String daysAbbrev[] =
   new DateFormatSymbols().getShortWeekdays();
...
```

Locale and Dates

As most Java developers are aware, the display of dates differs depending on the country. Various locales identify a specific country, and Java provides a rich API to support locale-specific formatting. If applications are coded correctly, they can let Java manage this locale-specific formatting for them.

The `Cal` class makes some use of locale by using `java.text.DateFormatSymbols` to generate the array of week day names. But note that the syntax used here loads these names when the class is loaded (since they are static final variables and thus belong to the class), not at runtime. Since the syntax for the `DateFormatSymbol` constructor does not specify a locale, the locale of the Java runtime environment will be used, not the locale of the user accessing the page.

A more robust implementation that needed to support multiple locales based on user logins would need to move the generation of these headings into the constructor for the `Cal` class and then set them based on the known locale of the user, as shown in the code fragment below.

```
...
private static final String[] months;
...
// constructor
public Cal( Locale loc) {
DateFormatSymbols(loc)
months = new DateFormatSymbols(loc).getMonths();
}
```

In this code fragment, the months array is declared `static` and `final` (a blank final variable) and must be initialized in the constructor (or all constructors if the constructor is overridden). The constructor is then called with a parameter of type `java.util.Locale`, which is used to set the values of the months array. This code assumes that the application has determined the correct locale of the user and passed this information to the constructor.

Internal members are also used to store the month, day, and year of the calendar to be created. A highlight color is defined for the color to use to highlight the current day (and a `setXX` method is available to change this property as needed).

```
// internal date
private int month;
private int day;
private int year;
private  String printHighLightColor = "grey";
private Calendar   mCalendar = null;   // internal calendar
private JspWriter mOut = null;          // response output stream
private boolean dateStringOnly = false;
```

The next block of code defines the bean methods to be used by the bean. A number of `set` methods are defined that can be used via `setProperty` tags in the JSP page. These methods allow the month, day, and year for the calendar to be defined, as shown below.

```
<jsp:setProperty name="Month" value="6" />
<jsp:setProperty name="Day" value="6" />
<jsp:setProperty name="Year" value="91" />
```

The responsibility of the `setXX` methods is to take arguments passed and to apply the value of those arguments to specific local data members (member variables of the class).

```
// Bean methods
public void setMonth( int month ) {
  this.month = month;
}
public void setYear( int year ) {
  this.year = year;
}

public void setDay( int day ) {
   this.day = day;
}
public void setHighLightColor ( String color ) {
   this.printHighLightColor = color;

}

public void setDateString( boolean flag ) {
 this.dateStringOnly = flag;

}

public void setCalDate( int month, int day, int year )
{
```

```
    mCalendar = new GregorianCalendar( year,   month, day );
}
public void setOut( JspWriter out ) {

    mOut = out;
}
```

The `set` method for the current date (`setCalCurrentDate`), as shown below, performs some additional work. The purpose of this method is to get the current date for the system and set the instance of the `calendar` class to that date. (Note that for a Web-based application, this will be the date of the server where the JSPs are running, not the date of the browser that invoked the HTTP request.)

The body of this method begins by creating an instance of `GregorianCalendar` and assigning that to the calendar for the instance. The methods `setDay`, `setMonth`, and `setYear` are then called to set the internal members to these values. Since the `Calendar.month` is zero-based, it is incremented to reflect the use of the month within this class (which is not zero-based but instead starts at the value 1).

```
public void setCalCurrentDate()
{

    mCalendar = new GregorianCalendar();

    setDay(    mCalendar.get( Calendar.DAY_OF_MONTH ));
    setYear(   mCalendar.get( Calendar.YEAR) );
    setMonth( mCalendar.get( Calendar.MONTH )+ 1 );


}
```

The `getXX` methods are used to wrap the private elements of the calendar and, in the case of the `getCurrentDate` method, provide convenient access to a date string within a JSP page.

```
// return the Current date (month day, year) as a string
public String getCurrentDate() {

if ( mCalendar == null )
    setCalCurrentDate();

return months[ this.month ] +
                "   " +
            this.day +
            "," +
                "   " +
            this.year;

}
```

The output of this class would be a text string with the current date. This could be used in a JSP page as follows. (It should be noted that the output of the `Cal.getCurrentDate` method is functionally equivalent to `DateFormat.getDateInstance(DateFormat.MEDIUM).format(mCalendar.getTime())`, which has the advantage of being non-locale specific. The approach shown here, however, is intended to take advantage of the internal members of the `Cal` class.)

```
...
<b>Today's Date:</b>    <jsp:getProperty name="myCal"
property="CurrentDate" />
...
```

The `printCal` method provides the output to produce calendar output in HTML format. This method takes as an argument the output stream for the response, which with JSP pages is the `JspWriter`. (This is actually an instance of a class that provides functionality similar to that of the `PrintWriter` class and is not a subclass of `PrintWriter`.) The `printCal` method uses the `JspWriter` output handle to output the resulting calendar. The calendar is produced based on the values of the internal members for the `Cal` class instance.

A local reference is used throughout the method; this is done for convenience and to allow for the easy substitution of a calendar object as a parameter in later revisions of this method. This local reference is first assigned to the internal calendar.

Since the calendar to be output will print all of the days of the month, the `printCal` method starts by setting the internal calendar to the first day of the month using the set method of the `GregorianCalendar` class.

```
public void printCal( JspWriter out ) throws ServletException {

Calendar cal = mCalendar;
String printAttr;

// set to the first day of the month
cal.set( Calendar.DAY_OF_MONTH, 1 );
...
```

A `try`/`catch` block is used to catch I/O exceptions for any of the statements that provide output to the `JspWriter` output stream. The output for the calendar is produced within this block.

The first output statement in this block is used to print a header for the calendar. This header displays the date in string format, using the `months` array (which contains the months of the calendar in string format), the `day` member (member variable of the `Cal` instance), and the year of the calendar.

```
...
try {

// print the header
out.println("<H2> " +
           months[ this.month ] +
           "  " +
           this.day +   // day of month
           "," +
           "   " +
           this.year +
            "</H2>" );
...
```

The next section of the method begins producing an HTML table for the calendar. This section of code currently contains hardcode table attributes, but could be expanded to add additional attributes for the table display.

A table row tag is used to denote the start of a week in the calendar output. Since a table header is needed for the calendar to display the days of the week, a for loop is used to loop for 7 days (0 to 6 inclusive) and display the days of the week. The days of the week are displayed in text format, using abbreviations stored in the daysAbbrev member variable.

```
...
out.println("<table border=3>");

// print the days of the week
out.print("<tr>");
for ( int n = 0; n <= 6; n++ )
    out.print("<td>" + daysAbbrev[n] + "</td>");

out.println("</tr>");
...
```

The next section of code shown below is used to display the days of the week in rows of 7 cells (one for each day). Since the first and last rows of output require cells to be produced that may not include a numerical day (i.e., days from the previous month and days from the next month), there is a block of logic that must determine whether or not a numerical day needs to be output. If a numerical day is not displayed, then a dash (-) is output. Additionally, if the day of the week being output is the current day for the calendar (this.Day), the day is output using the highlight color attribute. Since Sunday represents the end of the week (in the format used on this calendar), this represents the end of the row and must be output using the table row terminator tag (</tr>). Days of the week are represented as integer numbers ranging from 0 to 6.

```
...
// print blanks up to the start day
out.print("<tr>");

// if this is the day of the month highlight the table cell
// using the highlight display attribute
if (  Day == 1 )
    printAttr = "<td bgcolor=" + '"' + printHighLightColor + '"' + ">";
else
    printAttr = "<td>";


if ( cal.get( Calendar.DAY_OF_WEEK) > 1 ) {

    for ( int x = 0; x <= ( cal.get( Calendar.DAY_OF_WEEK) - 1); x++ ) {

        if ( x < ( cal.get(Calendar.DAY_OF_WEEK )-1) )
            out.print( "<td>" + "-" + "</td>" );
        else
                out.print( printAttr + "1" + "</td>" );

        if ( x == 6 ) {
            out.println("</tr>");
            out.print("<tr>");
        }
    }
}
else // day_of_week == 1 == 'Sunday'
    out.print( printAttr + "1" + "</td>" );
...
```

The next section of code stores the print attribute for the highlight block for the current day of the month in a string for convenience. A loop is then executed starting from the because at least one day of the month (the first day) has been printed in the control previous loop. This control loop will continue to process until the value of the loop control variable is greater than the maximum number of days in the month, at which time the loop will terminate.

As in the previous block of code, if the day of the week is the end of the week, as determined by the value of the call to get(Calendar.DAY_OF_WEEK), then the table row terminator will be printed.

```
...
printAttr = "<td bgcolor=" + '"' + printHighLightColor + '"' + ">";

for ( int n = 2; n <= cal.getActualMaximum( Calendar.DAY_OF_MONTH ); n++ ) {

    if ( n == Day ) // this is the day selected. let's highlight it
        out.print( printAttr + n + "</td>" );
    else
        out.print( "<td>" + n + "</td>" );
```

```
    // print <tr> at end of week
    cal.set( Calendar.DAY_OF_MONTH, n );
    if ( cal.get( Calendar.DAY_OF_WEEK) == 7) {
        out.println( "</tr>" );
        out.print( "<tr>" );
    }
}
...
```

At then end of the processing loop, two tags are output: the table row terminator and the table terminator. An `IOException` catch statement is required for the I/O performed by the `JspWriter` statement.

```
...
out.println( "</tr>" );
out.println("</table>");
}

catch (IOException e) {

    throw new ServletException("I/O Exception in Cal.printCal() " );

}

}

}
```

The complete code for the `Cal.java` class without breaks is shown in Appendix C.

USING CUSTOM TAGS IN JSP

With JSP version 1.1, *custom tag libraries* were introduced. These tag libraries provide a facility for creating custom JSP page tags. They provide a facility in which a common, well-understood approach to page programming, the page tag, can be used to access custom behaviors programmed in Java.

Tags provide a great deal of flexibility and are very effective in hiding the specifics of the operation from the user. For this reason, tags are an excellent mechanism for providing access to business logic to the HTML developer.

These tags resemble HTML tags in the use of a tag name, tag attributes, and a tag body, using the following syntax:

```
<myTag:tagName attribute1="value" attribute2="value">
optional tag body
</myTag:tagName>
```

A tag can be declared that can be inserted into a JSP page. When the JSP container encounters this tag as it preprocesses the page, the underlying code behind the tag will be invoked (in the servlet).

Custom tags provide additional value with the ability to perform programming flow-of-control functions within the JSP page. These are operations, such as loops or iterations, and execution of conditional statements.

Unlike HTML tags, which are just translated into a form that is then rendered on the browser, JSP tags can produce output based on input parameters and can iterate over output, producing various lists and tables in the resulting JSP page.

Coding Tags: Custom Tags and Business Logic

While tags offer many significant capabilities to the JSP page, they still do not eliminate the need for scripting. HTML was designed to provide for static page content; it does not provide programmatic flow-of-control statements that are required to perform robust rendering of dynamic content. For this reason, there are many reasons for placing scripting elements in a JSP page.

However, the developer must be careful not to confuse the coding of appropriate conditional logic to provide for the creation of the JSP page with the insertion of business logic into the JSP page. Business logic, logic that involves decisions concerning business rules (for example, a rule that indicates that region 1 should be excluded from district 4 totals if this report is for the first quarter), should be placed in *helper classes*, which should, if necessary, be called from within tag code. Decisions that involve the presentation of the page (for example, what color region 1 text should be, what color region 2 text should be) can be included in the page and may require some decision logic. But wherever possible, this logic should be placed in helper classes, thus providing a clear separation of roles and a much more manageable JSP page.

Using a Custom Tag Library: The JSP Calendar Utility

The following section of code uses the calendar creation code shown in the first JSP/JavaBean example to create a custom tag library to display calendar information in a JSP page. Using a JSP tag library requires the implementation of an interface (e.g., TagSupport) and the preparation of a configuration file in XML format, which provides information on the tag library (a .tld file). The XML descriptor file is referenced on the JSP page using the taglib directive, as shown below.

```
...
<%@ taglib uri="/jsp/TagCal.tld" prefix="tagcal" %>
...
```

This tag indicates that in the TOMCAT_HOME/webapps/jsp directory a .tld file named TagCal.tld is stored. This directs the Tomcat server to read the file and determine how to access the custom tag library that will be referenced on that page, using the `tagcal` prefix. (Note that the *TOMCAT_HOME* directory could instead be the `docBase` directory for the context.)

The tag library descriptor (TLD) file describes the JSP custom tag library to be used by the JSP page. The JSP page is made aware of the TLD by the `taglib` descriptor.

Since the TLD is an XML document, there is a corresponding document type definition (DTD) for the document. This first few tags in the document identify this DTD.

```
<?xml version="1.0" encoding="ISO-8859-1" ?>
<!DOCTYPE taglib
 PUBLIC "-//Sun Microsystems, Inc.//DTD JSP Tag Library 1.1//EN"
 "http://java.sun.com/j2ee/dtds/web-jsptaglibrary_1_1.dtd">

<!- a tag library descriptor ->

<taglib>
...
```

Additional elements are used to indicate the version of tag library being used, the JSP version being used. The short name for the tag library is identified followed by an alternative URI that this tag library may be mapped to. An informational tag provides an entry that describes the tag library.

```
<tlibversion>1.0</tlibversion>
<jspversion>1.1</jspversion>
<shortname>TagCal</shortname>
<uri></uri>
<info>
     Tag library for display of a calendar widget
</info>
```

The next block in the configuration file is shown below. This block is identified as the tag block and contains information usually provided by the developer, entries for the name of the tag, the `class` that will be loaded to implement the tag, and some general information about the tag. These entries are made on lines 3, 4, and 5 of the following listing.

The `class` entry identifies which Java class will be loaded to execute the tag. This class must provide an implementation of `BodyTag` or some other interface in the `javax.servlet.jsp.tagext` package. The name entry identifies the name that will be used to reference the tag.

A large portion of the remaining tag block on lines 7 through 28 is devoted to the various attributes that may be passed to the tag. The attribute is identified followed by a `required` tag, which indicates `true` or `false` whether or not the attribute is required for the tag.

The example below show the tags for each of the attributes passed to the TagCal calendar example, with tags for the optional attributes of month, day, year, out (output), and dateString (which sets the boolean dateString flag); each of these tags sets the required tag to false, since the attribute is optional.

The bodycontent tag is used to indicate whether or not the body of the tag will have content. In this example, it is empty.

```
1.
2.  <tag>
3.     <name>Calendar</name>
4.     <tagclass>JSPCal.TagCal</tagclass>
5.     <info> Display calendar</info>
6.
7.     <attribute>
8.         <name>month</name>
9.         <required>false</required>
10.    </attribute>
11.    <attribute>
12.        <name>day</name>
13.        <required>false</required>
14.    </attribute>
15.    <attribute>
16.        <name>year</name>
17.        <required>false</required>
18.    </attribute>
19.
20.    <attribute>
21.        <name>out</name>
22.        <required>false</required>
23.    </attribute>
24.
25.    <attribute>
26.        <name>dateString</name>
27.        <required>false</required>
28.    </attribute>
29.
30.    <bodycontent>EMPTY</bodycontent>
31.
32.  </tag>
33. </taglib>
```

The Java code for the tag library begins with a number of import statements, which are identical to the JavaBean code, with the exception of the statement to import the javax.servlet.jsp.tagext package used to specifically retrieve the tag library interfaces into the class namespace for the program.

```
package JSPCal;

import java.text.*;
import java.util.*;
import java.io.*;

import javax.servlet.*;
import javax.servlet.jsp.tagext.*;
import javax.servlet.jsp.*;
...
```

The major difference between this example and the JavaBean example is in the class definition. A JSP custom tag library must implement one of the interfaces in the `javax.servlet.jsp.tagext` package or extend one of the convenience classes in that package. In this example, the `TagSupport` class is extended, which provides empty body implementations for the methods in the `javax.servlet.jsp.tagext.Tag` interface and thus reduces the amount of work required to create the tag library.

```
public class TagCal extends TagSupport {

// array for months
private static final String months[] = new DateFormatSymbols().getMonths();

// array for days of week in string format
private static final String days[] = new DateFormatSymbols().getWeekdays();

// array for day abbreviations
private static final String daysAbbrev[] = new
DateFormatSymbols().getShortWeekdays();

// internal date
private int month;
private int day;
private int year;

private  String printHighLightColor = "grey";
private Calendar  mCalendar = null;   // internal calendar
private JspWriter mOut = null;        // response output stream
...
```

The tag library implementation also adds a boolean flag to indicate the behavior required of the `doStartTag` method. Specifically, this tag is used to indicate that the tag is being used to print the date as a character string and should not print the entire calendar.

Using Static Variables in JSP Pages

Because many JSP/servlet implementations allow servlet classes to be shared among sessions, the use of `static` variables could potentially create problems, since in Java `static` variables belong to the class, which would in turn be shared among multiple sessions.

But the use of `static` variables in the calendar JavaBean and tag library would not create a sharing conflict, since the variables declared `static` are also declared `final` (which indicate they cannot be changed once they are initialized). They are effectively constants that contain the calendar column headers—the names of the days of the week. As such, they can be shared among multiple objects or multiple JSP/servlet sessions without a problem.

```
...
private boolean dateStringOnly = false;
...
```

The `doStartTag` method is the method that is executed when the tag is encountered in the JSP page. The body of this tag is executed *after* the corresponding `setXX` methods have been called for the attributes in tag.

The body of the `doStartTag` method is shown below. This method acts as both a virtual constructor and a `main` program block for the tag. The first few lines of the method check the local members of the tag class to determine whether or not they have been set by the `setXX` methods of the tag (attributes that are not required to be set, as indicated in the TLD). These attributes indicate the date for the calendar to use. If the attributes have not been set, then the tag body assumes that the current date should be used and the `setCalCurrentDate` method is called. If the attribute values for the date have been set, then the `setCalDate` method is called to set the date for the calendar to the date specified in the attributes. Additionally, if the `JspWriter` output stream has not been specified in an attribute, the output stream is set to the output stream in the page context, as returned by `pageContext.getOut()`.

```
...
public int doStartTag() {

// use the current day as the default date
if ( ( mCalendar == null ) && ( this.month == 0 ) && ( this.day == 0 ) && (
this.year == 0 ) )
    setCalCurrentDate();

if ( ( this.month != 0 ) && ( this.day != 0 ) && ( this.year != 0 ) ) {
    this.month--; // GregorianCalendar expects 0 - based month
```

```
        setCalDate( this.month, this.day, this.year );
}

// set the default output stream to the JspWriter in the pageContext
if ( mOut == null )
    setOut( pageContext.getOut() );
...
```

An additional section of this code is shown below. Once all initialization has been done, a simple `if/else` block is used to determine the action to be performed by the tag. If the `dateStringOnly` flag has *not* been set, then the `printCal` method is called to output the HTML calendar for the date specified in the member variables of the calendar. If the `dateStringOnly` flag has been set, then the current date for the calendar (either the current date or the date specified in the attributes) is output as a text string. All of this work is performed in a `try/catch` block, which catches a `ServletException`.

```
...
try {

// print the calendar
if ( !dateStringOnly )
    printCal();
else // print the current date as a string
    mOut.println( getCurrentDate() );

}

catch (ServletException e) {

  System.out.println("TagCal error: " + e.getMessage() );

}
catch (IOException e) {
    System.out.println( "IOException in TagCal: " + e.getMessage() );
}
...
```

When work is complete, the `doStartTag` method returns a `SKIP_BODY` flag indicating that processing is complete (there are no additional iterations) and there is in fact no body to process for this tag.

```
...

// the tag shouldn't have a body to process
return (SKIP_BODY);
}
...
```

The class used to turn the calendar JavaBean into a custom tag has an additional method used to set a `dateStringOnly` flag indicating that the tag should display only the date as a string (and not display the full HTML formatted calendar). This class data member requires a `setXX` method to set the value of this flag, as shown below. With the exception of this method, the bodies of the two classes for the JavaBean and the tag library are virtually the same.

```
...
public void setDateString( boolean flag ) {

   this.dateStringOnly = flag;

}
...
```

JavaBeans or Custom Tag Libraries: Tips on Usage

JavaBeans and custom tag libraries are two different approaches to the same problem: how to extend the Java code on the JSP page. Since we would like to keep the use of scriptlets on the JSP page to a minimum, we need some mechanism to make use of Java helper classes on the JSP page. JavaBeans provide this capability in such a way that almost any valid Java class could be made into a JavaBean. The only requirement is that any properties accessed using the JSP `getProperty` or `setProperty` tag would require the coding of `get` and `set` methods in the class, using a specific naming convention, but this is not required.

The use of tag libraries with JSP pages is more restrictive in terms of the coding effort but in many ways is more powerful and provides easier access to the library methods on the JSP page. As we have seen here, JSP custom tag libraries require specific Java interfaces to be implemented, and various methods in these interfaces must coded in order for the tag to be executed properly from the JSP page. The integration of existing classes into custom tag libraries would therefore be more difficult than converting the same code into JavaBeans.

One approach to converting existing Java class libraries into custom tag libraries is through the creation of *wrapper classes*, classes that extend the class being converted using methods that consolidate and simplify one or more method call in the class being converted. These wrapper classes can make the conversion process simpler and can make the process of creating a custom tag library easier.

A custom tag library makes sense is when there is a requirement to perform an operation repeatedly within an application. This operation could be a general-purpose operation (for example, a calendar) that could be required across multiple applications, or it could be a business-specific operation such as retrieving customer or account information.

Creating a simple custom tag to perform an operation that must be executed repeatedly provides a better solution relative to performing the same operation with several lines of Java code (calling JavaBeans methods) in a scriptlet. Essentially, the custom tag approach will reduce the lines of Java code (in a scriptlet) that would be required with the JavaBeans approach, and reducing the amount of Java code on a JSP page improves the maintainability of the page and enhances the separation of roles between presentation and business logic. (While it is probably possible to write additional JavaBean methods and reduce the amount of scriptlet code required for a JavaBean approach to this same problem, the custom tag approach would still perform a better job of enhancing the separation of roles.)

The conclusion, then, is that JavaBeans work best with class libraries that map neatly into a `get/set` access approach, for instance, providing access to a database record or building a dynamic Web page based on a set of records. And custom tag libraries work best when an operation must be performed repeatedly (as opposed to only once) across many Web pages and the operation does not map easily into a simple get/set access approach.

SUMMARY

This chapter covered using JSP to create dynamic Web content. Since we know that we don't want to place too much Java code on the JSP page in scriptlets, we need to have a facility for moving Java code off the page. We have two basic approaches to doing this: using JSP with JavaBeans and using custom tag libraries.

Both approaches to using Java classes on JSP pages were covered in this chapter, using an example that created a set of calendar utilities. The first example used JavaBeans to display an HTML-formatted monthly calendar. Then, to demonstrate the same approach using a custom tag library, the code required to implement the calendar utility as a custom tag library was shown. Finally, we discussed the benefits and drawbacks of each approach and established some guidelines for the use of these two techniques.

COMING UP NEXT

Chapter 18 provides a more detailed example of JSP usage with the development of a threaded message list. The example shown in this chapter will be used throughout the next few chapters to demonstrate the development of more complex Web pages which require database access. Dynamic web pages will be created based on the contents of various database tables. The chapter also explains dynamic input forms, using session variables, forwarding requests, and using exceptions with JSP.

CHAPTER 18

JSP and JDBC in Development: A Discussion Group System

INTRODUCTION

There is no better way to learn the use of a technology than through example. While the Chapter 17 showed several simple examples to demonstrate some basic concepts, this chapter will detail the use of Java and JSP in a more complex example. The system developed in this chapter is a discussion group system designed to maintain a database of messages stored by topic. The system tracks message threads, and users of the system can start a message thread or add to existing message threads.

The code behind this system will be used to demonstrate login security, the creation of dynamic HTML tables, storing data in session variables, passing request parameters, and other important concepts.

A basic design strategy of separating presentation logic from business logic will be used. To maintain this separation of business logic from presentation logic, the use of Java scriptlets on the JSP page will be kept to a minimum and Java *design patterns* introduced will be applied whenever possible.

These design patterns will also be heavily used in the development of the classes for data access and workflow control. data access objects (DAOs) will be used to model and encapsulate database operations, and value objects will be used to encapsulate and model the logical data records used throughout the application. *facade patterns* will be used to manage the workflow control and marshal the resources of the DAOs to facilitate the creation of the dynamic Web pages.

Discussion Group System: Application Description

The application shown here is designed to allow users to enter messages. These messages can be part of a thread so that a user can enter an initial message and then users can add to that message, either providing additional information relative to the message or providing a reply to the message. These additional messages added to the initial message are referred to as *message threads*. This type of application is often referred to as a *threaded message list* or a *knowledge base* where knowledge or information is stored.

The Message

The focus of the discussion group system is the manipulation of messages posted to various discussion groups. These messages are tracked in the system using information on the user that entered the message, the date the message was entered, and the type and category of the message. This information about the message is used to store, manipulate, and sort the message when it is output on the message review pages.

Each message has a message type and message category. The valid message types and categories can be defined for a particular installation of the message system so that different installations of the message system can be used to track different types of messages. (This adds flexibility to the system but for us, the developers, implies additional work, since these dynamic values for the message types and message categories must be managed by the message system application.)

An example of the use of the flexibility of dynamic message types and message categories would be to use the message system to create a common problem-tracking system. This system would store information on problems as messages, and potential solutions to those problems could be posted as responses to the initial problem message. The initial problem message would be created with a message type of `problem`, and the message response, a message that is posted as a threaded message to the initial message, would be created with a message type of `resolution`.

Another use of the message system would be as a system to store online discussions. A message could be created with a message type of `post` for initial posted messages. Responses to the initial message, added as threaded messages, would be created with a message type of `reply` for replies to those messages.

Message Threads

A message that has been entered into the message system is either an initial message posting (or *base message* of a message thread) or a response type posting to an initial thread, also referred to as a *threaded message*.

Using the example for a problem-tracking system, a user may enter an initial message, perhaps identifying and explaining a particular problem identified. Another user of the message system may then read that initial message and add to the identification of the problem by adding to that message. At this point, two messages would be considered part of that message thread, the initial message or the *base* message entered by the user that identified the problem and the message that was added by the second user, a *threaded* message. Both of these messages could be entered with a message type of `problem`, indicating that they identified a problem as shown in Figure 18.1.

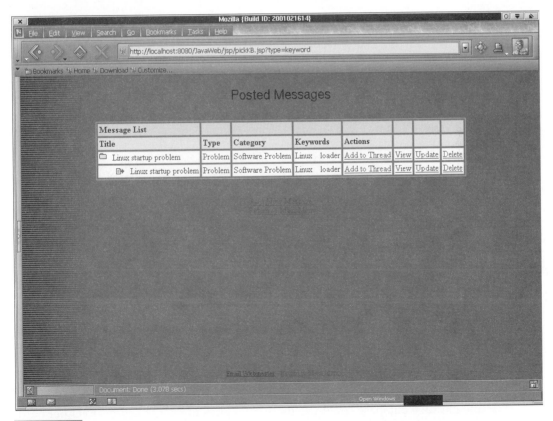

Figure 18–1 *Message Listing Page*

Finally, a message system user may read both messages and provide a resolution to the problem identified. This message would also be added as a thread of the initial message but would be added with a message type of `resolution`, indicating it provided a resolution to the problem identified by the other users.

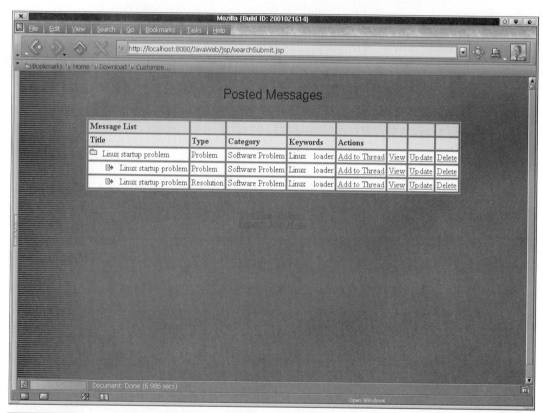

Figure 18–2   *Message Listing with Problem Resolution*

Message Categories

Each message is associated with a message *category*. This association is maintained in the database through a field in the message header that contains the category for that message. For a problem-tracking system, these categories could be `hardware` for hardware problems and `software` for software problems. Messages could be posted to either category, and dynamic JSP pages that searched or listed the message database could use these categories to restrict listings to either hardware or software problems.

Alternatively, the message system could be used for a discussion group, and these categories could be used as topics for discussions. Users could be allowed to add categories for different discussion topics. Other users could read these user postings and add additional postings. In essence, the message system application could provide a communication forum for a user community.

Database Structure

The message system uses a relational database to store configuration information for the system (message types, message categories), user login IDs and related security information, and messages and related information.

Each message entered in the message system has a primary key, known as a document key (`doc_key`). This primary key is automatically maintained by the database as a unique integer number. Maintaining the list of messages involves tracking the *base* key for the initial message in each of the threaded messages for that initial message.

Also stored with the message is the date the message was entered and the last date the message was modified. When the message list is displayed, it is sorted by the base document key and the date the message was entered, so that the initial message is at the top of the sorted list followed by the messages that have been posted to the initial message. The posted messages are displayed in the order in which they have been entered, based on the date they were entered and the last date they were modified.

APPLICATION FLOW FOR THE MESSAGE SYSTEM

Any Web application is constructed using a certain procedural flow, which assumes the user of the application is going to move through the application in a certain fashion. With larger Web sites, a great deal of consideration is applied to this process, creating large wireframe diagrams that detail the flow of the system.

The message system, though not as complex as some Web sites, does contain a number of pages that you would expect on a Web site: a login page, a main menu, a search page, a message listing page, a message view page, and a message input/update page. Taken together, these pages comprise the message system Web site.

But our Web site is not just static HTML pages; it includes JavaBeans code that supports these pages and a database and corresponding database schema. The JavaBeans code for this application comprises business objects, control objects, and database access objects.

Keeping the flow of the application in mind, our discussion of the message system will begin with a discussion of the pages of the message system in the order in which those pages would most likely be accessed. Following this discussion, the database schema for the message system will be discussed. This discussion will provide the framework for a discussion of the code behind the message system in Chapter 19.

Login Page

A login page on a Web site is used to perform several different functions. First, it should authenticate the user and verify his or her identity. This will usually involve checking a user ID and password entered by the user against a user ID and password stored on the system.

Next, a login page (or the processing behind the page) will retrieve some information about the user and retain this information for the user session. For many sites, this information includes the user name and user preference information. The message system performs these operations, though it does not collect the copious user preference and history information that many commercial sites may collect. The login page initially asks the user to enter a user ID and password (see Figure 18–3).

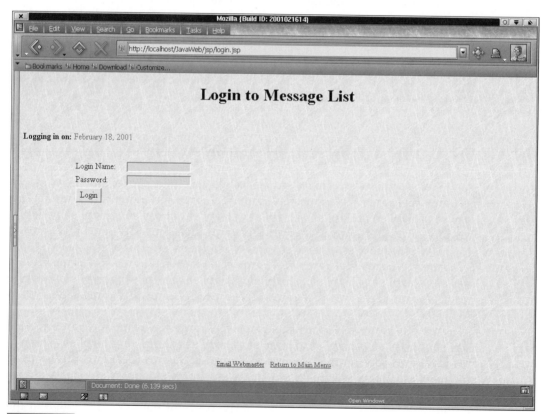

Figure 18–3   *Message Listing Page*

Once the user has entered his or her user ID and password on the login page (`login.jsp`), the form is posted to another page, which will process the information (`loginSubmit.jsp`). If the user login is successful (the user is known to the system and the password is valid) then the successful login page is shown (see Figure 18–4).

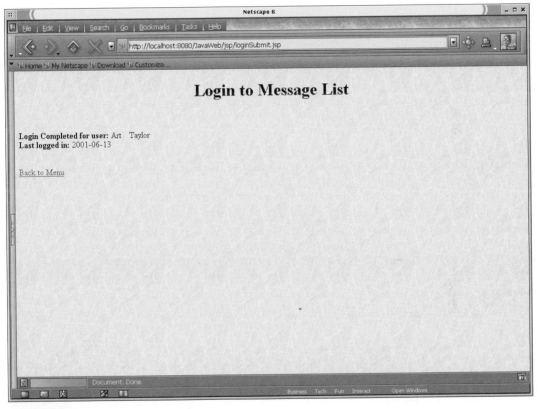

Figure 18–4   *Successful Login Page*

If the user login is not successful, then a Java exception is thrown; the error page (`ErrorPage.jsp`) is shown in Figure 18–5.

The message system does not require every user to log into the system. A user who is not logged in is allowed to review the messages on the message board, but is not allowed to post a message unless he or she has completed the login process.

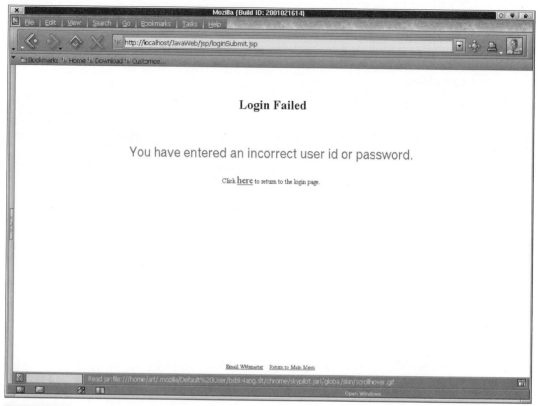

Figure 18–5 *Login Failure Page*

The login page retrieves user information (user name, location, last login date) from a database table and ultimately stores this information in a `session` object, an object available to all the pages in the user session (defined as pages called as part of a list of pages starting with the first page accessed). Other pages in the session will use the user information in the `session` object. Some pages will use the information to determine whether or not the user has logged in and whether or not he or she is a valid user. The message input/update page will use the user information to populate part of the input form for the user, information that will become part of the message record to be inserted or updated into the database.

The Main Menu

The main menu for the application is a simple static HTML page. This page will be accessed by the user through the Apache Web server, using server-side includes to display information on the current date and to retrieve the header and elements to be used throughout the application (see Figure 18–6). Since the page is static HTML, it can be served by the Apache server, which has the benefit of reducing some of the workload for the Tomcat server.

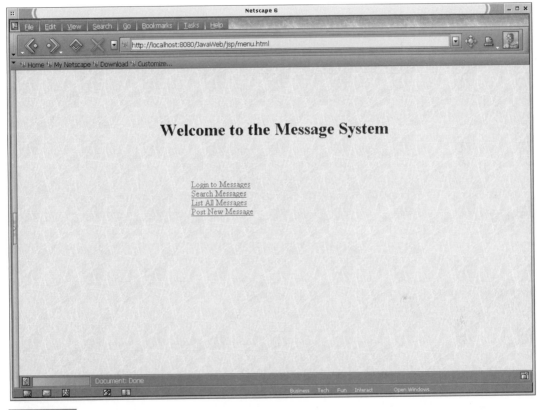

Figure 18–6   *Main Menu*

The options to search the message base, to list all messages, and to later view the contents of the message base do not require a valid login. The option to post a new message does, however, require a valid login. These options and their associated pages are explained in more detail in the following sections.

Post New Message

The post new message process allows the user to create a new message in the message database. This option will execute the `inputKB.jsp` page, which will require the user to have valid login entries in the JSP `session` object. If the user does not have a valid login, then he or she will be redirected (using a JSP forward) to an error page indicating that he or she must log in before posting a message. See Figure 18–7.

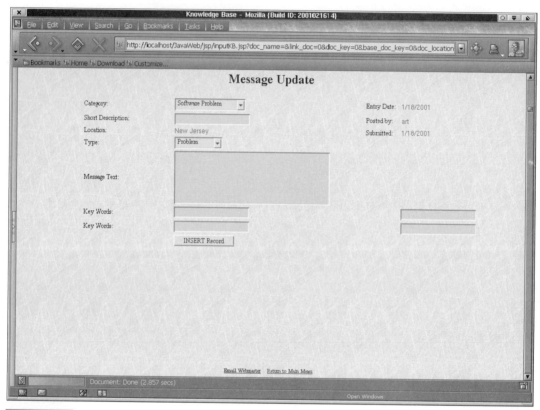

Figure 18–7 *Input New Message*

Note that some fields are displayed but cannot be changed by the user; these fields are either generated programmatically or obtained from the `session` object as part of the login record.

Search Existing Messages

The message search page allows messages to be searched using the keywords assigned to the messages. The page provides fields to input up to four keywords to be used to perform the search. See Figure 18–8.

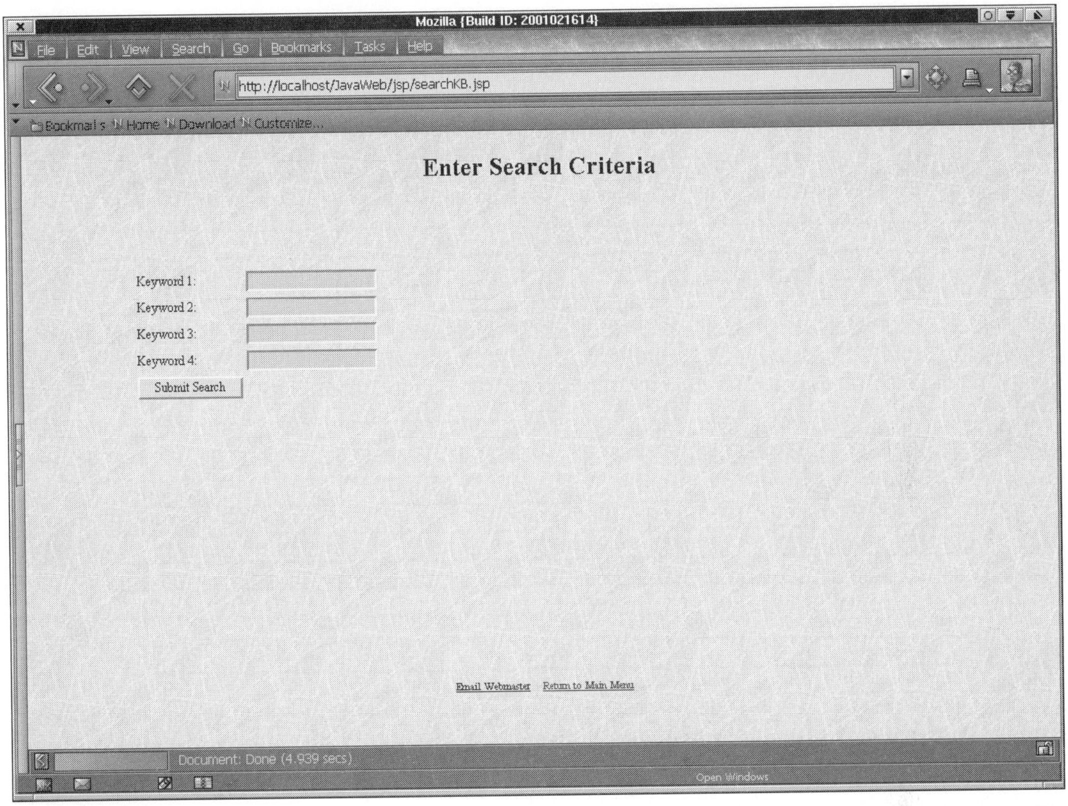

Figure 18–8 *Enter Search Criteria*

Once the keywords have been entered, the submit query button on the page is pressed by the user. This sends a request to the message listing page (`pickKB.jsp`), passing parameters that indicate that the user has requested a filtered list. The filter operation will select not only the messages that match the search criteria, but also the messages that are part of the message thread for those messages.

Message List: All Messages

The message list page provides a listing of all messages currently in the message database. (The current implementation of this feature displays all messages in the database. A more refined production version should limit the number of rows returned for efficiency purposes.) See Figure 18–9.

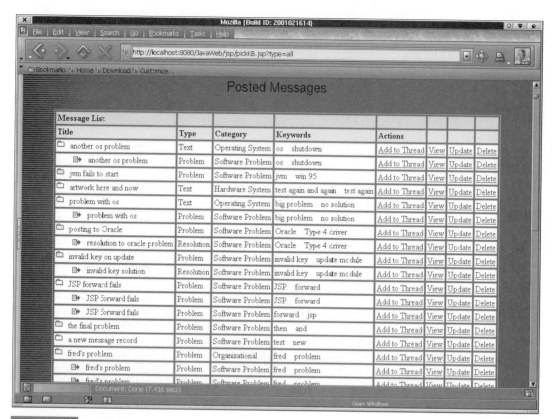

Figure 18–9 *List All Messages*

Message List: Filtered

The message listing for a filtered set of rows uses the same display as the listing for all rows but applies the filter before producing the page output. See Figure 18–10.

Update Message

The update message page is called with parameters that indicate the message document that should be displayed. The message document is then retrieved, and its contents are displayed in a form that allows the user to modify components of the record. Note that some fields are displayed but cannot be changed by the user;

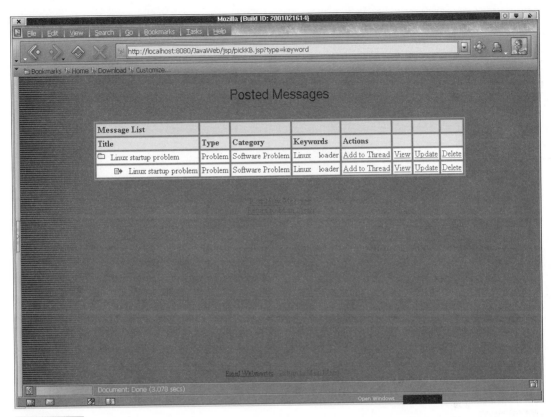

Figure 18–10 *Filtered Message List*

these fields are either generated programmatically or obtained from the `session` object as part of the login information. See Figure 18–11.

Delete Message

The delete message operation allows the user to delete a message but checks to determine that the user attempting to delete the message is actually the user that entered the message or is a user with permissions to delete the messages entered by another user (for example, a system administration user or a message group moderator). Messages are deleted using a link on the message listing page to the message view page. This process allows the user to view the message before it is deleted.

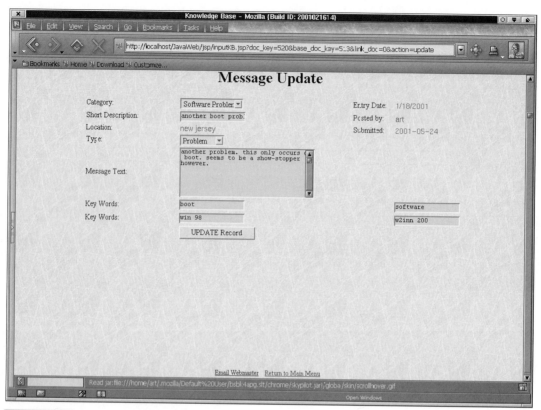

Figure 18–11   *Update Existing Message*

If the message delete operation is successful, a page is displayed indicating that the delete operation was successful. If the delete operation has failed, an exception is thrown, which displays the error page with a message about the failed delete operation. If the update is successful, then the page shown below is displayed.

THE MESSAGE SYSTEM: TECHNICAL DESCRIPTION

Previously we have discussed the concept of architectural tiers and design patterns applied to those architectural tiers. To effectively practice what we preach, the message system was designed using these architectural tiers, and it applies several of the design patterns discussed in that chapter.

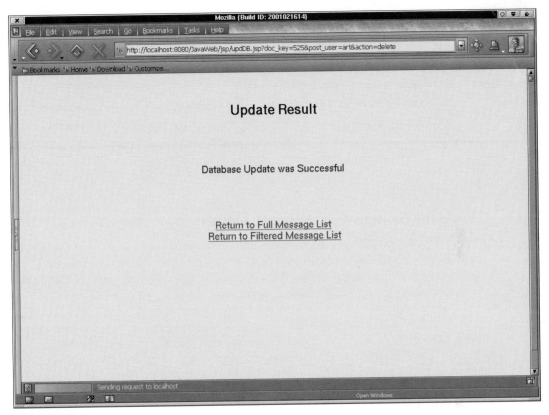

Figure 18–12 *Update Successful Message Page*

The logical tiers we have described are used to dictate the responsibilities of the components of the system. This applies structure to the design process and allows certain components to be used for what they do best. The tiers and the components used for those tiers are as follows.

- Client
- Presentation
- Business
- Integration
- Resource

For our purposes, the client tier is represented by a user with a Web browser. The resource tier is represented by the PostgreSQL relational database (or any relational database that supports SQL and JDBC). The tiers that are the focus of the next few chapters are described in Table 18–1.

Table 18–1   *Architectural Tiers*

Tier	Purpose	Components
Presentation	Creates the output for the page.	JSP
Business	Manages the business logic and application workflow.	JavaBeans
Integration	Manages database access, encapsulates database components.	JavaBeans

Message System Component Design

These *logical tiers* identify the responsibilities of the components (the JavaBeans and JSP pages) in the application. These responsibilities dictate the functions the components will perform within the application and are then used to dictate the lower level design details of these components.

The login process has the responsibility of authenticating the user and then directing the user to a particular view. This management of view is primarily a presentation issue and will therefore dictate that this component, the login component, is a presentation tier component. Some of the work of this component will involve database and workflow activity; this work will be managed by business tier components, which will be responsible for building the views that the login component will direct the user to.

The message application uses a number of *facade* classes on the business tier. The purpose of these facade classes is to manage the dynamic output of the pages. Their job is to marshal resources of the business objects and DAOs, send the value objects back and forth to the DAOs, and provide wrapper methods for the value objects. They are essentially the interface between one or more of the JSP pages and the database resources they access. They encapsulate the business logic of the application and control the flow of work being performed (see Figure 18–3). (While this use of these facade classes allowed the DAOs and value objects to remain focused on their tasks, it did create what was ultimately a very large and complex facade class for a number of the pages. A design revision would most likely include the use of multiple business objects by the facade classes to reduce the exposure of the facade class.)

These business tier objects are used by the JSP page to build the pages and perform the processing required of the pages. They are effectively helper classes for the JSP pages. To simplify the operations performed on the JSP page, a single session facade object, an instance of the `KnowledgeBaseFacade` class, is used by the various JSP pages in the application.

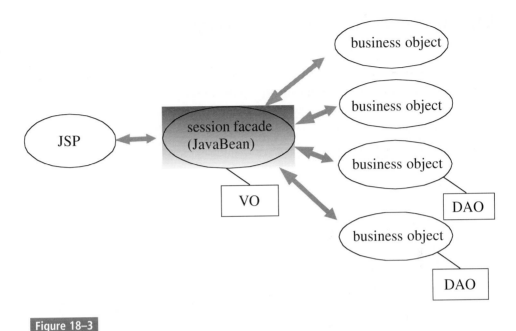

Figure 18–3

Two integration tier patterns are applied to the database operations. DAOs are used to provide access to the database, and value objects are use to encapsulate database objects in a form that can be conveniently passed from method to method in the application (these value objects are also used on the business tier). The use of these design patterns allowed database operations to be isolated, tested, validated, and then easily shared by other objects. This allowed the database resource to be protected and controlled in the application and provided a means of reducing the amount of work required to access the database. Code for database access is shared among the multiple business objects that access the database and, should the database vendor change (an all too common occurrence), the code change is isolated to a small set of classes.

The database operations are further abstracted in this application. A database utility class (dbUtil) is used to provide the low-level access to the database. This database utility class is accessed by the DAOs and contains virtually all JDBC database calls (with the exception of some ResultSet manipulation that appears elsewhere). This abstraction of database operations from the business classes of the application is used to encapsulate the low-level database operations and provide some flexibility in how they are managed. For instance, while the code used in this sample application does not use database connection pooling, it could easily be inserted into the database utility class in a manner that would be transparent to the rest of the application.

MESSAGE SYSTEM DATABASE DESIGN

The message system makes use of a number of relational tables to store pertinent information for the system. This information includes information about the system users, information concerning the messages that have been posted, the text of the messages, any keywords applied to the message, security information for the system, and message categories and message types. The design of the database is a relatively normalized relational structure with tables and descriptions, as detailed in Table 18–2.

Table 18–2   *Message System Database Tables*

Table	Description
message_user	Contains information on the users of the system, including the user name and their password.
base_keys	Contains the keywords associated with the messages in the system. Currently, messages can have up to for four entries in this table. Optionally, the message can have 0 no entries in this table (which is true for many threaded responses to existing message entries).
categories	Contains the categories of messages that exist on the system.
knowledge_base	Contains the *header* information for messages entered into the system.
knowledge_messages	Contains the message text for the message. This is a child table of the knowledge_base table, meaning that every record in this table must have a corresponding entry in this table.
message_types	Contains the types of messages that can be entered in the message system.
message_security	Security information for users of the message system, including the security role of the user.

These tables and their contents are explained in more detail in the following sections.

The knowledge_base Table

The `knowledge_base` table stores the base information for the message, the message header or parent in the parent-child relationship for the message database. This table uses a document key (`doc_key`) column as the primary key for the table—the column that uniquely identifies the row in the table. This column is an integer value that is automatically incremented and maintained by the database. (For the PostgreSQL database, this is managed using a `sequence` in the database; the Oracle database uses a similar approach, while the Informix database uses a `serial` column, and SQL Server and MySQL uses an `AutoNumber` column.)

The date the message was first entered is stored in the `date_submitted` field. This field indicates the date the message was submitted to the system. Like the `entry_date` field, this field is stored in the database as a `date` data type, but is managed by the JSP pages and Java code as a string.

The `knowledge_base` table stores the category of the message, the date the message was submitted, and the last date the message was updated (`entry_date`). The date columns are stored as `date` data types in the database, though for convenience and a certain amount of portability, they are treated as strings by the JSP/Java code, which uses the database to perform the conversion on inserts and updates.

The `knowledge_base` table also stores the location (`doc_location`) where the message document was entered and the user name of the user (`post_user`) that entered the message. This information appears in the `knowledge_base` record, but is not entered by the user. Instead, it is retrieved from the `session` object, where it has been populated based on the entries in the `message_user` table for the current user.

A short description of the document is contained in the `doc_name` field. This provides a description or *name* for the message.

The `level` field is intended to store the level of the message within the message threads for the initial posting. This field is currently not used. (Messages are displayed in the date order based on the date the message was first submitted or entered in the system.)

The `post_user` field is used to store the name of the user who first entered the message. This field is automatically inserted based on the user login information stored in the `session` object (which is stored in the `message_user` table). The user entering the message is not allowed to change this information.

The `link_doc` field is used to store the document to which this document is linked. (This field is not currently used.)

The `base_doc_key` field is used to store the base document key (`doc_key`) for the message thread to which this document belongs. This key is used to select and display message documents for a particular thread. The complete schema for this table is shown in Table 18–3.

Table 18–3 *Schema for the knowledge_base Table*

Column Name	Data Type	Description
doc_key	integer	Primary key for the message document.
doc_name	varchar(50)	Short name/short description for the message.
doc_location	varchar(50)	Location where the document was entered.
level	integer	Level of the message in the message thread list.
category	varchar(50)	Category for the message.
post_user	varchar(50)	User name for the user who posted the message.
date_submitted	date	The date the message was submitted (last changed).
link_doc	integer	The link document for this message; the message for which this document represents a response.
base_doc_key	integer	The document key for the base document in this message thread.
entry_date	date	The date this message document was entered.

The knowledge_messages Table

The knowledge_messages table stores the actual message text for the message. The message is stored using the doc_key as the primary key and foreign key for the corresponding header record in the knowledge_base table.

This message system stores the message as a variable length character data type with a limit of 500 characters (a varchar(500)). (The database, not the application, enforces the limit on the size of the message, so the size of the column could be increased at the database and the application would support the larger size.)

The message_type field is used to capture additional information about the message being stored. While the message category groups the message based on a category name, the message type indicates the general nature of the message. For example, the message type could be a post message or a response message for a message system that was providing a forum for discussion groups. Or the message type could be used to store a problem message to identify and describe a problem and a resolution message to describe a possible resolution for a problem. These message types are configurable and are contained in the message_types table in the database. The contents of this table are used to produce a list box for the message input page. The schema for this table is shown in Table 18–4.

Table 18–4	Schema for the knowledge_messages Table	

Column Name	Data Type	Description
doc_key	integer	The primary key for this message document.
message_txt	varchar(500)	The text of the message.
message_type	varchar(10)	The type of the message.

The message_user Table

The message_user table is used to store information on the users for the message system. This table stores the user first name and last name, the location of the user, and the user password. Information is also stored on the location of the user, the date the user login record was submitted, and the date of the last login for the user. The complete schema for this table is shown in Table 18–5.

Table 18–5	Schema for the message_user Table	

Column Name	Data Type	Description
login	varchar(20)	Login name for the user.
first_name	varchar(30)	First name for the user (given name).
last_name	varchar(30)	Last name for the user (surname).
location	varchar(50)	Location of the user.
date_submitted	date	Date login record was submitted by the user.
last_login	date	Last login date for the user.
pwd	varchar(15)	Password for the user.

The base_keys Table

The base_keys table is used to store the lookup keywords for the messages stored in the database. Currently, the system allows four keywords to be stored for each message (though there is nothing in the schema for this table that enforces a limit). The keywords are referenced using the doc_key column and there can be zero, one, or many entries in this table for a given message document key.

If a user enters no keywords for a message (this is common with threaded responses to an initial posting) then no entries would be stored in this table. The schema for this table is shown in Table 18–6.

Table 18–6   *Schema for the base_keys Table*

Column Name	Data Type	Description
doc_key	integer	The primary key for the message document.
keyword	varchar(50)	The keyword to be associated with the message document.

The categories Table

The `categories` table stores the various categories of messages that can be stored in the system. This provides some flexibility for the system, allowing categories to be customized for the particular installation. For instance, for a problem-tracking system, categories could be stored for hardware problems, software problems, installation issues, and so on. For a group discussion system, categories could be entered for politics, gardening, dogs, cats, and so on. This table contains a column for the category name and a column for a description of the category. The schema for this table is shown in Table 18–7.

Table 18–7   *Schema for the categories Table*

Column Name	Data Type	Description
category	varchar(20)	Category name.
description	varchar(30)	Description of the category.

The message_types Table

The `message_types` table stores additional information on the type of message being stored in the system. For instance for a problem-tracking system, the message type could be a `problem` message for a message that identifies a problem and a `resolution` for a message in the same thread that provides a resolution to the problem identified in the thread. The complete schema for this table is shown in Table 18–8.

Table 18–8	*Schema for the message_types Table*	

Column Name	Data Type	Description
message_type	varchar(20)	Message type.
description	varchar(50)	Description of message type.

Additional Database Components

The logical concept of a message document has no natural primary key, a field that uniquely identifies rows in the table. For this reason, a generated primary key was needed. This required a counter within the database that could be used to generate unique integer ID numbers. The PostgreSQL database (and other databases) provide this feature in the form of a `sequence`.

The `sequence` is created in the database and then accessed using certain database functions. The statement to create a sequence named `doc_key` with a starting number of 500 is as follows:

```
create sequence doc_key start 500;
```

To access the next value of a sequence, the `nextval('<sequence_name>')` function can be used. In the message system, the `insert` statement used to insert the message into the database makes use of this function. The value generated by the `nextval('doc_key')` function call is used as the primary key for the record being inserted.

Since the other records related to the message header must use the `doc_key` generated by the database `insert` operation, the insert function for the message header record (`knowledge_base`) must return the `doc_key` generated during the `insert` operation. This `doc_key` will then be passed to other methods to perform the insert operation.

Additionally, the system is designed to use a single database user ID to provide access to the data. For the message system shown in this example, the user ID is `puser`. This user is added to the PostgreSQL system with the following command:

```
create user puser;
```

This would create the user `puser` in the database. To allow the user `puser` to access specific tables in the database and perform specific database operations, the `grant` statement would be used as follows:

```
grant select on knowledge_base to puser;
grant update on knowledge_base to puser;
```

SUMMARY

This chapter laid the foundation for our discussion of a sample JSP application: the discussion group system. It detailed the design and page flow and also provided details on the database structure of this application.

COMING UP NEXT

Chapter 19 will provide the details behind the JSP pages shown in this chapter. The code behind the JSP pages in the discussion group will be shown and discussed, and the details of the Java code used to support the pages (in the form of JavaBeans and additional utility classes) will also be shown, so that the discussion of the pages will trace the execution of the page from the JSP page into the classes that support the page.

CHAPTER 19

JSP and JDBC in Development: Coding the Discussion Group System

INTRODUCTION

In Chapter 18, we introduced a sample JSP application, the discussion group system, and provided details on the design of the system. Now we will let the rubber hit the road and discuss the various components of the discussion group system—the JSP pages, the design of the database tables, and the classes that will perform the bulk of the work necessary to produce the dynamic pages of the discussion group system. The majority of this chapter is devoted to the JSP pages and the business tier JavaBeans classes that support those pages.

THE ORGANIZATION OF THE DISCUSSION GROUP SYSTEM

The code for the message system is divided into three distinct Java packages based on the functional responsibility of the code in those packages. These three packages are listed in Table 19–1.

481

Table 19–1	*Message System Packages*

Package Name	Description
JSPCal	General-purpose calendar classes.
db	Database utility access routines. This class is used to wrap the JDBC calls to the database.
knowledgebase	Classes used to manage the access to the message system, including the value object classes, the database access object classes, and the session facade classes.

Within the application there is a quite a bit of interaction between the classes in the db package and the knowledgebase package. The classes in the JSPCal package are used as needed throughout the system. The following sections explain these packages and their classes in more detail.

The JSPCal Package

The JSPCal class contains a number of utility methods to provide access to the current date and to display a calendar in HTML format. The two classes contained in this package are Cal and TagCal. The Cal class contains the methods listed in Table 19–2.

The TagCal class uses the same methods as the JSPCal class but wraps the calls to those methods using the methods that it must implement in order to be used as a custom tag library. The TagCal class extends the TagSupport class, which in turn implements the Tag interface and provides implementations for the various methods in that interface. The TagCal class as implemented here only provides an implementation for the doStartTag method which is executed when the custom tag is encountered. (Custom tag processing will also make use of the set methods in the TagCal class, but these methods also existed in the Cal class and were explained in Table 19–2.

The db Utility Package

The db utility package is used to abstract the details of low-level database access from the data access object (DAO) classes. While the DAOs are still used to manage the database access operations and return results in the form of value objects, the db utility class methods are used to load the database driver, open and close connections to the database, create prepared statements, and execute queries against the database.

These methods are fairly flexible in dealing with database connections; if a connection has not currently been made to the database, a connection is made.

Table 19–2   *JSPCal Class Methods*

Method	Description
`setMonth( int month )`	Set the month for the calendar.
`public void setYear( int year )`	Set the year for the calendar.
`public void setDay( int day )`	Set the day for the calendar.
`public void setHighLightColor ( String color )`	Set the highlight color to be used for the calendar.
`public void setDateString( boolean flag )`	A flag indicating whether or not to print a date string for the date. (This is used with the calendar tag.)
`public void setCalDate( int month, int day, int year )`	Set the day, month, and year for the calendar with a single method call.
`public void setOut( JspWriter out )`	Set the output stream for the calendar.
`public void setCalCurrentDate()`	Set the calendar to the current date on the server (the machine where the JSP page is executed).
`public String getCurrentDate()`	Retrieve the current date for the calendar (not necessarily the current date for the machine) as a string.
`public String getCurrentDate( String format )`	Retrieve the current date for the calendar as a formatted string. (The only format currently supported is mm/dd/yy.)
`public void printCal( JspWriter out ) throws ServletException`	Print the current calendar sending output to the `JSPWriter` passed to the method.

Likewise, if the database driver has not been loaded, the driver is loaded before an attempt is made to create a connection. This removes the responsibility of managing these low-level database details from the DAOs. All methods share the same active connection for the instance, thus avoiding the overhead of creating additional connections for each query. (Use of connection pooling reduces this overhead.) This class contains the methods listed in Table 19–3.

Table 19–3   *DBUtil Class Methods*

Method	Description
`public void getConnected() throws Exception`	Obtains a connection to the database if one has not currently been obtained.
`public void createDBStatement() throws Exception`	Creates a database statement from the current connection. Obtains a connection if one has not currently been made.

Table 19–3 *DBUtil Class Methods (cont.)*

Method	Description
`public PreparedStatement createPreparedStatement( String stmt ) throws Exception`	Creates a prepared statement from the query string passed to the method. Obtains a connection if one has not already been made.
`public ResultSet executePreparedStatement( PreparedStatement pstmt ) throws Exception`	Executes a prepared statement passed to the method. Obtains a connection if one is not currently active. Returns a JDBC `ResultSet`.
`public int executePreparedStmtUpd( PreparedStatement pstmt ) throws Exception`	Executes a prepared update statement and returns an integer indicating the number of database rows touched by the update. Obtains a connection if one is not currently active.
`public ResultSet executeDBQuery( String query ) throws Exception`	Executes a database query contained in the Sstring passed into the method. Obtains a connection if one is not currently active. Returns a `ResultSet` of rows returned by the query.
`public int executeUpdDBQuery( String query ) throws Exception`	Executes a database update query for the string passed into the method. Obtains a connection if one is not currently active. Returns an integer indicating the number of rows updated.
`public ResultSet getdbResultSet()`	Returns the current `ResultSet` used by the utility class.
`public String getdbDriverName()`	Returns the name of the database driver currently being used.
`public Connection getdbConnection()`	Returns the JDBC Cconnection being used by the utility class.
`public String getDbURL()`	Returns the URL of the database currently being used.
`public Statement getdbStatement()`	Returns the database statement currently being used.
`public void setdbDriverName ( String dbDN )`	Sets the driver to be used by the db utility class.
`public void setdbURL ( String dbURL )`	Sets the URL to be used by the db utility class.

The knowledgebase Package

The `knowledgebase` package contains the bulk of the code used by the message application. This package contains the facade classes, the value objects, and the DAOs, as described in Table 19–4.

Table 19–4 *knowledgebase Package Classes*

Class Name	Description
Base_keysDAO	The Data Access ObjectDAO for the `base_keys` table.
Base_keysVO	The Value Objectvalue object for the `base_keys` table.
CategoriesDAO	The Data Access ObjectDAO for the `categories` table.
CategoriesVO	The Value Objectvalue object for the `Ccategories` table.
Knowledge_baseDAO	The Data Access ObjectDAO for the `knowledge_base` table.
KnowledgeBaseFacade	The facade class for the `knowledge_base` system as a whole. This class controls the access to all Data Access ObjectDAOs and provides an interface for the presentation layer (the JSP pages) to the Data Access ObjectDAO.
Knowledge_baseVO	The Value Objectvalue object for the `knowledge_base` table.
Knowledge_messagesDAO	The Data Access ObjectDAO for the `knowledge_messages` table.
Knowledge_messagesVO	The Value Objectvalue object for the `knowledge_messages` table.
loginFacade	The facade class for the login process. Provides access to the Data Access ObjectDAOs used in the login process. Provides an interface for the presentation layer, the JSP pages.
Message_securityDAO	The Data Access ObjectDAO for the `message_security` table.
Message_securityVO	The Value Objectvalue object for the `message_security` table.
Message_typesDAO	The Data Access ObjectDAO for the `message_types` table.
Message_typesVO	The Value Objectvalue object for the `message_types` table.
Message_userDAO	The DAO for the `message_user` table.
Message_userVO	The value object for the `message_user` table.
searchFacade	The facade class for the search page. Encapsulates the search operation. Provides an interface for the search process and the database operations required for the search process.

The value objects in this package contain internal data members that mirror the attributes or columns of the database tables that they represent and 'get' and 'set' methods that are the accessor and mutator methods respectively for each of these class members. Each value object will not be covered in detail since the description of each method in these classes would quickly become redundant.

The methods listed in Table 19–5 are common to the DAOs used in this example.

Table 19–5   *Common Methods for DAOs*

Name	Description
`public int insertDAO( ) throws SQLException, Exception`	Inserts the current contents of the DAO into the database.
`public void updateDAO( ) throws SQLException`	Updates the current contents of the DAO into the database.
`public void deleteDAO( ) throws SQLException`	Deletes the current DAO from the database.
`public void loadDAO( int doc_key ) throws Exception`	Loads the DAO from the database using the key passed as a parameter.
`public void loadDAO( Knowledge_baseVO knowledge_base )`	Loads the values of the DAO from the value object passed as a parameter.
`public void setVO( Knowledge_baseVO vo ) throws Exception`	Sets the value object to the current contents of the DAO.
`public void createPreparedStatements( ) throws Exception`	Creates the prepared statements used by the DAO to perform database access.

A DAO may also contain `getXX` and `setXX` methods for retrieving and setting local members, though these are generally not used. The preferable method for setting or retrieving the values of the DAO is to pass a value object to set the values of the DAO and retrieve a value object reference from the DAO to get the values of the DAO. This is done using the `loadVO` and `setVO` methods.

The KnowledgeBaseFacade Class

The `KnowledgeBaseFacade` class provides an *interface* between the JSP pages used to provide the visual access to the message system and the logic and workflow required of the application. The division of responsibilities is that the JSP pages will manage the display, the facade class will manage business logic and workflow, and the DAOs and value objects will manage access to the resources of the system. The `KnowledgeBaseFacade` class includes the methods listed in Table 19–6.

Message System Application Flow

It is difficult, if not impossible, to understand the operation of a Web application without understanding the process flow of the system. With Web applications, this flow is indicated by the pages that are loaded as the user progresses through the

Table 19–6	*KnowledgeBaseFacade Class Methods*

Method	Description
`public void setRowsUpdated( int rows )`	Sets an internal member to the number of rows updated.
`public void setAction( String action ) throws Exception`	This method is used to define the action (add, update, insert) for the `inputKB.jsp` page.
`public void setSubmitTitle( String submitTitle )`	This is used to set the title for the submit button on the `inputKB.jsp` page.
`public void setNextKBVO( boolean val ) throws Exception`	This method is used to move to the next Value Objectvalue object in the list of value objects retrieved to populate the `pickKB.jsp` page.
`public Iterator getCategoryList()`	This method is used to retrieve a list of categories used to populate an HTML select list on the `inputKB.jsp` page.
`public Iterator getMessageTypesList()`	This method is used to retrieve a list of message types and is used to populate an HTML select list on the `inputKB.jsp` page.
`public String makeCategoryString( Object obj )`	This method is used to convert an `Object` parameter into a character string representing a category. (It essentially wraps a Java cast operation and avoids having to place this code into a JSP page.)
`public String makeMessageTypesString( Object obj )`	This method is used to convert an `Object` parameter into a character string representing a message type. (It essentially wraps a Java cast operation and avoids having to place this code into a JSP page.)
`public boolean isDefaultCategory( String category )`	Returns a boolean value indicating whether a category passed in is the default category.
`public boolean kbRecsHasMore()`	Returns a boolean value indicating whether or not there are more `knowledge_base` records to be retrieved.
`public void setFilterKBRecs( ServletRequest request, HttpSession session )`	Used by the `filterKB.jsp` page to pass the filter criteria for the JSP page.
`public void setFilterSelection( ServletRequest request, HttpSession session )`	Used to set the filter selection for the `pickKB.jsp` page. This method reads the 'type' parameter of the request and processes two selections: `'all'` for viewing all records, or `'keyword'` for a keyword filter.
`public void setAllKBRecs( boolean val ) throws Exception`	This method retrieves all message system records from the database. (The boolean parameter is currently not used.)

Table 19–6   *KnowledgeBaseFacade Class Methods (cont.)*

Method	Description
`public void insertKBRecs( ServletRequest request, HttpSession session )`	Used to insert message system records into the database. Data for the operation is contained in both the `request` object and `session` objects, which are passed as parameters.
`public void deleteKBRecs( ServletRequest request, HttpSession session )`	Used to delete message system records from the database. Data for the operation is contained in both the `request` object and the `session` objects.
`public void processParameters( ServletRequest request, HttpSession session ) throws Exception`	Used to process parameters for the operation.
`public void updateKBRecs( ServletRequest request, HttpSession session )`	Used to update message system records. Data for the operation is contained in both the `request` and `session` objects.
`public void doUpdate( ServletRequest request, HttpSession session )`	This method is called by the `updDB.jsp` page to perform database update operations.
`public void loadKnowledgeBase( int doc_key ) throws Exception`	Loads a message system (`knowledge_base`) record for the `doc_key` passed.

application. Therefore, to understand the message system application, the following sections detail the page flow through this system. For starters, Table 19–7 lists the pages used in the system.

Table 19–7   *JSP Pages in the Message System*

Page	Description
`pickKB.jsp`	Lists the existing messages in the system. Provides menu options for viewing, updating, and deleting any of the messages listed. Must choose a type of listing as either `'all'` to list all messages within the system, or `'keyword'` to filter on a set of keywords (as contained in a Ccollection in the `session` object).
`viewKB.jsp`	View all elements of a single message, including the message header (`knowledge_base`), message text (`knowledge_messages`), and keywords (`base_keys`). Provides menu options to delete the message (if allowed) and to return to the main menu.

Table 19–7 *JSP Pages in the Message System (cont.)*

Page	Description
inputKB.jsp	Provides data entry form for a new message, or to update a current message.
menu.html	The main menu for the message system.
login.jsp	Provides a form for to execute the login for the message system.
loginSubmit.jsp	Posted to by login.jsp. This page is used to process the login information and forward to an error page if the login failed.
ErrorPage.jsp	The error page for the message system.
updDB.jsp	Updates the database and forwards to the error page if there is an error during the update.
searchKB.jsp	Provides a search page using a form that allows searching the message system database based on four keywords. This page links to the pickKB.jsp page with the submission of the search criteria form.

The flow into the system begins with a user login. If the user successfully logs into the system, then the user can proceed to the main menu, which provides a number of choices:

- Login
- Search Messages
- List All Messages
- Post New Message

The most common course of action will be to proceed to the search page (searchKB.jsp). This page will allow the user to enter search criteria to narrow the search to a set of keywords. This page displays an input form, which will post to the pickKB.jsp page when the submit button is pressed. See Figure 19–1.

After the user enters search criteria, the message list page (pickKB.jsp) with a filtered list of messages is displayed. The pickKB.jsp page provides menu options with each message listed. These menu options allow the user to optionally display the contents of the message (viewKB.jsp), or to update or delete the message (updDB.jsp). See Figure 19–2.

If the user chooses to display the contents of the message, the message view page is displayed (viewKB.jsp). This page allows the user to view the complete contents of the message, including the message header, the text of the message, the message type, the message category, and the keywords for the message. See Figure 19–3.

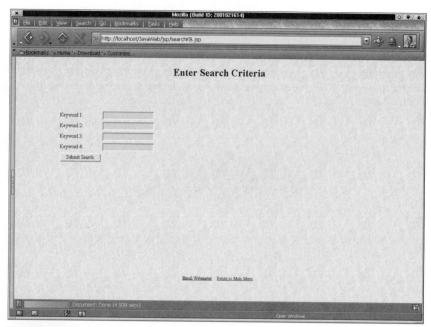

Figure 19–1   *Message System Input Form*

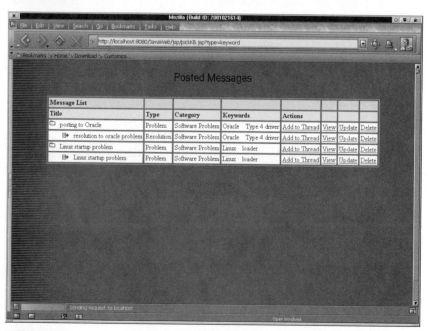

Figure 19–2   *Message Listing Page with Options*

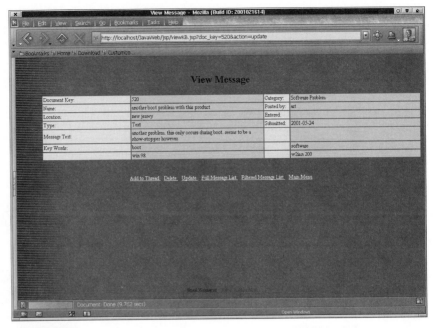

Figure 19–3 *Message View Page*

The menu options on this page allow the user to add a message to the message thread, delete the message, update the message, return to the message list, or return to the main menu. If the user chooses to update the message, then the message update page is displayed. See Figure 19–4.

The message update page displays an input form that allows the user to make changes to certain fields and then submit the form. The form provides a drop-down list box for the message category and message type. The user is allowed to change any field on the page. Once submitted, this form will post to the update page (updDB.jsp), which will perform the work necessary to update the changes to the database. If there is no error, then the updDB.jsp page will display a rows updated message indicating that the change was updated to the database. See Figure 19–5.

If the user chooses to input a new message, then the message input (inputKB.jsp) page is displayed with a blank form. (This is the same page used for the message update operation.) Once the user completes input for this form and chooses to submit, it is posted to the database update page (updDB.jsp) to send the changes to the database.

If the user chooses to delete an existing message, then the view message page is displayed, forcing the user to first view the contents of the page. At this point,

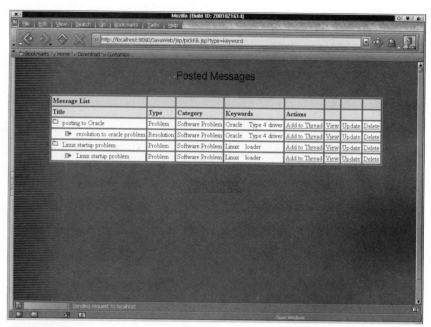

Figure 19–4 *Message Input Page*

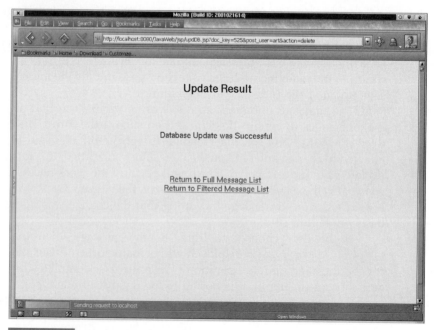

Figure 19–5 *Update Database Page*

the user must select the message delete link to delete the message from the database. The "delete" link on this page will submit a request to the updDB.jsp page to delete the message. If the message deletion is successful, then the message update page will output the number of rows updated message.

If an exception is thrown in any of these pages, the ErrorPage.jsp is invoked with the Exception that has been thrown. This page outputs the exception that was thrown and provides a menu option to allow the user to return to the main menu page. See Figure 19–6.

This page displays the contents of the exception that triggered the message and provides links to allow the user to move back to the main menu.

The preceding section explained the page execution that the user would use to move through the message system. This explanation provides a good basis for understanding how this system was developed. But now we need to examine these JSP pages in detail as well as examine the code behind the JSP page, the code that is executed when the JSP page is accessed.

Since we have kept close to the separation of roles concept in developing this application, the majority of the processing for a JSP page is performed by JavaBeans classes that are accessed by making a small number of method calls in the scriptlets on the JSP page. The following section will show both the JSP page and the Java code behind the page and provide a detailed explanation of both.

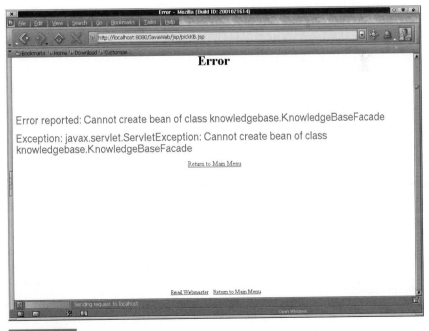

Figure 19–6 *Error Page*

THE REST OF THE STORY: JSP PAGES AND JAVABEANS CODE EXPLAINED

The page flow gives us half the story. At this point, we need to see the contents of the JSP page and understand the interaction of the page with the Java code behind the page, the JavaBeans. To understand the actions performed by the page and to understand the process for programming a JSP application, the code behind each of the pages will be explained *in-line* with the JSP page. This means that if a JSP calls a method, which in turn calls another method (as many of the facade class methods will do), then all of those methods will be examined at that point in the text. This means that some of the more complex JSP pages will be examined in fragments, while the code behind them is examined in detail. This will lead to a better understanding of the procedural flow of the application and of the reasoning behind the approach to coding the application.

Managing the Login Process: The login.jsp and loginSubmit.jsp Pages

The login page provides a simple input form for the user to enter his or her login name and the corresponding password. The bulk of this form is HTML, with the exception of the output of the current date on the top of the form. See Figure 19–7.

This date is output with the use of the `loginFacade` class, using the `currentDate` property, as shown in the following code. This is used to output the current date in a string format. The date is output using green text to indicate that the user does not need to enter this information.

The login.jsp Page

```
<html>
<!- <body bgcolor="#FFFFFF" background="/JavaWeb/img/bggradient.gif">  ->
<body bgcolor="#FFFFFF" background="/JavaWeb/img/bg2_grey.jpg">

<jsp:useBean id="loginFacade" class="knowledgebase.loginFacade" scope="page" />
<center>
<h1>Login to Message List</h1>
</center>

<br>
<br>
<b>Logging in on:</b> <font color="green"><jsp:getProperty name="loginFacade" prop-
erty="currentDate" /></font>
<br>
<br>
<br>
```

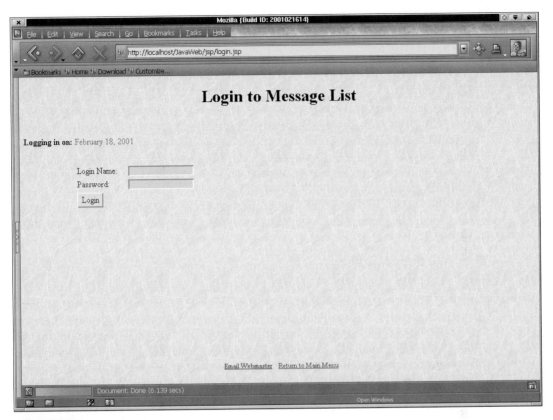

Figure 19–7   *The Login Submission Page*

```
<center>
<table border=0 width=100% >
<form method="post" action="loginSubmit.jsp">

<tr>
<td width=10%>   </td>
<td width=10%>Login Name: </td><td><input name="login" type="text" value=""></td>
</tr>

<tr>
<td width=10%>   </td>
<td width=10%>Password: </td><td><input name="pwd" type="password" value=""></td>
</tr>

<tr>
<td width=10%>   </td>
<td width=10%> <input name="submit" type="submit" value="Login" > </td>
```

```
</tr>

</form>
</table>
</center>
</body>
</html>
```

This page submits its contents to the `loginSubmit.jsp` page, which is responsible for processing the login information passed to it. If the login is successful, then a message is displayed indicating that the login succeeded.

If an error occurs, then the page forwards processing to an error page, which will indicate that the login failed and allow the user to return to the main menu, where he or she can choose the login option and try the login again. (Alternatively, the user can press the browser's Back button and move directly to the login page.)

The loginSubmit.jsp Page

The login page (`login.jsp`) will post the input from the form to the `loginSubmit.jsp` page, which will use the `loginFacade` class to process the information input on that page. The `handleSubmit` method is passed both the `request` object and `session` object as parameters. The information entered in the input form is available as request parameters, and the `session` object is used to store session parameters to be used elsewhere in the application. If the `handleSubmit` determines that there is a problem with the login—for example, the login name is not found in the database or the password entered is incorrect—then it will throw an exception and will forward processing to the error page for the `loginSubmit.jsp` page, the `errorPage.jsp` page. The JSP code for this page follows:

The loginSubmit.jsp Page

```
<html>
<body bgcolor="#FFFFFF" background="/JavaWeb/img/bg2_grey.jpg">

<%@ page errorPage="ErrorPage.jsp" %>

<jsp:useBean id="loginFacade" class="knowledgebase.loginFacade" scope="page" />
<center>
<h1>Login to Message List</h1>
</center>


<% loginFacade.handleSubmit( request, session ); %>

<br>
```

```
<br>
<b>Login Completed for user: </b> <jsp:getProperty name="loginFacade"
property="first_name" />    <jsp:getProperty name="loginFacade" proper-
ty="last_name" />
<br>
<b>Last logged in: </b> <jsp:getProperty name="loginFacade"
property="session_last_login" />
<br>
<br>
<br>
<a href="menu.html">Back to Menu</a>

</body>
</html>
```

The `handleSubmit` method performs the bulk of the processing for the login process. This method is part of the `loginFacade` class, which acts as a facade for the login process. This class creates a `message_user` value object named `message_userVO` and a `message_user` DAO named `message_userDAO`; both of these relate to the `message_user` table in the database. The calendar utility class `JSPCal` is imported, and a local `HttpSession` object reference is added as a local member of the class.

The loginFacade.handleSubmit Method

```
package knowledgebase;

import javax.servlet.*;
import javax.servlet.http.*;
import java.util.*;
import java.sql.*;

import db.*;
import JSPCal.*;

public class loginFacade {

Message_userVO      message_userVO;
Message_userDAO     message_userDAO;
Cal cal;
HttpSession localSession;

...
```

The `handleSubmit` method receives `ServletRequest` and `HttpSession` arguments. The local `HttpSession` reference is assigned to that of the `HttpSession` parameter. The login name has been passed as a parameter to the request, so this parameter is retrieved and then passed to the `message_userDAO.loadDAO` method as a parameter. This method will use the login passed (which is the primary key for the `message_user` table) and will load the DAO with the `message_user` table values for that login. The code for this section follows:

The loginFacade.handleSubmit Method

```
...
public void handleSubmit( ServletRequest request, HttpSession session) throws
Exception {

try {

localSession = session;

// load the user information
message_userDAO.loadDAO( request.getParameter( "login" ) );
message_userVO = message_userDAO.getVO();

// load the role for this user
// current implementation allows a single role
message_securityDAO.loadDAO( request.getParameter( "login" ) );
message_securityVO = message_securityDAO.getVO();
...
```

Once the login record has been retrieved, the password is checked to determine whether the password entered matches the password in the `message_user` table. If the password does not match, then an error message is written to the log file and the page is forwarded to an error page.

```
...
//
if (!(message_userVO.getPwd().trim()).equals(request.getParameter( "pwd" ).trim()))
{ // an invalid login

    System.out.println("Login error: " + message_userVO.getFirst_name() + " - " +
message_userVO.getLast_name() );
    throw new Exception( "Login error." );

}
...
```

As shown in the previous code example, if the login authentication is successful, then a series of `message_user` table attributes is stored in the `session` object, including the user name, location, login name, and date of the last login. Once the session attributes have been set, the database is immediately updated with the *new* user last login date (which would be the current date). Errors are caught in the `try/catch` block, where they are logged and then thrown to the calling method.

```
...

else {   // a valid login

   // store session information about the user
   session.setAttribute( "first_name", message_userVO.getFirst_name() );
   session.setAttribute( "last_name", message_userVO.getLast_name() );
   session.setAttribute( "last_login", message_userVO.getLast_login() );
   session.setAttribute( "location", message_userVO.getLocation() );
   session.setAttribute( "login", message_userVO.getLogin() );
   session.setAttribute( "role", message_securityVO.getRole() );

   // immediately update the database with the new last login date
   message_userVO.setLast_login ( getCurrentDate( "mm/dd/yy" ) );     // the new
last_login date
   message_userDAO.setVO( message_userVO );                          // update
the database
   message_userDAO.updateDAO();
}

...
```

This current implementation of the login page does not forward the user to a menu, which could easily be done using the JSP forward tag. Instead, it merely displays a message confirming that the login was successful, displays the last login date for the user, and provides a link that allows the user to proceed to the main menu.

```
...
<br>
<br>
<b>Login Completed for user: </b> <jsp:getProperty name="loginFacade"
property="first_name" />    <jsp:getProperty name="loginFacade" proper-
ty="last_name" />
<br>
<b>Last logged in: </b> <jsp:getProperty name="loginFacade"
property="session_last_login" />
<br>
<br>
<br>
<a href="menu.shtml">Back to Menu</a>
...
```

Storing Information in the session Object

Following the login operation, the message system now has a session object populated with separate attributes for the user first name, last name, location, login name, and security role. These session.setAttribute calls are a good example of how to add objects to the session object. The syntax for the `HttpSession.setAttribute` method is as follows:

```
setAttribute( String name, Object obj);
```

In this example. the `name` parameter is a string name, which will be associated with the object to be stored; this name will be used to retrieve the attribute. The `obj` parameter is an `Object` reference that contains the *value* to store for the attribute. Since an `Object` reference is being stored, and any Java object can upcast to an `Object` reference, this allows any Java object to be stored in the `session` object. Once this information is stored in the `session` object, it becomes global (visible) to the entire user session.

Note that while it would be easy to store a large amount of information in the `session` object, this should be avoided. It is a more modular and flexible solution to pass information via the `request` object as parameters than to use the `session` object.

Sessions and JSP

JSP pages ultimately use the HTTP protocol to communicate with the client. The HTTP protocol is stateless, meaning that connections to the client do not persist. But a session implies a persistent connection, a client state that persists and is maintained over multiple requests.

The servlet container within which the JSP page runs (once converted into a servlet and loaded by the server) must mimic a session by tracking requests that are made against the server. Each request is assigned a *session ID* and must communicate that session ID to the server through some mechanism. The default behavior is to have the client browser store a cookie on the browser and then send that cookie (along with others) to the server on each request. The servlet specification requires this cookie to be named `JSESSIONID`.

If for some reason the client does not allow a cookie to be added, then a URL rewriting mechanism will be used that adds the session ID to the URL so that it will appear as a request parameter each time the client browser sends a request to the server. The required name of the session ID request parameter is `jsessionid`. (Be sure to use the `HttpServletResponse.encodeURL` method to encode any forwarded URLs with the `jsessionid` if you think you may be using URL rewriting.)

Using Static HTML and Server-side Includes for the Main Menu

Once the user has completed the login process, he or she must choose a link to the main menu. The main menu is an HTML page that displays the various menu options available to the user, as in the following example:

The menu.shtml Page

```
1. html>
2. <body bgcolor="#FFFFFF" background="/JavaWeb/img/bg2_grey.jpg">
3. <!--#config timefmt="%A %B %d" -->
4. <br>
5. <br>
6. <center>
7. <h1>Welcome to the Message System</h1>
8. </center>
9. <br>
10. <h3>Date: <font color="blue"> <!--#echo var="DATE_LOCAL" --> </font>
11. <br>
12. <center>
13. <table width=100% border=0>
14.
15. <tr>
16. <td width=20%>
17. </td>
18. <br>
19. <br>
20. <td width=30%>
21. <font size=+2>
22. <br><a href="login.jsp">Login</a>
23. <br><a href="searchKB.jsp">Search Messages</a>
24. <br><a href="pickKB.jsp?type=all">List All Messages</a>
25. <br><a href="inputKB.jsp?doc_name=&link_doc=0&doc_key=0&base_doc_key=0&doc_loca-
tion=&action=insert">Post New Message</a>
26.
27. </font>
28. </td>
29. </table>
30. </center>
31. <br>
32. <br>
33. <br>
34. <br>
35. <!--#include file="footer.txt" -->
36. </html>
37. </body>
38.
```

The menu.shtml page uses *server-side includes* (SSI) to retrieve the current date for display on the main menu and to retrieve the footer for the page. (The footer.txt file is the same file included by the JSP pages for the footer.)

The highlighted tag on line 3 is an SSI directive used to set the format for the time to be displayed, using the DATE_LOCAL variable. This is the format used in the highlighted statement on line 10 to display the date. (This will be the date the page was served by the Apache server to the client browser, not the date on the browser's computer.)

On lines 21 through 24 in the listing, various menu options are displayed as links on the Web page. On line 33, an SSI directive is used to include the footer for the site into the page.

The discussion group menu provides the option of displaying a list of messages in the message database. The user can optionally list all messages or filter the message list for a listing of messages that contain a specific keyword. See Figure 19–8.

The user can optionally select one of the options from the menu page. The most common path would be to search the discussion group database based on search criteria. These search options will provide a listing that will be displayed, and then, based on what the user views in the listing, the user can choose to add to a thread or post a new message.

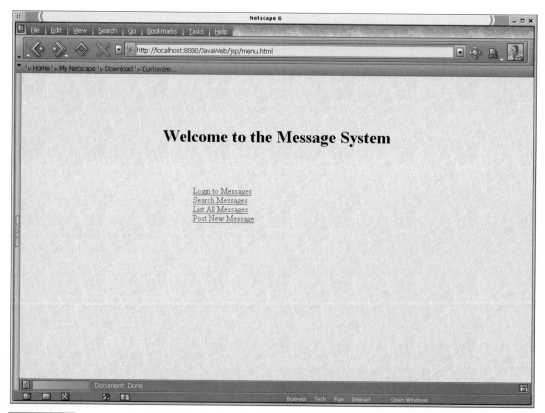

Figure 19–8   *Message Listing Page*

The following discussion proceeds with the assumption that a user has chosen to search the discussion group database for a particular set of topics and then review the listing that the search returns.

Collecting and Passing Search Criteria: The searchKB.jsp Page

If the user has selected the search option from the main menu, he or she will be allowed to search the message system database based on keyword entries. The searchKB.jsp page displays an HTML input form that allows the user to enter up to four search criteria. See Figure 19–9.

The page itself is a standard HTML input form with the exception of the one JSP directive, the JSP include directive highlighted at the bottom of the page, as the following code demonstrates. (This page could easily have been implemented in HTML by changing the JSP include directive at the bottom of the page to an SSI include directive and renaming the page with a .shtml extension.)

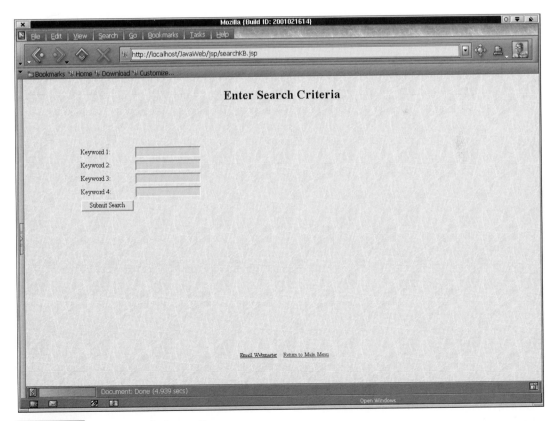

Figure 19–9   *Enter Search Criteria Page*

Alternative Menu Implementations

An alternative menu, and one very common with Web applications, would have the menu displayed on the left-hand side of the page in a frame or table cell and put some content on the right-hand side of the page. As the user moves through the site, the menu would remain displayed on the left-hand side of the page by either being included in the page or by remaining in an unchanging frame.

This approach to managing the menu has the benefit of allowing the user to continually see the available menu options and to select from those options. Implementing this different menu option would not require much work—simply changing the `menu.shtml` file to incorporate frames and then changing the links on the menu to work within the context of those frames.

The searchKB.jsp Page

```
<html>
<body bgcolor="#FFFFFF" background="/JavaWeb/img/bg2_grey.jpg">


<center>
<h1>Enter Search Criteria</h1>
</center>

<br>
<br>
<br>
<br>

<table border=0 width=100% >
<form method="post" action="searchSubmit.jsp">

<tr>
<td width=10%>   </td>
<td width=10%>Keyword 1: </td><td><input name="keyword1" type="text" value=""></td>
</tr>

<tr>
<td width=10%>   </td>
<td width=10%>Keyword 2: </td><td><input name="keyword2" type="text" value=""></td>
</tr>

<tr>
<td width=10%>   </td>
```

```
<td width=10%>Keyword 3: </td><td><input name="keyword3" type="text" value=""></td>
</tr>

<tr>
<td width=10%>   </td>
<td width=10%>Keyword 4: </td><td><input name="keyword4" type="text" value=""></td>
</tr>

<tr>
<td width=10%>   </td>
<td width=10%>           <input name="submit" type="submit" submit value="Submit
Search" > </td>
</tr>

</form>
</table>

<br>
<br>
<br>
<br>
<br>

<%@ include file="footer.txt" %>
</body>
</html>
```

Loading Request Parameters into a Collection

The search criteria that have been entered on the `searchKB.jsp` page are needed to execute the database query, so these parameters must have a way of making it to the DAOs that will ultimately interact with the database. While the parameters could have been forwarded as a request and then retrieved by the DAOs, we would prefer to completely shield the database access code (on the integration tier) from the details of the presentation, which certainly include the request object (an instance of `ServletRequest`). For this reason, we will place the contents of our filter criteria into a `Collection` object, which is added to the `session` object. Since we would like to be able to allow the user to move back to the filtered selection page and redisplay it using the same filter criteria (as when a user adds to an existing message thread and then wishes to continue examining the same filtered list for additional messages to read or respond to), we will store this filter criteria in the `session` object. With the criteria stored in the `session` object, when the user is linked to the posted messages page and the `type` parameter is set to `keyword`, the `session` object will be examined to determine if there is a `Collection` of keywords; if there is, we execute the query again with those keywords. If the query criteria were not stored in the `session` object, then it would be difficult to implement this functionality.

Aggregating and Forwarding Request Parameters

The `searchSubmit.jsp` page is responsible for aggregating or collecting the search criteria entered on the `searchKB.jsp` page and then forwarding processing to another page. This page demonstrates both the use of the session object for storing session-specific information and the use of the JSP forward directive to forward request processing to another page.

The request parameters from the `searchKB.jsp` page are loaded into a `Collection` object and processing is forwarded to the `pickKB.jsp` page to execute and display the results of the query. The code for this page is shown next.

This page uses the `searchFacade` class as a JavaBean; this is loaded using the `jsp:usebean` tag on line 6. Only one method in this class is called on line 12, and on line 16, processing is forwarded using the `jsp:forward` tag. If an error occurs in the `searchFacade handleSubmit` method, then an exception will be thrown and the error page declared for the page (`ErrorPage.jsp` declared at line 5) will be invoked. If no exception is thrown, then the `jsp:forward` statement at line 16 is called. This is passed a single request parameter, the type of which is set to the `keyword`, indicating that a keyword search should be conducted based on search parameters that have been stored.

The searchSubmit.jsp Page

```
1.<html>
2.<!-- <body bgcolor="#FFFFFF" background="/JavaWeb/img/bggradient.gif">  -->
3.<body bgcolor="#FFFFFF" background="/JavaWeb/img/bg2_grey.jpg">
4.
5.<%@ page errorPage="ErrorPage.jsp" %>
6.<jsp:useBean id="searchFacade" class="knowledgebase.searchFacade" scope="page" />
7.<center>
8.
9.<h1>Login to Message List</h1>
10.
11.</center>
12.
13.<!-- load the search criteria into a collection which is stored in the session
   object -->
14.<% searchFacade.handleSubmit( request, session ); %>
15.
16.<!-- forward to pickKB.jsp which will execute the query and display the results
   -->
17.
18.<jsp:forward page="/jsp/pickKB.jsp?type=keyword"/>
19.
20.<br>
21.<br>
22.<br>
23.
```

```
24.</body>
25.</html>
26.
27.
```

Storing Search Parameters: The searchFacade.handleSubmit Class

The `searchFacade` class is used by the `searchSubmit.jsp` page to manage the details of storing the search criteria collected on the `searchKB.jsp` page. This class contains a single method, the `handleSubmit` method, that is called on the `searchSubmit.jsp` page shown in the previous example.

This method is called with two parameters: the `request` parameter and the `session` parameter. The method merely creates a new `Vector` (which implements the `Collection` interface) and then adds the values of the four keyword parameters to the `Vector`.

We then want to add the `Vector` object into the `session` object for our session. This can be accomplished using the `setAttribute` method of the `HttpSession` class. This method takes two parameters: a `String` name and a corresponding `Object` reference. Once an object has been added using this method, calls to the `HttpSession.getAttribute` method can then be used to retrieve the attribute value, using the corresponding name that was used when it was added. In this example, the `Vector` object that has been loaded with the filter criteria is added to the `session` object and assigned the name `filter_criteria`. At this point, the `session` object has been populated with the filter criteria for our session and we are ready to execute the JSP page, which will ultimately execute the database query using these parameters and display the results.

The searchFacade Class

```java
package knowledgebase;

import java.util.*;
import javax.servlet.*;
import javax.servlet.http.*;


public class searchFacade {

public void handleSubmit( ServletRequest request, HttpSession session ) {

Vector v = new Vector();

v.add( request.getParameter("keyword1"));
v.add( request.getParameter("keyword2"));
v.add( request.getParameter("keyword3"));
v.add( request.getParameter("keyword4"));
```

```
session.setAttribute( "filter_criteria", v );

}

}
```

Building Dynamic HTML Tables with JSP: The Posted Messages Page

Because of the nature of page formatting with HTML, tables are often used to format and present content. So it is not uncommon when dealing with dynamic content to need to create an HTML page based on some combination of request parameters and the results of a database query. The creation of the posted message list is an example of just such a page. To understand this page, portions of the JSP code will be examined, and then the portions of the JavaBeans code that support the page will be shown, effectively tracing the program execution from the JSP page to the JavaBeans code and then back to the JSP page.

The posted message page (`pickKB.jsp`) provides a listing of a set of message from the discussion group database. As explained previously, this listing can be either a listing of all messages in the database or a filtered listing based on filter criteria that has been made available to this page.

This listing is an HTML table that is dynamically created with columns for the topic of the message, the keywords entered for the message, and links to pages that allow the user to view the message in full, to update the message, or to delete the message. This page will show links for update and delete even though the user may not have permission to perform these operations on the message (see Figure 19–10). Permissions are checked before the operation is attempted, and if the user does not have the appropriate permissions, he or she is not permitted to perform the operation.

This page provides a good example of techniques for building dynamic table output using JSP. The listing is sorted based on the primary key of the message document, the date the message was submitted, and the last date the message was changed. The message listing includes not only the messages selected, but threaded messages that were posted to the message selected, that is, posted to a *base message* or a *threaded message*. Any messages that are part of the message thread are indented from the left margin so that the base message appears flush with the left margin and all messages posted to the base message appear below the base message and are indented from the left margin. A different .gif image is also placed on each line of output, depending on whether the line being output is a base message or a threaded message.

Though this approach to creating the table with indented entries improves the readability of the table content, the code required to perform this indentation adds to the complexity of the control loop used to produce this table. The JSP code for this page (`pickKB.jsp`) is shown next.

The `pickKB.jsp` page performs its work using the `KnowledgeBaseFacade` class. The `KnowledgeBaseFacade` class is a JavaBean and is identified on the page (and assigned a reference ID) using the `JSP:useBean` tag on line 4. Through this tag, the `KBFacade` name is associated with the `knowledgebase.KnowledgeBaseFacade` class and is given the ID of `KBFacade`. Other HTML content is used to display the header and set the suggested font for some of the text on the page. On line 16, the controlling method for the page is called: `setFilterSelection`. This method is passed the reference for the `request` object for the page and the reference for the `session` object.

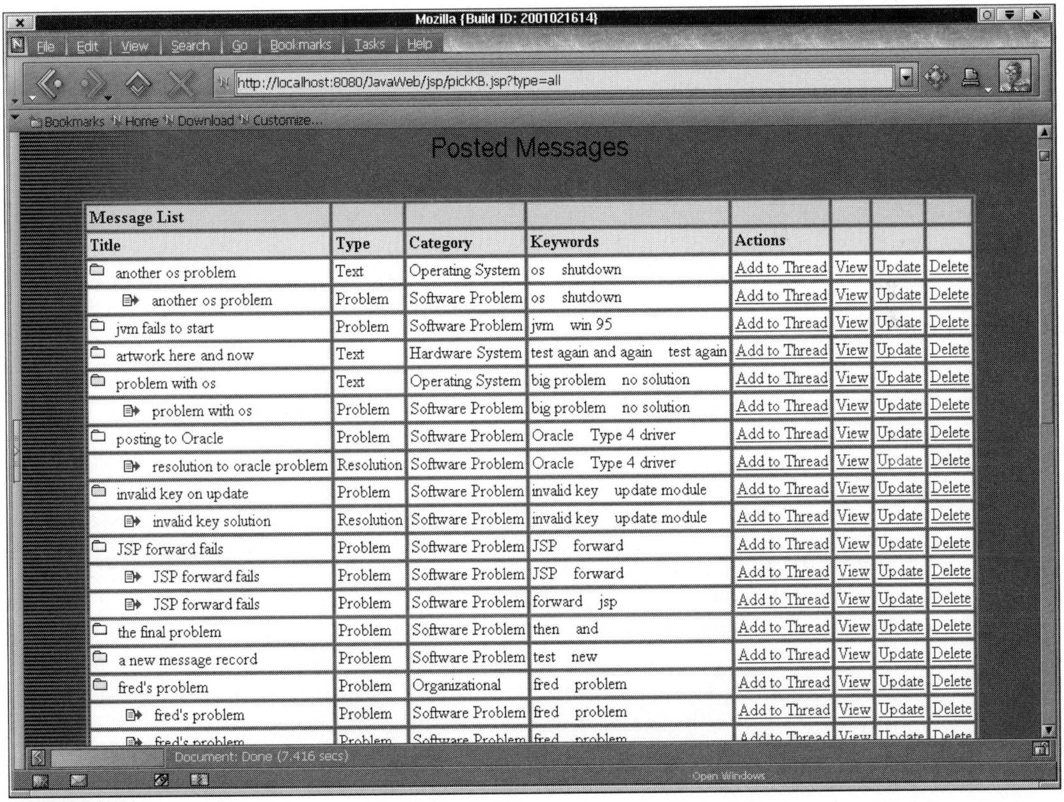

Figure 19–10 *Message Listing*

The pickKB.jsp Page

```
1.<HTML>
2.<body bgcolor="#FFFFFF" background="/JavaWeb/img/bg0020.gif">
3.<%@ page errorPage="ErrorPage.jsp" %>
4.<jsp:useBean id="KBFacade" class="knowledgebase.KnowledgeBaseFacade" scope="page"
/>
5.<br>
6.<font face="Helvetica, Sans-serif" size=+2 >
7.<center>
8.Messages
9.</center>
10.</font>
11.<br>
12.<br>
13.<center>
14.<font face="Helvetica, Sans-serif" size=+2 color="blue">
15.
16.<% KBFacade.setFilterSelection( request, session ); %>
17....
```

The setFilterSelection Method

The `setFilterSelection` method, shown next, is called from the `pickKB.jsp` page. This method is part of a facade class (`KnowledgeBaseFacade`) and as such is designed to reduce the coupling (the calls) between the JSP page and the business classes and DAOs that retrieve the data for the page. This method will perform a simple test of the requests passed into the `pickKB.jsp` page and determine what type of filter is to be used.

This method acts as a traffic cop of sorts, examining one of the request parameters passed to it and determining which action to perform (which method to call). If the `type` parameter is set to the value `all`, then all entries in the discussion group database are listed. This is achieved by calling the `setAllKBRecs` method with a boolean value of `true`.

If the request parameter is set to `keyword`, then a keyword filter will be applied to the database lookup operation using the `setFilterKBRecs` method and passing both the `request` and `session`. Since exceptions may be thrown up the call stack to this method, a `catch` block is used to trap and report messages. (The `setAllKBRecs` and `setFilterKBRecs` methods will in turn call methods in the `Knowledge_baseDAO` class to perform the low-level database operations required to retrieve the data; the code for these methods is shown later in this chapter.)

The setFilterSelection Method

```
...
public void setFilterSelection( ServletRequest request, HttpSession session ) {

try {
    if ( request.getParameter("type").equals("all") )
       setAllKBRecs( true );

    if  ( request.getParameter("type").equals("keyword") )
       setFilterKBRecs( request, session );
    }
    catch ( Exception e) {
       System.out.println("Exception in KnowledgeBaseFacade.setFilterSelection() : "
+ e );
    }
}
...
```

The setAllKBRecs and setFilterKBRecs Methods

The `setAllKBRecs` method takes a boolean argument and simply wraps a DAO method to retrieve the records necessary for the message listing of all message records. The method calls the `knowledge_baseDAO.getAll` method to retrieve all message records currently in the discussion group database and returns an `Iterator` object reference named `iterateKBList`, which is an instance member of the `KnowledgeBaseFacade` class.

The setAllKBRecs Method

```
...
public void setAllKBRecs( boolean val ) throws Exception {

iterateKBList = knowledge_baseDAO.getAll(); // get a collection of ValueObjects for
all knowledge_base records

}
...
```

The `setFilterKBRecs` method shown next is used to obtain a filtered list of messages based on the filter criteria contained in the `session` object (in code explained previously, the filter criteria is assembled as part of the processing for the `searchKB.jsp` and `searchSubmit.jsp` pages). This method wraps the `Knowledge_baseDAO.getFilteredList` method, which returns an `Iterator` reference that is assigned to the `iterateKBList` reference, which is part of the `KnowledgeBaseFacade` class.

Before the `getFilteredList` method is called, the `Collection` object stored in the `session` object must be retrieved, since this object stores filter criteria for the database query. This is performed on lines 7 and 8, where the `HttpSession.getAttribute` method is called.

As explained in the previous section, the session attribute `filter_criteria` stores an object of type `Collection` that contains the filter criteria for the page to use (see the description earlier in this chapter of the `searchSubmit.jsp` page processing that populates this collection). The `session.getAttribute` method is used to the retrieve the filter criteria on line 8. This method returns an `Object` reference, which is cast to a `Collection` reference and stored in an object named `filterCriteria`.

This object is passed to the `getFilteredList` method of the `Knowledge_baseDAO` class object on line 9. This method will access the database, retrieve the records that match the filter criteria, and place those records (in the form of value objects) into a Java `Collection` (a `Vector`). The `Vector` object is then converted to an `Iterator`, and the reference to the `Iterator` object is returned and stored in the `iterateKBList` reference of the `KnowledgeBaseFacade` class.

The setFilterKBRecs Method

```
1....
2.// use a filter to retrieve the list of knowledge base records
3.public void setFilterKBRecs( ServletRequest request, HttpSession session ) {
4.
5.try {
6.     // filter criteria passed as a Collection in the session object
7.
8.     Collection filterCriteria
9.        = (Collection) session.getAttribute( "filter_criteria" );
10.
11.     iterateKBList  = knowledge_baseDAO.getFilteredList(
12.            filterCriteria );
13.}
14.catch (Exception e)
15.   System.out.println("Exception in
16.KnowledgeBaseFacade.setFilterKBRecs(): " + e );
17.
18.}
19.
20.}
21....
```

Once the DAO `getFilteredList` method has returned the list of records (value objects) from the database, the `KnowledgeBaseFacade` object will see to it that the `Iterator` that has been returned (from the DAO) is kept internally.

This `Iterator` is later used by the JSP page to loop through the value object records stored in the `Collection` and to create the dynamic table output for the posted messages table.

Back to the pickKB.jsp Page

At this point, we have established the filter criteria for the page and have populated the `Iterator iterateKBList`, an instance variable of the `KnowledgeBaseFacade` class, with the results of the query operation. We now need to take the results in the `Iterator` and use them to create the results to be used in the `pickKB.jsp` page.

The approach shown in this example minimizes the use of scriptlet code and maximizes the use of JSP tags and directives. Since the `jsp:getProperty` tag can be used to retrieve values from a JavaBean using an HTML-like tag, we will use an approach that uses an instance member of the `KnowledgeBaseFacade` class to maintain a collection of records that have been returned from the database for display on the page. The `get` and `set` methods called by the `jsp:getProperty` tags return values or references to instance members of the `KnowledgeBaseFacade` class; we must set these instance members with the correct values from our collection of rows returned by the query. Since this collection is stored in an `Iterator`, we will use a loop increment method to move through the `Iterator`, and for each new row, we will set the instance members of the `KnowledgeBaseFacade` class to the same values as those in the `Iterator` row. The following code sample uses the `setNextKBVO` method to perform this operation.

As shown on line 5, the `hasNext` method is called to determine if there are more elements to the `Iterator`. If there are, then the `next` method is called to retrieve the value object from the `Iterator` and assign it to the instance member, `knowledge_baseVO`.

A call to the `NextKBVO` method of the `KnowledgeBaseFacade` class moves to the next element of the `Iterator` and sets the internal reference for the value object representing the current message (`knowledge_baseVO`) to the next value object within the list stored in the `iterateKBList Iterator`, as shown in the code below. A `catch` block is used to catch any exceptions that may be thrown by any of the methods called in this block.

The NextKBVO Method

```
1....
2./ increment the iterator and make the next knowledge_baseVO our current VO
3.public void setNextKBVO( boolean val ) throws Exception {
4.
5.
6.try {
```

```
7.
8.if ( iterateKBList.hasNext() ) {
9.    knowledge_baseVO = (Knowledge_baseVO) iterateKBList.next();
10.    loadKnowledgeBase( knowledge_baseVO.getDoc_key() );
11.   }
12.}
13.catch (Exception e) {
14.      System.out.println("Exception in
15.knowledgeBaseFacade.setNextKBVO(): " + e );
16.    throw new Exception("Exception in
17. knowledgeBaseFacade.setNextKBVO(): " + e );
18. }
19.}
20....
```

Building the Dynamic Table

The next task in creating the output for this listing is to create the HTML table to hold the listing. This table is created on line 3 in the JSP page fragment shown next. On line 5 in this listing, a row is created to hold a header describing the table, and on lines 8 through 15, empty cells are added to the table to provide a consistent, spreadsheet-like appearance to the table. On lines 18 through 29, another header row is created to output the columns headers for the table.

The pickKB.jsp Page (Continued)

```
1....
2.<!-- build table for output of selected messages -->
3.<table border=2 cellpadding=2 bgcolor="white">
4.
5.<tr>
6.<td bgcolor="#C0D9D9"><b>Message List<b></td>
7.
8.<td bgcolor="#C0D9D9" >     </td>
9.<td bgcolor="#C0D9D9" >     </td>
10.<td bgcolor="#C0D9D9" >     </td>
11.<td bgcolor="#C0D9D9" >     </td>
12.<td bgcolor="#C0D9D9" >     </td>
13.<td bgcolor="#C0D9D9" >     </td>
14.<td bgcolor="#C0D9D9" >     </td>
15.</tr>
16.
17.<!-- header row -->
18.<tr>
19.<td bgcolor="#E0E0E0" > <b>Title    </b> </td>
20.
21.
22.<td bgcolor="#E0E0E0" > <b>Type     </b> </td>
```

```
23.<td bgcolor="#E0E0E0" > <b>Category </b> </td>
24.<td bgcolor="#E0E0E0" > <b>Keywords </b> </td>
25.<td bgcolor="#E0E0E0" > <b>Actions  </b> </td>
26.<td bgcolor="#E0E0E0" > <b>    </b> </td>
27.<td bgcolor="#E0E0E0" > <b>    </b> </td>
28.<td bgcolor="#E0E0E0" > <b>    </b> </td>
29.</tr>
30....
```

Creating the Table Rows

The table is now ready to be constructed. Since there are multiple records to use, it makes sense to perform this operation within a loop. At the start of the loop on lines 4 and 5 in the listing, two control variables are set. These variables are used later in the loop to make decisions about whether or not to indent records based on their settings.

Within this loop, a `jsp:setProperty` tag is used to make a call to the `nextKBVO` method. This `jsp:setProperty` tag ultimately executes the `nextKBVO` method and moves to the next record in the internal list (`iterateKBList`). This process of moving the pointer in the list will set the internal `knowledge_base` value object to the next value object in the internal list of value objects so that once this call has been made, all calls to the `get` methods of the `KnowledgeBaseFacade` class will return the values of the current `knowledge_base` value object.

The contents of each `<td>` tag within the message listing table represents a column on that row. The contents of the columns for this table are now stored in instance members of the class and will be retrieved using `jsp:getProperty` tags (which will in turn call the `get` methods of the `KnowledgeBaseFacade` class). These tags are used on lines 22 through 28 and are used to retrieve the short description of the message document (`doc_name`), the message type of the message (`message_type`), and two of the keywords associated with the document (`keyword1` and `keyword2`).

The output of the columns is fairly straightforward, but the code on lines 13 through 21 requires more explanation. The purpose of this code is to provide the indentation of the output lines. This indentation is based on whether or not the line is a base message or a threaded message. If the message is a base message, then the short message description will not be indented and an image of a closed folder will be output on that line. If the message is a threaded message, then the short message description will be indented and a different image will be output on that line.

The determination of whether or not a message is a threaded message requires examination of the base document key (`base_doc_key`). A variable is used to track the current base document key and is set equal to the base document key of the current record at the end of each loop iteration. At the beginning of each loop iteration, the value of this current base document key is checked against the base document key of the record currently being output. If the base document key of the current record is the same as the current base document key, then this record is assumed to be a *threaded* message (since some previous record must have been used to set the current base document key to its value).

The first pass through the loop represents an exception to this rule. Since the value of the current base document key is not set until the end of the loop, on the first iteration of the loop, this value will not have been set. For our purposes, we assert that the first message in the loop is a base message and we ignore the setting of the current base document key.

```
1.<!-- columns -->
2.<!-- use program logic to indent threaded messages -->
3.<%
4.
5.    // start of loop
6.    int currBase_doc_key = 0;
7.    boolean firstLoop = true;
8.
9.while ( KBFacade.kbRecsHasMore() )   {
10.
11.%>
12.
13.
14.<jsp:setProperty name="KBFacade" property="nextKBVO" value="true" />
15.<tr>
16.<td> <% if ( !firstLoop && (currBase_doc_key == KBFacade.getBase_doc_key()) ) {
%>
17.
18.    <!-- indent if this is a thread off the base message -->
19.
20.               
21.<img src="/JavaWeb/img/quote.gif">  
22.
23.    <% } else { %>   <!-- not a thread - the base message - display a closed
folder -->
24.            <img src="/JavaWeb/img/folder_closed.gif" name="Base Folder"
align=left >  
25.
26.    <% } %>
27.
28.
29.    <jsp:getProperty name="KBFacade" property="doc_name" /> </td>
30.<td> <jsp:getProperty name="KBFacade" property="message_type" />
31.</td>
32.<td> <jsp:getProperty name="KBFacade" property="category" /> </td>
33.
34.<td> <jsp:getProperty name="KBFacade" property="keyword1" />
35.           <jsp:getProperty name="KBFacade" property="keyword2" />
```

```
36.      <jsp:getProperty name="KBFacade" property="keyword3" />
37.</td>
38.
```

Next to the output of the message header are table cells that contain the actions that can be executed for the message document in the row. The JSP code that produces these actions is shown below.

The cells in this output contain anchor references that reference other JSP pages in the application. Parameter values for these references are set according to the current message document key. These settings are made by using jsp:getProperty tags, which will retrieve the appropriate values for the current message document being processed.

Note that the jsp:getProperty tag can appear within the double quotes of the anchor href attribute, as follows:

```
<a href="viewKB.jsp?doc_key=<jsp:getProperty name="KBFacade" property="doc_key"
/>&action=update" >View</a>
```

The final section of this listing contains the termination of the loop that produces this table. On line 7 of the listing, the firstLoop flag is set to false, and on lines 10 through 13, a conditional statement is used to determine how to set the base document key. If the base document key is non-zero, then the base document key for the current record is used to set the current base document key variable on line 10. Alternatively, if the base document key is 0, then this code asserts that the document is in fact the base document and sets the base document key to the value of the document key for the current document (which is the base document for this thread).

On line 16, two links are provided to allow the user to return to the main menu or to post a new message.

```
1.<!-- actions -->
2.<td> <a href="inputKB.jsp?doc_key=0&action=insert&base_doc_key=<jsp:getProperty
name="KBFacade" property="base_doc_key" />&link_doc=<jsp:getProperty name="KBFacade"
property="doc_key"/>">Add to Thread</a> </td>
3.<td> <a href="viewKB.jsp?doc_key=<jsp:getProperty name="KBFacade"
property="doc_key" />&action=update" >View</a> </td>
4.<td> <a href="inputKB.jsp?doc_key=<jsp:getProperty name="KBFacade"
property="doc_key"/>&link_doc=0&base_doc_key=<jsp:getProperty name="KBFacade" proper-
ty="base_doc_key" />&action=update">Update</a> </td>
5.<td> <a href="viewKB.jsp?doc_key=<jsp:getProperty name="KBFacade"
property="doc_key"/>&base_doc_key=0&link_doc=0&action=delete">Delete</a> </td>
6.</tr>
7.
8.
```

```
9.<%
10. firstLoop = false;
11. if ( KBFacade.getBase_doc_key() > 0 )
12.     currBase_doc_key = KBFacade.getBase_doc_key();
13.else
14.     currBase_doc_key = KBFacade.getDoc_key(); // this IS the base
15.} %>
16.</table>
17.
18.
19.<br>
20.<br><a href="inputKB.jsp?doc_key=0&link_doc=0&base_doc_key=0&action=insert">Post
New Message</a>
21.<br><a href="menu.html">Main Menu</a>
22.
23.</font>
24.</center>
25.</BODY>
26.</HTML>
39.
```

The user of this page will have options to view the current document, add to the message thread, update the current document, or delete the document. The code for these pages is shown in the following sections. The full code for the posted messages page (`pickKB.jsp`) is shown in Appendix C.

Creating Read-Only Output: The View Message Page

If the user chooses to view an existing message, then the `viewKB.jsp` page will be displayed. Each message is composed of messages from a number of different tables. This page retrieves all related message records for a single message and displays them in a table. The page does not allow the user to update any of the information on the page. Menu options, however, are provided to allow the user to add to the message thread, update the message, delete the message, or to return to the main menu.

The coding of this page is fairly straightforward. The page merely needs to load the document key passed as the request parameters for the page and then use the `jsp:getProperty` tag on a JavaBean that contains all of the appropriate values. Fortunately, the `KnowledgeBaseFacade` class contains all of the necessary `get` and `set` properties to create the view page. Since only one message will be displayed, it isn't necessary to create a loop and iterate through multiple records as with the posted messages page (`pickKB.jsp`).

This page begins by using JSP directives to set the error page for this JSP page and to load the `KnowledgeBaseFacade` class and assign the class to a JavaBean named `KBFacade`. The document key for the message document to view is passed as part of the `request` parameter.

The contents of this page require data from a number of different tables in the message database. For this reason, the method that retrieves the data for this page must load not only the appropriate DAOs and value objects from the `knowl-edge_base` table, but also the `knowledge_messages` for the `message text` and `base_keys` for the message keywords tables.

The viewKB.jsp Page

```
<title>Message</title>

<center>

<%@ page import="java.util.*" %>
<%@ page errorPage="ErrorPage.jsp" %>

<jsp:useBean id="KBFacade" class="knowledgebase.KnowledgeBaseFacade" scope="page" />

<!- set the doc_key first, before setting 'action' ->
<% KBFacade.setDoc_key( Integer.parseInt( request.getParameter("doc_key").trim() ));
%>
<% KBFacade.setAction( request.getParameter("action")); %>

<br>
<br>
<H1>Message Display</H1>

</center>
```

Once the current message document has been loaded, it is then just a matter of describing the output of an HTML table, where the `<td>` tags will contain bodies that will use `jsp:getProperty` tags to retrieve the appropriate values for the document being viewed.

A table definition is made on line 2, and a blank cell is entered on line 4. On line 5, the document key for the document is entered using a `jsp:getProperty` tag for the output. (A space is added after every output on the page because some browsers will not render the cell color correctly if it does not interpret output for the table cell.) On lines 6 through 11, additional table rows and cells are created and output is generated using `jsp:getProperty` calls.

```
1....
2.<table border=0 cellpadding=2 >
3.
4.<tr>
5.<td width=5%><br></td>
6.<td width=5% bgcolor="#E0E0E0"> Document Key: </td> <td width=30%
7.bgcolor="#C0C0C0"> <jsp:getProperty name="KBFacade" property="doc_key" />  
</td>
8.
```

```
9.
10.<td width=5% bgcolor="#E0E0E0"> Category:       </td> <td width=30%
bgcolor="#COCOC0" > <jsp:getProperty name="KBFacade" property="category" />
 </td>
11.</tr>
12.
13.<tr>
14.<td width=5%><br></td>
15.<td width=5% bgcolor="#E0E0E0"> Name:          </td> <td width=30%
bgcolor="#COCOC0" > <jsp:getProperty name="KBFacade" property="doc_name" />
 </td>
16.<td width=5% bgcolor="#E0E0E0"> Posted by:    </td> <td width=30%
bgcolor="#COCOC0" > <jsp:getProperty name="KBFacade" property="post_user" />
 </td>
17.
18.
19.</tr>
20....
21.
```

The remainder of the table uses additional `jsp:getProperty` calls to retrieve data for the creation of the table. At the end of the table, a menu is created to allow the user to perform certain actions on the current message. The user can add to the current thread, delete the current record, update the current record, see a full listing of messages, or return to the main menu page. The references on lines 2, 3, and 4 of the following listing use the `jsp:getProperty` tag to retrieve the document key for the current message document.

Note that these options are output for this page regardless of whether or not the user has the appropriate permissions to perform these operations. The user permissions are checked but not until the user attempts to load the page to perform that operation; at that time permissions are checked, and if the user does not have permission to perform that operation, an exception is thrown and the page is not loaded.

```
1.<font color="white" family="times roman">
2.<p><a href="inputKB.jsp?doc_key=0&action=insert&base_doc_key=<jsp:getProperty
name="KBFacade" property="base_doc_key" />&link_doc=<jsp:getProperty name="KBFacade"
property="doc_key"/>">Add to Thread</a>   
3.<a href="updDB.jsp?doc_key=<jsp:getProperty name="KBFacade" property="doc_key"
/>&action=delete">Delete</a>   
4.<a href="inputKB.jsp?doc_key=<jsp:getProperty name="KBFacade" property="doc_key"
/>&base_doc_key=<jsp:getProperty name="KBFacade" property="base_doc_key"
/>&link_doc=0&action=update">Update</a>   
5.<a href="pickKB.jsp?type=all">Message List</a>   
6.<a href="menu.html">Main Menu</a> </p>
7.</font>
8.</center>
```

Performing Input with JSP: The Message Update Page

From the posted message list, the user who has requested the message list has various options available. If the requesting user is the user who entered the message, he or she will be allowed to change the text of the message, change the category or type of the message, or delete the message. Or, the user may choose to add to the message thread—that is, to add a new message under a specific base message. The `inputKB.jsp` page is used for all message updates, either to modify an existing message or to enter a new message as either a base message or an addition to a message thread.

The `inputKB.jsp` page uses an input form to insert a new message or update an existing message. The page uses the same HTML input form for insert or update, the difference being in how the existing field values are populated. If the page is being used for update, then the document that is being updated is loaded into the internal value objects. See Figure 19–11.

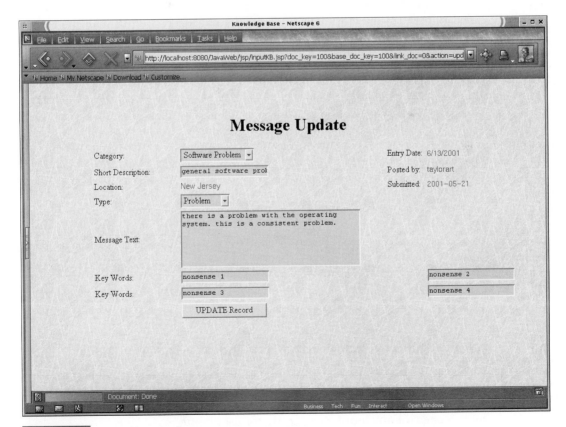

Figure 19–11 *Input Message Page*

If a new message document is being input, then default values are loaded into certain fields and the remaining fields are initialized to default Java values for the data types (this is done by nature of the fact that the JavaBean carrying these value objects is of page scope and is therefore created anew each time the page is loaded).

If an existing message document is being input, then the document key for the message document is passed into the page. The `KnowledgeBaseFacade` JavaBean will then load the corresponding document for the document key. If the page is a threaded message, then the message description will default to that of the base for the message thread, but the user is optionally allowed to override this text.

The `inputKB.jsp` JSP page begins by importing the `java.util` package (which contains collections used in scriptlets for the page) and identifying `ErrorPage.jsp` as the error page to be used if an exception is caught in the code generated for the page on lines 4 and 5. A `jsp:useBean` tag loads the `KnowledgeBaseFacade` JavaBean class and associates it with the `KBFacade` name for the page on line 6 of the listing.

On line 8, the `KnowledgeBaseFacade.processParameters` method is called to perform the work necessary for the page to be output with the HTML form. This method is passed the `request` and `session` objects for the page.

The inputKB.jsp JSP Page

```
1.<html>
2.
3.<body bgcolor="#FFFFFF" background="/JavaWeb/img/bg2_grey.jpg">
4.
5.
6.<%@ page import="java.util.*" %>
7.<%@ page errorPage="ErrorPage.jsp" %>
8.
9.<jsp:useBean id="KBFacade" class="knowledgebase.KnowledgeBaseFacade" scope="page"
/>
10.
11.<!-- the 'action' parameter indicates whether or not this is an insert,update or
delete operation -->
12.<% KBFacade.processParameters( request, session );   %>
13.
14....
```

Prepare Input Form: KnowledgeBaseFacade.processParameters Method

The `processParameters` method of the `KnowledgeBaseFacade` performs the work necessary to prepare the `inputKB.jsp` page for processing. For that reason, it is useful to look at the code for this method to understand what is required to get this page (or any input page) ready for user input.

This page is called at the start of the `inputKB.jsp` page and is passed the `HttpRequest` object for the page (`request`) and the `HttpSession` object (`session`) for the page (and for the session). The method begins by creating a new `Calendar` object using the `Cal` convenience class described in Chapter 17. The parameters passed into the method are checked at line 6, specifically, the parameter `doc_key`, which should always be passed to the method.

The document key (`doc_key`) value is an integer but is sent in the `request` parameter as a `String` data type. It must therefore be converted using the `Integer.parseInt` method, as shown on line 7. The results of this conversion are immediately passed to the `setDoc_key` method of the `KnowledgeBaseFacade` class. This will set the document key for the local value object to the converted value of the request parameter.

At line 11, the same test is performed for the `request` parameter for the `link_doc` (the document key for the document to which this document is linked). This converted value is passed to the `setLink_doc` method of the `KnowledgeBaseFacade` class. (Though this is stored in the value object and stored in the `knowledge_base` database table, the value of this column is currently not used.)

Beginning on line 13, a number of the values are stored in the `session` object to be passed to the `updDB` page, which will perform the database update for the values entered on this page. The document key (`doc_key`), the link document key (`link_doc`), and the base document key (`base_doc_key`) are stored as `Integer` object values in the `session` object. (Alternatively, these values could have been entered as hidden form fields and passed as `request` parameters.)

The next block of code on lines 18 through 23 is used to set the default date for the `entry_date` field on the form (and ultimately in the database record). The definition of the entry date field is the date when the record was last updated, so logically this field should be set to the current date. On lines 19 and 20, a conditional statement evaluates the `action` parameter to determine if an `insert` or `update` is being performed. (Currently, these are the only two valid actions for the page, but this conditional testing allows different actions to be added at a later time.) If the conditional statement tests true, then an `entry_date` attribute is set using the current date as returned by the `Cal` class `getCurrentDate` method. The `setEntry_date` method for the internal knowledge base value object is also called to set this date to the current date.

The remainder of the method is used to set default values for the form fields, depending on the action being performed.

KnowledgeBaseFacade.processParameters

```
. . .
1.// called by inputKB.jsp at the start of the input page
2.
3.public void processParameters( ServletRequest request, HttpSession session )
```

```
throws Exception {
4.
5.Cal cal = new Cal();
6.int doc_key = 0;
7.
8. // assert these parameters are always passed to inputKB.jsp which will call this
method
9.  if ( request.getParameter("doc_key") != null )
10.        setDoc_key( Integer.parseInt( request.getParameter("doc_key").trim() ));
11.
12.// set action will load the DAOs and the value objects for the knowledge_base
(in loadKnowledgebase() )
13.  if ( request.getParameter("action") != null )
14.        setAction( request.getParameter("action"));
15.
16. if ( request.getParameter( "link_doc" ) != null )
17.       setLink_doc( Integer.parseInt( request.getParameter("link_doc").trim() ));
18.
19.
20.   // add some of these to our session object, since they may not be passed via
the input form
21.   session.setAttribute( "doc_key", new Integer(
request.getParameter("doc_key")));
22.   session.setAttribute( "link_doc", new Integer(
request.getParameter("link_doc")) );
23.   session.setAttribute( "base_doc_key",
24.                          new Integer(request.getParameter("base_doc_key")));
25.
26.// store the dates as String ... let the database perform conversion
27.  if ( request.getParameter("action").equals("insert") ||
28.        request.getParameter("action").equals("update")   )   {
29.       session.setAttribute( "entry_date", cal.getCurrentDate( "mm/dd/yy" )); //
date last changed
30.       knowledge_baseVO.setEntry_date( cal.getCurrentDate( "mm/dd/yy" ));
31.  }
32.
33....
```

The next block of code in the following listing is executed only for an insert operation - action.equals('insert') - and is used to set a number of default values for the insert operation. A number of these fields are set in the internal value object and in the session object to be sent to the updDB.jsp page for the database update operation. On line 3, for example, the date_submitted field of the knowledge_base value object is set to the current date. The same value is placed in the date_submitted attribute at line 2.

At lines 4 and 5, the user name (login) and the user location (location) are retrieved from the session object where they were placed by the login process.

They are placed in the appropriate fields in the current `knowledge_base` value object (`post_user` and `doc_location` respectively).

The next block of code deals with the contingency that the message being inserted is a threaded message. Since this is a threaded message, the short description of the message will most likely be the same as the short description for the base message for the thread. In this application, then, the default short description for a threaded message should be the short description for the base message, but this is not a requirement. This block of code will get the short description from the base message and then use that description for the current message. (This description will be placed in the input field, and the user will have the option of optionally changing the description.)

On line 10, the contents of the document key for the base message for the thread (`base_doc_key`) are examined. If this is currently set to 0, then the value of the link document is used and is retrieved on line 7. Otherwise, the value of the base message document key (`base_doc_key`) is retrieved on line 9. A local `Knowledge_baseDAO` object is created on line 10 and uses the document key (`doc_key`) populated on the previous lines to load the DAO with the database values for that document key, which will be the base document for this message thread. The short name for the local message document is then set to the short name from the base message `knowledge_base` DAO on line 12.

On line 14, a series of security checks are performed to determine whether or not the user has permission to perform the operation he or she has requested. This block of code checks to determine if the user is performing an update operation (`action='update'`), and if so, whether he or she is the user who created the document or the system administrator (which is currently *hardcoded* as a user role of `admin`). Lines 15 and 16 perform these validations, examining the `session` object attributes of `login` and `role`. If the user does not have correct permissions, then an exception is thrown at line 17.

KnowledgeBaseFacade.processParameters (Continued)

. . .

```
1.  if ( request.getParameter("action").equals("insert") ) {
2.
3.      // date first entered (submitted)
4.      session.setAttribute( "date_submitted", cal.getCurrentDate( "mm/dd/yy" ));
5.      knowledge_baseVO.setDate_submitted( cal.getCurrentDate( "mm/dd/yy" ));
6.
7. // get the user name and location from the login information stored in the ses-
sion object
8.      knowledge_baseVO.setPost_user( (String) session.getAttribute( "login") );
9.      knowledge_baseVO.setDoc_location( (String) session.getAttribute( "location" )
);
10.
11.// if this is a threaded message, get the doc_name from the base_doc_key record
12.// since this is an insert, knowledge_baseVO has not been loaded, so need to
```

```
create a DAO to
13.        // get the base_doc_key
14.
15.        // no base_doc_key value passed
16.     if ( Integer.parseInt(request.getParameter("base_doc_key").trim()) == 0   )
17.           // then use the link_doc
18.         doc_key = Integer.parseInt( request.getParameter("link_doc"));
19.     else
20.         doc_key = Integer.parseInt( request.getParameter("base_doc_key"));
21.
22.     Knowledge_baseDAO baseDAO = new Knowledge_baseDAO( );
23.     baseDAO.loadDAO( doc_key );
24.     knowledge_baseVO.setDoc_name( baseDAO.getDoc_name() );
25.
26.  }
27.
28.
29.  // if this is an update or delete, does the user have permission to do this
30.if ( request.getParameter("action").equals("update") ) {
31.
32. // if this isn't the user that posted the message
33.if ( (!((String) session.getAttribute("login")).equals(
34.           knowledge_baseVO.getPost_user() )) ||
35.    (!((String) session.getAttribute("role")).equals( "admin" ) ) ) {   // this is
the sysadmin
36.
37.         throw new Exception("You do not have permission to perform this func-
tion.");
38.
39.
40.     }
41.     }
42.}
43.
```

The inputKB.jsp Page (Continued)

The next section of the `inputKB.jsp` page outputs a header and then starts the HTML table that will house the input form. The table is created at line 7, and a form tag that directs the output of the form as a `post` operation to the `updDB.jsp` page is created at line 10.

On lines 11 and 12, hidden fields are created to store the action and the link document as `request` parameters. (Though still included on a number of these pages, the `link_doc` field is not currently used by the discussion group application.)

```
1.<title>Knowledge Base</title>
2.<center>
3.<br>
```

```
4.<br>
5.<H1>Message Update</H1>
6.</center>
7.<table border=0 width=100% >
8.<tr>
9.   <td width=10%><br></td>
10.<form method="post" action="updDB.jsp">
11.<input name="action"   type="hidden" value="<jsp:getProperty name="KBFacade"
property="action"/>" >
12.<input name="link_doc" type="hidden" value="<jsp:getProperty name="KBFacade"
property="link_doc"/>" >
13.
14.<td width=10%> Category: </td> <td width=20%>
15.
16....
```

The next section of the page displays a list box of categories, which must be dynamically created. In order to format the form fields, including the list box, the list box is placed in table cell using the <td> tag on line 1.

To dynamically create the list box based on the current contents of the database table containing the categories, the getCategoryList method retrieves the contents of the message_categories table (by calling a method in the message_categoriesDAO) and returns the results as an Iterator on line 9.

The while loop starting on line 10 loops through this Iterator and converts the members to a String data type on line 11.

A conditional test is performed on line 12 to determine if the category is the default category. If this conditional test is true, then the category will be displayed as the selected list box item (an option), as shown in the output on line 13. If the category is not the default category, then the output on line 12 is produced.

The inputKB.jsp Page(Continued)

```
...
1.<td width=10%> Category: </td> <td width=20%>
2.<!-- create category list box -->
3.<select name="category"
4.<%
5.String category = null;
6.
7.// iterate through category list to create a listbox of categories
8.
9.Iterator i = KBFacade.getCategoryList();
10.while ( i.hasNext() )  {
11. category = KBFacade.makeCategoryString( i.next() );
12. if ( KBFacade.isDefaultCategory( category ) ) { %>
13.   <option selected> <%= category %>
14.<% } else { %>
15.     <option> <%= category %>
```

```
16.<%
17.     }
18.   }
19.   %>
20.</select>
21.</td>
22....
```

Following the creation of the category list box, a series of input fields are produced by the JSP. As shown below, in order to provide some spacial formatting for the fields on the form, each field is enclosed in a table cell. Since the `entry_date` field being output is not an input field, it is output in a different color than the fields that allow input. A `jsp:getProperty` tag is used to retrieve the contents of the `entry_date` field in the current `knowledge_base` value object in the `KnowledgeBaseFacade JavaBean`.

Additional input fields are also defined using a `jsp:getProperty` tag to provide a value for the field. The value of the `doc_name` field is used to provide a value for the short description field. Using this JSP tag, the contents of the `doc_name` field in the current `knowledge_base` value object is output as part of the value attribute for this field. The contents of the `doc_location` field are also retrieved using the same manner.

The `date_submitted` field does not allow user input (it is retrieved from the database), so the contents of this field are output as simple text, without an input field. To clarify that this field is not like the other fields on the form and does not allow input, the contents of this field (as returned by the `jsp:getProperty` tag) is output in a different font color. The code fragment for this processing is shown below.

The inputKB.jsp Page (*Continued*)

```
...
<td width=5%> Entry Date: </td> <td width=20%><font face="helvetica, sans-serif"
color="green">
<jsp:getProperty name="KBFacade" property="entry_date" />
</font></td>
</tr>

<tr>
<td width=10%><br></td>
<td width=15%> Short Description: </td> <td width=20%>
<input name="doc_name" type="text" value="<jsp:getProperty name="KBFacade" proper-
ty="doc_name" />"> </td>
<td width=5%> Posted by:    </td> <td width=20%> <input name="post_user" type="text"
value="<jsp:getProperty name="KBFacade" property="post_user" />"> </td>
</tr>
```

```
<tr>
<td width=10%><br></td>
<td width=15%> Location:        </td>
<td width=20%> <input name="doc_location" type="text" value="<jsp:getProperty
name="KBFacade" property="doc_location" />"> </td>

<td width=5%> Submitted: </td> <td width=20%> <font face="helvetica, sans-serif"
color="green"> <jsp:getProperty name="KBFacade" property="date_submitted" />
</font>
</td>
</tr>
...
```

The `message_type` field also requires the user to choose from multiple selections. This is accomplished using the list box created in the JSP scriplet code shown below. A call is made to the `getMessageTypesList` method to retrieve the values needed to populate the list box. This call returns an `Iterator` that is used to iterate through the contents of the `message_types` table.

The `while` loop is used to iterate through the contents of the iterator. The page output should have a list box which has selected the current message type of the message being displayed. To make sure the page is formatted so that this is accomplished, a conditional statement is used to select the message type of the current record in the select list. This is done by comparing the contents of the message type value object contained in the `KnowledgeBaseFacade` class with the contents of the `message_types` list being used. If the message type of the current record is found, then it is output as the selected item. If the message type of the current record is not the message being iterated in the list, then alternative output is provided.

```
...
<td>
<select name="message_type">

<%
// iterate through message types list to create a listbox of message types
String message_type=null;
i = KBFacade.getMessageTypesList();
while ( i.hasNext() )   {
      message_type = KBFacade.makeMessageTypesString(
                             i.next());
if ( (KBFacade.getMessage_type() != null ) && (
   KBFacade.getMessage_type().equals(message_type) ) ) {
%>
   <option selected><%= message_type %>
 <% } else {   %>
   <option><%= message_type %>
 <% }
   }
%>
```

```
</select>
...
```

The remainder of the `inputKB.jsp` page contains a series of form fields for the input or update of the message. The form fields are wrapped in table cells and contain values retrieved using `jsp:getProperty` tags as shown in the listing below. A submit button is created for the page and since the page is used for both inserts and updates, the button title is generated based on the action for which the page is being used. This is accomplished by retrieving the value of the `submitTitle` property.

The inputKB.jsp Page *(Continued)*

```
<tr>
<td width=10%><br></td>
<td width=15%> Message Text: </td> <td width=20%> <textarea name="message_txt"
cols=40 rows=5 wrap><jsp:getProperty name="KBFacade" property="message_txt"
/></textarea> </td>
</tr>

<tr>

<td width=5%> <br>
<td width=2%> Key Words: </td> <td width=2%> <input name="keyword1" type="text"
value="<jsp:getProperty name="KBFacade" property="keyword1" />"> </td>
<td width=5% align="left"> </td> <td width=5%> <input name="keyword2" type="text"
value="<jsp:getProperty name="KBFacade" property="keyword2" />"> </td>
</tr>

<tr>
<td width=5%> <br>
<td width=2%> Key Words: </td> <td width=2%> <input name="keyword3" type="text"
value="<jsp:getProperty name="KBFacade" property="keyword3" />"> </td>
<td width=5% align="left"> </td> <td width=5%> <input name="keyword4" type="text"
value="<jsp:getProperty name="KBFacade" property="keyword4" />"> </td>
</tr>

<tr>
<td width=10%><br></td>
<td width=10%><br></td>

<td width=5%> <input name="submit" type="submit" value="<jsp:getProperty
name="KBFacade" property="submitTitle" />" >
</td>
</tr>

</form>
</table>
```

```
</body>
</html>
</tr>

</form>
</table>

</body>
</html>
```

Performing Database Updates

This page is posted to by the `inputKB.jsp` page and is responsible for performing the database update operations required by any input done on that page. The page contains very little presentation output, and the bulk of the work performed is done by the `KnowledgeBaseFacade.doUpdate` method. If the update succeeds, then the page produces output indicating the number of rows updated. If some part of the update operation throws an exception, then the error page is displayed with information about the error. If the update fails to update any rows (which usually indicates a problem, since at least one row should have been updated), the current implementation of this page will simply indicate that 0 rows have been updated.

The `errorPage` directive is used at line 3 to indicate that the error page will be `ErrorPage.jsp`. On line 4, the `jsp:useBean` tag is used to indicate that the bean to be used for this page will be the `knowledgebase.KnowledgeBaseFacade` class and will be identified on the page using the `KBFacade`.

A header is output on lines 6 through 10, and then on line 13, the `doUpdate` method of the `KnowledgeBaseFacade` class is called to perform the database update operations required for this method. This method is the workhorse of this page, performing the relatively complex processing required to update the message database with form input it has received. (The processing performed by this method will be detailed in the next section.)

Following the call to the `doUpdate` method, a value is placed in the `rowsUpdated` member of the `KnowledgeBaseFacade` bean. This value indicates how many rows have been updated by the page. The current implementation merely reports this number using a `jsp:getProperty` tag, without comment, on line 17. (An alternative implementation would be to interpret a "no rows updated" condition as an error condition and forward control to an error page.) On lines 20 and 21, links are provided to allow navigation back to the main menu page or to return to a full listing of all messages.

The full processing of this page is performed off the page, in the `doUpdate` method. You can't really understand the processing being performed without examining the code behind this method. The next section provides the details of this method.

The updDB.jsp Page

```
1.<html>
2.<body bgcolor="#FFFFFF" background="/JavaWeb/img/bkg.gif">
3.<%@ page errorPage="ErrorPage.jsp" %>
4.<jsp:useBean id="KBFacade" class="knowledgebase.KnowledgeBaseFacade" scope="page"
/>
5.<br>
6.<font face="Helvetica, Sans-serif" size=+2 >
7.<center>
8.<h1>Update Completed</h1>
9.</center>
10.</font>
11.<br>
12.<br>
13.<% KBFacade.doUpdate( request, session ); %>
14.<center>
15.<font face="Helvetica, Sans-serif" size=+2 color="blue">
16.
17.<br>Updated <jsp:getProperty name="KBFacade" property="rowsUpdated" /> Rows.
18.<br>
19.<br>
20.<br><a href="pickKB.jsp?type=all">Return to Message List</a>
21.<br><a href="menu.html">Return to Main Menu</a>
22.</font>
23.</center>
24.</body>
25.</html>
26.
```

Updating the Database: The KnowledgeBaseFacade.doUpdate Method

The `doUpdate` method is responsible for updating the database with the input from the HTML form generated by the `inputKB.jsp` page in the following code listing. This method receives two parameters: the `request` object (`HttpRequest`) and the `session` object (`HttpSession`).

This method is responsible for marshaling the resources of other methods within the `KnowledgeBaseFacade` class to execute the update and for enforcing security. A great deal of code within the method is spent validating that the user has permission to perform the update operation he or she is requesting.

On lines 9 through 13, the document key is examined to determine whether or not it has been set correctly. Since the document key is the primary key for any messages, we must have a document key to be able to perform any update operations. If the `doc_key` is found, it will be converted into an integer and stored in a local variable, where it can be used later without having to perform an integer conversion.

On line 16, the method checks to see if the `doc_key` is 0 and the action is an update. If this condition is true, then an exception is thrown, since we cannot perform an update without a `doc_key`.

On lines 22 and 23, we check to see if an `insert` operation is being performed. If an insert is being performed, then the user must be logged into the system. If the user is not logged in and is not attempting an insert, an exception will be thrown.

On line 28, the method checks again to determine whether or not the user is logged in, and on lines 31 through 34, the method checks to determine whether or not the logged in user is allowed to perform the operation he or she has requested. If the user is neither a system administration user or the user who entered the message, then he or she is not allowed to perform the operation, and an exception is thrown.

If the user arrives at line 40, he or she is allowed to perform the update operation. The `request getParameter` method is used to retrieve the `action` parameter. The content of this parameter indicates which update action the user wishes to use. On line 41, if the user has permissions to perform the operation, then the `insertKBRecs` method is called and is passed both the `request` and `session` objects. The method will return immediately once the `insert` operations have been performed.

On lines 45 through 49, the update option is handled. A session attribute is assigned for the `doc_key`, and the `updateKBRecs` method is called with both the `request` and `session` objects.

On lines 51 through 54, the delete option is managed. A session attribute is assigned for the `doc_key`, and the `deleteKBRecs` method is passed both the `request` object and the `session` objects.

If the method arrives at line 57, then it has not received appropriate parameters. It will log an error and then throw an exception, thus returning control to the calling method.

KnowledgeBaseFacade.doUpdate Method

```
1....
2.
3.public void doUpdate( ServletRequest request, HttpSession session ) throws
Exception {
4.int doc_key=0;
5.
6.try {
7.
8.// let's make sure we have a doc_key
9.if ( request.getParameter("doc_key") != null )
10.    doc_key = Integer.parseInt( request.getParameter("doc_key").trim() );
11.else
12.    if ( session.getAttribute("doc_key") != null )
13.        doc_key = ((Integer) session.getAttribute("doc_key")).intValue();
```

```
14.
15.// if our doc_key is still 0 and this isn't an insert, throw an exception
16.if (( doc_key == 0 ) && ( request.getParameter("action").equals("update")) )
17.    throw new Exception ("Invalid document key.");
18.
19.// update can be an insert,update or delete operation
20.// check security before allowing an update
21.// user must be logged in to perform an insert
22.if ( request.getParameter("action").equals("insert") ) {
23.    if ( session.getAttribute("login") == null ) // the user has not logged in
24.        throw new Exception("User must log in to add a message.");
25.}
26.// if user is performing an update or delete, then
27.// this must be the user that posted the message
28.if ( session.getAttribute("login") == null ) // user has not logged in
29.    throw new Exception("User must login to perform this operation." );
30.
31.if ( request.getParameter("action").equals("update") ||
32.        request.getParameter("action").equals("delete") ) {
33.    if ( (!((String) session.getAttribute("login")).equals(
request.getParameter("post_user") )) ||
34.        (!((String) session.getAttribute("role")).equals( "admin" ) ) ) {   //
this is the sysadmin
35.        throw new Exception("User does not have permission to perform this func-
tion.");
36.    }
37.}
38.
39.// security is ok, so perform the update
40.if ( request.getParameter("action").equals("insert") ) {
41.    insertKBRecs( request, session );
42.    return;
43.}
44.
45.if ( request.getParameter("action").equals("update") ) {
46.    session.setAttribute("doc_key", new Integer( doc_key ) );
47.    updateKBRecs( request, session );
48.    return;
49.}
50.
51.if ( request.getParameter("action").equals("delete") ) {
52.    session.setAttribute("doc_key", new Integer( doc_key ) );
53.    deleteKBRecs( request, session );
54.    return;
55.}
56.
57.// if at this point, then we have not been passed a valid action
58.// log an error and throw an exception
59.System.out.println("knowledge_baseFacade.doUpdate() called with invalid action: "
+
60.                       request.getParameter("action"));
61.throw new Exception( "KnowledgeBaseFacade.doUpdate called with an invalid action
```

```
" +
62.                              request.getParameter("action"));
63.
64.}
65.catch (Exception e) {
66.  System.out.println("Exception in KnowledgeBase.doUpdate(): " + e );
67.  throw new Exception ("Exception in KnowledgeBase.doUpdate(): " + e );
68.}
69.
70.
71.
72.}
73....
74.
```

All of the update methods in the message system facade class use the DAOs for the various tables involved in the update operation. These objects encapsulate the insert, update, and delete operations for the database tables they represent. (Note that DAOs do not need to wrap a single relation but can in fact map to multiple relations, though that is not done in this example.)

Since the doUpdate method can optionally call either the insertKBRecs, updateKBRecs, or deleteKBRecs methods, this is a good point to discuss the code behind these methods. Each of these methods uses one or more DAOs to manipulate the database. So that we can focus on the business logic of the facade class, the detailed operation of these DAOs is not covered in this chapter. The following sections will discuss each of the insertKBRecs, updateKBRecs, and deleteKBRecs methods in turn.

Inserting Records: The insertKBRecs Method

The insertKBRecs method in the KnowledgeBaseFacade class is used to insert records into the database. Since discussion group messages are stored in multiple tables, this method is responsible for managing these multiple inserts into several tables, using DAOs for each of the tables.

The insertKBRecs method shown below is passed the request (HttpRequest) object and the session (HttpSession) object from the JSP page. The first order of business is to set the DAO members with the values from the input form. This is done on lines 8 through 25. Data values are retrieved from the request object on lines 8 through 12.

Lines 16 and 17 retrieve values from the session object, data values that are not entered in the input form that provides the data for this method. Lines 20 through 22 provide some conditional logic to set the base document key (the base message document for a threaded message) if it has not yet been set. The result of this logic is that if the base document key is not set and the link document key is set, then the link document key is used as the base document key for this message.

Lines 24 and 25 are used to retrieve the date submitted and the entry date for the message from the `session` object.

Note that up to this point the document key (`doc_key`) for the message document has not been set. The reason for this is that the document key for the discussion group database is a database-generated unique key. Its value is set by the DAO (ultimately by the database) as part of the insert operation into the `knowledge_base` table. But since there are a number of related tables that must be updated as part of the message insert operation, this unique key generated by the database must be returned to this method to be used in `insert` operations for the related tables. This is done on line 27, where the `Knowledge_baseDAO.insertDAO` method is called. This method returns an integer corresponding to the document key (`doc_key`) of the `knowledge_base` record just inserted.

The remainder of the method is devoted to updating the multiple tables related to the `knowledge_base` table. On lines 32 through 35, the `knowl-edge_messages` table is updated. On line 32, the document key (`doc_key`) from the `knowledge_base` update operation is used to set the document key for the `knowledge_messages` table. The data for the `knowledge_messages` fields is retrieved from request parameters, and on line 35, the `insertDAO` method of the `Knowledge_messagesDAO` class is called to perform the database insert.

The insertKBRecs Method

```
1.public void insertKBRecs( ServletRequest request, HttpSession session ) {
2.
3.int doc_key;
4.
5.try {
6.
7.// use the request to get the values for our DAO members
8.knowledge_baseDAO.setDoc_location( request.getParameter( "doc_location" ) );
9.knowledge_baseDAO.setDoc_name( request.getParameter( "doc_name" ) );
10.knowledge_baseDAO.setCategory( request.getParameter( "category" ) );
11.
12.knowledge_baseDAO.setPost_user( request.getParameter( "post_user" ) );
13.
14.
15.// these parameters aren't in the form, they're stored in the session object
16.knowledge_baseDAO.setLink_doc( ((Integer) session.getAttribute( "link_doc"
)).intValue() );
17.knowledge_baseDAO.setBase_doc_key( ((Integer) session.getAttribute(
"base_doc_key" )).intValue() );
18.
19.
20.if ( knowledge_baseDAO.getBase_doc_key() == 0 )
21.    if ( knowledge_baseDAO.getLink_doc() > 0  )
22.        knowledge_baseDAO.setBase_doc_key( knowledge_baseDAO.getLink_doc() ) ;
```

```
23.
24.knowledge_baseDAO.setDate_submitted( (String) session.getAttribute( "date_submit-
ted") );   // only set on initial insert
25.knowledge_baseDAO.setEntry_date( (String) session.getAttribute( "entry_date" ) );
26.
27.doc_key = knowledge_baseDAO.insertDAO();
28.
29.// should throw an execption if we get a 0 back from knowledge_baseDAO.insertDAO
30.
31.// knowledge_messages
32.knowledge_messagesDAO.setDoc_key( doc_key );
33.knowledge_messagesDAO.setMessage_txt( request.getParameter( "message_txt" ) );
34.knowledge_messagesDAO.setMessage_type( request.getParameter( "message_type" ) );
35.knowledge_messagesDAO.insertDAO();
36....
```

The next set of statements performs the `insert` operation for the `base_keys` table. In the current implementation, four keywords are stored in this table. These keywords are each inserted into the table in separate insert operations on lines 2 through 16. The document key from the `knowledge_base` insert operation is used for the document key for these records and is set in the DAO on lines 2, 6, 10, and 14. Each `insert` operation on lines 4, 8, 12, and 16 inserts a separate row into the database, using the values from the keyword parameter values retrieved on lines 3, 7, 11, and 15. Lines 18 through 25 catch various exceptions that may be thrown.

No specific success or failure flags are returned by this method; if any part of the database `update` operation fails, an exception would be thrown by the `insertKBRecs` method, which would be caught and then thrown to `doUpdate` method, which will in turn throw an exception to the JSP page that called it. (Note that the current implementation does not use a transaction for these multiple updates, so it could leave the database in an inconsistent state.)

```
...
1.// base_keys - the keywords for our message
2.base_keysDAO.setDoc_key( doc_key );
3.base_keysDAO.setKeyword( request.getParameter( "keyword1" ) );
4.base_keysDAO.insertDAO();
5.
6.base_keysDAO.setDoc_key( doc_key );
7.base_keysDAO.setKeyword( request.getParameter( "keyword2" ) );
8.base_keysDAO.insertDAO();
9.
10.base_keysDAO.setDoc_key( doc_key );
11.base_keysDAO.setKeyword( request.getParameter( "keyword3" ) );
12.base_keysDAO.insertDAO();
13.
14.base_keysDAO.setDoc_key( doc_key );
```

```
15.base_keysDAO.setKeyword( request.getParameter( "keyword4" ) );
16.base_keysDAO.insertDAO();
17.}
18.catch (SQLException e) {
19.    System.out.println( "SQLException caught in
KnowledgeBaseFacade.insertKBRecs(): " + e.getMessage() );
20.
21.}
22.catch (Exception e) {
23.    System.out.println( "Exception in KnowledgeBaseFacade.insertKBRecs(): " +
e.getMessage() );
24.}
25.
26.}
```

The updateKBRecs Method

The `updateKBRecs` method is responsible for updating the records updated on the `inputKB.jsp` page. This method, like the other update methods, receives the `request` object and the `session` object as parameters.

For updates, the document key (`doc_key`) must be known. The value of the current document key is stored in the `doc_key` attribute of the session object as an `Integer` object reference. This object reference is retrieved and converted into its integer value and stored in a local integer variable on line 8.

On lines 11 through 16, the values of the `knowledge_base` DAO are set to the corresponding parameter values from the input form. On line 17, the `entry_date` for the `knowledge_base` record is set to the current date, as stored in the `session` object attribute `entry_date`.

Beginning on line 21, the `knowledge_messages` table is prepared for the `update` operation that occurs at line 24. The processing for the table that stores the keywords for the messages (`base_keys`) begins on line 28. Since there is no primary key for this table, and to simplify the update logic, it is *updated* by deleting all existing rows for the document key and inserting the values that have been returned by the input form into the table. The deletion is accomplished by first setting the value of he DAO on line 29, and then calling the `deleteDAO` method made on line 30.

On lines 49 through 56, various exceptions are caught. These exceptions are processed by creating and throwing a new exception, which contains information on where the failure occurred and appends the message text from the message that was caught. This exception will be caught in the `doUpdate` method, which will in turn throw the message back to the JSP page, which will forward page processing to the `ErrorPage.jsp` page (as indicated by the `page` directive `errorpage` attribute on the JSP page). (Note that the implementation shown here does not use transactions, which could potentially leave the database in an inconsistent state if one or more of the `update` operations fails.)

The updateKBRecs Method

```
1.public void updateKBRecs( ServletRequest request, HttpSession session ) {
2.int doc_key = 0;
3.
4.
5.
6.try {
7.
8.doc_key = ((Integer) session.getAttribute("doc_key")).intValue();
9.
10.// use the request to get the values for update
11.knowledge_baseDAO.setDoc_key( doc_key );
12.knowledge_baseDAO.setDoc_name( request.getParameter( "doc_name" ) );
13.knowledge_baseDAO.setPost_user( request.getParameter( "post_user") );
14.knowledge_baseDAO.setDoc_location( request.getParameter( "doc_location") );
15.knowledge_baseDAO.setLink_doc( Integer.parseInt( request.getParameter( "link_doc"
)) );
16.knowledge_baseDAO.setCategory( request.getParameter( "category" ) );
17.
18.knowledge_baseDAO.setEntry_date((String) session.getAttribute( "entry_date")); //
date last changed
19.
20.// knowledge_messages
21.knowledge_messagesDAO.setDoc_key( doc_key );
22.knowledge_messagesDAO.setMessage_txt( request.getParameter( "message_txt" ) );
23.knowledge_messagesDAO.setMessage_type( request.getParameter( "message_type" ) );
24.knowledge_messagesDAO.updateDAO();
25.
26.// base_keys - the keywords for our message
27.// no true primary key in this table - it's just a list
28.// so delete all existing recs and then insert them again
29.base_keysDAO.setDoc_key( doc_key );
30.base_keysDAO.deleteDAO();
31.
32.base_keysDAO.setDoc_key( doc_key );
33.base_keysDAO.setKeyword( request.getParameter( "keyword1" ) );
34.base_keysDAO.insertDAO();
35.
36.base_keysDAO.setDoc_key( doc_key );
37.base_keysDAO.setKeyword( request.getParameter( "keyword2" ) );
38.base_keysDAO.insertDAO();
39.
40.base_keysDAO.setDoc_key( doc_key );
41.base_keysDAO.setKeyword( request.getParameter( "keyword3" ) );
42.base_keysDAO.insertDAO();
43.
44.base_keysDAO.setDoc_key( doc_key );
45.base_keysDAO.setKeyword( request.getParameter( "keyword4" ) );
46.base_keysDAO.insertDAO();
47.
48.}
```

```
49.catch (SQLException e) {
50.    System.out.println( "SQLException caught in
KnowledgeBaseFacade.updateKBRecs(): " + e + " - " + e );
51.    throw new Exception( "Database exception in updateKBRecs." + e.getMessage()
);
52.
53.}
54.catch (Exception e) {
55.    System.out.println( "Exception in KnowledgeBaseFacade.updateKBRecs(): " + e
);
56.    throw new Exception( "Database exception in updateKBRecs." + e.getMessage()
);
57.
58. }
59.
60.}
61.
```

The deleteKBRecs Method

The deleteKBRecs method is responsible for deleting all references to a specified message in the discussion group database. The method only needs the document key to the message to accomplish this, but for consistency it receives both the request and session objects as parameters.

The first step is to extract the document key for the message to delete. This is accomplished on line 8, where the document key (doc_key) is retrieved from the session object. The Object reference returned by the session object is cast as an Integer reference (its *real* type), and then the reference resulting from that cast is used to call the intValue method to the return a primitive integer value. This integer value is stored in a local variable and is then used throughout the method to reference the message being deleted.

On line 11, the loadDAO method of the Knowledge_baseDAO class is used to load the message header for the document key passed to the method. Once the DAO has been set to this document key, the deleteDAO method is called to delete the referenced message document from the knowledge_base table.

On lines 15 and 16, the knowledge_messages table, which is used to store the text of the discussion group message, is processed. On line 15, the setDoc_key method of the knowledge_messages DAO is called to set the document key to the value of the document key that is passed. On line 16, the knowledge_messages records for that document key are deleted using the deleteDAO method.

On lines 19 and 20, the base_keys table, used to store the keywords for a discussion group message, is processed. The Base_keysDAO.setDoc_key method is called to set the document key to that of the message to be deleted. Once this has been set, the deleteDAO method of the DAO can be called to delete all references to the message in the base_keys table.

The deleteKBRecs Method

```
1.// delete this knowledge_base record and all of the related records
2.public void deleteKBRecs( ServletRequest request, HttpSession session ) {
3.int doc_key;
4.
5.
6.try {
7.
8.doc_key = ((Integer) session.getAttribute( "doc_key" )).intValue();
9.
10.// knowledge_base
11.knowledge_baseDAO.loadDAO( doc_key );
12.knowledge_baseDAO.deleteDAO( );
13.
14.// knowledge_messages
15.knowledge_messagesDAO.setDoc_key( doc_key );
16.knowledge_messagesDAO.deleteDAO();
17.
18.// base_keys - the keywords for our message
19.base_keysDAO.setDoc_key( doc_key );
20.base_keysDAO.deleteDAO();
21.
22.}
23.catch (SQLException e) {
24.    System.out.println( "SQLException caught in
KnowledgeBaseFacade.deleteKBRecs(): " + e.getMessage() );
25.    throw new Exception( "Database exception in deleteKBRecs." + e.getMessage()
);
26.}
27.catch (Exception e) {
28.    System.out.println( "Exception in KnowledgeBaseFacade.deleteKBRecs(): " +
e.getMessage() );
29.    throw new Exception( "Database exception in deleteKBRecs." + e.getMessage()
);
30.}
31.
32.}
33.
```

The Error Page: ErrorPage.jsp

The ErrorPage.jsp page is, as the name implies, used to handle exceptions that are thrown on various JSP pages in the application. This page displays a message concerning the error and provides links through the page footer that allow the user to return to the main page. (See Figure 19–12).

As shown in the following listing, this page does little more than display the error message as contained in the exception object and then displays output for

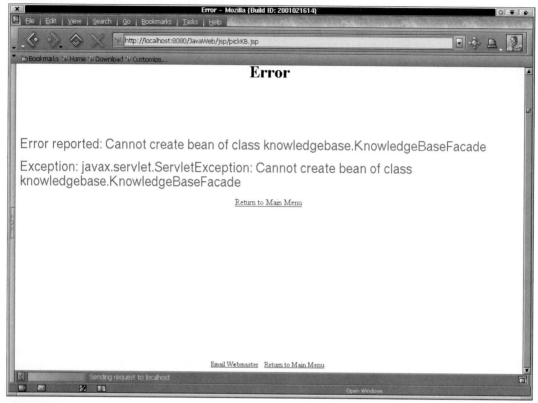

Figure 19–12
Error Page

the exception object by printing the object (which will eventually call the toString method on the object). A link in the middle of the page allows the user to return to the menu page. A JSP include page directive is used to include the footer.txt file (which contains a page footer used throughout the discussion group application) into the page.

ErrorPage.jsp

```
<%@ page isErrorPage="true" %>
<html>
<body bgcolor="#FFFFFF">
<head>
<title>Error</title>
</head>
</body>
```

```
<br>
<br>
<center>
<H1>Error</H1>
</center>
<br>
<br>
<br>
<br>
<font face="helvetica,sans-serif" size=+3 color="red">
<p>Error reported: <%= exception.getMessage() %>
<p>
<p>Exception: <%= exception %>
</font>
<center>
<a href="menu.shtml">Return to Main Menu</a>
</center>

<br>
<br>
<br>

<%@ include file="footer.txt" %>

</html>
```

Using the JSP include Directive: Inserting a Page Footer

It is not uncommon to include a footer on an HTML page. This footer would most likely include links to other sites that may be of interest to the user of your site. The insertion of the footer.txt file for the JSP include provides an example of just such an approach.

The file footer.txt is inserted at the bottom of most of the pages in the discussion group application, as shown in the following code. Using this file provides a consistent look for the application and, though it appears trivial in this example, on larger projects with more complex pages, this could save a significant amount of work by allowing some portion of the site to be duplicated code to be shared among developers.

The text in this file contains HTML and provides a link to the menu page as well as a link to send email to a specified email address (this is done using the URL mailto as the reference for the link).

The footer.txt File

```
<center>
<br>
<br>
```

```
<br>
<br>
<font size=-1>
<a href="mailto:webmaster@nowhere.com">Email Webmaster</a>    <a
href="menu.shtml">Return to Main Menu</a>
</font>
<center>
```

Summary

This chapter examined JSP in practice. Sections in the chapter reviewed many of the design issues and principles that had been laid out in previous chapters. This chapter provided examples of how to implement these design principles with a detailed code example for an application that delivers a discussion group system. This system uses numerous JSP pages, which provide examples of a form-based login process that uses a database, the creation of dynamic HTML tables based on database content, and `update` and `delete` operations on multiple related tables.

In order to make the discussion clear and thorough, the JSP pages were presented and discussed, and the Java code called within the pages was also discussed in detail.

Coming Up Next

The extensible markup language has become the tool of choice for data interchange. Most database applications have some need to move data between systems or between components of systems. XML and the various parsers and transformation technologies that are available make this task easier. The next chapter provides a discussion and examples of using XML with JDBC.

CHAPTER 20

Transforming JDBC Data to XML

INTRODUCTION

The use of the Extensible Markup Language (XML) is an important part of the current IT environment. Though originally touted as a "silver bullet" that would solve all of IT's data interchange issues, it has now settled into being a useful and widely supported standard for encoding data and moving it between applications.

JDBC applications can use XML documents in two ways. The application may read an XML document, parse the contents, and store the results in a relational database. The process of parsing an XML document with an XML parser such as Sax or using JAXP is involved (though by no means difficult) and is beyond the scope of this text.

The second way that JDBC applications can use XML documents is by taking the result of a SQL query and converting it into some useful XML representation. This chapter demonstrates that process and then takes it one step further, demonstrating the process of transforming the XML output into a useful HTML presentation document.

WHY PERFORM TRANSFORMATION

XML documents in and of themselves are not particularly useful; they represent encoded data. Encoded data must be converted and transformed to be useful. This transformation could involve writing a parser application to parse the contents of a document and perform operations on the data, or it could involve parsing the contents and producing output from the results.

The example shown here takes the results of a SQL query and encodes those results in an XML format. The resulting XML document is then transformed using the SAXON transformation API to convert the contents of the XML document into an HTML document, which will display an HTML table.

The SAXON transformation API uses Extensible Stylesheet Language (XSL) transformation to indicate how the transformation of the XML document should take place. This XSL stylesheet is a flat file containing instructions on how to convert the data passed in the form of an XML document. Using this technique, the format of the output, even how the output will be filtered, can be specified in the XSL document and does not require changing Java code.

Since we would like to ultimately produce an HTML document and output it to a Web browser, a Java servlet represents a useful candidate for performing these tasks. This example uses a Java servlet to access the database, retrieve and then convert the data, and call the SAXON API to produce the HTML output. The SAXON API will transform the XML document and send its output to the specified location. In this example, the output of the transformation will be sent to the `PrintWriter` response stream for the servlet (the data sent back to the Web browser). The output from this example is shown in Figure 20–1.

JDBC TO XML: THE CONVERSION CLASS

The process of converting the results of a SQL query to an XML encoded format is not complex and can be accomplished with a few lines of code. This is not a process that would benefit from any complex object relationships, so we simply create a class to perform an XML conversion for a `ResultSet` and expose a pair of static methods to perform the conversions. These methods simply accept a `ResultSet` parameter and iterate through the contents of the `ResultSet`. One method will accept the `ResultSet` parameter and a file location where the results of the XML encoding should be written. The other method accepts the `ResultSet` as a parameter and returns a string containing the XML document. The class declaration for this XML conversion class is shown below.

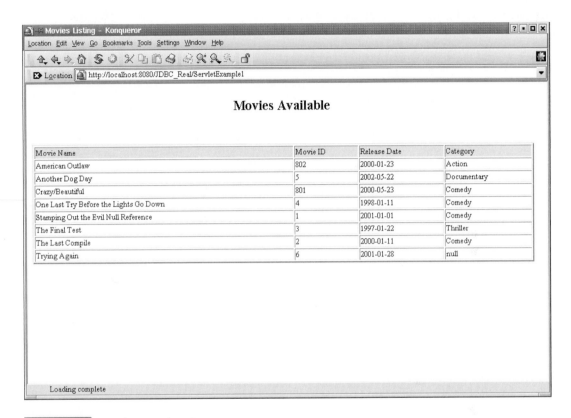

Figure 20–1 *ServletExample1 Output*

The JDBCXML Class

```
package jdbcutil;

import java.sql.*;
import java.io.*;
import db.*;

public class JDBCXML {


public static String toXMLString( ResultSet rs ) {
StringBuffer buffer = new StringBuffer(1024);

buffer.append( "<ResultSet>\n" );

try {
```

```
ResultSetMetaData rsmd  = rs.getMetaData();

while ( rs.next() ) {
buffer.append( "  <row>\n");
    for ( int n = 1; n <= rsmd.getColumnCount(); n++ ) {

        buffer.append( "    <Column>\n" );
        buffer.append(
          "      <Name>" ).append( rsmd.getColumnName(n) ).append( "</Name>\n" );
        buffer.append(
          "      <Table>" ).append( rsmd.getTableName(n) ).append( "</Table>\n" );
        buffer.append(
        "      <Type>" ).append( rsmd.getColumnTypeName(n) ).append( "</Type>\n" );

        //
        // must manage null object references
        //
        Object o = rs.getObject( n );
        if ( rs.wasNull() ) {
            buffer.append( "      <Data>null</Data>\n");
        }
        else {
            buffer.append(
                "      "<Data>").append(o.toString()).append("</Data>\n");

        }
        buffer.append( "    </Column>\n" );

    }
buffer.append( "  </row>\n");

}

buffer.append( "</ResultSet>\n" );

}
catch (SQLException e) {
    System.out.println( "SQLException thrown in toXMLString " + e.getMessage()
);

}

finally {
if ( buffer != null )
   return buffer.toString();
else
   return null;
}
```

```
}

// ————————————————————————————

public static void toXMLFile( ResultSet rs, Writer writer ) {
//StringBuffer buffer = new StringBuffer();

try {

BufferedWriter out = new BufferedWriter( writer );

//
// write the XML document to the output stream and close it
//
out.write( toXMLString( rs ) );
out.close();

}
catch (IOException e) {
        System.out.println( "IOException thrown in toXMLString " + e.getMessage() );

}

}

}
```

Within the JDBCXML class, two methods are declared. The toXMLString method takes a ResultSet parameter and encodes the data in the ResultSet into XML format. The toXMLFile method takes a ResultSet reference and a Writer reference as parameters and writes the XML document to the file referenced by the Writer parameter.

The toXMLString method executes a while loop to iterate through the contents of the ResultSet. A ResultSetMetaData object is retrieved from the ResultSet and will be used to identify the column names for the XML document.

A StringBuffer (a more efficient mechanism for continually concatenating strings) is created and used throughout the while loop to build the XML document representing the rows in the ResultSet.

The toXMLFile method accepts a ResultSet parameter and a java.io.Writer object parameter. A BufferedWriter object is then created on the Writer object to create the output for the method to use. The write method for the output BufferedWriter is then called, and the toXMLString method is called using the ResultSet parameter passed into the method. This string is then passed directly to the write method to output the contents of the XML document to the output Writer. The method concludes by calling the close method on the Writer object.

The XML structure of the document resulting from processing using these methods produces output as shown in the following listing. This output includes an outermost element tag of `ResultSet`, and then nested elements for the `row` and `column` elements. For each `column` tag, the column attributes of `name`, `table`, `type`, and `data` are nested.

XML Document Output from the `JDBCXML toXMLFile` **Method**

```
<ResultSet>
  <row>
   <Column>
      <Name>movie_id</Name>
      <Table>movies</Table>
      <Type>LONG</Type>
      <Data>1</Data>
   </Column>
   <Column>
      <Name>movie_name</Name>
      <Table>movies</Table>
      <Type>VARCHAR</Type>
      <Data>Stamping Out the Evil Null Reference</Data>
   </Column>
...
  </row>
  <row>
   <Column>
      <Name>movie_id</Name>
      <Table>movies</Table>
      <Type>LONG</Type>
      <Data>801</Data>
   </Column>
   <Column>
      <Name>movie_name</Name>
      <Table>movies</Table>
      <Type>VARCHAR</Type>
      <Data>Crazy/Beautiful</Data>
   </Column>
   <Column>
      <Name>release_date</Name>
      <Table>movies</Table>
      <Type>DATE</Type>
      <Data>2000-05-23</Data>
   </Column>
   <Column>
      <Name>movie_desc</Name>
      <Table>movies</Table>
      <Type>BLOB</Type>
      <Data>Clever, witty, slow paced</Data>
   </Column>
   <Column>
      <Name>special_promotion</Name>
      <Table>movies</Table>
      <Type>TINY</Type>
```

```
        <Data>1</Data>
      </Column>
      <Column>
        <Name>update_date</Name>
        <Table>movies</Table>
        <Type>DATE</Type>
        <Data>2002-01-28</Data>
      </Column>
      <Column>
        <Name>category</Name>
        <Table>movies</Table>
        <Type>VARCHAR</Type>
        <Data>Comedy</Data>
      </Column>
    </row>
  </ResultSet>
```

JDBC TO XML: THE SERVLET

We will use a servlet to access the XML document and produce the HTML output. The role of the servlet in this operation is that of a *controller* object; the real work to access the database, create XML, and transform the XML to HTML is being done by the objects the servlet has created. The result is a compact servlet focused on the task of creating a presentation component and delivering it to the browser that has generated the request.

The servlet retrieves the query to execute from an initialization parameter in the servlet web.xml file (shown in the next code example). The transformation is done using an XSLT script located in a disk file. The end result of this application design is that the composition and content of the HTML table displayed by this servlet can be changed without altering a single line of servlet code. The code for this servlet is shown in the sections below.

The ServletExample1 Class: The doGet Method

The servlet class declaration includes a number of imports for the various packages used within the servlet. Since this servlet responds to an HTTP GET request, it includes a declaration for the doGet method, as shown in the following code:

The ServletExample1 Class

```java
package examples.servlets;

import java.io.*;
import java.util.*;
```

```java
import javax.servlet.*;
import javax.servlet.http.*;

import java.sql.*;
import javax.sql.*;

import java.net.*;
import java.io.*;

import javax.naming.*;
import java.rmi.*;

import db.*;
import jdbcutil.*;
import movies.ejb.*;

import com.icl.saxon.trax.*;
import org.xml.sax.*;

public class ServletExample1 extends HttpServlet {

ServletConfig        config;
ServletContext       context;

//
// for Saxon XML transformations
//
Processor       processor;
Templates       templates;
Transformer transformer;

PreparedStatement    pstmt;
Connection                con;

String            defaultStyleSheet =
"file:/web/xslt/rs.xsl";


public void doGet(HttpServletRequest request,
HttpServletResponse response)
throws IOException, ServletException
{
PrintWriter out = response.getWriter();

out.println("<html>");
out.println("<head>");

out.println("<title>Movies Listing</title>");
out.println("</head>");
out.println("<body bgcolor=\"white\">");
```

```
try {

//
// only need to prepare the query if it hasn't been
// prepared before
//
if ( pstmt == null ) {      // need to prepare the query

  //
  // get the query from an environment parameter
  //
  String query = context.getInitParameter( "Query2" );

  //
  // prepare the query
  //
  pstmt = con.prepareStatement( query );

}


//
// execute the prepared query and retrieve the results
// results are formatted as an XML document
//
String xmlDoc = getQueryResults();

//
// transform the XML to the format for our output
// (an HTML table)
//
transformer.transform(
new InputSource( new StringReader( xmlDoc ) ),
new Result( out ) );

out.println("</body>");
out.println("</html>");
}
catch (Exception e) {
log( "Exception in doGet: " + e.getMessage() );
}


}
```

The servlet begins by importing various packages needed for operation, including the standard servlet packages, the JNDI packages (for `DataSource` usage), Java I/O packages, and the JDBC packages. Packages used for the SAXON XSLT transformer are also imported, as are various local packages used in the servlet.

The XSLT transformer will use a *processor*, a *template*, and a *transformer* to perform its work. A processor is created from a factory method (`newInstance`) and is then used to create a template. The template is created based on the transform to be done and receives the name of the transform stylesheet to process. The stylesheet contains the script that indicates how to process the document. Once the template has been created (using the transform stylesheet), a transformer can be retrieved from the template. It is this transformer which will then be used to perform that actual transformation (see Figure 20–2).

The point of all this is that since we are using the same XSLT transformation for all of the work being performed by this servlet, we do not need to recreate the transformer each time it is called; that would not be very efficient. It is better to create the transformer (through the processor and template) in the servlet `init` method, which is called when the servlet instance is first loaded by the container. In the servlet `doGet` method, which is called when an HTTP `GET` is executed on the servlet page, the transformer is simply called to perform the transformation. (The transformer object can be considered the equivalent or analogue of a prepared SQL statement.)

The template, processor, and transformer references are declared as instance members for the servlet class. This means that they will be shared among instances of the servlet (potentially by different users), but since they represent static information for the servlet—information that will not change based on the user or invocation of the servlet—having them shared among servlet instances does not present a problem. (Had they represented some information that would change per invocation, they should be declared and set within the appropriate method to be called by the servlet engine—for example, the `doGet  or  doPost` method.)

In the code example, the standard declaration for the `doGet` method is declared. Since the servlet is responding to an HTTP request and will respond with the HTTP response, we see declaration parameters that represent the HTTP

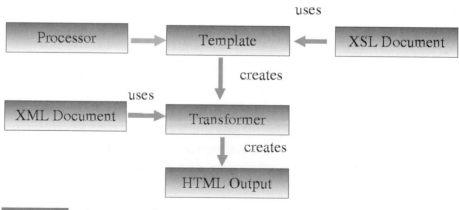

Figure 20–2   *The XSLT Transformation Process*

request (`HttpServletRequest`) and the HTTP response (`HttpServletResponse`). We would like to write our transformed XML document to the response stream, so we obtain the response writer with a call to the `HttpServletResponse getWriter` method.

The code block then contains several statements outputting HTML statements to format the page. A `try/catch` block is started, and the query string for the query to be executed is retrieved with a call to the `ServletContext getInitParameter` method. The value for this parameter is retrieved from the `web.xml` file (shown later in this chapter) declaration for the `context param` entry for `Query2`. By storing the query string in the `web.xml` configuration file, we create a flexible servlet that, when combined with the use of the XSLT style sheet, allows us to change the operation of the servlet with very little effort.

The query is prepared, and a `PreparedStatement` object is created. The `getQueryResults` method is then called and this method (shown later) uses the `PreparedStatement` (`pstmt`) instance member to execute the query and convert the `ResultSet` to an XML document format. If the `pstmt` object is not null, then the code to prepare the statement will not be executed.

At this point, the XML document containing the query results is in the string `xmlDoc` and the `Transformer transform` method is called. This method accepts a `java.io.Reader` parameter and a `Result` (part of the SAXON package) parameter as arguments. The `Reader` argument in this case is created by wrapping a `StringReader` around our `xmlDoc` string, and the `Result` parameter is created by wrapping the `Result` class around the output `PrintWriter` (from our `HttpServletResponse`). This method will use the XSLT transform stylesheet to transform the XML document (in `xmlDoc`) and produce HTML output that will be written to the output `PrintWriter` (`out`). The remaining code in this program block outputs HTML to complete the formatting of the HTML page and provide `catch` blocks for the exceptions that may be thrown in the method.

The ServletExample1 Class: The getQueryResults Method

The `getQuery` method performs the task of executing the query and transforming the results into an XML document. The execution of the query simply involves executing the prepared statement that was prepared in the `doGet` method and converting the `ResultSet` into XML format using the `JDBCXML toXMLString` method (as shown previously in this chapter).

The `executeQuery` method is called in a `try/catch` block, and the conversion to the XML document is performed in the `finally` block, which is used to return the XML document string. Should there be a failure in the execution of the XML statement, the empty or null `ResultSet` will be passed to the `JDBCXML toXMLString` method, which will return an invalid XML document. This will lead to a parser error in the transformation process in the `doGet` method. (Though not shown in this example, a more involved error-checking scheme would determine that the prepared statement execution had failed and return a value to the calling method that would terminate processing at that point.) The code for this method is shown next.

The ServletExample1 Class: The getQuery Method

```
public String getQueryResults() {
ResultSet rs = null;
try {
        rs = pstmt.executeQuery( );

}
catch (SQLException e) {
        //context.log("RemoteException in ServletExample2.getQueryResults: " +
e.getMessage() );
        System.out.println("SQLException in ServletExample2.getQueryResults: " +
e.getMessage() );
}
finally {
      return JDBCXML.toXMLString( rs );
}

}
```

The ServletExample1 Class: The init Method

A servlet runs within a container, a runtime environment for the servlet, usually provided as part of a Web server or application server. The container is responsible for providing various services for the servlet, such as security and a Java Virtual Machine (JVM) to run the class files. When the servlet is first loaded, the `init` method for the servlet class is called by the servlet container as implemented by the Web server. Per the servlet specification, the `init` method is called only once.

The `init` method is therefore a good location to provide initialization code for the servlet, much as a constructor is used in a conventional class. In this example, the `init` method is used to obtain a connection to the database and to prepare the template and create a processor for the XSLT transformation service. The code for this method is shown next.

The ServletExample1 Class: The init Method

```
1.
2.public void init( ServletConfig config ) {
3.try {
4.          super.init( config );
5.
6.          this.config = config;
7.      this.context = config.getServletContext();
```

```
8.
9.         //
10.        // get the location of the xslt stylesheet
11.          // from an init parameter parameter
12.        //
13.        String styleSheet = context.getInitParameter(
14.                                "XsltQuery2" );
15.
16.        //
17.        // build the URL for the stylesheet
18.        //
19.        if ( styleSheet == null )
20.            styleSheet = defaultStyleSheet;
21.            else
22.            styleSheet = "file:" + styleSheet;
23.
24.          //
25.        // create the objects we need for the XSL transformation
26.        //
27.        processor = Processor.newInstance("xslt");
28.
29.          //
30.        // get an InputStream from the URL
31.          //
32.        templates = processor.process(new InputSource(
33.                    new URL( styleSheet ).openStream() ) );
34.
35.        transformer = templates.newTransformer();
36.
37.         //
38.        // prepare data access
39.        //
40.          InitialContext init = new InitialContext( );
41.          //
42.          // tomcat 4.02 requires a two step lookup
43.          //
44.          Context ctx  = (Context) init.lookup(
45. "java:comp/env/jdbc" );
46.          DataSource ds = (DataSource) ctx.lookup( "moviesmysql" );
47.
48.        con = ds.getConnection();
49.
50.
51.}
52.catch (SQLException e) {
53.        context.log("SQLException in ServletExample2.init: " +
54.                        e.getMessage() );
55.}
56.catch (ProcessorException e) {
57.        context.log("ProcessorException in ServletExample2.init: "
58.                        + e.getMessage() );
59.}
```

```
60.catch (RemoteException e) {
61.    context.log("RemoteException in ServletExample2.init: " +
62.                        e.getMessage() );
63.}
64.catch (NamingException e) {
65.    context.log("NamingException in ServletExample2.init: " +
66.                        e.getMessage() + " - " + e );
67.}
68.catch (ServletException e) {
69.    context.log("ServletException in ServletExample2.init: " +
70.                        e.getMessage() );
71.}
72.catch (Exception e) {
73.        context.log("Exception in ServletExample2.init: " +
74.                        e.getMessage() );
75.}
76.}
77.
78.}
```

The `init` method is passed the servlet configuration (`ServletConfig`). This is used on line 7 to obtain the servlet context, which provides access to such useful operations as the log device for the servlet engine. The servlet context also provides access to the initialization parameters for the servlet environment, and this is used on line 13 to obtain the name of the XSLT stylesheet script to use to transform the XML document.

Lines 19 through 22 are used to build a URI name for the stylesheet, and on line 27, a new instance of the SAXON transformation processor is obtained. The processor then uses the name of the stylesheet to create a template on lines 32 and 33. The template is used to create the last `object` reference needed to perform the transformation, the *transformer* on line 35.

On lines 40 through 48, we see the code we have seen many times before in this text—the code used to obtain a `DataSource` and ultimately a JDBC connection through a JNDI resource.

THE SERVLETEXAMPLE1 CLASS: THE WEB.XML FILE

As defined by the Java servlet specification, the `web.xml` file contains configuration information for a servlet context, or what is also referred to as a Web application. In this example, the `web.xml` file is used to store the initialization parameters used by the servlet, specifically the XSLT stylesheet and the query to execute. The partial contents of this file are shown below.

Annotated web.xml File with Parameters

```xml
<?xml version="1.0" encoding="ISO-8859-1"?>

<!DOCTYPE web-app
    PUBLIC "-//Sun Microsystems, Inc.//DTD Web Application 2.3//EN"
    "http://java.sun.com/dtd/web-app_2_3.dtd">

<web-app>

        <context-param>
            <param-name>Query1</param-name>
            <param-value>select knowledge_base.doc_key, base_doc_key, doc_name, mes-
sage_txt
                from knowledge_base, knowledge_messages
                where knowledge_base.doc_key = knowledge_messages.doc_key
                order by knowledge_base.doc_key, base_doc_key
            </param-value>
        </context-param>

        <context-param>
            <param-name>Query2</param-name>
            <param-value>select  movie_name, movie_id, release_date, category
                from  movies
                order by movie_name
            </param-value>
        </context-param>

        <context-param>
            <param-name>XsltQuery2</param-name>
            <param-value>/stdApps/Useful/rsQuery2.xsl</param-value>
        </context-param>

        <context-param>
            <param-name>XsltStyleSheet</param-name>
            <param-value>/lin/home/art/JDBC_Real/Code/Dynamic/rsQ1.xsl</param-value>
        </context-param>

    <servlet>
        <servlet-name>
            ServletExample2
        </servlet-name>
        <servlet-class>
            ServletExamples.ServletExample2
        </servlet-class>
    </servlet>

    <servlet>
        <servlet-name>
            ServletExample1
        </servlet-name>
        <servlet-class>
```

```
        ServletExamples.ServletExample1
    </servlet-class>
</servlet>

<servlet>
    <servlet-name>
        BlobView
    </servlet-name>
    <servlet-class>
        ServletExamples.BlobView
    </servlet-class>
</servlet>

...

</web-app>
```

The `context-param` tag is used to identify a parameter definition that can be retrieved through a call to `ServletContext getInitParameter`. The definitions highlighted in the previous listing and used in the `ServletExample1` servlet are for the `XsltQuery2` parameter, which identifies the full path to the XSLT stylesheet, and for the `Query2` parameter, which identifies the SQL `select` query to run.

There are other options for passing parameters into servlets. A common approach is to pass the parameters to the servlet as `request` parameters, meaning that they would appear as part of the URL requesting the servlet, as follows:

```
http://www.asite.com/ServletExamples/ServletExample2?Query2=select+movie_id+from+movi
es&XsltQuery2=/stdApps/Useful/rsQ1.xsl
```

As shown in this example, parameters are passed to the servlet for the `Query2` parameter and the `XsltQuery2` parameter. There are a few issues with this approach. The first is that the parameters for the query and the XSLT stylesheet are not expected to change between invocations, so there is no strong, compelling reason to pass them in as parameters. Another issue is that the parameters for a SQL query could quickly become tedious to view and debug when spread across the command line, and certain characters used in SQL queries may not be allowed as part of URLs.

Yet another issue, and a serious issue at that, is a security issue. The problem with these request parameters is that they expose the data resources of the enterprise to the general user population. If parameters are passed as shown previously, then any user able to execute the servlet could access any table visible in the database. Opening freely accessible Web applications to generalized queries must be carefully considered. Using the approach shown in this example, where a limited number of queries is available to the user, adds a layer of security to the processing of the data.

The ServletExample1 Class: The XSLT Stylesheet

An XSLT stylesheet describes the transformation process for the XML document being processed. The example shown below is the stylesheet for our transformation.

The complete syntax for this document is beyond the scope of this text. The script is shown here to demonstrate that minor modifications can be made to this file to accommodate changes to the XML source document (and the source for the XML document, the SQL `select` query).

The portions in the XSLT stylesheet highlighted in bold in this example represent the syntax that is specific to the SAXON transformation tool. All other tags in the stylesheet are HTML and allow the presentation of the data to be modified without impacting Java code.

The rsQ1.xsl File

```
<html
 xmlns:xsl="http://www.w3.org/1999/XSL/Transform"
 xsl:version="1.0"
 xmlns:saxon="http://icl.com/saxon">
 <body>
        <Center>
        <H1>Movies Available</H1>
         </Center>
        <br></br>
        <br></br>
        <br></br>
        <table width="100%" border="2">

           <tr>
                <td bgcolor="E0E0E0">Movie Name</td>
                <td bgcolor="E0E0E0">Movie ID</td>
                <td bgcolor="E0E0E0">Release Date</td>
                <td bgcolor="E0E0E0">Category</td>
           </tr>


           <xsl:for-each select="ResultSet/row">
             <tr>
               <xsl:for-each select="Column">
                <td><xsl:value-of select=".//Data"/></td>
               </xsl:for-each>
             </tr>
           </xsl:for-each>
        </table>
  </body>
 </html>
```

The highlighted `xsl:for-each` tag is executed for each occurrence of the identified `select` tags. For the first occurrence of the `for-each` tag, the

`ResultSet/row` nested tag is identified. Since the `ResultSet` tag is the outer-most tag in the XML document we have produced, there will be only a single occurrence of this tag in the file. There will, however, be a row tag for the multiple rows of our XML document (one for each row in the `ResultSet` that was used to produce the document).

For each `row` tag encountered in the XML document, the XSL stylesheet specifies that the HTML `<tr>` tag will be output, indicating a table row, so we are creating a single row in the HTML table for each row in the XML document.

Within the outer `for-each` loop, there is a nested `xsl:for-each` tag for each column in the row. Within the block of this `for-each` loop, there is an `xsl:value-of` tag, which selects the contents of the `data` element. Since we have formatted the XML document to place the column data with `data` element tags, this has the effect of outputting the column data at this point in the transformed (HTML) document; this is done between HTML `<td>` tags (for *'table data'*). At the termination of the inner `for-each` loop, a `</tr>` tag is inserted, indicating the end of the HTML table row. After the termination of the outer `for-each` loop, the HTML table is terminated with a `</table>`. The end result is an HTML table displayed as seen earlier in Figure 20–1.

Summary

The XML language has become the standard for data interchange, so it is worth-while to examine how this tool can be used with JDBC. We know that XML is useful if we can encode our data as XML. This was demonstrated in the first example with static methods in the `JDBCXML` class. These methods take a `ResultSet` as an argument and convert the contents of the `ResultSet` into an XML document.

The next useful step is to transform that XML data in some way. This could be done with an XML parser, which, though it provides a great deal of flexibility, can involve some effort. An easier approach is to use XML transformation tools to transform the data into a useful format based on an XSL specification or script. This was demonstrated with the `ServletExample1` Java servlet, which used the SAXON transformation API to transform the XML document we produced earlier in the chapter into an HTML table.

Transformation could be used to produce other output—for example, transforming an XML document into an EDI format for interaction with a legacy system. Some, though not all, Web browsers also support XSL transformations, allowing the processing of transformations to be offloaded to client machines (where, given the power of today's CPU chips, there are an incredible number of free CPU cycles to work with). Note that this browser XSL support is not universal, and support for specific XSL versions varies.

COMING UP NEXT

The binary large object (BLOB) allows the storage of large binary or text fields in relational databases. These data types are widely supported, and JDBC provides a very useful mechanism for dealing with these columns using Java streams and writers. Chapter 15 showed how objects could be saved to the database using this mechanism. Chapter 21 will demonstrate the storage and retrieval of graphical data to these columns and provide code examples using a servlet that displays a graphic object to a browser.

JDBC and BLOBs

INTRODUCTION

The JDBC API makes the use of binary large objects (BLOBs) a relatively simple task. By allowing Java streams and writers to be associated with a BLOB column, any data that can be written to a stream or writer can be stored and manipulated in a BLOB field. This was demonstrated in Chapter 15, where a Java object was persisted using a BLOB column.

While it is common to store large blocks of text in a BLOB field (usually in a CLOB, or character large object, field), it is also very common to store graphics images in BLOB fields. This chapter demonstrates several applications that make use of BLOB fields with Web applications.

THE BENEFITS OF THE BLOB

The BLOB is a data type for a database column in a relational database. Whereas other data types, such as the integer and decimal types, may have a fixed length, BLOB column data generally does not have a known size.

BLOB columns are useful for storing large text fields or binary data. Though there is some debate about the performance impact of using BLOBs, for many applications the convenience benefits of being able to store BLOB data in a database far outweigh any performance impact.

The advantages of storing graphics and text information in BLOBs are directly related to the features of relational databases: easy searches and manipulation and data integrity features. There are some who feel that graphics should always be stored in disk files, but anyone who has had to search a complex directory structure for a file knows that this can be a very limiting environment. With databases, it is a simple task to create a BLOB field and associate various columns of information with that BLOB merely be creating columns in the same table. More complex relationships can then be formed by creating additional related tables.

Java streams are represented by the Java classes `java.io.InputStream` and `java.io.OutputStream`. These classes provide low-level I/O for bytes and are generally used for I/O operations with binary data. This makes them the logical choice for the manipulation of BLOB fields being used to store graphical images. Alternatively, `java.io.Reader` and `java.io.Writer` are associated with character streams.

As developers, we must usually not only retrieve the data but also present it to the user. This chapter demonstrates the storage of thumbnail graphic images in a BLOB field and the retrieval of those images using a servlet. Using a small number of API calls, the servlet will retrieve the column and send it back to the browser for display. This servlet will then be combined with a JSP page, which will present both text and graphical information, all of which are retrieved from the database.

The BlobView Servlet

The `BlobView` class is a servlet that receives a single parameter that represents an ID number for a movie stored in the database. The ID number is used to find the BLOB record in the database, retrieve it, and write it to the output stream for the HTTP response. Figure 21–1 shows the ouput of this servlet in a browser window.

The movie ID number (`movie_id`) is retrieved from a command-line parameter, so the URL to call the `BlobView` servlet is as follows:

```
http://serverName/ServletExamples/BlobView?movie_id=801
```

The job of finding and retrieving the BLOB and writing it to the output stream is left to an associated class (`BlobWriter`) so that the servlet is really only responsible for retrieving the request parameter and calling the methods in the associated class to perform the other work required. The code for the `BlobView` servlet is shown in the following example:

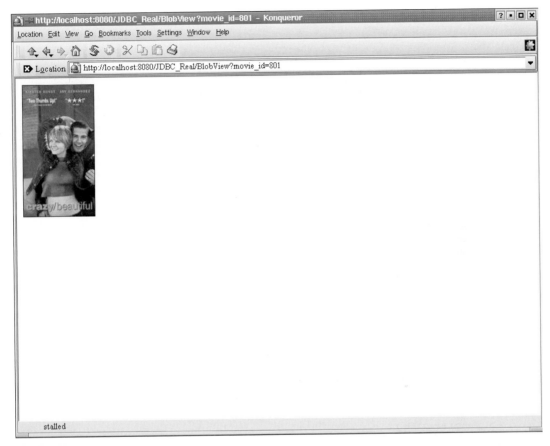

Figure 21–1 *The BlobView servlet*

BlobView Servlet: BlobView.java

```java
package examples.servlets;

import java.io.*;
import javax.servlet.*;
import javax.servlet.http.*;

import java.sql.*;

import java.net.*;

// our packages
import db.*;
import movies.blobs.*;
```

```java
public class BlobView extends HttpServlet {

ServletConfig        config;
ServletContext       context;

BlobWriter               blobwriter;


    public void doGet(HttpServletRequest request,
                        HttpServletResponse response)
        throws IOException, ServletException
    {

        //
        // get the output stream for our response
        //
        OutputStream out = response.getOutputStream();

        //
        // set the content type for our graphic file to return
        //
        response.setContentType("image/jpeg");

        try {

            //
            // this will retrieve the Blob referenced by the movie_id
            // and write it to the OutputStream parameter passed in
        //
        blobwriter.getBlob(
                Integer.parseInt(
                    request.getParameter( "movie_id" ) ), out );

        }
        catch (Exception e) {
                log( "Exception in doGet: " + e.getMessage() );
        }

    }


public void init( ServletConfig config ) {

    //
    // BlobWriter will open the connection and create
    // a PreparedStatement to perform the database i/o
    //
    blobwriter = new BlobWriter( "jdbc/moviesmysql " );
```

```
//
// save the servlet context
//
context   = config.getServletContext();


}



}
```

The `BlobView` servlet uses the `init` method to create a new instance of the `BlobWriter` class, the class that will perform the work necessary to retrieve and display the graphic image. The `BlobWriter` class is passed the JNDI name of the `DataSource` to use to retrieve the images. The servlet context is also obtained in the `init` method.

The `doGet` method retrieves the output stream for the HTTP response by making a call to the `HttpServletResponse getOutputStream` method. The content type for the output is then set to `image/jpeg`, indicating that the response contains a JPEG format graphic image. The `BlobWriter getBlob` method is then called and passed two arguments: an integer for the `movie_id` record to retrieve and the `OutputStream` reference for the response output stream. The work performed by the `getBlob` method is explained in the next section.

THE BLOBWRITER CLASS

The `BlobWriter` class is the utility class used by the `BlobView` servlet. This class contains the methods that perform the task of retrieving the BLOB column for viewing. Unlike some of the other utility classes, this class takes on the responsibility of establishing a connection to the database and creating the prepared statement to use in the database operation. The code for this class is shown in the next few sections.

The BlobWriter Class: The Class Declaration and the main Program Block

The main class declaration for the `BlobWriter` class performs the imports we expect to access JNDI naming services and to use the JDBC API. For convenience, instance members are created for a JDBC `Connection` reference and for a `PreparedStatement` reference.

The `getBlob` method is the method exposed to the client objects. This method takes two parameters: an integer for the `movie_id` record to retrieve and an `OutputStream` reference for the output stream where the BLOB should be written. The `movie_id` is used to set the parameter for the first element in the prepared statement and then executes the `writeBlob` method to perform the task of retrieving the BLOB and writing it.

The BlobWriter Class: Class Declaration and the main Program Block

```
import java.rmi.*;
import javax.naming.*;
import javax.rmi.*;

import java.sql.*;
import javax.sql.*;

import java.util.*;
import java.io.*;

import db.*;


public class BlobWriter {

private Connection              con;
private PreparedStatement   prepStmt;



public void getBlob(int movie_id, OutputStream out ) {

try {

  prepStmt.setInt( 1,movie_id );

  writeBlob( out );



}
catch (SQLException e) {
    System.out.println("SQLException in getBlob: " + e.getMessage());
    throw new Exception( "SQLException in getBlob: " + e.getMessage());
}
catch (Exception e) {
    System.out.println("Exception in getBlob: " + e.getMessage());
    throw new Exception( "Exception in getBlob: " + e.getMessage());
}
}
```

The BlobWriter Class: The writeBlob Method

The writeBlob method performs the core work of the BlobWriter class. This private method receives an OutputStream reference where the contents of the BLOB should be written. It creates a byte array buffer with a fixed size (tuned to the size of the graphics we know are stored in the column).

The method executes the query for the prepared statement, and if no rows have been found, it goes no further; a message is displayed indicating the error condition, an exception is thrown, and the method returns (by nature of the exception being thrown).

The getBinaryStream method is then used to obtain an InputStream on the BLOB column (which is column two in the ResultSet). The InputStream is then used in a loop to perform read operations on the stream, reading bytes from the InputStream and writing all bytes read to the OutputStream. This is done until the byte count from the read operation is less than zero (–1). Before the method returns, both the InputStream and the OutputStream are closed. The code for this method follows:

The BlobWriter Class: The writeBlob Method

```
private void writeBlob( OutputStream out )throws Exception {
int byteCount = 0;
byte[] buffer = new byte[1024*5];

try {

//
// execute the query. Throw exception and return if no rows found
//
ResultSet rs = prepStmt.executeQuery();
if ( !(rs.next()) ) {
    System.out.println("Blob row not found.");
    throw new Exception( "Blob row not found.");
}

//
// get the InputStream for the Blob column
//
InputStream input = rs.getBinaryStream( 2 );

//
// read till bytes read == 0. Write all bytes to the
// OutputStream
//
byteCount = input.read( buffer );
while ( byteCount > 0 ) {

        out.write( buffer );
```

```
    byteCount = input.read( buffer );

}

input.close();
out.close();
}
catch( IOException e) {
      System.out.println( "IOException in writeBlob: " +
                             e.getMessage() );
         throw new Exception(  "IOException in writeBlob: " +
                             e.getMessage() );
}
catch( SQLException e) {
      System.out.println( "SQLException in writeBlob: " +
                             e.getMessage() );
         throw new Exception(  "IOException in writeBlob: " +
                             e.getMessage() );
}


}
```

The BlobWriter Class: The prepareStatement Method

The prepareStatement method performs the task of preparing the SQL statement to be executed to retrieve the BLOB. In this example, the query is hardcoded into the application code. (A different implementation would potentially store the query in a properties file and extract the value of the query at runtime.) The code for this method is shown below.

```
private void prepareStatement() {

try {
   prepStmt = con.prepareStatement(
                 "select movie_id, movie_image " +
                 " from movie_images " +
                 " where movie_id = ?" );

}
catch (SQLException e ) {
      System.out.println("SQLException in prepareStatement: " +
                          e.getMessage() );
}

}
```

The BlobWriter Class: The getConnected Method

The `getConnected` method creates, as the name implies, a connection to the database. This method is overloaded using a no-argument version to create a connection to a default `DataSource`. A version that uses a string parameter allows a specific `DataSource` name to be specified. This version performs the work of obtaining the `InitialContext` and executing the `lookup` method to find the specific `DataSource` requested. The code for this method is shown next.

The BlobWriter Class: The getConnected Method

```
private void  getConnected() {

 getConnected( "movies" );

}


private void getConnected(String dataSourceName ) {

try {

     InitialContext context = new InitialContext( );

     DataSource ds = (DataSource) context.lookup( dataSourceName );

     con = ds.getConnection();

   }
catch (SQLException e) {
     System.out.println("SQLException caught in getConnected: " +
                        e.getMessage() );
}
catch (NamingException e) {
     System.out.println("NamingException caught in getConnected: " +
                        e.getMessage() + " - " + e );
     System.out.println("Resolved Name: " + e.getResolvedName()   );

}
catch (Exception e) {
     System.out.println("Exception caught in getConnected: " +
                        e.getMessage() );

}


}
```

The BlobWriter Class: The Constructor

The constructor for the `BlobWriter` class prepares the class for usage by establishing a connection to the data source and preparing the SQL statement. The `getConnected` method is used to obtain the connection to the data source, and the `prepareStatement` method is used to prepare the SQL statement to be used in the servlet. The constructor is overloaded to include a no-argument version that constructs the class with a default data source name. The code for this constructor follows:

The BlobWriter Class: The Constructor

```
public BlobWriter() {
   //
   // create a connection to the database
   // using the default DataSource
   //
   new BlobWriter( "moviesmysql" );
}

public BlobWriter( String dataSourceName ) {

   // create a connection to the database
   getConnected( dataSourceName );

   // prepare the sql statement
   prepareStatement();

}

}
```

THE LISTMOVIES JSP PAGE

The `BlobView` servlet does not have much utility as a standalone servlet, but when placed as an element in a Web page, this provides a useful mechanism for retrieving specific graphic images for the page based on the `movie_id` being requested. The `ListMovies` JSP page does just that, as shown in Figure 21–2.

The `ListMovies` JSP page accepts a parameter for a `movie_id` and uses this parameter to extract information on the specified movie from a database, information that includes the image of the video box for the movie. The code for this JSP page is shown next.

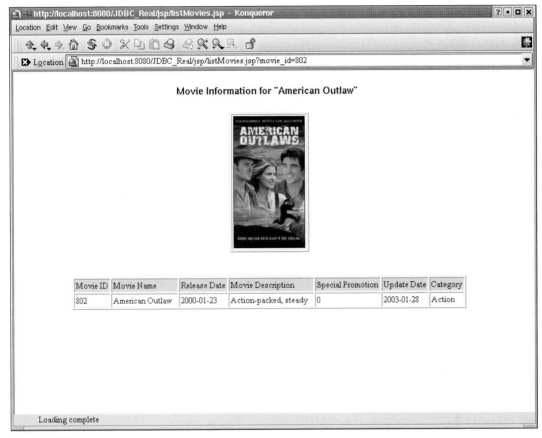

Figure 21–2 *Movie Listing with Video Box Image*

ListMovies.jsp

```
<HTML>
<BODY bgcolor="white">

<jsp:useBean id="moviesBean" class="movies.beans.MoviesBean" scope="session" />

<!- load the bean with the request parameter ->
<% moviesBean.loadBean( request.getParameter( "movie_id" ) ); %>

<br>
<font face="Helvetica, Sans-serif" size=+3 >
<center>
```

```html
<b>Movie Information for "<jsp:getProperty name="moviesBean" property="movie_name"
/>" </b>
</center>
</font>
<br>
<br>


<center>
<table border=1 cellpadding=2 bgcolor="white">
<tr>
<td>
<img src="http://localhost:8080/JDBC_Real/BlobView?movie_id=<%=
request.getParameter("movie_id") %>" name="Box Picture" align=center >
</td>
</tr>
</table>
</center>

<br>
<br>
<br>

<center>

<font face="Helvetica, Sans-serif" size=+2 color="blue">

<table border=1 cellpadding=2 bgcolor="white">

<tr>
<td bgcolor="#C0D9D9">Movie ID</td>
<td bgcolor="#C0D9D9">Movie Name</td>
<td bgcolor="#C0D9D9">Release Date</td>
<td bgcolor="#C0D9D9">Movie Description</td>
<td bgcolor="#C0D9D9">Special Promotion</td>
<td bgcolor="#C0D9D9">Update Date</td>
<td bgcolor="#C0D9D9">Category</td>

</tr>

<tr>
<td> <jsp:getProperty name="moviesBean" property="movie_id" /> </td>
<td> <jsp:getProperty name="moviesBean" property="movie_name" /> </td>
<td> <jsp:getProperty name="moviesBean" property="release_date" /> </td>
<td> <jsp:getProperty name="moviesBean" property="movie_desc" /> </td>
<td> <jsp:getProperty name="moviesBean" property="special_promotion" /> </td>
<td> <jsp:getProperty name="moviesBean" property="update_date" /> </td>
<td> <jsp:getProperty name="moviesBean" property="category" /> </td>

</tr>

</table>
```

```
</font>
</center>

<br>
<br>

<br>
<br>

</HTML>
</BODY>
```

The `ListMovies` JSP page begins by using the JSP `usebean` tag to declare a JavaBean for inclusion in the page. This bean is declared to be an instance of the `MoviesBean` class, which extends a value object class (`MoviesVO`) for the `movies` table. This class is shown in detail in the next section. It is worth mentioning at this point that, being an instance of a value object, the `MoviesBean` will have the `get` and `set` methods that allow it to be used as a `JavaBean` in this page.

Two HTML tables are used on the page. The first table is simply used to frame the image of the movie video box. Within this table, the `BlobView` servlet shown previously is used with an HTML `src` tag to display the image for the movie selected. The call to retrieve the image uses the request parameter as an argument to specify the `movie_id` for the `BlobView` servlet to display.

The text information on the movie is displayed in the second table. Within this table, the `MovieBean` JavaBean is used via the JSP `getProperty` tag to display the information about the movie that is being requested. The `movieBean` `JavaBean` has been loaded with this information using the call to its `loadBean` method, which received the `movie_id` as an argument.

THE MOVIESBEAN JAVABEAN

The `MoviesBean` class is used as a `JavaBean` in the `ListMovies` JSP page. This class is responsible for retrieving the information about a particular movie from the database. It does not perform this task directly, but instead uses an Enterprise Java Bean (EJB) component to perform the work for it. EJBs will not be explained in detail in this chapter, but will be shown in more detail in the next few chapters. Their inclusion here provides an opportunity to demonstrate how these components will be used in client code.

As mentioned previously, this class extends the value object class created for the `movies` table, the `MoviesVO` class, and thus has access to all of the `get` and `set` methods of the super class—a useful feature considering this will be used as a JavaBean that expects `get` and `set` methods. The code for this class is shown in the sections below.

The MoviesBean Class: The Class Declaration and Constructor

The class declaration for the MoviesBean class is shown below. A number of imports are performed to provide access to the classes used for EJBs. Instance members for the home and remote objects for the EJBs are declared within the class declaration (the next chapter will explain the purpose of these; right now, just consider them a facility for accessing the EJB).

All data access for the JavaBean will be provided through the EJB, so the constructor takes on the job of obtaining access to the EJB. EJBs are accessed in a two-step process. First, a reference to the home object for the EJB is obtained. Then, using the home object, a reference to the remote object for the EJB is obtained. It is through the remote object that the bean is accessed using various EJB methods that have been exposed to the client code (using the remote interface).

A Hashtable object is created in the constructor and is used to store various parameters required to have the InitialContext access the JNDI name server for the application server that will provide access to the EJB we need. (In this case, it is the JBoss open-source application server.) Once the InitialContext has been obtained, the home object is retrieved using a lookup method call.

The home object reference is stored in the instance member for the movies entity bean home. This reference will be used to retrieve instances of the movies bean for a specific movie_id. The code for this class declaration and constructor are shown next.

The MoviesBean Class: Class Declaration and Constructor

```
package movies.beans;

// ejb
import java.rmi.*;
import javax.naming.*;
import javax.rmi.*;
import javax.ejb.*;

import java.util.*;

// our packages
import db.*;
import movies.ejb.*;

public class MoviesBean extends MoviesVO {

InitialContext context;

MoviesEntityRemote    movies;
```

```
MoviesEntityHome        moviesHome;


public MoviesBean() {

try {
    Hashtable env = new Hashtable();

    //
    // get a connection to the EJB
    // the InitialContext in Tomcat will not access the JBoss JNDI context
    // by default, so we set the environment explicitly to get to JBoss
    //
    env.put( "java.naming.factory.initial",
               "org.jnp.interfaces.NamingContextFactory");
    env.put( "java.naming.provider.url",
               "jnp://localhost:1099");
    env.put( "java.naming.factory.url.pkgs",
               "org.jboss.naming:org.jnp.interfaces");

    context = new InitialContext( env );

    moviesHome = (MoviesEntityHome) PortableRemoteObject.narrow(
                    context.lookup("ejb/MoviesEntityBean"),
                    MoviesEntityHome.class );
}
catch (NamingException e) {
      System.out.println(
               "NamingException in MoviesBean constructor: " +
               e.getMessage() );
}
catch (Exception e) {
      System.out.println(
                  "Exception in MoviesBean constructor: " +
                  e.getMessage() );
}

}
```

The MovieBean Class: The loadBean Method

The loadBean method is passed an argument containing the movie_id of the bean to load. Since we are using EJBs to provide database access, we only need to take the movie_id and pass it to the EJB component to retrieve the information for the movie.

The entity bean is a special type of EJB component designed to interact with a database or some type of data store. The findByPrimaryKey method, which has been defined for the movie entity bean, accepts an integer argument representing the movie_id for the movie. The findByPrimaryKey method will return a reference to the movie EJB `remote` object, the object that will provide access to the methods in the EJB.

The `movies remote` object is used to call the `getMoviesVO` method, which returns a value object for the `movies` table. In this case, it returns the value object that represents the `movie_id` passed to the `findByPrimaryKey` method.

Once the `movies` value object has been retrieved, the `setMoviesVO` method is called to set the internal values of our `MoviesBean` value object (which extends the `MoviesVO` value object) to the values of the value object returned by the `getMoviesVO` method. This sets the state of our JavaBean to match that of the EJB that is performing the database access. The code for this method follows:

The MoviesBean Class: The loadBean Method

```
public void loadBean( String movie_id ) {

try {

    //
    // lookup this movie_id
    //
    movies = moviesHome.findByPrimaryKey(new Integer( movie_id ));

    //
    // set this object to look like the VO populated by the lookup
    //
    MoviesVO vo = movies.getMoviesVO();

    setMoviesVO( vo );

}
catch (RemoteException e) {
        System.out.println("RemoteException in MoviesBean loadbean: " +
                            e.getMessage() );
}
catch (FinderException e) {
        System.out.println("FinderException in MoviesBean loadbean: " +
                            e.getMessage() );
}
catch (Exception e) {
        System.out.println("Exception in MoviesBean loadbean: " +
                            e.getMessage() + " - " + e  );
}
catch (Throwable e) {
        System.out.println("Exception in MoviesBean loadbean: " +
                            e.getMessage() + " - " + e  );
}


}
```

SUMMARY

This chapter provided a demonstration of using database BLOBs with JDBC and J2EE. The first example showed the creation of a Java servlet. The servlet used a helper class to obtain a database connection, prepare a SQL statement, and execute a query. The helper class also included a method that was passed a `movie_id` for the movie image to retrieve and an `OutputStream`. The method then obtained the contents of the BLOB and wrote them to the `OutputStream`.

The second example took the usage of BLOBs one step further and merged the servlet from the first example into a JSP document that displayed textual information about the movie in conjunction with a graphic display of the movie image. This example used an EJB to provide access to the textual information about the movie. Given the brevity of the code in that example, it is clear that EJBs can reduce the quantity of code for client objects and can help to streamline the development process. The next few chapters will explain EJBs, the primary business tier component for Java, and will demonstrate how EJBs use JDBC to provide database access.

COMING UP NEXT

The next few chapters, in fact the final chapters of the book, provide details on the use of EJBs. EJBs are at the core of the J2EE specification, providing specifications for developing middleware components using Java. As we will see, there are several different types of components in the EJB specification, and JDBC can technically be used in most of them. But good design practice, as detailed in Java design patterns for J2EE and as explained and demonstrated in the next few chapters, suggest that JDBC code should be isolated in certain types of EJBs.

CHAPTER 22

Enterprise JavaBeans Architecture

INTRODUCTION

Enterprise JavaBeans (EJBs) lie at the core of the J2EE architecture. They represent the middleware component specification for Java. The pure object-oriented nature and platform independence, security, and network I/O features of Java made it a natural for the development of distributed components.

Following the release of the first EJB specification, the specification was quickly embraced and implemented by a number of application server vendors, and at last count, there were over 20 J2EE application servers available with varying costs and compliance levels (not all are J2EE-certified by Sun Microsystems).

This chapter presents an overview of EJBs and serves as an introduction to the next chapter of the book, which covers using JDBC with EJBs. In-depth coverage of EJBs, their various properties, and detailed examples is beyond the scope of these two remaining chapters. The purpose here is to demonstrate how the JDBC API should be used with EJB components.

EJBs Defined

If we consider applications to be composed of a set of components within our multitiered architecture, then Java Server Pages and servlets are *presentation tier* components, components that are used to create Web pages (HTML). If a JSP is a component, then an application is composed of one or, in most cases, more than one of these components. The JavaBeans used to support these Web pages are also components, though we would not consider them Web tier components. Since they manage the business logic of the application, we consider them *business tier* components.

The combination of JSP and JavaBeans running in a Web server is adequate for a large range of applications. But this combination does have its limits. The scalability, transaction, and failover features of standalone Web servers are generally not as robust as those of application servers.

Scalability and Failover

The *scalability* of an application represents the application's ability to handle an increase in usage without a significant drop in performance. For a Web site, usage is generally represented by the number of concurrent users or the number of page hits for the site for some increment of time (day, hour, minute, second). Scalability is usually provided using a feature known as *load balancing,* where a dispatcher can dispatch requests over one or more servers. Load balancing can be done using various algorithms, from a simple *round-robin* algorithm, where requests are distributed evenly among all available servers, to a *weighted average* form of load balancing, where requests are distributed among servers based on some statistical weight. See Figure 22–1.

Even more complex load balancing algorithms are used by some servers. These load balancing algorithms evaluate the system load on the servers in the cluster in real time and load balance according the actual system load on the servers rather than using the static parameters of round-robin or weighted average.

Application servers may also provide some form of *fail-over* capabilities. The fail-over capabilities of a server represent the server's ability to survive a failure of some sort caused by either the server hardware or the operating system. Specifically, fail-over generally applies to the ability of session activity to survive the failure of one of the servers in the cluster. This fail-over may be transparent, meaning that if the server on which the session is running fails, the other servers in the cluster will manage its workload transparent to the client application.

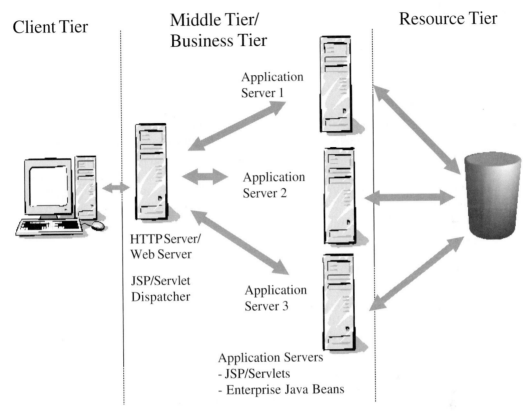

Client Tier

Middle Tier/
Business Tier

Resource Tier

Application
Server 1

Application
Server 2

HTTP Server/
Web Server

JSP/Servlet
Dispatcher

Application
Server 3

Application Servers
- JSP/Servlets
- Enterprise Java Beans

Figure 22-1 *Scalability with multiple servers.*

EJBs

The J2EE specification provides for EJB components. These components are special Java objects that can be invoked and run remotely by a client application. These components run within a *container* that provides various services for the components and represents the runtime environment for the component. The J2EE specification for EJBs details the services the container is expected to provide, though it does not detail how the container will provide the services.

This use of distributed software components is not new; the ability to create those components with a standard API and a standard, widely adopted cross-platform language is new. Many of the features J2EE-compliant application servers provide for EJBs would need to be developed with custom, proprietary code working with other components.

Flavors of EJBs

EJBs come in three flavors as of the EJB 2.0 specification: *session beans, entity beans,* and *message-driven beans*. Each has its specific benefits and will be discussed in the following sections.

Session Beans

Session beans represent a session between a client and an EJB, a client conversational state. Using the service model, a client will request a service from the bean through some conversation, and the bean will respond with a result.

     This communication between the client process and the bean may or may not require the EJB to retain state information between invocations. If a session bean retains state between invocations, then it is considered a *stateful session bean*. If a session bean does not retain state between invocations, then it is considered a *stateless session bean*.

     Any stateless session bean, since it does not retain state between invocations, should not use instance members or class members, because they will not be guaranteed to have sensible values, values specific to a client session, between invocations. In this vein, stateless session beans should receive a request, perform all work necessary to complete the request, and then return results for the request, all within the space of the invocation (the method call).

Entity Beans

Entity beans represent a unique element in a persistent data store. They represent persistent data and, in relational database terms, they are said to represent a row in a database table (or potentially, a unique record composed of a join across multiple tables).

     Since it represents a unique relation in a persistent data store, an entity bean is represented by a *primary key*, a unique representation for the entity bean. A primary key can be represented by one or more columns in the underlying table.

     An entity bean does not need to be mapped into a relational database. An entity bean could be mapped into a legacy database system or even into a set of files, though the most common implementation is that of object-relational mapping, using the entity bean to represent some portion of a relational database.

     Entity beans must remain synchronized with the persistent data store. This is accomplished using a set of methods that must be implemented by the entity bean (methods defined in the `EntityBean` interface). Specifically, the `ejbLoad` method is used to load the bean from the database, and the `ejbStore` method is used to synchronize the bean with the database.

     Either an entity bean developer can write the code for the `ejbLoad` and `ejbStore` methods (and a few others) or the application server vendor can provide a tool that will write the code for these methods. If the developer provides the code for the entity beans database synchronization, then the bean is using *bean-managed persistence* (BMP). If the developer allows the application server tool to create the code for the entity bean persistence, then the entity bean is using *container-managed persistence* (CMP).

As part of the EJB 2.0 specification, additional features have been added to entity beans to improve performance, address some of the limitations of the previous specification, and enhance the implementation of CMP. A query language has also been added (EJB-QL), which allows internal selects and the navigation of related beans, values, and dependent objects.

Message-Driven Beans

Message-driven beans have been added as part of the EJB 2.0 specification. These beans represent a useful integration of the Java Messaging Service (JMS) and the EJB. A message-driven bean allows asynchronous invocation of an EJB component. The message-driven bean is stateless and is invoked by the container upon the arrival of a message.

The EJB Container

With EJBs, the container is implemented by what is commonly called an *application server*. Application server vendors and development groups may add additional services above and beyond the EJB specification and have some discretion on how services are implemented, but in order to be compliant, they must provide a core set of services:

- security
- transactions
- naming
- scalability
- life-cycle management

These services and some background information on how they may be implemented are discussed in the following sections.

Security

EJB application servers must implement a specific role-based security model and must provide a role reference facility that allows a role reference name to be established for the role. Role permissions are then associated with methods and can be assigned to all methods within a component.

EJB security does not deal with authentication—the expectation is that this is managed in the presentation tier or the client tier. EJB security is concerned with the user's role and whether or not the user has permission to perform the action he or she is attempting to perform (executing a method or accessing a resource).

Transactions

The EJB specification provides for transactions related to components and for transaction managers that transparently manage transactions with a single data source or with multiple data sources combined. Transactions can be managed either by the container using *container-managed transactions* or programmatically through specific method calls using *bean-managed transactions*.

Components may run within a transaction and may propagate transactions down the call chain. This means that a method may have one transaction mode and call another method. That method being called may elect to use the transaction of the method that called it or not, depending on the configuration of the component. This provides an easy mechanism to manage transactions based on component boundaries.

The transactional rules for entity beans are more stringent than for session beans. Entity beans must run within a transaction, so only container-managed transactions may be used for entity beans. (Using bean-managed transactions would allow a programmer to eliminate transactions for an entity bean through exclusion of transaction code, and that is not allowed by the specification.)

Naming

The naming services provided by the EJB application server allow the component to use a JNDI name server to access resources. These resources could be an EJB component, a data source, or an environment entry that provides configuration information for the component. The naming service allows entries to be retrieved as `object` references, which may be cast, or *narrowed*, to their specific Java type.

Scalability

The EJB server should provide scalability features that should be enjoyed by the components transparently. The EJB specification does not provide details on what these scalability features should be or how they should be implemented (though it does specify that pooling of EJB components may be done and provides callback methods to allow some control over the process). Virtually all EJB application servers provide some type of scalability feature, though the type and sophistication varies.

Life-Cycle Management

The EJB server should provide life-cycle management services for the component. This means that the application server should find the bean when it is requested and should be able to return a home `object` reference for the bean. When the home object attempts to create or locate the bean, the application server should create or access the remote `object` reference and return it to the client that requested the component.

Life-cycle management also includes the *passivation* of EJBs. If an EJB component has not been accessed for some time, the application server can elect to passivate the bean. When the EJB component is later requested, the application server must be able to find the bean and restore its state.

EJBs can be instantiated before use and kept in a *pool*. Then, when an EJB is requested by a client, it is simply retrieved from the pool and made available to the client, thus avoiding the overhead of object instantiation (for the EJB) at run-time. See Figure 22–2.

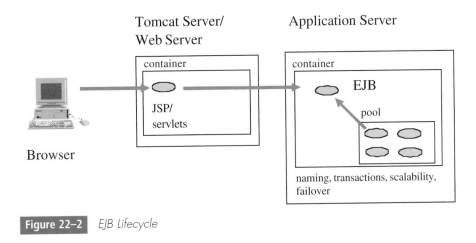

| Figure 22–2 | *EJB Lifecycle* |

EJBs and Transactions

One of the services provided by the EJBs container is transactional control. Transactions can be controlled either programmatically by the developer or declaratively by the container. If transactions for a bean are controlled by the container, they are considered *container-managed transactions* (CMTs) and are declared by making entries in a configuration file used to deploy the EJB application. If the transactions for a bean are controlled by programmatic instructions, then they are considered *bean-managed transactions* (BMTs).

Since entity beans are guaranteed to be synchronized with a persistent data store, they are considered transactional by nature. With session beans, transactions are optional, but with entity beans, transactions are required. Therefore, entity beans must be defined to use CMTs

Developing EJBs

What should be noted about EJBs is that an application server is required to develop and deploy these components. The Sun J2EE download from its Web site includes a development version of an application server, but this is not considered appropriate for a production environment. Application servers range in price from nothing for open-source products (JBoss) to the mid-range prices (JRun and WebLogic) to the high range (IPlanet and WebSphere). (The Web site *www.flashline.com* has a very good application server matrix, which includes a comparison of application servers, their EJB compliance, their prices, and most importantly, user reviews.)

Not all application servers that support the development of EJBs are considered EJB-compliant. Compliance is important in providing portability of EJBs so that an EJB developed and deployed on the application server of one vendor can easily be deployed onto another application server vendor.

EJBs require a very specific coding paradigm. Two interfaces must be coded for the EJB, and the actual bean class must implement a specific interface. Table 22–1 elaborates on these details.

Client applications that access EJBs do not access the EJB directly; they access the bean indirectly through a *proxy* object. A client application will use a naming service to look up the home interface (an `EJBHome` implementation) for the EJB. Once the home interface object is obtained, it is then used to access a remote object for the EJB. Using this remote object, the client application can then interact with the EJB by calling the business methods of the EJB using the object. In this way, the client uses the EJB indirectly via the remote object, the proxy for the actual EJB. See Figure 22–3.

Table 22–1　*EJB Client Communication*

EJB	Extend Interface	Implement Interface
Session Bean	EJBHome EJBObject	SessionBean
Entity Bean	EJBHome EJBObject	EntityBean

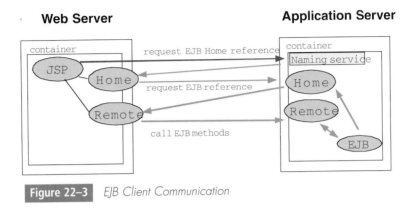

Web Server   **Application Server**

Figure 22–3   *EJB Client Communication*

EJB Code Sample

EJBs require a specific development process. This process is required because of the nature of EJBs, where components must run within a container. Since the container must be able to communicate with the component, there are certain methods the component must implement in order to be able to work within the container.

The following example demonstrates the process of creating an EJB and how multiple beans can communicate. The `myBean` class is being developed as a session bean and therefore must implement the `javax.ejb.SessionBean` interface. This bean will access the `Cust` bean to retrieve customer information.

The `ejbCreate` method is required for the implementation and in this example is an empty-body method. For session beans, this method performs like a constructor, being called once when the bean is created by the container. Were there some initialization activity that needed to be done when the bean was started, the code for it would go in this method.

The `ejbPassivate` method is called when the bean is passivated and is potentially sent to the ready pool, a pool of available EJB components. Likewise, the `ejbActivate` method is called when the bean is retrieved from the ready pool and is set to the appropriate state (its members are set to the appropriate value) for the bean. Since there is no specific code for this bean to implement before it is passivated or when it is activated, these methods have a blank body. If the bean were managing a database connection, we may want it to make a call to the `close` method of the `Connection` class when the bean is passivated and the `ejbPassivate` method is called, and have it establish a new connection in the `ejbActivate` method when the bean is activated.

The `setSessionContext` method is called and passed a parameter for the `SessionContext` for the EJB. It is good practice to save this reference for future use. The `SessionContext` provides methods to implement programmatic security and for programmatic management of transactions.

The ejbRemove method is called when the remove method is executed on the home interface or when the bean no longer has any active connections and the application server is removing the resources associated with the EJB. This is where the component may want to clean up its environment and close any open resources. This implementation does not require any work in this method, and so it has an empty body.

The myBean Class

```
import javax.ejb.*;
import javax.naming.*;
import javax.rmi.*;


public class myBean implements SessionBean {
SessionContext sc;

// SessionBean interface methods

public void ejbCreate() { }


public void ejbPassivate() { }
public void ejbActivate() { }
public void setSessionContext( SessionContext sc ) {
this.sc = sc;
}

public void ejbRemove() {}
```

The myBean Class: The getCustData Method

The getCustData method uses a lookup method call to access another EJB and is therefore a client to another bean. This method obtains the InitialContext and then performs a lookup to obtain the home object for the Cust bean. The object reference obtained by the InitialContext cannot simply be cast to the appropriate type (this is because of the underlying implementation for the lookup call and for backwards compatibility with existing middleware). The PortableRemoteObject narrow method must be used to convert the object reference obtained to the appropriate type.

Once the home object has been converted into the correct type, that of the CustHome class, the home object can be used to create references for the remote object for the Cust bean, acting as a factory for the bean, which is what is done in this method. The remote object reference is then used to call the getCustData method on the Cust bean and return the results to the client bean that accessed myBean. The code for this method is shown next.

The myBean Class: The getCustData Method

```
public String getCustData() {

CustRemote cr   = null;
CustHome    ch  = null;
String retval   = null;

try {

//
// get the InitialContext
//
InitialContext ic = new InitialContext();

//
// lookup our home object
//
Object obj = ic.lookup("Cust");

//
// special cast for home object
//
ch = (CustHome) PortableRemoteObject.narrow( obj,
                                             CustHome.class );
//
// create our remote object
//
cr = ch.create();


//
// call our 'business method'
//
retval = cr.getCustData();


}
catch (NamingException e) {

System.out.println("NamingException caught in getData(): " +
                                    e.getMessage() );
throw new EJBException("naming exception");

}
catch (Exception e) {

System.out.println("Exception caught in getCustData(): " +
                                    e.getMessage() );
throw new EJBException("naming exception");
```

```
}
finally {

   return   retval;


}
}


}
```

The EJBHome Interface

As discussed previously, every EJB created requires a home and remote interface be defined. The `EJBHome` interface represents an implementation of the `Factory` design pattern, since this interface controls the creation of remote objects for the EJB. Using the home interface allows the container to intercede in the creation process and manage pooled resources and perform other housekeeping operations for the bean.

The EJB developer must create a specific interface that extends the `EJBHome` interface, as shown in the following code. A signature for the `create` method must be declared to return the type of the remote interface for the EJB.

It is the responsibility of the application server vendor to provide an implementation for this interface. This is usually done during the deployment process.

The myHome Interface

```
import javax.ejb.*;
import javax.naming.*;
import java.rmi.*;

public interface myHome extends EJBHome {

public myRemote create() throws CreateException, RemoteException ;

}
```

The EJBObject Interface (the Remote Interface)

A remote interface must be declared for the EJB to extend the `EJBObject` interface. This interface must provide signatures for all of the business methods in the EJB class that are to be accessed from the client.

As with the `EJBHome` interface, it is the responsibility of the application server vendor to provide an implementation for this interface during deployment. The remote interface for this example is shown next.

The myRemote.java Interface

```
import javax.naming.*;
import javax.ejb.*;
import java.rmi.*;

public interface myRemote extends EJBObject {

public String getData() throws RemoteException;
public String getCustData() throws RemoteException;


}
```

Deploying the EJB

Once the interfaces and classes for the EJB have been declared, they must be *deployed* into the application server. This deployment process reads a deployment descriptor, an XML-encoded document that describes various properties of the EJB. These properties include but are not limited to transactional behavior, whether a session bean is stateful or stateless, and whether an entity bean is using CMP or BMP.

The application vendor is expected to provide a tool that will perform the deployment process. The process will include reading the deployment descriptor, finding the classes and interfaces, possibly generating implementation code for the interfaces, and making entries into the name server.

EJB Client Code

The client application for an EJB must obtain two `object` references to be able to access the EJB. The first reference it must obtain is the *home* object, the implementation of the `EJBHome` interface for the EJB. Once it has a reference to the home object, it can call the `create` method on the home object (or possibly the `findByPrimaryKey` or other *finder* method if using an entity bean) to receive a reference to the *remote* object. The remote object is an implementation of the `EJBObject` interface that will provide a proxy to the actual EJB running on the application server. For all practical purposes, it is used as though it were a reference to the actual EJB.

The home `object` reference is usually found using the *name server* provided as part of the J2EE-compliant application server. This name server allows name/value pairs to be stored in a lightweight, hierarchical database. The J2EE specification provides that this name server will be provided by the application server vendor, and access to the name server will be provided using the Java JNDI (Java Naming and Directory Interface).

The name/value pairs that can be stored in the name server include the ability to store references to objects. Part of the deployment of an EJB application involves placing a JNDI lookup name and the `object` reference for the home interface into the JNDI namespace.

In this code example, a command-line parameter is optionally passed in to provide the lookup name for the home interface. If a name is not supplied on the command line, then a default name is supplied.

The usual process for an EJB client is to obtain an *initial context* using a call to the `InitialContext` method. This provides access to the name server and allows the `lookup` method to be called, passing a string that corresponds to the name for the home interface (as declared during the deployment process).

The `InitialContext lookup` method will return an `object` reference that must be converted into the appropriate type for the home interface of the EJB. Because of the nature of the underlying communication mechanism for EJBs, the `PortableRemoteObject.narrow` method is used to perform the conversion of the object reference to the type of the home interface.

Now that the home interface has been obtained, a call can be made to the `create` method of the home interface. The `create` method will return a reference to the remote object for our EJB. Once we have this remote object, we can then make calls to the business methods of our EJB. The code for this client program follows:

The TestClient Class

```
import javax.naming.*;
import java.rmi.*;
import javax.rmi.*;

public class testClient {

public static void main( String args[] ) {

//
// home object
//
myHome mh = null;

//
// remote object
//
myRemote mr = null;

try {

//
```

```
// may pass the bean name on the command line
//
String lookupName =null;
if (args.length > 0 )
    lookupName=args[0];
else
    lookupName = "myBean";

//
// get the InitialContext
//
InitialContext ic = new InitialContext();
System.out.println("InitialContext found. " );

//
// get the bean name
//
Object obj = ic.lookup(lookupName);
System.out.println("myBean found. Performing narrow ... " );

//
// get the home object
//
mh = (myHome) PortableRemoteObject.narrow( obj, myHome.class );

//
// create the remote object from the home object
 //
mr = mh.create();
System.out.println("Customer Data: " + mr.getCustData() );

}
catch (Exception e) {
    System.out.println("Exception in main: " + e.getMessage() );
}


}


}
```

When to Use EJBs

EJBs have their place in server-side development. For applications that require high scalability and a some level of session failover capabilities, EJBs are a good fit. This includes sites with a heavy user load and/or the need for transactions to failover transparently to the end user. But for sites that don't have these requirements, the need for using EJBs is not as clear.

EJBs provide the capability to create an application with components that can then be accessed fairly easily from remote locations. Using EJBs, a client application running on a modest hardware platform can access a complex, expensive processing routine and, through the architecture of EJBs, the processing routine will run on the remote hardware platform (where the EJBs are deployed). With this architecture, the resource-intensive processing will be done on the remote machine, which will have the hardware processing to manage the load; it will not be done on the modest client machine.

Many would argue that the centralized, middleware architecture of EJBs provides a better development and deployment paradigm for software in general. Using this architecture, the information technology department maintains a high degree of control of the development and deployment of the component software. Since the EJBs will reside on a centralized platform, the IT department will have control over these machines and the development and runtime environment. Client applications, such as Web applications, can have a much smaller footprint, since they will not need to carry the complex code that will reside in the EJBs on the central server. The messy process of deploying software to client machines is minimized or, depending on departmental responsibilities, possibly even eliminated.

Counter to this argument would be that the deployment of a Web application with JSPs, servlets, and JavaBeans has the same low deployment cost profile as the same application with an EJB application server and does not incur the expense of installing and running the application server.

Overengineering with EJBs

It should be noted that EJBs are not a good fit for every application. In fact, there are a significant number of applications where EJBs are not needed and would represent *over-engineering* the application.

EJBs exact a cost, in terms of both application software for the server and code development time. EJBs require additional software to run, software that could prove expensive if some of the more robust, high-end servers are selected. EJBs also require additional coding effort, since component interfaces must be written, beans must extend interfaces and provide implementations, and then components must be deployed, retested, and often redeployed when the components change (not unusual during development).

EJBs, therefore, exact a higher development cost and a higher production cost that must be justified by the requirements of the application. For applications that do not have stringent failover requirements, can endure having a client restart a session if it fails, and do not have to scale up to 100,000 page hits per day with 3,000 concurrent users, using JSP and JavaBeans may be the preferred solution.

SUMMARY

EJBs are the distributed software component for the Java language and are at the core of the J2EE specification. These components run within in an abstract container implementation provided by an application server. Application servers that are J2EE-compliant provide a set of services that now represent the standard, the basic set of services expected of application servers.

This chapter provided a brief summary of EJBs and discussed how these components are developed with Java. A sample application was used to demonstrate this process.

COMING UP NEXT

The next and final chapter of this book will revisit EJBs and examine more closely how JDBC might be used to provide database access in these components. This discussion will come back to the Java design patterns we saw earlier in the book, specifically data access objects, to provide a useful encapsulation of the data access process. We will see that by applying these design patterns and others, we can reduce the amount of binding, the *collusion* between our EJB components and client applications and between the EJB components and the business tier.

CHAPTER 23

JDBC and Enterprise JavaBeans

INTRODUCTION

As explained in Chapter 22, Enterprise JavaBeans (EJBs) provide a facility for creating a component-based application with Java. EJB components operate within a logical environment, a *container*, which is implemented by an application server. The application server implements the container, which provides the runtime environment for the component.

JDBC IN EJBS

The EJB specification provides for several different types of bean components, including *session beans*, which represent a user session—a user conversational state—and *entity beans*, which are a unique representation of persistent data.

Given these definitions, the entity bean is clearly where JDBC code should be located. Common EJB coding practice suggests that database access code be contained in an entity bean using *bean-managed persistence* (BMP), though this is not a requirement and is not enforced by any existing application servers. In fact, in many cases session beans are used with various associated objects, such as data access objects (DAOs), to provide database access; this is an approach demonstrated in this chapter.

The latest specification for entity beans, the EJB 2.0 specification, details a number of changes in entity beans. These changes are designed to improve performance and to allow better implementations of container-managed persistence (CMP). The use of CMP, where the container manages database access, of course precludes the use of JDBC and is therefore out of scope and not a topic for a JDBC book.

This chapter details the use of EJBs, both session beans and entity beans, and how JDBC code should be used with these components. We will begin the discussion with entity beans.

Entity Beans and JDBC

Since entity beans represent persistent data, data that resides in a data store, this is where you would expect to find JDBC code. But the entity bean specification makes no commitment to JDBC and makes some effort to provide for object-relational mapping through these components using CMP. Instead, we would expect to find JDBC code in the alternative to CMP: Bean Managed Persistence.

An entity bean that is declared to use **container-managed persistence** will allow the container to control persistence, letting the container determine how the runtime content of the bean will be read from or written to the database. With this approach, the developer will not need to provide any code for the persistence. Instead, the application server will provide a tool to describe how this persistence will be managed. Obviously, JDBC is not needed here.

An entity bean may also be declared to use **bean-managed persistence,** where the developer must write the database code to manage persistence for the bean. Using this type of persistence, developers must create instance members for the bean and must write the code to load data from the database and apply these values to the instance members for the bean and to write updated instance members to the database.

If CMP works and works well, then there is no compelling reason to write database access code for an entity bean. But there is the catch. As application queries grow more complex, the more likely it is that CMP tools which provide the object-relational mapping for the application will fail or will result in sluggish performance. For this reason, it is still common to find JDBC being used in EJB applications.

Connecting EJBs to Presentation Tier Components

As we have discussed in a number of previous chapters, design patterns provide useful abstractions to help guide the development process. These patterns represent proven solutions for recurring problems. One pattern that has proven useful in the development of EJB solutions is the *session facade* design pattern. Using this design pattern, the EJB session bean provides a layer of control between the objects it works with and the client code accessing it. The EJB client invokes the session bean and submits requests. The session bean is responsible for gathering any resources needed, using various helper objects. The facade object also plays a controller role, managing the work flow and formatting the results to return to the client. See Figure 23–1.

The following example illustrates the use of the *session facade* design pattern using a session bean that provides the help desk status information for a servlet. This bean exposes a simple interface, a single method, which is accessed by the client servlet. Much of the work being performed by the EJB has been isolated in the helper objects so that ultimately the code needed to create the session facade

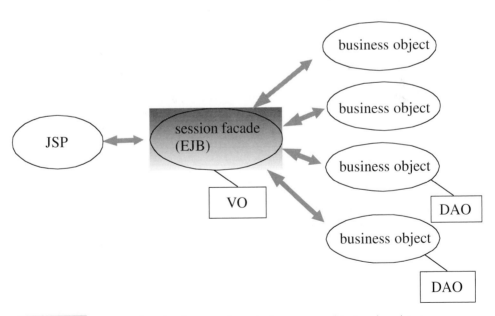

Figure 23–1   *Session facade object works with data access object, value objects and business objects*

EJB is relatively simple. The following sections provide an explanation of the code for the session bean and its interfaces and for the helper class used in the example. See Figure 23–2.

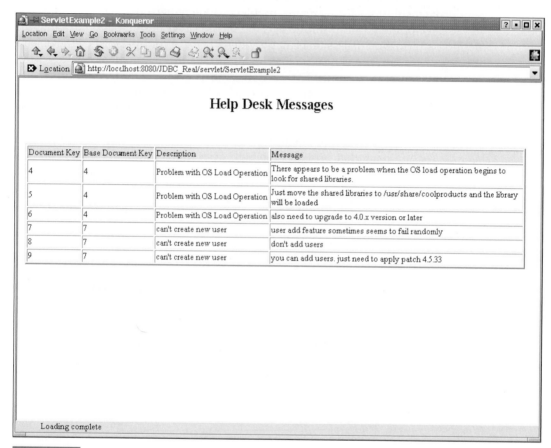

Figure 23–2   *ServletExample2 Output*

THE SERVLETEXAMPLE2 CLASS DECLARATION

The `ServletExample2` servlet receives an XML document and uses the Saxon transformation API to transform the XML document into an HTML table (as demonstrated in Chapter 20).

The servlet uses an EJB component to access the database and encode the data as an XML document. The first code block shown here simply declares the class and various instance members needed to perform its work.

The ServletExample2 Class: Class Declaration

```
package ServletExamples;

import java.io.*;
import java.text.*;
import java.util.*;
import javax.servlet.*;
import javax.servlet.http.*;


import java.sql.*;
import java.net.*;
import java.io.*;

// j2ee
import javax.ejb.*;
import javax.naming.*;
import java.rmi.*;
import javax.rmi.*;
import java.io.Serializable;

// our packages
import db.*;
import jdbcutil.*;
import movies.ejb.*;

// saxon
import com.icl.saxon.trax.*;
import org.xml.sax.*;

public class ServletExample2 extends HttpServlet {

ServletConfig      config;
ServletContext     context;

MoviesFacadeRemote moviesEJB;

//
// for Saxon XML transformations
//
Processor   processor;
Templates   templates;
Transformer transformer;

String             defaultStyleSheet = "file:/stylesheets/xslt/rs.xsl";
...
```

The ServletExample2 Class: doGet Method

The next code block shows the implementation of the `doGet` method for the servlet. This method is called by the servlet container to respond to the HTTP `GET` request. The code sample shown here obtains the `PrintWriter` object from the response and displays some HTML formatting elements to the output writer. The `getQueryResults` method is then called and returns an XMLformatted document, as a string, containing the results of the query.

Once the XML document has been returned, it is transformed into an HTML table, using the SAXON transformation API, as was done in Chapter 20. `transform` method accepts the XML document as a `Reader` (`java.io.Reader`) by wrapping the string with a `StringReaderPrintWriter` as a `Result` (part of the SAXON API) class.

The ServletExample2 Class: The doGet Method

```
public void doGet(HttpServletRequest request,
                  HttpServletResponse response)
   throws IOException, ServletException
{
    PrintWriter out = response.getWriter();

    out.println("<html>");
    out.println("<head>");

   out.println("<title>ServletExample2</title>");
    out.println("</head>");
    out.println("<body bgcolor=\"white\">");

    try {

    //
    // retrieve the query results as an XML document
    //
    String xmlDoc = getQueryResults();

    //
    // transform the XML to the format for our
    // output (an HTML table)
     //
      Transformer transformer = templates.newTransformer();
      transformer.transform( new InputSource(
                                   new StringReader( xmlDoc ) ),
                              new Result( out ) );


      out.println("</body>");
```

```
        out.println("</html>");
    }
   catch (Exception e) {
        log( "Exception in doGet: " + e.getMessage() );
   }


   }
```

ServletExample2 Class: The getQueryResults Method

The getQueryResults method is called in the doGet method to return an XML document moviesEJB, and calls the getHelpDeskStatus method. This returns a string containing the XML formatted document, which is returned to the calling method.

```
...
public String getQueryResults() {
String retVal = null;
try {
     retVal = moviesEJB.getHelpDeskStatus();
}
catch (RemoteException e) {
        //context.log(
        "RemoteException in ServletExample2.getQueryResults: " +
        e.getMessage() );
        System.out.println(
        "RemoteException in ServletExample2.getQueryResults: " +
        e.getMessage() );
}
finally {
   return retVal;
}


}
...
```

The ServletExample2 Class: The init Method

The init method is responsible for initializing the servlet to be used in the eb application. This method is called once when the servlet is first loaded and will not be called again. The init method is, as the name implies, a good location to perform initialization work, work which for performance reasons we do not want to be doing each time the servlet is invoked. The code for this method is shown next.

The init Method

```
public void init( ServletConfig config ) {

Hashtable env = new Hashtable();

        this.config = config;
      this.context = config.getServletContext();

        //
        // get the location of the xslt stylesheet from a
            // context parameter
        //
        String styleSheet = context.getInitParameter(
                            "XsltStyleSheet" );

try {
        //
        // build the URL for the stylesheet
        //
        if ( styleSheet == null )
            styleSheet = defaultStyleSheet;
         else
            styleSheet = "file:" + styleSheet;

            //
        // create the objects we need for the XSL transformation
        //
        processor = Processor.newInstance("xslt");

            //
         // get an InputStream from the URL
            //
        templates = processor.process(new InputSource(
                        new URL( styleSheet ).openStream() ) );

        transformer = templates.newTransformer();

          //
          // get a connection to the EJB server
        //
            env.put( "java.naming.factory.initial",
                        "org.jnp.interfaces.NamingContextFactory");
            env.put( "java.naming.provider.url",
                        "jnp://localhost:1099");
             env.put( "java.naming.factory.url.pkgs",
                        "org.jboss.naming:org.jnp.interfaces");

        InitialContext init = new InitialContext( env );

          //
```

```
            // get the home object
            //
            Object obj =    init.lookup("ejb/MoviesFacade");


            //
            // perform a special 'cast' on the home object
            //
            MoviesFacadeHome home = (MoviesFacadeHome)
                PortableRemoteObject.narrow( obj, MoviesFacadeHome.class );


            //
            // create our remote reference
            //
            moviesEJB = home.create();

}
catch (ProcessorException e) {
        System.out.println(
            "ProcessorException in ServletExample2.init: " +
            e.getMessage() );
}
catch (NamingException e) {
        System.out.println(
            "NamingException in ServletExample2.init: " +
            e.getMessage() + " - " + e );
}
catch (Exception e) {
        System.out.println(
            "Exception in ServletExample2.init: " +
            e.getMessage() );
}



}

}
```

This code performs much of the initialization work seen in the ServletExample1 class shown in Chapter 20: the XSLT stylesheet is chosen and the transformer, template, and processor are created. What is different about this init method is the work performed to act as a client to an EJB bean. Environment entries are stored in a Hashtable, which is then passed into the InitialContext constructor as a parameter. This is done because the servlet is running within the Tomcat server and would default to accessing Tomcat's JNDI name server; we need to access the application server (JBoss) at this point.

Once the InitialContext is obtained, the lookup method is executed to find the home object for the MoviesFacade bean. For backwards compatibility and to maintain portability, this home object must be cast using a special method,

PortableRemoteObject narrow method. The result of the narrow call is the appropriate home object for the MoviesFacadeBean EJB.

This home object for the bean then acts as a factory for obtaining references to the remote object for the MoviesFacadeBean EJB. The create method for the home object acts as the factory method, returning an object reference for the remote object (moviesEJB).

The remote object is technically a proxy; it is not the EJB, since that is running on the server. But the remote object gives us complete access to the EJB through the methods we have exposed to client code by defining them in the remote interface (MoviesFacadeRemote), which we will examine shortly.

THE MOVIESFACADEBEAN CLASS

The MoviesFacadeBean class provides the actual business methods for the EJB. Since it is a session bean, it must implement the SessionBean interface. Because of the internal operation of the helper class for the session bean, we need to declare it to be a *stateful* session bean.

The methods in any class implemented as an EJB can perform a wide range of operations but for maximum portability they should not access local resources (disk files, open network connections), should not use threads, and should have serializable arguments if they are going to be exposed to client code by defining the signature in the remote interface. The code for the MoviesFacadeBean class is shown next.

MoviesFacadeBean **Class: The Class Declaration**

```
package movies.ejb;

import javax.ejb.*;
import java.rmi.*;
import java.io.Serializable;

import java.sql.*;
import javax.sql.*;
import javax.naming.*;

import db.*;
import jdbcutil.*;

public class MoviesFacadeBean implements SessionBean {

EJBHome    ejbHome;
Handle     ejbHandle;

DBUtil     dbutil;
```

```
StatusDAO statusDAO;

PreparedStatement statusQuery1;

SessionContext context;
...
```

The MoviesFacadeBean Class: Method Declarations

This EJB class contains a single method definition that is exposed to the client code: the `getHelpDeskStatus` method, as shown in the following code example. The *helper object*, the `statusDAO` DAO, to retrieve general status information for a hypothetical help desk. Since the `getGeneralStatus` method of the `statusDAO` object retrieves all active help desk messages, it does not require any parameters be passed to express filter criteria.

The `getGeneralStatus` method of the `StatusDAO` class returns a `ResultSet`. Since we have created a servlet that uses an XSLT transformer to render output based on XML input, we would prefer to have the results formatted in an XML document. This is accomplished through the use of a helper class, the `JDBCXML` class. The `ResultSet` returned from the `statusDAO` object is passed to the `JDBCXML toXMLString` method, which returns a string containing an XML document based on the `ResultSet`.

The `ejbCreate` method, which is invoked each time a session bean is created, is used to create the `statusDAO` object, passing in an argument for the name of the `DataSource` to use to the `statusDAO` constructor.

The `setSessionContext` method is called when the session bean is created and at other times during the life of the bean. This associates the bean with the container in which it is running. The common practice is to save the context to an instance member, as is shown in this example. The `SessionContext` object is used to access security information, obtain a home object reference, and obtain a transaction control object. The code for these methods is shown next.

The MoviesFacadeBean Class Methods

```
//
// return XML formatted string of help desk status
//
public String getHelpDeskStatus() {

        // getGeneralStatus returns a ResultSet which we
        // will convert/transform to an XML formatted string
        //
        return JDBCXML.toXMLString( statusDAO.getGeneralStatus() );
  }
```

```
public void ejbCreate() throws CreateException {

  //
  // give constructor the name of the DataSource to use
  //
  statusDAO  = new StatusDAO( "java:/knowledgebase" );

}

public void setSessionContext(SessionContext sc) {

      //
      // store the SessionContext
      //
      this.context = sc;
}


// ** required, but not used **
public void remove() {}
public void ejbPostCreate() { }
public void ejbRemove() { }
public void ejbActivate() { }
public void ejbPassivate() { }

public MoviesFacadeBean() {}

}
```

The MoviesFacadeBean Helper Objects: The StatusDAO

Using the session facade design pattern, the session facade object is responsible for marshaling and coordinating the resources needed to accomplish its task. In this example, this is accomplished using a single DAO to perform the low-level specifics of data access.

The StatusDAO class represents a simple DAO which provides status information to the facade bean. The code for this class is shown in the following example.

The StatusDAO class approaches the execution of the status query in a manner similar to that shown in previous examples. The actual query to be executed is not hardcoded into the program but is instead stored in a environment entry that can be easily retrieved by the component. Thus, changing the query does not require the component (the MovieEntityBean EJB) to be changed and redeployed.

The constructor for the StatusDAO class establishes a connection to the database using the DBUtil helper class (see Chapter 16). The InitialContext is then accessed to obtain the environment entry for the status query to execute. With EJBs, as indicated in the EJB specification, environment entries are available using a JNDI lookup, as shown in this example. The value of the query is retrieved as a string and is stored in an instance member for the EJB.

The final step in the constructor is to call the `prepareQueries` method. As shown in the code listing below, this will prepare the single query that has just been stored in the instance member (`statusQuery1`).DBUtil `createPreparedStatement` method simply creates a prepared statement on its internal connection; it returns a `PreparedStatement` reference.

The `getGeneralStatus` method, the method called by the `MoviesFacadeBean` to retrieve the help desk status, executes the internal prepared statement and returns the result as a `ResultSet`. Because this method expects to have an active `PreparedStatement` reference (it expects the underlying connection for the `PreparedStatement` to be active), the session bean must be declared to be a stateful session bean, meaning that the container will ensure the state of the member variables of the session bean will be retained even if the bean has been passivated. Since the `MoviesFacadeBean` contains an instance of the `StatusDAO` class and expects to be able to use it after it has been created (in the `ejbCreate` method of the bean), then we must ensure that the container restores the proper reference for the `StatusDAO` class when the `MoviesFacadeBean` is invoked; defining the bean as a stateful session bean will accomplish this.

The StatusDAO Class Definition

```
package db;

import java.sql.*;
import javax.naming.*;

public class StatusDAO {

DBUtil                          dbutil;
PreparedStatement   generalStatusQuery;

String statusQuery1;


public StatusDAO( String dataSourceName ) {

try {

    dbutil =  new DBUtil( dataSourceName );

    //
    // get the query from an environment entry - don't hardcode it
    //
```

```java
    InitialContext ctx = new InitialContext();
    statusQuery1 = (String) ctx.lookup("java:comp/env/statusQuery1");

    //
    // create a prepared statement for the query
    //
    prepareQueries();

}
catch (Exception e) {
    System.out.println("Exception in StatusDAO.constructor: " +
                        e.getMessage() );
}

}

private void prepareQueries() {

try {

    generalStatusQuery = dbutil.createPreparedStatement(
                            statusQuery1 );

}
catch (Exception e) {
    System.out.println(
            "Exception in StatusDAO.prepareQueries: " +
            e.getMessage() + " - " + e );
}

}

public ResultSet getGeneralStatus( ) {
//
// return a ResultSet with the results of the general status query
//
ResultSet rs = null;

 try {

    rs =  generalStatusQuery.executeQuery();

  }
  catch (SQLException e ) {
        System.out.println(
            "Exception caught in StatusDAO.prepareQuery: " +
            e.getMessage() );
  }
  finally {
        return rs;
```

```
        }

      }

}
```

The MoviesFacadeHome and MoviesRemote Interfaces

The home and remote interfaces for the `MoviesFacadeBean` are shown below. These interfaces are required to create the EJB. The methods identified in the remote interface are the methods that will be visible to the client. The home interface for session beans declares the `create` methods for the bean and can optionally declare `create` methods with multiple arguments, though that is not done here. Each `create` method declared in the home interface must have a corresponding `ejbCreate` method declared in the session bean class.

The MoviesFacadeHome Interface

```
package movies.ejb;

import javax.ejb.*;
import java.io.Serializable;
import java.rmi.RemoteException;

public interface MoviesFacadeHome extends EJBHome {

  MoviesFacadeRemote create() throws RemoteException, CreateException;


}
```

The MoviesFacadeRemote Interface

```
package movies.ejb;

import javax.ejb.*;
import java.io.Serializable;
import java.rmi.RemoteException;

public interface MoviesFacadeRemote extends EJBObject {
    public String getHelpDeskStatus() throws RemoteException;
}
```

THE MOVIESENTITYBEAN EJB

The entity bean is an EJB that represents a unique instance of an entity in a permanent data store. Each entity bean is represented by a unique ID: a primary key. Unlike session beans, which are usually created for use, an entity bean represents persistent data and is therefore usually found and retrieved from the data store.

The previous example showed the use of JDBC in a helper object for a session bean. The helper object implemented the DAO design pattern, which isolates and encapsulates the data access activity into a coarse-grained object. By using this design pattern, the details of the data and the data access are isolated from the session facade bean.

DAOs can also have utility when used with entity beans, specifically entity beans using BMP. With this approach, the entity bean simply *wraps* the DAO. The following code sample demonstrates this approach.

The `ListMovies` JSP page (shown below) used the `MoviesBean` JavaBean to access an entity bean. In this example, the `MoviesBean` acted as a presentation tier *business object*. The business object is sometimes referred to as a *business object* design pattern. This is a generalized category for an object that takes on the responsibility of managing business logic, thus removing that responsibility from some other object or component.

On the presentation tier, where we have JSPs and servlets creating the presentation for the user, it is useful to remove business logic from these components and allow their development to be focused on creating a presentation. This is just what was done with the `ListMovies` JSP page. Using the `MoviesBean` object, the only Java code exposed on the JSP page was a call to the `MoviesBean` `loadBean` method, which was passed the `movie_id` for the bean to load. All other interaction with the JavaBean on the JSP was through JSP `useBean` tags, the preferable method of accessing Java code on JSP pages as shown below.

The ListMovies JSP Page

```
<HTML>
<BODY bgcolor="white">

<jsp:useBean id="moviesBean" class="movies.beans.MoviesBean" scope="session" />

<!- load the bean with the request parameter ->
<% moviesBean.loadBean( request.getParameter( "movie_id" ) ); %>

<br>
<font face="Helvetica, Sans-serif" size=+3 >
<center>
<b>Movie Information for "<jsp:getProperty name="moviesBean" property="movie_name"
/>"   </b>
</center>
```

```
</font>
<br>
<br>


<center>
<table border=1 cellpadding=2 bgcolor="white">
<tr>
<td>
<img src="http://localhost:8080/JDBC_Real/servlet/BlobView/?movie_id=<%=
request.getParameter ("movie_id") %>" name="Box Picture" align=center >
</td>
</tr>
</table>
</center>

<br>
<br>
<br>

<center>

<font face="Helvetica, Sans-serif" size=+2 color="blue">

<table border=1 cellpadding=2 bgcolor="white">

<tr>
<td bgcolor="#C0D9D9">Movie ID</td>
<td bgcolor="#C0D9D9">Movie Name</td>
<td bgcolor="#C0D9D9">Release Date</td>
<td bgcolor="#C0D9D9">Movie Description</td>
<td bgcolor="#C0D9D9">Special Promotion</td>
<td bgcolor="#C0D9D9">Update Date</td>
<td bgcolor="#C0D9D9">Category</td>

</tr>

<tr>
<td> <jsp:getProperty name="moviesBean" property="movie_id" /> </td>
<td> <jsp:getProperty name="moviesBean" property="movie_name" /> </td>
<td> <jsp:getProperty name="moviesBean" property="release_date" /> </td>
<td> <jsp:getProperty name="moviesBean" property="movie_desc" /> </td>
<td> <jsp:getProperty name="moviesBean" property="special_promotion" /> </td>
<td> <jsp:getProperty name="moviesBean" property="update_date" /> </td>
<td> <jsp:getProperty name="moviesBean" property="category" /> </td>

</tr>

</table>
</font>
</center>
```

```
<br>
<br>

<br>
<br>

</HTML>
</BODY>
```

THE MOVIESBEAN JAVABEAN

The `MoviesBean` JavaBean was presented in Chapter 21 and is shown here again just to identify the portions of the class that pertain to the retrieval of entity beans. This code is explained after the listing.

The MoviesBean JavaBean

```
package movies.beans;

import java.rmi.*;
import javax.naming.*;
import javax.rmi.*;
import javax.ejb.*;
import java.util.*;

import db.*;
import movies.ejb.*;

public class MoviesBean extends MoviesVO {

InitialContext context;

MoviesEntityRemote movies;
MoviesEntityHome    moviesHome;


public MoviesBean() {

try {
    Hashtable env = new Hashtable();

    //
    // get a connection to the EJB server (Jboss)
    //
    env.put( "java.naming.factory.initial",
             "org.jnp.interfaces.NamingContextFactory");
    env.put( "java.naming.provider.url", "jnp://localhost:1099");
    env.put( "java.naming.factory.url.pkgs",
```

```
                 "org.jboss.naming:org.jnp.interfaces");
    context = new InitialContext( env );


    //
    // get the movies entity bean
    //
    moviesHome = (MoviesEntityHome) PortableRemoteObject.narrow(
                                context.lookup("ejb/MoviesEntityBean"),
                                MoviesEntityHome.class );

}
catch (NamingException e) {
      System.out.println(
            "NamingException in MoviesBean constructor: " +
            e.getMessage() );
}
catch (Exception e) {
      System.out.println("Exception in MoviesBean constructor: " +
                        e.getMessage() );
}

}

public void loadBean( String movie_id ) {

try {

    //
    // lookup this movie_id
    //
    movies = moviesHome.findByPrimaryKey(new Integer( movie_id ));

    //
    // set this object to look like the VO populated by the lookup
    //
    MoviesVO vo = movies.getMoviesVO();

    //
    // set our Value Object to look like the
    // value object returned  by the getMovies method
    //
    setMoviesVO( vo );

}
catch (RemoteException e) {
      System.out.println("RemoteException in MoviesBean loadbean: " +
                        e.getMessage() );
}
catch (FinderException e) {
      System.out.println("FinderException in MoviesBean loadbean: " +
                        e.getMessage() );
```

```
}
catch (Exception e) {
      System.out.println("Exception in MoviesBean loadbean: " +
                              e.getMessage() + " - " + e );
}
catch (Throwable e) {
      System.out.println("Exception in MoviesBean loadbean: " +
                              e.getMessage() + " - " + e );
}


}


}
```

The MoviesBean constructor calls the InitialContext constructor, using various environment entries to indicate how to access the name server of the JBoss application server. This is required because the JSP page will be executing inside the Tomcat Web server and the default InitialContext will not access the JBoss server. (Other application servers or Web servers, and the use of JBoss with the embedded Tomcat server, may offer a federated namespace that does not require the environment to be set or that sets the environment using different entries; the access of the InitialContext shown here is in no way universal.)

The MoviesEntityBean home object is then obtained through a call to the InitialContext (which is accessing the JBoss server namespace). For reasons explained previously, the home object must be narrowed in order to be accessible as a normal Java object. The constructor then stores the home object reference in an instance member for the entity bean.

The loadBean method, the method called from the ListMovies page, calls the findByPrimaryKey method of the home object (referred to as a *finder* method). The method call returns the remote object for the entity bean, specifically for the entity bean referenced by the movie_id passed into the findByPrimaryKey method.

This remote object is stored in an instance member and is then used to call the getMoviesVO method on the entity bean. This will return a reference to the internal value object of the entity bean, but since this is being done with remote object communication, the value object will be passed by value and copied into the local JVM memory space. The value object reference is then passed to the setMoviesVO method for the MoviesBean class (which is a subclass of MoviesVO). This method will set the internal members of the MoviesBean class to those of the value object of the entity bean, thus synchronizing the MoviesBean to the entity bean.

At this point, the internal members of the MoviesBean (as inherited from the MoviesVO value object) are set to the correct values. The MoviesBean is ready to be accessed by the ListMovies page through the JSP useBean tags. When the JSP page is invoked, the occurrences of the useBean tags on the page will be mapped to the MoviesBean object.

THE MOVIESENTITYBEAN CLASS

The `MoviesEntityBean` class provides an entity bean wrapper for the `MoviesDAO` class, which implements the DAO design pattern. As with previous examples, the details of the data access are encapsulated in the DAO. The implementation of the entity bean class merely maps the entity bean methods called by the application server (the callback methods) to the appropriate `MoviesDAO` methods. The code listing for the class declaration and `findByPrimaryKey` method is shown next.

The MoviesEntityBean Class Declaration and findByPrimaryKey Method

```
package movies.ejb;

import javax.ejb.*;
import java.rmi.*;
import java.io.Serializable;

import java.sql.*;
import javax.sql.*;
import javax.naming.*;

import db.*;
import jdbcutil.*;

public class MoviesEntityBean implements EntityBean {

EJBHome     ejbHome;
Handle      ejbHandle;

EntityContext context;

MoviesDAO moviesDAO;
MoviesVO    moviesVO;

//
// return XML formatted string of help desk status
//
public Integer ejbFindByPrimaryKey( Integer movie_id) throws FinderException {

Integer retVal = null;

try {
        // getGeneralStatus returns a ResultSet which we
        // will convert/transform to an XML formatted string
        //

    //
    // load our DAO using this movie_id
```

```
//
if ( moviesDAO == null ) {
    moviesDAO = new MoviesDAO("java:/moviesmysql");
    moviesVO  = new MoviesVO();
  }


  moviesDAO.loadDAO( movie_id.intValue() );

//
// if the movie_name has not been set, then no movie
// was found for this primary key
//
if ( moviesDAO.getMoviesVO().getMovie_name()!= null )   {
    retVal = movie_id;
}


}
catch (Exception e) {
      System.out.println("Exception in findbyPrimaryKey: " +
                            e.getMessage() + e );
}

finally {

    //
    // return the primary key
    //
    return retVal;
}

}
```

The class declaration for the MoviesEntityBean class provides instance members for a MoviesDAO DAO and a MoviesVO value object. A reference for the EntityContext is also declared.

The ejbFindbyPrimaryKey method takes an integer argument for the primary key of the movie to find. The purpose of this method is simply to establish whether or not the record exists in the database. It verifies whether or not the record exists. and if the record does not exist, it returns a null reference. If the record does exist, it returns the primary key for the record.

The method code checks to determine whether or not the MoviesDAO exists. If it does not, then a MoviesDAO object is created and assigned to the instance member for the entity bean, and an instance of the MoviesVO object is also created.

Since the DAO we have defined does not have a specific locate method, we simply call the loadDAO method and attempt to load the DAO for the movie_id that has been passed. After loading the DAO, we test the movie_name for a null value. If the movie_name field is not null, then we assert the DAO has been loaded and the primary key for the entity bean does exist. (A more efficient implementation would simply do a quick database lookup or select a count of records from the database to determine the records existence.)

Note that the code for the `ejbFindByPrimaryKey` method is not expected to load the entity bean; the `ejbLoad` method will be called by the container to perform that function.

The MoviesEntityBean Class: The getMoviesVO, set MoviesVO and ejbCreate Methods

The `getMoviesVO` method performs the simple task of returning the internal value object for the entity bean. The `setMoviesDAO` method takes a `MovieVO` object reference as an argument and calls the `MoviesDAO loadDAO` method to set the internal value object for the `MoviesDAO` to the values of the `MoviesVO` value object passed as an argument.

The `ejbCreate` method performs the work of adding a new movie record to the persistent data store for the method parameters that have been passed in. The method code creates a new `MoviesDAO` object and a new `MoviesVO` object and assigns the `MoviesVO` instance members to the values that have been passed into the method. (This example does not set all fields of the movie record.)

The `MoviesDAO loadDAO` method is then called to set the members of the `MoviesDAO` to the values of the value object. The `insertDAO` method is then called to insert the contents of the DAO into the database. The code for these methods is shown next.

The MoviesEntityBean Class: The getMoviesVO, set MoviesVO and ejbCreate Methods

```
public MoviesVO getMoviesVO() {
//
// return the internal Value Object
//

   return moviesDAO.getMoviesVO();

}

public void setMoviesVO( MoviesVO moviesVO) {

   //
   // set the internal value object for the DAO
   // to that of the value object being sent
   //
   moviesDAO.loadDAO( moviesVO );

}
```

```
public Integer ejbCreate(int movie_id, String movie_name, String category) throws
CreateException {
//
// create a record for this primary key in the permanent data store
//

try {

    //
    // this is a new entity, so we require a new DAO
    //
    moviesDAO = new MoviesDAO("java:/moviesmysql");
    moviesVO  = new MoviesVO();

    //
    // set our elements to the parameter being passed in
    //
    moviesVO.setMovie_id( movie_id );
    moviesVO.setMovie_name( movie_name );
    moviesVO.setCategory( category );

    //
    // set the DAO to match our Value Object
    //
    moviesDAO.loadDAO( moviesVO );

    //
    // insert into the database
    //
    moviesDAO.insertDAO();

}
catch (SQLException e) {
    System.out.println("Exception in ejbCreate: " + e.getMessage() );
}
finally {
    return new Integer( movie_id );
}

}
```

The MoviesEntityBean Class: The ejbLoad and ejbStore Methods

The `ejbLoad` and `ejbStore` methods are called by the container when it determines it needs to synchronize the bean with the database. Exactly when the methods will be called is implementation-specific, but the developer can be assured they will be called to perform database synchronization.

The `ejbLoad` method loads data from the permanent data store (the database) to the entity bean. The `ejbLoad` method shown below simply maps the call to the `MoviesDAO loadDAO` method after checking to be assured that there is in fact an active instance of the DAO to use. The code in the method should not assume that the primary key value of the current state is the correct primary key. Good coding practice uses the primary key value as made available through the entity context. Since the primary key has been defined to be an instance of `java.lang.Integer` and the `loadDAO` method expects an integer primitive, we call the `intValue` method of the `Integer` class to get the correct form for the method argument.

The `ejbStore` method writes the current contents of the entity bean to the data base. This method can assume that the current values of the entity bean are set correctly and simply needs to write its contents to the database. This is done by calling the `MoviesDAO updateDAO` method.

The ejbLoad and ejbStore Methods

```
public void ejbLoad() {
//
// load the entity bean from the database
//
try {

if ( moviesDAO == null ) {

    //
    // DAO constructor receives name of DataSource to use
    //
    moviesDAO = new MoviesDAO("java:/moviesmysql");
    moviesVO  = new MoviesVO();

}

    //
    // synch with the database using the primary key value
    // passed as a parameter
    //
    moviesDAO.loadDAO(
        ((Integer) context.getPrimaryKey()).intValue() );
}
catch (Exception e) {
    System.out.println("Exception in ejbLoad: " +
                        e.getMessage() + " - " + e );
}


}
```

```
public void ejbStore() {
//
// store the contents of the Entity Bean in the permanent data store
//
try {

    //
    // assert our current state is correct
    //
    moviesDAO.updateDAO();

}
catch (SQLException e ) {
    System.out.println("Exception in ejbLoad: " + e.getMessage() );
}

}
```

The MoviesEntityBean Class: The ejbRemove and ejbPostCreate Methods

The `ejbRemove` method is called when the `remove` method of the home object is called by client code; it is not called indirectly by the container. The result of executing this method is to remove the corresponding record for the entity bean from the database.

The implementation of `ejbRemove` shown here maps to the `MoviesDAO` `deleteDAO` method. This method takes an argument for the primary key of the movie to delete. This method cannot be sure that the state of the bean contains the correct primary key, so the primary key is retrieved from the `EntityContext`.

The `ejbPostCreate` is called by the container after the entity bean has been created. Since there is no specific action required for this entity bean, this implementation is left empty.

The MoviesEntityBean Class: The ejbRemove and ejbPostCreate Methods

```
public void ejbRemove() {
//
// remove the record in the permanent data store which relates to
// this entity bean
//
try {

    moviesDAO.deleteDAO(
        ((Integer) context.getPrimaryKey()).intValue() );

}
catch (SQLException e ) {
```

```
       System.out.println( "SQLException in ejbRemove: " + e.getMessage() );
}


}
```

```
public void ejbPostCreate(int movie_id, String movie_name, String category) throws
CreateException { }
```

The MoviesEntityBean Class: The ejbActivate, ejbPassivate, unsetEntityContext, and setEntityContext Methods

The `ejbActivate` and `ejbPassivate` methods are called when the bean is moved in and out of the pool of available entity beans. Since we require no specific action to be taken for this bean, we do not need to provide an implementation.

The `setEntityContext` method is used as an initialization point for the bean. The `ejbCreate` method is called if a new entity bean is being created. But the `setEntityContext` method is called before most other callback methods are called. This is therefore a good place to locate initialization code for an entity bean.

This example tests for whether or not the `MoviesDAO` and `MoviesVO` instance members have been created. If they have not been created, then they are instantiated. The method also stores the `EntityContext` passed into the method in an instance member.

The `unsetEntityContext` is available to perform certain actions before an entity context is removed from the active list in the container. This could be used to release database resources or perform similar actions. Since we have no specific resources to release, we do not provide an implementation for this method.

The ejbActivate, ejbPassivate, unsetEntityContext, and setEntityContext Methods

```
public void ejbActivate() { }
public void ejbPassivate() { }

public void setEntityContext(EntityContext ec) {
//
// perform our initialization here.
//

    //
    // create the Data Access Object and Value Object
    //
    if ( moviesDAO == null ) {
       moviesDAO = new MoviesDAO( "java:/moviesmysql" );
       moviesVO  = new MoviesVO();
    }
```

```
//
// store the session context
//
this.context = ec;

}


public void unsetEntityContext( ) {}

}
```

The MoviesEntityBean Home Interface

The home and remote interfaces for the `MoviesEntityBean` are shown next. These interfaces are required by the EJB specification and are used to allow the container to create a proxy object (the remote object) and a home object (a factory object) for the entity bean.

The home interface defines all of the `create` methods and `finder` methods the entity bean will be exposing to the client. This example uses a single finder, the `findByPrimaryKey` method, and a single `create` method.

The remote interface extends the `EJBObject` interface and contains the one method this entity bean exposes to the client: the `getMoviesVO` method.

The MoviesEntityHome Interface

```
package movies.ejb;

import javax.ejb.*;
import java.io.Serializable;
import java.rmi.RemoteException;

public interface MoviesEntityHome extends EJBHome {

    public MoviesEntityRemote create(int movie_id,
                                     String movie_name,
                                     String category )
              throws RemoteException, CreateException;
    public MoviesEntityRemote findByPrimaryKey( Integer movie_id ) throws
RemoteException, FinderException;

}
```

The MoviesEntityRemote Interface

```
package movies.ejb;

import javax.ejb.*;
import java.io.Serializable;
import java.rmi.RemoteException;

import db.*;

public interface MoviesEntityRemote extends EJBObject {

    public MoviesVO getMoviesVO() throws RemoteException;
}
```

THE DEPLOYMENT DESCRIPTOR

The EJB *deployment descriptor* is an XML document that provides configuration, deployment, and assembly information on EJB components. J2EEcompliant application servers must provide support for deployment descriptors (though it is not common to require information to be stored elsewhere).

The deployment descriptor provides basic information about the EJB components, the beans being deployed. This information includes the name of the bean and the classes that constitute the bean. If the EJB is a session bean, the deployment descriptor must indicate whether or not the bean is stateful or stateless.

Environment entries can also be made in the deployment descriptor. These values can be retrieved (but not modified) by beans that have been invoked within the container. The entire deployment descriptor for the EJBs is shown below.

EJB Deployment Descriptor

```
<?xml version="1.0" encoding="ISO8859_1"?>
<!DOCTYPE application PUBLIC '-//Sun Microsystems, Inc.//DTD J2EE Application
1.2//EN' 'http://java.sun.com/j2ee/dtds/application_1_2.dtd'>
<application>
  <display-name>JDBC_Real</display-name>
  <description>Demonstration EJBs for JDBC book</description>
  <enterprise-beans>

    <session>
     <ejb-name>MoviesFacade</ejb-name>
     <ejb-class>movies.ejb.MoviesFacadeBean</ejb-class>
     <home>movies.ejb.MoviesFacadeHome</home>
     <remote>movies.ejb.MoviesFacadeRemote</remote>
     <session-type>Stateful</session-type>
```

```
     <transaction-type>Bean</transaction-type>

     <env-entry>
       <env-entry-name>statusQuery1</env-entry-name>
       <env-entry-value> select knowledge_base.doc_key, base_doc_key, doc_name,
message_txt
          from knowledge_base, knowledge_messages
          where knowledge_base.doc_key = knowledge_messages.doc_key
          order by knowledge_base.doc_key, base_doc_key </env-entry-value>
       <env-entry-type>java.lang.String</env-entry-type>
     </env-entry>

   </session>

   <entity>

     <ejb-name>MoviesEntityBean</ejb-name>
     <ejb-class>movies.ejb.MoviesEntityBean</ejb-class>
     <home>movies.ejb.MoviesEntityHome</home>
     <remote>movies.ejb.MoviesEntityRemote</remote>
     <persistence-type>Bean</persistence-type>
     <prim-key-class>java.lang.Integer</prim-key-class>
     <reentrant>False</reentrant>

   </entity>

 </enterprise-beans>

 <assembly-description>
        <container-transaction>
                <method>
                        <ejb-name>MoviesEntityBean</ejb-name>
                        <method-name>*</method-name>
                </method>
                <trans-attribute>Required</trans-attribute>
        </container-transaction>
   </assembly-description>
</application>
```

SUMMARY

EJBs are used in J2EE to represent business tier components. These components run within a container, which provides a number of services for the component.

This chapter provided a set of examples of using JDBC with EJBs. Building on the introductory material of the previous chapter, examples demonstrated the use of EJBs with presentation tier components, such as servlets and JSP pages.

JDBC 3.0

INTRODUCTION

The JDBC 3.0 revision involves the bundling of the 'standard extension' features into the regular JDBC package and the addition of a number of features. The introduction of some of these features is directed at driver developers and will therefore be transparent to most users. In this section, we will review several of the more important visible features of this revision.

RETRIEVING AUTO-INCREMENTED VALUES

The use of auto-incrementing fields is now a common value-added feature of relational databases. But the implementation of this feature varies among database vendors, with some using database 'sequences' to provide the functionality, and others creating 'serial' fields or 'auto-increment' fields. Not only does the implementation vary, but the process of retrieving the values varies, with some vendors storing the value in an `SQLWarning` and others sometimes neglecting to provide for retrieval of the value using JDBC. (The use of 'sequences' allowed distinct values to be retrieved and used SQL syntax, so SQL statements could simply be executed to provide the values.) Since the JDBC API did not dictate how these values could be accessed, these were still JDBC compliant drivers.

With the release of the JDBC 3.0 specification, a facility for retrieving auto-increment values (referred to in the specification as 'auto-generated keys') has been added to the API. What has resulted is a nice, vendor-neutral facility for retrieving the value of an auto-incremented field.

The support for auto-incremented fields has been added to the `Statement` interface by adding additional methods and overloading several existing methods. The `executeUpdate` method has been overloaded to support an integer argument which specifies the type of auto-generated keys facility to use. The type of support is one of the following listed in the table below.

Table A–1   *Auto-Generated Key Support Constants*

Constant Value	Description
NO_GENERATED_KEYS	Indicates generated keys (auto-incremented values) will not be available to be retrieved.
RETURN_GENERATED_KEYS	Indicates that generated keys (auto-incremented values) will be available for retrieval.

The following code demonstrates the retrieval of auto-generated keys.

Retrieving Auto-Generated Keys

```
...
//
// execute the update which will insert an
// auto-increment value
//
int updateCount = stmt.executeUpdate(
          "insert into users values (0, 'Joe Smith')",
                              Statement.RETURN_GENERATED_KEYS );

//
// get the auto-increment value
//
ResultSet rs = stmt.getGeneratedKeys();

//
// in this case, we know there is only one key
```

```
//
int userID=0;
if ( rs.next() )
    userID = rs.getInt(1);
...
```

In this example, the `executeUpdate` method is called with an argument that indicates that it should return auto-generated keys. The `Statement` class `getGeneratedKeys` method is called to return a `ResultSet` with the generated keys. The `ResultSet` allows more than one auto-generated key to be returned. In this example, only one key is returned and that is retrieved using the `ResultSet` `getInt` method.

If there are multiple auto-generated key columns in the table, then it is possible that the return of all values may not be of interest to the application performing the update. In this case, it could be useful to specify only specific key columns to return from the update operation as shown in the following example.

Retrieving Auto-Generated Keys

```
...
String key[] = {"USER_ID"};
...

//
// execute the update which will insert an
// auto-increment value specify the auto-generated
// key field to return
//
int updateCount = stmt.executeUpdate(
        "insert into users values (0, 'Joe Smith')",
        key);

//
// retrieve the generated keys
//
ResultSet rs = stmt.getGeneratedKeys();

//
// we know there is only one key
//
int userID=0;
if ( rs.next() )
    userID = rs.getInt("USER_ID");
...
```

In this example, the 'USER_ID' column is specified as the auto-increment (auto-generated key) to return. This array is then passed as a parameter to the executeUpdate method. The value of the auto-increment field is then retrieved using the ResultSet getInt method.

There are some restrictions on retrieving auto-generated key values. The concurrency type of the cursor (the ResultSet) returned by the getGeneratedKeys method must be of type java.sql.CONCUR_READ_ONLY. The ResultSet type must be one of either java.sql.TYPE_FORWARD_ONLY or java.sql.TYPE_SCROLL_INSENSITIVE.

RESULTSET HOLDABILITY

When a commit operation is executed using the Connection commit method, the cursors created (the ResultSet objects) using that connection may or may not be closed. The default behavior for the ResultSet is implementation-dependent, which means that it can vary depending on the JDBC driver being used. This has often led to issues with JDBC code being ported from one database to another. The DatabaseMetaData supportsOpenCursorsAcrossCommit method provides an indication of how cursor holdability is supported in the JDBC driver being used.

With the release of JDBC 3.0, there is now a means to specify the behavior of cursors after database commit operations. The Connection createStatement method has been overloaded to support an argument which indicates the type of cursor hold behavior. Cursor holdability is specified using the java.sql.ResultSet constants as shown in Table A-2.

Table A–2   *Cursor Holdability Constants*

Argument Value	Description
CLOSE_CURSORS_AT_COMMIT	Cursors will be closed after a commit on the associated connection
HOLD_CURSORS_OVER_COMMIT	Cursors will remain open after a commit on the associated connection

The createStatement method can now be used to specify how cursors will behave as shown in the following code snippet.

Specifying Cursor Holdability

```
...
Connection con = ds.getConnection( );
```

```
Statement stmt = con. CreateStatement(
         ResultSet.TYPE_SCROLL_INSENSITIVE,
         ResultSet.CONCUR_READ_ONLY,
         ResultSet.CLOSE_CURSORS_AT_COMMIT );
...
```

SETTING SAVE POINTS

Save points are used to provide a fine-grained control over the delineation of transactions in a database update. A *save point* represents a distinct point in the database work being performed. Using specific JDBC methods an application may choose not to rollback the entire transaction but instead to rollback work to a given save point. As of JDBC 3.0, a JDBC driver may save points through the implementation of several methods in the `Connection` interface.

Not all databases support save points and JDBC compliance does not require that they do. The `DatababaseMetaData` method `supportsSavePoints` returns a boolean true if the database does provide save point support. The following code demonstrates the use of save points with JDBC.

Save Points Sample

```
Statement stmt = con.createStatement();

//
// begin the transaction
//
con.setAutoCommit(false);

//
// update the sales tables
//
try {

stmt.executeUpdate( "insert sale_status (stock_id, quantity) " +
                    " values( 12355, 10 )");

stmt.executeUpdate("update sales " +
                    " set quantity = quantity - 10 " +
                    " where stock_id = 12355" );

// set a savepoint
Savepoint savePoint1 = con.setSavepoint("SAVEPOINT_1");

}
catch (SQLException e ) {
```

```
        con.rollback(); // rollback everything
}        return;

//
// update the commission tables
//
try {

stmt.executeUpdate( "update commissions " +
                    " set commission_flag = 'X' " +
                    " where employee_id = 20" );

stmt.executeUpdate( "update sales_employee " +
                    " set regional_sales =  regional_sales + 1 " +
                    " where employee_id = 20" );

Savepoint savePoint2 = con.setSavepoint("SAVEPOINT_2");
}
catch (SQLException e) {
  // retain the sales
  // commission will be caught in the next job run
  // this will invalidate savePoint2
  //
     conn.rollback( savePoint1 );
}
...
```

In this code snippet, a sale is being updated to the database. This requires that a series of tables be updated—tables which update stock information and tables that update the salesman's commission status. These update operations are divided into two groups: the update of the stock information and the update of the salesman's commission. The two update groups are allowed to update separately since businesses treat them as distinct operations. This means that a sale is allowed to ship even though the commission has not been paid. (Commissions are usually paid quarterly, so there is usually plenty of time to match sales to salesman.) The assumption is that some later balancing operation will indicate that commissions have not been paid on the sale and will rectify the situation.

For our purposes, based on assumed business rules, we want product to ship in a timely fashion (so customers will pay in a timely fashion) so we allow a rollback of the commission updates to the point first savepoint: `savePoint1`.

The rollback to the first save point, `savePoint1`, will invalidate the second save point, `savePoint2`. It will not rollback the work of `savePoint2`, it will just invalidate the save point. Closing or committing a transaction will also invalidate any save points. Any attempt to reference a released save point transaction will cause an `SQLException` to be thrown.

Java Servlets

INTRODUCTION

J2EE provides not one but two technologies for creating dynamic web page content: servlets and Java server pages. As we will see, Java Server Pages (JSP) are built on top of servlet technologies.

In order to understand how to write a web application you need to understand how the internet works. This would entail some knowledge of networking and then some knowledge of how the internet uses networking, specifically the Hyper Text Transport Protocol. Once we have developed an understanding of the networking foundation of servlets, we will then focus our discussion on servlets including several basic servlet examples.

THE NETWORK: TCP/IP

Though we may not know the specifics, we all know that the world wide web is just a network. A rather extensive and pervasive network, but just a network never the less.

A web application runs on a network. The network is the *wire* through which the application operates and if it were not present, the Web application which requires remote users to connect to a Web server would not run. (A Web application can be run locally on a machine and not use a physical network, but it will nevertheless be using local network loopback mechanisms to mimic the operation of the network on the local machine.)

Networks are composed of a series of *nodes* or points on the network. Networks provide high speed data communications between the nodes using a *protocol*, a pre-determined language for communication, and a pre-determined format for a *data buffer* or information *packet*. The protocol is used by the two nodes in the communication process to determine what information is being conveyed. The data buffer or packet is what is transmitted between the two nodes and is a combination of the actual data being transmitted and information about the data packet contained in the packet header. To transmit a packet, a node may set a flag in the packet header indicating that the packet is being transmitted to a specific target; the target address will also be included in the header. The packet will then be transmitted and may travel to a number of different nodes until it is received at the node to which it was sent. The source and destination nodes may exchange additional packets of data to ensure delivery of the data packet; this exchange of additional packets is part of a handshaking protocol used to provide some control over the transmission process.

At any given point a large number of data packets may be coursing through a network. These packets are sent to their correct destination via *routers*. The routers examine the packet and try to make a determination about where the packet is bound as shown in Figure B-1.

The World Wide Web uses the TCP/IP protocol for communication. This combination of acronyms stands for Transmission Control Protocol and Internet Protocol and represents one of the most common protocols for network communication.

TCP/IP is actually two protocols: TCP and IP. The IP protocol stands for Internet Protocol and provides routing information, information on how to find the address of the resource being requested. The IP protocol splits the data into packets and attaches a source and destination address to the packet. This information is then used to route the packet from the source to the destination.

The TCP protocol uses the IP layer protocol to provide routing services. TCP establishes the connection and provides a handshaking mechanism to ensure that data gets to its destination. TCP provides guaranteed delivery of data (unlike other protocols which do not) and for this reason provides some level of error correction and integrity for data transmission.

But TCP/IP communication alone does not make the Web. As mentioned previously, the HTTP protocol provides a layer of communication above the TCP/IP layers. This protocol uses a small number of handshaking directives to transmit resources from the server to the client.

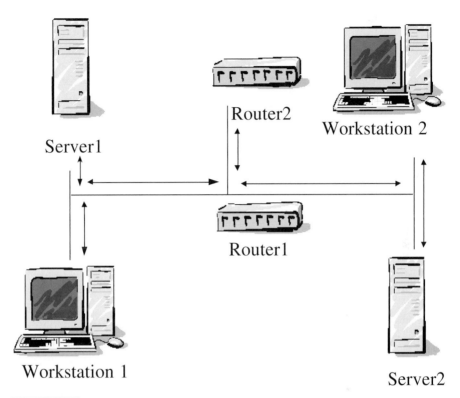

Figure B–1   *The Data Network*

In respect to the World Wide Web infrastructure, TCP/IP and HTTP are part of a network protocol layer framework known as the Open Systems Interconnection (OSI) developed by the International Standards Organization (ISO). The framework provides for seven layers and though vendors have implemented parts of this framework, rarely is the entire standard adhered to in a product. TCP/IP combined with HTTP comprise the part of this layer model used in this book (see Table B-1).

Table B–1

OSI Layer	Type	Description
HTTP	Application	Hyper Text Transport Protocol
TCP	Transport	Transport Control Protocol
IP	Internet	Internet Protocol
Ethernet, ISDN, PPP, SLIP	Data Link	Network packet transmission

At the lowest level, a layer exists to move the network packets from one point to another. This layer has only rudimentary knowledge of the contents of the packets; higher level protocols such as IP provide the routing of the packets. Above IP, the TCP layer provides for the communication between network nodes and ensures accuracy, using the IP layer for routing. And above all other layers, the HTTP layer executes the handshaking between client and server with some knowledge of the information being transmitted. It is this HTTP layer that we are concerned with as web developers.

THE NETWORK: HTTP

HTTP is one of several network protocols the common web browser uses. When a web browser requests a page it makes this request in the form of a URL, a Uniform Resource Locator. This URL contains valuable information about the resource being requested using the following syntax.

```
<protocol>://<server name>[:<port number>]/<location>
```

The *protocol* requested can be one of many different protocols, but most commonly is either HTTP for *hypertext transport protocol*, ftp for *file transfer protocol*, or file for a file on the local machine. Table B-2 is a more complete list of protocols that most browsers will accept.

Table B–2   *Network Protocols*

Protocol	Description
http://	World Wide Web server
ftp://	FTP server (file transfer)
https//	Secure HTTP
news://	Usenet newsgroups
mailto://	e-mail
wais://	Wide Area Information Server
gopher://	Gopher server
file://	file on local system
ldap://	directory server request
telnet://	applications on network server
rlogin://	applications on network server
tn3270://	applications on mainframe

The server name can alternatively be an IP address. This identifies for the browser the server which will manage the request it is going to submit. Optionally this designation of the server can include a network port number. If the URL designates the protocol as http and the server name portion of the URL contains a port number, the browser will attempt a connection for HTTP services on the designated server at the specified port number. If no port number is specified, then the browser will attempt communication with the server at the default port for HTTP communications, port 80.

Name Resolution

When a server name is specified in a URL, this name alone is not adequate to achieve a connection to the server. The name must be resolved to an IP address. The resolution of the server name involves either retrieving the name from a local `hosts` file which contains a list of server names and related IP addresses, or more commonly, the use of a *name server*, or *domain name server*.

The job of the name server, which usually resides on the local network, is to take query for a server name and return an IP address. Since the Internet is large and dynamic the process of determining the correct IP address for an internet domain name can involve querying several name servers on the Internet. To avoid the overhead of Internet name resolution, local name servers will often make an effort to *cache* Internet domain names so that the name can be resolved on the local network rather than the external Internet.

Note that if the use of a name server is required, the network software where the browser is running must be configured to use the domain name server or else the request for the URL will fail. Alternately, a local configuration file (usually named hosts) can be configured to map domain names to IP addresses, but these files are used infrequently on client machines.

HTTP transactions operate in a *request/response* cycle. Once an HTTP request is sent, it will course through the network, whether it be an internal intranet or the Internet, and ultimately arrive at a server. An HTTP request is commonly processed by an *HTTP server* (Apache, IIS) or *web server* which would be listening for a connection on a well-known port (port 80 for HTTP). The web server will accept the connection and then retrieve the URL for processing.

In its simplest form, processing a request is a simple task for an HTTP server, a task which involves little more than retrieving the HTML page and returning it to the client pre-pending HTTP headers in the process.

But it is not uncommon for a Web server to provide additional services for developers to use. For instance, web servers usually provide some form of realm authentication, which requires a user to enter a user name and password to access

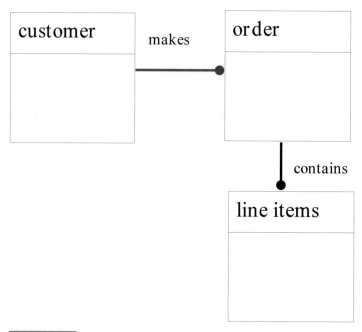

The HTTP Communication Protocol

a portion of the web site. It can also map short names for directories within a site into full directory paths and provide the capability to run web components such as servlets, or perform the processing required to transform JSPs into HTML.

The processing or requests and responses within the web server is a stateless transaction. Once a request is sent by a browser to a web server, the connection to the web server is usually not retained. Each request to a web server requires another connection.

This type of request/response cycle is efficient. A web server can handle a large number of users because it does not need to maintain physical connections to each of those users. Since the web server is delivering a page to the client browser, the page delivered to the browser by the web server is considered *self-sustaining* in that the page sent to the client does not need to communicate with the server while the user is processing the page. This relatively low network overhead allows web servers to manage a heavy user load relative to the more heavyweight network access required by traditional client-server.

The HTML Standard

A standard that resides separately from the other portions of the Web infrastructure is that of the Hyper Text Markup Language. Though separate, it is by no means unimportant and its origin and purpose speak directly to the need for server-side scripting in Web development.

HTML is not a programming language and as such has been sorely stretched to perform the work necessary to create complete applications on the web. HTML is a *presentation language* derived from Standard Generalized Markup Language (SGML) and is comprised of tags that define how the text they surround will be rendered. But these tags combined with links, the ability to input data into data entry forms and the ability to execute external programs with Common Gateway Interface (CGI), provide some level of functionality and thus provide the ability to create working applications which operate over the Web.

But this combination of tools and components (HTML, links and CGI) has distinct limitations. To implement business logic is difficult and clumsy and the performance of CGI solutions has generally been poor.

The logical solution to this problem was to somehow extend HTML to provide for many of the shortcomings of the original presentation language. Vendors originally did this in such a way as to address the shortcomings of HTML and CGI and to provide a proprietary solution that would lock the user into their product. These solutions usually used tag extensions that would be embedded into the HTML page and would be executed at the server (not the browser client), providing a server-side scripting solution. To implement these solutions, the infrastructure of the web was also extended, often adding an application server to manage the execution of the vendor's server-side script. This application server would work together with the HTTP server to parse, execute and serve the HTML page to the browser.

The Execution of Java Servlets

Java servlets are instances of a Java class which operate as a web component. They are invoked (not necessarily instantiated) to manage a request. They can optionally (but are not required to) generate a response to the request.

Java servlets operate within a container, an abstraction of an operating environment for the component. This container is usually provided by the web server but could be provided by some other environment, for instance a number of application servers provide servlet containers in addition to providing EJB containers.

The servlet container is responsible for providing certain services to the servlet, services such as life-cycle management, security and maintenance of context properties. With life-cycle management the container is responsible for creation of the component if necessary, and makes the component available to manage a request. The container also manages the security of the components, restricting access to the local operating environment and providing authentication services. The container is also responsible for mapping a request to a servlet component and makes an environment available to the component.

The design of the servlet environment reflects the stateless nature of the HTTP protocol. The servlet is essentially stateless; there is no guarantee that any instance members of the servlet class will retain their values from one invocation to the next. There are facilities for maintaining session state within servlets, but they do not include using instance members.

As multiple requests are handled by the servlet container, multiple threads of activity will be executing servlet code. As a developer, we need to be aware of both the lifecycle and state activities of the servlet container in this multi-threaded environment and program accordingly. Thread safe issues can often lead to coding errors with inexperienced servlet developers. If you are aware from the start that certain portions of servlet code are not thread-safe, then these coding errors can be avoided.

The servlet API

The servlet API reflects the HTTP protocol with which these components will be used. The servlet component is subject to the life cycle imposed by the container. The servlet will be initialized once and then be invoked multiple times to handle incoming requests. The web server will map URLs to servlets through the servlet container. When the container determines that the servlet is no longer needed (usually through a timeout parameter) the servlet will be destroyed. This lifecycle is shown in Figure B-3.

As the diagram showed, there are servlet methods called by the container for each of these lifecycle events. The classes in the servlet API reflect a delineation between a generic servlet and a servlet which will operate under the HTTP protocol. The most common implementation used is the HTTPServlet. Figure B-4 describes these relationships.

The init Method

The `init` method is called to initialize a servlet component. This method is called only once by the container before any requests are handled by the servlet. This method is usually used in a manner similar to that of a constructor, performing the various initialization tasks that a component may require before it is used. These tasks usually include accessing any resources that may be needed by the servlet and initializing servlet state. For instance, creating a JDBC connection to use or loading an XML translation template.

The `init` method is overloaded to include an `init` method with no arguments and an init method with a `ServletConfig` argument. Since the `GenericServlet` and the `HTTPServlet` both implement `ServletConfig`,

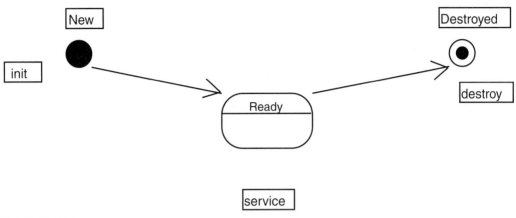

Figure B–3 *Servlet Lifecycle (init, service, destroy)*

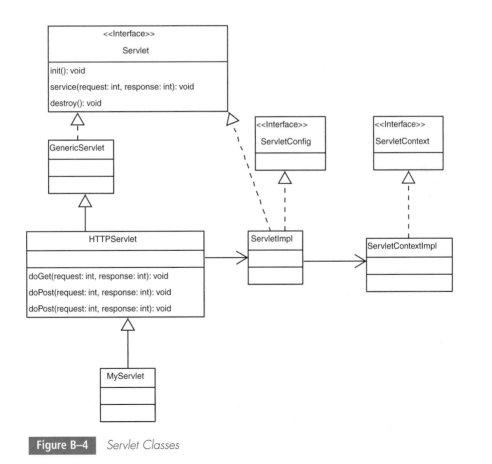

Figure B–4 *Servlet Classes*

there is technically no reason to obtain a reference to the `ServletConfig` being used by the servlet, though this is sometimes done for programming clarity. The init method with no arguments is a convenience method that is often used to perform initialization.

The `init` method is overridden if initialization tasks need to be performed by the servlet. Since most servlets need to perform some type of initialization, it is not uncommon to see this method overridden. Any `HTTPServlet` implementation overriding the `init` method with the `ServletConfig` argument should be sure to call the superclass `init` method (`super.init(ServletConfig)`) since the `GenericServlet` implementation needs a reference to the `ServletConfig` object.

The service Method

The service method is called by the container to dispatch an incoming request. This method usually calls the `doGet` or `doPost` method depending on the method being used by the sender.

This method could be overridden by an implementation in order to provide some form of custom processing, but that is not usually done. It is more common to override the `doGet` or `doPost` method and take whatever actions are necessary in those methods.

The destroy Method

The `destroy` method is called by the container when it is preparing to destroy the servlet component and free the resources being used by the servlet. The destroy method would be overridden to free any resources used by the servlet that the container was not aware of, for instance a JDBC database connection reference or a message queue reference.

Initialization Parameters

The J2EE servlet specification provides for initialization parameters. These parameters are static values which can be retrieved by a servlet but cannot be set.

This provides a very useful mechanism for setting various application properties, for example the URL of an error page for a specific type of error, or the email address of the web administrator. The values of the parameters are set in the servlet `web.xml` configuration file as shown below. Two types of parameters are available: servlet initialization parameters and servlet context parameters.

Servlet initialization parameters are defined in the servlet configuration file as part of the servlet initialization and are thus only visible to the servlet for which they were defined. The following provides an example of the declaration of a servlet initialization parameter in the `web.xml` file.

```
...
<servlet>
  <servlet-name>MyServlet</servlet-name>
   <servlet-class>MyServlet.class</servlet-class>
   <init-param>
            <param-name>site-name</param-name>
            <param-value>Movies-R-Us</param-value>
   </init-param>
</servlet>
...
```

This example declares a parameter named site-name for the servlet MyServlet. Within the body of the MyServlet class, a call to the getInitParameter method could be used to retrieve the value of the site-name parameter as follows.

```
...
   String siteName = getInitParameter( "site-name" );
...
```

Alternatively, a servlet context parameter is defined as part of the context for the servlet, a portion of the web application. This parameter is thus visible to all servlets within that context, not just a single servlet as with the servlet initialization parameters. The following provides an example of the declaration of a context parameter in the web.xml file.

```
<web-app>
    <context-param>
            <param-name>stock-server</param-name>
            <param-value>delaware</param-value>
    </context-param>
</servlet>
<context-param>
  <param-name>XsltQuery2</param-name>
  <param-value>/stdApps/Useful/rsQuery2.xsl</param-value>
</context-param>

  <servlet>
    <servlet-name>AServlet</servlet-name>
        ...
```

In this example several parameters are defined for the context in which one or more servlets are defined. In the body of any of those servlets, the following code could be used to retrieve the context parameter stock-server.

```
...
   server = getServletContext().getInitParameter("stock-server");
...
```

The ServletConfig Implementation

The `ServletConfig` implementation of the `ServletConfig` interface provides access to initialization parameters for the servlet, the servlet name and the `ServletContext`. The methods in this class are commonly used to retrieve the initialization values for the servlet and to access the `ServletContext`. The `ServletConfig` instance being used for a servlet is passed into the `init` method for the servlet and can be stored at that time, or since the `GenericServlet` and the `HTTPServlet` implement this interface, the methods defined in the interface can be called directly from the servlet component.

The ServletContext Implementation

The `ServletContext` implementation contains methods that provide access to global attributes, values which can be retrieved by any servlet running in the container. As with any global variable, these attributes should be used sparingly. The general rule of thumb about using the narrowest scope available still applies with servlets. In many cases, a context parameter could be used in place of a `ServletContext` attribute. Also note that these attributes are not thread safe.

The `ServletContext` also provides access to the logging facility for the context. A string message may be passed to the `log` method which has also been overloaded to accept a string message and a corresponding object which implements the `Throwable` interface.

The `GenericServlet` abstract class provides methods for retrieving the `ServletContext` (`getServletContext`) and the `ServletConfig` (`getServletConfig`), so technically a servlet does not need to retain a reference to these objects. But there are some developers who feel it is useful to avoid the overhead of the method call and retain a reference to the `ServletContext` and the `ServletConfig` for the servlet.

Maintaining Session State

Even though HTTP is a stateless protocol, it is possible for a servlet to maintain state information for a session. This is provided through an implementation of the `HtttpSession` interface which is obtained through the request being processed - the `HttpServletRequest` reference passed to the `doXXXX` method (for example: `doGet`).

A servlet may store any arbitrary object of interest using the `HttpSession` reference, the *session object*. As long as the session is active, the corresponding session object is available. Objects are stored with the session object through a call to the `setAttribute` method as follows.

Saving a Session Attribute

```
...
public void doGet( HttpServletRequest request,
                        HttpServletResponse response )
    throws IOException, ServletException  {
...
//
// create a Hashtable of customer shopping cart information
//
java.util.Hashtable customer = new java.util.Hashtable();

customer.put( "customer-name", "Fred Fleller" );
customer.put( "customer-number", "139039" );
customer.put( "customer-shopping-cart-number", "333909339" );

request.getSession().setAttribute( "customer-info", customer );
...
```

Retrieving the session object uses the `HttpServletRequest getSession` method. Since the `getSession` method returns an object, a cast is required to provide a useful reference as shown below.

Retrieving a Session Attribute

```
...
//
// get the session object
//
HttpSession session = request.getSession();

//
// retrieve our Hashtable
//
Hashtable customerInfo = (Hashtable)
        session.getAttribute("customer-info");
....
out.println("<p>customer-name: " +
                    customerInfo("customer-name"));
```

The session information is visible only to servlets within the current session. These values are not visible to servlets in another context. Additionally, the client may choose to implement features which restrict the container's ability to create a session. A servlet can determine that the container cannot maintain a session by calling the `isNew` method. If a servlet is trying to retrieve a value placed by a previous servlet in the and this method returns true, then the value will not be available (since a session is not active).

A container implementation may elect how to manage session information. A common implementation is to use cookies to store a reference number for the client and have the container create an internal `Hashtable` to store the session information with the reference number as the key.

Since not all browsers will accept cookies, URL rewriting is another approach to managing session information. This approach has the client send a session id as a request parameter with each request. If a container is using this approach, as developers we must be certain to use the `encodeURL` method of the `HttpServletResponse` class to be sure that any forwarded requests will contain the session id if it is needed.

Yet another approach to maintaining session information is to use cookies to store all of the relevant session information. This is a relatively simple approach but for security reasons not all clients will allow this. As a developer we need to be aware that cookies stored on a client machine may be accessible to the determined hacker.

As touched on previously in this section, a safer approach to using cookies is one that does not store the actual information on the client's machine and instead stores a reference ID. The relevant information is stored elsewhere in a secure environment and can only be retrieved by specific servlets using the session id.

For instance, a a reference ID could be a customer ID which references a customer record on a server, or a shopping cart ID which references a shopping cart stored on the server. While a hacker may be able to get the reference ID from the cookie on the client's machine, the ID is of little use to them.

You should be aware that there is a limit to the number of cookies a browser will store for a server, usually around 20 per web server. And the size of the cookie is usually restricted to less than 4 KB each.

The client cookie is available through the request and response objects passed to the doXXX methods. The cookie can be set using the `addCookie` method of the `HttpServletResponse` implementation and it can be retrieved using the `getCookie` method of the `HttpServletRequest` implementation.

A cookie is represented by the `Cookie` object (`java.servlet.http.Cookie`). This class contains methods to get and set various relevant parameters for the cookie such as the value of the cookie and age (expiration time) for the cookie. Cookie values are always represented as strings. To set a cookie for a client session, the following code would be used.

```
...
public void doGet( HttpServletRequest request,
                            HttpServletResponse response )
    throws IOException, ServletException {

...
response.addCookie( new Cookie( "customer-id", "093092309" ) );
...
```

Cookie retrieval requires a little more work as demonstrated in the following code snippet.

```
...
public void doGet( HttpServletRequest request,
                              HttpServletResponse response )
    throws IOException, ServletException {

...
response.addCookie( new Cookie( "customer-id", "093092309" ) );
...

Cookie[] cookieArray = request.getCookies( );

// load our cookies into a Hashtable
java.util.Hashtable cookies = new Hashtable();

//
// if we didn't get any cookies, we'll get a null reference
//
if ( cookieArray != null ) {
    for ( int n = 0; n < cookieArray.length; n++ ) {
        cookies.put( cookieArray[n].getName(), cookieArray[n] );
    }
}

//
// output our customer ID
//

String customerID = null;
if ( cookieArray != null ) {
    if ( cookies.get("customer-id" ) != null ) {
        customerID =
          ((Cookie) cookies.get( "customer-id" )).getValue();
        response.getWriter().println(
            "<p>Customer ID: " + customerID );
    }
}
if ( customerID == null) {
    response.getWriter().println(
        "<p>Could not retrieve customer ID." );
```

We must retrieve the cookies as an array of all the cookies sent with the request. Since we prefer to only examine specific cookies instead of constantly iterating the entire array, we load the array into a Hashtable which associates the cookie name with the cookie reference (and through that the cookie value). After storing our cookies in the Hashtable, we use the get method to retrieve the appropriate cookie and display its value.

Thread Safety and Concurrency Management

As servlet developers we need to be aware of the process flow for servlets. By default, any given servlet may be executed by one or more clients so that the code for the servlet is effectively shared among clients. This behavior allows multiple clients to concurrently execute code within a servlet `service` method.

This standard behavior can be overridden using the `SingleThreadModel` (`javax.servlet.SingleThreadModel`) interface. Any servlet which implements this interface is guaranteed that no two clients will execute its `service` method concurrently.

As developers we need to be aware what is threadsafe and what is not threadsafe. Table B-3 illustrates the attributes which are available to us as developers and indicates whether or not they are considered threadsafe by default.

Table B–3

Attribute/Variables	Threadsafe
request attributes	yes
session attributes	no
context attributes	no
instance members	no
class variables	no
local variables	yes

As we can see from this table, it is fairly easy to remember what is thread safe and what is not. Other than request attributes and local variables, all other attributes and variables are not thread safe by default.

Session attributes are not thread safe within the context of the client session. Session content will not be accessible to other threads from other clients, so there is no risk of that. But should a client session have multiple browser windows open on the same page, there is the possibility session information could become corrupt. This can be prevented by disallowing multiple browser windows for the same page. (A simple check of the session attributes could be used to determine this.)

Generally speaking, instance members should only be used for data which will not change over the duration of the servlet's life. They should be read only, having their values set in the initialization method and remaining unchanged over the life of the servlet. Given this rule of thumb, it would be appropriate to declare these members final variables.

Any information that may change over the client session should be manipulated in local variables and then stored in the session object where it can be retrieved later by other servlets participating in the session.

Servlet Exception Handling

The servlet is somewhat restricted in the exceptions it can throw. In fact, it can only throw two exceptions: an `IOException` and a `ServletException`. This is not a very restrictive requirement when you consider that the client accessing the servlet (the browser) is really not expected to handle any exceptions. Exceptions are ultimately caught in the service method where they are handled by branching to a named error page or generating an error page. A robust application should handle exceptions by producing useful log entries and returning a user-friendly error page to the client.

Any checked exception generated by the execution of a servlet must be wrapped in a `ServletException` before execution returns to the `service` method. This requirement suggests the exceptions should be handled locally in the method whenever possible and log entries should generated at that point. Once that processing is complete, a `ServletException` should be thrown to the caller.

A servlet will generate a default error page if none is declared. An entry can be made in the `web.xml` file to allow error handling to be directed to another page. The error-page element allows error pages to be identified to handle specific checked exceptions, with one page declared for each exception type.

Application Security

There are two types of security we are concerned with in servlet programming: authentication and authorization. With authentication, we need to determine that a user is who they say they are. This is usually done with some type of password security.

With authorization, we need to determine that an authenticated user is allowed to perform the action they are requesting.

A user is considered a principal and once authenticated, a principal may be mapped to certain roles. The security in the servlet ultimately maps certain permissions to certain roles. Consequently, a facility is required that maps the principal (our authenticated user) to a role. The servlet security realm matches a user (principal) to a role. Exactly how the security realm is implemented is vendor-specific. Common implementations in use today use a database to provide authentication information or allow an LDAP server to provide this information. Authentication can take one of the forms listed in Table B-4.

| Table B–4 | *Servlet Authentication Techniques* |

Authentication	**Description**
BASIC	HTTP Basic authentication. Sends an 'authenticate' request to the browser which displays a user name/password dialog box to the user. The password is returned as a base64 encoded string; it is not encrypted.
DIGEST	HTTP Digest authentication. Sends an 'authenticate' request to the browser which displays a user name/password dialog box to the user. The password is returned in encrypted form. (Not widely used. Containers are not required to support this form of authentication.)
FORM	An HTML form is used to request a user name and password. Password is returned unencrypted. User name field must be named j_username, and user password field j_password.
CLIENT-CERT	Uses SSL over HTTP (HTTPS) which requires the use of public key certificate. Only servlet containers that are J2EE compliant are required to support this protocol.

HTTP Basic Security involves widely supported HTTP protocol to have the browser generate a dialog box to query the user for a user name and password. Once the user enters the name and password, the results are sent back to the HTTP server. The problem is that when the results are returned to the server, the password is not encrypted, it is encoded using base64 encoding. Unfortunately, it is a fairly simple task to decode a base64 encoded string.

Used alone, HTTP Basic security is not very secure when used over the Internet. When augmented with a very strong security mechanism like HTTPS (HTTP with SSL), this becomes a much more attractive authentication mechanism. In fact, this is the approach used by a large number of web sites today.

With HTTP Digest Security the server sends the client browser a request to authenticate the user. As with HTTP Basic Security, the browser displays the password dialog and returns the data results to the server. But unlike Basic Security, the browser encrypts the password.

HTTP Digest Security involves a security mechanism that is not as strong has HTTPS and is not widely supported among browsers. Servlet containers are encouraged but are not required to support this type of authentication.

Basic Security login involves the user of a simple login dialog. For many users, this dialog may be confusing. Form Based Security provides some flexibility in the presentation of the login to the user. With this approach, a login form page and and error page are identified for a protected web resource. When the user attempts to access the secure resource, the login form is sent to the client. When the login form is posted back to the server, the user name and password are retrieved and validated. If an error is encountered (the user name or password are invalid) then control is forwarded to an error page.

The final form of authentication specifies the use of strong security using SSL with HTTP. SSL combines both symmetric and asymmetric security, in a sense providing the best of both worlds. It is widely supported, relatively simple to implement and highly secure.

Programmatic and Declarative Application Security

Application security can be handled programmatically or declaratively. With *programmatic security* management, method calls can be made to determine whether or not a user is in a specific role. Application code can then restrict the user to certain actions.

Programmatic security provides a very finely grained level of security. Certain actions within a servlet or within a class used by a servlet can be restricted based on a role.

But the programmatic approach is also prone to error. A programmer who misplaces a curly bracket could leave an application with a gaping security hole.

Alternatively, with declarative security entries in a deployment descriptor (`web.xml`) relate roles to secure resources (as referenced by an URL).

SERVLET EXAMPLE

As mentioned previously, servlets are one type of J2EE web component. JSPs are the other. After introducing JSPs and tag libraries and EJBs, we will come back to the web component and demonstrate how servlets and JSPs can be used together to create a cohesive application. Servlet examples shown later will demonstrate the manipulation of graphics with servlets, applying a service-to-worker design patter and using a servlet as a control object (model 2), and using servlets with EJBs. The following example demonstrates creating a simple servlet to perform an XML transformation that ultimately produces an HTML page which is returned to the client browser. This is a servlet that will be used later in the text as part of the demonstration application.

JDBC to XML: The servlet

We will use a servlet to access the XML document and produce the HTML output. The role of the servlet in this operation is that of a *controller* object; the real work to access the database, create XML, and transform the XML to HTML is being done by the objects the servlet has created. The result is a compact servlet focused on the task of creating a presentation component and delivering it to the browser that has generated the request.

The servlet retrieves the query to execute from an initialization parameter in the servlet `web.xml` file (shown in the next code example). The transformation is done using an XSLT script located in a disk file. The end result of this application design is that the composition and content of the HTML table displayed by this servlet can be changed without altering a single line of servlet code. The code for this servlet is shown in the sections below.

The ServletExample1 Class: The doGet Method

The servlet class declaration includes a number of imports for the various packages used within the servlet. Since this servlet responds to an HTTP `GET` request, it includes a declaration for the `doGet` method, as shown in the following code:

The ServletExample1 Class

```
package examples.servlets;

import java.io.*;
import java.util.*;
import javax.servlet.*;
import javax.servlet.http.*;

import java.sql.*;
import javax.sql.*;

import java.net.*;
import java.io.*;

import javax.naming.*;
import java.rmi.*;

import db.*;
import jdbcutil.*;
import movies.ejb.*;

import com.icl.saxon.trax.*;
import org.xml.sax.*;

public class ServletExample1 extends HttpServlet {

ServletConfig      config;
ServletContext     context;

//
// for Saxon XML transformations
//
Processor       processor;
```

```
Templates       templates;
Transformer transformer;

PreparedStatement    pstmt;
Connection                con;

String             defaultStyleSheet =
"file:/web/xslt/rs.xsl";


public void doGet(HttpServletRequest request,
HttpServletResponse response)
throws IOException, ServletException
{
PrintWriter out = response.getWriter();

out.println("<html>");
out.println("<head>");

out.println("<title>Movies Listing</title>");
out.println("</head>");
out.println("<body bgcolor=\"white\">");


try {

//
// only need to prepare the query if it hasn't been
// prepared before
//
if ( pstmt == null ) {     // need to prepare the query

  //
  // get the query from an environment parameter
  //
  String query = context.getInitParameter( "Query2" );

  //
  // prepare the query
  //
  pstmt = con.prepareStatement( query );

}

//
// execute the prepared query and retrieve the results
// results are formatted as an XML document
//
String xmlDoc = getQueryResults();

//
// transform the XML to the format for our output
```

```
//  (an HTML table)
//
transformer.transform(
new InputSource( new StringReader( xmlDoc ) ),
new Result( out ) );

out.println("</body>");
out.println("</html>");
}
catch (Exception e) {
log( "Exception in doGet: " + e.getMessage() );
}


}
```

The servlet begins by importing various packages needed for operation, including the standard servlet packages, the JNDI packages (for `DataSource` usage), Java I/O packages, and the JDBC packages. Packages used for the SAXON XSLT transformer are also imported, as are various local packages used in the servlet.

The XSLT transformer will use a *processor,* a *template,* and a *transformer* to perform its work. A processor is created from a factory method (`newInstance`) and is then used to create a template. The template is created based on the transform to be done and receives the name of the transform stylesheet to process. The stylesheet contains the script that indicates how to process the document. Once the template has been created (using the transform stylesheet), a transformer can be retrieved from the template. It is this transformer which will then be used to perform that actual transformation (see Figure B-5).

The point of all this is that since we are using the same XSLT transformation for all of the work being performed by this servlet, we do not need to recreate the transformer each time it is called; that would not be very efficient. It is better to create the transformer (through the processor and template) in the servlet `init` method, which is called when the servlet instance is first loaded by the container. In the servlet `doGet` method, which is called when an HTTP `GET` is executed on the servlet page, the transformer is simply called to perform the transformation. (The transformer object can be considered the equivalent or analogue of a prepared SQL statement.)

The template, processor, and transformer references declared on lines 37, 38, and 39 are declared as instance members for the servlet class. This means that they will be shared among instances of the servlet (potentially by different users), but since they represent static information for the servlet—information that will not change based on the user or invocation of the servlet—having them shared among servlet instances does not present a problem. (Had they represented some information that would change per invocation, they should be declared and set within the appropriate method to be called by the servlet engine—for example, the `doGet` or `doPost` method.)

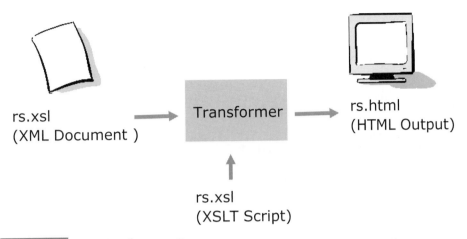

Figure B–5 *XSLT Transformation Process*

On lines 48 through 50, the standard declaration for the `doGet` method is declared. Since the servlet is responding to an HTTP request and will respond with the HTTP response, we see declaration parameters that represent the HTTP request (`HttpServletRequest`) and the HTTP response (`HttpServletResponse`). We would like to write our transformed XML document to the response stream, so we obtain the response writer on line 52 with a call to the `HttpServletResponse` `getWriter` method.

The code block then contains several statements outputting HTML statements to format the page. A `try/catch` block is started on line 62, and the query string for the query to be executed is retrieved on line 72 with a call to the `ServletContext getInitParameter` method. The value for this parameter is retrieved from the `web.xml` file (shown later in this chapter) declaration for the `context param` entry for `Query2`. By storing the query string in the `web.xml` configuration file, we create a flexible servlet that, when combined with the use of the XSLT style sheet, allows us to change the operation of the servlet with very little effort.

The query is prepared on line 77, and a `PreparedStatement` object is created. The `getQueryResults` method is then called on line 88. This method (shown later) uses the `PreparedStatement (pstmt)` instance member to execute the query and convert the `ResultSet` to an XML document format. If the `pstmt` object is not null, then the code to prepare the statement will not be executed.

At this point, the XML document containing the query results is in the string `xmlDoc`. The `Transformer transform` method is called on lines 94 through 96. This method accepts a `java.io.Reader` parameter and a `Result` (part of the SAXON package) parameter as arguments. The `Reader` argument in this case is created by wrapping a `StringReader` around our `xmlDoc` string, and the

Result parameter is created by wrapping the Result class around the output PrintWriter (from our HttpServletResponse). This method will use the XSLT transform stylesheet to transform the XML document (in xmlDoc) and produce HTML output that will be written to the output PrintWriter (out). The remaining code in this program block outputs HTML to complete the formatting of the HTML page and provide catch blocks for the exceptions that may be thrown in the method.

The ServletExample1 Class: The getQueryResults Method

The getQuery method performs the task of executing the query and transforming the results into an XML document. The execution of the query simply involves executing the prepared statement that was prepared in the doGet method and converting the ResultSet into XML format using the JDBCXML toXMLString method (as shown previously in this chapter).

The executeQuery method is called in a try/catch block, and the conversion to the XML document is performed in the finally block, which is used to return the XML document string. Should there be a failure in the execution of the XML statement, the empty or null ResultSet will be passed to the JDBCXML toXMLString method, which will return an invalid XML document. This will lead to a parser error in the transformation process in the doGet method. (Though not shown in this example, a more involved error-checking scheme would determine that the prepared statement execution had failed and return a value to the calling method that would terminate processing at that point.) The code for this method is shown next.

The ServletExample1 Class: The getQuery Method

```
public String getQueryResults() {
ResultSet rs = null;
try {
        rs = pstmt.executeQuery( );

}
catch (SQLException e) {
        //context.log("RemoteException in ServletExample2.getQueryResults: " +
e.getMessage() );
        System.out.println("SQLException in ServletExample2.getQueryResults: " +
e.getMessage() );
}
finally {
     return JDBCXML.toXMLString( rs );
}

}
```

The ServletExample1 Class: The init Method

A servlet runs within a container, a runtime environment for the servlet, usually provided as part of a Web server or application server. The container is responsible for providing various services for the servlet, such as security and a Java Virtual Machine (JVM) to run the class files. When the servlet is first loaded, the `init` method for the servlet class is called by the servlet container as implemented by the Web server. Per the servlet specification, the `init` method is called only once.

The `init` method is therefore a good location to provide initialization code for the servlet, much as a constructor is used in a conventional class. In this example, the `init` method is used to obtain a connection to the database and to prepare the template and create a processor for the XSLT transformation service. The code for this method is shown next.

The ServletExample1 Class: The init Method

```
1.// ---------------------------------------------------
2.public void init( ServletConfig config ) {
3.try {
4.        super.init( config );
5.
6.          this.config = config;
7.          this.context = config.getServletContext();
8.
9.      //
10.     // get the location of the xslt stylesheet
11.         // from an init parameter parameter
12.     //
13.     String styleSheet = context.getInitParameter(
14.                             "XsltQuery2" );
15.
16.     //
17.     // build the URL for the stylesheet
18.     //
19.     if ( styleSheet == null )
20.         styleSheet = defaultStyleSheet;
21.       else
22.         styleSheet = "file:" + styleSheet;
23.
24.        //
25.     // create the objects we need for the XSL transformation
26.     //
27.     processor = Processor.newInstance("xslt");
28.
29.        //
30.     // get an InputStream from the URL
31.        //
```

```
32.      templates = processor.process(new InputSource(
33.                      new URL( styleSheet ).openStream() ) );
34.
35.      transformer = templates.newTransformer();
36.
37.        //
38.     // prepare data access
39.     //
40.       InitialContext init = new InitialContext( );
41.       //
42.       // tomcat 4.02 requires a two step lookup
43.       //
44.       Context ctx   = (Context) init.lookup(
45.                          "java:comp/env/jdbc" );
46.        DataSource ds = (DataSource) ctx.lookup( "moviesmysql" );
47.
48.      con = ds.getConnection();
49.
50.
51.}
52.catch (SQLException e) {
53.    context.log("SQLException in ServletExample2.init: " +
54.                         e.getMessage() );
55.}
56.catch (ProcessorException e) {
57.    context.log("ProcessorException in ServletExample2.init: "
58.                         + e.getMessage() );
59.}
60.catch (RemoteException e) {
61.    context.log("RemoteException in ServletExample2.init: " +
62.                         e.getMessage() );
63.}
64.catch (NamingException e) {
65.    context.log("NamingException in ServletExample2.init: " +
66.                         e.getMessage() + " - " + e );
67.}
68.catch (Exception e) {
69.    context.log("Exception in ServletExample2.init: " +
70.                         e.getMessage() );
71.}
72.
73.}
74.
75.}
```

The init method is passed the servlet configuration (ServletConfig). This is used on line 7 to obtain the servlet context, which provides access to such useful operations as the log device for the servlet engine. The servlet context also provides access to the initialization parameters for the servlet environment, and this is used on line 13 to obtain the name of the XSLT stylesheet script to use to transform the XML document.

Lines 19 through 22 are used to build a URI name for the stylesheet, and on line 27, a new instance of the SAXON transformation processor is obtained. The processor then uses the name of the stylesheet to create a template on lines 32 and 33. The template is used to create the last `object` reference needed to perform the transformation, the *transformer* on line 35.

On lines 40 through 48, we see the code we have seen many times before in this text—the code used to obtain a `DataSource` and ultimately a JDBC connection through a JNDI resource.

THE SERVLETEXAMPLE1 CLASS: THE WEB.XML FILE

As defined by the Java servlet specification, the `web.xml` file contains configuration information for a servlet context, or what is also referred to as a Web application. In this example, the `web.xml` file is used to store the initialization parameters used by the servlet, specifically the XSLT stylesheet and the query to execute. The partial contents of this file are shown below.

Annotated web.xml File with Parameters

```
<?xml version="1.0" encoding="ISO-8859-1"?>

<!DOCTYPE web-app
    PUBLIC "-//Sun Microsystems, Inc.//DTD Web Application 2.3//EN"
    "http://java.sun.com/dtd/web-app_2_3.dtd">

<web-app>

        <context-param>
            <param-name>Query1</param-name>
          <param-value>select knowledge_base.doc_key, base_doc_key, doc_name,
message_txt
                from knowledge_base, knowledge_messages
                where knowledge_base.doc_key = knowledge_messages.doc_key
                order by knowledge_base.doc_key, base_doc_key
            </param-value>
        </context-param>

        <context-param>
            <param-name>Query2</param-name>
          <param-value>select  movie_name, movie_id, release_date, category
                from  movies
                order by movie_name
            </param-value>
        </context-param>
```

```
<context-param>
    <param-name>XsltQuery2</param-name>
    <param-value>/stdApps/Useful/rsQuery2.xsl</param-value>
</context-param>

<context-param>
    <param-name>XsltStyleSheet</param-name>
    <param-value>/lin/home/art/JDBC_Real/Code/Dynamic/rsQ1.xsl</param-value>
</context-param>

<servlet>
    <servlet-name>
        ServletExample2
    </servlet-name>
    <servlet-class>
        ServletExamples.ServletExample2
    </servlet-class>
</servlet>

<servlet>
    <servlet-name>
        ServletExample1
    </servlet-name>
    <servlet-class>
        ServletExamples.ServletExample1
    </servlet-class>
</servlet>

<servlet>
    <servlet-name>
        BlobView
    </servlet-name>
    <servlet-class>
        ServletExamples.BlobView
    </servlet-class>
</servlet>

...

</web-app>
```

The `context-param` tag is used to identify a parameter definition that can be retrieved through a call to `ServletContext getInitParameter`. The definitions highlighted in the previous listing and used in the `ServletExample1` servlet are for the `XsltQuery2` parameter, which identifies the full path to the XSLT stylesheet, and for the `Query2` parameter, which identifies the SQL `select` query to run.

There are other options for passing parameters into servlets. The most common approach is to pass the parameters to the servlet as `request` parameters, meaning that they would appear as part of the URL requesting the servlet, as follows:

```
http://www.asite.com/ServletExamples/ServletExample2?Query2=select+movie_id+from+movi
es&XsltQuery2=/stdApps/Useful/rsQ1.xsl
```

As shown in this example, parameters are passed to the servlet for the `Query2` parameter and the `XsltQuery2` parameter. There are a few issues with this approach. The first is that the parameters for the query and the XSLT stylesheet are not expected to change between invocations, so there is no strong, compelling reason to pass them in as parameters. Another issue is that the parameters for a SQL query could quickly become tedious to view and debug when spread across the command line, and certain characters used in SQL queries may not be allowed as part of URLs.

Yet another issue, and a serious issue at that, with passing these parameters as part of the URL is a security issue. The problem with these request parameters is that they expose the data resources of the enterprise to the general user population. As this servlet example stands, any user able to execute the servlet could access any table visible in the database. Opening freely accessible Web applications to generalized queries must be carefully considered. Using the approach shown in this example, where a limited number of queries is available to the user, adds a layer of security to the processing of the data.

XML Basics and Processing with JAXP

INTRODUCTION

When the XML standard was first released it quickly became one of the hot topics of the IT industry. Many felt that this standard and its related technologies (which at the time were largely incomplete) would revolutionize data interchange and easily solve all existing problems.

Developers who scrambled to learn the language soon discovered that it wasn't a programming language but a markup language like HTML. And while XML did provide significant benefits for data interchange, it didn't necessarily solve many long-standing problems with schema-incompatibilities and the corresponding semantic issues that data modelers had been struggling with for years.

Despite its shortcomings, the technologies surrounding XML have had an immense impact on the IT field. As a standard markup language, it is free, flexible and easy to learn. The documents described with XML can, to varying degrees, be *self-describing* and *self-validating*. The related parsing tools are also free and have a short learning curve. The SOAP protocol is itself an extension of the XML standard and HTTP.

As we will see in this appendix, XML alone is of little use. It is the parsers that provide the value. Parsing involves taking the XML document and processing its contents. In many cases the result of the processing is output of the information in a different format; this is a process known as *transformation*. Adding to the value of using XML are corresponding transformation standards for XSLT (Extensible Stylesheet Language for Transformation). The emerging standards for Web Services, most notably SOAP, also build on these toolsets to provide for both point-to-point and asynchronous messaging using XML documents.

Uses of XML

XML is used for a variety of purposes wherever data must be defined in an open, platform-neutral and application-neutral manner. XML is also language independent and can be used with C, C++, Visual Basic or any other language which has the required parsing and transformation libraries.

XML is now widely used to exchange information in business-to-business (B2B) applications and for formatting data for presentation and has become something of a de facto standard for configuration files (deployment information in J2EE).

In business-to-business applications, XML is replacing EDI (Electronic Data Interchange) format documents for transferring information between applications. XML provides a more understandable and expressive language for this purpose combined with a richer toolset for processing the data.

The formatting of data for presentation allows a single format to be output and then formatted as needed for HTML or WAP applications, or for transmitting the information to another system. This allows for further abstraction of presentation information providing a more focused, cohesive application architecture. The XSLT and XPATH standards provide the basis for XML transformation tools as demonstrated in the examples in this chapter.

What It is and What It Isn't

XML and its related technologies certainly has made its mark in the IT world, and will no doubt continue to transform the industry. But it is not, and never has been, a cure-all, a silver-bullet solution to all of IT's data interchange ills. Applications must have some knowledge of the data being interchanged to be able to use it, and often proper use of that knowledge involves subtleties in the data that must be managed in the application. Semantic issues (i.e., 'closing date', 'date of closing' and 'closed date' may or may not mean the same thing), data formatting issues and locale issues are just some of the problems that are not solved by the XML standard.

XML is also not HTML. HTML is a Standard Generalized Markup Language (SGML) extension that is used to describe the formatting of Web pages. It is not extensible, is not case sensitive and allows that improperly structured pages, pages that don't conform completely to the HTML syntax, may be displayed. Whitespace, non-printing characters, is not preserved in the formatted output.

Conversely, XML is an extensible markup language and is not limited to the tags that have been defined. XML is also case sensitive and documents must be well-formed, conforming to the syntax of XML. Documents which are not *well-formed* having balanced end-tags and not allowing interleaved tags, should not be parsed by XML parsers. Whitespace in XML documents is preserved in the parsed output.

XML: Applying Order to Data

XML is a markup language that provides information about data in a document. This information is conveyed through a series of tags that are spread throughout the document. But unlike HTML, XML tags are structured in a hierarchical format. This structure, in concert with the tags themselves, conveys meaning about the data.

For instance, information about a customer would include a name and address for the customer. But the customer may have more than one address: a home address and a billing address. The information about the customer could also include the customer's billing information and the customer's buying history. All of this information could very succinctly be described in a hierarchical fashion. The customer could represent the outer most part of this structure, with the address information being nested within the customer information. The address information could also contain nested information for the two customer addresses: the home address and the business address. The customer's billing information could also involve nested information, containing cash purchase billing information and credit purchase information as shown in Figure C-1.

XML involves placing tags into a text document. The tags use the same basic format as HTML with an open tag symbol, the tag name, tag attributes, tag values and content, and a closing tag. Tag content can be any textual information and unlike HTML which ignores *white-space* (blanks, tabs and various text formatting characters), XML preserves white-space.

XML documents are self-describing through the nature of their structure. They may optionally be self-validating partially through that structure and partially through the use of Document Type Definitions (DTD). Though somewhat

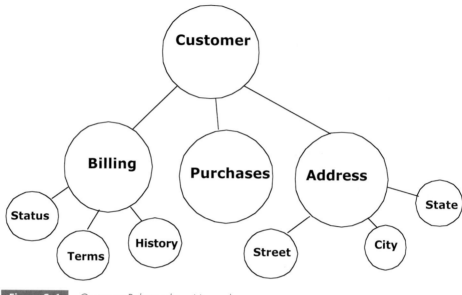

Figure C–1 *Customer Relationships Hierarchy*

limited in their current capabilities, the DTD can be used to provide some validation of an XML document. DTDs will be explained in more detail in a later section.

XML documents must be *well-formed,* meaning the document conforms to the
syntax of XML, in essence it has begin and end tags, is organized in a hierarchical
structure and does not have nested tags. Additionally, a document may be considered valid if it has DTD and conforms to the syntax and structure defined in
that DTD. An XML parser may optionally validate an XML document against a
DTD. Such a parser would be considered a validating parser. But XML parsers are
not required to perform validations (and many XML documents do not use DTDs)
so many parsers are non-validating parsers and do not validate an XML document
against a DTD.

Certainly a very good way to understand an XML document is to examine
one. The following document provides just such an example.

ResultSet Output XML Document

```
<?xml version="1.0" encoding="ISO-8859-1"?>
<!DOCTYPE ResultSet FILE "rs.dtd">

<resultSet run_date="01-02-2001" user="fred">
  <row>
    <column>
      <name>movie_id</name>
```

```
    <table owner="admin">movies</table>
    <type>LONG</type>
    <data>1</data>
</column>
<column>
    <name>movie_name</name>
    <table owner="admin">movies</table>
    <type>VARCHAR</type>
    <data>Stamping Out the Evil Null Reference</data>
</column>
<column>
    <name>release_date</name>
    <table owner="admin">movies</table>
    <type>DATE</type>
    <data>2001-01-01</data>
</column>
<column>
    <name>movie_desc</name>
    <table owner="admin">movies</table>
    <type spec="true">BLOB</type>
    <data>** not provided **</data>
</column>
<column>
    <name>special_promotion</name>
    <table>movies</table>
    <type>TINY</type>
    <data>1</data>
</column>
<column>
    <name>update_date</name>
    <table>movies</table>
    <type>DATE</type>
    <data>2002-01-14</data>
</column>
<column>
    <name>category</name>
    <table>movies</table>
    <type>VARCHAR</type>
    <data>Comedy</data>
</column>
</row>
<row>
 <column>
    <name>movie_id</name>
    <table>movies</table>
    <type>LONG</type>
    <data>801</data>
 </column>
 <column>
    <name>movie_name</name>
    <table>movies</table>
    <type>VARCHAR</type>
```

```
      <data>Crazy/Beautiful</data>
    </column>
    <column>
      <name>release_date</name>
      <table>movies</table>
      <type>DATE</type>
      <data>2000-05-23</data>
    </column>
    <column>
      <name>movie_desc</name>
      <table>movies</table>
      <type>BLOB</type>
      <data>Clever,witty, slow paced</data>
    </column>
    <column>
      <name>special_promotion</name>
      <table>movies</table>
      <type>TINY</type>
      <data>1</data>
    </column>
    <column>
      <name>update_date</name>
      <table>movies</table>
      <type>DATE</type>
      <data>2002-01-28</data>
    </column>
    <column>
      <name>category</name>
      <table>movies</table>
      <type>VARCHAR</type>
      <data>Comedy</data>
    </column>
  </row>
</resultset>
```

Using JDBC, the results of a query are stored in an object of type `ResultSet`. This document demonstrates the use of an XML document to encapsulate the information gained from executing a query against a database table. The data retrieved by the query is the partial contents of a table used to store information on movies.

Even without knowing the specifics of XML, it is possible to read this document and gain some understanding of the contents. Based on the indentation of the rows and the names of the tags, it appears that some type of hierarchy exists in the document. Between the start tags and end tags, there is tag body content which undoubtedly relate to the tags. In all, this represents a rather clean expression of data encoding, relative to other more complex and arduous methods that preceded XML.

Rather than attempting to dissect this document at this point the following sections will explain XML documents in more detail. Following these sections the contents of this document should become clearer.

XML Standards

The XML standard was created by the World Wide Web Consortium. This standards body created the specification based on input from a number of individuals and organizations. Additional standards have been developed with the XML standard and loom large in any discussion of using the technology. These standards are shown in Table C-1.

Table C–1 *XML and Related Standards*

Standard	Description
XML	Document markup language. Hierarchical description of the enclosed data.
XML Namespaces	Namespace definition for elements of an XML document.
XSL-FO	Document and page description formatting definition for XML.
XSL	XML style sheet language. Describes how to transform an XML document.
XPATH	A language definition for describing a path to a location in the hierarchy of the XML document.
XLinks	Describes the linkages of XML documents.
XPointer	In combination with XLINKS describes how XML data in other documents can be linked.
XMLSchema	Data type definition for an XML document.

The complete description of XML and the tools used for XML processing are beyond the scope of this text. This text will focus on the more common usage of XML in a J2EE application: data description and formatting. This will entail coverage of the XML parsing and transformation APIs:XML, XSL and XPATH. These APIs and standards will be described and demonstrated in this chapter.

JAVA XML PACKAGES

The capabilities of XML lend it to a number of tasks from messaging to informational registries. In order to use XML correctly, we also require class libraries to help perform some of the common tasks required such as describing data correctly and parsing and transforming XML data to more useful structures. The various Java XML packages currently or soon to be available provide these capabilities as shown in Table C-2

Table C–2   *Java XML Packages*

Package	Description
JAXP	XML parsers and transformation libraries
JAXB	Conversion of XML to data program structures
JAXM	XML for messaging (SOAP)
JAXR	XML for registries
JAX-RPC	XML for messaging using remote procedure calls (RPC). Provides web services using this mechanism

The JAXP package provides the ability to read and understand the contents of an XML document, an important step to any XML processing. The JAXP package provides two types of parsers—event based and object-based, and transformation APIs that understand stylesheets and can use the stylesheets to transform documents into virtually any format needed by the developer.

The JAXB package provides classes and tools which translate a DTD into corresponding Java classes. The resulting Java classes can parse XML documents described by the DTD and produce objects representing the parsed data as described in the DTD. The class can also handle the details of formatting an XML document based on the contents of the object.

The JAXM package allows Java applications to participate in XML messaging using the SOAP protocol. A SOAP server can be created to receive SOAP messages, or a Java application can generate a SOAP message which can be sent to a SOAP server.

An XML registry is an information repository containing information on available Web Services. There are currently a number of different standards for XML registries. The JAXR package provides access to a variety of XML registries using a unified interface.

The JAX-RPC package allows XML messaging to be performed using the RPC protocol and SOAP. Communication is, as the name implies, over the Remote Procedure Call mechanism.

The XML Document

The XML document or data packet is considered an XML entity. Within the XML document, various tags similar to HTML tags are used to delineate content. These tags represent elements which form a hierarchy.

XML has been designed for internationalization so that documents may be represented in different encoding formats. This requires that the case of characters in the document be preserved so markup in an XML document is case-sensitive.

XML Names

An XML document creates structure, applies order to data. Structures within an XML document are always named, usually using markup tags. Certain rules apply to the choice of names in XML document creation. Names must begin with a letter, underscore or colon and must continue with a sequence of characters that are considered valid name characters: letters, underscores, colons, digits, hyphens, periods. The colon character can be used in a name, but is generally reserved for delimiting *namespaces* (a naming facility that reduces ambiguity in the use of names in an XML document).

The "XML" prefix for names in a document is reserved for special syntax. The string literal "XML"cannot be used as the beginning of XML names including both upper case and lower case versions of the string.

The colon character can be used in a name, but this is usually reserved for a namespace delimiter. Parsers make no specific assumption about the use of the colon character in names.

XML Document Parts

An XML document is composed of three parts as follows.

* A prolog
* A body
* An epilog

Only the body of the document is required—all other parts are optional. The parts must appear in order.

The optional prolog contains processing instructions and encoding information about the document. The prolog contains processing instructions for the document, usually just the version of XML used and possibly identification of a DTD to use during parsing, as follows.

```
<?xml version="1.0"?>

<!DOCTYPE ResultSet SYSTEM "file:/processing/transform/resultset.dtd">
```

The body contains the elements of the XML document structured as a hierarchy of elements and may also contain character data. The optional epilog contains comments, processing instructions or white space that follows the elements of the document.

The optional epilog may include comments, processing instructions or white space. The epilog or miscellaneous section is considered a design error by some and should not be included in a document unless absolutely necessary since forward compatibility may be an issue.

Elements in an XML Document

Elements are used to define the structure of an XML document. Elements are the basic unit of markup in XML and are defined by tags in the document. They must form a hierarchy. Elements in turn may contain other elements, character data, processing instructions or CDATA sections.

Elements are identified using *tags* which contain a tag name within the current namespace. The syntax of tag representation is similar to that of XML as shown in the document fragment below.

```
...
  <book>
    <title>Hello World and Other Stories</title>
    <publisher>Small World Press</publisher>
  </book>
...
```

XML documents are represented as a hierarchy. This hierarchy is composed of elements and their tags with a single required root element which represents the document as a whole. This root element is known as the *document entity* (it represents the entire entity). It is also referred to as the *document root*.

The document root contains a child element that is the root of all elements in the XML document. This element is known as the *document element* and it would have one or more child elements representing the content of the document. Figure C-2 illustrates this concept.

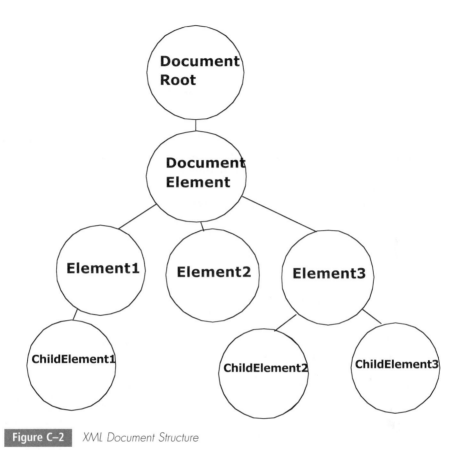

Figure C–2   *XML Document Structure*

An element in an XML document must have a *start tag* and an *end tag*. A special form of an XML tag, an empty content tag, can be used as a shorthand to indicate the tag has no content. (Such tags are often used to indicate a flag setting within an application, or to convey properties through attributes as discussed shortly.) Start and end tags must be consistent and balanced—any start tag must have a corresponding end-tag.

A document is considered *well-formed*, if among other requirements, tags are nested correctly and each start tag has an appropriate end tag. An XML document must be well-formed in order to be parsed, indicating the every start tag has a corresponding end tag and start and end tags are not interleaved as in the following example.

```
<!- this would fail to parse ->
<tag1>
    <tag2>
```

```
</tag1>
    </tag2>
```

In this example, the `tag1` element has a nested `tag2` element. After the start of the `tag2` element, the innermost element at this point is `tag2` and `tag2` must have an end tag before an end tag for `tag1` is encountered. That is not the case in the above example and the document is not well-formed; an XML standards compliant parser would abort the parsing of this document.

Any text that is not part of the tags used to identify elements, processing information, or to insert comments into a document is considered to be character data by XML syntax. The XML standard currently has no concept of a numeric data type. This does not mean that numbers cannot be stored in XML documents —they can. What this means is that XML parser validations will not validate that data is formatted correctly for various primitive data types. Applications parsing the XML documents must manage any formatting exceptions that may occur.

Elements may optionally have attributes. Attributes provide property information about an element and use the form as follows.

```
...
<car color="red" make="Chrysler" model="300 M" mileage="low"/>
...
```

This tag defines an element of car and then provides various attributes to describe the car. Note that this is information that could be conveyed using nested tags as shown below.

```
...
<car>
    <color>read</color>
    <make>Chrysler</make>
    <model>300 M</model>
</car>
...
```

By definition, XML parsers will preserve white space. The term white space is usually applied to character data that is used to create formatting in text. Space characters or tab characters are the more common types of white space. As shown in Table C–3, the XML specification defines the four hexadecimal characters to be white space in an XML document.

Comments can be placed in an XML document using the same comment tag used in HTML. This tag is shown below.

```
<!- this is a comment  ->
```

A comment may be extended over multiple lines in the document but a comment cannot be used in an element tag (within the brackets).

Table C–3	Allowed XML Whitespace Characters

Method	Description
9	Horizontal tab
0A	Line feed
0d	Carriage return
20	ASCII space character

A CDATA section can be declared in an XML document to indicate that the text in that section should not be parsed and should be passed to the output as is. The syntax for a CDATA tag is as follows.

```
<! [CDATA [ this is escaped text ... ]]>
```

Usually a CDATA section would be used to include text in a document as markup that should not be parsed.

```
...
<! [CDATA  [

Markup should be as follows:

  <customer>
   <name>Fred Flinstone</name>
   <country>US</country>
   <street-address>222 Stony Place Ct</street-address>
  </customer>

]]!>
```

Well-Formed Documents

Any data object that conforms to the XML syntax specification is considered to be a *well-formed* document, also known as a stand-alone document. A well-formed document does not require a DTD to be parsed by XML parsers. The criteria for a well-formed document are as follows.

- syntax is compliant with the XML specification;
- the elements in the document form a hierarchical tree; and
- no references to external entities with the exception of a DTD

Parsers which read a well-formed document should throw a fatal exception if an error in the well-formed elements is detected. This fatal error should be expected to stop the execution of the application.

XML Parsers

XML documents are converted into a usable form using *parsers*. Parsers take an XML document and, based on how the user has programmed the application using the parsing API.

XML parsers come in two flavors: *non-validating* and *validating*. A non-validating parser would allow any well-formed document to be parsed and no DTD would be used. Alternatively, a validating parser would require access to a DTD for the document and would validate the XML document against the DTD. Most parsers provide a method call which allows parsers to alter the validating behavior of the parser to be either validating or non-validating.

Describing the XML Document: The DTD

As mentioned previously, the XML document is both *self-describing* and *self-validating*. The degree to which the document provides these features can vary depending partly on whether or not the document identifies a corresponding Document Type Definition (DTD). The DTD describes the type, order, frequency and relationship of elements in an XML document. In the current release of the XML-DTD specification, data types are limited to variations of character data.

An XML document is composed of elements in a specific order or structure, a hierarchy. These elements may optionally contain attributes which further describe the elements. The element may also contain corresponding values. We would therefore expect the DTD to allow some or all of this structure to be described.

The DTD uses tags which begin with "<!'" and then describe some portion of the XML document. The DTD contains two primary tags for describing the XML document: the `ELEMENT` tag to describe, as you might have guessed, the elements in the document, and the `ATTLIST` tag to describe the list of attributes for an element.

The DTD specification allows the number of occurrences of an element, and the order of any child elements to be described using the `ELEMENT` tag. An example of this tag is shown below.

```
<!ELEMENT resultset     (row)+>
```

This example shows that the element 'resultset' can contain a child element 'row'. The plus sign '(+)' after the child element (which must appear in parentheses) indicates the number of occurrences for this element. In this case, the plus sign indicates that the element may appear one or more times. Other characters placed after an element or group of elements that indicate the number of occurrences are as shown in Table C-4.

Table C–4 *DTD Special Characters*

Character	Description
+	One or more occurrences
*	Occurs 0 or more times
?	Occurs 0 or 1 time
<no	Occurs 1 time

The Element Tag

The data type of an element can also be described in the DTD. This is most commonly #PCDATA for text data as shown below.

```
<!ELEMENT name    (#PCDATA)>
```

An element can be composed of a set of child elements. The order of these elements can be specified as follows.

```
<!ELEMENT name (first, last, middle-initial)>
```

In this case, the name element will be composed of one occurrence of the 'first', 'last' and 'middle-initial' elements. Alternatively, the element definition could specify a choice as follows.

```
<!ELEMENT interior-seat-covers (cloth | leather | vinyl )>
```

The element of 'interior-seat-covers' allows a choice of either the 'cloth', 'leather' or 'vinyl' element as a child element. Only one of the set can be used and there will only be one occurrence of the element. A list can also be specified to indicate that all of the indicated elements should follow the defined element as shown in the example below.

```
<!ELEMENT name (first, last, middle-initial)>
```

This indicates the name element will contain one and only one occurrence of the 'first', 'last' and 'middle-initial' elements. To indicate multiple occurrences of child elements, the following syntax could be used.

```
<!ELEMENT car (luxury*, mid-size*, sedan*)>
```

In this example, a 'car' element may contain zero or more occurrences of the 'luxury' element, zero or more occurrences of the 'mid-size' element and zero or more occurrences of the 'sedan' element. Using the syntax shown above, the order specified must be used or a validating parser would reject the XML document. To provide more flexibility, a set of alternative definitions could be provided as shown in the listing below.

Car XML Document DTD

```
<!ELEMENT car (( luxury*, mid-size*, sedan*) |
   (mid-size*, sedan*, luxury*) |
   (sedan*, luxury*, mid-size*) |
   (luxury*, mid-size*, sedan*) |
   (luxury*, sedan*,  mid-size* ))>
```

This example provides for variations of the car element, allowing the order of the child elements to be any of the alternatives listed. The '|' which separates the alternatives indicates that a choice of one of the alternatives is allowed.

The ATTLIST Tag

The ATTLIST tag is used to describe attributes for an element. The tag definition allows the tag names and default values to be identified using the following syntax.

```
<!ATTLIST element-name attribute-name element-data-type default-declaration>
```

The data type is usually CDATA and the default declaration can be one of the following values as shown in Table C–5.

Table C–5

Default Declaration	Description
#REQUIRED	Attribute and value must always be present in the document
#IMPLIED	If the attribute is not present, then no value will be used
'string value'	If the attribute is not provided, then use the 'string value' provided as a default value

An example of the use of this tag is as follows.

```
<!ATTLIST resultset run_date CDATA #IMPLIED>
```

In this example, the attribute `run_date` will be provided with the `result-set` element. Since the attribute is identified with the '#IMPLIED'default declaration, then if the attribute is not provided, no value will be used. A complete DTD for the `resultset` XML document is provided in the code below.

The resultset DTD: resultset.dtd

```
<!— DTD for ResultSet XML document    —>
<!ATTLIST resultset run_date CDATA #IMPLIED>

<!ELEMENT resultset     (row)+>
<!ELEMENT row     (column)+>
<!ELEMENT column (name?, table?, type?, data?))>
<!ELEMENT name     (#PCDATA)>
<!ELEMENT table    (#PCDATA)>
<!ELEMENT type     (#PCDATA)>
<!ELEMENT data     (#PCDATA)>
```

This DTD describes the XML document file layout for an XML document that will be used to capture JDBC `ResultSet` output. The DTD indicates that the `resultset` document will contain one or more `row` elements and a `row` will contain one or more `column` elements (indicated by the '+' sign following the element name). (While technically a valid `ResultSet` which was the product of a query which found no rows would contain 0 rows, but would not be valid for our purposes.)

Within the `column` element a number of child elements are allowed in the order specified: `name`, `table`, `type` and `data`. Per this DTD, the child elements are not required—they may occur 0 or one time as indicated by the '?' after the element name. The element types are then identified in the DTD as PCDATA indicating that it is text data.

(The `ResultSet` object type in JDBC represents the results of a query or the execution of a stored procedure directed against a relational database using JDBC.)

JAXP OVERVIEW

The Java SDK supports XML through a set of classes consolidated under JAXP package. But XML manipulation with Java is not limited to these packages. Open source efforts such as Apache XML project (`xml.apache.org`) provide the very robust Crimson and Xerces parsers and the JDom parser effort (www.jdom.org) also provides an alternative to using the parsers provided with the Sun JDK. These packages are not covered in this text (though the usage is similar). Instead, in this chapter we will focus on the packages provided by Sun.

The Java SDK provides a number of packages to support the XML processing. The classes and interfaces in these packages are generally divided based on the functionality provided by the package, distinguishing between parsing the XML document and transforming the document into another format. These packages are subpackages of the javax.xml package as shown in Table C–6.

Table C–6 *The javax.xml Packages*

Package	Description
javax.xml.parsers	Provides the basic classes needed to perform XML parsing
javax.xml.transform	Provides the classes for the transformation of XML documents using XSL instructions
javax.xml.transform.sax	Provides for the transformation of XML documents using the Sax parser
javax.xml.transform.dom	Provides for the transformation of XML documents using the DOM parser
javax.xml.transform.stream	Allows sources and results of transformation processing to be implemented using a Java stream

Classes are also divided based on the standard which defined them. The classes defined by the World Wide Web Consortium (W3C) XML standards are placed in the org.w3c.dom and org.w3c.sax packages as detailed in Table C–7

Table C–7 *Additional XML Packages*

Package	Description
org.w3c.dom	Defines the interfaces which must be implemented to use the Document Object Model (DOM)
org.xml.sax	Defines the interfaces which must be implemented to provide the Simple API for XML (SAX)
org.xml.sax.ext	Provides extension classes for SAX parsing
org.xml.sax.helpers	Provides helper classes for SAX parsing

XML parsers work with a *source*. A source can be either an input source or an output source. Though the input and output source are commonly different objects, they could conceivably be the same. For XML parsing, the source represents an XML document that provides the input for the parsing operation. With DOM, the result of the parsing operation is an object representation of the XML document. The DOM object contains a hierarchical series of nodes that represents the XML structure of the document as illustrated in Figure C–3.

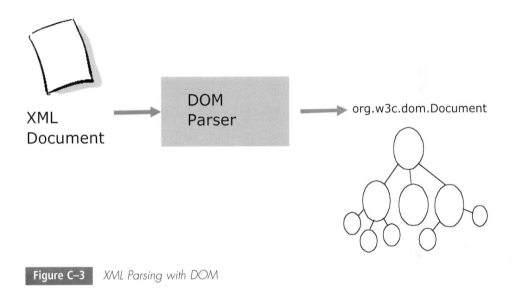

Figure C–3   *XML Parsing with DOM*

Alternatively, an event-based parser such as SAX could be used. This type of parser is provided a set of methods to handle the events triggered by the parsing operation. As the parser reads the XML document and as XML nodes are encountered, it calls the various handler methods to manage the content of the XML document. Figure C-4 illustrates this process.

In many cases a document is being parsed as a means of converting it from one format, in this case an XML document, into another format. This process is referred to as *transformation* and is often used to convert XML documents into HTML documents (as demonstrated in this chapter and in the sample application). XML transformations involve the use of a style sheet to describe the transformation process as shown in Figure C-5.

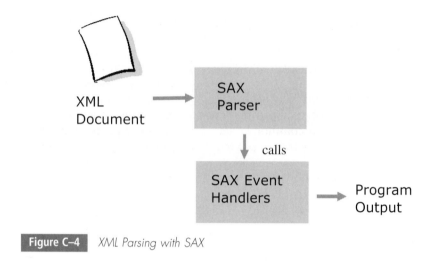

Figure C–4   *XML Parsing with SAX*

Because it is in some ways easier to use and more amenable to object-oriented development, the DOM package is more commonly used. This package makes use of the SAX parser under the covers.

The conversion of a document from one format into another, the process of transformation, can be performed using the classes in the `javax.xml.transform` package. Using a stylesheet language such as XML, a document can easily be transformed into a complex and robust output format using minimal code. An example below will demonstrate this process.

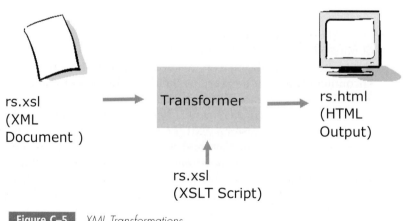

Figure C–5   *XML Transformations*

XML Parsing and Transformations

To be useful to an application, XML documents are generally converted into another format through either *parsing* or *transformation*. Transformation is effectively the parsing and conversion of a document combined into one process. The result of a transformation is the output of a document in a different format.

Parsing involves the disassembling of a target document into useful elements. Parsing is a common practice in computer processing. One of the most common examples is that of parsing a computer program during the compilation process. One of the first steps taken when a computer program is compiled is the parsing of the program. This involves applying a grammar, a set of rules for the structure of the program. Failure to follow the rules of the grammar results in a failed compilation. Successful parsing will generally move the compilation into the next process where lower-level processing instructions are created based on the computer program being compiled. The ultimate output from this process of computer program compilation will be an executable program.

XML documents are parsed in a similar manner though the process is not referred to as compiling. The more common term applied to the parsing of XML documents is *transformation* since the documents are being transformed into another form. Many applications are being designed to return the data from the business tier in XML format. The presentation layer will then take this XML formatted data and transform it into the correct format depending on the application component that made the request. For instance, a web-based application may transform the data into an HTML page and a Swing GUI application may parse the data into an internal object using DOM. Alternatively, an application running on a handheld (PDA) may transform the data into WML format to provide an appropriate user presentation for the device where it will be rendered.

The following sections will first examine the process of parsing and transforming an XML document, covering first the parsers and then the transformation processing using XSLT.

Parsing an XML Document

A number of parsers are available for parsing XML with Java. As of J2SE version 1.4, parsers are included with the Sun JDK. There are two primary types of parsers available: event-driven parsers and tree-based parsers.

Event-driven parsers process the XML document as a stream and generate events as elements are encountered. Developers must implement event handlers to manage the parsing process. These parsers are fast, efficient and lightweight. The most common example of this parser is the Simple API for XML (SAX) developed by members of the XML-DEV mailing list and led by David Megginson.

Tree-based parsers take the target document, parse its contents and create an internal object tree to reflect the contents of the document. Developers must then write code to traverse the object tree to find the content or perform the transformation desired. These parsers are not as fast and require more system resources for larger documents than event-based parsers. The most common of these parsers is the document object model developed by the W3C (World Wide Web Consortium) which will be demonstrated in the next section.

Using the DOM Parser API

The DOM parser with the JDK provides the implementations of the various abstract classes and interfaces needed to parse a document and obtain output using the Document Object Model. The most common classes used are shown in Table C–8.

Table C–8   *DOM Classes and Interfaces*

Class	Description
`javax.xml.parsers.DocumentBuilderFactory`	Implements a factory pattern for the creation of DocumentBuilder objects. Used to set various attributes for the parser including its validating behavior.
`javax.xml.parsers.DocumentBuilder`	Provides methods to perform the parsing to create an internal DOM representing the XML document
`org.w3c.dom.Document`	Represents the document root or document entity. An element which contains the constituent (all child) elements of the document
`org.w3c.dom.Node`	A single node in the document tree. A node can be an element, an attribute, an entity, document or text node.
`org.w3c.dom.NodeList`	An ordered enumeration of nodes.
`javax.xml.transform.Source`	Represents a location for a source for a parsing or transformation operation.
`javax.xml.transform.Result`	Represents a location for the results of a transformation or parsing operation.

Processing an XML Document with DOM

The processing of an XML document with DOM involves the creation of a small number of objects to manage much of the process. The task of parsing the document then involves iterating over the various nodes in the document tree to obtain the information needed.

The DOM API makes use of the *factory* design pattern. The `DocumentBuilderFactory` class allows a number of properties for the parser to be determined and set before the parser is created. This simplifies the usage of the resulting parser object. The expectation is that the creation of the factory and the document builder (`DocumentBuilder`) would be performed once for the duration of the application since the builder object will retain its properties. The following code example demonstrates the usage of the DOM API.

This code example will execute an SQL statement which will read rows from a database used to store information about movies. The results of this SQL query will be stored in a JDBC `ResultSet` object. The `ResultSet` object will then be converted into an XML document that will encapsulate the results of the query. This XML document will be stored internally in a string.

The string containing the XML document will then be parsed using the DOM API. We cannot parse the contents of the string directly using DOM, so we must wrap the string with an appropriate object.

The program will parse the XML document and then call a method recursively, parsing a node and then parsing all child nodes, until the parse operation is complete. For convenience and simplicity, the results of the parsing operation are written to the console.

The XMLDemo1 Class: Declarations and main Program Block

The program begins by instantiating an instance of itself and then calls its `getConnected` method. The `getConnected` method will perform the task of looking up and connecting to the `DataSource`. At this point, the instance members for the JDBC Statement (`stmt`) will have an active reference and the call to the `processQuery` method (which will use the `stmt` reference) will return a valid `ResultSet`. This `ResultSet` object reference (`rs`) is then passed to the `JDBCXML.toXMLString` method to convert the contents of the `ResultSet` to an XML document. The XML document is stored in the String reference (`s`).

The `parse` method takes an `InputSource` object reference as an argument (overloaded versions of the `parse` method take other arguments, but the `InputSource` is the most convenient for parsing of this XML document). The `String` object reference is wrapped with a `StringReader` which is then wrapped with an `InputSource` object.

For simplicity, the majority of the work involved in creating the parsers is performed in the `main` program block. In practice, this is work that is best done in a constructor or an initialization method. First a call is made to get the `DocumentBuilderFactory`. The `DocumentBuilderFactory` instance is then used to create `DocumentBuilder` object. This is the object that will be used to perform the parsing operation.

The `DocumentBuilder parse` method is then used to parse the `InputSource`. The result of this call is a reference to a `Document` object which represents the *document root* of the parsed document. The `Document normalize` method is then called to simplify the parsing operation and ensure only structure separates text nodes.

The `getDocumentElement` method is then called to retrieve the root element of the document tree; all other elements will reside under this element. The root element is then passed to the `parseNode` method to begin the parsing operation. The code for this section of the application follows.

The XMLDemo1 Class: Declarations and main Program Block

```
package examples.jaxp;

import java.sql.*;
import java.io.*;

import javax.naming.*;
import javax.sql.*;

import javax.xml.transform.*;
import javax.xml.parsers.*;

import org.w3c.dom.*;
import org.apache.log4j.Category;

import jdbcutil.JDBCXML;
import service.LoggingService;


public class XMLDemo1 {

private static Category logger = LoggingService.getLogger(
                         "examples.XMLDemo1" );
private Statement  stmt;
private Connection con;

private String pad = "                        ";

public static void main( String args[] ) {
Document doc=null;
```

```
try {

   XMLDemo1 xmldemo = new XMLDemo1();

   //
   // connect to the database
   //
   xmldemo.getConnected();

   //
   // retrieve a JDBC ResultSet
   //
   ResultSet rs = xmldemo.processQuery();

   //
   // convert the ResultSet into an XML document
   // and store it in a string
   //
   String s = JDBCXML.toXMLString( rs );

   //
   // parse the XML document
   //
   // create an InputSource around the string document
   //

   StringReader in = new StringReader( s );
   org.xml.sax.InputSource source =
              new org.xml.sax.InputSource( in );

   //
   // get the DOM Factory
   //
   DocumentBuilderFactory dbf =
                   DocumentBuilderFactory.newInstance();
   DocumentBuilder db = dbf.newDocumentBuilder();


   //
   // parse the XML source
   //
   doc = db.parse( source );
   doc.normalize();

   //
   // recursively parse the XML document starting at the root
   //
   org.w3c.dom.Node root = doc.getDocumentElement();
   xmldemo.parseNode( root, 0 );

}
catch (Exception e) {
```

```
      logger.error("Exception e: " + e );
 }
}
```

The XMLDemo1 Class: getConnected and processQuery Methods

The getConnected method performs the task of obtaining the InitialContext and performing a lookup to obtain the appropriate DataSource. A connection to the DataSource is then obtained and a JDBC Statement object is created which will then be used by the processQuery method to execute a query against the DataSource.

The processQuery method will execute a query and return a ResultSet containing the results of the query. It simply calls the executeQuery method of the JDBC Statement class, captures and returns the ResultSet resulting from that operation.

the getConnected and processQuery Methods

```
public void getConnected() {

try {

InitialContext ctx = new InitialContext();
DataSource ds = (DataSource) ctx.lookup( "movies" );

con = ds.getConnection();

stmt = con.createStatement();


}
catch (Exception e) {
 logger.error("Exception e: " + e );
}

}

// --

protected ResultSet processQuery() {

ResultSet rs=null;

try {
```

```
rs = stmt.executeQuery("select * from movies");

}
catch (SQLException e) {
    logger.error("Exception e: " + e );
}

finally {

    return rs;
}

}
```

The XMLDemo1 Class: The parseNode Method

In XML documents, the node name and corresponding value reside in different nodes, so that a node containing a customer name would have a child node containing the value of the customer name in a text node. For this reason, parsing a DOM object involves iterating through various child nodes to find the appropriate content. The parseNode method does this using recursion, the ability of a method to call itself using the wonders of program call stacks.

The parseNode method performs the parsing operation for this application. It does not look for any specific element names in the document, it merely outputs all node names and node values for any nodes found in the document. The output for the node name and the corresponding value will be output on one line.

In practice, an application would look for specific nodes and their corresponding values and perform processing on those nodes. Other examples in this text will demonstrate that process.

The parseNode method will output each node to the console and will indent based on the depth of the node in the document tree hierarchy. For this reason, it accepts two arguments: the node to parse and an integer representing the depth into the hierarchy. A string will be used to perform the indentation, padding output using a substring of the string based on the depth into the document hierarchy. This string is created as a local variable for the method and a substring is created at the start of processing based on the depth into the tree hierarchy.

The Node getNodeName method is called to determine the name of the node and to determine if the node is a text node ("#text") and is not a blank or a null reference it is output. Note that the PrintWriter print method is used to perform the output since the expectation is that the node name would have been printed on the previous call to this method.

If the node is not a text node, then a test is performed to determine whether or not the node contains a valid node name. If it does, the node name is output to the console.

Following the test to determine whether or not node content or node name needs to be output, a test is performed to determine if there are any child nodes for this node. If there are, then those nodes must be examined. If there are child nodes a call is made to obtain the list of child nodes. Then, for each of the child nodes, a call is made to this same method, indicating that the next level of the hierarchy is being used by passing the `depth+1` as a parameter to the method.

The XMLDemo1 Class: The parseNode Method

```
public void parseNode( org.w3c.dom.Node node, int depth ) {

//
// create a string for output padding
//
String outputPad = pad.substring(0, depth*2 );

//
// if this is a text node, it has our value
//

if ( node instanceof Text ) {
    String value = node.getNodeValue();
    //
    // if it isn't whitespace, then print it
    //
    if ( ( value != null ) && ( value.trim().length() > 0 ) )
       System.out.print("- value: " + node.getNodeValue() );
}
else {
   //
   // if this isn't a text node, it may have our node name
   //
   if ( node.getNodeName() != null )
      System.out.print( "\n" +
                           outputPad +
                           node.getNodeName() + ": " );
}

//
// parse any child nodes
//
if ( node.hasChildNodes() ) {
   NodeList list = node.getChildNodes();
   for ( int n = 0; n < list.getLength();n++)   {
       parseNode( list.item(n), depth + 1 ); } }

}
```

```
}
```

The result of running the XMLDemo1 program would be the output shown below.

XMLDemo1 Program Output

```
resultset:
  row:
    column:
      name: - value: movie_id
      table: - value: movies
      type: - value: LONG
      data: - value: 1
    column:
      name: - value: movie_name
      table: - value: movies
      type: - value: VARCHAR
      data: - value: Stamping Out the Evil Null Reference
    column:
      name: - value: release_date
      table: - value: movies
      type: - value: DATE
      data: - value: 2001-01-01
    column:
      name: - value: movie_desc
      table: - value: movies
      type: - value: BLOB
      data: - value: ** not provided **
    column:
      name: - value: special_promotion
      table: - value: movies
      type: - value: TINY
      data: - value: 1
    column:
      name: - value: update_date
      table: - value: movies
      type: - value: DATE
      data: - value: 2002-01-14
    column:
      name: - value: category
      table: - value: movies
      type: - value: VARCHAR
      data: - value: Comedy
  row:
    column:
      name: - value: movie_id
      table: - value: movies
      type: - value: LONG
```

```
    data: - value: 801
column:
  name: - value: movie_name
  table: - value: movies
  type: - value: VARCHAR
  data: - value: Crazy/Beautiful
column:
  name: - value: release_date
  table: - value: movies
  type: - value: DATE
  data: - value: 2000-05-23
column:
  name: - value: movie_desc
  table: - value: movies
  type: - value: BLOB
  data: - value: ** not provided **
...
```

Math Functions

Function	Description
ACOS(float)	Returns the arccosine
ABS(number)	Returns the absolute value
ASIN(float)	Returns the arcsine
ATAN(float)	Returns the arctangent
ATAN2(float1, float2)	Returns the arctangent of the x and y coordinates represented by float1 and float2
CEILING(number)	Returns the smallest integer greater than or equal to number
COS(float)	Returns the cosine
COT(float)	Returns the cotangent
DEGREES(number)	Returns the number of degrees
EXP(float)	Returns the exponential value of float
FLOOR(number)	Returns the largest integer less than or equal to number
LOG(float)	Returns the log

Function	Description
LOG10(float)	Returns the base 10 logarithm
MOD(integer1, integer2)	Returns the modulus of integer1 divided by integer2
PI()	Returns the constant value of pi as a floating point number
POWER(number, power)	Returns the value of number to integer power
RADIANS(number)	Returns the number of radians converted from degrees
RAND(integer)	Returns a random floating point value
ROUND(number, places)	Returns a numeric expression rounded to integer expression places to the right of the decimal point
SIGN(number)	Returns the sign of number; -1 if less than 0, 0 if number equals 0, 1 if greater than 0
SIN(float)	Returns the sine
SQRT(float)	Returns the square root
TAN(float)	Returns the tangent
TRUNCATE(number, places)	Returns the number of truncated places to the right of the decimal point

String Functions

Function	Description
ASCII(string)	Returns the integer ASCII code of the leftmost character value for the character string
CHAR(code)	Returns the character that has the ASCII code value specified by code
CONCAT(string1, string2)	Returns the string that is the result of concatenating string2 to string1
DIFFERENCE(string1, string2)	Returns an integer value that represents the difference between the SOUNDEX values of string1 and string2
INSERT(string1, start, length, string2)	Returns a character string where length characters have been deleted from string1 beginning at start and where string2 has been inserted into string1 at start
LCASE(string)	Returns all characters in string converted to lowercase
LEFT(string, count)	converts all lowercase characters in the string to uppercase
LENGTH(string)	Returns the length of the string in bytes excluding trailing blanks and the string termination character
LOCATE(string1, string2, start)	locates string1 in string2. Begins searching at the start of string2 unless the optional start parameter is specified, in which case it would start searching at start position in string2
LTRIM(string)	Eliminates leading blanks from string

Function	Description
REPEAT(string, count)	Returns a string composed of string repeated count times
REPLACE(string1, string2, string3)	Replaces all occurrences of string2 in string1 with string3
RIGHT(string, count)	Returns the rightmost count of characters of string
RTRIM(string)	Eliminates trailing blanks from string
SOUNDEX(string)	Returns a data source dependent character string representing the sound of string
SPACE(count)	Returns a string of count spaces
SUBSTRING(string, start, length)	Returns a substring of string starting at start and running for length characters
UCASE(string)	Returns all characters in string in uppercase

Date Functions

CURDATE()	Returns the current date
CURTIME()	Returns the current time
DAYNAME(date)	Returns the name of the current day (Monday, Tuesday …)
DAYOFMONTH(date)	Returns the day of the month as an integer (1-31)
DAYOFWEEK(date)	Returns the day of the week as an integer (1-7)
DAYOFYEAR(date)	Returns the day of the year as an integer value (0-366)
HOUR(time)	Returns the hour of time as an integer value (0-23)
MINUTE(time)	Returns the minute as an integer value (0-59)
MONTH(time)	Returns the month as an integer value (0-1-12)
MONTHNAME(date)	Returns the name of the month
NOW()	Returns the current date and time as a timestamp value
QUARTER(date)	Returns the quarter in date as an integer value (1-4)
SECOND(time)	Returns the second in time as an integer value (0-59)
TIMESTAMPADD (interval_type, interval, timestamp)	Returns the timestamp created by adding timestamp to interval of interval_type
TIMESTAMPDIFF (interval_type, timestamp1, timestampt2)	Returns the difference between the timestamps of type interval_type
WEEK(date)	Returns the week number of the date as an integer (1-53)
YEAR(date)	Returns the year of the date as an integer

Function	Description
Database Functions	
DATABASE()	Returns the name of the database corresponding to the current connection
IFNULL(expression, value)	If expression is null, then the value is returned. If the expression is not null, then expression is returned
USER()	Returns the current user name

INDEX